7/04

ENCYCLOPEDIA OF AMERICAN MILITARY HISTORY

ENCYCLOPEDIA OF AMERICAN MILITARY HISTORY

VOLUME I
A TO F

Spencer C. Tucker, General Editor

ASSOCIATE EDITORS
David Coffey
John C. Fredriksen
Justin D. Murphy

Facts On File, Inc.

Encyclopedia of American Military History

Facts On File, Inc.
132 West 31st Street
New York NY 10001

Library of Congress Cataloging-in-Publication Data

Encyclopedia of American military history / Spencer C. Tucker, general editor ; associate editors David Coffey, John C. Fredriksen, Justin D. Murphy.
   p. cm.
   Includes bibliographical references and index.
   ISBN 0-8160-4355-8 (set)—ISBN 0-8160-4352-3 (vol. 1) —
   ISBN 0-8160-4353-1 (vol. 2) — ISBN 0-8160-4354-X (vol. 3)
   1. United States—History, Military—Encyclopedias. I. Tucker, Spencer, 1937–

E181 .E63 2003
355′.00973′03—dc21   2002029658

Text design by Joan M. Toro
Cover illustration by Nora Wertz
Cover design by Cathy Rincon
Maps by Dale Williams and Jeremy Eagle

Printed in the United States of America

VB TB 10 9 8 7 6 5 4 3 2 1

This book is printed on acid-free paper.

Contents

List of Entries

Contributors List

Dr. William Allison
Weber State University

Ms. Erica Ardolino
Virginia Military Institute

Dr. Joseph (Geoff) Babb
US Army Command
and General Staff
College

Mr. Joshua Lee Bandy
Virginia Military Institute

Mr. Alhaji S. Bangura
Virginia Military Institute

Mr. Daniel P. Barr
Kent State University

Mr. Mark A. Bauserman
Virginia Military Institute

Ms. Lisa L. Beckenbaugh
University of Arkansas

Mr. Robert Beeks
McMurry University

Col. Dr. Daniel Randall
Beirne, USA, Rtd.

Dr. Alexander M.
Bielakowski
University of Findlay

Mr. Ryan M. Blake
Virginia Military Institute

Mr. Christian Blanch
Virginia Military Institute

Mr. Scott Blanchette
Naval Information Security
Program

Daniel K. Blewett
The College of DePage

Mr. Jason S. Boncher
Virginia Military Institute

Ms. Anna Boros
Zrínyi Miklós National
Defense University
Hungary

Mr. William M. Boulware
Virginia Military
Institute

Dr. Carl Boyd
Old Dominion University

Mr. Walter Boyne

Mr. Matthew B. Brady
Virginia Military Institute

Mr. Anthony Bravo
Virginia Military Institute

Mr. Jonathan Breyfogle
Florida State University

Brig. Gen. Dr. Charles
Brower IV
Virginia Military Institute

Dr. Shannon A. Brown
Smithsonian National
Museum of American
History

Professor Thomas C.
Buckley
University of Minnesota—
General College

Dr. Robert J. Bunker
California State University
at San Bernardino

Mr. Matthew Burgess
Virginia Military Institute

Mr. Michael L. Butterfield
Virginia Military Institute

Dr. Michèle Butts
Austin Peay State University

Mr. Mark N. Calandra
McMurray University

Mr. Roger W. Caraway
McMurry University

Mr. Samuel D. Carney
Virginia Military Institute

Dr. Stanley Carpenter
U.S. Naval War College

Dr. Michael S. Casey
Graceland University

Ms. Adrienne Caughfield
Texas Christian University

Mr. Nathan Charles
Virginia Military Institute

Dr. Paul C. Clark, Jr.

Mr. Edwin Clarke
Virginia Military Institute

LTC Steven E. Clay
U.S. Army Command
and General Staff
College

Mr. Craig T. Cobane
Culver-Stockton College

Dr. Don Coerver
Texas Christian
University

Dr. David Coffey
The University of
Tennessee at Martin

Mr. David W. Coffey
Virginia Military Institute

Mr. Justin V. Cole
Virginia Military Institute

Dr. Paolo E. Coletta
U.S. Naval Academy

Ms. Kristin Collins
Florida State University

Mr. Jared M. Conrad
Virginia Military Institute

Mr. Howard J. Cook III
Virginia Military Institute

Mr. David Corlett
College of William and
   Mary

Dr. Dallas Cothrum
University of Texas at Tyler

Ms. Lisa L. Crutchfield
College of William and
   Mary

Mr. Brian A. Cummings
Virginia Military Institute

Mr. George H. Cushman
Virginia Military Institute

Mr. Andrew L. Dawson, Jr.
Virginia Military Institute

Mr. John J. Dempsey
Virginia Military Institute

Dr. Keith Dickson
Armed Forces Staff College

Ms. Rebecca J. Dodson
McMurry University
Abilene, Texas

Mr. Richard H. Donohue
Virginia Military Institute

Dr. David R. Dorondo
Western Carolina University

Mr. John W. Downs
Virginia Military Institute

Dr. Blake Dunnavent
Idaho State University

Ms. Jean A. Ebbert

Col. Lawyn C. Edwards
U.S. Army Command
   and General Staff
   College

Brig. Gen. Uzal W. Ent,
   PNG, Rtd.

Mr. John E. Foley
Austin Peay State
   University

Mr. Thomas M. Forsyth
Virginia Military Institute

Dr. Arthur T. Frame
U.S. Army Command and
   General Staff College

Mr. Brian D. Frank
Virginia Military Institute

Dr. John C. Fredriksen

Mr. Derek Frisby

Dr. Michael P. Gabriel
Kutztown University

Mr. Aric Gerke
Virginia Military Institute

Mr. Ray F. Girman, Jr.
Virginia Military Institute

Mr. Milton Goldin

Mr. Kevin Gould

Mr. David Green

Mr. Jack Greene

Mr. Joseph W. Gunter
Virginia Military Institute

Mr. Justin Guy
Virginia Military Institute

Mr. Jason M. Halin
Virginia Military Institute

Ms. Marie-Beth Hall

Mr. Richard C. Halseth

Mr. Marshall J. Hardy
Virginia Military Institute

Dr. Theodore Harris
University of Minnesota

Mr. Alex Haseley
Virginia Military Institute

Mr. Benjamin K. Hassell
Virginia Military Institute

Mr. Brian Head

Dr. William Head
U.S. Air Force

Mr. Benjamin L. Huggins

Dr. Lance Janda
Cameron University

Mr. Patrick R. Jennings
National Park Service

Mr. Sven Jensen
Virginia Military
   Institute

Dr. James R. Jewell
West Virginia University

LTC Kim M. Juntunen
U.S. Army Command and
   General Staff College

Mr. Benjamin Kaler
Virginia Military
   Institute

Mr. Stephen J. Kaufman
Virginia Military
   Institute

Mr. Jim M. Kerbow
McMurry University

Ms. Angela Kidd
McMurry University

Dr. Jeff Kinard

Maj. Dr. Curtis S. King
U.S. Army Command and
   General Staff College

Ms. Nichole E. Kramer
Virginia Military Institute

Mr. Joseph Kupsky

Mr. Jared W. Lapp
Virginia Military Institute

Mr. Ryan J. Lapsley
Virginia Military Institute

Mr. Eric P. Lauer
Virginia Military Institute

Dr. Wayne E. Lee
University of Louisville

Mr. Paul Leicht
University of Illinois

Dr. Adrian R. Lewis
University of North Texas

Dr. E. Raymond Lewis

Ms. Sarah H. List

Ms. Rebecca Livingston
National Archives

Mr. Adam T. Love
Virginia Military Institute

Ms. Rachel J. Love
Virginia Military Institute

Dr. Jack McCallum
Texas Christian University

Mr. Matthew J. McKee
Virginia Military Institute

Dr. James McNabb

Dr. John McNay

Mr. Rodney Madison
Texas Christian University

Mr. Michael J. Manning
U.S. National Park Service

Mr. Jason R. Maslow
Virginia Military Institute

Mr. Brandon R. Matthews
Virginia Military Institute

Mr. Brian Melton
Texas Christian University

Mr. Alexander Mendoza
Texas Tech University

Dr. Major Jay Menzoff,
   Columbia College of
   Missouri, Ft. Worth
   Campus

Mr. Matthew Meyers
Virginia Military Institute

Mr. Benjamin J. Midura
Virginia Military Institute

Mr. Devon S. Miller
Virginia Military Institute

Mr. Mark D. Mills
Virginia Military Institute

Dr. Dan Monroe

LTC Forrest Morgan, USAF
School of Advanced
   Airpower Studies

Mr. Troy Morgan

Brig. Gen. John W.
   Mountcastle, USA Rtd.

Dr. Malcolm Muir, Jr.
Austin Peay State
   University

Dr. Justin Murphy
Howard Payne University

Mr. Shane Nall
McMurry University

Dr. Cynthia Clark
   Northrup
Texas Christian University

Dr. Eric Osborne
Virginia Military Institute

Mr. Ryan N. Peay
Virginia Military Institute

Dr. Galen Perras
Bishop's University Canada

Dr. James D. Perry

Mr. Dwight Peveler

Mr. Jim Piecuch
William & Mary University

Mr. Trevor Plante
National Archives and
   Records Administration

Dr. Max Plassmann
Universitäts-und
   Landesbibliothek
   Düsseldorf, Germany

Mr. Brandon Polk

Mr. Christopher Preble
Temple University

Mr. David L. Preston
College of William and Mary

Dr. Peter Rainow

Maj. Steven J. Rauch
U.S. Army Command
   and General Staff
   College

Dr. John David Rausch
West Texas A&M
   University

Ms. Mary S. Rausch

Dr. David Rezelman

Mr. Jon B. Rhiddlehoover, Jr.
McMurry University

Mr. Christopher J. Richman
Virginia Military Institute

Dr. Priscilla Roberts
University of Hong Kong

Mr. Todd Rodriguez
McMurry University

Mr. Christopher S. Roman
Virginia Military Institute

Mr. Joseph R. Rubin
Virginia Military Institute

Dr. Gordon Rudd
United States Marine
   Corps University

Dr. Aldo E. Salerno
Staff Historian
U.S. Army Space and
   Missile Defense
   Command

Dr. Stanley Sandler

Mr. Stuart W. Sanders

Dr. Elizabeth D. Schafer

Dr. Frank Schumacher
University of Erfurt
   Germany

Mr. Nicholas Shallcross
Virginia Military
   Institute

Mr. James G. Sheldon
Virginia Military Institute

Ms. Tracy M. Shilcutt
Texas Christian University

Mr. Donald G. Shomette

Dr. David J. Silbey
Bowdoin College

Dr. David C. Skaggs
Bowling Green State
   University

Mr. Steve Skakandy
Virginia Military Institute

Mr. Adam P. Stanley-Smith
Virginia Military Institute

Mr. James B. Smith
Virginia Military Institute

Col. Dr. Jeffrey G. Smith
U.S. Army

Mr. Michael Thomas Smith

Dr. David L. Snead
Texas Tech University

Mr. Puthyvuth Sok
Virginia Military Institute

Dr. Lewis Sorley

Mr. Kenneth Cavanagh
   Stein
Virginia Military Institute

Mr. John J. Stewart
Virginia Military Institute

Lt. Thomas J. Stuhlreyer,
   USCG

Dr. Bruce Tap

Mr. David R. Tavvener
Virginia Military Institute

Dr. Jack W. Thacker
Western Kentucky
   University

Mr. Ryan Thiel
Virginia Military Institute

Mr. Toby Thompson
McMurry University

Mr. Frank Luis Trigueros
Virginia Military Institute

Mr. David Troxell
Virginia Military Institute

Dr. Spencer C. Tucker
Virginia Military Institute

Mr. Brandon H. Turner
Virginia Military Institute

Mr. David Ulbrich
Kansas State University

Dr. Gregory J. W. Urwin
Temple University

Dr. Mark D. Van Ells
Queensboro Community
College

Dr. Thomas D. Veve
Dalton State College

Mr. Erik J. Vik
Virginia Military
Institute

Dr. Gilmar E. Visoni
Queensborough
Community College

Dr. John F. Votaw
Cantigny First Division
Foundation

Mr. Stephen P. Ward
Virginia Military Institute

Dr. Andrew Jackson Waskey
Dalton State College

Mr. Stephen A. Wiegel
Virginia Military Institute

Mr. Duane Wesolick
737 Crestmont Drive
Waynesville, NC 28786

Mr. Gregory Collin Wheal
Virginia Military Institute

2d Lt. Ronald White, Jr.,
USMC
Virginia Military Institute

Dr. LTC James Willbanks,
USA Rtd.
U.S. Army Command and
General Staff College

Mr. Joseph M. Williams
Virginia Military
Institute

Dr. Alan F. Wilt
Iowa State University

Mr. Bradford Wineman
Texas A&M University

Dr. Laura Wood
Tarrant County College

Dr. Steven Woodworth
Texas Christian University

Mr. Justin Wouters
Virginia Military Institute

Mr. Joshua L. Wright
Virginia Military Institute

Mr. Luke Charles
Wullenwaber
Virginia Military Institute

Brig. Gen. David Zabecki,
USAR

Mr. Kyle F. Zelner
College of William and
Mary

Introduction

The United States has enjoyed a rich and varied military history. From the first English settlements in North America to the present, the U.S. military has evolved from poorly trained militia formations into the world's most powerful professional military establishment. During that time the United States has fought almost every type of war, from guerrilla actions to global conflicts.

In many ways the U.S. military establishment reflects the society from which it comes; in more recent years, especially, the military has also had its impact on civilian society. Understanding the history of America's wars and its military establishment helps us understand ourselves and our world a bit better.

It is quite impossible, even in a three-volume encyclopedia of more than 600,000 words, to include all information about U.S. military history. I have tried to center the encyclopedia entries on key individuals; overviews of the causes, courses, and effects of America's wars; key technological developments; and overviews of weapons systems. The encyclopedia covers the period from the colonial wars to the horrible events of 11 September 2001, which like 7 December 1941, will probably stand as a major turning point in our history. In the encyclopedia we have tried to pay due attention to minorities and women, both of which have contributed significantly to American military success.

The glossary defines basic military terms. The bibliography is, because of space restraints, selective. For ease of access it is divided into general reference works, monographs by chronological period, and encyclopedias and atlases.

I am especially indebted to my three associate editors. Dr. David Coffey, a professor at the University of Tennessee at Martin, wrote many of the entries and supervised the writing of many more. Dr. Justin D. Murphy, professor at Howard Payne University, and Dr. John C. Fredriksen, an independent scholar, also wrote many entries. All three read the entire manuscript and made numerous editing suggestions. I hope that among the four of us, we have caught the great majority of errors. I take full responsibility for any that might still appear, however.

Dr. Donald Frazier provided information for the maps. Both area maps and those of specific battles are included.

I am also most grateful to my colleagues Dr. Eric W. Osborne and Dr. Malcolm Muir, Jr., each of whom wrote entries and read others to answer specialized technical questions. Former VMI cadets Alexander D. Haseley and Richard H. Donohue, Jr., have assisted me throughout this process, helping to research facts or bibliographies and xeroxing and sending materials. They and former cadet Jason Halin, who helped locate and order photographs, have been invaluable. I am most appreciative to the Virginia Military Institute for funding, associated with the Biggs Chair of Military History, that has made such assistance possible.

Finally, I am most indebted to Dr. Beverly Tucker and to Max Tucker for their patience and understanding in this long and sometimes tedious process.

— Spencer C. Tucker

ENTRIES
A TO F

Abrams, Creighton W., Jr. (1914–1974) *U.S. Army general, commander of U.S. forces in Vietnam, and army chief of staff*

Born on 15 September 1914, at Springfield, Massachusetts, Creighton Williams Abrams grew up in nearby Agawam in a family of modest means. Graduating from the U.S. Military Academy, WEST POINT, in 1936, he was assigned to the horse-mounted 7th Cavalry Regiment at Fort Bliss, Texas.

During World War II Abrams commanded the 4th Armored Division's 37th Tank Battalion (the first unit to cross the Moselle River, and the first element of Lieutenant General George S. PATTON's Third Army to reach the Rhine). Abrams's 37th Tank Battalion relieved the 101st Airborne Division when it was surrounded at Bastogne during the Battle of the BULGE. In the process Abrams won two Distinguished Service Crosses, two Silver Stars, and a battlefield promotion to colonel.

Subsequently Abrams headed the Armor School's Department of Tactics at Fort Knox, Kentucky, then returned to Germany to command the 63d Tank Battalion and then the 2d Armored Cavalry Regiment. During the KOREAN WAR he served successively as chief of staff of all three U.S. corps deployed there. Selected for brigadier general in 1956, Abrams served a Pentagon staff tour in reserve affairs before returning to Germany as assistant commander of the 3d Armored Division and later (promoted to major general) as its commander.

Returning to Washington and the army staff, Abrams received a succession of delicate, special missions involving overseeing troops assigned to a number of civil rights crises. He gained a reputation for coolness and common sense that marked him for greater responsibilities and resulted in promotion to lieutenant general and command of V Corps in Germany.

In 1964 Abrams was promoted to full general and was assigned as army vice chief of staff. During three years in that post he played a key role in the rapid expansion of the army and deployment of much of it to Vietnam. Abrams was himself assigned to Vietnam in May 1967 as deputy to General William C. WESTMORELAND. During 13 months in that role, he devoted himself primarily to improving the Republic of Vietnam's armed forces.

In June 1968 Abrams became commander, U.S. Military Assistance Command, Vietnam. In close cooperation with Ambassador Ellsworth Bunker and, before long, William Colby, who directed pacification support, Abrams stressed the necessity of conducting "one war" of combat operations, pacification, and improvement of South Vietnamese forces, all of equal importance—this in contrast to Westmoreland's preoccupation with combat operations.

The measure of merit now became, instead of "body count," the percentage of South Vietnam's rural population living in relatively secure hamlets and villages. "Clear and hold" missions replaced "search and destroy" combat operations, and the large-scale maneuvers of the earlier period gave way to thousands of small-unit patrols and ambushes, both day and night. These and other initiatives constituted a more fruitful approach to the conduct of the war, even as U.S. forces were progressively withdrawn.

In the last major battle of his four-year command, the "Easter Offensive" of 1972, Abrams disposed primarily air and naval forces to help greatly improved South Vietnamese forces repulse a massive North Vietnamese conventional invasion.

Named army chief of staff, Abrams worked to rebuild an army badly damaged by the long conflict in Vietnam, stressing combat readiness and taking care of soldiers while developing key combat systems. General John Vessey later noted, "When Americans watched the stunning success of our armed forces in DESERT STORM, they were watching the Abrams vision in action. The modern equipment, the effective air support, the use of the reserve components and, most important of all, the advanced training which

1

taught our people how to stay alive on the battlefield were all seeds planted by Abe." Abrams died of cancer in Washington, D.C., on 4 September 1974.

See also ARMY, U.S.; VIETNAM WAR, COURSE OF.

Further reading: Sorley, Lewis. *Thunderbolt: General Creighton Abrams and the Army of His Times.* New York: Simon & Schuster, 1992; Sorley, Lewis. *A Better War: The Unexamined Victories and Final Tragedy of America's Last Years in Vietnam.* New York: Harcourt Brace, 1999.

— Lewis Sorley

African Americans in the military

Men and women of African descent have participated in every major conflict in U.S. history and have contributed meaningfully to the nation's armed forces in numerous combat and support roles. In the course of their service they have encountered varying degrees of racism and resistance from white officers and comrades, reflecting the nation's cultural attitudes regarding race. Often recruited only at times of manpower shortage, African Americans historically found themselves considered to be unequal and inferior to white troops. Antagonism between black and white soldiers and from civilian populations near military bases led to a number of violent encounters. African-American military service, however, has been an important factor in the civil rights movement in American society at large.

African Americans participated in colonial military actions as slaves or servants of white masters, performing a variety of duties. Because British colonists were concerned about attacks by the French and Spanish settlers on their Indian allies, free African Americans and slaves were encouraged to join colonial militia units to defend British settlements. But many colonies passed laws forbidding African Americans from peacetime military service, because colonists feared slave rebellions.

Approximately 5,000 African Americans, both freedmen and slaves, fought in the American Revolutionary War. Many African Americans allied themselves with the British and Loyalists in the hope of securing their freedom, as promised by Virginia's royal governor, LORD DUNMORE, who established the Ethiopian Regiment.

In May 1776 the Continental Congress declared that only free males could join the CONTINENTAL ARMY. Worried about slave uprisings, colonists tried to restrict African Americans from fighting, but the shortage of white soldiers provided opportunities for blacks. In January 1776, Rhode Island passed the Slave Enlistment Act, which created a slave battalion, the 1st Rhode Island Regiment. In 1778, 800 blacks fought in the 1778 Battle of MONMOUTH COURT HOUSE. African Americans also served aboard Commodore John Paul JONES'S *BONHOMME RICHARD* in its engagement with HMS *Serapis*.

The American Revolution was the catalyst for Vermont to abolish slavery in 1777 and for New Jersey to initiate gradual emancipation in 1804. In the South, however, conditions for blacks became more restrictive. In 1792 Congress passed the MILITIA ACT, which prohibited blacks from militia service. The Marine Corps, on its creation in 1798, also excluded African Americans. On the other hand, the U.S. Navy encouraged blacks to serve.

African Americans played notable roles in the U.S. Navy during the War of 1812, constituting 10 percent of U.S. Navy personnel strength by war's end.

Racial discrimination increased in peacetime, and in 1820 the army declared that African Americans would not be accepted as recruits. By 1839, the navy had limited blacks to 5 percent of the force. Most African Americans who fought in the FIRST and SECOND SEMINOLE WARS were "maroons" (escaped slaves) who joined the Native Americans' forces. Most blacks who participated in the MEXICAN-AMERICAN WAR were the servants of white officers.

The CIVIL WAR addressed issues, specifically slavery, that directly concerned African Americans. Federal officials initially refused to enlist black soldiers because they were concerned that this might provoke border states to join the Confederacy. Some Union commanders, however, employed African Americans as laborers. Congress finally approved the use of black troops in 1862, and ultimately some 200,000 African Americans fought for the Union (10 percent of the army and 25 percent of the navy). An unknown number of enslaved African Americans accompanied masters into the field and thus unofficially fought for the Confederacy, which officially approved the use of African-American troops in March 1865, too late to have any impact on the war.

During the war many slaves ran away from their Southern masters to join invading Union forces as cooks, nurses, or sentries. Initially classified as "contraband of war," some of these escaped slaves were organized into such units as the 1st South Carolina Colored Volunteers (1862). In January 1863 the Emancipation Proclamation, freeing slaves in those parts of the Confederacy still in rebellion, brought more blacks into the military. In May 1863 regiments composed of African-American soldiers and white officers were mustered into the U.S. Colored Troops organization, a branch of the volunteer army.

During the war Union African-American soldiers fought in 449 military engagements in all theaters. By war's end, they constituted two-thirds of the Mississippi Valley forces. African-American soldiers endured minuscule pay (their pay was not made equal to that of whites until June 1864), strenuous assignments, and humiliating, often

African Americans have made important contributions to all U.S. wars. This photograph shows members of an African-American regiment on leave in France during World War I.   *(National Archives)*

abusive, treatment from whites. Few blacks were promoted to officer ranks. Segregated units experienced 35 percent higher losses than white troops because many Confederate troops targeted black soldiers, and some declined to take African Americans as prisoners. More than 100 black soldiers, who had surrendered, were killed in the FORT PILLOW massacre.

Black troops formed part of the Reconstruction occupation forces in the South until 1867. Two beneficial results of the Civil War were the Fourteenth (1868) and Fifteenth (1870) Amendments to the Constitution, which promised African Americans citizenship and provided suffrage for black males. Consequently, however, racism intensified in the late 19th century, as manifested in stricter social segregation, de facto disenfranchisement, and lynchings.

African-American military achievements during the Civil War were denigrated, and the first black U.S. Military Academy cadets, James Webster Smith and Henry O. FLIPPER, endured racial persecution. Despite reduced defense budgets, Congress mandated African-American regiments for the postwar regular army, which resulted originally in six but finally four permanent units: the 24th and 25th Infantry and the 9th and 10th Cavalry. Known by the Indians as the BUFFALO SOLDIERS, African Americans fought in the American West, Mexico, Cuba, and the Philippines. The navy, meanwhile, reduced the number of its black sailors, claiming that it needed specialists, such as engineers, for its new steamships.

War again changed the atmosphere, and World War I offered African Americans more military opportunities.

Approximately 200,000 black soldiers served with the AMERICAN EXPEDITIONARY FORCES (AEF), although some 90 percent of them were in service and labor battalions behind the front lines. Two black army combat divisions, the 92d and 93d Divisions, were organized, however. The 93d Division served with the French army, which proved more receptive to black soldiers. Enduring 191 days at the front, the 93d had a 35 percent casualty rate.

Because of antagonism toward black cadets at the service academies, the National Association for the Advancement of Colored People (NAACP) promoted the creation of the Colored Officers' Training Camp at Fort Dodge, Des Moines, Iowa. During World War I, 639 African-American officers completed officer candidate school. Although African Americans made up 13 percent of troop strength, slightly less than 1 percent of the officer corps was black. Acceptance of African-American troops also suffered because of the Houston Mutiny of 23 August 1917, in which soldiers from the 3d Battalion of the 24th Infantry engaged in a riot in which 20 people, most of them whites, died. This led to courts-martial; 19 African-American soldiers were executed.

Racism intensified during the postwar period and depression. World War II again opened opportunities for the achievement of black military aspirations, chiefly because of the extensive manpower needs. On 25 June 1941, President Franklin D. ROOSEVELT signed Executive Order 8802, which created the Fair Employment Practice Commission. It prohibited government agencies from practicing racial discrimination in hiring for defense work. Integration was not immediate, and blacks still encountered segregation and racism.

The NAACP promoted a "Double-V campaign," demanding victory against both fascism abroad and racism at home. At first, the army's black military population was limited to 6 percent, in primarily noncombat positions. In 1940 President Roosevelt had arranged for each military branch to have both combatant and noncombatant African-American units. The first such unit was the 758th Tank Battalion. Early the next year, the U.S. Army Air Corps commissioned the first black pilots (the acclaimed Tuskegee Airmen). Also, the Marine Corps admitted its first African-American recruits; ultimately almost 20,000 African-American marines trained at Montford Point during the war. Black soldiers accounted for a maximum of 8.7 percent of army strength, 15 percent of them seeing combat. Black American sailors constituted 5 percent of the navy. The navy commissioned its first black officers in 1944 and assigned them to the destroyer escort USS *Mason* (DE 529), which had an African-American crew. Black American women were also permitted to join the Women's Army Auxiliary Corps (WAAC).

During the war the army initiated integration of officer candidate schools, transportation, and recreational facilities. In the desperate circumstances of the Battle of the BULGE, 2,600 black soldiers were integrated with white troops. Nine black soldiers received the Distinguished Service Cross during World War II; seven of these were upgraded to the Medal of Honor in 1997.

Veterans, frustrated upon returning home to encounter increased prejudice and intolerance, demanded the abolishment of segregation in the military. On 26 July 1948, President Harry S. TRUMAN signed Executive Order 9981, mandating the integration of armed forces and creating the President's Committee on Equality of Treatment and Opportunity in the Armed Services. Thus the military became the first large institution in the United States to integrate.

The first integrated U.S. combat units fought in the KOREAN WAR, and almost 90 percent of African-American soldiers fought in integrated units when the war concluded. The final segregated unit was terminated in 1954. Success in racial integration in the military had a profound impact on the 1960s Civil Rights movement in American society at large.

During the VIETNAM WAR, conscription fell disproportionately on poor African Americans, who also believed they were assigned the most dangerous duties. Some African-American leaders began to question the national commitment to racial equality. Following the Vietnam War, the U.S. military set out to improve race relations and to enhance promotion opportunities for African Americans. General Colin L. POWELL, who directed the military buildup to the Persian Gulf War, was the first African-American chairman of the Joint Chiefs of Staff.

Many African Americans saw the peacetime volunteer military as an opportunity to secure economic and educational goals, and they joined in numbers greater than the proportion of blacks to the general population. By 1996 African Americans represented almost 22 percent of the total enlisted military forces: 30.2 percent of the army, 18.5 percent of the navy, 17.1 percent of the marines, and 16.8 percent of the air force. Their presence has been an asset to the U.S. military.

Further reading: Davis, Lenwood G., and George Hill. *Blacks in the American Armed Forces 1776–1983: A Bibliography.* Westport, Conn.: Greenwood, 1985; Nalty, Bernard C. *Strength for the Fight: A History of Black Americans in the Military.* New York: Free Press, 1986; Voelz, Peter M. *Slave and Soldier: The Military Impact of Blacks in the Colonial Americas.* New York: Garland, 1993; Westheider, James E. *Fighting on Two Fronts: African Americans and the Vietnam War.* New York: New York University Press, 1991.

— Elizabeth D. Schafer

Aguinaldo, Emilio (1869–1964) *Filipino independence leader and president of the first Philippine Republic, 1899–1902*

A mestizo of Chinese and Tagalog descent, Emilio Aguinaldo was born 23 March 1869 near Cavite, Luzon, in the Philippines. He became Kawit City's mayor in January 1895 and soon afterward joined the anti-Spanish Katipunan independence movement, achieving several military successes. Factional differences soon weakened Aguinaldo's proclaimed revolutionary government, and in a negotiated settlement in early 1898 he and 40 followers agreed to leave the Philippines for Hong Kong in exchange for $400,000.

Both parties soon reneged on their agreement. Aguinaldo made contact with American diplomats and naval officers in Hong Kong and Singapore, including the commander of the U.S. Pacific Squadron, Admiral George DEWEY. The outbreak of the SPANISH-AMERICAN WAR soon brought Dewey's victory over the Spanish in the Battle of MANILA BAY, whereupon he despatched a ship to restore Aguinaldo to the Philippines.

Aguinaldo assumed command of the revived indigenous anti-Spanish revolutionary movement, routing Spanish troops throughout the archipelago and proclaiming an independent Philippine republic. The arrival of large American forces in July 1898 and Spain's cession of the Philippines to the United States soon triggered outright Philippine-American hostilities. Aguinaldo led an often-effective anti-American guerrilla independence movement until his capture in March 1901 by troops under Brigadier General Frederick FUNSTON.

Aguinaldo subsequently swore allegiance to the United States, accepted an American pension, and ran unsuccessfully for the Philippine presidency in 1935. However, from 1941 to 1945 he collaborated with the Japanese occupation forces; this action and Aguinaldo's earlier involvement in the deaths of several revolutionary rivals severely tarnished his reputation as a Philippine independence hero. He died on 6 February 1964 at Quezon City.

See also PHILIPPINE-AMERICAN WAR.

Further reading: Achútegui, Pedro S. de, and Miguel A. Bernard. *Aguinaldo and the Revolution of 1896: A Documentary History.* Manila: Ateneo de Manila, 1972; Brands, H. W. *Bound to Empire: The United States and the Philippines.* New York: Oxford University Press, 1992; De los Santos, Epifanio. *The Revolutionists: Aguinaldo, Bonifacio, Jacinto.* Edited by Teodoro A. Agoncillo. Manila: National Historical Commission, 1973; Saulo, Alfredo B. *Aguinaldo: Generalissimo and President of the First Philippine Republic—First Republic in Asia.* Quezon City: Phoenix, 1983.

— Priscilla Roberts

Ainsworth, Frederick C. (1852–1934) *U.S. Army adjutant general*

Born on 11 September 1852 at Woodstock, Vermont, Frederick Crayton Ainsworth briefly attended Dartmouth College. He then trained as a physician, graduating in 1874 from the University of the City of New York. That September Ainsworth became an assistant surgeon in the army, serving in Alaska, Arizona, and Texas before his appointment in 1885 as recorder of the Army Medical Examining Board in New York City.

In December 1886 Ainsworth was named head of the Records and Pensions Division in the surgeon general's office, moving permanently to Washington, D.C. He demonstrated exceptional administrative and organizational ability in streamlining and consolidating medical and service records, materials previously in such disorder that they had proved unequal to the growing demands that generous Civil War–related legislation—pensions and medical benefits to Union army veterans—imposed on them. Ainsworth transferred data from fragile paper files to a centralized card-index system, introduced new business procedures, and soon cleared a substantial backlog of cases. Impressed by his success, Congress in July 1889 established a broader Record and Pension Division of the War Department as part of the office of the secretary of war, merging Ainsworth's existing bureau with portions of the office of adjutant general. Heading the new division, Ainsworth repeated his earlier successes, establishing orderly administration and eliminating the backlog.

In 1892 Congress created a separate Record and Pension Division, headed by Ainsworth, who won promotion to colonel and directly controlled more than half the War Department's employees. Since his office gradually assumed responsibility for records from U.S. wars, Ainsworth's work contributed substantially to the holdings and ultimate establishment of the National Archives. In 1904 the division merged with the Adjutant General's Office to become the Military Secretary's Department, which Ainsworth headed, retaining his position in 1907 when its name reverted to Adjutant General's Office.

Although Ainsworth hoped in 1910 to become army chief of staff, that position went to Leonard WOOD. Friction between the two men over reorganization led to Ainsworth's suspension; in 1912 he resigned rather than face court-martial. In retirement he continued to advise many military officers, and he played a substantial role in drafting the 1916 NATIONAL DEFENSE ACT. Ainsworth died at Washington, D.C., on 5 June 1934.

See also ROOT, ELIHU; STIMSON, HENRY L.

Further reading: Deutrich, Mabel E. *Struggle for Supremacy: The Career of General Fred C. Ainsworth.* Washington, D.C.: Public Affairs Press, 1962; Riepma,

Siert F. "A Soldier-Archivist and His Records." *American Archivist* 4 (July 1941), 178–87.

— Priscilla Roberts

airborne forces *Troops dropped by parachute from aircraft*

Airborne operations seek to place forces on the ground in enemy rear areas to seize key points, destroy logistics and communications, and facilitate a simultaneous attack by other forces to the enemy front. Airborne forces rely on surprise and local superiority to overwhelm defenders, and they can produce psychological effects disproportionate to their numbers. But since airborne forces are usually lightly armed, they can be destroyed before they can be relieved by friendly ground forces, should defending forces learn the enemy offensive plan or happen to have armor prepositioned near where they land.

Italy and the USSR pioneered the airborne concept. In the 1920s, Italy formed an airborne company and developed the "static line" parachute, which opens automatically as the soldier exits the plane. The Soviets developed an extensive airborne doctrine in the late 1920s and utilized airborne forces on a small scale against insurgents in Central Asia. By 1936 they had essentially established an airborne doctrine. France established an airborne school near Avignon and created two airborne companies in 1938 but soon disbanded them. Italy established an airborne school in Libya in 1938 and then in Italy proper. The small, defensively oriented armies of Britain and the United States conducted no serious airborne work before 1940.

German strategists understood the impact that airborne forces could have on blitzkrieg warfare. Major General Kurt Student formed the 7th Flieger Division in July 1938. His troops saw action in Poland, in Norway, and most notably in the invasion of the Low Countries in May 1940. They captured key defensive positions and bridges, holding them until conventional forces could come up. Their last major deployment was in the invasion of Crete in May 1941. In that attack, thanks to ULTRA, the British knew in advance the German drop zones and exacted a terrible price from the airborne forces; more than 5,000 parachute and glider troops died. The Germans were ultimately successful. Adolf Hitler, however, concluded that the days of airborne forces were over and thereafter used his parachute units only as elite infantry.

In response to the German invasion of France and the Low Countries, the Soviets formed five airborne corps of three brigades each before June 1941. Crete had helped convince the Soviets, British, and Americans of the utility of such units. Britain first created battalion-sized raiding units and then the 1st Airborne Division.

The U.S. Army also experimented with airborne techniques, beginning with 50 men in June 1940 at Fort Benning, Georgia. By mid-1941 the army had established four battalions. Beginning in August 1942, the U.S. 82d and 101st Divisions underwent conversion into airborne units. That same year the United States formed its first glider regiment at Fort Bragg, North Carolina. Tension arose between traditionalist infantry commanders and the airborne leaders over the longer training time necessary for the parachute troops, the utilization of airborne units, and the length of their deployment in battle. There was even discussion prior to OPERATION TORCH, the November 1942 Anglo-American invasion of North Africa, of disbanding the 82d and 101st and converting them to infantry divisions.

U.S. airborne forces were first employed in the war during Operation Torch, when a battalion of the 82d Airborne dropped into Algeria. Things did not go well; there were problems locating the drop zones. The July 1943 Allied invasion of SICILY witnessed the first U.S. Army regimental-sized parachute drop. Paratroopers dropped behind Axis lines to protect the invasion beaches from counterattack became a key element of the Allied plan. High winds and a night drop again produced wide dispersion, but this dispersion confused the defenders as to actual Allied objectives and led them to believe they were confronting a much larger force than was actually the case.

In June 1944 the U.S. 82d and 101st Airborne Divisions and the British 6th Airborne Division participated in the NORMANDY INVASION (Operation Overlord). Dropped the night before the beach landings, they shielded the invasion sites from German counterattack, fighting on the ground for several weeks. The wide dispersion of the drop again confused the Germans, and the airborne forces played an important role in the Allied success.

In August 1944 an ad hoc division dropped into southern France to support Operation Dragoon. Many of these men were dropped too soon and were lost in the Mediterranean Sea. Another problem was the weight of equipment. The Germans dropped their paratroops without weapons, which left them largely defenseless on the ground until they could locate their bundles of weapons; U.S. paratroops carried 100-pound loads, including a reserve chute. They were the only Allied airborne forces to have reserve chutes.

In September 1944 the 82d and 101st Divisions, the 1st British Division, and a Polish brigade dropped on Holland as the airborne element of OPERATION MARKET-GARDEN. An airborne carpet 50 miles long was to secure key bridges, enabling the British XXX Corps to race to Arnhem. The ground forces were unable to move as swiftly as planned, however; German units reacted more swiftly, denying the Allies their objective, a bridgehead over the

Rhine. The British 1st Division, dropped at Arnhem, was stymied by German tank divisions. Dropped some distance from its objective, most of the division was unable to reach it because of the panzers.

The 82d and 101st fought as infantry in the Battle of the BULGE (Ardennes) in December 1944–January 1945.

The last major airborne drop of the war was Operation Varsity. On 24 March 1945, the British 6th and U.S. 17th Airborne Divisions dropped to support the Rhine crossing. In terms of troops, planes, and gliders employed, Varsity was an even larger single drop than Market-Garden. Casualties were heavy, but there were a number of accurate drops, and the airborne forces then advanced across Germany until May. There was discussion of using the 82d Airborne Division for a drop into Berlin, but General Dwight EISENHOWER opposed the plan, which would have been costly in terms of casualties. Another U.S. airborne division, the 13th, arrived in France in February 1945, but it never saw combat.

The Pacific theater was generally unsuitable for large-scale airborne drops, although Japan employed airborne battalions in Indonesia in early 1942. The U.S. 11th Airborne Division participated in the Retaking of the PHILIPPINES, fighting on Leyte Island after November 1944 and then dropping onto Luzon Island in January 1945. The 11th fought on Luzon until June and afterward participated in the occupation of Japan.

After the war, attempts were made by traditionalists to disband U.S. airborne units. This effort failed, but gliders were eliminated entirely, their place being taken by helicopters.

During the KOREAN WAR the U.S. Army conducted two brigade-sized airborne drops, but airmobile (helicopter-transported) forces proved more effective. Airmobile units such as the 101st Airborne served with distinction in Vietnam. The 173d Airborne Brigade made the only major airborne drop of the VIETNAM WAR, in Tay Ninh Province in February 1967. The 3d Brigade of the 82d served in Vietnam from February 1968 until December 1969.

Airborne forces continued to serve as quick-reaction formations. The 82d intervened in the Dominican Republic (1965), in GRENADA (1983), and in PANAMA (1989). The 82d and 101st deployed to Saudi Arabia during OPERATION DESERT SHIELD in response to Iraq's 1990 invasion of Kuwait. During OPERATION DESERT STORM in 1991 the two divisions screened the flanks of the "left hook" when ground combat began. They remain elite units, available for global deployment at short notice.

See also GAVIN, JAMES M.; RIDGWAY, MATTHEW B.; TAYLOR, MAXWELL, D.

Further reading: Ambrose, Stephen E. *Pegasus Bridge, June 6, 1944.* New York: Simon & Schuster, 1985; Blair, Clay. *Ridgway's Paratroopers: The American Airborne in World War II.* New York: Quill, 1985; Gavin, James M. *Airborne Warfare.* Washington, D.C.: U.S. Government Printing Office, 1947; Hickey, Michael. *Out of the Sky: A History of Airborne Warfare.* New York: Scribner, 1979.

— James Perry and Spencer C. Tucker

aircraft, fixed-wing *Survey of the most important aircraft used by the armed services*
At Kitty Hawk, North Carolina, on 17 December 1903, Orville and Wilbur WRIGHT conducted the world's first manned airplane flight. The Wright brothers believed that the airplane would soon gain military acceptance for reconnaissance and possibly serve as a deterrent to future wars.

In 1908 the Wrights signed a contract with the War Department to produce the Wright Military Flyer for the army SIGNAL CORPS. Eight planes of the First Aero Squadron served in the PUNITIVE EXPEDITION INTO MEXICO in 1916–17, one of them crashing on its maiden flight. Congress ultimately appropriated $500,000 for the Air Service to buy 24 new planes, although none arrived in Mexico in time to be useful.

The army came to see the airplane's potential for battlefield reconnaissance and bombing missions. The Curtiss Company became the chief supplier of U.S. military aircraft. When the United States entered World War I, the army had only 250 aircraft and five balloons in its inventory. The priority was on getting men, as opposed to heavy equipment, to Europe, and this led to a U.S. reliance on British and French aircraft.

During World War I the most impressive U.S. aircraft was a trainer, the Curtiss JN-4 Jenny. A collaboration between Glenn CURTISS and British engineer B. D. Thomas of Sopwith, it began as a trainer for the army and navy. The Jenny had a long service life, from 1915 to 1927; more than 6,000 were produced for the Army Air Service, U.S. Navy, Royal Flying Corps, and the Royal Canadian Air Force.

Curtiss also produced many reconnaissance and bomber aircraft to deal with the German U-boat threat in the Atlantic. One of the most important of these was the H-12 Large America flying boat, an impressive aircraft for its day. It was designed in collaboration with the Royal Naval Air Service, but when the United States entered the war the U.S. Navy purchased 20 for the North Atlantic. More than 500 were in use by the end of the war, principally in convoy protection. The H-12 was also the first American-manufactured plane to shoot down an enemy aircraft and the first to destroy a submarine. It remained in service until 1921.

The United States also utilized the British de Havilland D.H.4 (DH-4, U.S. designation) Liberty as a reconnaissance

Two Army Service Curtiss JN-4 Jennys   *(San Diego Aerospace Museum)*

aircraft and light bomber. The American version replaced the British engine with a 400-horsepower Liberty engine. A total of 4,864 were built for the U.S. Army. It was the only American-built airplane to fly over German-held territory in World War I, and it flew the most bombing missions of any U.S.-manufactured plane, more than 150. After the war the Liberty remained the principal U.S. Army bomber; upgrades included new and more powerful engines. In 1923 army aviators flying the DH-4 shattered the world's endurance record for time aloft. The DH-4 remained in service as a utility aircraft until 1932.

In 1921 the U.S. Army operated nearly 3,000 aircraft. These included 1,500 Curtiss Jennies (JN-4) trainers; 1,100 DH-4Bs for observation; 179 SE-5 pursuit aircraft (a British design); and 12 Martin MB-2s. The Martin was an American-designed and -built twin-engined bomber, the first indigenous design adopted into service.

With military budgets sharply reduced and in light of rapid technological advancement, the army decided to put 25 percent of its aviation budget into research and development for new types of aircraft and engines. Most World War I aircraft had been biplanes covered with linen. Changes after the war included the introduction of monoplanes, all-metal fuselages, and far more powerful engines.

In the late 1920s the U.S. Navy received the Boeing F2B fighter, intended as both a fighter and bomber. The navy employed this agile aircraft in its first-ever acrobatic team, the Three Seahawks. In service only from 1928 to 1932, the F2B was a biplane, with a fabric-covered fuselage.

The F2B was replaced by a series of Grumman biplanes that set a long-term trend in naval fighter design. The Grumman FF-1, which entered service in 1933, was the first U.S. naval fighter equipped with retractable landing gear, the placement of which produced a rotund

A North American B-25C Mitchell. This excellent medium bomber provided excellent service during World War II and was the most widely exported U.S. bomber.   *(San Diego Aerospace Museum)*

fuselage appearance. The fuselage itself was all-metal and had one of the first enclosed canopies. The FF-2, an improved FF-1, was Grumman's first single-seat fighter. Able to climb quickly and highly maneuverable, the FF-2 was in service during 1935–40. The F3F was the navy's last biplane fighter. An improved F2F, it served from 1936 to 1940. The series of three Grumman biplane fighters led directly to the F4F Wildcat and F6F Hellcat.

In 1939, the Grumman biplanes were followed by the Brewster F2A Buffalo, the navy's first monoplane in squadron service. Slow and insufficiently maneuverable, it was completely outclassed by the Bf-109 Messerschmitt and Japanese Zero. The bulk of the 507 planes produced went to Britain, Finland, and the Netherlands. In the U.S. Navy, the F2A was taken out of service after the 1942 Battle of MIDWAY.

The army's first all-metal monoplane entered service in 1934. The Boeing P-26 Peashooter was the last U.S. Army Air Corps fighter designed with an open cockpit and fixed landing gear. The P-26 was also the first U.S. military aircraft to exceed 225 mph, and its relatively high landing speed of 75 mph required that it be fitted with flaps. The Peashooter remained in service with the Army Air Corps until 1939. It also served in the Philippines air force during the Japanese invasion of 1941.

The Curtiss P-40 Warhawk entered service in 1940 and was the most important aircraft in America's first two years in the war. The P-40 was exported to Great Britain, where it was known as the Kittyhawk or Tomahawk. It lacked the speed and altitude capabilities of the Me-109, although the P-40 gained fame with the American Volunteer Group (Claire CHENNAULT's Flying Tigers) in China. With a speed

Boeing B-17 Flying Fortress. The B-17 was one of the most famous bombers in U.S. history. This photograph shows a B-17G of the 385th Bomb Group, Eighth Air Force, c. 1944.   *(San Diego Aerospace Museum)*

of 352 mph, it was far heavier than the Zero. It was solidly built, and Chennault's tactics made effective use of its capabilities. It went through 10 models until 1944, when it was withdrawn from production. By the end of the war 28 countries employed the aircraft.

The Bell P-39 Aircobra was another first-line U.S. Army aircraft; it entered service in early 1941. The P-39's design developed around its unique armament of one 37-mm cannon, firing through the propeller shaft. The P-39 also had a retractable tricycle landing gear, the first time such an arrangement had been used in a U.S. fighter. No match for the Zero in one-on-one combat, the P-39 excelled in ground-support operations. Of 9,558 P-39s produced during the war, half went to the Soviet Union, which used them for tactical air support.

The twin-engine, twin-boom design Lockheed P-38 Lightning (9,923 produced) entered service in 1942.

Developed to meet the Army Air Corps's need for a long-range interceptor, the P-38 was heavily armed and fast. One of the best fighters and the largest single-seat aircraft of the war, it was not as maneuverable as other fighters, but it was highly versatile. It shot down more Japanese aircraft than any other U.S. airplane. Reconnaissance versions remained in service until 1949.

The Republic P-47 Thunderbolt first flew in 1941. It could outdive any German plane and was a fine high-altitude fighter, but it also excelled as a ground-support fighter-bomber. The P-47 had the largest production run, 15,683 planes, of any American single-engine aircraft of World War II. P-47 pilots thought it was the best single-engine heavy fighter of the war, and it continued in service thereafter in the air forces of a dozen countries.

The premier U.S. fighter was the North American P-51 Mustang, which first flew in 1940. Developed for Britain, the original model was, however, underpowered. The British replaced its Allison engine with a Rolls-Royce engine, and the resulting aircraft outperformed all other piston-engine fighters in the European theater of operations. It may have been the best fighter aircraft of the war. Fitted with drop tanks, the Mustangs and Thunderbolts could escort bomber formations on raids deep into the industrial heart of Germany, drastically reducing bomber losses. The Mustang remained in service through the KOREAN WAR, during which it was employed as a close-support aircraft. By 1945, 15,686 had been produced. Ultimately 55 countries employed the Mustang in their air forces.

By the time of the U.S. entry into World War II, the navy had largely replaced the Buffalo with the Grumman F4F Wildcat fighter. The F4F served in the early cam-paigns of the Pacific theater. Overmatched in maneuverability and speed by the Japanese Zero, it was nonetheless ruggedly built. By the time it was removed from service in 1944, the Wildcat had achieved a seven-to-one kill ratio against Japanese planes, chiefly the result of superior U.S. pilot training and tactics.

In 1940 Vought conceived the gull-wing F4U Corsair fighter for the navy. The F4U entered service in 1942 and saw action throughout the Pacific. Initially flown solely from land bases, it was fitted with arresting gear for operations from an aircraft carrier. The Marine Corps flew the F4U; VMF 214 (the Black Sheep Squadron), flying over the northern Solomons and Rabaul, produced at least 10 aces. The F4U remained in production after the war and saw combat in Korea, where it scored against jet aircraft. By the end of its service life in 1952, 12,681 had been produced.

A Douglas C-47 Skytrain, military version of the DC-3, belonging to the 98th Troop Carrier Squadron, 440th Troop Carrier Group, Ninth Air Force, based at Devon, England, in 1944 *(San Diego Aerospace Museum)*

The other chief front-line navy fighter during World War II was the Grumman F6F Hellcat, in service from 1943 to 1952. It had the highest kill ratio of any U.S. aircraft in World War II—19:1. The F6F could outclimb and outrun (at 376 mph) the Zero. Strongly built, it was also the navy's first night-fighter. A total of 12,275 F6Fs were built, many of which remained in service through the Korean War.

Navy requirements for a torpedo bomber were met by the Douglas Aircraft Corporation's TBD Devastator, which entered service in 1940. A single-engine, low-wing aircraft with a three-man crew, it was quickly outdated as a consequence of its slow speed and difficulty in handling. Thirty-six of 41 TBDs sent against the Japanese fleet in the Battle of MIDWAY were shot down; shortly thereafter the navy retired the airplane.

Douglas also produced the navy's principal carrier dive-bomber, the SBD Dauntless. It entered service in 1940 and saw service until the end of the war. It sank more than 300,000 tons of Japanese shipping; in the Battle of the CORAL SEA and at Midway it sank a total of five Japanese aircraft carriers. A ruggedly built aircraft, the SBD could absorb substantial punishment. A total of 5,321 SBD Dauntless aircraft were produced for the navy.

The Grumman TBF Avenger, meanwhile, had replaced the Devastator in 1942 and had become the navy's best torpedo bomber of the war. The Avenger featured a patented Grumman system of rearward-folding wings for stowage on board of aircraft carriers. The TBF had a ball turret in the rear of the fuselage and an enclosed bomb bay. The TBF saw action in every major battle in the Pacific after 1943 and helped to sink the Japanese battleships *Musashi* and *Yamato.* Grumman and General Motors produced a total of 9,836. After the war only a few were retained in service, transformed into antisubmarine aircraft.

U.S. Air Force F-100 Super Sabre in flight over South Vietnam, September 1970   *(U.S. Air Force photograph)*

Paratroopers of the 187th Regimental Combat Team put on parachutes and "Mae West" life preservers before boarding a 483d Troop Carrier Wing U.S. Air Force C-119 "Flying Boxcar," en route to Korea from southern Japan.   *(National Archives)*

The Curtiss SB2C Helldiver was the primary navy dive-bomber later in the war. It entered service in 1943, and 7,002 were produced. The Helldiver had an internal bomb bay and could carry a payload under its wings as well. However, it was difficult to handle and plagued with mechanical problems; its crews dubbed it "the beast."

Of medium bombers employed by the army, the most important was the North American B-25 Mitchell. This twin-engined aircraft had a crew of three to six men and could carry 3,000 pounds of bombs. It carried out the celebrated April 1942 raid on TOKYO and was the most widely exported U.S. bomber. Great Britain, China, Australia, and the Soviet Union were among those employing the B-25 in the war. More than 11,000 were built, and some stayed in service up to 1959 as trainers.

The twin-engine Martin B-26 Marauder, in service from 1941 to 1946, sustained the lowest loss ratio of any U.S. bomber in World War II. It was also the only U.S.

Army plane rigged to drop torpedoes. By war's end, some 5,200 of the speedy M-26s had been built. An additional 272 served the navy (under the designation JM) as target tugs.

The most successful army light bomber of the war was the Douglas A-20 Havoc, which entered service at the end of 1941. A total of 7,385 were produced. Armed with four nose-mounted .50-caliber machine guns and capable of carrying 2,600 pounds of bombs, it was a formidable ground-support aircraft. The French, British, and Russians all flew the Havoc, with 3,000 A-20s going to the Soviet Union alone.

Prior to World War II, leaders of the Army Air Corps believed emphatically in STRATEGIC BOMBING and devoted most of the branch's research and development resources to a heavy bomber. The first U.S. heavy bomber was the Boeing B-17 Flying Fortress. Sold to Congress as a coast-defense weapon, the B-17 first flew in 1935; it entered

Two F-14A Tomcats of Fighter Squadron 14 from the carrier USS *John F. Kennedy*   *(San Diego Aerospace Museum)*

service with the Army Air Corps in 1937. The four-engine B-17 had a crew of nine men and could carry a bomb load of up to 4,000 pounds. Designed to be self-defending, along the lines of Guilio Douhet's "Battle Plane," it had 10 to 13 .50-caliber machine guns mounted in turrets on the top and the bottom of the fuselage and in side mounts that could cover the rest of the plane from enemy fighters. The B-17 was designed to withstand heavy punishment from antiaircraft fire and enemy aircraft. Appearing in many variations, it formed the backbone of the American strategic bombing campaign against German industrial targets in the war. A total of 12,371 were produced. It was arguably the most celebrated U.S. plane of the war.

The twin-finned Consolidated B-24 Liberator entered service in 1941. Intended as a complement to the B-17, its design was begun only in 1939. It had a crew of eight to 10 men; it was armed with 10 .50-caliber machine guns. The Liberator was a remarkable aircraft; a total of 18,188 were produced—more than any other bomber of World War II. Its exceptionally long range enabled the B-24 to play a key role in antisubmarine warfare in the Atlantic (the navy version was known as the PB4Y Privateer). By the end of 1944

the U.S. Army Air Forces operated more than 6,000 B-24s in the Pacific theater.

The Boeing B-29 Superfortress was the most sophisticated aircraft produced until that time and the best heavy bomber of World War II. Development began in 1941; the B-29 entered production in 1943. It was deployed only in the Pacific theater, arriving at bases in India and China in 1944. The four-engine B-29 was the first production bomber to have a pressurized fuselage. It could carry a payload of 20,000 pounds, although the usual load for long distances was half that amount. With a 32,000-foot ceiling, the B-29 could fly above most Japanese fighter aircraft. Flown by a crew of 10 men, it was armed with one 20 mm tail cannon and 10 .50-caliber machine guns in optically controlled power turrets. In addition to strategic bombing of the Japanese home islands, B-29s were used with great effectiveness to lay mines. In May and June 1945, B-29-laid mines sank an estimated half-million tons of Japanese shipping. In all, 3,970 B-29s were produced. Two were used to deliver atomic weapons against Hiroshima and Nagasaki, respectively, in August 1945.

The B-29 subsequently saw action during the Korean War as a strategic bomber against Communist lines of communication and supply, as well as other strategic targets, principally in North Korea. Vulnerable to the MiG-15 jet fighter, however, the B-29s were ultimately withdrawn from daylight service and ended their days in reconnaissance and weather duties.

The Douglas C-47 Skytrain, or "Gooney Bird," was the main U.S. transport aircraft. It entered service in 1940 and saw action in every theater of World War II, transporting personnel and material, deploying airborne forces, and performing medical evacuation. Notably, it was used to supply Chinese forces from India, crossing the "hump" of the Himalayan mountain range. More than 10,000 C-47s were built, and the aircraft remained in service with the air force until 1976. Many continue to fly today.

The Douglas C-54 Skymaster was the army's first four-engine transport. Originally designed as a passenger transport, it was quickly adapted for military use. The C-54 entered service in 1942 and served capably in World War II and during the subsequent BERLIN BLOCKADE.

Among patrol bombers, one of the finest was the Consolidated PBY Catalina flying boat. It entered service in 1941. Armed with four machine guns, it could carry up to 4,000 pounds of bombs, two torpedoes, or four depth charges. More PBYs (3,290) were produced than any other reconnaissance aircraft of the war. It was also widely used for search and rescue.

The Piper L-3 Grasshopper saw extensive use by the army in reconnaissance, liaison missions, and artillery spotting. It could take off and land almost anywhere, and it could operate off an aircraft carrier. It is still in use today as a private aircraft.

The piston-engine Douglas A-1 Skyraider joined the navy in 1946, too late for service in World War II. It was the principal navy attack aircraft during the Korean War. The Skyraider could carry 8,000 pounds of rockets and bombs and stay airborne for as long as 14 hours without refueling. Its usefulness was such that it was kept in service after the Korean War and was employed in the VIETNAM WAR by the U.S. and Republic of Vietnam air force for ground attack, search and rescue of downed pilots, and close-in support of ground units. This workhorse retired only in 1974.

The close of World War II witnessed the first widespread application of jet engine technology. The U.S. Air Force Lockheed F-80 Shooting Star, in development at the end of World War II, became the first mass-produced U.S. jet fighter. First introduced in 1946, it did not incorporate the swept-wing design, which put it at a disadvantage when facing the MiG-15. Some 1,700 were built. The F-80 served in Korea as a fighter-bomber in support of ground troops. In November 1950, though obsolete, it become the first jet fighter to shoot down another jet in combat. It was finally retired in 1956.

The mainstay of the air force in the Korean War and throughout the 1950s was the North American F-86 "Sabre." The first U.S. fighter produced with a swept-wing design, it entered service in 1949. During the Korean War it established an overall kill ratio of 10 to one against Soviet-made MiG-15 fighter aircraft (792 MiGs destroyed in combat, as opposed to only 76 Sabres). The Sabre remained in service with National Guard units until 1960.

The Navy McDonnell F2H Banshee was a highly maneuverable fighter employed during the Korean War to escort B-29 bombers and to attack ground targets. It entered production in 1947, and more than 800 were built. The F2H was very rugged and able to absorb punishment and yet return to base. It remained in service with the navy as reconnaissance aircraft until 1959.

Another navy aircraft to see action in Korea was the Grumman F9F Panther. With long, straight wings, the Panther was an ideal carrier plane, and more than 1,300 were produced for the navy. It was used largely as a fighter-bomber. A later version, the swept-wing F9F Cougar, became the first jet aircraft flown by the Blue Angels. It was retired in 1957.

Two other important aircraft entered service during this period. The Boeing B-47 Stratojet, which joined the air force in 1951, was the core of the STRATEGIC AIR COMMAND throughout the 1950s. It was the first heavy bomber to have such a small crew—three men. Stratojets could fly faster than many fighters and could be refueled in flight for extended range. With a payload of 20,000 pounds, the B-47 remained in service until 1966. Other reconnaissance models served longer; several were shot down gathering military intelligence along the peripheries of the Soviet Union.

One of the first aerial-refueling aircraft was the Boeing KC-97 Stratotanker, replacing the KB-29s. It began as a military transport, and 76 were built for that role, but when the Strategic Air Command needed a tanker for aerial refueling, Boeing added a fueling boom. A total of 812 KC-97s were built, and they remained in service with National Guard units until 1977.

In the category of post–World War II transport aircraft, in 1949 the air force introduced the twin-engine C-119 Flying Boxcar, the most famous cargo plane developed exclusively for military use. Known to its crew members as the Dollar Nineteen (for 119), it saw extensive use in the Korean War. A total of 1,112 were built, including 99 that went to the Marine Corps as R4Qs.

The Lockheed C-130 Hercules four engine transport entered service with the air force in 1956. It featured a shoulder-mounted wing and an inclined cargo door at the rear of the fuselage. More than 2,000 C-130s have been built, and it continues in service today.

Lockheed produced an innovative and important reconnaissance plane in 1956, the U-2. This aircraft was developed to overfly the Soviet Union at altitudes above 90,000 feet, requiring its pilot to wear a space suit. A U-2 flown by Francis Gary POWERS produced an international crisis when it was downed over the Soviet Union on a reconnaissance flight in May 1960. The U-2 provided important intelligence information during the 1962 CUBAN MISSILE CRISIS, and it remains in service.

The next steps in the advance of aviation technology were the guided weapons, improved onboard radar, increased speed and altitude, and greater performance. Weapons carried by the new aircraft became more precise and automated. Fighter aircraft became faster and possessed greater striking power.

One of the first of the new fighters was the Lockheed F-104 Starfighter. First introduced to the air force in 1958, it was a high-altitude interceptor. Some 300 of these planes were built, but because the F-104 suffered from a lack of range, it did not fulfill hopes as an interceptor. It was used briefly as a ground-attack aircraft. About 400 of these planes were exported as the F-104G, and many European countries were licensed to build it. The final version, the F-104S, is still flown by the Turkish air force. The F-104 was taken out of U.S. service in 1975.

The Convair F-102 Delta Dagger and F-106 Delta Dart were designed to protect the continental United States from Soviet bomber attack. The Delta Dart was the world's first delta-wing supersonic interceptor aircraft. Highly automated, the plane could be directed to its target by a ground defense network via a sophisticated fire-control system. More than 2,200 F-102s were manufactured, and the plane was in service from 1956 to 1976. The F-106 began as a modification of the F-102 but underwent so many changes, including a far more powerful engine, that a new designation was warranted. It too was highly automated. A total of 320 fighters and trainers were built. The F-106 entered service in 1959 and served until 1968.

The mainstay of the U.S. Air Force during the 1960s and 1970s was the McDonnell Douglas F-4 Phantom II. One of the finest military aircraft ever built, it was first produced for the navy. It could deliver 16,000 pounds of bombs, yet it was an excellent air-superiority fighter. The only two U.S. pilot aces of the Vietnam War, including Randall CUNNINGHAM, flew F-4s. During Operation ROLLING THUNDER, the bombing campaign against North Vietnam, the Phantom was employed in the "Wild Weasel" role (to locate and suppress ground antiaircraft sites) in the suppression of surface-to-air missiles (SAMs). Some 5,000 of the planes were produced for the navy, Marine Corps, air force, and foreign customers.

The air force's Republic F-105 Thunderchief was used as both as a fighter-bomber in the bombing of North Vietnam and in ground-support missions within South Vietnam. Entering service in 1958, the Thunderchief could carry 14,000 pounds of ordnance at high speed close to the ground. It could attain speeds greater than Mach 2, and it flew a majority of the bombing missions over Vietnam. One of the first all-weather aircraft, 833 F-105s were produced for the air force. A two-seat version of the plane was used in a "Wild Weasel" role. Even though it was primarily a ground-attack plane, the F-105 shot down 25 MiGs. It was retired from service in 1980.

The navy's principal light bomber throughout the Vietnam War was the Douglas A-4 Skyhawk. Though the smallest warplane of its era, it could carry a 9,000-pounds payload. The A-4 was tough and fast. A total of 2,960 were built for the navy and Marine Corps, and it was widely exported to other countries. It was retired in 1990 but is still widely employed around the world.

The navy Douglas A3D "Skywarrior" was the largest catapulted airplane of its time, designed to deliver nuclear weapons from an aircraft carrier. A total of 280 were built for the navy. The A3D had a 12,000-pound payload. During the Vietnam conflict it was used as an aerial-refueling platform and for reconnaissance and electronic surveillance. It was removed from service in 1993.

Grumman met the navy's need for an all-weather attack aircraft with the A-6 Intruder, which entered service in 1963. More than 700 were built for the navy and Marine Corps, and it became the backbone of navy attack forces. The A-6 could carry an 18,000-pound payload and had a crew of two. In its day it was the world's most versatile carrier aircraft. The A-6 served through the Gulf War and was then replaced by the F/A-18.

The General Dynamics F-111 Aardvark was a revolutionary long-range, high-speed airplane and the first production aircraft with swing-wing technology. The pilot could adjust the angle of the wing sweep in fight, depending on the speed he wished to attain. The F-111 entered the Vietnam War in 1968 without adequate testing; four crashed, probably as a consequence of the failure of their terrain-following radar. The Aardvark has a 31,500-pound payload. The last version, the FB-111, was a strategic deep-strike aircraft capable of carrying nuclear weapons.

The navy required in the 1960s a new aircraft for the combat-support role. Vought built the A-7 Corsair II to do this job. It was an excellent aircraft, capable of precise delivery of ordnance. The navy replaced the A-4 Skyhawk with the Corsair II in 1967. More than 1,500 were built for the navy; it was the primary carrier-based navy bomber until 1993, when it was replaced by the F/A-18 Hornet.

New heavy bombers were produced during this period as well. The most important of these was the Boeing B-52 Stratofortress. It entered service with the Strategic Air Command in 1955 and remains in service. It can carry approximately 70,000 pounds of mixed ordnance: bombs, mines, and missiles. In Vietnam it was used to carpet-bomb enemy positions in direct support of ground troops. Late in the war it was employed against North Vietnam in the LINEBACKER I and LINEBACKER II raids. B-52s are also employed in reconnaissance and mine laying, to attack shipping. The B-52 is the first warplane to remain in active service for half a century; in 2001 94 B-52s were still in operation.

The B-58 Hustler, built by Convair, was introduced in 1960 as a supersonic heavy bomber that could carry 7,000 pounds of bombs at Mach 2 speed over great distances. Some 116 of these planes were manufactured, but high maintenance costs led to their replacement with the FB-111 in 1969.

Another aircraft of the Vietnam era was the Grumman EA-6 Prowler. This version of the Intruder was equipped for electronic countermeasures. The Prowler was introduced in 1971 and has a crew of four. Its mission is to accompany bombers and suppress enemy air-defense radar sites. It carries six jamming pods. The EA-6 can also attack shipping by means of the Harpoon antiship missile. The navy currently has nine squadrons of EA-6 Prowlers.

Another important navy plane is the Grumman E-2 Hawkeye. First deployed in 1964, the airborne early-warning plane has a large rotating radar dome on top of its fuselage. Its radar systems can track 600 targets at once and vector 40 planes to those targets. It is still active in carrier battle group defense.

An important reconnaissance plane is the Lockheed SR-71 Blackbird. Entering service in 1966, the Blackbird is a high-speed, high-altitude reconnaissance aircraft (capable of achieving speeds of more than 2,300 mph and altitudes of 80,000 feet). It was developed after the shooting down of a U-2 piloted by Francis Gary Powers over the Soviet Union during the COLD WAR. The plane is made of heat-resistant titanium able to stretch up to 11 inches to allow for heat expansion during high-speed flight. The SR-71 was retired in 1991, but three were reactivated in 1995.

The Boeing KC-135 Stratotanker, first introduced in 1957, was the first jet designed specifically for aerial refueling. The KC-135 was adapted from the Boeing 387-80, a model of the 707. It can carry up to 31,000 gallons of jet fuel. It is still in service with air force and National Guard units.

The Grumman F-14 Tomcat was the first of the new breed of American fighter aircraft. It entered service in 1972 as a long-range interceptor and boasts a swept-wing design, with onboard computers that change the wing angle as required. The radar in the nose, the Hughes AWG-9, is capable of tracking 24 targets simultaneously; AIM-54 Phoenix missiles allow the Tomcat to engage targets at a range of 100 miles. Some 700 Tomcats form the backbone of navy fighter squadrons.

The air force's front-line fighter, the McDonnell-Douglas F-15 Eagle, entered service in 1974, replacing the F-4 Phantom II. The Eagle was designed as the first air-superiority fighter since the F-86 Sabre. A single-seat fighter, it has two engines and more thrust than weight, enabling it to accelerate in a vertical climb. The air force flies more than 1,000 Eagles. The Israeli air force has also utilized the F-15, with deadly effectiveness. The F-15E is a two-seat, all-weather strike fighter.

To complement the F-15, the General Dynamics Corporation began production of the F-16 Fighting Falcon in 1980. This is a low-cost supplement to the Eagle. It was the first "fly-by-wire" aircraft (that is, whose control surfaces are linked to the cockpit by digital systems) produced for the air force. It is a dual-role aircraft, being both a fighter and a ground-attack fighter. The F-16 can carry 20,540 pounds of ordnance. Since it is highly maneuverable and can attain nine Gs in a turn, the pilot's seat is at a 30-degree angle so that he will not pass out. Some 2,400 serve the U.S. Air Force. It is also exported to many European countries.

The navy sought to replace its aging fleet of combat aircraft with a single type that could be used for all of those roles. McDonnell-Douglas produced the F/A-18 Hornet in 1983 for this purpose. It was adopted into both the navy and Marine Corps to replace the F-4, F-14, A-7, A-4, and A-6. The F/A-18, now built by Boeing, has the latest fly-by-wire technology. A total of 1,168 have been built to date. The Hornet flew more than 5,000 sorties during the Gulf War, with only two being lost to hostile fire.

The most recent addition to the air force complement of fighters is the Lockheed Martin F-22 Raptor. It incorporates all innovations emerging since the F-15 entered service. It is largely invisible to radar and has super-cruise ability, enabling it to fly above the speed of sound without afterburners. The air force has ordered 339 Raptors. Initial operating capability is projected for 2003.

Perhaps the best ground-attack aircraft ever built is the Fairchild A-10 Thunderbolt II, affectionately known by its pilots as the Warthog. Entering production in 1975, it is a very rugged platform with numerous redundant systems, including two engines, two tail fins, and duplicate controls. The cockpit is encased in a titanium tub to protect the pilot from ground fire. The A-10's chief armament is a nose-mounted gatling gun capable of firing 4,000 rounds per minute. The Thunderbolt II played a key role in Operation DESERT STORM but was retired from active service thereafter. It is still utilized by the National Guard.

The principal Marine Corps ground-support aircraft is currently the McDonnell Douglas AV-8 Harrier, the sole vertical take-off and landing aircraft in the U.S. arsenal. This was adapted from the British Hawker-Siddley design of the same name. The AV-8 has vectored-thrust nozzles under the fuselage, enabling it to take off and land in small spaces. It saw action in the Gulf War, destroying Iraqi armor and mechanized units in support of marine ground units.

The most advanced ground-attack fighter is the Lockheed Martin F-117A Nighthawk. The first stealth aircraft produced, it entered service in 1983. It can carry 4,000 pounds of ordnance in internal bomb bays. The multifaceted angles in the structure of its fuselage deflect and diffuse radar beams. Thus far, 64 of the planes have been built. During the Gulf War the F-117 was the first plane to attack Iraqi radar and communication installations.

In October 2001, following a five-year competition between Boeing and Lockheed Martin, the Department of Defense awarded a contract for the new Joint Strike Fighter (JSF) to Lockheed Martin. The JSF is radar evading and capable of short takeoffs and vertical landings. It is also an attempt to provide a standard aircraft for the U.S. Navy, Air Force, and Marines. A total of 3,202 JSFs are to be produced for the United States and Britain at a cost of up to $200 billion: 1,763 planes for the air force, 609 for the marines, and 480 for the navy, as well as 90 for the Royal Air Force and 60 for the Royal Navy.

New heavy bombers in the air force inventory include the North American Rockwell B-1B Lancer and the Northrop Grumman B-2A Spirit. The Lancer can carry 59,000 pounds of bombs, nuclear or conventional. It has a very small radar cross section and flies at high speeds at low altitudes to deliver its payload. It is the only U.S. heavy bomber to have a swing-wing design. Powered by four jet engines set in pairs under each wing, the B-1 entered service in 1986, with 100 being purchased.

Northrop Grumman manufactured the B-2A Spirit, the first stealth heavy bomber. Built for high-altitude penetration of hostile airspace, the B-2A has a payload of 40,000 pounds of conventional or nuclear weapons. It is capable of flying anywhere in the world with only a few aerial refuelings. Only 21 have been built to date because of the high cost per plane.

Transport aircraft also play a key role in the modern air force. The Lockheed C-141 Starlifter was the world's first all-jet transport aircraft. Entering service in 1965 with the MILITARY AIR TRANSPORT SERVICE (MATS), the C-141 provided the United States with strategic transport capacity. Modifications enabled the C-141B to carry up to 200 combat troops or loads of more than 94,000 pounds. The C-141 continues in service with the Air Force Reserve and National Guard.

The Lockheed C-5 Galaxy heavy transport, introduced into the air force inventory in 1969, is a four-engine aircraft capable of carrying any piece of equipment in the army's inventory. The C-5 has both front and rear-loading ability. A total of 131 of the planes have been produced.

The C-5 was the backbone of the air force's airlift capability, but it is now being supplemented by the McDonnell-Douglas C-17 Globemaster, which entered service in 1993. A total of 120 C-17s have been ordered. The Globemaster is able to take off and land on a very rough, short runway and still carry a large payload of 170,000 pounds. It too is capable of transporting anything in the army's inventory.

The newest versions of fighter, bomber, and transport aircraft employ the most recent advances in aircraft design and performance. Many planes today have radar-evasion abilities and can employ stand-off weapons. Most of their engines are capable of greater thrust than the planes actually weigh. New "fly-by-wire" electronics let the pilot fly the plane while computers adjust the settings of the planes' wings and engines. These latest innovations give the United States the most powerful and versatile air force in the world.

See also DE SEVERSKY, ALEXANDER P.; HELICOPTERS; MITCHELL, WILLIAM; WORLD WAR I, U.S. ROLE IN; WORLD WAR II, EUROPE; WORLD WAR II, PACIFIC.

Further reading: Biddle, Wayne. *Barons of the Sky: From Early Flight to Strategic Warfare: The Story of the American Aerospace Industry.* Baltimore, Md.: Johns Hopkins University Press, 2001; Fredriksen, John C. *Warbirds: An Illustrated Guide to U.S. Military Aircraft, 1915–2000.* Denver, Colo.: ABC-Clio, 1999; Johnson, Herbert A. *Wingless Eagle: U.S. Army Aviation through World War I.* Chapel Hill: University of North Carolina Press, 2001; Mauer, Mauer. *Aviation in the U.S. Army, 1919–1939.* Washington, D.C.: Office of Air Force History, 1987; Van Wyen, Adrian O. *Naval Aviation in World War I.* Washington, D.C.: U.S. Government Printing Office, 1979; Wagner, Ray. *American Combat Planes.* New York: Doubleday, 1982.

— Thomas M. Forsyth, Spencer C. Tucker, and Walter J. Boyne

aircraft carriers *Ships with flight decks on which aircraft may be launched and landed*

The history of U.S. naval aviation vessels can be traced as far back as the CIVIL WAR, during which the navy utilized observation balloons moored to ships. Experiments with heavier-than-air craft aboard ships began in 1910 with the first successful launch of a biplane from a temporary deck erected on the cruiser *Birmingham,* followed two months later by a landing on a similar deck aboard the armored cruiser *Pennsylvania.* In 1911 Congress made its first appropriation for naval aeronautics, and the navy ordered its first airplane.

Carriers entered the fleet following World War I. The navy's first carrier, the converted collier *Langley,* was an experimental vessel designed to test new concepts. The 1921 Washington Naval Disarmament Treaty had a direct

USS *Essex* (CV 9) underway in May 1943. Among planes on deck are SBDs, F6Fs, and TBMs.   *(Naval Historical Foundation)*

effect on American carrier development. Because of tonnage limitations, the navy converted two battle cruisers then under construction into the aircraft carriers *Lexington* and *Saratoga*. At 38,500 tons displacement when launched in 1927, the two vessels remained the largest aircraft carriers in the world until 1945. Their large size also accounted for more than half of the total tonnage allowed the United States for aircraft carriers under the Washington Treaty. As a result, a debate developed within the Navy Department concerning the displacement of future carriers. The navy's next carrier, the *Ranger*, commissioned in 1934, was much smaller, at 14,500 tons. While smaller size meant that more carriers could be spread throughout the fleet, the General Board determined that the small carrier did not meet the navy's needs. The subsequent *Yorktown* class, launched in the late 1930s, was therefore much larger, at more than 25,000 tons.

During the 1920s and 1930s the navy undertook several war games to determine the best means of applying airpower to naval scenarios. Many admirals believed the aircraft carrier to be, at best, a scouting platform for the fleet's BATTLESHIPS. In contrast, aviation advocates saw the games as a means of establishing the superiority of aircraft. Fleet Problem IX, conducted in 1929, proved a watershed in carrier tactics. It was the first year in which the *Lexington* and the *Saratoga* participated. In the exercise, the *Saratoga,* acting as the center of an independent strike force, laid the groundwork for the fast carrier task force tactics employed against Japan.

Aircraft carrier technology and tactics matured during WORLD WAR II. Two primary carrier types developed. The first was the attack carrier (CV), epitomized by the Essex class. These carriers displaced 27,100 tons and normally carried 90-plane air groups. Essex-class carriers acted as

USS *John F. Kennedy* taking on fuel and ammunition from the USS *Joshua Humphreys* in the Red Sea during the Persian Gulf War   (*US Air Force*)

the navy's primary offensive weapon against the Japanese fleet. The following Midway class was much larger, at 45,000 tons displacement; however, the first unit was not commissioned until eight days after the formal Japanese surrender.

To fill the gap before arrival of the bulk the *Essex* class in late 1943 and 1944, President Franklin D. ROOSEVELT pressed for an emergency carrier program. This led to the nine *Independence*-class CVLs based on Cleveland-class cruiser hulls, then on the way. These light carriers displaced 10,662 tons and normally carried 30 aircraft. They entered service in 1943.

Another type of carrier perfected during the war was the escort carrier (CVE). The CVE design was forced on the navy by President Roosevelt, who demanded a small aviation ship capable of ferrying assembled aircraft. But it had originated with the British, who ordered them in order to provide aircraft protection for the Atlantic convoys. The bulk of the escort carriers of the war were built on merchant hulls and generally displaced between 10,000 and 20,000 tons. The CVE was very successful as an antisubmarine warfare (ASW) platform in the Battle of the ATLANTIC, working in hunter-killer groups; it served also as a platform for ground-attack sorties in the Pacific.

Although World War II proved the supremacy of the carrier, its postwar future was uncertain. The advent of the atomic bomb led many in Washington to question the utility of the navy as a whole. The primary role of the navy since Alfred Thayer MAHAN had been sea control. Echoing the arguments of Brigadier General William MITCHELL 20 years earlier, air force proponents argued that the need for sea control was superfluous in the atomic age, wherein strategic bombing would decide any future war quickly and decisively.

To secure a role in the escalating COLD WAR, the navy scrambled to find a means of delivering atomic weapons from carriers. That search led to the development of a new supercarrier, the *United States*, but only days after the new ship's keel was laid, Secretary of Defense Louis JOHNSON canceled the program. As a result of shrinking budgets, navy ready forces continued to decline until the KOREAN WAR. The ability of carriers to respond quickly was then reaffirmed, and when Dwight D. EISENHOWER became president in 1953, hostility against the navy declined.

Eisenhower considered the carrier an ideal platform from which to project U.S. power overseas without causing undue diplomatic strain. For the remainder of the cold war, U.S. carriers fulfilled the role of power projection.

During the 1950s the navy undertook the construction of the *Forrestal.* Commissioned in 1955, it displaced more than 59,000 tons and was the first to ignore the size limits imposed by the Panama Canal. The existing carrier fleet also underwent an extensive modernization program to bring the vessels into the jet age. Upgrades included angled flight decks, steam catapults, mirror landing systems, and improved electronics. The British had devised many of the new innovations, but the results reached maturity in the U.S. fleet. More powerful aircraft and miniaturization also allowed the navy finally to end the air force's atomic monopoly.

The next revolution in aircraft carrier design arrived in 1961 with the nuclear-powered *Enterprise.* With a powerplant designed by Admiral Hyman RICKOVER, it displaced 75,700 tons and operated 70–100 aircraft. Nuclear power also radically increased the cost of the ship; following carriers were oil fired until the *Nimitz* class ships entered production in 1968. In the early 1970s, Admiral Elmo ZUMWALT proposed the construction of "sea control ships" (SCS), essentially a modern interpretation of the CVE concept. The SCS would embark helicopters for infantry assault or ASW work, as well as Harrier jump-jets for close air support. Congress refused funding.

At the beginning of the 21st century, the future of the large aircraft carrier is once again under debate. With defense budgets being retrenched, smaller, more versatile designs are being explored to find better means to meet the requirements of low-intensity conflicts in restricted waters. Regardless of future developments, the aircraft carrier remains the ultimate platform for projecting U.S. military power on a global scale.

See also CORAL SEA, BATTLE OF; FLETCHER, FRANK J.; HALSEY, WILLIAM F., JR.; LEYTE GULF, BATTLE OF; MIDWAY, BATTLE OF; MOFFETT, WILLIAM A.; NIMITZ, CHESTER W.; PHILIPPINE SEA, BATTLE OF; VIETNAM WAR, COURSE OF.

Further reading: Belotte, James H., and William M. Belotte. *Titans of the Seas: The Development and Operations of Japanese and American Carrier Task Forces during World War II.* New York: Harper & Row, 1975; MacDonald, Scot. *Evolution of Aircraft Carriers.* Washington, D.C.: Office of the Chief of Naval Operations, 1964; Musciano, Walter A. *Warbirds of the Sea: A History of Aircraft Carriers & Carrier-Based Aircraft.* Atglen, Pa.: Schiffer, 1994; Roscoe, Theodore. *On the Seas and in the Skies: A History of the U.S. Navy's Air Power.* New York: Hawthorn Books, 1970.

— Rodney Madison

Air Force, U.S. *One of the principal armed services of the U.S. Department of Defense*
The U.S. Air Force has primary responsibility for air warfare, air defense, airlift, military space operations, and related research and development. It also provides air and space support to the other military services.

The air force was created as an independent service by the National Security Act of 26 July 1947. A 1949 amendment to that act established the Department of the Air Force as a military department within the executive-branch Department of Defense. However, the roots of air force history go back decades earlier and parallel the development of American military aviation.

U.S. military forces first exploited the vertical dimension during the CIVIL WAR when the North and South used balloons for reconnaissance. Observation balloons also were employed in the SPANISH-AMERICAN WAR and WORLD WAR I, but true military aviation did not begin until the Wright brothers demonstrated powered flight of a heavier-than-air machine in 1903 and sold the army SIGNAL CORPS its first airplane on 10 February 1908.

Congress passed the first appropriation for aeronautics in 1911 and created the Aviation Section of the Signal Corps in 1914, but American airpower developed slowly during its first decade. Aircraft proved unreliable when used for the first time in the PUNITIVE EXPEDITION INTO MEXICO in 1916–17, and the army had only one ill-equipped squadron when the United States entered WORLD WAR I the following year.

World War I triggered a rapid expansion of U.S. Army aviation. When the U.S. declared war on Germany on 6 April 1917, the Army Signal Corps owned only 250 airplanes. By the end of the war, the army had moved air warfare responsibilities to the newly created Army Air Service and had taken delivery of about 11,000 of the 27,000 planes Congress had funded for the conflict. However, less than 4,000 of these planes were combat aircraft, and only 196 of those reached the front before the 11 November 1918 armistice. American aviators flew mostly British and French models in combat.

The end of the war challenged U.S. Army aviators to find an appropriate role for airpower in the face of rapid demobilization. Influenced by wartime contact with Air Marshal Sir Hugh Trenchard, head of Britain's newly independent Royal Air Force (RAF), and by the writings of Italian airpower theorist Giulio Douhet and U.S. brigadier general William MITCHELL, many army aviators concluded that airpower would be preeminent in the future, making armies and navies obsolete and costly land wars unnecessary. However, they believed the nation could realize this potential only if it created an independent air force.

Despite technological challenges, resistance from a conservative military establishment, and an isolationist

American public, airmen worked toward that vision. They kept aviation in the public eye by performing air shows and sponsoring teams that repeatedly set new speed, distance, and altitude records. Advances in aircraft technology provided more powerful engines and eventually replaced the flimsy wood-and-canvas biplanes of the war era with all-metal monoplanes that were able to carry heavy payloads. Most important, army aviators established the Air Corps Tactical School, where they developed a theory of war contrary to existing army doctrine. Instructors there theorized that a modern air force could defeat an enemy nation by bombing key nodes of its industrial-economic system. Believing that bombers were superior to pursuit aircraft (fighters), they advocated the building of a bomber force to conduct unescorted, high-altitude, precision, daylight bombardment. Throughout the 1930s the school indoctrinated pilots in this theory of victory through airpower.

Faith and persistence paid off. After shrinking dramatically immediately after the war, the Air Service gradually expanded in personnel and new equipment; the War Department reorganized it as the Army Air Corps on 2 July 1926. Subsequent realignments produced General Headquarters Air Force on 1 March 1935 and on 20 June 1941 the U.S. Army Air Forces (USAAF) as an autonomous command within the army.

The USAAF realized the opportunity to apply its STRATEGIC BOMBING theory when the United States entered World War II in December 1941. With France defeated and the British Expeditionary Force driven off the continent, airpower was one of the few weapons that American and British commanders could wield against Germany while they gathered forces to invade Europe. The USAAF conducted limited operations in 1942 while it built up its strength, but in June 1943 it committed itself to a combined bomber offensive with the RAF. In that effort the British conducted nighttime area bombing of industrial sectors of German cities while the USAAF attempted precision daylight bombing against industrial targets in Germany and Axis-occupied areas. The USAAF also provided air defense, interdiction bombing, and close air support for Allied operations in North Africa and the Mediterranean area of operations.

The USAAF achieved mixed success with daylight strategic bombing in Europe, and it adjusted its doctrine accordingly. Because of strong fighter defenses, technological limitations on bombing accuracy, and the resilience of German industry, the Allies were unable to end the war simply by destroying nodes of the German industrial-economic system. Yet American participation in the combined bomber offensive and other air operations contributed significantly to defeating the European Axis by eliminating enemy air forces, inhibiting ground maneuver and resupply, and destroying German fuel-refining capability.

The USAAF drew three fundamental lessons from its wartime experience in North Africa, the Mediterranean, and Europe. First, land and air forces are coequal and interdependent. Second, air superiority is the first requirement in battle. Third, air operations should be controlled centrally in each theater by an air commander. The air force internalized these lessons as enduring doctrinal principles.

The USAAF experience in the Pacific was somewhat different. Because of the geographic expanse of that theater and Japan's control over much of China and the western Pacific, the air force was unable to employ concentrated strategic bombing against the Japanese home islands until late in the war. During the first few years, USAAF operations mainly consisted of bombing Japanese forces on the mainland from austere bases in southwestern China, airlifting supplies from India over "the hump" (the Himalayas) to support those bases and Chinese ground forces. The capture of the MARIANA ISLANDS in November 1944 provided the air force a platform from which to launch a strategic bombardment campaign, but weather conditions over Japan and payload limitations made high-altitude bombing with high explosives ineffective. Consequently, in March 1945 the air force switched to low-altitude, nighttime, area incendiary bombing. The campaign had great destructive effect; by midyear more than 60 major Japanese cities had been burned. Yet Japan did not surrender until August 1945, when the USAAF dropped ATOMIC BOMBS on Hiroshima and Nagasaki and the Soviet Union declared war on Japan.

The end of the Pacific war convinced the USAAF and many political leaders that the promise of strategic bombing finally had been fulfilled in the marriage of airpower and atomic weapons. Consequently, the U.S. Air Force (USAF), which achieved independence in 1947, soon became the dominant service in terms of funding and political support, and the STRATEGIC AIR COMMAND (SAC), responsible for atomic (later nuclear) bombardment, emerged as the most influential command in the U.S. defense establishment. Because atomic-armed airpower was seen as the preeminent war-winning force, SAC grew dramatically while conventional forces within the air force and in the other services languished in the postwar demobilization.

The KOREAN WAR presented a thorny problem for the new air force. Contrary to assumptions that future wars would be won by large-scale strategic bombardment with atomic weapons, Korea was a limited war against an adversary with little industrial development. War materials and economic goods were shipped into North Korea from the Soviet Union and the People's Republic of China, which were off limits to attack as Washington did not want to widen the war. Yet American airpower inflicted heavy casualties on North Korean forces when they invaded in June 1950 and on Chinese forces after they entered the war in November. Also in November, the world's first air-to-air combat between jet aircraft took place over Korea—a USAF F-80 shot down a Chinese MiG-15. As the war progressed, USAF pilots in F-86s achieved a 13-to-one kill ratio over adversaries flying the Soviet-built jets. Ultimately, while strategic bombing played only a limited role in the conflict, the pressure the air force applied by bombing dikes in North Korea late in the war probably contributed to the Communist decision to sign an armistice on 27 July 1953.

Believing the Korean War to have been an anomaly, however, air force officials and political leaders continued to assume that future wars would be large-scale nuclear conflicts. Consequently, throughout the 1950s and early 1960s, they increasingly focused on deterring the Soviet Union and the Warsaw Pact from attacking Western Europe and the United States. The American political climate was fiscally conservative, so conventional war-fighting capabilities withered while SAC continued to grow. In these years, the USAF replaced its inventory of propeller-driven heavy bombers with jets, such as the B-47 and B-52. The United States launched its first intercontinental BALLISTIC MISSILE (ICBM) in 1957, and nuclear-armed ICBMs entered SAC's operational inventory soon afterward.

The VIETNAM WAR challenged the nuclear paradigm once again. As in Korea, the United States found itself in a limited war against an adversary who, lacking a developed industrial base, depended on the Chinese and Soviets for logistical support. Between 1963 and 1973, the USAF conducted various operations against targets in North and South Vietnam and in Laos. But the difficulties of using airpower against unconventional forces in jungle terrain prevented the air force from interdicting supplies to communist insurgents operating in South Vietnam. This failure, and political constraints on the effort against North Vietnam, made it impossible to compel Hanoi to stop its military intervention in South Vietnam. Yet the air force contributed significantly to defeating conventional Communist attacks, such as the 1967 siege of KHE SANH and the TET OFFENSIVE in 1968. In 1972 the USAF played a major role in turning back North Vietnam's massive Easter offensive and in persuading Hanoi to agree to a peace settlement. When negotiations broke down, 11 days of heavy bombardment around Hanoi and Haiphong persuaded North Vietnamese leaders to sign a cease-fire (in January 1973).

Drawing lessons from the Vietnam experience and exploiting advances in air and space technology, the USAF underwent significant reform in the 1970s and 1980s. Knowledge gained from air battles in the skies over Vietnam guided the development of new tactics and a new generation of air-superiority fighters. Advances in PRECISION GUIDED MUNITIONS and stealth technology promised the USAF an ability to penetrate enemy defenses and destroy small, hardened targets, using a fraction of aircraft and airmen needed to perform comparable missions in earlier

wars. Developments in air- and space-based intelligence, reconnaissance, command and control, and navigation provided air commanders unprecedented awareness of the battlespace and an ability to network multiple systems together in closely coordinated, high-tempo operations. Most importantly, the Vietnam experience motivated the air force to reconsider the nature of modern warfare and to reemphasize the role of airpower in conventional operations and limited war, thus inspiring a new generation of air force doctrine.

These advances prepared the air force well for challenges in the post–COLD WAR world. On 16 January 1991 the USAF, along with air components of other U.S. and allied forces, launched a coordinated offensive against Iraq as part of an effort to evict that country's military forces from Kuwait. During the next 40 days, coalition air forces conducted the most intense aerial bombardment in the history of war. These actions significantly contributed to the success of a 100-hour ground offensive that crushed the world's fourth-largest army with fewer than 100 coalition combat fatalities. As the decade progressed, the USAF enforced United Nations–sanctioned "no-fly" zones in Iraq and the Balkans and conducted several humanitarian airlift operations. The air force also performed combat operations in support of successful coercive diplomacy to curb Serbian aggression in Bosnia in 1995 and human rights violations in Kosovo in 1999, and it conducted operations against Afghanistan in 2001.

See also AIRCRAFT; CHINA-BURMA-INDIA THEATER; ARNOLD, HENRY H.; DESERT SHIELD, OPERATION; DESERT STORM, OPERATION; DOOLITTLE, JAMES H.; LEMAY, CURTIS E.; LINEBACKER I, OPERATION; LINEBACKER II, OPERATION; MITCHELL, WILLIAM; NUCLEAR AND ATOMIC WEAPONS; ROLLING THUNDER, OPERATION; TOKYO, RAID ON.

Further reading: Dick, Ron. *American Eagles: A History of the United States Air Force.* Charlottesville, Va.: Howell, 1997; Futrell, Robert Frank. *Ideas, Concepts, Doctrine: Basic Thinking in the United States Air Force.* Vol. 1, *1907–1960,* and Vol. 2, *1961–1984.* Maxwell Air Force Base, Ala.: Air University Press, 1989; Lambeth, Benjamin S. *The Transformation of American Air Power.* Ithaca, N.Y.: Cornell University Press, 2000; Nalty, Bernard C., ed. *Winged Shield, Winged Sword: A History of the United States Air Force.* 2 vols. Washington, D.C.: Air Force History and Museums Program, 1997.

— Forrest E. Morgan

Air Force Nurse Corps   *Established in 1949, having evolved from the Army Nurse Corps*
During World War II approximately 1,500 nurses served in the aviation environment. They cared for the sick and

wounded during air evacuations, administering emergency medical treatment as needed. Thirteen flight nurses survived for two months after their plane was downed 850 miles behind Axis lines in the Balkans, concluding their escape with a 27-hour forced march to the Adriatic Sea. Seventeen flight nurses were killed during the war, most of them in aircraft crashes.

In 1949 a number of the army's flight nurses became the nucleus of the Air Force Nurse Corps, helping to pioneer aviation nursing practices. Some served with the Medical Air Evacuation Squadron in the KOREAN WAR. During the VIETNAM WAR the air force at first declined to send female nurses to the war zone, but it was forced to do so when too few male nurses became available. Sixteen female air force nurses reported for duty at the 12th Air Force Hospital in Cam Ranh Bay in 1966. They were soon followed by more, usually acting as senior medical officers on medical evacuation flights that hopped from base to base, picking up casualties en route.

Today, air force nurses deploy where needed. They served in PANAMA in 1989, in Saudi Arabia during Operations DESERT SHIELD and DESERT STORM, and in medical units in the Balkans.

See also ARMY NURSE CORPS; NURSING.

Further reading: Holm, Jeanne M., and Sarah Wells. "Air Force Women in the Vietnam War." In *Celebration of Patriotism and Courage.* Washington, D.C.: Vietnam Women's Memorial Project, 1993; Sarnecky, Mary, "Army Nurse Corps." In *In Defense of a Nation,* edited by Jeanne M. Holm. Washington, D.C.: Women's Military Press, 1997.

— Jean Ebbert and Marie-Beth Hall

Aisne-Marne counteroffensive (18 July–2 August 1918) *Allied World War I counteroffensive*

The German army had risked everything on its series of offensives from 21 March through July 1918. Although six had been planned, only five were executed because the final effort, "Hagen," was preempted by the reaction of the Allied armies to the threat posed on the western front. German field commanders were initially skeptical of the fighting spirit and effectiveness of the rapidly arriving Americans, but the sharp engagements at CANTIGNY and CHÂTEAU-THIERRY/BELLEAU WOOD in May and June proved them wrong.

The Second Battle of the MARNE salient, 15–18 July, was the beginning of the end for the Central Powers. The quartermaster general (deputy chief of staff) of the German army, Erich Ludendorff, had thrown two armies against the southeastern face of the penetration perimeter beginning on 15 July, intending to take Reims. The plan had been compromised, and the French were well prepared to meet it. Within three days the German High Command ended the offensive.

Even as the battle for Reims raged, the Allied commander in chief, General Ferdinand Foch, husbanded a reserve of 20 divisions. As soon as the Allies had the strategic initiative, Foch unleashed them. On 18 July he launched a counteroffensive against the western face of the salient, with supporting attacks in the southwest and southeast. Four French armies participated in the attack. Two American divisions, the 1st and 2d, along with the 1st Moroccan Division, constituted the XX (French) Corps, which was charged with driving against the west face of the salient toward the east, just south of Soissons, to cut the major rail and road connection between it and Château-Thierry. Three more American divisions, the 3d, 4th, and 26th, participated in the main effort. Four others—the 28th, 32d, 42d, and 77th—were in reserve. The I (U.S.) Corps controlled the actions of the 26th (U.S.) and the 167th (French) Divisions, and the III (U.S.) Corps was in reserve to provide administrative support to American divisions in the Tenth (French) Army.

A U.S. division was twice as large as, and substantially more powerful than, its European counterparts. The most battle-experienced divisions of the AMERICAN EXPEDITIONARY FORCES (AEF), the 1st and 2d, committed more than 50,000 infantrymen, artillerymen, and engineers to the attack. These two divisions, with the Moroccans sandwiched between them, spearheaded the assault, pushing forward for nearly four days in the face of withering German fire and through gas-filled ravines. American junior officers and noncommissioned officers fell in large numbers and were replaced by less-experienced leaders from within the units. The resilience and cohesion of the American units bent but never fractured. This test marked the maturing of the AEF. The 1st Division took 3,500 German prisoners and 90 guns from the seven German divisions with which it came into contact. It suffered 1,752 killed and 5,289 wounded. The 2d Division took 2,900 prisoners and 75 German guns while suffering 4,392 total casualties. In all, some 310,000 Americans participated in the offensive, and 67,000 became casualties. The Allied offensive wiped out the Marne salient and forced Ludendorff to call off his planned Flanders offensive.

The American contribution was important in the Allied success. The offensive revealed the truth of the maxims that a combination of arms is essential for the success of tactical actions and that cooperation among allied nations is essential for victory. The Allied nations of World War I learned that lesson; the Central Powers and their Axis successors did not.

See also WORLD WAR I, U.S. INVOLVEMENT.

Further reading: Johnson, Douglas V., II, and Rolfe Hillman, Jr. *Soissons*. College Station: Texas A&M Press, 1999; Wise, Jennings C. *The Turn of the Tide: American Operations at Cantigny, Château Thierry, and the Second Battle of the Marne*. New York: Henry Holt, 1920.

— John F. Votaw

Aix-la-Chappelle, Treaty of (18 October 1748)
Treaty that ended the 1740–48 War of the Austrian Succession

In regard to the European settlement, Prussia by this treaty was confirmed in its acquisition of Silesia; the European powers recognized Francis Stephen (husband of Maria Theresa) as Holy Roman Emperor and confirmed Maria Theresa's inheritance of the Habsburg lands; Spain gained the Italian duchies of Parma, Piacenza, and Guastalla for Don Philip, the second son of Philip V; France returned the Austrian Netherlands (modern Belgium and Luxembourg) to Austria and the fortification of Dunkirk to England, recognized the Hanoverian dynasty, and agreed to expel the Pretender (the Stuart claimant to the English throne); and Austria confirmed the cession of the Ticino frontier to Sardinia-Piedmont.

The colonial provisions of the treaty were less conclusive. Much to the chagrin of its New England colonists, Britain agreed to return Louisbourg in Nova Scotia in exchange for France's returning Madras in India, but negotiators failed to resolve boundary disputes in North America. Instead, a special Anglo-French commission, which first met in 1750, was charged with settling the boundary of Acadia. The French and British also agreed that Dominica, St. Lucia, St. Vincent, and Tobago in the Lesser Antilles should forever constitute a neutral zone, possessed by their native inhabitants (Great Britain would seize them all in 1759). Although Spain confirmed the *asiento*, England's right to ship slaves to the Spanish colonies, and extended colonial trading rights to England for four years, the treaty failed to resolve the "right of search" issue that had started the concurrent War of Jenkins' Ear.

See also KING GEORGE'S WAR.

Further reading: Dorn, Walter L. *Competition for Empire, 1740–1763*. New York: Harper & Row, 1963; Simmons, R. C. *The American Colonies: From Settlement to Independence*. New York: Norton, 1976.

— Justin D. Murphy

Alabama, CSS *Confederate navy commerce raider, the most famous of the Civil War*

Built under contract for the Confederate government by John Laird & Sons at Liverpool, England, the ship was launched in May 1862 as the *Enrica*. Outfitted in the Azores, in August it was commissioned there by Captain Raphael SEMMES as the *Alabama*.

The *Alabama* was a three-masted, bark-rigged sloop. Built of oak with copper sheathing, it was probably the finest cruiser of its day. The *Alabama* displaced 1,050 tons, was 220 feet long and 31 feet, nine inches in beam, and had a 14-foot depth of hold. It was capable of 13 knots under steam and sail and 10 knots under sail alone. The *Alabama* had a crew of 148 and mounted six 32-pounders in broadside and two pivot guns amidships—a seven-inch 110-pounder rifled Blakeley and a smoothbore eight-inch 68-pounder.

From August 1862 to June 1864 the *Alabama* cruised the Atlantic, the Caribbean, and the Pacific, all the way to India. In all, it sailed 75,000 miles, took 66 prizes, and sank the Union schooner *Hatteras*. Twenty-five Union warships searched for the *Alabama*, and its exploits greatly boosted Confederate morale.

With his ship badly in need of an overhaul, however, Semmes sailed the *Alabama* to Cherbourg, France. There it was cornered by the Union steam sloop *Kearsarge,* and on 19 June 1864, Semmes took his ship out to do battle. In the engagement the *Kearsarge* sank the *Alabama*.

In 1984 the French navy located the wreck within French territorial waters, and in 1989 the U.S. Congress passed a preservation act to secure the *Alabama*'s remains.

See also ALABAMA V. KEARSARGE.

Further reading: Robinson, Charles M., III. *Shark of the Confederacy: The Story of the CSS* Alabama. Annapolis, Md.: Naval Institute Press, 1995; Semmes, Raphael. *Memoirs of Service Afloat, during the War between the States*. Baltimore: Kelly, Piet, 1869. Reprint, Secaucus, N.J.: Blue and Grey Press, 1987; Summersell, Charles G. *CSS* Alabama: *Builder, Captain, and Plans*. University: University of Alabama Press, 1985; Tucker, Spencer C. *Raphael Semmes and the* Alabama. Abilene, Tex.: McWhiney Foundation Press, 1996.

— Spencer C. Tucker

Alabama v. Kearsarge (19 June 1864) *Civil War naval engagement*

On 12 June 1864 the Confederate commerce raider *Alabama*, under Captain Raphael SEMMES, arrived at Cherbourg, France. In nearly two years of cruising, the *Alabama* had covered 75,000 miles, captured 66 Union prizes, and sunk the Union warship *Hatteras*. Semmes hoped to utilize the French navy dry dock there to effect needed repairs. Captain John A. Winslow of the U.S. Navy screw sloop *Kearsarge*, then in the English Channel, learned of the *Alabama*'s presence and immediately took his ship to Cherbourg.

Engagement between the CSS *Alabama* and the USS *Kearsarge,* 19 June 1864 (painting by Xanthus R. Smith)   *(Naval Historical Center)*

Sensing that time would only bring more Union ships, Semmes resolved to fight and issued a challenge to the *Kearsarge.* On 19 June the *Alabama* exited Cherbourg, accompanied by the French ironclad *Couronne,* to ensure that the engagement occurred beyond the three-mile French territorial limit.

The two ships were well matched, throwing roughly the same weight of shot, although the *Alabama*'s Blakeley rifled gun outranged the *Kearsarge*'s Dahlgrens. The Confederate ship was in poor repair, however, and its bottom was foul. Semmes knew that chain protected the vitals of the Union sloop, but he had made no effort so to equip his own vessel, being confident of victory.

The ensuing battle was one of the most dramatic of the Civil War at sea. Some 15,000 people endeavored to watch it from the shore, although most could see little, as the battle began six or seven miles offshore. The entire action lasted a bit more than an hour. At 10:57 A.M. Semmes opened with a broadside at somewhat less than a mile. It was several minutes, after two or three Confederate broadsides (all of which passed overhead), before the *Kearsarge* replied, at a range of about a half-mile. Winslow ordered a

port turn to try to position his ship to rake the *Alabama.* Semmes veered his vessel to port to avoid that threat, but his maneuver allowed Winslow to close the range. The *Alabama* turned back to starboard, and the *Kearsarge* mirrored the movement. Winslow employed his ship's superior speed to narrow the range further; thus the ships described circles that grew progressively smaller, from one-half to one-quarter of a mile in diameter, each ship firing its starboard batteries only.

Most of the *Alabama*'s shots went high, and a number of shells failed to explode, likely because of defective fuses, including one that lodged in the *Kearsarge*'s sternpost but did not detonate. Union gunnery was far superior; most of the shells from the *Kearsarge* struck the hull of the *Alabama,* which was soon flooding. Semmes tried to disengage and run for the French coast, but his ship was too badly damaged. He finally struck his colors. Winslow continued firing for a time, claiming that another flag had been raised at the *Alabama*'s stern.

As the *Alabama* sank, Winslow ordered boats lowered to rescue survivors. A British yacht, the *Dearhound,* which was nearby to observe the action, rescued 42 survivors, including Semmes, and transported them to Britain. London refused subsequent demands by Washington that they be handed over. The *Alabama* lost nine killed in the engagement, 12 drowned, and 21 wounded. The *Kearsarge* reported only one dead and two wounded.

See also CIVIL WAR, NAVAL OVERVIEW.

Further reading: Marvel, William. *The* Alabama *and the* Kearsarge: *The Sailor's Civil War.* Chapel Hill: University of North Carolina Press, 1996; Robinson, Charles M., III. *Shark of the Confederacy: The Story of the CSS* Alabama. Annapolis, Md.: Naval Institute Press, 1995; Tucker, Spencer C. *Raphael Semmes and the* Alabama. Abilene, Tex.: McWhiney Foundation Press, 1996.

— Rodney Madison

Alamance, Battle of (16 May 1771) *Intracolonial battle in North Carolina before the American Revolution*
The North Carolina Regulators, primarily small farmers (estimated at more than 6,000) from the frontier counties of Rowan, Anson, and Orange were organized in the late 1760s to protest a lack of proportional representation in the provincial assembly and local governments, as well as corruption by Crown-appointed officials. Outright acts of defiance, including flogging of officials and interruption of courts and legal proceedings by armed mobs, by the Regulator movement prompted royal governor William Tryon to call up North Carolina militia (with the payment of bounties) and to push the "Bloody Act" of 15 January 1771 through the colonial assembly, declaring Regulator activity treasonous.

The Regulators responded to the legislation by forming forces, large but loosely organized and poorly armed. As tension mounted, Regulators gathered on the Alamance River, just east of present-day Greensboro. Governor Tryon took the field in April to restore order by armed force. He advanced from New Bern, the colonial capital, toward Hillsboro with 1,000 militiamen. Another militia force, under General Hugh Waddell, advanced to Salisbury to rendezvous with the governor at Hillsboro. Tryon reached Hillsboro unopposed, but Waddell had been delayed by Regulator opposition. Despite a numerical disadvantage, Tryon marched toward Salisbury on 11 May and by 14 May was at the Alamance River, some five miles from an encampment of about 2,000 Regulators.

Lacking well-defined leadership, artillery, and sufficient arms, the Regulators could not resist effectively Tryon's assault on 16 May. After initially refusing demands for complete submission, the Regulators argued among themselves as to whether to stand their ground or simply to make a show of resistance so as to induce concessions from the royal governor. Tryon, a former professional army officer, did not hesitate. Forming his force into two lines in the accepted tactic of the day, he pummeled the Regulators with artillery fire. Their crudely formed and ill-disciplined defensive line quickly disintegrated when the governor's troops advanced. Although the Regulators wounded more than 60 of the opposing militia, perhaps reflecting the skills learned in hunting on the frontier, the better trained, disciplined, and armed royal militia did not waver. Driven from the field in chaos after an hour's fight, the Regulators collapsed, even though only nine died on each side. Tryon executed one Regulator leader the following day on the battlefield and six others in Hillsboro on 19 June. Many Regulators fled west to new settlements.

Despite their military defeat and subsequent suppression at the hands of the royal government, many former Regulators remained loyal to the Crown during the upcoming American Revolutionary War. More than 200 Regulators took part in the abortive Loyalist rising that ended in defeat at Moore's Creek Bridge in February 1776.

See also MILITIA, ORGANIZATION AND ROLE OF.

Further reading: Chidsey, Donald Barr. *The War in the South: The Carolinas and Georgia in the American Revolution.* New York: Crown, 1969; Kay, Marvin L. Michael and Lorin Lee Cary. "Class, Mobility and Conflict in North Carolina on the Eve of the Revolution." In *The Southern Experience in the American Revolution,* edited by Jeffrey J. Crow and Larry E. Tise. Chapel Hill: University of North Carolina Press, 1978; Maier, Pauline. *From Resistance to Revolution: Colonial Radicals and the Development of American Opposition to Britain, 1765–1776.* New York: Alfred A. Knopf, 1972.

— Stanley D. M. Carpenter

Alamo, Battle of (5 March 1836) *Major battle in the Texas War of Independence (1835–36)*
The Alamo was originally established in 1718 as the Mission San Antonio de Valero but was abandoned in 1793. From 1803 to 1835 it served almost continuously as a fortress, first under Spanish control then later under Mexican authority. When Texans revolted in October 1835, they laid siege to San Antonio and the Alamo, where Mexican general Martín Perfecto de Cos had concentrated his troops. Texan forces attacked San Antonio on 5 December 1835, forcing Cos to surrender and allowing him to withdraw after promising to move south of the Rio Grande.

The Texans occupied San Antonio and the Alamo, but most of the volunteers soon departed for home. The revolutionary government decided to maintain a garrison at the Alamo to control one of the two main roads leading from Mexico into Texas. Lieutenant Colonel James Clinton Neill—a regular officer and artillery expert—assumed command of the garrison. Sam HOUSTON, commander of all Texas forces, considered the Alamo indefensible and wanted to withdraw the troops and destroy the fortifications. The provisional government overruled him and ordered the garrison to remain, promising that additional troops and supplies would be forthcoming. All involved knew that the Alamo—stripped of many of its men and supplies for an attack on Matamoros that never took place—could be held only if substantial reinforcements arrived.

In early 1836, reinforcements began to dribble into the Alamo: On 19 January James Bowie with 30 men arrived from Goliad; Lieutenant Colonel William B. Travis and his "Legion of Cavalry" (actually 29 horsemen) came in on 3 February; a few days later Davy Crockett appeared with a dozen volunteers from Tennessee. On 11 February, Neill took personal leave to attend to his ailing family, believing that he would be able to return before Mexican forces appeared in the area. He left Travis, an officer in the regular Texas forces, as acting commander. When the volunteers at the Alamo objected, a compromise was reached—Bowie would command the volunteers and Travis the regulars.

Travis, expecting Mexican forces only in mid-March, had to withdraw inside the Alamo when Mexican forces under General Antonio López de Santa Anna arrived on 23 February. The Mexicans at first were content to lay siege to the Alamo. Travis received the last of his reinforcements on 1 March—32 men from Gonzales. This meant that some 200 Texan defenders faced as many as 6,000 Mexican troops. On 5 March—with the siege apparently working, and over the objections of his officers—Santa Anna abruptly decided to stage a frontal assault on the Alamo. Santa Anna wanted not only to teach the Texans a lesson but also to intimidate his opponents in other parts of Mexico. Early on the morning of 6 March, Santa Anna sent some 1,800 of his troops against the Alamo. The fighting lasted about 90 minutes before the Alamo was completely overrun. Reportedly, a few defenders—perhaps as many as seven, including Crockett—survived the assault but were immediately executed. Approximately 30 noncombatants—women, children, and slaves—survived the fall of the Alamo. Mexican casualties numbered approximately 600.

The military implications of the stand at the Alamo continue to be debated. The delaying of Santa Anna's march provided time for the Texans to organize additional military forces; it also permitted a convention to issue a declaration of independence and to draft a constitution for the new Republic of Texas. Santa Anna's decision to lay siege but then stage an assault combined the bad results of both approaches: delay and heavy casualties. The bloody fall of the Alamo temporarily terrorized the Texans, precipitating a flood of refugees before the advancing Mexican forces. However, it also motivated at least some Texans to stiffer resistance, realizing that they were in a no-quarter war. The brief but bitter struggle for the Alamo soon acquired a mythic and symbolic significance beyond any military significance it might have had.

See also MEXICAN-AMERICAN WAR, CAUSES OF; SAN JACINTO, BATTLE OF; TEXAS WAR OF INDEPENDENCE.

Further reading: Hardin, Stephen L. *Texian Iliad: A Military History of the Texas Revolution.* Austin: University of Texas Press, 1994; Kilgore, Dan. *How Did Davy Die?* College Station: Texas A&M University Press, 1978; Long, Jeff. *Duel of Eagles: The Mexican and United States Fight for the Alamo.* New York: Morrow, 1990.

— Don M. Coerver

Albany Conference (1 May 1690) *Intercolonial conference during King William's War*
A French and Indian raiding party having burned Schenectady, New York, on 9 February 1690, representatives from New York, Massachusetts, Connecticut, and Plymouth convened in Albany on 1 May 1690 to organize militarily. The three most influential leaders of the conference were Jacob Leisler (leader of LEISLER'S REBELLION in New York), Connecticut governor John Winthrop, and Massachusetts governor Simon Bradstreet.

The conference adopted an ambitious plan, calling for Sir William PHIPS, who was leading a successful expedition against Port Royal (captured on 11 May 1690), to lead also an assault up the St. Lawrence River against Quebec and for Governor Winthrop's son, Fitz, a former major general of militia under the Dominion of New England, to lead a joint New York–Connecticut force through the Lake Champlain corridor against Montreal.

Although this strategy would prove ultimately successful in the FRENCH AND INDIAN WAR, the colonies lacked sufficient resources to achieve success in 1690. An outbreak of smallpox halted Winthrop's expedition before it reached Lake Champlain. Although Phips's expedition of 32 ships and approximately 1,500 militia from Massachusetts and Plymouth (commanded by John Walley) reached Quebec in early October, the colonists lacked supplies and guns for a long siege and were forced to withdraw after a few weeks.

Although its plans failed, the Albany Conference was significant because it revealed that colonial leaders could and would take the initiative in their defense. Its strategic objective provided a blueprint for future wars.

See also KING WILLIAM'S WAR.

Further reading: Craven, Wesley Frank. *The Colonies in Transition, 1660–1713.* New York: Harper & Row, 1968; Millett, Allan R., and Peter Maslowski. *For the Common*

Defense: A Military History of the United States of America.
New York: Free Press, 1984.

— Justin D. Murphy

Aleutian campaign (1943) *Pacific theater campaign of World War II*

On 15 August 1943, 35,000 U.S. and Canadian troops assaulted the Aleutian island of Kiska, which had been occupied by Japan since June 1942. Although Japanese forces covertly withdrew at the end of July, several dozen invaders died—victims of friendly fire and Japanese mines—and 70 sailors perished when their destroyer struck a mine. Noted British strategist Basil Liddell Hart later described the use of more than 100,000 American servicemen in this trivial task as a flagrant abuse of the principle of economy of force and a good example of the distraction that can be caused by a diversionary effort with a slight expenditure. U.S. naval historian Samuel Eliot Morison later averred that no operations in this region of almost perpetual mist and snow accomplished anything of great importance or had any appreciable effect on the war's outcome.

When the Japanese attacked the Aleutians, raiding Dutch Harbor twice on 3–4 June 1942 before occupying Kiska and Attu, they sought only to extend their defensive perimeter while guarding the MIDWAY operation's northern flank. But after their decisive Midway defeat, Japanese leaders, who had planned only a brief presence in the western Aleutians, resolved to remain indefinitely for fear that America would employ the islands to attack across the North Pacific.

Badly defined command procedures (the U.S. Navy would not accept unity of command unless an invasion of mainland Alaska seemed imminent), poor interservice cooperation, and a shortage of ships and aircraft plagued the American effort to retake the two islands. Moreover, by September 1942, after weeks of arguing about strategic options, both the Alaskan army head, General Simon Bolivar BUCKNER, Jr., and his naval counterpart, Admiral Robert Theobald, were nearly relieved by the Joint Chiefs of Staff. It was a temporary respite for Theobald, as he was removed the following December by Admiral Ernest KING, destroying their decades-long friendship.

U.S. forces seized the islands of Adak and Atka on 30 August and 16 September, turning Adak into a major base to support air assaults upon Kiska and Attu. Amchitka, visible from Kiska on a clear day, was seized on 11 January 1943. Then, with the reluctant approval of the Joint Chiefs (General George C. MARSHALL, dealing with British concerns that too many resources were Pacific-bound, had limited Aleutian operations at the January 1943 Casablanca Conference), Major General Albert Brown's U.S. 7th Division was selected to invade Attu in mid-May 1943. The division, allotted three days to take the island, took three weeks to do so because of poor weather, rough terrain, ill-suited clothing and boots that led to hundreds of cases of frostbite, and a spirited defense by the Japanese. Unhappy with the slow progress, Admiral Thomas KINKAID relieved Brown on 16 May. Two weeks later, after the remnants of the 2,500-man Japanese garrison had been destroyed in a suicidal banzai attack, Attu was secure. It had cost 549 American lives plus another 3,000 casualties.

Facing an estimated 10,000 Japanese on Kiska, the Western Defense Command chief, General John DeWitt, gathered more than 35,000 soldiers, including some 5,000 Canadians, for the next assault. But Japan removed Kiska's garrison in a daring naval foray in late July. Once Kiska was secure, DeWitt and his Alaskan commanders, taking their cue from geopolitical theories of Alfred Thayer MAHAN and William "Billy" Lendrum MITCHELL that the Aleutians were stepping stones to Asia, pushed hard to attack the Japanese-held Kurile Islands, perhaps with the participation of Soviet forces. While such notions had the support of King and senior planners, Marshall and others, worried by the region's dismal climate and the potentially huge logistical requirements (10 to 20 American divisions, dozens of warships, and hundreds of aircraft), were uninterested, especially when the Soviets declined to abandon their neutrality pact with Japan as long as Germany remained unbowed.

So long ignored prior to 1941, the Aleutians faded back into the strategic mists after 1945, emerging only occasionally—for example, when President Bill Clinton declined in late 2000 to build a ballistic missile defense system that would have placed a sophisticated radar installation on the bleak island of Shemya.

Further reading: Chandonnet, Fem, ed. *Alaska at War, 1941–1945: The Forgotten War Remembered.* Anchorage: Alaska at War Committee, 1995; Cloe, John Hafle. *The Aleutian Warriors: A History of the 11th Air Force & Fleet Wing 4.* Missoula, Mont.: Pictorial Histories, 1991; Garfield, Brian. *The Thousand-Mile War: World War II in Alaska and the Aleutians.* New York: Bantam Books, 1969; Goldstein, Donald M., and Katherine V. Dillon. *The Williwaw War: The Arkansas National Guard in the Aleutians in World War II.* Fayetteville: University of Arkansas Press, 1992.

— Galen Roger Perras

Allen, Ethan (1737–1789) *American militia officer and American Revolutionary War leader*

Born on 10 January 1737 at Litchfield, Connecticut, Ethan Allen served briefly in 1757 as a volunteer during the FRENCH AND INDIAN WAR. He then operated an iron forge at Salisbury, Connecticut.

Warned out of Salisbury and then Northampton, Massachusetts, because of his deism, in 1770 Allen moved to the Green Mountains, then belonging to New York. He soon became the leader of the "Green Mountain Boys," a vigilante force formed to defend the New Hampshire Grants (later Vermont) against the claims of New York. Allen was an active propagandist in this cause, and by 1774 he had in effect nullified New York control over the area.

During the American Revolutionary War, however, Allen made common cause with New Yorkers against the British Crown, leading a force of the Green Mountain Boys, of which he was the self-appointed colonel commandant, to capture FORT TICONDEROGA.

One of the most important strategic points in North America, Ticonderoga was located on a gateway between Canada and the colonies, the juncture of Lake George and Lake Champlain. Originally constructed by the French in 1755, it had been taken by the British at the end of the French and Indian War but had been allowed to deteriorate. The British planned to rebuild it, but Allen struck before this could be carried out.

In the early morning of 10 May 1775, Ethan Allen, with Benedict ARNOLD in company, led a small group of men against the south wall, surprised the sentinel there, and took the fort. The capture was both an important morale boost to the Patriot cause and a source of substantial numbers of cannon, which were sent to Boston. Their employment forced the British from that place in March 1776.

Allen led 90 men that summer to the northern end of Lake Champlain to take St. John's, but they were surprised by a British force and driven back. Undaunted, Allen and Major John Brown planned to take Montreal with a pitifully small force. On 24 September 1775 Allen's attack failed, and he was captured. Allen spent almost three years as a prisoner in North America and England. In May 1778 he was paroled in New York and exchanged for a British lieutenant general. He spent 1779 writing a vivid account of his role in the war and his captivity. *A Narrative of Colonel Ethan Allen's Captivity* proved a masterful propaganda document and a boost to colonial morale.

Between 1778 and 1784 Allen commanded Vermont's military forces but did not see further action. A fervent supporter of the rights of Vermont, he wrote editorials, pamphlets, and books, most of which advocated its independence from New York. Allen did not live to see Vermont enter the Union in 1791 as the 14th state. He died in Bennington on 12 February 1789.

See also AMERICAN REVOLUTIONARY WAR, LAND OVERVIEW.

Further reading: Bellesiles, Michael. *Revolutionary Outlaws.* Charlottesville: University Press of Virginia, 1993;

Graffagnino, J. Kevin, ed. *Ethan and Ira Allen: Collected Works.* 3 vols. Benson, Vt.: Chalidze, 1992. Jellison, Charles A. *Ethan Allen, Frontier Rebel.* Syracuse, N.Y.: Syracuse University Press, 1969.

— Mark A. Bauserman

Allen, Henry T. (1859–1930) *U.S. Army general*

Born on 13 April 1859 at Sharpsbury, Kentucky, Henry Tureman Allen graduated from the U.S. Military Academy at WEST POINT in 1882. In 1884 he became aide-de-camp to General Nelson A. MILES. On Miles's orders he undertook a demanding seven-month expedition to Alaska. Allen's report, published in 1887, brought international recognition for his geographical achievements. Fluent in Russian, German, and French, he taught at West Point and in 1890 was the first American military attaché to St. Petersburg, spending five years there and two more in Berlin.

Brief service in Cuba during the 1898 SPANISH-AMERICAN WAR was followed by seven years in the Philippines as chief of the new Philippine Constabulary. Allen, as a temporary brigadier general, developed the constabulary into a highly efficient force. In 1910 he joined the General Staff in Washington as acting chief of cavalry under General Leonard WOOD, spending four years there (without regaining his general's star).

At the beginning of World War I, Allen's diplomatic expertise led to his appointment as senior military member of a delegation sent to Europe to help repatriate more than 50,000 American civilians trapped there. Having viewed some of the fighting and visited most major European capitals, Allen submitted a report predicting the war's likely course and advocating great increases in U.S. defense expenditures and training. Allen then commanded a cavalry unit at Fort Oglethorpe, Georgia. His unit took part in the PUNITIVE EXPEDITION INTO MEXICO of 1916, in which he worked closely with Brigadier General John J. PERSHING.

After American intervention in the world war, Pershing appointed Allen commander of the 90th Division ("Texas-Oklahoma"), which arrived in France in spring 1918, participating in the SAINT-MIHIEL OFFENSIVE and MEUSE-ARGONNE OFFENSIVE. After hostilities ended, Allen commanded the occupying U.S. forces in Germany, often serving as the senior American diplomatic (as well as military) representative in Germany. Later, as Franco-German tensions increased, Allen frequently sympathized with Germany and attempted to persuade the French to moderate their demands, deploring their 1922 occupation of the Ruhr and publicly calling for lower German reparations payments.

After retirement in 1923, Allen spoke and wrote extensively on international affairs, publishing two books on his German experiences, forcefully advocating American membership in the League of Nations, and raising funds to alleviate hunger in Germany. He dabbled in politics, unsuccessfully attempting to win the Democratic vice-presidential nomination for 1928. He died at his country home at Buena Vista Springs, Pennsylvania, on 30 August 1930.

See also WORLD WAR I, U.S. INVOLVEMENT.

Further reading: Allen, Henry T. *My Rhineland Journal.* Boston: Houghton Mifflin, 1923; ———. *The Rhineland Occupation.* Indianapolis, Ind.: Bobbs-Merrill, 1927; Bullard, Robert L. *Fighting Generals.* Ann Arbor, Mich.: J. W. Edwards, 1944. Twichell, Heath, Jr. *Allen: The Biography of an Army Officer, 1859–1930.* New Brunswick, N.J.: Rutgers University Press, 1974.

— Priscilla Roberts

Allen, Terry de la Mesa (1888–1969) *U.S. Army general*

Born on 1 April 1888, at Fort Douglas, Utah, Terry Allen entered the U.S. Military Academy at WEST POINT in 1907 but failed math. In his fifth year he again failed, this time in gunnery, and had to leave the academy. He graduated from Catholic University of America in Washington, D.C., in 1912 and was commissioned in the cavalry. His World War I service, as a captain, was in the 90th Division, in which he was wounded and was commended for his conduct in battle. After the war Allen graduated from the Command and General Staff School in 1926 and from the Army War College in 1935, rising to the rank of lieutenant colonel. Allen was promoted to brigadier general in 1940 without ever holding the intervening rank of colonel. As a new major general in June 1942 he took command of the 1st Infantry Division (the "Big Red One") and led it through the North African campaign, including the Battle of the KASSERINE PASS, and in SICILY.

General Omar N. BRADLEY relieved Allen from command in August 1943 following the battle for Troina, Sicily. This action has been attributed to Bradley's dislike of Allen's leadership style, Allen's apparent subordination of teamwork to the parochial interests of his Big Red One, and concerns that he allowed discipline in his division to slacker.

One of very few general officers assigned to command a division in combat after having been relieved for cause, Allen proved his mettle and worth to the army by assuming command of the new 104th Infantry Division ("Timberwolves"), training it to peak efficiency, and then leading it in combat in the European theater of operations a year later. The division served ably until VE Day.

Allen was an unconventional commander and a master of night-fighting tactics. Despite his brilliant performance with the 104th, Allen was forever marked by his relief from command of the 1st Infantry Division. He retired in 1946 to El Paso, Texas, and lived to see his son, Terry, Jr., killed in action in Vietnam. Allen died at El Paso on 12 September 1969.

See also WORLD WAR II, U.S. INVOLVEMENT, EUROPE.

Further reading: Hoegh, Leo A., and Howard J. Doyle. *Timber Trucks: The History of the 104th Infantry Division, 1942–1945.* Washington, D.C.: Infantry Journal Press, 1946; Hurkala, John. *The Fighting First Division, A True Story.* New York: Greenwich Book, 1957.

— John F. Votaw

Alliance, USS (1777) *Continental navy warship of the American Revolutionary War*

The American-built 36-gun frigate *Alliance* was built in 1777 at Salisbury Point on the Merrimack River, Massachusetts, by William and James Hackett. *Alliance* was 151 feet in length of lower deck, 36 feet in beam, and 12 feet, 6 inches in depth of hold; it mounted 28 12-pounders and 12 9-pounders. In 1779 the *Alliance* joined three other vessels, accompanying the flagship of John Paul JONES, *BON-HOMME RICHARD,* on a cruise along the British coast. Under Captain Pierre Landais, the *Alliance* participated in the 23 September action off Flamborough Head in which the *Bonhomme Richard* took the British frigate *Serapis.* During the battle Landais circled the two vessels, firing on both indiscriminately.

The *Alliance* then cruised the coasts of Spain before returning to L'Orient, France, where Benjamin Franklin relieved Landais of his command, replacing him with Jones. While Jones was ashore, Landais seized control of the ship and sailed for America. The officers removed him from command before the ship reached Boston on 16 August 1780. Sailing again in 1781 under Captain John BARRY, the *Alliance* took several prizes and on 29 May fought a hard battle with the British ship *Atlanta* (16 guns) and brig *Trepassy* (14) off Nova Scotia. Barry was severely wounded but kept up the fight and took both British vessels.

Again under Barry, the *Alliance* sailed from New London, Connecticut, in August 1782 and took a half-dozen prizes before refitting at L'Orient. Carrying a cargo of specie and escorting the *Duc de Lauzun* (20) from Havana, Barry was chased by the British frigates *Alarm and Sybil* and sloop *Tobago.* The *Duc de Lauzun* was a slow sailer, so Barry ordered most of its guns thrown overboard to increase its speed. The British still gained, but the fortunate appearance of a French 50-gun ship caused two of the British ships to break off the pursuit. The *Sybil,* however, engaged the *Duc de Lauzun.* Barry placed the *Alliance* between the two, allowing the *Duc de Lauzun* to escape. After a 45-minute fight the *Sybil* broke off the action.

The *Alliance* was the last ship of the war to be decommissioned. The frigate was sold in Philadelphia in June 1785.

See also AMERICAN REVOLUTIONARY WAR, NAVAL OVERVIEW; *BONHOMME RICHARD*, USS, V. HMS *SERAPIS*.

Further reading: Chapelle, Howard I. *The History of the American Sailing Navy. The Ships and Their Development.* New York: Norton, 1949; Miller, Nathan. *Sea of Glory: The Continental Navy Fights for Independence, 1775–1783.* New York: David McKay, 1974.

— Cynthia Clark Northrup and Spencer C. Tucker

Almond, Edward M. (1892–1979) *U.S. Army general*

Born on 12 December 1892 at Luray, Virginia, Edward Mallory Almond attended the Virginia Military Institute, graduating in 1915. Commissioned in the army, during World War I Almond was a first lieutenant with the 4th Division in France and was wounded in the AISNE-MARNE COUNTER OFFENSIVE. He taught military science at Marion Institute, Alabama, from 1919 until 1923. In 1923 Almond attended the Infantry School at Fort Benning and remained there as an instructor until 1928. He then served in the Philippines.

In July 1942, following U.S. entry into World War II, Almond was promoted to temporary brigadier general and given command of the 92d Division (Negro). During training, Almond's command was investigated by Brigadier General Benjamin O. DAVIS, who issued a report critical of Almond's leadership. In 1944 Almond led the 4th Division in Italy, where it advanced through Pisa and Genoa to the Franco-Italian border.

When his division was disbanded at the end of the war, Almond assumed command of the 2d Infantry Division. In June 1946, he joined General Douglas MACARTHUR in Japan as his deputy chief of staff for personnel. In December 1946 he became deputy chief of staff of the Far East Command. He was promoted to major general in 1948. Almond became MacArthur's chief of staff in February 1949. By June 1950, when North Korea invaded South Korea, he was considering retirement.

The KOREAN WAR offered Almond a chance to rejuvenate his career. In August 1950, MacArthur placed him in charge of planning an invasion behind North Korean lines at Inchon and then gave him command of the invasion force, X Corps. The 15 September 1950 INCHON LANDING was highly successful; X Corps captured Seoul within two weeks. On 7 October, X Corps made another amphibious landing, on the northeast coast near Wonsan, and pushed north. Following the massive Chinese intervention at the end of November, Almond directed the evacuation of United Nations forces from northeastern Korea, principally through the port of HUNGNAM.

Washington insisted that the system of divided command be ended, and Eighth Army absorbed X Corps on 26 December. Almond remained its commander, being promoted to lieutenant general. He left Korea in July 1951. After the war, Almond supported MacArthur in criticizing U.S. policy that did not allow UN troops to invade China.

Almond served as commandant of the Army War College until he retired in January 1953. He then engaged in public relations for an insurance company in San Antonio, Texas. He also served as a member of the VMI Board of Visitors from 1961 to 1968. Almond died on 11 June 1979 in San Antonio.

See also CHANGJIN/CHOSIN RESERVOIR, BATTLE AND RETREAT FROM.

Further reading: Appleman, Roy E. *Escaping the Trap: The US Army X Corps in Northeast Korea, 1950.* College Station: Texas A&M University Press, 1990; Stanton, Shelby L. *America's Tenth Legion: X Corps in Korea, 1950.* Novato, Calif.: Presidio, 1989.

— John David Rausch, Jr.

American Expeditionary Force (AEF) *U.S. military force sent to France in World War I*

When the United States declared war on Germany in April 1917, it was militarily unprepared. American leaders faced a daunting task, as the Entente powers desperately needed help on the western front. However, for some time there was little the United States could do in terms of ground forces. Its regular army of 127,000 men ranked 16th in the world in size. To make matters worse, this small force was poorly trained and equipped. The force would have to be expanded and properly trained, and equipped. Fortunately, there was sufficient time for American resources to play an important role and help turn the tide of war.

In May 1917 President Woodrow WILSON, working with Secretary of War Newton BAKER, chose General John J. "Blackjack" PERSHING to lead the American Expeditionary Force (AEF). Although not the most senior officer in the army, Pershing had an impressive record of service in the American West, the SPANISH-AMERICAN WAR, and the Philippines. A thoroughly professional officer, a strong administrator, and a doggedly persistent man, Pershing was a superb choice to lead the AEF.

To raise the necessary troops, Congress passed the Selective Service Act in May 1917. Under this legislation, the army grew from slightly more than 200,000 men, including federalized National Guardsmen, in April 1917 to 3,685,458 by November 1918. Of this total, almost 2.2 million were draftees. Of the 29 divisions (1,000 officers and 27,000 men each) that saw action in France, only 11 were draftee divisions, however. The remainder were seven regular and 11 National Guard divisions, all volunteer.

As the number of troops expanded, Baker and his staff faced the daunting task of training them. Modern weapons and equipment had to be found, and then the men had to be transported to France. All were difficult problems, not easily solved. When the United States declared war, the army had housing for only 124,000 men. In a matter of months, the number of beds needed to be increased more than tenfold. Baker instituted a crash building program to expand existing facilities and construct more than 30 new training camps. Equipping the men was equally difficult; simply acquiring clothing was a major task. Military equipment of all kinds was in short supply. The army had only 800,000 rifles of two different types on hand in 1917, and these could not be mass-produced easily. Ultimately the AEF adopted a modified version of the British Enfield rifle because it could be manufactured quickly.

American field artillery units were largely dependent on the French 75 mm gun, and aviation units relied on foreign aircraft; not only was it impossible to produce the American equivalents quickly, but ships were crammed with troops as a first priority. By the end of the war, not a single U.S.-manufactured tank had gone into action. Only about 500 of the 3,500 artillery pieces used in action by the AEF were U.S. made.

The army had its own air arm. The First Aero (later 1st Bombardment) Squadron had been organized in 1913 and served during the PUNITIVE EXPEDITION INTO MEXICO. The air service had only 65 officers, of whom just 35 could fly. In France it was amalgamated with the American volunteers of the LAFAYETTE ESCADRILLE in the French army and began combat duty in March 1918. Soon the Americans had three air squadrons providing reconnaissance and even doing some bombing behind enemy lines. The U.S. Army had only 55 planes when the war began. When hostilities ended it had 3,227 de Haviland DH-4 aircraft (a British design), of which 1,885 had been shipped to France.

Training the men of the AEF took an average of eight months before action. The lack of experienced officers and noncommissioned officers greatly complicated this process. It was not unusual for an officer to have learned a drill the night before having to teach it to recruits. There were also other difficulties. Pershing wanted the AEF trained in open-warfare techniques. His vision was of the AEF using concentrated rifle fire and infantry rushes to break through the German defensive positions and reach open territory beyond. Allied leaders, however, insisted on trench-warfare training, for which intensive preparation was essential.

The 1st Infantry Division arrived in time to parade in Paris on 4 July 1917. It was soon divided into smaller components for training. By the end of 1917 there were 180,000 U.S. soldiers in France. At that time the strategic situation was desperate. Italian forces had been smashed at Caporetto, and Russia and Romania were soon to drop out of the war, enabling the Germans to shift resources from the eastern front and prepare for a massive offensive in the west to win the war. A desperate "race to France" of American manpower began.

Wilson's directive to Pershing stated simply that he was "vested with all necessary authority to carry on the war vigorously." Wilson instructed him to cooperate with the forces of the other countries employed against Germany but to keep U.S. forces as "a separate and distinct component of the combined forces, the identity of which must be preserved." Wilson, Baker, and Pershing were determined that the AEF should be a separate entity. However, in the desperate situation caused by the German offensive of March 1918, Wilson ordered Pershing to place all his forces at the disposal of the new Allied supreme commander, General Ferdinand Foch, who dispersed them among the Allied armies where they were most needed. Foch promised that once the German drive had been contained, an independent American army would hold a sector of the front.

However insufficient their training, the Americans had to be used, and they proved themselves in savage fighting at CANTIGNY and CHÂTEAU-THIERRY/BELLEAU WOOD. In the 15–18 July Second Battle of the MARNE, American forces were critical in blunting the German drive. They further distinguished themselves in the 12–16 September SAINT-MIHIEL OFFENSIVE and the 26 September–11 November MEUSE-ARGONNE OFFENSIVE. Without the AEF's timely intervention the Allies might well have lost the war.

American losses in World War I were slight compared to those of the other powers. Out of 1,390,000 American troops and sailors committed to active combat, 49,000 were killed in action or died of wounds; 230,000 more were wounded. Yet as in previous wars, deaths from disease, 57,000, exceeded those from fighting, mostly from an influenza-pneumonia pandemic that swept the camps in America and France in the fall of 1918. The total of 106,000 military dead for the United States pales alongside the 947,000 for Britain and 1,400,000 for France.

See also AISNE-MARNE COUNTEROFFENSIVE; ARMISTICE; BLISS, TASKER H.; MARCH, PEYTON C.; PARIS PEACE SETTLEMENT; SELECTIVE SERVICE; WORLD WAR I, CAUSES OF U.S. ENTRY; WORLD WAR I, COURSE OF U.S. INVOLVEMENT.

Further reading: Coffman, Edward M. *The War to End All Wars: The American Military Experience in World War I.* Madison: University of Wisconsin Press, 1986; Farwell, Byron. *Over There: The United States in the Great War, 1917–1918.* New York: Norton, 1999; Hallas, James H. *Doughboy War: The American Expeditionary Force in World War I.* Boulder, Colo.: Lynne Rienner, 2000;

Stallings, Laurence. *The Doughboys: The Story of the AEF, 1917–1918.* New York: Harper & Row, 1963.
— David L. Snead and Spencer C. Tucker

American Indian wars, overview *The military confrontation between Euro-American settlers and the indigenous population of North America*

The American Indian wars lasted from the early 17th to the late 19th centuries. In nearly 2,000 separate engagements, the Indian tribes were defeated militarily, and the continent was made accessible for white settlement. Most of the campaigns were driven by white settler desires for land and wealth and were justified by a social Darwinist and expansionist worldview. They were also characterized by one-sided demonstrations of Euro-American technological supremacy and superior social organization.

The Indian nations had for thousands of years fought among themselves for hunting grounds, revenge, and personal aggrandizement. They were familiar with guerrilla warfare techniques, and many regarded warfare as the only suitable occupation for males. Euro-American society thus did not introduce war to North America but rather presented a new kind of military challenge for the indigenous population, one that ultimately proved insurmountable.

The colonial period was marked by almost continuous warfare. Those conflicts were characterized not only by settlers' desire for land but also by a contest for empire between Britain and France in which Indian tribes were used as allies. The tribes' knowledge of the land and their ability to sustain numbers of warriors in a hostile environment made them valuable to the belligerent powers.

By the late 18th century, the military power of the Indians east of the Mississippi was already in sharp decline because of their long involvement in colonial wars with British, French, and Spanish settlers and because of European diseases, for which the Native Americans had no immunity.

After early reversals under Josiah HARMAR and Arthur ST. CLAIR, the new republic won victories over the Indians in the Northwest in the Battle of FALLEN TIMBERS (1794) and the Battle of TIPPECANOE (1811). These effectively ended the ability of tribes in the Northwest Territory to challenge white intrusion.

Between 1812 and the 1840s, the U.S. government relocated the eastern tribes to territories west of the Mississippi thus far untouched by white settlement. It was assumed that this territory, at the time called the Great American Desert, was largely unfit for white settlement. These removals were met by occasional military resistance. The most prominent campaigns were the SEMINOLE WARS (1817–18, 1835–42, 1856–58) and the Black Hawk War, when the Sac and Fox Indians refused to quit their homelands.

Despite legislation intended to prohibit white migration to the Indian territory (the Indian Intercourse Act of 1834), conflict was inevitable as new territories came under the control of the U.S. government. After the MEXICAN-AMERICAN WAR and the Oregon settlement, Indian country no longer marked the effective western boundary of the United States but rather divided it in two. The California gold rush of 1848–49 produced massive migration through Indian country. The trails not only violated laws but radically altered the ecological balance of the territory as settlers and migrants began to reduce the buffalo herds that served as the economic and cultural basis of many tribes.

The government approached the Indian question with a mixture of negotiation and military force. The primary military objective was to keep the travel routes to the West open, through a system of military outposts. Hostile tribes were crushed in a number of campaigns such as the Rouge River War, the Yakima War, and the campaign of 1858, which eliminated Indian military resistance in the Oregon Territory.

The Civil War temporarily diverted Washington's military energies, but local volunteers replaced Federal troops departing the Indian frontier. A number of tribes participated in the war on both sides. Most of the western tribes, however, used the opportunity of a militarily divided United States to attack along the frontier. Warfare in the West dramatically increased in brutality, as demonstrated by the 1862 Sioux uprising in Minnesota and the 1864 SAND CREEK MASSACRE in Colorado.

After the Union victory in the Civil War, the U.S. Army was reorganized for peacetime duties, such as policing the South and controlling the Plains Indians. By the time the regulars returned to the frontier, the policy of a permanent Indian country had been abandoned. The Homestead Act of 1862 had opened farmland, and railroads were working their way westward through Indian country. The army's mission was to clear the way for settlement by forcing the Indians onto, or back onto, reservations. Initially outnumbered and outgunned, the army took advantage of new transportation and communications technology to carry out coordinated military operations against the remaining hostile western tribes.

In the fall of 1868, Major General Philip SHERIDAN, commander of the Department of the Missouri, initiated a new strategy of forcing four southern nations onto reservations. He waged his campaign in winter when the food supply was lowest for the Indians and their mobility at a low point. The alternative to starvation was surrender.

The U.S. Grant administration's "peace policy" did not bring peace, however. The most spectacular of the conflicts that resulted were those with the SIOUX and the Cheyenne of the northern plains between 1876 and 1881. This period saw the Battle of the LITTLE BIGHORN (1876), the RED

RIVER WAR (1874–75), the MODOC WAR (1872–73), and the APACHE WARS, ending with the defeat of GERONIMO in 1886. The final military engagements took place at WOUNDED KNEE (1890) and in Minnesota, with a military expedition against the Ojibwa in 1898.

With those last engagements, more than two centuries of military confrontation between Native Americans and Euro-American settlers ended. The tribes had been defeated by superior Euro-American social organization, the railroad, the repeating rifle, the telegraph, and destruction of the buffalo. The strategy of annihilation employed by many army commanders in the post–Civil War period had seriously threatened the survival of many tribes. Army casualties between 1866 and 1891 amounted to 932 killed and more than 1,000 wounded. Native American casualties are unknown. The military defeat ended Native American control over vast stretches of North America. For the U.S. Army, the Indian wars provided a proving ground for future colonial warfare, such as the PHILIPPINE-AMERICAN WAR.

See also BLACK HAWK; CRAZY HORSE; CREEK WAR; CUSTER, GEORGE A.; DUTCH-INDIAN WARS; FETTERMAN DISASTER; FRENCH AND INDIAN WAR; GREAT SWAMP FIGHT; HARMAR'S EXPEDITION; HORSESHOE BEND/TOHOPEKA, BATTLE OF; IROQUOIS WAR; KING PHILIP'S WAR; MACKENZIE, RANALD S.; MILES, NELSON A.; OPECHANCANOUGH, CHIEF; OSEOLA; PEQUOT WAR; PONTIAC'S REBELLION; POWDER RIVER EXPEDITION; POWHATAN; RED CLOUD, CHIEF; ROSEBUD RIVER, BATTLE OF; ST. CLAIR'S EXPEDITION; SALTCREEK PRAIRIE RAID; SHERMAN, WILLIAM T.; SHERIDAN, PHILIP H.; SIOUX WARS; SITTING BULL; TECUMSEH; TUSCARORA WAR; WASHITA RIVER, BATTLE OF; WAYNE, ANTHONY.

Further reading: Starkey, Armstrong. *European and Native American Warfare, 1675–1815.* Norman: University of Oklahoma Press, 1998; Utley, Robert M. *Frontier Regulars: The United States Army and the Indian, 1866–1891.* New York: Macmillan, 1973; ———. *The Indian Frontier and the American West, 1846–1891.* Albuquerque: University of New Mexico Press, 1997; Wooster, Robert. *The Military and United States Indian Policy, 1865–1903.* New Haven, Conn.: Yale University Press, 1988.

— Frank Schumacher

American Red Cross (1868–Present) *Humanitarian organization founded for the purpose of assisting wounded soldiers, civilians, and prisoners of war during periods of conflict*

Over the course of time, the goals of the group have expanded to include providing assistance to victims of natural disasters, epidemics, and famine.

In 1863, the Swiss philanthropist Jean Henri Dunant, appalled by the effects of war, issued an appeal for leaders in Europe to form an organization to aid wounded soldiers. The first committee, a group of five Swiss citizens, founded the International Red Cross in Geneva. It held its first international conference in October 1863, with representatives from 16 nations attending. The delegates agreed to the Geneva Convention, a document that established rules governing the treatment of the wounded and provided protection for medical personnel. The committee adopted a white flag with a red cross as the symbol of the organization (the red cross would later be changed in non-Christian countries). Additional conferences in the 20th century expanded the rules to offer protection to all noncombatants.

Clarissa (Clara) BARTON founded the American Red Cross in 1881. Having served as a nurse during the U.S. Civil War, Barton recognized the need for this type of humanitarian effort. The Congress issued a charter for the organization in 1900, granting a second charter in 1905 when Mabel Thorp Boardman reorganized the Red Cross according to modern business management principles.

The Red Cross is charged with the responsibility to act as a conduit of information between service personnel and their families. It also aids victims suffering from pestilence, flood, fire, and other disasters. Specific programs include counseling services as well as emergency financial assistance, the largest blood-donor program in the world, clinical research, tissue services, the operation of the first U.S. bone marrow registry, nursing and health services, and first-aid instruction.

During WORLD WAR II the American Red Cross recruited nurses for the military, and it coordinated efforts of social workers to assist families of men drafted into the

Poster depicting a nurse to promote the American Red Cross during World War II   *(National Archives)*

armed services. The Red Cross also assisted European civilians who were victims of Nazi Germany. When the KOREAN WAR began on 25 June 1950, the Red Cross served military personnel by relaying emergency messages from families and by delivering personal packages. The blood-donor program provided military medical personnel with blood and plasma for the wounded. The Red Cross also took an active role in efforts to arrange prisoner-of-war exchanges during the war. Another program focused on providing entertainment for service personnel, while civilians with missing loved ones could turn to the organization to locate friends and family separated during the conflict. Fulfilling the same functions during the VIETNAM WAR, the Red Cross also initiated Operation Babylift in 1975, rescuing 2,000 orphaned babies and toddlers from that war-torn country. Another Red Cross program, Operation New Life, assisted more than 100,000 refugees from Southeast Asia, operating refugee camps in Guam and the United States and arranging for refugee resettlement.

In 1962 the Red Cross sent its first paid staff to Vietnam, where 480 field directors, hospital personnel, and recreation assistants provided services to soldiers. The recreation assistants, usually young female college students, boosted the morale of service personnel in remote areas and military hospitals. Approximately 280,500 soldiers a month participated in programs at 20 different locations. In 1976, budget reductions ended these programs in military hospitals.

The Red Cross also established health clinics in South Vietnam to assist refugees. It provided instruction in such areas as hygiene, while volunteers assisted in building and sanitation programs. Arrangements for emergency leave for soldiers because of the death or serious illness of immediate family members remained a high priority. Another important function performed by the Red Cross involved assisting returning service personnel to readjust to civilian life and to fill out paperwork so they could receive benefits.

During OPERATION DESERT SHIELD and OPERATION DESERT STORM, the Red Cross once again served as an intermediary between families and soldiers and provided financial assistance to those adversely affected by the deployment of a family wage-earner to the Middle East. After the conflict the Red Cross joined other groups, such as the Red Crescent, to assist refugees and third-country nationals fleeing the area.

During intervals of international peace the American Red Cross continues to participate in humanitarian efforts around the world. In 1985, the Red Cross initiated the African Relief Campaign to feed millions of starving people in the sub-Saharan region. After the Armenian earthquake in 1988, the organization operated a massive relief effort. Between 1992 and 1993, Somalia and other African nations received tons of food as the result of Red Cross efforts. After the 1994 massacre of Tutsis in Rwanda, the Red Cross assisted victims and their families. Civilians in the former Yugoslavia have received assistance from the Red Cross since 1996. The Red Cross also played a prominent role in assisting survivors and the families of victims in the 11 September 2001 terrorist attacks in New York City and Washington, D.C.

Originally intended to alleviate the plights of soldiers and victims of disasters, the Red Cross has continued to fulfill its mission. Millions of people have received assistance from the Red Cross, and nations around the world realize the need for, and extend recognition to, this nonpolitical relief agency.

See also AIR FORCE NURSE CORPS; ARMY NURSE CORPS; NAVY NURSE CORPS; NURSES.

Further reading: Berry, Nicholas O. *War and the Red Cross: The Unspoken Mission.* New York: St. Martin's Press, 1997. Forsythe, David P. *Humanitarian Politics: The International Committee of the Red Cross.* Baltimore: Johns Hopkins University Press, 1977; Hutchinson, John F. *Champions of Charity: War and the Rise of the Red Cross.* Boulder, Colo.: Westview, 1996; Moorehead, Caroline. *Dunant's Dream: War, Switzerland, and the History of the Red Cross.* New York: Carroll and Graf, 1999.

— Cynthia Clark Northrup

American Revolution, causes of

Interpretations of the causes of the American Revolutionary War have changed over time. Contemporaries of the Founding Fathers and many 19th-century historians emphasized the devotion of the colonists to Enlightenment principles and ideology. Early 20th-century historians stressed the economic self-interests of the many upper-class merchants and landowners who were at the forefront of revolutionary activity. The ideological interpretation has also received a powerful impetus in Bernard Bailyn's *The Ideological Origins of the American Revolution* (1967). Recently, New Left historians have added a class dimension to the debate. They see the revolution as not only a war to gain independence but also a means to advance the interest of the lower classes against upper-class exploiters within the colonies. Another interpretation is that over time the attitudes of the colonials came to differ markedly from those of the mother country and that the politicians in London were slow to realize this fact.

Conflict between Great Britain and the American colonies began to accelerate at the conclusion of the 1754–63 FRENCH AND INDIAN WAR. Fought and won largely by British regulars, the war had been costly. London now proposed stationing 10,000 British regulars in North America and called on the American colonists to partly subsidize this expense. A variety of money-raising measures followed: the Sugar Act of 1764, the Stamp Act of 1765, and the Townshend Duties of 1767. The colonists resisted each in turn. The Americans in practice enjoyed a degree of tax exemption within the empire, paying only such taxes as were imposed by their colonial legislatures. American leaders including Patrick Henry, John Dickinson, Samuel Adams, and others argued the theme of "no taxation without representation." London pointed out that the Americans did enjoy representation, that they might come to Britain to stand for the House of Commons like any other Englishman; Parliament represented the interest of all British subjects. For Americans, this concept of political sovereignty—often called virtual representation—was anathema.

As events unfolded in the late 1760s and early 1770s, many Americans became convinced that the British government, particularly Parliament, was plotting to extinguish colonial rights and liberties. Colonial dissent borrowed heavily from 18th-century British Whig thinkers who had criticized the Crown for corrupting the political process. Others, such as Samuel Adams, were heavily influenced by Puritan religious ideas that held that all authority had to be scrupulously kept in check lest citizens be unfairly deprived of liberties.

Events in the early 1770s were interpreted through this conspiratorial lens. Patriots saw the Boston Massacre of 5 March 1770 as an unprovoked attack on innocent citizens by royal soldiers, many of whom were "moonlighting" and taking the jobs of colonials. The Tea Act of 1773, while it lowered the price of tea, established a monopoly of the British East Indies Company and harmed a number of colonial tea merchants, such as John Hancock. In retaliation for the Boston Tea Party, the Coercive (Intolerable) Acts of 1774, which closed the port of Boston and substituted martial law for the authority of the Massachusetts legislature, were seen as unjustified intrusions into the internal affairs of a colony. What had been inflicted on Massachusetts could be applied to other colonies. Finally, the Quebec Act of 1774, which recognized the rights of Roman Catholics in an enlarged province of Quebec, raised anti-Catholic fears, particularly in New England; its definition of the boundaries of Canada as extending to the Ohio River conflicted with the western land claims of many of the colonies.

Even after the Battles of LEXINGTON AND CONCORD in April 1775, only a minority of Americans wanted separation from Great Britain. Indeed, many fought only to force London to change its course toward the American colonies. London's decision to bring the colonies to heel by armed might, for which King George III shared responsibility with Parliament, changed the minds of many in America. Increasing bloodshed hardened positions on both sides and forced reluctant colonists to choose between them. On 5 July 1775, the Continental Congress passed the Olive Branch Petition. Written by John Dickinson, it asked the king to take up the cause of the colonies against his ministers and Parliament. When King George III refused to receive the petition (a decision that became known to the colonists in November 1775), many reluctant revolutionaries felt they had little choice but to fight for independence.

See also AMERICAN REVOLUTIONARY WAR, LAND OVERVIEW; AMERICAN REVOLUTIONARY WAR, NAVAL OVERVIEW.

Further reading: Bailyn, Bernard. *The Ideological Origins of the American Revolution.* Cambridge, Mass.: Harvard University Press, 1967; Wood, Gordon S. *The American Revolution: A History.* New York: Modern Library, 2001; Young, Alfred F., ed. *The American Revolution: Explorations in the History of American Radicalism.* Dekalb: Northern Illinois University Press, 1976.

— Bruce Tap

American Revolutionary War, land overview
(1775–1783)

The American Revolutionary War on land presented each side with different problems. The theater of war was a long, relatively thin, and for the most part sparsely populated area, stretching 1,200 miles between the St. Lawrence River and Florida. Lacking roads and still largely undeveloped, it was strategically excellent defensive country and would be difficult to subdue. It also lacked strategic centers, the taking of which might decide the war. Perhaps a third of the population supported the British; another third favored independence; the remaining third was ambivalent.

The northern sector included New Hampshire, Massachusetts, Rhode Island, Connecticut, and New York; the central sector, New Jersey, Pennsylvania, Delaware, Maryland, and Virginia; and the southern sector, the Carolinas and Georgia. The British lacked the resources to take all at once, and the northern sector was the most important politically; it was also the easiest to invade because the British could use Canada as a base. If the rebellion could be put down in New England and New York, the probability was that even if the central and southern sectors continued to hold out, they could in time be subdued piecemeal. Thus the northern sector was the key.

The American Patriots had to create a military establishment from scratch, and they lacked military equipment of all kinds, especially cannon and powder. The British, on the other hand, faced staggering logistical problems in conducting land warfare. Britain had few human resources immediately available; most of its troops and supplies would have to be transported 3,000 miles across the Atlantic

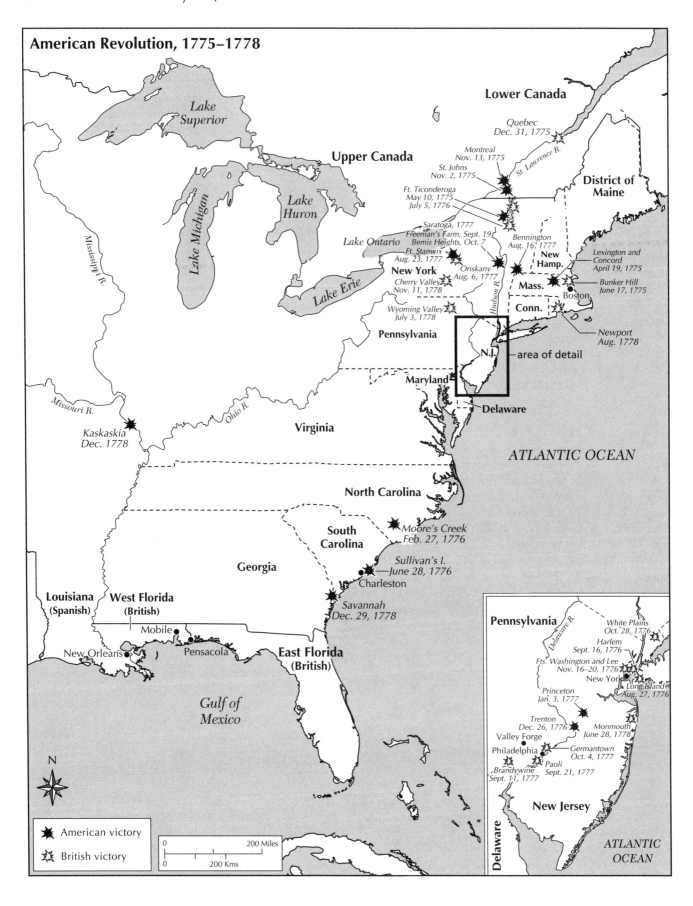

American Revolution, 1775–1778

Lake Superior

Lake Michigan

Lake Huron

Upper Canada

Lake Ontario

Lake Erie

Mississippi R.

Missouri R.

Ohio R.

Lower Canada

Quebec
Dec. 31, 1775

Montreal
Nov. 13, 1775

St. Johns
Nov. 2, 1775

St. Lawrence R.

District of Maine

Ft. Ticonderoga
May 10, 1775
July 5, 1776

Saratoga, 1777
Freeman's Farm, Sept. 19
Bemis Heights, Oct. 7

Ft. Stanwix
Aug. 23, 1777

New York

Oriskany
Aug. 6, 1777

Cherry Valley
Nov. 11, 1778

Wyoming Valley
July 3, 1778

Pennsylvania

Bennington
Aug. 16, 1777

New Hamp.

Hudson R.

Mass.

Conn.

Lexington and
Concord
April 19, 1775

Bunker Hill
June 17, 1775

Boston

Newport
Aug. 1778

N.J. —area of detail

Maryland

Delaware

Virginia

Kaskaskia
Dec. 1778

North Carolina

South Carolina

Moore's Creek
Feb. 27, 1776

Sullivan's I.
June 28, 1776

Charleston

Georgia

Savannah
Dec. 29, 1778

Louisiana
(Spanish)

West Florida
(British)

Mobile

New Orleans

Pensacola

East Florida
(British)

Gulf of Mexico

ATLANTIC OCEAN

N

★ American victory

✳ British victory

| 0 | | 200 Miles |
| 0 | | 200 Kms |

Pennsylvania

Delaware R.

White Plains
Oct. 28, 1776

Harlem
Sept. 16, 1776

Fts. Washington and Lee
Nov. 16–20, 1776

New York

Long Island
Aug. 27, 1776

Princeton
Jan. 3, 1777

Trenton
Dec. 26, 1776

Valley Forge

Philadelphia

Germantown
Oct. 4, 1777

Monmouth
June 28, 1778

Paoli
Sept. 21, 1777

Brandywine
Sept. 11, 1777

Delaware

New Jersey

ATLANTIC OCEAN

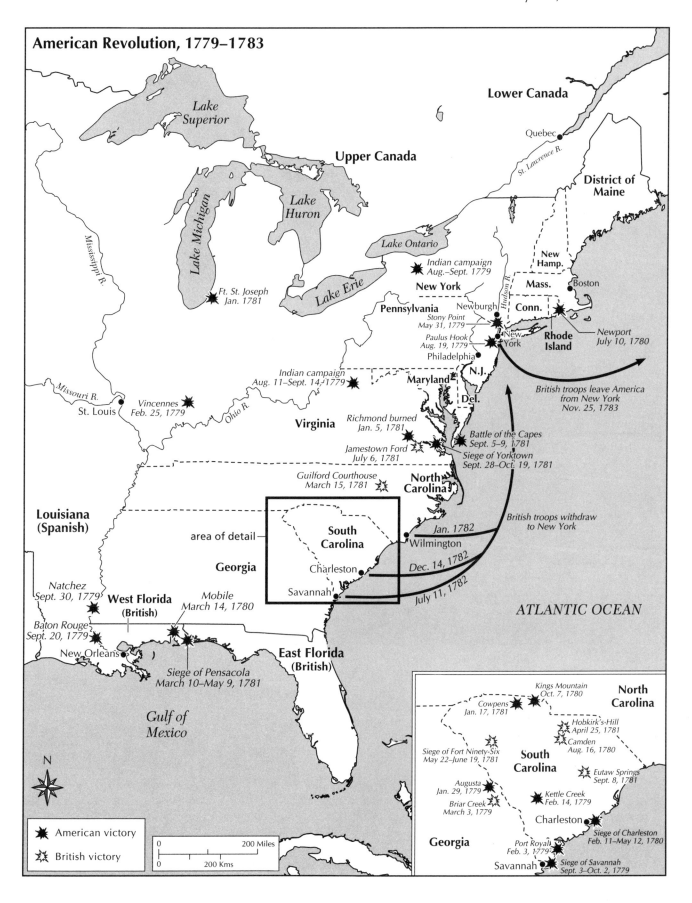

American Revolution, 1779–1783

Lower Canada

Lake Superior

Upper Canada

Lake Michigan

Lake Huron

Lake Erie

Lake Ontario

Quebec

St. Lawrence R.

District of Maine

New Hamp.

Mass.

Boston

Indian campaign Aug.–Sept. 1779

New York

Ft. St. Joseph Jan. 1781

Mississippi R.

Newburgh

Stony Point May 31, 1779

Paulus Hook Aug. 19, 1779

Pennsylvania

New York

Philadelphia

Conn.

Rhode Island

Newport July 10, 1780

Hudson R.

Missouri R.

Vincennes Feb. 25, 1779

St. Louis

Ohio R.

Indian campaign Aug. 11–Sept. 14, 1779

Maryland

N.J.

Del.

British troops leave America from New York Nov. 25, 1783

Virginia

Richmond burned Jan. 5, 1781

Jamestown Ford July 6, 1781

Battle of the Capes Sept. 5–9, 1781

Siege of Yorktown Sept. 28–Oct. 19, 1781

Guilford Courthouse March 15, 1781

North Carolina

Louisiana (Spanish)

area of detail

South Carolina

Jan. 1782

Wilmington

British troops withdraw to New York

Georgia

Charleston

Savannah

Dec. 14, 1782

July 11, 1782

ATLANTIC OCEAN

Natchez Sept. 30, 1779

West Florida (British)

Mobile March 14, 1780

Baton Rouge Sept. 20, 1779

New Orleans

Siege of Pensacola March 10–May 9, 1781

East Florida (British)

Gulf of Mexico

N

★ American victory

✺ British victory

0   200 Miles

0   200 Kms

Inset (area of detail):

Kings Mountain Oct. 7, 1780

North Carolina

Cowpens Jan. 17, 1781

Hobkirk's Hill April 25, 1781

Camden Aug. 16, 1780

Siege of Fort Ninety-Six May 22–June 19, 1781

South Carolina

Eutaw Springs Sept. 8, 1781

Augusta Jan. 29, 1779

Kettle Creek Feb. 14, 1779

Briar Creek March 3, 1779

Charleston

Siege of Charleston Feb. 11–May 12, 1780

Georgia

Port Royal Feb. 3, 1779

Savannah

Siege of Savannah Sept. 3–Oct. 2, 1779

and on to the fighting front. Although British control of the sea allowed the movement of troops at will along the Atlantic and Gulf of Mexico coasts, once British troops moved inland from coastal enclaves they could be cut off and destroyed. The British did not anticipate these difficulties or the magnitude of resistance. London thought in terms of a police action, in which a small force would arrest the troublemakers, after which the majority of Americans would rally to the Crown. The Patriots themselves did not anticipate a long war.

Fighting began on 19 April 1775 when British commander and captain general of Massachusetts Thomas Gage ordered 700 men from Boston to seize arms and ammunition stored by the Patriots at Concord. Forewarned, American minutemen prepared to meet the British. Fighting erupted at LEXINGTON. The British destroyed the stores, but their column suffered heavy casualties from colonial militia fire during its return to Boston. In May, the Second Continental Congress voted to raise an American army, named Virginian George WASHINGTON as its commander, dispatched an expedition to bring Quebec into the revolutionary effort, and entered into talks with France and other European powers. Meanwhile, encircling colonial militia laid siege to Boston. Also, on 10 May colonials took FORT TICONDEROGA in New York and its 120 cannon.

Gage had requested 20,000 troops. With half that figure he might have snuffed out the rebellion, but by June he had received only 3,500. Pressure from newly arrived Major Generals William Howe, Henry Clinton, and John Burgoyne led to British action. On 17 June Howe led an assault on the Charlestown peninsula, near Boston. On a third attempt the British took Breeds Hill and then went on to secure BUNKER HILL but with unacceptably heavy losses. The Americans drew the false impression from this that militia could stand up against a regular force.

During the winter of 1775–76, the cannon from Ticonderoga were transported to the Patriot works around Boston. These were emplaced by early March, and the British evacuated their 9,000-man garrison in mid-March, ending the first phase of the war.

While Boston was still under siege, Washington launched an invasion of Canada. Colonel Benedict ARNOLD with some 1,000 men worked through Maine toward Quebec. The expedition commander, Brigadier General Richard MONTGOMERY, with 1,200 more men, pushed up Lake Champlain to Montreal, which he occupied in November. Unfortunately for the Patriots, the British learned of American plans and fortified Quebec in time to prevent its capture; a desperate late-December assault was repulsed. The effort simply lacked sufficient support. Had it succeeded, it could have united Canada to the lower thirteen colonies and changed the course of the war.

London, meanwhile, looked to Europe for mercenaries. Most were German, and many were from Hesse, hence the term *Hessians*. During the conflict, some 30,000 Germans fought in the war, representing 37 percent of British forces deployed in America.

In 1776 the British pushed the remaining colonial forces from Canada. In June 1776 General Howe, with 32,000 men, set out from Halifax by sea. Howe's invasion of New York began the second phase of the war. In early July the British disembarked on Staten Island. During the New York campaign Howe repeatedly failed to press a series of victories, and Washington escaped each time. In August Howe landed on Long Island, but again Washington eluded him. In September Howe crossed to Manhattan and was again victorious in the Battles of KIP'S BAY and HARLEM HEIGHTS, and at WHITE PLAINS in October.

To culminate this awful campaign, Washington left an isolated garrison in FORT WASHINGTON on the Manhattan side of the Hudson River. On 16 November, with naval support from the Hudson, Howe stormed the fort and took 3,000 prisoners, 100 cannon, and a huge quantity of munitions. The same thing almost happened at FORT LEE, across the Hudson in New Jersey, a few days later. Warned, Washington and his army got away just in time. Washington now withdrew to the interior, pursued without much enthusiasm by the British, who ignored the Hudson River. Howe might have gone up it, instead of after Washington, and in the process split off New England from the rest of the colonies. If instead the destruction of the colonial army was his primary goal, Howe may be criticized for his failure to bag Washington's army and for his dilatory pursuit. Washington now withdrew behind the Delaware River for the winter.

General Guy Carleton had planned a secondary British offensive down the Lake Champlain corridor from Canada, but Brigadier General Arnold countered with a small flotilla of gondolas and fought two naval battles, VALCOUR ISLAND and Split Rock, on Lake Champlain in October. Although defeated, Arnold thereby delayed Howe's secondary thrust just long enough to cause its cancellation It was thus an important, and often overlooked, effort. A third thrust, against CHARLESTON, South Carolina, under Henry Clinton, met rebuff before a sturdy palmetto-log fortification commanded by William Moultrie.

Meanwhile the British had gone into winter quarters along the Delaware River line, which was covered by a line of posts, of which the most important was at Trenton, held by 1,300 Hessians. Washington's force was ravaged by sickness, with many enlistments about to expire. He therefore decided on a desperate gamble. On Christmas Day, Washington and his men recrossed the icy Delaware. The next morning Washington defeated the Hessians at TRENTON. He followed this victory by taking PRINCETON in early January. These two small victories fanned the dying embers of American independence into flame and established Washington's military reputation.

The year 1777 saw two conflicting British offensives. The minister of colonies, Lord George Germain, who was actually running the war, approved two contradictory British plans, one by Howe and the other by Burgoyne. Burgoyne planned a renewed effort to cut off New England, severing the northern colonies along the Lake Champlain corridor. Lieutenant Colonel Barry St. Leger, meanwhile, would move west, then south down the Mohawk Valley, uniting with Burgoyne. Burgoyne expected Howe to send a force up the Hudson to meet him at Albany. Howe, however, wanted to take the Patriot capital of Philadelphia, believing that Washington would fight to defend it and be destroyed. Germain approved both plans.

Burgoyne quickly captured the primary American defensive position at Fort Ticonderoga, but St. Leger was rebuffed at FORT STANWIX and ultimately withdrew. Undaunted, and though Howe informed him that he would be sending only one corps north up the Hudson (it got to the vicinity of present-day Hyde Park), Burgoyne continued on, unsupported. Washington sent reinforcements north in the hopes of cutting off and destroying a British army in the interior. The Americans defeated part of Burgoyne's force in the Battle of BENNINGTON and forced the surrender of the remainder in the September and October battles of SARATOGA. This was one of the most important battles of the war, for it brought France openly into the conflict on the American side.

Meanwhile, Howe had transported a large force into Chesapeake Bay, disembarked them, and driven on Philadelphia from the south. Washington moved to meet him, taking up position at BRANDYWINE CREEK. Here the Americans were again defeated, but they managed to withdraw in good order. Howe occupied Philadelphia, though it was of no strategic importance. Meanwhile, the Americans spent a difficult winter at VALLEY FORGE near Philadelphia. Here, however, the army finally received European-style training, from Fredrich von STEUBEN.

With the end of winter in 1778, Henry Clinton succeeded Howe. Clinton evacuated Philadelphia, and Washington attacked the withdrawing British at MONMOUTH, New Jersey, a battle that proved inconclusive. Clinton then withdrew to New York. To the west, the Americans launched a small but effective campaign to secure the Ohio River Valley. A militia force under the command of George Rogers CLARK captured important towns along the Mississippi and eventually captured a British fort at Vincennes (in present-day Indiana).

In 1779 Germain decided to concentrate on the South, without abandoning the Hudson. The South had the advantage of being close to British bases in the West Indies. The British also hoped to use the southern slaves as political tools to destabilize the region, issuing proclamations that offered protection to slaves who ran away from their masters. This only caused whites slave owners in the South to unite against the British. In a supreme irony, the Revolution came to defend slavery, a legacy that would haunt the new nation.

The British also attempted to turn over more of the fighting to the Loyalists. They would send in a small force of regulars to subdue an area, then arm Loyalists and encourage them to rise up and hold it. The British ended up igniting a cruel civil war, in which both sides were guilty of barbarities.

Germain proposed to conquer Georgia, next the Carolinas, and finally Virginia. He assumed that isolation of the northern states would lead them to collapse through exhaustion. From this point on the American South was the main theater of the war.

The British captured Savannah in December 1778 and by the end of February 1779 had taken all of Georgia. Inconclusive fighting followed. Then in 1780 Clinton put together the largest British offensive force since 1777, some 14,000 men, laying siege to CHARLESTON in March. In May Major General Benjamin LINCOLN surrendered the city with the loss of nearly 5,500 men and 400 cannon, the greatest disaster to befall the Patriot cause during the war.

Clinton believed South Carolina to be fully conquered. Leaving Major General Charles Cornwallis with 8,500 men, he returned to New York early in June. Congress, without consulting Washington, appointed Major General Horatio GATES, victor at Saratoga, to take command of the southern army. He set out to seize the British post at CAMDEN, South Carolina. Cornwallis rushed up to meet him, utterly routing the Americans that August. This marked a low point in the Patriot cause. Paper money was now all but worthless, and Washington's army had suffered greatly in the winter of 1779–80 at MORRISTOWN, New Jersey. States would not furnish supplies or men, the supply system broke down, regiments of the Continental army mutinied in 1780 and 1781, and in September 1780 Benedict Arnold turned traitor at West Point.

Despite these disasters, the tide of battle was about to turn. Washington replaced Gates with Major General Nathaniel GREENE, with Steuben as second in command. Greene would yield territory while he rebuilt his force, splitting his army into small bands. Cornwallis followed suit. After Camden, new British mounted forces successfully employed irregular tactics and achieved tactical mobility equal or superior to that of the rebels themselves. However, the British never had anything approaching the number of men necessary to pacify the region. Neither side was able to protect its civilian supporters, and a ferocious guerrilla war spread through the South. In 1781 Cornwallis shifted priorities and concentrated his mobile forces in order to destroy the rebel army.

In October 1780 at KING'S MOUNTAIN, a Patriot militia force surrounded and annihilated a Loyalist force. Greene, meanwhile, assumed the offensive, although he wisely restricted himself to guerrilla warfare. At the beginning of 1781, in order to support Cornwallis, Clinton sent Brigadier General Arnold, now in British service, and 1,600 men to the Chesapeake. In reply, Washington sent Major General Marie-Joseph de LAFAYETTE and a smaller force to oppose him.

In January 1781 Patriot forces under Brigadier General Daniel MORGAN, operating in the vicinity of King's Mountain, defeated a British force under Lieutenant Colonel Tarleton in the Battle of COWPENS, South Carolina. Morgan then retreated and rejoined Greene, pursued by Cornwallis's fast-moving and superior force through North Carolina and into southern Virginia and then back into North Carolina. Finally, the two armies came together at GUILFORD COURTHOUSE. Greene was defeated, but the battle cost the British 25 percent casualties. Cornwallis now decided to abandon the interior and march to the coast at Wilmington. He then moved north to join some 2,500 men Clinton had sent to establish a base in Virginia at YORKTOWN.

For Washington, 1781 opened disastrously. First the Pennsylvania Line regiment and the New Jersey Line mutinied. Washington still hoped to drive the British from New York. His main forces were posted at White Plains, now reinforced by 4,000 French troops under Lieutenant General Jean-Baptiste Donatien de Vimeur, comte de Rochambeau.

Early in May 1781, French admiral Jacques Melchoir Saint-Laurent, comte de Barras, sailed into Newport, Rhode Island, with a small squadron. He brought news that Admiral the count de Grasse was on his way from France with a powerful fleet. The war at sea was being fought mainly in the West Indies around the Lesser Antilles, but the French fleet would be available northward during the hurricane season.

Meanwhile, actions by Arnold and his British forces in the Chesapeake Bay and along the James River all the way to Richmond had caused Washington to send 1,200 troops under Lafayette to try to trap him. Cornwallis now came up and took over command of what amounted to 7,000 men, approximately one-quarter of the British armed strength in North America.

Then came news, in mid-August, that de Grasse would not come to New York but instead to the Chesapeake and that he would arrive later that month and remain there until 25 October. Washington saw immediately the possibility of a strategic concentration of forces on land while de Grasse held the bay. If this could be accomplished before Clinton could relieve the situation, Washington could destroy the British force at Yorktown. Washington now ordered Lafayette to contain Cornwallis and sent 2,000

American and 4,000 French soldiers south, leaving only 2,000 Continentals to watch Clinton in New York. Not until 2 September did Clinton grasp what had happened. He promised Cornwallis a diversion, but this consisted only of sending General Arnold against New London, Connecticut.

Meanwhile, at the end of September the French and Americans assembled near Williamsburg. Before this, however, the most important naval battle of the war occurred. An early September standoff between de Grasse and Admirals Alexander Hood and Samuel Graves in the Battle of the CHESAPEAKE left the French in control of the bay. During the battle, Barras was able to slip in with siege artillery.

When Washington's army arrived at Yorktown on 26 September, the French fleet was in full control of the bay, blocking Cornwallis's sea route of escape. Washington had 9,000 Americans, 3,000 of them militia, and 6,000 French. Cornwallis surrendered on 17 October. The British, having lost control of the American seaboard for one brief period, lost the war. The conflict continued, however, for two more years. Greene and Washington maintained their armies in position near Charleston and New York, but the only fighting to occur was some skirmishing in the South.

Yorktown brought down the British government and ushered in a policy of cutting losses immediately. In London's view, France was the real enemy, and British strategy shifted to that of befriending its former foe in order to prevent it from falling into the French orbit. This found expression in the 1783 TREATY OF PARIS.

See also AMERICAN REVOLUTIONARY WAR, NAVAL OVERVIEW; CONTINENTAL ARMY, OVERVIEW; FRANCE AND THE AMERICAN REVOLUTION; MILITIA, ORGANIZATION AND ROLE OF; MINUTEMAN.

Further reading: Black, Jeremy. *War for America: The Fight for Independence, 1775–1783*. Stroud, U.K.: Alan Sutton, 1991; Higginbotham, Don. *The War of American Independence: Military Attitudes, Policies, and Practice, 1763–1789.* New York: Macmillan, 1971; Middlekauff, Robert. *The Glorious Cause: The American Revolution, 1763–1789.* New York: Oxford University Press, 1982; Royster, Charles. *A Revolutionary People at War: The Continental Army and the American Character, 1775–1783.* Chapel Hill: University of North Carolina Press, 1979; Ward, Christopher. *The War of the Revolution.* Edited by John R. Alden. 2 vols. New York: Macmillan, 1952.

— Patrick R. Jennings and Spencer C. Tucker

American Revolutionary War, naval overview
(1775–1783)
American and allied seapower was vital in the outcome of the American Revolutionary War. With 28 warships

originally blockading the East Coast from Halifax to Florida, Britain could keep its trade routes open and operate out of Halifax and New York throughout the war and, for limited periods, from Chesapeake Bay, Boston, Newport, Charleston, and Savannah. When the colonists revolted, however, they denied Britain some 2,000 ships and 18,000 seamen. Moreover, colonists were handy with rifles, knowledgeable about building at least small sailing ships, and had gained wartime experience at sea during the FRENCH AND INDIAN WAR (1754–63). It was with these strengths that the Continental Congress created the Continental navy on 23 October 1775, placing it under the jurisdiction of the newly appointed American Naval Committee, headed by Richard Morris.

The American Naval Committee selected Esek HOPKINS to command the small fleet it created by converting a number of merchant vessels to warships. Hopkins had captained a number of merchant ships and had commanded a privateer during the French and Indian War. The Continental navy's first ships were two sloops; at its apogee it had 57 ships. Of 13 frigates authorized by Congress, four were destroyed to avoid their falling into British hands, three were blockaded in ports by British fleets, one blew up, and the rest were captured. The committee also called upon the states to fill quotas for military service. Eleven of the 13 founded navies, mostly of small craft, but they failed to fill the committee's quotas. The main tasks of the state navies were to import supplies and defend America's coastline. In addition to creating navies, states also issued letters of marque to privateers. While they were primarily interested in making a profit, privateers contributed to the ultimate American victory by seizing some 600 British ships by war's end.

In the Continental navy's first major action of the war, Hopkins landed a force at New Providence in the Bahamas in early March 1776. Although he succeeded in obtaining badly needed powder, Hopkins could not thereafter field a task force because of British opposition and because privateering proved more attractive to seamen than did naval service.

Unfortunately for Britain, its navy also displayed various weaknesses. In addition to the disadvantage of having to cross 3,000 miles of ocean to reach the rebels and secure logistic support, many ships of the line used during the Seven Years' War had rotted in reserve by 1776, and a desire for economy had kept new ships smaller than they should have been. To replace American masts, inferior Baltic fir was substituted. Most naval officers opposed the war; some resigned rather than fight the colonists, and sailors who had been impressed had no heart for the struggle. The Royal Navy at sea also divided its attention when France entered the American Revolutionary War.

Despite these disadvantages, Britain held a huge naval advantage over the Continental navy. In 1775 Britain had converted 131 warships from merchantmen and would have 608 such ships in 1783. As a result, Continental captains opted for a GUERRE DE COURSE strategy of raiding British merchant ships. Among the best of about 1,597 of these captains, some of whom operated in British waters, were Nicholas BIDDLE, Lambert Wickes, Gustavus Conyngham, and John Paul JONES. They forced the British to escort their merchant ships and troopships, emptied many British ships of their supplies, and seized prizes worth some $18 million. British commercial losses stimulated demands at home to end the war. These captains also established much of the fighting tradition inherited by the U.S. NAVY.

British naval power contributed greatly to its military successes in 1776. Able to land forces at will on the American coast, Britain gained a military superiority that allowed it to drive the Continental army commander, General George WASHINGTON, from New York. On the other hand, British efforts to invade New England and upstate New York from Canada were delayed by Brigadier General Benedict ARNOLD, who had assembled 15 small ships on Lake Champlain. Although Arnold was forced to allow the 30 British ships to sail by and was defeated in the Battle of VALCOUR ISLAND, he delayed the British long enough to force them called off their invasion. As a result, the Americans gained a year's time with which to prepare to counter new forces led by Major General John Burgoyne.

The only other major action involving the Continental Navy came in the PENOBSCOT campaign in August 1779. Anxious to defend itself from the 700 British troops brought by ship from Halifax and stop Britons from seizing timber, Massachusetts called upon Commodore Dudley Saltonstall to attack the British garrison in the Penobscot River area of Maine. Including three Continental warships based in Boston Harbor and 12 privateers, Saltonstall had a total of 19 armed vessels, 20 or more transports, 200 guns of various calibers, more than 2,000 seamen, and 1,500 militia. Unfortunately, he knew nothing about conducting amphibious operations and failed to heed the admonition of Massachusetts to cooperate with the military leaders, who in any case proved equally deficient. Upon arriving at the mouth of the Penobscot River, Saltonstall ordered nine of his ships in three divisions to attack three sloops that Captain Henry Mowat had stationed across it, and four fireships behind them. Much firing followed, but no damage occurred. American troops got ashore but were driven back. American ships got the worse of an exchange of cannon fire the next day. When the Navy Board notified Saltonstall that a British relief force was approaching and that he should attack, he planned a full sea and land assault on 13 August. Informed next day that four heavy and three light relief ships were approaching, he signaled his ships to scatter and find safety where they could. Most ships ran aground, but some were blown up by their crews. Fourteen ships were destroyed and 28 were captured, 500 Americans were either killed or captured, and an estimated $7 million had been wasted. For his actions in one of the saddest spectacles in American naval history, Saltonstall was court-martialed and dismissed from the service.

Although the Penobscot campaign was a disaster for the Continental navy, it was more than compensated for by the success of American diplomacy, which had brought France, and more important, the French navy, into the American Revolutionary War. After its defeat in the Seven Years' War (1756–63), France had rebuilt its navy and awaited an opportunity to avenge itself against Britain. After Burgoyne surrendered at SARATOGA on 17 October 1777, French and American diplomats negotiated a Franco-American alliance, which was signed on 8 February 1778. Aggravated by British arrogance, Spain and Holland would also enter the American Revolutionary War. By 1779 Britain faced a worldwide war, and her 72 ships of the line faced 92 French and Spanish.

Although corruption and indifference had reduced British naval power during the first two years of the war, French intervention forced the British to go all-out to furnish good ships and crews. Nonetheless, the British failed to see the need to blockade Brest and Toulon, from which French warships reached American waters. Some British naval operations, such as the taking of the Dutch West Indies island of St. Eustatius, were undertaken for profit rather than for a strategic purpose.

Although France and Spain squandered much energy in capturing them, the British overseas territories proved crucial to the American cause by providing ammunition, harassing British seaborne commerce, and supporting American military operations. With the appearance of a fleet—20 ships of the line, 13 frigates, and transports carrying 6,000 troops—commanded by a "general at sea," Charles-Henri-Hector, comte d'Estaing, British Major General Henry Clinton evacuated Philadelphia for New York, where d'Estaing bottled him up. Rather than attack Clinton there, d'Estaing operated in the West Indies and off the southern American coast, but his mere presence caused the British to evacuate Philadelphia and Newport, eased the grip of British ships on American merchants, and provided Washington the intelligence he needed to determine future British moves. In June 1781, for example, Washington learned that Admiral François-Joseph-Paul, comte de Grasse, would be sailing to the Chesapeake, where British Lieutenant General Charles, Lord Cornwallis had established his headquarters at YORKTOWN to await reinforcements and resupply.

Beginning on 5 September 1781, in the Second Battle of the CHESAPEAKE, de Grasse sparred for five days with a British fleet under Admirals Sir Samuel Hood and Sir Thomas Graves. Either disobeying or misunderstanding orders from Graves, Hood failed to "close up" with him, and a chance for success was perhaps lost. Meanwhile, Commodore compte Barras de Saint Laurent, stationed at Newport, slipped into the Chesapeake and landed French reinforcements and artillery. de Grasse sped back to the Chesapeake to join Barras; Graves, with 19 ships, could not hope to defeat 36 French ships. He abandoned Cornwallis, who surrendered at Yorktown on 19 October with one-third of the British army in North America, dashing hopes for victory.

Although the United States might have eventually won the war anyway, naval power certainly determined the timing of its victory. Even though American and allied seapower had helped win the war, the first U.S. Congress sold off its navy. Those who wished to pursue a naval career, such as John Paul JONES, were obliged to do so in other countries.

See also AMERICAN REVOLUTIONARY WAR, LAND OVERVIEW; FRANCE IN THE AMERICAN REVOLUTION; SPAIN IN THE AMERICAN REVOLUTION.

Further reading: Allen, Gardner W. *A Naval History of the American Revolution.* 2 vols. Boston: Houghton, Mifflin, 1913. Reprint, Williamstown, Mass.: Cornerhouse, 1970; Balch, Thomas. *The French in America during the War of Independence of the United States, 1777–1783.* 2 vols. Philadelphia: Porter & Oates, 1891–95; Bird, Harrison. *Navies in the Mountains: The Battles on the Waters of Lake Champlain and Lake George, 1609–1814.* New York: Oxford University Press, 1962; Chadwick, French Ensor, ed. *The Graves Papers and Other Documents Relating to the Naval Operations of the Yorktown Campaign July to October 1782.* New York: Naval History Society, 1916; Preston, Antony, D. Lyon, and John H. Batchelor, eds. *Navies of the American Revolution.* Englewood Cliffs, N.J.: Prentice Hall, 1975; Syrett, David. *The Royal Navy in American Waters, 1775–1783.* London: Scholar, 1989.

— Paolo E. Coletta

Anaconda Plan *Civil War Union military strategy designed in effect to strangle the Confederacy*
Drafted in May 1861 by the commander of the army, Brevet Lieutenant General Winfield SCOTT, the strategy promised to win the war by blockading the more than 3,000 miles of the Confederacy's Atlantic and Gulf coasts, then bisecting the South by means of its rivers. Scott's plan called for a combined naval gunboat/army offensive to seize control of the Mississippi River, splitting off the Trans-Mississippi West from the remainder of the Confederacy. Scott hoped his limited offensive strategy could achieve a restoration of the Union by demonstrating Northern strength.

Scott, a native Virginian, came under attack from critics who saw him as somehow defending his native South. They sought immediate Union action against Confederate forces forming at Manassas Junction and had no patience for a time-consuming buildup of naval and land forces. Few saw the war lasting long enough for Scott's elaborate plan to reach fruition. In Northern newspapers, Scott's plan became derisively known as the Anaconda Plan, in reference to the giant snake that slowly strangles its victim.

The First Battle of BULL RUN/MANASSAS led both sides to take the long-term steps necessary for an expanded war. Over the next four years, as various Union offensives succeeded or failed, Scott's plan emerged as the basis for eventual northern victory. However, while the Anaconda Plan advanced a naval blockade and capture of the Mississippi, both important to the eventual Union success, its passive nature undermines historical claims to be the full blueprint for the Northern victory.

See also CIVIL WAR, LAND OVERVIEW; CIVIL WAR, NAVAL OVERVIEW.

Further reading: Beringer, Richard E., et al. *Why the South Lost the Civil War.* Athens: University of Georgia Press, 1986; Johnson, Timothy D. *Winfield Scott: The Quest for Military Glory.* Lawrence: University Press of Kansas, 1998.

— Thomas D. Veve

Anderson, Robert (1805–1871) *U.S. Army general*
Born on 14 June 1805 near Louisville, Kentucky, Robert Anderson graduated from the U.S. Military Academy in 1825. Commissioned into the 3d Artillery, he served at a variety of posts and saw action in the Black Hawk War and in the Second SEMINOLE WAR. Serving under Major General Winfield SCOTT during the MEXICAN-AMERICAN WAR, he was wounded in the Battle of MOLINO DEL REY, for which he earned one of his two brevets for gallantry. Anderson then performed routine administrative duties and translated French artillery manuals, rising through the ranks to major in the 1st Artillery by 1857.

In November 1860, during the mounting secession crisis, Anderson assumed command of the three Federal forts (Castle Pinckney, Fort Moultrie, and the yet-unfinished Fort Sumter) in Charleston Harbor. Anderson took his station at Fort Moultrie, where he stayed until South Carolina's secession on 20 December rendered Moultrie untenable. Anderson moved his two-company garrison to Fort Sumter on 26 December; South Carolina officials regarded the movement as a hostile act.

A proslavery Kentuckian, Anderson nonetheless remained loyal to the Union. He hoped to avoid war but would not yield his now-isolated post. He refused to return fire when in January 1861 South Carolina batteries turned back the relief ship *Star of the West.* The new Confederate government demanded Sumter's surrender, while the incoming administration of Abraham LINCOLN vowed to maintain the fort. On 11 April Anderson rejected a final Confederate demand for surrender but indicated that without supplies he would be obliged to abandon the fort within days. Confederate authorities chose not to risk the arrival of a relief expedition and informed Anderson that an attack was forthcoming.

At 4:30 on the morning of 12 April, Confederate batteries opened on FORT SUMTER. Unable to respond effectively, Anderson and his men endured a devastating bombardment for the next day and a half. At noon on 14 April, Anderson surrendered.

The first Union war hero, Anderson was promoted to brigadier general in the regular army. He assumed command of the Department of Kentucky (later the Department of the Cumberland), but failing health forced him to retire in October 1863. He was breveted major general for his actions at Sumter.

On 14 April 1865, four years after he surrendered, Anderson raised the U.S. flag at recaptured Fort Sumter. He died in Nice, France, on 26 October 1871.

See also CIVIL WAR, CAUSES OF.

Further reading: Garrison, Webb B. *Lincoln's Little War.* Nasville, Tenn.: Rutledge Hill Press, 1997; Klein, Maury. *Days of Defiance: Sumter, Secession, and the Coming of the Civil War.* New York: Knopf, 1997; Swanberg, W. A. *First Blood: The Story of Fort Sumter.* New York: Scribner, 1957.

— Shane Nall

Andersonville *Infamous Civil War prisoner-of-war (POW) camp where thousands of soldiers died of malnutrition and disease*
In fall 1863, Confederate authorities decided to move Northern prisoners away from the vicinity of Richmond. The area's food supply was already strained, and the prisoners could be a liability in the event of a new Federal invasion. Officials discussed several possible sites before settling on the small town of Andersonville, near Americus, in Sumter County, Georgia.

The land, cleared by slaves, was a good place for the prison. Its design was simple; a large stockade of hewn pine logs originally surrounded some 16.5 acres, although this was subsequently expanded. Sentry boxes sat perched on the wall about every 88 feet, and earthen redoubts to defend against Federal cavalry were constructed at the corners. A small creek, later called Stockade Branch, passed through the center of the site, providing water and waste

Union prisoner-of-war compound, Andersonville, Georgia   *(U.S. Army Military History Institute)*

disposal. In theory, if well supplied, Andersonville could hold around 8,000 men.

Capt. Henry Wirz, who had been wounded in the Battle of SEVEN PINES/FAIR OAKS and upon recovering had run the Richmond military prison, took command of the new facility. Confederate authorities were far from ready when the first prisoners began to arrive. This was aggravated by the refusal of Lieutenant General Ulysses S. GRANT to exchange prisoners. Each successive trainload of men increased problems at the prison exponentially, and its population soon surpassed the theoretical maximum capacity. Mismanagement by Confederate authorities compounded the problems. Difficulties in obtaining lumber prevented the construction of barracks for the prisoners; the men scraped together what they could to build crude huts to shelter themselves from cold winter rain and blistering summer sun. Food was also scarce in the area.

Stockade Branch soon overflowed with waste, which, coupled with the deficiencies in nutrition, led to serious outbreaks of scurvy and dysentery. Desperate for water, the Confederates allowed prisoners to dig wells, which some used as escape tunnels. Soldiers died by the thousands and were buried outside the walls in the prison cemetery.

All told, some 41,000 men were held at Andersonville, as many as 30,000 at one time in a facility designed to hold less than a third that number. More than 14,000 men died there. Eventually, the movement of Major General William T. SHERMAN into Georgia, coupled with a review of the prison conditions, led to a decision to move the majority of the men away from Andersonville. In the fall of 1864, Confederate authorites transferred many of the prisoners to Millen (Georgia) and Florence (South Carolina).

After the end of hostilities, Major Wirz was made a scapegoat for the evils of Andersonville. Tried and convicted, he gained the dubious distinction of becoming the only person hanged for war crimes during the Civil War.

See also CIVIL WAR, LAND OVERVIEW.

Further reading: Futch, Ovid L. *History of Andersonville Prison.* Gainesville: University of Florida Press, 1968;

Marvel, William. *Andersonville: The Last Depot.* Chapel Hill: University of North Carolina Press, 1994.

— Brian C. Melton

Andrews, Frank M. (1884–1943) *Army Air Corps general and aviation pioneer*

Born on 3 February 1884 at Nashville, Tennessee, Frank Maxwell Andrews graduated from the U.S. Military Academy at WEST POINT in 1906 and was commissioned in the cavalry. He then held routine assignments in the West, Hawaii, and the Philippines. In 1917 Andrews transferred to the Aviation Section of the Signal Corps. He completed flight training in 1918, too late to fly in combat in France, but in 1920 he succeeded Brigadier General William MITCHELL as the air service officer of the American Army of Occupation in Germany.

Andrews returned to the United States in 1923 and commanded the 1st Pursuit Group, establishing speed and altitude records until leaving to assume staff posts. In March 1935 the U.S. Army Air Corps underwent a major reorganization; Andrews was promoted to temporary brigadier general and named to command the newly created General Headquarters (GHQ) Air Force. For the first time, all the U.S. Army's air strike elements were under a single commander. Subsequently promoted to temporary major general, Andrews molded GHQ Air Force into the offensive combat arm that became the model for the U.S. Army Air Forces in World War II.

In 1937 Andrews ran afoul of the army general staff when he strongly advocated an independent air force during testimony before the House Military Affairs Committee. In 1939 he was exiled to Fort Sam Houston, Texas, and reverted to his permanent rank of colonel. Within a few months, however, new chief of staff of the army, General George C. MARSHALL, returned Andrews to Washington as assistant chief of staff of the army for training and operations. Andrews was the first aviator to hold that important general staff position.

In 1941 Andrews assumed command of the Caribbean Defense Command as a lieutenant general, becoming the first U.S. air officer to command a theater. In November 1942 he took command of all U.S. forces in the Middle East. In February 1943 Andrews received supreme command of all U.S. forces in the European theater of operations—a tacit recognition that the majority of American forces in Europe were air rather than ground units. Three months later, on 3 May 1943, Andrews died at the controls of a B-24 bomber, which crashed while he was attempting a low-visibility landing in Iceland.

Frank Andrews was America's great "might have been" of World War II. At the time of his death, many observers considered him the leading candidate to command the invasion of France. He had the total confidence of General Marshall, and he possessed an almost ideal balance of intellect, character, courage, and military skill. Andrews Air Force Base in Maryland was later named for him.

See also AIR FORCE, U.S.

Further reading: Copp, DeWitt. *A Few Great Captains: The Men and Events That Shaped the Development of U.S. Air Power.* New York: Doubleday, 1980; Frisbee, John L., ed. *Makers of the United States Air Force.* Washington, D.C.: Air Force History and Museums Program, 1987; McClendon, R. Earl. *The Question of Autonomy for the U.S. Air Arm.* Maxwell Air Force Base, Ala.: Air University, 1950.

— David T. Zabecki

Anglo-Dutch Wars (1652–1654, 1665–1667, 1672–1674) *Series of naval conflicts between England and the United Provinces of the Netherlands over maritime rights, trade, and colonial rivalries*

Angered by Dutch refusal of an alliance based on common Calvinist religious beliefs, the English Commonwealth Parliament passed the Navigation Act (October 1651), severely curtailing Dutch trade with England. Other irritants included Dutch poaching on traditional fishing grounds and refusal to salute the English flag.

English naval forces under Robert Blake attacked a Dutch East Indies convoy off Dover for refusing an inspection (May 1652), sparking the First Anglo-Dutch War. Further naval engagements (Kentish Knock in September 1652 and Dungeness in November 1652) demonstrated the superiority of English tactics, armament, and ship tonnage. Attacks on merchant convoys proved devastating to the Dutch economy. English adoption of the line-ahead (line of battle), combined with superior leadership and firepower, carried the day in battles off Gabbard Bank (June 1653) and Texel (August 1653). Despite English tactical victories, however, the cost of the war and damage to commerce induced negotiations, resulting in the Treaty of Westminster (April 1654), whereby the Dutch agreed to fishing restrictions, to the Navigation Act, and to salute English warships.

Colonial and commercial rivalries, particularly in India, West Africa, and the Americas prompted the Second Anglo-Dutch War. The Stuart Restoration (1660) had brought to the throne the anti-Dutch Charles II, with his aggressive and militant brother James, duke of York, as Lord High Admiral. English forces attacked Dutch West African slave-trading stations (October 1663), thus initiating the war. Early English successes included the capture of the New Amsterdam colony (September 1664), subsequently renamed New York. The first major naval engagement occurred off Lowestoft (June 1665), with almost 300 warships engaged. Within months, both Denmark and France had joined the Dutch cause. Forced to divide naval forces to cover both ends of the English Channel, Monck proved unable to prevent Dutch control of the Thames Estuary (1666); he eventually broke the blockade and raided the Dutch coast.

Financial and political strains stemming from the plague and the Great Fire of London induced Charles to negotiate. Despite an agreement to stay in their bases, the Dutch under Admiral Michiel Adrienszoon de Ruyter sailed into the Thames, destroying commercial shipping and raiding the naval dockyard at Chatham. Nonetheless with both sides exhausted, peace came at the Treaty of Breda (July 1667).

Following a failed English-Swedish-Dutch alliance in the 1660s to check further French conquests in the Spanish Netherlands, Charles allied himself with King Louis XIV of France against the Dutch in the secret Treaty of Dover (1670). English warships subsequently attacked a Dutch merchant convoy, sparking the Third Anglo-Dutch War. Anglo-French strategy called for combined fleet operations in support of an amphibious invasion. But de Ruyter had dramatically improved Dutch tactics and soundly defeated Anglo-French fleets at Sole Bay (May 1672), Schoonvelt Channel (May 1673), and Texel (August 1673), and he again blockaded the Thames. Faced with public and Parliamentary dislike for the French (Catholic) alliance, Charles concluded a separate peace (Treaty of Westminster, February 1674), acknowledging Dutch victory.

Further reading: Boxer, Charles R. *The Anglo-Dutch Wars of the 17th Century, 1652–1674.* London: H.M. Stationery Office, 1974. Capp, Bernard S. *Cromwell's Navy: The Fleet and the English Revolution, 1648–1660.* Oxford, U.K.: Clarendon Press, 1989; Jones, James R. *Britain and Europe in the Seventeenth Century.* New York: Norton, 1967; Warner, Oliver. *The British Navy: A Concise History.* London: Thames and Hudson, 1975.

— Stanley D. M. Carpenter

Anglo-Powhatan War (1609–1614) *First major conflict between the Powhatan Indians and the Virginia colonists*

In August 1609, the Powhatan Indians under their war chief OPECHANCANOUGH killed nearly half of the English colonists at Nansemond and Nonsuch, the outposts most distant from the center of Virginia settlement, Jamestown. The triggers for the Indian attacks were the arrival of 250 new settlers (which nearly tripled the number of English in Virginia), the colonists' refusal to confine their activities to the immediate Jamestown area, and the departure for England of Captain John Smith, the Englishman whom the Indians saw as the most trustworthy.

Beginning in November 1609, the Powhatans laid siege to the Jamestown fort itself. Without sufficient provisions for the winter, more than two-thirds of those within the fort succumbed to famine and disease or combat. The only recorded instances of cannibalism in colonial Virginia occurred at Jamestown during this winter, which was known as the Starving Time.

The siege was lifted in May 1610, and more than 600 new settlers arrived during the summer, saving the colony from extinction. Among the new arrivals was Sir Thomas West, third baron De La Warr, who had been sent to serve as the colony's governor and captain general. De La Warr instituted martial law in Virginia, as described in his *Lawes Divine, Morall, & Martiall.*

Sporadic conflicts between colonists and Indians continued over the next four years until a truce was achieved and sealed by the marriage of Pocahontas, daughter of Wahunsenacawh, the emperor of the Powhatan Confederation, to colonist John Rolfe. (The Indian princess had been taken captive by a renegade tribe of the Powhatans and turned over to the English a few months earlier.)

It is estimated that between 1609 and 1614 more than 350 (nearly one-fourth) of the English colonists were killed, as compared to 250 deaths among their Powhatan opponents. Some authorities refer to this first conflict as the First Anglo-Powhatan War and consider the concerted Indian attacks of 1622 and 1644 as the beginnings of the Second and Third Anglo-Powhatan Wars.

See also AMERICAN INDIAN WARS, OVERVIEW.

Further reading: Fausz, J. Frederick. "'An Abundance of Blood Shed on Both Sides': England's First Indian War, 1609–1614." *Virginia Magazine of History and Biography* 98, no. 1 (1990): 3–56; Gleach, Frederic W. *Powhatan's World and Colonial Virginia: A Conflict of Cultures.* Lincoln: University of Nebraska Press, 1997; Morgan, Edmund S. *American Slavery, American Freedom: The Ordeal of Colonial Virginia.* New York: Norton, 1975.

— David W. Coffey

Ansell, Samuel T. (1875–1954) *U.S. army colonel and lawyer*

Born on 1 January 1875 at Coinjock, North Carolina, Samuel Tilden Ansell was commissioned a second lieutenant of infantry in 1899 on graduation from the U.S. Military Academy at WEST POINT. In 1904 he earned a law degree from the University of North Carolina. He was an instructor in law and history at West Point from 1902 to 1904 and from 1906 to 1909, and he was the prosecuting attorney for Moro Province in the Philippines from 1909 to 1911.

Ansell then performed special legal work for the War Department in Washington and New York, and from 1913 to 1917 he represented the Philippine and Puerto Rican governments in U.S. federal courts and served as counsel for the War Department. Promoted brigadier general in 1917, that August he was appointed acting judge advocate general of the army.

On Ansell's initiative, the army issued General Order No. 75, abolishing all distinctions between the regular army, national army, and National Guard. All land forces were to be denominated the Army of the United States. Ansell also established a system of review and revision of court-martial procedures. This revision made the administration of military justice similar to that of civilian justice.

In February 1919, Ansell attacked before a Senate committee the entire system of courts-martial, calling it responsible for "terrible, gross injustice." He was relieved of his duties as acting judge advocate general a short time later but was appointed head of the judicial Board of Review, with his pre–World War I rank of lieutenant colonel. After five months of review, the board remitted the sentences of more than 5,000 prisoners. This led to a contest of wills between Ansell and Senator G. W. Chamberlain, attacking the existing court-martial system, and Secretary of the Army Newton BAKER and General Enoch Herbert Crowder defending it.

At Baker's request, the American Bar Association appointed a committee to investigate the army's court-martial procedure. After lengthy investigation the committee delivered a divided report, in which the majority supported the existing system. Ansell publicly attacked the report (which was put in abeyance) at a session of the American Bar Association in August 1919.

Aided by Representative Royal Johnson, Senator Chamberlain, and many other lawyers, Ansell continued to push for reformation of the military code and correction of court-martial abuses. In June 1920 Congress enacted the Articles of War, which featured Ansell's reforms.

Ansell resigned from the army in July 1919 and established with Edward Bailey what became the prominent law firm of Ansell and Bailey. He died in Washington, D.C., on 27 May 1954.

Further reading: Generous, William T. *Swords and Scales: The Development of the Uniform Code of Military Justice.* Port Washington, N.Y.: Kennikat, 1973; Snedeker, James. *Military Justice under the Uniform Code.* Boston: Little, Brown, 1953.

— Adam P. Stanley-Smith

Antietam/Sharpsburg, Battle of (17 September 1862) *Pivotal Civil War battle*

After defeating Union forces in the Second Battle of BULL RUN/MANASSAS, the Army of Northern Virginia comman-

der General Robert E. LEE decided on an invasion of the North. Accordingly, on 4 September Lee set his army of approximately 40,000 men in motion, crossing the Potomac and moving east of the Blue Ridge Mountains. Arriving at Frederick, Maryland, on 7 September, Lee gambled boldly, dividing his army into five separate parts. Three columns were to converge on HARPERS FERRY and take that vital communications point, while another column moved to Hagerstown, Maryland, and the final segment to Boonsboro.

Meanwhile, President Abraham LINCOLN restored Major General George B. MCCLELLAN to command of the Federal Army of the Potomac. McClellan moved out of Washington with 80,000 men to find and destroy Lee's army. Near Frederick, Maryland, soldiers of the 27th Indiana Infantry discovered a copy of Lee's Special Order No. 191, which revealed the disposition of Lee's forces.

Despite this vital information, McClellan moved with his usual glacial speed. Waiting a full 16 hours, McClellan finally pushed through the Blue Ridge Mountain passes. Unable to stop the surge of Federal troops, Lee ordered his army to consolidate at the village of Sharpsburg, Maryland. Although initially inclined to retreat, Lee decided to face Federal forces on a low ridge extending about four miles north to south, just east of the village.

On 16 September Lee had only 18,000 troops in position. Had McClellan attacked that day, he would have destroyed his adversary. McClellan failed to attack, and Lee's force grew to 30,000 men with the arrival of troops under Major General Thomas J. "Stonewall" JACKSON from Harpers Ferry. Meanwhile, McClellan carefully positioned his men and guns. He planned a simultaneous double envelopment, keeping two corps in the center to reinforce either wing if a breakthrough was achieved, or attack the Confederate center should Lee weaken it to reinforce either wing.

Early on the morning of 17 September, Major General Joseph HOOKER's 12,000-man I Corps opened the battle with a vigorous attack against Jackson's troops on the Confederate left. Hooker's men drove the Confederates back into a wooded portion of the battlefield known as the West Woods. Lee avoided disaster only through the action of Brigadier General John Bell HOOD's Texas Brigade, which moved up to repulse the Union attack. Successive Union attacks, by Major General Joseph Mansfield's XII Corps and Brigadier General Edwin Sumner's II Corps, also failed to break the Confederate left.

At the Confederate center a crisis developed while the fight raged on the left. Some 3,000 Confederates under Major General Daniel H. Hill fought desperately to hold the Sunken Road, which came to be known as Bloody Lane. Major General William B. Franklin's Federal VI Corps launched three separate attacks against the brigades

Battle of Antietam/Sharpsburg, 17 September 1862   *(Library of Congress)*

of Brigadier Generals Robert Rodes and George Anderson. All were beaten back after savage combat. Amid the confusion on the battlefield, two Union regiments managed to position themselves so as to enfilade the Confederate position on the Sunken Road. Rodes and Anderson were forced to fall back, leaving a gap between the Confederate center and left; to prevent disaster, General D. H. Hill personally led 200 men to fill the hole and ordered an artillery barrage. To relieve pressure on Hill, Lee ordered Jackson to counterattack the Union right, an attack that proved unsuccessful. Characteristically, McClellan failed to take advantage of the situation, deciding not to commit his reserve, thus surrendering the initiative to Lee's smaller army.

Union forces on the left also struggled. Ordered to seize a bridge across Antietam Creek and then assault the Confederate right, Major General Ambrose BURNSIDE, commanding IX Corps, wasted the morning trying to carry the bridge. Eventually Union forces crossed the creek farther south via fords. Anticipating a flanking attack, Confederate forces moved back to higher ground

and awaited the arrival of Major General Ambrose P. HILL's division, the only portion of Lee's army not yet at Sharpsburg. By the time Burnside was ready to attack, Hill's men had arrived after a forced march from Harpers Ferry. Despite exhaustion, they hit Union forces with vigor, driving Burnside's men back to their original position. The battle of Antietam was over. McClellan had failed to commit an entire corps.

In the battle the Union sustained 2,108 dead, 9,540 wounded, and 753 missing. Confederate losses came to 1,546 dead, 7,752 wounded, and 1,018 missing. Antietam was the bloodiest day in American military history; more Americans died there than on any other. Although Lee's invasion of the North was thwarted, he was confident enough that McClellan would not move and that he waited a day before retreating across the Potomac. McClellan was content to allow Lee's army to retreat across the Potomac unmolested; Lincoln was furious and soon removed McClellan from command. Nevertheless, the battle had important results for the North. Lee's defeat weakened Confederate hopes to secure recognition from Britain

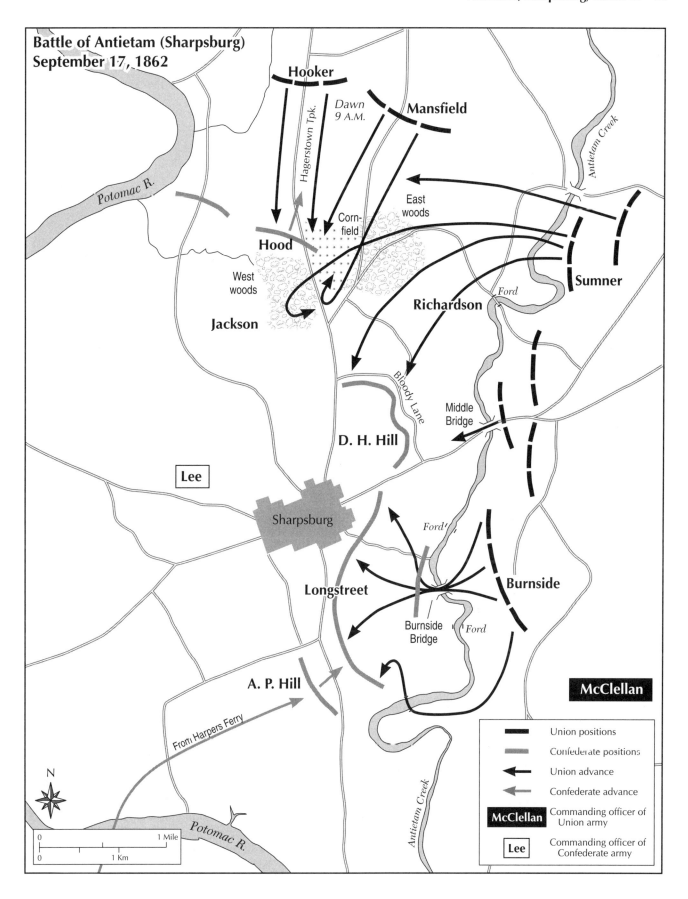

Battle of Antietam (Sharpsburg)
September 17, 1862

Potomac R.

Hooker

*Dawn
9 A.M.*

Mansfield

Hagerstown Tpk.

Antietam Creek

East
woods

Corn-
field

Hood

West
woods

Jackson

Ford

Sumner

Richardson

Bloody Lane

Middle
Bridge

D. H. Hill

Lee

Sharpsburg

Ford

Longstreet

Burnside

A. P. Hill

Burnside
Bridge

Ford

From Harpers Ferry

McClellan

N

Potomac R.

Antietam Creek

▬▬	Union positions
▬▬	Confederate positions
←	Union advance
←	Confederate advance
McClellan	Commanding officer of Union army
Lee	Commanding officer of Confederate army

0   1 Mile

0   1 Km

and France, and it allowed Lincoln an opportunity to issue the Preliminary Emancipation Proclamation, which transformed a war for the Union into a war for human freedom.

See also CIVIL WAR, LAND OVERVIEW.

Further reading: Gallagher, Gary W., ed. *Antietam: Essays on the 1862 Maryland Campaign.* Chapel Hill: University of North Carolina Press, 1999; Sears, Stephen. *Landscape Turned Red: The Battle of Antietam.* New York: Ticknor and Fields, 1983.

— Bruce Tap

Anzio invasion (22 January–4 March 1944)
Unsuccessful World War II Allied attempt to end the military stalemate in Italy by an amphibious landing behind German lines

After the conclusion of the SALERNO battles in mid-September, Allied forces advanced up the Italian Peninsula. By late October, however, they had been halted by a German defensive line anchored at MONTE CASSINO, where Allied attacks were repeatedly repulsed. Allied planners hoped that a landing behind the enemy positions would cut German supply lines, forcing them to abandon Cassino, and possibly permit the quick capture of Rome. Anzio was chosen as the invasion site because it was close to a major supply route, had suitable invasion beaches, and had a small port.

Major General John Lucas's VI Corps, part of Lieutenant General Mark CLARK's Fifth Army, constituted the invasion force. The corps consisted of Major General W. R. C. Penney's British 1st Division, Major General Lucian K. TRUSCOTT's U.S. 3d Division, and Colonel William DARBY's U.S. Rangers. Penney's troops were to land north of Anzio, Truscott's to the south, and the Rangers at the port itself. Clark's original orders to Truscott were to secure the beachhead, then occupy the Alban Hills to control the road to Rome, and be prepared to march on Rome if opportunity offered. Clark later modified the orders, requiring only an advance toward the Alban Hills and eliminating any mention of Rome.

The Allied invasion force landed at Anzio on 22 January 1944. Operation Shingle achieved complete surprise and met almost no opposition. Of the 36,000 troops put ashore that day, only 13 were killed, and the port facilities were captured intact. A jeep patrol from the 36th Engineer Regiment drove to the outskirts of Rome without being observed by the Germans. By the end of the second day Lucas had expanded the bridgehead to a depth of seven miles and had 50,000 troops on hand. But he focused his energies on securing a defensive perimeter instead of undertaking a rapid advance, even though the town of Cisterna was only 14 miles northeast of Anzio. A key objective,

in Allied hands it would have blocked the road linking the eastern part of the German defensive line to Rome.

Meanwhile, the German commander in Italy, Field Marshal Albert Kesselring, refused to consider abandoning the Cassino line. His original intention was to keep the Allies from reaching the Alban Hills. However, Lucas's caution gave the Germans time to assemble forces from throughout the Mediterranean theater, and Kesselring soon believed that he could destroy the Allied forces at Anzio.

On 24 January Lucas sent a reconnaissance force toward Cisterna, but it was driven back. More determined efforts to reach the town were undertaken on 26 and 27 January, when the Germans repulsed 3d Division infantry attacks supported by tanks. The British, on the left, were more successful, capturing the towns of Carroceto and Aprilia. Further advances were halted by German counterattacks, and Lucas delayed resuming the offensive until 30 January when elements of the U.S. 1st Armored Division had arrived. But Lucas had allowed the Germans too much time to reinforce, and the Allies were halted, though not before the 3d Division had pushed to within a mile of Cisterna (1 February). In these actions an entire U.S. Ranger battalion was annihilated, with only six of 767 men escaping death or capture.

With the Allied advance stalled, Kesselring seized the opportunity to strike a counterblow. Between 3 and 9 February the Germans launched a series of limited attacks, retaking some ground and driving the British from Aprilia. On 16 February, after a week-long lull in which Lucas organized his defenses and the Germans received additional reinforcements, Kesselring mounted a major counteroffensive, supported by air attacks on Allied shipping offshore. For three days the Germans continued their assault, spurred on by Adolf Hitler's belief that the destruction of the Anzio invaders would force the Allies to abandon any attempts to make an amphibious landing in France. They drove the Allies back along much of the front and nearly achieved a breakthrough on 18 February. However, the last serious German threat was checked by the U.S. 45th Division. When further attacks on 18 February gained some ground but could not achieve a breakthrough, Kesselring broke off the effort.

On 23 February Clark dismissed Lucas from command of VI Corps and replaced him with Truscott. Five days later the Germans attacked the 3d Division, but Allied resistance and bad weather ended the attempt; a final German effort was checked by 3d Division on 3 March, after which the Germans went over to the defensive. The front remained relatively static until 23 May, when VI Corps attacked to link up with Fifth Army, which had at last broken through at Cassino. The next day the Germans at Anzio began to withdraw, and on 25 May VI Corps finally met elements of the U.S. II Corps advancing from the south.

Allied losses at Anzio were approximately 7,000 killed and 36,000 wounded, captured, or missing. The Germans suffered an estimated 40,000 total casualties.

See also WORLD WAR II, U.S. INVOLVEMENT, EUROPE.

Further reading: D'Este, Carlo. *Fatal Decision: Anzio and the Battle for Rome.* New York: HarperCollins, 1991. Lamb, Richard. *War in Italy, 1943–1945: A Brutal Story.* New York: St. Martin's Press, 1993.

— Jim Piecuch

Apache Wars (1848–1886) *Native American struggle against the United States, the last major campaign of the American Indian Wars*
With the arrival of the Spanish in the New World, the nomadic, autonomous Southern Athapaskan bands in the Southwest came to be called Apache, meaning "enemy" (in Zuñi) or "raccoon" (in Nahuatl). Formidable military opponents and possessed of great endurance, the Apache never united but fought as individual tribes or bands.

During the long Spanish period, military officers endeavoring to control the Apache employed all the military techniques later employed (successfully) by the U.S. Army. Their superiors would tolerate no innovation, however. The Mexican government and the Apache carried on sporadic warfare. During the 1846–48 MEXICAN-AMERICAN WAR, the Apache distinguished between Anglo-Americans and Mexicans, welcoming the former into the Southwest as allies. When Brigadier General Stephen KEARNY reached New Mexico, Mangas Coloradas promised friendship, but the Apache learned that as a consequence of the U.S. victory over Mexico in the war, Washington now claimed their lands, which Mexico had never conquered, and expected the Apache to stop raiding into Mexico.

With no official policy, unregulated settlement, and unratified treaties, Anglo-Apache relations deteriorated. Campaigns against the Gila, Jicarilla, and Mescalero forced many Apache to settle on reservations, but they reserved the right to raid Mexico to acquire food and the goods and skills their culture required.

After years of generally peaceful relations with Anglo-Americans, Chiricahua resentment exploded when miners attacked a Mimbres River *ranchería* in December 1860, and 2d Lieutenant George Bascom seized and executed Chiricahua leader COCHISE's relatives at Apache Pass in February 1861. With start of the Civil War and U.S. Army's withdrawal to the East, the Confederate orders to kill Apache on sight escalated the conflict. Following Cochise's attack on Captain Thomas Roberts's detachment of Brigadier General James Carleton's column of California Volunteers on 15 July 1862 in Apache Pass, Carleton launched a war of extermination against all Apache. The murder of Mangas Coloradas on a peace mission on 8 January 1863 unified

Apache warriors, Geronimo at center on horse   *(Library of Congress)*

Chiricahua under Cochise. Carleton's campaigns drove Gila Apache into their mountain haunts in Arizona and Sonora, and Mescalero onto the Bosque Redondo Reservation.

Following the Civil War, President Ulysses S. GRANT's peace policy assigned bands to individual reservations, but most Apache preferred their traditional nomadic lifestyle. After Tucson vigilantes massacred peaceful Arivaipa Pinaleño at Camp Grant in 1871, the Apache no longer considered Anglos trustworthy. When Brigadier General Oliver O. HOWARD's peace treaties failed to curtail raids, Brigadier General George CROOK launched a nine-column winter campaign in 1872–73 into the Tonto Basin, forcing the western bands into submission. Although Crook gained the support of those favoring peace, mismanagement created unrest as agents and officers quarreled, tribes were concentrated on the San Carlos reservation, Anglos stole reservation land, and corrupt officials sent inadequate food and shoddy goods.

Hungry and forced to settle next to their enemies at San Carlos, Victorio's band fled on 2 September 1877 but later surrendered at Fort Wingate, hoping to return to Warm Springs. When orders came in 1879 to return them to San Carlos, Victorio and Nana raided their way into Mexico, where 150 Chiricahua, Comanche, Lipan, Mescalero, and Navajo joined them. Victorio eluded a relentless pursuit by U.S. mounted units, including the black "buffalo soldiers" of the 9th and 10th Cavalry. Ultimately, Mexican troops under Colonel Joaquín Terrazas cornered and killed Victorio, along with most of his warriors, in October 1880 at Tres Castillos in Chihuahua. Away on an ammunition raid at the time, Nana dashed back across the Rio Grande later that year to raid unscathed more than a thousand miles before returning to the Sierra Madre.

Convinced in 1881 that their shaman could bring two leaders back to life if all the Anglos were dead, Coyotero gathered at Cibecue for the prerequisite ceremonies. On 30 August, 100 warriors attacked a force sent to arrest the shaman, killing Captain E. C. Hentig and six troopers; their shaman also died in the fighting. The Coyotero attacked Fort Apache and raided across the Tonto Basin before Colonel Ranald MACKENZIE's troops forced them back onto the reservation. To avoid arrest, two rebel chiefs fled to Mexico with Juh, GERONIMO, Chatto, Nachee, and 70 others. Sixty Cibecue rebels attacked San Carlos Agency on 6 July 1882, but troops from Fort McDowell converged on them and forced the survivors to return.

General Crook had the most success against the Apache. He employed friendly Apache as scouts, used mule trains for supply rather than road-bound wagons, and pursued the Apache wherever they went, even into Mexico. Upon resuming command of Arizona in September 1882, Crook corrected sources of discontent on the reservation, enlisted 250 Apache scouts, and the following May crossed into Mexico to apprehend the Chiricahua. After Apache scouts attacked Chato's camp, 325 Apache surrendered and accompanied Crook back to Arizona, while Geronimo, Chihuahua, Nachee, Mangas, and Chato promised to return "soon," independently. Chafing under reservation restrictions, Geronimo, Nachee, Mangas, and Nana headed south again in 1885. Quickly placing cavalry at every spring or waterhole along the border, Crook sent Captain Emmett Crawford into Mexico with a large force of Apache scouts, followed by two troops of the 4th Cavalry under Captain Wirt Davis and a company of White Mountain scouts under Lieutenant Charles Gatewood. The expedition was forced to return without the Chiricahua. To punish the peace seekers and scouts, Chihuahua's brother Josanie attacked the reservation in November and raided 1,200 miles across Arizona before reentering Mexico.

Committed to the use of Apache scouts, Crook sent Crawford back into Mexico with them in December, assisted by Lieutenant Marion Maus. After surprising Geronimo's camp on the Río Aros (Haros River) and beginning negotiations, Crawford was fatally shot by Mexican scalp hunters, who then demanded mules and rations for Maus's release. The holdouts agreed to meet Crook and accepted two-years' imprisonment before returning to San Carlos, but Lieutenant General Philip SHERIDAN overruled Crook (who then requested to be relieved) and ordered Chihuahua, Nana, and the 60 Chiricahuas who had accompanied Maus to Fort Bowie be sent on to Fort Marion, Florida.

Despite utilizing 5,000 troops, a mobile strike force, and heliograph stations, Crook's replacement, Brigadier General Nelson MILES, quickly realized that regular troops could not keep up with Apache. Miles sent two Apache familiar to Geronimo, Kieta and Martine, along with Gatewood to persuade the war leaders to surrender. Coordinating with Captain Henry Lawton's column on the Río Aros, Gatewood located the Apache camp and arranged a parley. Unwilling at first to submit to incarceration, Geronimo was worn down by his men's desire to see their families, who were being held at Fort Marion. During a meeting at Skeleton Canyon on 3 September 1886, Miles falsely offered protection, reunion with their families, and a well-supplied reservation and thus obtained the surrender of the Apache, but at Fort Bowie Miles shipped them east, disobeying orders to imprison them for trial. President Grover Cleveland ordered the men imprisoned at Fort Pickens, Florida, and the families held at Fort Marion. The only group remaining at large, Mangas's band, was captured near the Black Mountains in October and was also sent to Florida. The Apache Wars were over.

See also AMERICAN INDIAN WARS, OVERVIEW.

Further reading: Cole, D. C. *The Chiricahua Apaches, 1846–1876.* Albuquerque: University of New Mexico Press,

1988; Gunnerson, Dolores A. *The Jicarilla Apaches.* DeKalb: Northern Illinois University Press, 1974; Ogle, Ralph H. *Federal Control of the Western Apaches, 1848–1886.* Albuquerque: University of New Mexico Press, 1970; Sweeney, Edwin R. *Cochise: Chiricahua Apache Chief.* Norman: University of Oklahoma Press, 1991; ———. *Mangas Coloradas: Chief of the Chiricahua Apaches.* Norman: University of Oklahoma Press, 1998; Worcester, Donald E. *The Apaches: Eagles of the Southwest.* Norman: University of Oklahoma Press, 1979.

— Michèle Butts

Appomattox (3–9 April 1865) *Site of the surrender of General Robert E. Lee's Army of Northern Virginia to Union forces under Lieutenant General Ulysses S. GRANT*

The Appomattox campaign began after the Confederate defeat at FIVE FORKS on 1 April 1865, where Robert E. LEE hoped to break free from Petersburg and link up with Confederate forces in North Carolina.

Lieutenant General Ulysses S. GRANT had anticipated Lee's plan and organized his forces for a pursuit. Major General George C. MEADE's Army of the Potomac was to apply direct pressure on the Confederates, while Major General E. O. C. Ord's Army of the James moved to block the Confederate retreat. Major General Philip H. SHERIDAN's Union cavalry was to harass the retreating Confederates.

Lee's columns converged on Amelia Court House on 4 April, but there were no rations there for his troops. Lee stayed for one day in a vain attempt to forage for food before resuming his retreat on 5 April. He found his path to the south blocked by the Union V Corps, which forced him to detour north. By the morning of 6 April, Lieutenant General James LONGSTREET's leading elements were separated from trailing units, slowed by wagons and artillery. In the late afternoon, the lagging Confederate units were caught by Union cavalry and the Federal VI Corps near Saylor's Creek. The Northern forces smashed the Confederates, destroying one-quarter of Lee's army.

The remainder of the Confederate forces continued to the west. They found provisions at Farmville but could only pause briefly. Lee pushed on toward Appomattox Court House in one last desperate attempt to get around the Federals, but Sheridan's cavalry again blocked the route. On 9 April the Confederates penetrated the Union cavalry line, but infantry from Ord's army formed behind Sheridan's cavalry, and Lee was trapped. Later that day, Lee agreed to meet with Grant to discuss surrender terms.

Lee and Grant met in the home of Wilmer McLean in Appomattox. Ironically, McLean had owned a farm on the battlefield of BULL RUN and he had moved his family to Appomattox to escape the turmoil of war. Grant and Lee met in the McLean parlor and set the conditions for the surrender of the Army of Northern Virginia. Grant's terms were generous and did not treat the Confederates as traitors. Officers could keep their sidearms, and enlisted men could retain their horses and mules for spring planting. Grant also ordered the release of rations for the Confederate soldiers. Lee left the McLean house for an emotional meeting with his army. Both sides conducted the surrender ceremony with admirable dignity. Both Lee and Grant deserve credit for a just and humane end to the fighting in the main theater of war.

See also CIVIL WAR, LAND OVERVIEW.

Further reading: Calkins, Chris. *The Battles of Appomattox Station and Appomattox Court House, April 8–9, 1865.* Lynchburg, Va.: H. E. Howard, 1987; Catton, Bruce. *A Stillness at Appomattox.* Garden City, N.Y.: Doubleday, 1953; Chamberlain, Joshua Lawrence. *The Passing of the Armies.* Dayton, Ohio: Morningside Bookshop, 1982; Davis, Burke. *To Appomattox: Nine April Days.* New York: Rinehart, 1959; Hendrickson, Robert. *The Road to Appomattox.* New York: J. Wiley, 1998.

— Curtis S. King

Ardennes offensive   See BULGE, BATTLE OF THE.

Argus, USS, v. HMS Pelican (14 August 1813)
Naval engagement of the War of 1812

Built in 1803, the 16-gun U.S. brig *Argus* had, from October 1812 to 3 January 1813, conducted along the eastern American seaboard a series of coastal patrols that resulted in the capture of six valuable prizes. Ordered to operate in European waters under Master Commandant William Allen, the *Argus* conducted highly successful anticommerce raids in June and July 1813.

On the morning of 14 August the *Argus* was in the St. George Channel, off England, when its crew, preoccupied with the capture of an English merchant ship, sighted nearby the British warship *Pelican*, an 18-gun sloop under Captain John Maples, who had been ordered to hunt down the U.S. warship. Maples now maneuvered to gain the wind advantage. Allen, a veteran of several fights who had boasted that he could take any British sloop, even one somewhat larger and more heavily gunned than his own, shortened sail to allow the *Pelican* to close. A few minutes before 6:00 A.M. both crews hoisted their colors.

Realizing that he would not get to windward of *Pelican*, Allen turned toward his adversary and fired at very close range. Maples responded with a powerful broadside that severely damaged the main braces and sails on the American brig. A second broadside from *Pelican* carried away one of

Allen's legs and injured several crewmen. Allen remained at his station but he soon passed out from loss of blood. Lieutenant William Watson took command.

Maples attempted to pass behind the American ship, but Watson managed to cut the *Pelican* off while at the same time returning a raking fire. Maples soon was able to rake his opponent as well, 45 minutes after the first shots had been fired, the Americans hauled down their colors and surrendered.

The *Pelican* had suffered two killed and five wounded out of a crew of 113, apparently all, save one, to U.S. Marine musket fire. The ship itself was largely undamaged. The *Argus* suffered six killed and 18 wounded out of a crew of 125. Allen's leg was amputated, and he died four days later at Mill Prison hospital. Maples took his prize to England, where, after repairs, it entered British service.

See also ARGUS, USS; WAR OF 1812, NAVAL OVERVIEW.

Further reading: Dye, Ira. *The Fatal Cruise of the Argus: Two Captains in the War of 1812.* Annapolis, Md.: Naval Institute Press, 1994. Silverstone, Paul. *The Sailing Navy, 1775–1854.* Annapolis, Md.: Naval Institute Press, 2001.

— Patrick R. Jennings

Armistice (11 November 1918) *Armistice ending World War I*

By late September 1918 it was clear that Germany had lost the war. On 30 September Bulgaria signed an armistice, and one was concluded with Austria-Hungary on 3 November. On 29 September quartermaster general (deputy chief of staff) of the German army, Erich Ludendorff, asked that a new German government be formed to begin immediate negotiations with the Allies. On 3 October, Prince Max of Baden became chancellor of a new, liberal German government; he sent President Woodrow WILSON of the United States a note requesting peace on the basis of the Fourteen Points. In late October Ludendorff resigned. On 28 October a mutiny broke out in the High Seas Fleet at Kiel on word that the admirals planned a last-ditch foray at sea. By early November the rising had spread to other German seaports, where councils of workers and soldiers were formed.

In these circumstances Allied leaders at Paris discussed the options of concluding an armistice or continuing the offensive until Germany surrendered. An armistice would merely halt the fighting, with the understanding that peace negotiations would follow. The British government supported an armistice, as did many of the French. Supreme Allied Commander General Ferdinand Foch was disappointed; he and President Raymond Poincaré wanted total victory. Foch believed that two additional weeks of fighting would force a German surrender. Some British and French leaders sought an armistice because prolonging the war might strengthen American influence over the peace settlement. Indeed, if the war had continued into 1919, the AMERICAN EXPEDITIONARY FORCE (AEF) commander, General John J. PERSHING, would have commanded an army larger than either the French or British.

While Wilson supported an armistice, his commander in the field did not. Meeting with other Allied commanders on 25 October, Pershing spoke in favor of continuing the war until Germany surrendered unconditionally. But Pershing was overruled, and on the morning of 8 November Foch received a German armistice delegation in the former royal hunting preserve of Compiègne.

To spare the German army the onus of defeat, the chief of the German General Staff, Field Marshal Paul von Hindenburg, insisted that a civilian head the German delegation; the chancellor named Catholic Center Party leader Mathias Erzberger. The German delegation was astonishingly low-level—an army major general and two captains and a navy captain.

Meeting with the Germans in his special train at Compiègne, Foch instructed General Maxime Weygand to read the armistice terms one by one, interrupted only by another officer who read them in German. The Germans were given 72 hours to accept the terms, on threat of resumption of the war. After several days of negotiations and frantic telegrams back and forth to Berlin, the parties reached agreement. The Germans signed the armistice at 5 A.M. on 11 November.

The agreement provided that the Germans would within two weeks evacuate all captured territory, as well as Alsace and Lorraine. Within four weeks German troops were to be gone from the left (west) bank of the Rhine River and pull back from its right bank to a depth of 30 kilometers (20 miles). Allied troops would occupy that territory and control crossing points over the Rhine at Cologne, Coblenz, and Mainz. The true nature of the arrangement was revealed when Germany was forced to turn over sufficient armament to ensure it could not resume the war. This included the bulk of its surface navy (10 battleships, six battle cruisers, eight light cruisers, and 50 destroyers), all its submarines, 5,000 artillery pieces, 25,000 machine guns, and 1,700 aircraft. Germany would also have to surrender 5,000 locomotives and 150,000 railway cars, along with 5,000 trucks. Germany would have to make reparation for war damages, and all Allied prisoners of war were to be returned immediately, without reciprocity. The most controversial provision was the continuation of the naval blockade, which had exacted such a high price on German civilians, until a peace agreement was signed, although London did promise to allow such provisioning of the German people as it deemed necessary.

The Allied failure to insist on German surrender undoubtedly saved lives at the time but had momentous

consequences. The fact that Germany had been spared invasion during the war—the German armies marched home in good order, with drums beating and battle flags flying—led many in Germany to believe the lie that began to circulate about "a stab in the back"; that is, many, perhaps most, Germans believed their armies had not been defeated in the field but had been betrayed by corrupt politicians, Jews, war profiteers, or disaffection on the home front. Later this provided grist for Adolf Hitler's hate mill, especially when leading German generals testified that the "stab in the back" was factual. This experience would lead President Franklin ROOSEVELT during World War II to insist on "unconditional surrender."

The war was at last over. At 11:00 A.M. on 11 November the guns on the western front fell silent. Soldiers on both sides came out of the trenches and cheered.

See also PARIS, PEACE SETTLEMENT OF; WORLD WAR I, U.S. INVOLVEMENT.

Further reading: Brock-Shepherd, Gordon. *November 1918*. Boston: Little, Brown, 1981; Weintraub, Stanley. *A Stillness Heard Round the World: The End of the Great War, November 1918*. New York: Dutton, 1985.

— Spencer C. Tucker

Armstrong, John (1758–1843) *U.S. secretary of war*

Born on 23 November 1758, at Carlisle, Pennsylvania, John Armstrong, Jr., was the son of a distinguished Indian fighter. He became active in revolutionary politics while attending Princeton College in 1775, and the following year he served as aide de camp under Brigadier General Hugh Mercer. In 1777 Armstrong transferred to the staff of Major General Horatio GATES and was present at the decisive American victory in the campaign and Battles of SARATOGA.

In 1782 the Revolutionary War was effectively over, and a small cabal of officers under Gates began pressing the Continental Congress for back pay. Armstrong, a talented writer, subsequently penned the anonymous "Newburgh Addresses" of 10–11 March 1782, which demanded that the army not disband until just compensation was secured. General George WASHINGTON personally intervened to quash the so-called NEWBURGH CONSPIRACY, but thereafter Armstrong—the suspected author—was denigrated as having a sinister, conniving personality.

Elected to the U.S. House of Representatives in 1787, Armstrong cemented his political fortunes two years later by marrying Alida Livingston of New York. He used his literary skills effectively during the 1800 election campaign, which saw Thomas JEFFERSON chosen president. In 1804 Jefferson appointed him ambassador to France. There Armstrong clashed frequently with Napoleon over the issue of seized American ships.

When the War of 1812 commenced against England in June 1812, Armstrong returned to the United States as a brigadier general in the U.S. Army. Disastrous wartime events forced Secretary of War William EUSTIS to resign from office. In February 1813 President James Madison appointed Armstrong to fill the vacancy, although Republican statesmen protested what they perceived as Armstrong's overweening ambition to win the presidency.

In office, Armstrong proved an energetic, capable administrator, compared to his predecessor. He was responsible for promoting such talented military figures as Winfield SCOTT, Jacob BROWN, George IZARD, and Eleazar W. Ripley to high command. However, his strategy proved vacillating. Willing to strike a blow at the main British supply base at Montreal, he was continually urged by Major General Henry DEARBORN to carry the war westward on Lake Ontario. By the time Armstrong finally settled on a campaign against Montreal, his choice of generals, James WILKINSON and Wade Hampton, proved disastrous and culminated in the twin defeats of CRYSLER'S FARM and CHATEAUGUAY.

In the spring of 1814, Armstrong turned his focus westward again, launching Brown's spectacular but futile 1814 Niagara campaign. Armstrong then compounded his error by ordering Izard from Plattsburg to Niagara in support, just as a major British invasion was developing. But Armstrong's biggest failure was neglecting the defenses of Washington, D.C., against British attack. When that threat materialized in August 1814, the poorly prepared American militia were routed in the Battle of BLADENSBURG; the capital was occupied and its government buildings burned. Public outrage led to Armstrong's resignation, and he returned to private life.

Armstrong remained in seclusion for the next 31 years, penning a vitriolic set of memoirs that attempted to exonerate himself and excoriated his enemies. He died at Red Hook, New York, on 1 April 1843.

See also FORT NIAGARA IN THE WAR OF 1812; WAR OF 1812, LAND OVERVIEW.

Further reading: Quimby, Robert S. *The U.S. Army in the War of 1812: An Operational and Command Study*. 2 vols. East Lansing: Michigan State University Press, 1997; Skeen, C. Edward. *John Armstrong, Jr., 1758–1843: A Biography*. Syracuse, N.Y.: Syracuse University Press, 1981.

— John C. Fredriksen

Army, U.S.

The U.S. Army is a reflection of the society it represents. The settlers who established the North American English colonies in the early 17th century were imbued with the

strong belief, traditional in the mother country, that standing armies posed a threat to liberty. The colonists relied on locally raised militias to fight the Native Americans. Apart from a few British regulars and a major British military presence late in the 1754–1763 FRENCH AND INDIAN WAR, militias constituted the major military force in the American colonies until the Revolutionary War. Myth has the militia playing the key role in both the Revolutionary War and the WAR OF 1812, although in fact professional armies carried the brunt of the fighting in both wars. Nonetheless, the tug and pull between the professional army and the militia continued well, even remains something of an issue today between the U.S. Army and the National Guard.

Because of the Atlantic Ocean and lack of a major continental military threat, most Americans saw a large standing army as unnecessary and actually pernicious, a threat to the republic. President Thomas JEFFERSON reflected this attitude. Although he established the U.S. Military Academy at WEST POINT, New York, in 1802, he saw it as a "meritocracy" and "peace academy," useful primarily for the training of engineers in the new republic.

Typically, the American military has been unprepared for wars. As a result, at the beginning of conflicts the United States has usually fared poorly. This was certainly true of the American Revolutionary War and the War of 1812. It is somewhat surprising that Americans have ignored this fact and continued to express unbounded confidence in their ability to prevail in war, regardless of the circumstances. Americans have assumed that because, in their view at least, their causes have been just, they would triumph.

The U.S. Army has traditionally proven remarkably resilient and adaptable. Unlike, for example the Soviet and Japanese armies in World War II, the U.S. Army has been quick to adopt new strategies and tactics when the old ones failed.

Americans early on democratized war, making it the business of all adult male citizens. Thus militia practice followed that of Britain, incorporating most free adult males between the ages of 16 and 60. Americans also believed that everyone should take his turn at service. This led to disastrous short-term enlistments, the norm in the American Revolutionary War, War of 1812, MEXICAN-AMERICAN WAR, and the CIVIL WAR.

Traditionally, at the conclusion of wars, the American people have insisted on demobilization. For instance, ground forces after the Civil War went from more than a million men under arms in April 1865 to only 25,000 men by the end of 1866. This has usually meant that when war again comes, the army is unprepared, as it was at the start of the 1898 SPANISH-AMERICAN WAR.

In their wars Americans have placed a high premium on the value of their fighting men, which has weighed heavily on decisions to commit the military to action, especially in recent years, in the debate over U.S. involvement in the Balkans. In Vietnam this led to infantry serving as a fixing force while artillery and airpower acted as the killing forces. More recently the American way of war has meant high-technology and stand-off weapons in order to minimize casualties on the ground.

Americans fought the Revolutionary War with both a regular army and colonial militias. Militiamen fought the opening Battles of LEXINGTON AND CONCORD and BUNKER HILL, but while they performed well in these actions, it was clear that a regular military force was necessary. On 4 June 1775, Congress voted to accept into the regular forces New England militia forces then besieging Boston and to raise 10 companies of riflemen. This date marks the beginning of the U.S. Army. On 15 June Congress selected Virginian George WASHINGTON to command the Army of the United Colonies (CONTINENTAL ARMY), as it was then known. Militia forces continued to play the important roles of providing local security, forcing uncommitted colonists to choose sides (especially after the Declaration of Independence), harassing British lines of communication and supply, and engaging small British units when they ventured away from coastal enclaves. But militiamen were not well trained, and when they were called up and employed with regular units in pitched battles, as was often the case, they invariably broke and ran, often causing Patriot defeat.

Washington had terrible problems simply maintaining an army in the field. The Continental army fluctuated wildly in size, from 5,000 to 20,000 men, and it was difficult to feed and equip. Early in the war, Washington adopted a strategy of refusing set-piece battles, in which his army might be destroyed. He carefully selected his opportunities, knowing full well that the revolutionary cause rested on the survival of the army. Thanks to Friedrich Wilhelm, baron von STEUBEN, his simplified drill manual, and the crucible of VALLEY FORGE, by 1778 the army was able to engage the British on the basis of something like parity. Still, French support was crucial, especially in providing small arms, artillery, gunpowder, equipment, and eventually units of the French army and navy. A powerful French fleet and 6,000 French ground troops made the Continental victory in the Battle of YORKTOWN possible.

After the Revolutionary War the army shrank in size dramatically. It at least fared better than the navy, which was done away with entirely. Congress rejected Washington's call for a standing force of 2,600 officers and men. Stating that standing armies in times of peace were inconsistent with the values of republican states, Congress reduced the army to just 80 enlisted men and the requisite number of officers, none above the rank of captain. Administration was in the hands of one clerk. In 1784 the army was

increased to an authorized strength of 700 men, to be raised from state militias. Even this number proved totally inadequate to deal with the threat posed by British occupation of forts in the Old Northwest and by the Indian resistance to white settlers' encroachments on their lands.

In 1785 Henry KNOX was appointed to the post of secretary of war. He established the army's first ARSENAL at Springfield, Massachusetts. Militia, not the army, defended the arsenal the next year during SHAYS'S REBELLION, although Congress did vote in its wake to increase the army to 2,040 men.

Concern over the inadequate military was one of the factors that prompted the CONSTITUTION OF 1789. It established civilian control of the military. The president became commander in chief of the armed forces of the United States, but Congress retained the power to declare war, raise and support armies, call out the militia, make rules and regulations governing the army and land warfare, and approve officers recommended by the president for commissions. The states were allowed to maintain militia forces, and to ensure their readiness, citizens retained the right to keep and bear arms.

Even so, the new U.S. Army proved totally inadequate in size. It was also abysmally trained and led, as was demonstrated by sound defeats in wars with the Indians in 1790 and 1791. These disasters led to the creation of the LEGION OF THE UNITED STATES, a force of some 5,000 men commanded by Major General Anthony WAYNE. After thoroughly training this force, Wayne led it into Indian territory and defeated the Native Americans in the 1794 Battle of FALLEN TIMBERS. Many regard this engagement as the birthright of the U.S. Army and Wayne as the father of the army. Soon afterward, however, the army again shrank in size.

Although the army gradually expanded before the War of 1812 to an authorized strength of 10,000 men, it was again poorly trained and appallingly led. In 1812, when the United States went to war with Britain and attempted to invade Canada, the army was defeated in detail by a smaller force of British regulars.

After training, and with inefficient officers weeded out, a virtually new army took the field in 1813 and fought well in the remainder of the war. Despite the fiasco of the Battle of BLADENSBURG, popular myth attributed much of the military success of American arms in the war to the militia, especially after the Battle of NEW ORLEANS. But as the encounters at CHIPPEWA and LUNDY'S LANE demonstrated, regular American infantry, properly led and trained, fully equaled their European counterparts.

Army reduction followed the War of 1812, but this time there was a concurrent search for professionalism. Secretary of War John C. CALHOUN (1817–25) established the post of commanding general of the army, the rudiments of a general staff system, and in 1824 the first postgraduate

institution, in the Artillery School of Practice at Fortress Monroe. Calhoun also established a number of military posts in the western United States. But with the Atlantic Ocean as protection and no major continental enemies with which to contend, Congress reduced the size of the army to 6,000 men.

As part of the drive toward professionalism, the army sent officers to Europe to study. One of them was Dennis Hart MAHAN, who founded the American branch of the study of military theory as a professor at West Point. The 1830s also saw the appearance of the first U.S. professional military journals, and the army undertook exploration of the West.

The new professional army and its West Point–trained officers performed well during the 1846–48 Mexican-American War. Many Civil War generals earned their spurs in this conflict. The Civil War a decade later was the first modern industrial war. Generalship of Federal and Confederate forces during the Civil War was as professional as in the armies of Europe, and the Union staff system that evolved during the conflict was as fine as anything in the world until the German General Staff later in the century. Both North and South raised large numbers of volunteer regiments to fight in the Civil War; the regular U.S. Army remained small.

After the war the U.S. Army was reduced to about 25,000 officers and men. This force had to man coastal defenses, garrison the South during Reconstruction, and fight the 1,000 or so actions of the AMERICAN INDIAN WARS (1866–90). This period was also marked by a push for greater military professionalism, with the creation of additional military schools, including the General Service and Staff College (today the Command and General Staff College) at Fort Leavenworth.

Tremendous advances in military technology were taking place. The machine gun, self-recoiling artillery, smokeless powder, the internal combustion engine, and the airplane were but a few of the revolutionary changes. Although the army early led in military aviation, generally it was slow to adopt the new technologies. The 1898 Spanish-American War, for example, caught the army without a modern, breechloading, repeating rifle. In that war the United States acquired an empire from Spain and had to put down an uprising in the Philippines, in the PHILIPPINE-AMERICAN WAR. As part of its expanding world reach, the army also took part, for the first time since the Yorktown campaign of the American Revolutionary War, in a multinational operation—the suppression of the BOXER UPRISING in China.

The PUNITIVE EXPEDITION INTO MEXICO of 1916–17 helped prepare the army for World War I. The army experimented with military aviation, the machine gun, and truck transport. This operation, however, was hardly war as it was being waged in France on the western front. The NATIONAL

DEFENSE ACT OF 1916 led to an expansion of the army and established reserve components, the RESERVE OFFICERS TRAINING CORPS (ROTC), and reformed the National Guard. Even so, on U.S. entry into the war in April 1917 the army and National Guard together totaled only 200,000 men.

Congress quickly adopted conscription, and during the war the army expanded to 4 million men, 2.1 million of whom were shipped to France, 1.4 million of whom saw action. Of the 29 divisions (1,000 officers and 27,000 men each) that fought in France, only 11 were draftee divisions; the remainder were seven regular and 11 National Guard divisions, all volunteer. Still, it took eight months to train a recruit for combat. Fortunately for the Allies, the war was prolonged sufficiently for the AMERICAN EXPEDITIONARY FORCES (AEF) to contribute meaningfully.

A massive reduction followed World War I as the United States retreated into isolation, convinced that involvement in the war had been a mistake. In September 1939, at the beginning of World War II, the army numbered only 190,000 men, smaller than that of Portugal. Time was again vital in allowing U.S. resources to gear up; the more than two years between the outbreak of the war and U.S. entry in December 1941 gave the nation the time it needed to prepare. Congress again adopted conscription, but equipment was in short supply, and much of what was available was obsolescent.

Originally the army planned a force of 215 maneuver divisions, of which 61 were to be armored, 61 mechanized, 54 infantry, four cavalry, 10 mountain, and seven airborne. It actually fielded only 89 divisions during the war, compared to 100 for Japan and 300 for the Soviet Union. But a significant portion of America's available men, and women as well, were working in equally important war industries. The United States became the great "Arsenal of Democracy," supplying the sinews of war to all powers fighting the Axis. During the war the United States expended considerable resources in the air and on the sea. By the end of the war the army had 16 numbered air forces, and the navy had more ships than all the other navies of the world combined.

In 1947 the U.S. Air Force was established, split off from the army as a separate service. A year later, President Harry S. TRUMAN published an executive order integrating the armed forces, although this did not become reality in the ranks until the KOREAN WAR.

With the onset of the COLD WAR, the army found itself stretched thin, deploying forces overseas in occupations of Germany and Japan. In June 1950, on the outbreak of the Korean War, the army was down to less than 600,000 officers and men. It was also desperately short of equipment, but resources hurriedly rushed to scene stemmed the North Korean invasion of South Korea.

The Korean War rejuvenated the American defense establishment. On the conclusion of the 1953 armistice,

for the first time after a war, the United States did not disarm. The army, however, did find itself losing out to the air force and the navy, due to President Dwight EISENHOWER's reliance on nuclear weapons and strategic delivery systems.

The U.S. Army came out of the prolonged VIETNAM WAR badly shaken. Ground troops had fought there from 1965 to 1973, and for a variety of reasons, some self-inflicted, the army had performed unevenly. It was riddled with careerism, racism, insubordination, and drug use. President Richard NIXON's abolition of the draft, carried out to win support of the middle class for his Vietnam War policy, dramatically changed the army. The war led to a rethinking of the services from top to bottom. That this effort succeeded was made abundantly clear in OPERATION DESERT STORM, the 1991 Persian Gulf War.

More than a decade after the end of the cold war, the U.S. army finds itself again stretched thin. Authorized manpower is shrinking, and with the George W. Bush administration pushing national missile defense at the expense of training, conventional weapons, and ammunition stockpiles, the army will be even more hard pressed to fulfill its multiple roles, which now include a variety of peacekeeping assignments around the world under the auspices of the NORTH ATLANTIC TREATY ORGANIZATION (NATO) and the United Nations and the war against terrorism, including Operation Enduring Freedom in Afghanistan.

See also AMERICAN REVOLUTIONARY WAR, LAND OVERVIEW; CASUALTIES; CIVIL WAR, LAND OVERVIEW; CONTINENTAL ARMY; KOREAN WAR, COURSE OF; MILITARY ACADEMIES; MILITIA ACT (1794); MILITIA, ORGANIZATION AND ROLE OF (1603–1815); UPTON, EMORY; WAR OF 1812, LAND OVERVIEW.

Further reading: Coffman, Edward M. *The Old Army: A Portrait of the American Army in Peacetime, 1784–1898.* New York: Oxford University Press, 1986; Doughty, Robert A., and Ira A. Gruber, eds. *American Military History and the Evolution of Western Warfare.* Lexington, Mass.: Heath, 1996; Heller, Charles E., and William A. Stofft. *America's First Battles, 1776–1995.* Lawrence: University Press of Kansas, 1986; Mansoor, Paul R. *GI Offensive in Europe: The Triumph of American Infantry Divisions, 1941–1945.* Lawrence: University Press of Kansas, 1999; Weigley, Russell F. *History of the United States Army.* Bloomington: Indiana University Press, 1984.

— Adrian R. Lewis and Spencer C. Tucker

Army Nurse Corps *Organization of nurses serving the U.S. Army*

Established in 1901, the Army Nurse Corps (ANC) was preceded by the Army Nursing Corps, formed by the U.S.

Army during the CIVIL WAR. In 1898, during the SPANISH-AMERICAN WAR, the army employed trained nurses under contract. The AMERICAN RED CROSS, chartered by Congress in 1900, fostered the birth and early years of the ANC. It helped purchase army nurse uniforms, and it strongly encouraged the military forces to enroll only trained graduate nurses. Initially, army nurses were neither enlisted nor commissioned, although they were generally treated as officers. They were instead given "relative rank," which established pay grades and levels of seniority but defined only anomalous status within the army hierarchy.

The ANC proved its value during the PUNITIVE EXPEDITION INTO MEXICO (1916–17), which helped prepare it for the great demands of WORLD WAR I. From 1917 to 1923 army nurses served in military hospitals throughout the nation as well as in Europe, sometimes under hostile fire. Of 102 army nurses who died overseas in World War I, about 100 succumbed to the influenza pandemic.

In mid-1941 the ANC numbered nearly 5,500 personnel. This increased to more than 56,000 during WORLD WAR II. Again army nurses were called to overseas service, often working in medical units in combat zones, some quite close to front lines. Of 215 army nurses who died in service, 16 were killed in action or died of wounds. More than 60 army nurses spent three years as prisoners of war after being captured by the Japanese in January 1942. In 1947 the Army-Navy Nurses Act granted permanent commissioned status to military nurses.

During the KOREAN WAR, army nurses served in a new development in combat nursing—mobile army surgical hospitals (MASH). Such units were further developed during the 11 years (1963–74) in which 5,500 army nurses served in the VIETNAM WAR. During those years, advances in nursing practice, coupled with the nurses' dedication, greatly reduced the average length of stay at medical facilities. One army nurse was killed by hostile fire; seven Nurse Corps officers also died in the war.

In 1970 the army promoted Anna Mae Hayes to brigadier general, the first woman in the army to achieve that rank. Army nurses have also pioneered advances in nursing practices and professional training that have enhanced medical service in the field.

See also AIR FORCE NURSE CORPS; MEDICINE, MILITARY; NAVY NURSE CORPS; NURSING.

Further reading: Sarnecky, Mary T. *A History of the Army Nurse Corps.* Philadelphia: University of Pennsylvania Press, 1993. Tomblin, Barbara. *G.I. Nightingales: The Army Nurse Corps in World War II.* Lexington: University Press of Kentucky, 1996; West, Iris J. "The Women of the Army Nurse Corps during the Vietnam War." *In Celebra-*

tion of Patriotism and Courage. Washington, D.C.: Vietnam Women's Memorial Project, 1993.

— Jean Ebbert and Marie-Beth Hall

Arnold, Benedict (1741–1801) *American Revolutionary War general and traitor*

Born on 14 January 1741 in Norwich, Connecticut, Benedict Arnold experienced a troubled early life. Of 10 siblings, only one sister lived to adulthood. His alcoholic father lost the family fortune, and Arnold deserted both an apprenticeship and his military unit (twice) during the 1754–63 FRENCH AND INDIAN WAR. Nonetheless, he gained positive notice for his physical strength and restless energy.

Shortly after the early fights at LEXINGTON AND CONCORD during the American Revolutionary War, Arnold won a Massachusetts commission as a colonel of militia and helped organize the seizure of FORT TICONDEROGA. After raiding St. Johns, Canada, he obtained CONTINENTAL ARMY commander General George WASHINGTON's approval to attack QUEBEC. Arnold's overland march across Maine to the St. Lawrence despite appalling hardships must rank

Benedict Arnold   *(Library of Congress)*

among the great feats of leadership and endurance in U.S. history.

Seriously wounded in his right leg during the failed 31 December 1775 assault on Quebec, Arnold won promotion in January 1776 to brigadier general. Retreating from Canada, he next organized the small American fleet on Lake Champlain, which, while defeated at VALCOUR ISLAND in October, forced the British to postpone their assault on the Hudson River Valley. In early 1777 Arnold was outraged when Congress promoted over him five officers he considered to be of lesser ability and attainment. Washington persuaded him to stay in the army, and Arnold, with a scratch militia force, harassed the British during their DANBURY RAID in April. Finally promoted to major general in May, he played a key role in wrecking the 1777 British offensives in New York. First, he organized the relief of FORT STANWIX, then he figured prominently in both battles at SARATOGA, where he suffered a second serious wound in his right leg. Congress recognized his contribution by voting him a formal thanks and by backdating his major general's commission, giving him seniority over his rivals.

Hobbled by his wounds, Arnold in June 1778 took a sedentary assignment as military governor of Philadelphia. Marrying Peggy Shippen, of a prominent Tory family, Arnold became embroiled in local politics and shady business dealings, which led a court-martial to find him guilty of financial peculation in January 1780. Washington gave him a mild reprimand.

By this point, Arnold was deep into treasonous correspondence with British lieutenant general Sir Henry Clinton. Arnold, pleading his wounds, asked Washington for the garrison command at WEST POINT. He planned to turn over the fort and even Washington himself to the enemy, but the plot was uncovered with the capture of Major John André.

Arnold narrowly escaped to New York City, where he was commissioned a brigadier general in the British army. His record in his new uniform was mixed. He proved as energetic as ever, leading raids into Connecticut and Virginia, but he found his new associates chilly and his Tory followers few. In December 1781 Arnold moved to London, where, unable to obtain a field command, he turned unsuccessfully to commerce. He died there on 14 June 1801.

As a daring tactician and leader, Arnold had few peers. Had he remained loyal, his name would probably have ranked second only to Washington among American Revolutionary War military leaders.

See also AMERICAN REVOLUTIONARY WAR, LAND OVERVIEW; BENNINGTON, BATTLE OF.

Further reading: Brandt, Clare. *The Man in the Mirror: A Life of Benedict Arnold.* New York: Random House, 1994; Flexner, James Thomas. *The Traitor and the Spy.* 2d ed. Syracuse, N.Y.: Syracuse University Press, 1975; Martin, James Kirby. *Benedict Arnold, Revolutionary Hero: An American Warrior Reconsidered.* New York: New York University Press, 1997; Randall, Willard Sterne. *Benedict Arnold: Patriot and Traitor.* New York: Morrow, 1990; Van Doren, Carl. *Secret History of the American Revolution.* New York: Viking, 1941.

— Malcolm Muir, Jr.

Arnold, Henry H. ("Hap") (1886–1950) *Army Air Forces and Air Force general, commander of U.S. Army Air Forces during World War II*

Born on 25 June 1886 at Gladwyne, Pennsylvania, Henry Harley Arnold graduated from the U.S. Military Academy at WEST POINT in 1907. He spent four years in the Philippines and at Governors Island, New York, before volunteering for flight training with Wilbur and Orville WRIGHT as one of the army's first military aviators. In June 1912 Arnold won the first Mackay Trophy for setting a world altitude record of 6,540 feet. Arnold then served in the Philippines, temporarily renouncing flying because of its danger, but in October 1916 he rejoined the Army's Aviation Section.

Following U.S. entry into World War I, Arnold, then commanding the 7th Aero Squadron in Panama, was assigned to Washington as assistant director of military aeronautics, responsible for training and the acquisition of flying bases in the United States. He rose to the rank of colonel, but his success kept him from France until after the armistice. After the war Arnold reverted to his permanent rank of captain.

Between the wars Arnold remained a convinced advocate of air power, testifying in 1926 in support of Brigadier General William MITCHELL's contention that the military's neglect of aviation jeopardized national security. Arnold wrote or coauthored five books on airpower, worked closely with scientists at the California Institute of Technology on aviation development, and in 1934 won a second Mackay Trophy when he led a flight of B-10 bombers from Washington to Alaska and back.

In February 1935 Arnold won promotion to brigadier general and took command of 1st Wing, General Headquarters (GHQ) Air Force. That December he became assistant chief of staff of the air corps, and in September 1938 he was promoted to temporary major general and chief of staff of the air corps.

As World War II approached, Arnold forcefully advocated a major expansion of U.S. airpower, a view that had already led President Franklin D. ROOSEVELT to appoint him assistant chief of the air corps in 1936 and chief two years later. In spring 1940 Roosevelt set a target of 50,000 aircraft to defend the Western Hemisphere, and in 1941 Congress appropriated $2.1 billion for this effort—a vast expansion, which Arnold oversaw. At their wartime height, the Army Air Forces comprised almost 2.5 million personnel in 243 combat groups operating more than 63,000 aircraft around the world.

In October 1940 Arnold became acting deputy chief of staff of the army for air matters. In June 1941 he became chief of the renamed U.S. Army Air Forces and was promoted to temporary lieutenant general that December. From March 1942 Arnold was commanding general of army air forces. He was promoted to temporary general in 1943.

From 1941 onward, Arnold, health permitting, attended all the wartime conferences of the Allied leaders as the army's aviation representative on the Joint Chiefs of Staff and Combined Chiefs of Staff, helping to formulate wartime strategy. Arnold was a staunch supporter of massive STRATEGIC BOMBING against both Germany and Japan. He drove his subordinates hard toward that end, directing operations from the Pentagon. In December 1944 he became one of only four American generals to receive five-star rank. In August 1945 he urged employment of the ATOMIC BOMB against Japan.

Ill health forced Arnold's retirement in 1946. His successor, General Carl A. SPAATZ, drove for an independent air force, a goal that Arnold's policies, particularly the effective autonomy with which his command had operated, had enormously facilitated. In retirement Arnold continued, privately and publicly, to campaign for a strong national defense in which airpower would be a vital component. In May 1949 he was named first General of the Air Force, the father of which force he could plausibly claim to be. Arnold died at Sonoma, California, on 15 January 1950.

See also AIR FORCE, U.S.

Further reading: Arnold, Henry H. *Global Mission.* New York: Harper and Brothers, 1949; Coffey, Thomas M. *Hap: The Story of the U.S. Air Force and the Man Who Built It, General Henry H. "Hap" Arnold.* New York: Viking, 1982; Daso, Dik Alan. *Hap Arnold and the Evolution of American Air Power.* Washington, D.C.: Smithsonian Institution Press, 2000; Hayes, Grace P. *The History of the Joint Chiefs of Staff in World War II: The War against Japan.* Annapolis, Md.: Naval Institute Press, 1982; Sherry, Michael S. *The Rise of American Air Power: The Creation of Armageddon.* New Haven, Conn.: Yale University Press, 1987.

— Priscilla Roberts

arsenal system   *Stores or manufactories for weapons*
During the early modern period, European states gradually developed administrative machineries that supervised arsenals to ensure the production and storage of standardized small arms and artillery pieces of sufficient quantity and quality for their military establishments. In the 19th century, arsenals assumed a public character.

During the American Revolutionary War, the Continental army's military stocks were stored in rented private buildings. Under the influence of France, attempts were made to regularize calibers of the small arms. Following the war, in 1785 the new secretary of war, Henry KNOX established the first federal arsenal at Springfield, Massachusetts. SHAYS'S REBELLION of 1786, in which disgruntled farmers protesting taxes and foreclosures tried to seize the Springfield Arsenal, helped lead to a new and strengthened federal constitution. In 1796 President George WASHINGTON selected HARPERS FERRY (then Harper's Ferry), Virginia, as the site for a second federal arsenal.

The War of 1812 found the U.S. military woefully unprepared for the conduct of sustained military operations. As a consequence, efforts were undertaken to regularize arrangements whereby large forces could be armed in future conflicts. Early muskets were largely handmade, and their lack of standardization posed severe problems for military logistics.

Efforts were then undertaken to develop simple weapons of identical calibers using interchangeable parts so that repairs might easily be undertaken in the field. This would also standardize ammunition, thus easing the strain on primitive logistics. In the 1820s, under the direction of John H. Hall, Harper's Ferry had considerable success in the standardization of firearms for the military. Techniques developed here also had a considerable impact on civilian manufacturing.

The Ordnance Department, founded in 1812 and reorganized in 1815, had responsibility for the production, storage, and supply of weapons and ammunition. Thus it also was interested in standardization of small arms.

By 1816, in addition to Springfield and Harper's Ferry, there were three additional federal arsenals: Watervliet, New York (artillery and ammunition); Watertown, Massachusetts (small arms and gun carriages); and Frankford, Pennsylvania (ammunition). Two new arsenals were added in the second half of the 19th century: Rock Island Arsenal, Illinois (production of small arms); and Picatinny Arsenal, New Jersey (production of powder). During World War II a tank arsenal was established in Detroit, Michigan.

In 1839 the Ordnance Board was established within the Ordnance Department as a division for research and development. It worked especially on the establishment of a uniform artillery system. By the mid-1850s both small arms and artillery had been largely standardized. In 1859, when John Brown attempted to incite a slave revolt, he tried but failed to capture the federal arsenal at HARPERS FERRY and arm freed slaves with its weapons. The importance of such arsenals was shown in April 1861 when Southern troops stormed Harpers Ferry and managed to prevent destruction by its defenders of its machinery, which was then transported to Richmond and used to produce weapons for the Confederacy.

In the 20th century the federal arsenals were insufficient to produce all the weapons required for the two world wars, so wartime needs were met through private industry. The arsenals undertook specialized functions, monitoring standardization and interchangeability.

See also WHITNEY, ELI.

Further reading: Smith, Merrit Roe. *Harpers Ferry Armory and the New Technology. The Challenge of Change.* Ithaca, N.Y.: Cornell University Press, 1977; Smith, Merrit Roe, ed. *Military Enterprise and Technological Change. Perspectives on the American Experience.* Cambridge, Mass.: Massachusetts Institute of Technology Press, 1987.

— Max Plassmann

Articles of Confederation (1777) *First plan of government for the United States*

When the Continental Congress appointed a committee to draft the Declaration of Independence, it authorized another committee to draft a plan of government for the new nation. Chaired by John Dickinson of Pennsylvania, it drew up the Articles of Confederation. Debate in Dickinson's committee was lengthy, and Congress did not pass the final version of the articles until November 1777. It was not ratified until 1781.

A number of assumptions influenced the character of the central government that the articles sought to establish. Since many colonists had rebelled in the belief that London's authority was too expansive and arbitrary, the articles placed serious limitations on the power of the central government. All power was vested in Congress; there was no independent executive or judiciary. Congress exercised these functions through committees.

Congress was vested with authority to declare war and negotiate peace; it would conduct both foreign and Indian affairs; it could also establish a system of weights and measures as well as establish a government post office. Yet Congress had no power to tax, remaining totally at the mercy of the states for the national revenue. Congress also lacked authority to control or regulate interstate commerce; each state, in effect, was free to adopt its own commercial policies.

The framers of the articles ignored the pleas of the Continental army commander, General George WASHINGTON, for a standing army of some 2,600 men and a small navy. The army established under the articles consisted of just 80 men and a few officers, none above the rank of captain. The navy was totally disbanded. This force was totally inadequate for the new nation, and in 1784 states' righters pushed through a plan to increase the army to 700 men. Each state was to contribute men for one year on a quota system based on wealth and population. Only Pennsylvania, which feared the Indian threat the most, fulfilled its assigned total.

Despite differences in population, each state was entitled to one vote in Congress. Important matters of legislation—for instance, the ratification of treaties—would require a two-thirds majority of state delegations. Perhaps the biggest problem for the articles was the limitation on amendments. Each state had to agree; the vote of a single state could frustrate the wishes of all the others.

The government established under the articles saw the new nation through the war, though not officially ratified until 1781. Shortly after the end of the war, with the limitations of the articles all too apparent, a number of important political figures advocated either amending or abolishing it altogether. Ultimately a constitutional convention drafted a new document, the constitution that went into effect in 1789.

While the Articles of Confederation did have a number of drawbacks, notable success was achieved under it in the area of land policy, especially the Northwest Ordinances of 1785 and 1787.

See also CONSTITUTION OF 1789.

Further reading: Dougherty, Keith L. *Collective Action under the Articles of Confederation.* Cambridge, U.K.: Cambridge University Press, 2001; Jensen, Merrill. *The Articles of Confederation: A Interpretation of the Social-Constitutional History of the American Revolution, 1774–1781.* Madison: University of Wisconsin Press, 1970.

— Bruce Tap

artillery, land

Fire and maneuver are the two primary elements of land combat power. From the late Middle Ages to the early years of the 20th century, artillery was the most significant source of land-based firepower. Even after the appearance of machine guns, tanks, and rotary and fixed-wing attack aircraft, artillery remained a major force on the battlefield.

Throughout history, firepower and mobility technology have been in a constant tug-of-war. Rarely has one achieved a significant advantage over the other, but whenever one has, the results have been devastating. World War I is an example—a period during which firepower eclipsed mobility. The result was trench warfare. By World War II the technological balance had been restored. Artillery also played a significant role in the 20th-century transformation from a linear, two-dimensional battlefield to a deep, three-dimensional battlefield.

A 15-inch Rodman coast defense gun at Port Royal, South Carolina *(Library of Congress)*

Weapons

Tube artillery pieces are broadly classified by the behavior of the projectiles they shoot. The three basic categories of tube artillery have not changed in the last 300 years, although the individual technologies have undergone significant changes. Guns fire projectiles at a very high velocity on a relatively flat trajectory; they have the greatest range. Mortars deliver relatively light projectiles at short ranges, and only at high angles of fire (above 45 degrees). The howitzer is an extremely versatile weapon, capable of firing at both high and low angles; its muzzle velocity and range are less than a gun of comparable size, but it is far more accurate. Most field artillery pieces today are howitzers, although some field guns do exist. All tanks are armed with guns. Although technically artillery pieces, most mortars today are considered infantry weapons.

All forms of artillery in the late 18th century were smooth-bore, muzzle-loading, black-powder affairs. They had poor mobility, and artillerymen engaged their targets only by direct fire—they had to see and aim directly at the target. Starting in the middle half of the l9th century, artillery began to make large technological strides, including improved metallurgical and manufacturing techniques, rifled bores, breach-loading mechanisms, fire control instruments, and perhaps most importantly, recoil mechanisms.

Modern recoil mechanisms, introduced in the years prior to World War I, allowed the artillery piece to remain in its position on the ground after a round was fired. This in turn permitted artillery to fire at a far more rapid rate and meant that guns did not have to be reaimed after each round. These improvements in accuracy and repeatability, combined with modern optics and fire control techniques, made indirect fire possible. Indirect fire allows a gun to fire at a target unseen by the gun crew. It extended the effective range of artillery fire, which led to the concept of deep battle, in which targets for behind the lines are engaged. The first artillery piece with modern fire control and recoil systems was the French 75 mm Model 1897. American units used this gun extensively in WORLD WAR I.

In World War I, effective indirect fire required a forward observer who could see the target and transmit the targeting information to the battery. Aerial observers appeared near the end of World War I. (These target-acquisition techniques are still very much in use today; others include radar and electronic sensors.) In the late 1930s the U.S. Army was the first to introduce the concept of the fire direction center, which controlled the firing of an entire battery or even a battalion. Originally equipped with manual and graphical means of computation, modern fire direction centers are completely computerized. Prior to World War I, the only way to mass artillery effects was to concentrate the guns physically. Today, the fire of an entire division or even a corps can be brought to bear on a single point, regardless of where the guns are deployed.

Up through World War I, field artillery was horse-drawn. During the interwar years the horse gave way to the truck as the artillery's prime mover in the U.S. Army; many armies, including the German and Soviet, would rely heavily on horses until the end of World War II. Self-propelled (SP) artillery—guns mounted on wheeled or tracked carriages—also came into its own in that conflict. (The U.S. Army today uses a combination of SP and towed artillery pieces. SP artillery is designed to keep up with the fast-moving armored vehicles of heavy divisions; towed artillery can be transported by air to deploy globally with light divisions.)

Shortly after World War I, the U.S. Army started design work on a rugged and reliable 105 mm towed howitzer. The resulting M-2A1 howitzer served throughout WORLD WAR II as the mainstay of American divisional artillery. Modified slightly after the war, it became the M-1O1A1 howitzer and continued as the backbone of American artillery through Korea and Vietnam. The most successful and widely used artillery weapon in history, it was adopted by at least 35 armies. The last M-1O1A1 was withdrawn from U.S. service in the l990s, but at the start of the 21st century it remained in service in many parts of the world.

Rockets and missiles represent a fourth category of land-based artillery. Rockets actually predate cannon, but they were not servicible until William Congreve introduced military rockets into the Royal Artillery in the early 19th century. Used against the Americans with minor effect in the WAR OF 1812, the military rocket was really little more than a psychological tool through the end of World War I. By World War II, field artillery rockets had developed into moderately effective area-saturation weapons. The Germans, Soviets, and Americans all fielded various models of towed and SP multiple rocket launchers.

Following World War II, the U.S. Army concentrated on field artillery rockets with nuclear warheads. In the middle of the COLD WAR the truck-mounted, rail-fired "Honest John" delivered either a small nuclear or a large high-explosive warhead. Despite its sophistication, it was still essentially a free-flight rocket that simply went where pointed. Reacting to advances in Soviet systems, the U.S. Army in the mid-1980s reintroduced a multiple rocket launcher system. The technologically sophisticated Multiple Launch Rocket System (MLRS) is mounted on its own purpose-built, fully tracked chassis, which has an inertial positioning system and fires a family of rockets with various types of conventional warheads.

Missiles, rockets with onboard guidance systems do not have to be pointed before they are fired. Though generally considered to be strategic weapons, field artillery versions of guided missiles do exist. Deployed in the latter years of the cold war, the nuclear-tipped Pershing and Pershing-II missiles were U.S. Army field artillery weapons. Many analysts today consider the deployment of Pershings in Europe a significant factor in the collapse of the Soviet system and the end of the cold war.

Ammunition

The British Royal Artillery has a saying that the real weapon of the artillery is the projectile—the gun merely delivers it to its target. This has become more true as artillery projectiles have become increasingly diverse and sophisticated since the end of World War II. During the black-powder era, the three basic categories of artillery projectiles were solid, scatterable, and exploding. Solid shot was just that—a solid iron ball that tore gaps into tightly packed ranks of men and horses at a distance. As an attacking enemy closed, gun crews changed to grape shot, tightly packed clusters of iron balls, each about an inch and a half in diameter. When an enemy was within musket range, artillery crews switched to canister (or case shot), literally cans packed with musket balls, which turned the cannon into a huge shotgun. Exploding rounds (called shells, or bombs) were hollow projectiles packed with gunpowder and triggered by powder-burning fuses. A shell had a relatively small effective bursting radius, and the fuse was extremely difficult to time correctly. Mortars fired only exploding rounds; guns generally fired solid or scatterable shot; howitzers could fire either. Exploding rounds for guns became more common from the middle of the 19th century onward.

The first truly modern innovation in artillery ammunition came in 1784, when Lieutenant Henry Shrapnel of the Royal Artillery introduced the spherical case round. Essentially, it was a hollow sphere packed with musket balls and an explosive charge, triggered by a powder-burning time fuse. Shrapnel's round effectively extended the lethal range of canister (case) shot to that of solid shot. It also was the first of what today are called cargo-carrying rounds, which deliver submunitions to the target. By 1914, shrapnel was the round of choice for field artillery throughout the world. In World War I, however, it was relatively ineffective against dug-in and well-protected defensive positions.

Until almost the end of World War I, high-explosive (HE) artillery rounds produced only a blast effect. The metallurgy of the shell and the chemical characteristics of the explosive charge produced very large shell pieces which gave a relatively insignificant fragmentation effect. By 1918 the metallurgical and chemical balances finally had been perfected to produce both blast and fragmentation effects from an HE round. From that point on, the shrapnel round quickly disappeared from the arsenals of the world's armies (though to this day, HE shell fragments are incorrectly called shrapnel).

Smoke and illumination rounds both came into wide use during World War I. Smoke was (and still is) used to impede enemy observation and conceal friendly movements; illumination was and is used to facilitate friendly observation and mark targets at night. World War I also the saw the first (and so far only) large-scale use of artillery gas rounds. During the German 1918 Ludendorff offensive, Colonel Georg Bruchmüller made skillful use of combinations of lethal and nonlethal gas and of persistent and nonpersistent gas rounds. Although artillery gas rounds were not used in World War II, all major armies had them in their arsenals. The U.S. Army started demilitarizing its gas rounds only in the early 1990s.

The U.S. Army introduced nuclear artillery rounds in the 1950s. The ultimate symbol of the cold war, these "battlefield nukes" were intended primarily to stop massed armored formations, either at the Korean Demilitarized Zone or along the inter-German border. Nuclear rounds existed for both the 155 mm and 8-inch howitzers. Following a decision by President George H. W. BUSH, the U.S. Army pulled the nuclear artillery rounds out of its arsenal in the early 1990s.

A rapid growth of increasingly diverse and sophisticated artillery projectiles began in the 1960s. The first was the Improved Conventional Munition (ICM), which in many ways reached back to Shrapnel's original concept. The ICM is a cargo-carrying round containing antipersonnel "bomblets." The round explodes in the air, scattering the bomblets, which float to earth. A small explosive charge throws each bomblet back up into the air a few meters, where the main charge explodes. The effect is similar to that of the "bouncing Betty" mine of World War II. First introduced in Vietnam, the ICM later was replaced by the dual purpose ICM (DP-ICM), which contains a mix of antipersonnel and antiarmor bomblets.

The basic concepts of the canister round and the cannon as a huge shotgun were revived during Vietnam. The antipersonnel round—called the "beehive round" by GIs—contains thousands of "flechettes." It was fired virtually point-blank into charging masses of troops attacking firebases or gun positions. Such combat was common in Vietnam.

One of the most sophisticated and lethal of modern American artillery rounds is the Copperhead. It is a terminally guided antitank round, capable of pinpoint accuracy never before achieved with artillery. Once in the air, the round is guided directly to its target by a forward observer using a laser designator to mark the target. Sensing and steering mechanisms in the round guide it in flight. The observer can "designate" the target either from a ground position or from a helicopter. A remotely piloted vehicle (a robotic drone) also can be used to designate the target.

Other sophisticated artillery rounds include projectiles that lay minefields, emplace battlefield sensors, jam enemy radio transmissions, and home in on enemy radars.

The fuse is one of the most critical elements of an artillery round. Up until World War I, fuse timing was achieved by a burning powder train. Fuses were imprecise, which made it difficult to fire successive rounds with the same aim or achieve accurate heights of burst. Those problems were solved with the introduction of the mechanical time fuse near the end of World War I. Near the end of World War II, the U.S. Army introduced the *proximity fuse* for field artillery work, adapted from antiaircraft artillery. Also called the variable-time (VT) fuse, it contains a small radar transmitter and receiver that produces a perfect 20-meter height of burst every time. Point-detonating fuses include quick, superquick (which is so sensitive that a tree branch will set it off), delay, and concrete-piercing.

Organization

Henry KNOX was the first American chief of artillery, during the American Revolutionary War. Despite the heavy influence of French advisers and volunteers in the CONTINENTAL ARMY, Knox organized, equipped, and trained four regiments of artillery along British lines. After the Revolution, the standing army was almost completely disbanded. The only unit left on active duty was an artillery company originally raised by Alexander Hamilton, assigned to guard military stores at West Point. (That unit is today the 1st Battalion, 5th Field Artillery, the only regular U.S. Army unit with unbroken service since the Revolution.)

As the U.S. Army slowly rebuilt in the 1790s, the artillery and the engineers at first were combined in a single branch. By the War of 1812, there were four artillery regiments, although many of the cannoneers fought as infantry. After the War of 1812, the U.S. Army entered a long period of reliance upon French artillery doctrine and organization—largely under the long shadow of Napoleon Bonaparte in France; that phase would continue through the end of World War I. In the years leading up to the CIVIL WAR, most artillerymen were assigned to large garrisons or coastal forts, manning large and immobile guns. Although all artillery was part of a single branch, most artillery units were designated as either *heavy* or *light* (or *field*). The *horse* (or *flying*) artillery units of the MEXICAN-AMERICAN WAR period were specially organized and equipped, with each cannoneer mounted. Many heavy artillery units were raised during the Civil War, but most fought as infantry. In 1902, the artillery split into coast and field artillery branches.

On the eve of World War I, American artillery was undermanned, underequipped, and poorly trained. Despite the establishment of the Field Artillery School at Fort Sill, Oklahoma, in 1911, most artillery officers had never seen an entire battery fire "for effect" (to destroy a target). The standard American artillery piece, the three-inch field gun, was completely inadequate for modern warfare. Upon entering the war, the United States provided scrap iron as raw material from which France manufactured more of its standard guns for arriving American units. Early in 1918 Major General William J. Snow was appointed the U.S. Army's first chief of field artillery and given the responsibility to equip, organize, and train that branch for war. As the U.S. Army rapidly expanded, new cannoneers and officers received rudimentary training in the United States and more advanced training under French instructors once they landed in Europe. American batteries were then assigned to French units in the line for short periods to gain experience.

The German army revolutionized artillery tactics in World War I. During the interwar years, the Americans and Soviets, especially, studied the German lessons; in the United States a young artillery officer, Maxwell TAYLOR, translated one of Bruchmüller's books into English. Building on and expanding the German World War I techniques, both the Americans and the Soviets fielded artillery systems in World War II that vastly overmatched those of the Germans.

Although coast artillery was a separate branch throughout World War II, large coastal guns did not play a significant role in the war. Coast artillery units were heavily involved, however, as antiaircraft artillery; Virtually all of the air-defense artillery function evolved under the coast artillery; the airplane, however, made large coastal guns obsolete. Those guns were eliminated from the arsenal following World War II, and in 1950 the coast and field branches merged. Officers and soldiers, however, tended to specialize in either field or air-defense artillery, with the former training at Fort Sill and the latter at Fort Bliss, Texas. The newly combined branch added a missile to the traditional crossed-cannons branch insignia of the field artillery.

Increasing technical complexities and the need for specialization soon forced field and air-defense artillery into separate branches, in 1968. The air-defense artillery branch retained the crossed-cannons-and-missile insignia the combined branch had used; the field artillery reverted to its traditional crossed cannons (first authorized in 1834).

The modern American field artillery community encompasses both the army and the Marine Corps. When the Marine Corps established marine divisions prior to World War II, specific marine regiments were designated as artillery units. Presently the 10th, 11th, 12th, and 14th Marines are artillery units (the 14th Marines is the only Marine Corps Reserve artillery regiment). Marine Corps artillery units are organized and equipped similarly to army units, and their tactics are virtually identical. Marine and army artillerymen train side by side at Fort Sill, with the marines providing a certain percentage of the instructors and staff. The official title of the field artillery professional association—the United States Field Artillery Association—makes it clear that it is a joint army-marine organization.

See also AMERICAN REVOLUTIONARY WAR, LAND OVERVIEW; ARMY, U.S.; BALLISTIC MISSILES, COAST DEFENSE; MORTARS; PARROTT, ROBERT P.

Further reading: Bailey, Jonathan B. A. *Field Artillery and Fire Power.* Oxford, U.K.: Military Press, 1989; Birkheimer, William E. *Historical Sketch of the Organization, Administration, Matériel, and Tactics of The Artillery, United States Army.* Washington, D.C.: Chapman, 1884; Comparato, Frank E. *The Age of Great Guns.* Harrisburg, Pa.: Stackpole, 1964; Dastrup, Boyd L. *The Field Artillery: History and Sourcebook.* Westport, Conn.: Greenwood, 1994; Downey, Fairfax. *Sound of the Guns: The Story of the American Artillery.* New York: McKay, 1956; Grotelueschen, Mark E. *Doctrine under Trial: American Artillery Equipment in World War I.* Westport, Conn.: Greenwood, 2001; Snow, William J. *Signposts of Experience.* Washington, D.C.: United States Field Artillery Association, 1941; Zabecki, David T. *Steel Wind: Colonel Georg Bruchmüller and the Birth of Modern Artillery.* Westport, Conn.: Praeger, 1994.

— David T. Zabecki

Atkinson, Henry (1782–1842) *U.S. Army general*

Born in 1782 in Person County, North Carolina, Henry Atkinson was commissioned a captain in the U.S. Army in 1808. He served actively throughout the War of 1812 but saw no fighting; he remained in the peacetime establishment as colonel of the 6th U.S. Infantry Regiment. Atkinson first gained national recognition in command of the ill-fated 1819 Missouri River Expedition, which was abandoned at Council Bluffs (in present-day Iowa) after mechanical difficulties with its steamboats. Fort Atkinson, a siqnificant frontier post, was erected there. Atkinson next commanded the 9th Military District, which encompassed a large part of the northwestern frontier. In this capacity he spent several years constructing roads and fortifications and concluding treaties with various Native Americans tribes. In 1820 Atkinson also dispatched to the Rocky Mountains an expedition headed by Major Stephen H. Long.

In 1825 Atkinson gained promotion to brigadier general and was directed to lead another expedition up the Yellowstone River.

He proceeded 100 miles upstream in paddle-driven keelboats, signed treaties with numerous tribes, and opened vast sections of the northern plains and Rocky Mountains to trade. The following year Atkinson returned to St. Louis, Missouri, where he took charge of locating a site for Jefferson Barracks, the army's only infantry school. In 1827 Atkinson directed Colonel Henry LEAVENWORTH to construct in the neighboring Kansas Territory a post that subsequently became known as Fort Leavenworth.

During the next 15 years Atkinson was preoccupied with frontier pacification and containing Indian unrest. In 1827 he directed operations to quell a possible uprising by the Winnebago tribe, and in 1832 he fought actively in the successful BLACK HAWK war. On 2 August 1832, Atkinson crushed the Indians at the Battle of Bad Axe, which restored peace to the frontier and removed an obstacle to white settlement. Thereafter he and the soldiers of his command were increasingly utilized for Indian removal across the Mississippi River. Atkinson died at Jefferson Barracks on 14 June 1842, the most influential frontier officer of his generation. A new post, Fort Atkinson, Nebraska, was named in his honor.

See also AMERICAN INDIAN WARS, OVERVIEW.

Further reading: Ney, Virgil. *Fort on the Prairie: Fort Atkinson on the Council Bluffs.* Washington, D.C.: Command Publications, 1978; Nichols, Roger L. *General Henry Atkinson: A Western Military Career.* Norman: University of Oklahoma Press, 1965.

— John C. Fredriksen

Atlanta campaign (5 May–1 September 1864)
Major campaign of the Civil War

In March 1864, when Lieutenant General Ulysses S. GRANT assumed command of all Union forces, Major General

William T. SHERMAN took charge of the Military Division of the Missouri. Grant ordered him to destroy General Joseph E. JOHNSTON's Confederate Army of Tennessee, then arrayed near Dalton, Georgia. Confederate president Jefferson DAVIS hoped that Johnston would move before Union forces could concentrate, but Johnston, claiming inadequate resources, refused to take the offensive. On 5 May Sherman began a campaign that would end four months later with the capture of Atlanta.

Moving southward from Chattanooga, Tennessee, Sherman's amalgamated force included Major General George THOMAS's 73,000-man Army of the Cumberland (IV, XIV, XX Corps), Major General James B. MCPHERSON's Army of the Tennessee (25,000 men in the XV, XVI, and XVII Corps), Major General John SCHOFIELD's Army of the Ohio (XXIII Corps), and a large cavalry corps—in all, some 110,000 soldiers and 250 guns.

At Dalton, General Johnston commanded 47,000 men in the infantry corps of Lieutenant General William J. HARDEE and Lieutenant General John Bell HOOD and 8,000 troopers in Major General Joseph WHEELER's excellent cavalry corps. Soon Lieutenant General Leonidas POLK arrived with his Army of Mississippi—adding an infantry corps and a cavalry division, and bringing Johnston's total strength to roughly 70,000 men.

After two months of campaigning, the combination of Sherman's strong flanking maneuvers and Johnston's predilection for strategic withdrawal brought the two forces to the outskirts of Atlanta. Although there had been some intense clashes—at New Hope Church and Pickett's Mill, for example—both commanders avoided a general engagement until 27 June when an impatient Sherman attacked Johnston's prepared position at KENNESAW MOUNTAIN with heavy losses. On 9 July Johnston's army crossed the Chattahoochee and moved into Atlanta's outer defenses.

President Davis demanded to know Johnston's plans for holding the vital railroad and manufacturing center. Johnston's vague responses seemed to indicate a further retreat (Johnston later claimed that he was preparing to fight a major battle for Atlanta, but nothing he said or did at the time indicated such). If Johnston would not fight for Atlanta, Davis needed a general who would. After much deliberation, Davis relieved Johnston on 17 July and appointed the 33-year-old Hood, who had offered much negative commentary, to lead the Army of the Tennessee.

One of the best combat commanders of the war, Hood had suffered a disabled arm at GETTYSBURG and lost a leg at CHICKAMAUGA. He now planned to strike Sherman's armies in much the same way that Robert E. LEE had driven the Federals from Richmond in 1862. McPherson and Schofield, Hood's friends at West Point, warned Sherman that Hood would be aggressive, even rash. Nonetheless, Sherman's forces pressed closer to Atlanta.

Hood planned to attack the slow-moving Army of the Cumberland as it crossed Peachtree Creek north of Atlanta. On 20 July the two Confederate corps of Hardee and Lieutenant General A. P. STEWART (who had replaced the fallen Polk) struck the center of Thomas's army south of the creek. The attack fell mostly on Major General Joseph HOOKER's XX Corps, which rallied from the initial shock to turn back the attackers, inflicting about 2,400 casualties while suffering some 1,600 of its own. Sherman, traveling with McPherson's army, was unaware of the battle until it had been decided. Although unsuccessful, the attack slowed the Union advance.

Two days later Hood launched a more ambitious assault on McPherson's army, east of Atlanta. After an all-night march, Hardee's corps hit McPherson's exposed southern flank, achieving some success before Federal resistance solidified. McPherson was killed by Confederate skirmishers as he worked to secure his line. In late afternoon Hood sent Major General Benjamin F. Cheatham's corps (Hood's own former corps) against the main Federal line, and Hardee resumed his attack. Major General John Logan, now commanding the army, rallied his own XV Corps to contain Cheatham's breakthrough. By nightfall the desperate attack was over. The Confederates had come close to achieving a stunning victory and had stymied another Federal approach, but Hood's attacking corps had suffered 6,000 casualties, while inflicting some 4,000. Sherman now became more cautious, settling for a semisiege as his armies worked to isolate Atlanta.

On 28 July Lieutenant General Stephen D. Lee, who replaced Cheatham, initiated a battle with the Army of the Tennessee, now commanded by Major General Oliver O. HOWARD, west of Atlanta near Ezra Church. Hood had planned another flanking attack for the next day, but Lee having engaged, he allowed the battle to continue. It was another loss and cost another 3,000 casualties, but it temporarily halted a move against Hood's rail communications. Meanwhile, Wheeler's horsemen dealt Sherman a stunning blow, virtually destroying two Federal cavalry divisions raiding south of Atlanta.

During August, Sherman continued his effort to encircle Atlanta, but Hood's forces managed to thwart each foray. Finally, Sherman moved with most of his force against Hood's lines of communication. Hood sent Hardee to Jonesboro to protect the road to Macon, but Hardee could not counter the overwhelming attacking force and after two days of fighting settled for blocking the road. Meanwhile, Union brigadier general Jacob Cox's division, from XXIII Corps, cut the railroad between Atlanta and Jonesboro. On 1 September Hood evacuated Atlanta, destroying tons of valuable supplies trapped in the city.

Hardee withdrew to Lovejoy's Station, where he was soon joined by Hood and the balance of the army. Sherman led most of his force in pursuit while on 2 September Atlanta's mayor surrendered the city to Major General Henry W. SLOCUM of XX Corps. Disengaging at Lovejoy's, Sherman returned to Atlanta. Hood soon marched his army northward, hoping to draw Sherman out of Georgia. Sherman refused to oblige, sending a portion of his command to deal with Hood while he prepared to cut a swath through Georgia in a MARCH TO THE SEA. Hood then launched an invasion of Tennessee, which ended in disaster at NASHVILLE. Sherman's victory at Atlanta capped one of the great campaigns of the Civil War and contributed mightily to President Abraham LINCOLN's reelection that November.

See also CIVIL WAR, LAND OVERVIEW.

Further reading: Castel, Albert. *Decision in the West: The Atlanta Campaign of 1864.* Lawrence: University Press of Kansas, 1992; Coffey, David. *John Bell Hood and the Struggle for Atlanta.* Abilene, Tex.: McWhiney Foundation Press, 1998; McMurry, Richard. *Atlanta 1864: Last Chance for the Confederacy.* Lincoln: University of Nebraska Press, 2000.

— David Coffey

Atlantic, Battle of the (World War I) *Struggle between the Allies and the Central Powers for control of North Atlantic shipping lanes, particularly around the British Isles, from 1914 to 1918*

Following the 1916 Battle of Jutland, the Germans shifted their campaign at sea away from large surface actions in favor of wholesale submarine warfare. German U-boats and surface raiders attempted to cut off Britain and France from the raw materials, industrial production, and military support of the United States, Canada, and overseas colonial possessions. The Battle of the Atlantic saw extensive use of the submarine in combat for the first time and ushered in a new era of naval warfare.

When war began in August 1914, Britain possessed the world's largest merchant marine. At nearly 20 million tons, it represented half of the world's total tonnage. Britain also possessed the world's largest and most powerful navy. The naval and merchant fleets of Britain, France, Russia, Japan, and later the United States gave the Allies an advantage at sea that was overwhelming. This maritime superiority provided access to world resources and markets, while it could deny similar access to the Central Powers.

Britain declared a blockade of Germany that threatened to strangle the Central Powers economically and hinder their ability to wage a protracted war. The British blockade ultimately included not only war matériel but all raw materials and foodstuffs. In February 1915 Germany responded by declaring the waters around the British Isles a war zone and commenced unrestricted submarine warfare against Allied and neutral vessels. The strategy was intended to retaliate against the increasingly effective British blockade and to cut off Britain and France from overseas support. Germany's use of unrestricted submarine warfare risked the loss of American lives and ships, however, which could bring the United States into the war.

Germany began its submarine offensive in 1915 with only 29 U-boats. The destruction of passenger liners and neutral vessels, most notably the sinking of the British liner *LUSITANIA* by *U-20* in May 1915, with 124 Americans among the 1,201 passengers killed, brought considerable diplomatic pressure on Germany to cease its U-boat campaign. In early June 1915, the German Admiralty instructed U-boat commanders not to sink passenger liners on sight. On 18 September 1915, Berlin suspended the unrestricted submarine warfare campaign. During 1915, German U-boats had sunk 850,000 gross tons of shipping, but the British had launched more than 1.3 million tons. After much debate in Germany, Kaiser Wilhelm II approved the resumption of submarine warfare in 1916; the single restriction was that only armed merchant ships would be sunk without warning. German policy wavered under diplomatic pressure during 1916 when U-boats were having moderate success against Allied shipping.

The Allies immediately labeled the German U-boat campaign illegal and barbaric. U-boat commanders attempted to conduct themselves according to the traditional rules of cruiser warfare, but technology had overtaken custom and law. Surfacing to warn vessels and allowing crews to abandon ship before sinking them could prove fatal to U-boats. Merchant vessels were often armed, and a wireless radio broadcast could alert nearby warships. Consequently, U-boats increasingly relied on submerged attacks made without warning.

In truth, the U-boat offensive was no more a violation of international law than was the British blockade. Both infringed on the rights of neutrals to trade with belligerents. Until April 1917, when the United States joined the war against Germany, British violations of American neutral shipping rights through the detention and inspections of neutral vessels were far more numerous than violations by German U-boats. However, as Allied propaganda vividly illustrated, German mistakes cost lives, while British mistakes cost only money and time and could largely be rectified in Admiralty court.

Despite the diplomatic risks, on 1 February 1917 Berlin again instituted a policy of unrestricted submarine warfare. German naval planners believed if the U-boats could sink 600,000 tons of shipping per month, Britain would be driven from the war and the Allies would be forced to seek peace on German terms. German leaders believed that the United States, an inconsequential land power, would not be able to make a meaningful contribution on the ground in

France before Germany had won the war. As expected, the policy pushed the United States to declare war against Germany in April 1917. However, the great success of the U-boats did threaten Britain and France with defeat. Sinkings rose precipitously to an unprecedented 860,000 tons in April 1917; in three months, more than 2 million tons of Allied and neutral shipping had been sent to the bottom. The Allies could not replace lost tonnage fast enough. At the same time, U-boat losses were low.

While improvements in technology and tactics were available to help meet the U-boat menace, the real solution was the CONVOY SYSTEM. Vessels carrying essential cargoes, from ammunition to foodstuffs, gathered at key ports and were escorted in large groups by Allied warships. The British Admiralty had initially avoided the convoy system because, among other things, it believed there were not sufficient destroyers to escort convoys and protect the Grand Fleet in the North Sea at the same time. The U-boat emergency of 1917 raised the importance of merchant-vessel protection and forced a closer look that showed the escort problem was not insurmountable.

The assistance of the U.S. Navy made implementation of the convoy system even more complete. When Congress declared war on Germany in April 1917, the Navy Department sent Rear Admiral William S. SIMS to London to consult with the Admiralty, and Sims quickly became a proponent of the convoy system. Although he met widespread resistance in both London and Washington, he pushed for full U.S. integration into the system as soon as possible. By August, 35 U.S. Navy destroyers were engaged in convoy duty, operating out of Queenstown, Ireland. They represented more than one-third of the total number of destroyers engaged in Atlantic escort duty. Soon U.S. warships were regularly escorting convoys between Halifax, New York, Hampton Roads, Gibraltar, and the British Isles.

Although full implementation of the convoy system took time, sinkings from U-boats immediately began to drop. The protection offered by escorts and the lower probability that U-boats would intercept a target (when compared the likelihood of finding one of hundreds of ships sailing alone) yielded immediate results. It would not be until the spring of 1918 that sinkings would fall below 300,000 tons a month, but the Allies had reversed the deadly trend of early 1917 and had won the Battle of the Atlantic.

See also NAVY, U.S.; WORLD WAR I, U.S. INVOLVEMENT.

Further reading: Halpern, Paul G. *A Naval History of World War I.* Annapolis, Md.: Naval Institute Press, 1994; Hough, Richard. *The Great War at Sea, 1914–1918.* New York: Oxford University Press, 1983.

— Thomas J. Stuhlreyer

Atlantic, Battle of the (World War II) *One of the critical campaigns of World War II, often marginalized in larger histories of the conflict*

Without Allied success against U-boats attacking the Atlantic convoys, the Allied invasions of western Europe could not have occurred. It took almost four years to overcome the German U-boat campaign against Allied seaborne lines of communication.

Because Adolf Hitler had informed the German navy commander Admiral Erich Raeder that war would not occur before 1944, Raeder had been busy building a balanced fleet. Thus Germany, as in World War I, had the wrong mix of combatants when the war began in 1939. On 1 September 1939, Germany had just 57 U-boats, of which 27 were oceangoing types rather than the 300 that the commander of submarines, Admiral Karl Dönitz, believed were needed. On the other hand, in contravention of the Treaty of Versailles, Germany in the 1930s established a naval school for submariners and had submarines designed and built in various friendly countries. Also, thanks to the Anglo-German Naval Agreement of June 1935, Germany could have 45 percent of British submarine tonnage and, in special cases, 100 percent. When Germany went to war in 1939, then, it had only the newest type craft.

Operations in the Atlantic Ocean and Baltic Sea were directed personally by Dönitz, while his office directed those in the North Sea and the Indian Oceans. Subordinate commands handled matters in the Mediterranean, the Arctic, and off southeastern Norway. This organization lasted until March 1943 when U-boat operations devolved upon the Navy's Operations Bureau.

Dönitz was able to take advantage of German code-breaking operations to direct his boats to where he believed enemy ships would be. With about double the speed of the eight-knot convoys, U-boats could trail until dark and then attack. It did not take the British long, however, to locate the boats via radio-direction-finding stations in ships or ashore and to reroute the convoys even if they failed to break Dönitz's communications code.

By May 1941 German surface ships had destroyed 885,493 tons of enemy shipping, but U-boats had sunk 3,758,766 tons. After Marshal Hermann Göring's Luftwaffe failed in 1940 to defeat Britain, a few surface warships and a growing number of U-boats were left to attack its trade. Dönitz surprised the British by having his boats operate in "wolf packs," attack while surfaced at night, and operate for extended periods far out at sea, resupplied from 1940 on by supply boats ("milch cows"). British Admiral of the Fleet Sir Andrew B. Cunningham deemed Dönitz the most dangerous opponent since Michael A. de Ruyter, a 17th-century Dutch admiral. Helping to build his reputation were such U-boat "aces" as Otto Kretschmer, Gunther Prien, Joachim Schepke, Herbert Schultze, and others through

U-118 under attack by planes from the USS *Bogue* (CVE 9) in the Central Atlantic, 12 June 1943. *U-118* was sunk in this action. Note German crew members by conning tower.   *(Naval Historical Foundation)*

1941, when individual operations largely gave way to wolf packs.

Also, for at least two years U-boats were favored because they could operate farther to the west than Britain at the time could escort its convoys; British air could not cover all the western Atlantic. Unfortunately for Germany, radar sets fitted to U-boats as early as 1934 were inefficient, and crews relied upon hydrophones (primitive passive sonar) instead. Both Britain and Germany, and then the United States, suffered until at least 1943 from faulty torpedoes. On the other hand, Dönitz obtained a great boon when the fall of France in July 1940 enabled him to construct strongly built submarine pens along the Bay of Biscay coast at Bordeaux, Brest, St. Lorient, La Pallice, and St. Nazaire. The shortened time it accordingly took U-boats to reach operating areas in the Atlantic permitted the submarines, particularly the Type VII boats, to remain much longer on station. The German occupation of Norway similarly facilitated U-boat operations.

In May 1940 Prime Minister Winston Churchill asked President Franklin D. ROOSEVELT, who had moved from neutrality to cobelligerency with Britain, to supply 50 World War I–vintage destroyers. In turn, Britain gave the United States sites for bases in its territories in the Western Hemisphere. Roosevelt then made Britain a prime recipient of matériel in his LEND-LEASE program. In addition, staff talks with the British resulted in plans to have the United States, once at war, make the defeat of Hitler its prime objective, protect friendly shipping in the western approaches to the United Kingdom, and immediately start building escort ships for the British.

The British countered the U-boat threat by using convoys, improving the training of escort personnel, building escort craft, fitting radar as well as sonar to escorts, using radio-direction-finding stations to locate wolf packs, integrating the planes of Coastal Command into antisubmarine work, operating long-range planes from Greenland and Iceland to cover the last vestiges of the central Atlantic (the

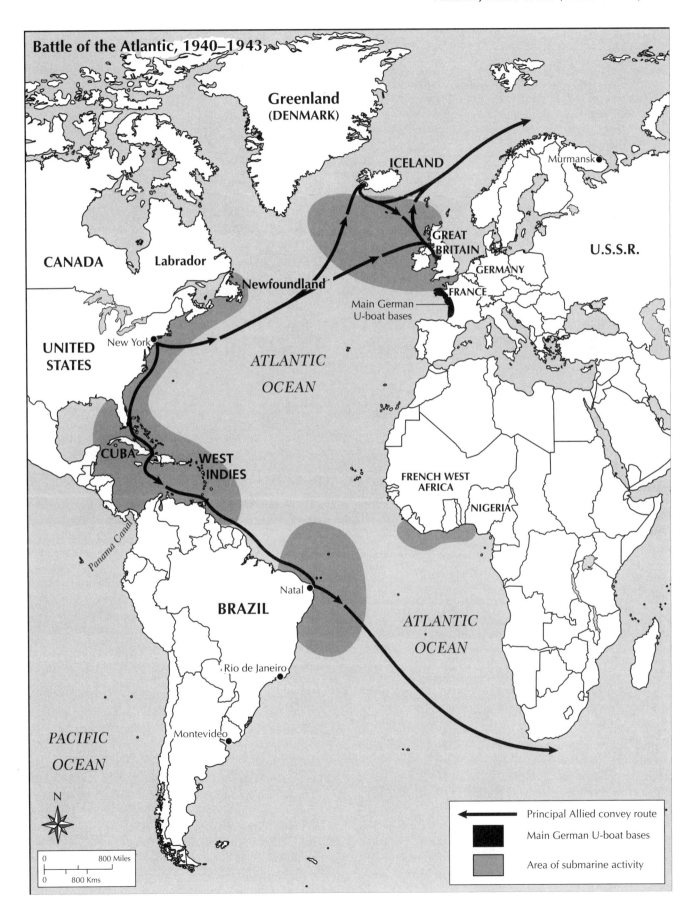

Battle of the Atlantic, 1940–1943

Greenland
(DENMARK)

ICELAND

Murmansk

CANADA   Labrador

Newfoundland

GREAT
BRITAIN

GERMANY

FRANCE

U.S.S.R.

Main German
U-boat bases

UNITED
STATES

New York

ATLANTIC
OCEAN

CUBA

WEST
INDIES

FRENCH WEST
AFRICA

NIGERIA

Panama Canal

BRAZIL

Natal

ATLANTIC
OCEAN

Rio de Janeiro

PACIFIC
OCEAN

Montevideo

N

0   800 Miles

0   800 Kms

Principal Allied convey route

Main German U-boat bases

Area of submarine activity

"Black Pit"), and finally, reading the German navy's communications when it salvaged Enigma machine from the damaged *U-110*. Moreover, the captured *U-570* revealed many of the German submarines' secrets. Finally, with Canadian ships shepherding convoys in the western zone, British ships could turn about and escort eastbound vessels. By May 1941, with the 50 American destroyers on duty, escorts, including some from of the U.S. Navy, could stay with a convoy all the way across the Atlantic.

Following the Japanese air attack on PEARL HARBOR on 7 December 1941 and Germany's declaration of war on the United States, U.S. Chief of Naval Operations, Admiral Ernest KING directed that unrestricted war begin against Japan, and on 8 December against Germany as well.

With his own boats busy elsewhere, it was not until January 1942 that Dönitz issued orders for Operation *Paukenschlag* (drumroll) along America's east coast. The original six U-boats in those waters soon became 19, and all had a "happy time" sinking ships, especially tankers, silhouetted against the lighted shoreline. In a reverse Lend-Lease, the British offered the use of 22 trawlers for convoy work and advised that convoying was the only way to protect shipping. Shipping finally sailed only by day and sought shelter in protected anchorages at night, and a blackout was imposed. Nonetheless, 81 ships were sunk before Dönitz transferred his boats to the Caribbean and the Gulf of Mexico, as well as some large boats to the South Atlantic and Indian Ocean.

Following Germany's invasion of the Soviet Union in June 1941, Roosevelt offered the Soviet Union Lend-Lease supplies. Some American, but mostly British, ships in convoys from Iceland or Scotland delivered supplies to Murmansk via Arctic waters, at terrible cost. The most savage attack was that made by German planes from northern Norway and U-boats on convoy PQ. 17 in late June and early July 1942. Twenty-six of 33 ships were lost.

With more than 300 U-boats in the North Atlantic, Dönitz enjoyed another happy time between May 1942 and March 1943, destroying another 1,770,000 tons of shipping in the nadir of the convoy experience. By the end of May 1943, however, the Allies had staged a comeback.

Long-range Allied aircraft now covered the Black Pit, hunter-killer groups (escort carriers with destroyer or destroyer escorts) sought U-boats at focal points, and Admiral King created a think tank, the Tenth Fleet, that did very helpful antisubmarine analysis work. In mid-March 1943 the 63 U-boats in the North Atlantic destroyed 22 ships, and it appeared that Dönitz was winning the battle. But since 1 January 1943 he had lost 40 boats, among them many milch cows, and he suffered additional heavy losses in May and thereafter. Particularly effective was Allied use of aircraft fitted with shortwave (10 cm) radar (which the Germans could not receive), aircraft fitted with

high-powered searchlights, improved shipboard torpedoes, and ahead-thrown small depth charges and rockets. Dönitz failed to keep pace with losses and could not obtain improved boats, such as the Type XXI and Type XXIII. Moreover, the Allies countered with acoustic torpedoes and radar that could detect snorkels. Also, Dönitz's constant use of radio permitted Allied radio direction finding to locate his boats, which would then be attacked by hunter-killer groups.

In the end, the ability of the Allies, particularly of the United States, to produce so many antisubmarine craft and weapons simply overwhelmed the U-boats. Important also was the cooperation of Allied civilian scientists with naval personnel in devising new tactics, the destruction of German shipbuilding and other facilities by Allied bombing, and the loss of the French coastal U-boat bases after the Allies landed in Normandy.

During the war, U-boats sank 2,775 merchant ships totaling 14,573,000 tons, but 300,000 voyages across the Atlantic were successful.

See also NAVY, U.S.

Further reading: Bekker, Cajus D. *Hitler's Naval War.* Translated and edited by Frank Ziegler. Garden City, N.Y.: Doubleday, 1974; Blair, Clay. *Hitler's U-boat War.* 2 vols. New York: Random House, 1996, 1998; Dönitz, Karl. *Memoirs: Ten Years and Twenty Days.* Translated by R. H. Stevens and David Woodward. Annapolis, Md.: Naval Institute Press, 1990; Hessler, Gunter. *The U-Boat War in the Atlantic, 1939–1945.* 3 vols. London: H.M. Stationery Office, 1989.

— Paolo E. Coletta

atomic bomb, decision to employ (1945)

Almost immediately after President Harry S. TRUMAN ordered atomic bombs employed against Japan, Americans began to take sides on the issue. Initially, people assumed that the administration had acted primarily out of military necessity. Stories circulated of potential U.S. casualties of up to 1 million Americans in an invasion of Japan. Tokyo seemed as intransigent as ever, and kamikaze attacks on U.S. ships in the struggle for OKINAWA seemed to support the conclusion that the Japanese would fight to the last. Thousands of GIs believed emphatically that U.S. lives were spared by employing the atomic bomb.

Soon, however, historians began to question this interpretation. They pointed out that contrary to popular belief, many key individuals had opposed its employment, notably General Dwight D. EISENHOWER. They attacked the idea that the decision had been motivated by military necessity and pointed out that the projection of casualties in an invasion of Japan had come only after the fact. Japan had already initiated peace overtures with the Soviet Union. Had the United States but softened its terms, they reasoned, Japan would probably have accepted. Indeed, many on the Japanese council voting for peace said they were more impressed with Soviet entry into the war than by the atomic bombs.

Revisionist historians, including Gar Alperovitz, asserted that Truman was motivated entirely by political reasons. With the COLD WAR looming, he wanted to intimidate the Soviets.

More recent scholarship holds that the primary motivation for employing the bomb was indeed military. Although there was never an estimate of a million U.S. casualties in an invasion of Japan, there were clearly studies positing significant numbers. As far as Japanese attempts to end the war by diplomatic means were concerned, these amounted to little, as the ruling council was deadlocked. Even after the second bomb was dropped on Nagasaki, it took Emperor Hirohito's personal intervention to resolve the issue, and even so he was nearly overthrown in a military coup.

This current view is more balanced. While allowing that Truman's chief concern was military necessity, it acknowledges that he had secondary diplomatic goals in mind. The fact that the United States had a nuclear monopoly and a strategic air force to deliver the bombs could not help but impress Stalin and deter him from putting pressure on Japan for territorial acquisitions.

Finally, it is worth noting that the conflict in the Pacific was war to the knife hilt. The most destructive air raids in history were not Hiroshima or Nagasaki but the February 1945 firebombing of Dresden and the March 1945 firebomb raid on TOKYO.

At the time, employment of the atomic bomb simply was not a controversial issue.

See also NUCLEAR AND ATOMIC WEAPONS.

Further reading: Alperovitz, Gar. *The Decision to Use the Atomic Bomb and the Architecture of an American Myth.* New York: Knopf, 1995; Davis, Raymond. *Clear Conscience: The Atom Bombs v. The Super Holocaust.* Paducah, Ky.: Turner, 1999; Hogan, Michael J., ed. *Hiroshima in History and Memory.* New York: Cambridge University Press, 1996; Walker, J. Samuel. *Prompt & Utter Destruction: Truman and the Use of Atomic Bombs against Japan.* Chapel Hill: University of North Carolina Press, 1997.

— Brian C. Melton

B

Bacon's Rebellion (10 May–December 1676)

A rebellion against the Virginia government's Indian policies and growing elitism

Bacon's Rebellion was directed against the Virginia government as personified by longtime colonial governor Sir William BERKELEY. The immediate trigger for the revolt was the belief among settlers along the frontier of the colony (the fall line and the Potomac) that Governor Berkeley, desiring to continue to profit from his trade with the Indians, had turned a deaf ear to their desires to subdue the Indian population and thus eliminate its frequent attacks against English settlements.

Significantly, many of the disgruntled frontiersmen were former indentured servants who had been unable to obtain land in older sections of the colony, where the Indians were no longer a threat. Other causative factors included the increasing haughtiness of the governor and his inner circle and the passage in 1671 of a requirement that property ownership be a prerequisite for voting, thus eliminating universal manhood suffrage that had been in effect in Virginia since 1619.

Nathaniel Bacon (1647–76), a newly arrived, well-educated, and wealthy English gentleman, became the leader of a band of indentured servants, ex–indentured servants, and slaves who supported Bacon's efforts to obtain a commission from Berkeley to lead a company against the Indians along the frontier. Although a few of Bacon's supporters, such as William Byrd, were of the colony's elite, the vast majority were of the class referred to by Bacon's opponents as "the giddy multitude."

Bacon, who had been appointed to the Governor's Council shortly after coming to Virginia in 1674, was initially denied a commission by Berkeley, but the governor relented when confronted in Jamestown by Bacon and a contingent of armed supporters. However, when Bacon's band confiscated horses and other supplies from the Gloucester County militia on its way to meet the Indians on the frontier, Berkeley rescinded the commission and declared Bacon an outlaw.

In the sporadic fighting that ensued, Bacon's supporters burned the colony's capital village of Jamestown and looted and pillaged the property of those loyal to the governor. During the summer of 1676, when Bacon effectively controlled the colony, the legislature convened to restore universal male suffrage and took other steps to democratize the colonial government.

Bacon's death of dysentery ("the bloody flux") on 26 October 1676 destroyed the rebellion's momentum. By the end of the year the governor and his forces had suppressed the rebellion. Significantly, the last of Bacon's rebels to surrender their weapons were a small number of indentured servants and slaves.

The aftermath of the rebellion saw the Crown void the actions of the legislature when it had been under Bacon's sway, recall Berkeley, and eventually return to the status quo prior to the revolt.

Further reading: Morgan, Edmund S. *American Slavery, American Freedom: The Ordeal of Colonial Virginia.* New York: Norton, 1975; Washburn, Wilcomb E. *The Governor and the Rebel: A History of Bacon's Rebellion in Virginia.* Chapel Hill: University of North Carolina Press, 1957; Webb, Stephen Saunders. *1676, the End of American Independence.* New York: Knopf, 1984; Wertenbaker, Thomas Jefferson. *Torchbearer of the Revolution: The Story of Bacon's Rebellion and Its Leader.* Princeton, N.J.: Princeton University Press, 1940.

— David W. Coffey

Bainbridge, William (1774–1833) *U.S. naval officer*
Born on 7 May 1774 at Princeton, New Jersey, William Bainbridge joined the merchant service at 15. By 1794 he was in command of his own ship, which battled British

privateers in undeclared hostilities during the years 1796–97. In 1798, upon the reestablishment of the U.S. NAVY during the 1798–1800 QUASI-WAR WITH FRANCE, Bainbridge received both a commission as a lieutenant and command of the schooner *Retaliation* (ex-French privateer *Le Croyable*). His ship was captured by French privateers in September 1798, Bainbridge becoming the first U.S. Navy officer to surrender without a shot fired.

Imprisoned in Guadeloupe, Bainbridge was freed in 1799 and cleared by a court of inquiry. He then took command of the brig *Norfolk,* serving as escort for an American convoy sailing from the West Indies to the United States. In October 1800, as captain of the frigate *George Washington,* Bainbridge delivered overdue tribute to the dey of Algiers and consented to deliver Algiers's own tribute to Istanbul, making the first American official visit (although under the Algerian flag) to Turkey.

Bainbridge then commanded the frigate *Essex* in Commodore Richard DALE's squadron before joining Edward PREBLE's squadron in the frigate *Philadelphia* in August 1803. On 31 October 1803, during the TRIPOLITAN WAR, the *Philadelphia* ran aground, forcing Bainbridge to surrender it to the Tripolitans. Until June 1805, Bainbridge

Captain William Bainbridge with USS *Constitution* and HMS *Java* in the background   *(Naval Historical Foundation)*

and his crew languished in a Tripolitan prison. Lieutenant Stephen DECATUR led a daring raid that burned the *Philadelphia* in Tripoli Harbor.

Following the end of the war with Tripoli, Bainbridge and his men were released from prison. Bainbridge then left the navy and resumed merchant service. Following the 22 June 1807 CHESAPEAKE-LEOPARD AFFAIR, which seemed to portend war with Britain, he returned to duty in the U.S. Navy. Assigned to the frigate CONSTITUTION, he exchanged ships with Captain Isaac HULL to command the *President* from 1808 to 1810 before returning to the merchant service.

In February 1812 Bainbridge again rejoined the navy, serving on shore as commander of the Charlestown Navy Yard in Boston, Massachusetts, until the WAR OF 1812 began. Assigned to the *Constitution* after Hull's defeat of HMS *Guerrière,* Bainbridge's lukewarm reception by its crew prompted him to try to exchange with Captain John RODGERS for command of *President.* However, on the *Constitution* Bainbridge and his crew won lasting fame for engaging and sinking HMS *Java* on 29 December 1812 off the coast of Brazil, the third defeat of a British frigate in less than five months. Bainbridge received a gold medal from Congress and $7,500 in prize money.

In February 1813, Bainbridge resumed command at the Charlestown Navy Yard, supervising the building of ship of the line *Independence,* which he then commanded during a Mediterranean cruise in 1815.

Bainbridge held various shore posts from 1815 to 1820, establishing a school for naval officers in Charlestown in 1817, before assuming command of the Philadelphia Navy Yard. During the years 1820–21 he commanded the ship of the line *Columbus* in the Mediterranean. He served in a series of shore posts from 1821 to 1831, then as president of the Board of Naval Commissioners from 1832 until his death in Philadelphia on 27 July 1833.

See also NAVY, U.S.

Further reading: Allison, Robert J. *The Crescent Obscured: The United States and the Muslim World, 1776–1815.* Chicago: University of Chicago Press, 2000; Long, David F. *Ready to Hazard: A Biography of Commander William Bainbridge, 1774–1833.* Hanover: University of New Hampshire Press, 1981; Martin, Tyrone G. *A Most Fortunate Ship: A Narrative History of Old Ironsides.* Annapolis, Md.: Naval Institute Press, 1997.

— Sarah Hilgendorff List

Baker, Newton D. (1871–1937) *Secretary of war*
Born on 3 December 1871 at Martinsburg, West Virginia, Newton Diehl Baker qualified as a lawyer and in 1897 joined the Cleveland firm headed by ex-Congressman Martin Foran, a prominent Ohio politician. Baker himself soon became

Secretary of War Newton Baker *(Library of Congress)*

active in Democratic politics as assistant director of the city's law department and as city solicitor before running successfully for mayor as a progressive, reformist Democrat in 1913.

In March 1916, shortly after Baker's mayoral term ended, President Woodrow WILSON appointed him secretary of war, replacing the forceful Lindley M. Garrison, who had resigned over differences with the president as to how best to strengthen national preparedness to meet the threat of potential European war. Baker, known for his pacifist leanings, had effectively no defense experience. This facilitated his acquiescence in both presidential direction and in passage of the NATIONAL DEFENSE ACT of 1916, which expanded both the regular army and the NATIONAL GUARD, but he rejected the army's proposed large federal volunteer reserve force.

Shortly after his appointment Baker reacted vigorously to Mexican raids on the United States, directing Brigadier General John J. PERSHING to undertake the PUNITIVE EXPEDITION INTO MEXICO. When the United States entered World War I in April 1917, its army was still largely unready for the conflict. Baker oversaw its expansion from 95,000 to 4,000,000 men, instituting a program of national conscription, which he, like the Wilson administration, had previ-

ously opposed. Baker's well-known antimilitary tendencies made the draft somewhat more palatable to American liberals. Baker's antiracist and pro–civil libertarian tendencies helped to restrain some of the worst excesses of wartime superpatriotism, although abuses still occurred.

In early 1918, the tardiness with which the Wilson administration initially prepared for war generated a Senate investigation and heavy congressional criticism. Baker responded by recruiting several able, energetic, and well-qualified civilians into the War Department to organize industrial mobilization, concentrating procurement in the General Staff. He reorganized the overburdened and inadequate General Staff into several functional "G" divisions, handling personnel, intelligence, and supply, and temporarily asserted its authority over the War Department's various bureaus (although the National Defense Act of 1920 was to reverse this development).

When the AMERICAN EXPEDITIONARY FORCES (AEF) arrived in Europe, Baker supported Wilson and Pershing, its commander, in maintaining the force's integrity rather than amalgamating its troops into experienced Allied units. On two visits to Europe he negotiated agreements that determined the American contingent's strength and provided it with shipping. Baker deplored but loyally supported Wilson's 1918 decision to contribute American troops to the Allied intervention in Russia. In autumn 1918, when Pershing attempted to undercut Wilson's efforts to negotiate an armistice with Germany, Baker was ready to assert civilian control by firing the recalcitrant commander if necessary.

After leaving office in 1921, Baker once again practiced law, while remaining active in Democratic politics. A strong supporter of U.S. membership in the League of Nations and the World Court, he was a founder of the Council on Foreign Relations and a leading Democratic internationalist, consciously representing the principles set forth by Wilson. Baker died in Cleveland on 25 December 1937.

See also RUSSIA, U.S. INTERVENTION FOLLOWING WORLD WAR I; WORLD WAR I, COURSE OF U.S. INVOLVEMENT.

Further reading: Baker, Newton D. *Why We Went to War.* New York: Harper & Brothers, 1936; Beaver, Daniel R. *Newton D. Baker and the American War Effort, 1917–1919.* Lincoln: University of Nebraska Press, 1966; Cramer, C. H. *Newton D. Baker: A Biography.* Cleveland: World, 1961; Palmer, Frederick. *Newton D. Baker: America at War.* 2 vols. New York: Dodd, Mead, 1931.

— Priscilla Roberts

Balangiga Massacre (28 September 1901) *Battle on the island of Samar during the Philippine-American War*
In August 1901 U.S. Army intelligence intercepted a letter indicating that the people of Balangiga intended to profess

their support for the U.S. occupation and then strike against the Americans at an opportune moment. For some reason, army authorities failed to act on this information.

Captain Thomas W. Connell's C Company of the 9th Infantry Regiment was sent to Samar to assist in putting down the Filipino insurgents there. To win the support of the people of Balangiga, Connell announced plans to clean the town plaza. Insurgents in the countryside used this project as an excuse to enter the town in the guise of poor farmers working off tax bills.

On the morning of 28 September 1901, the inhabitants of Balangiga surprised and attacked the unsuspecting members of C Company at mail call after breakfast when most of the men were without firearms. The attackers used makeshift weapons, including axes, knives, picks, and shovels, to hack to death many of the Americans, including all three officers. The surviving soldiers then rallied and drove the insurgents into the jungle. The troops then burned everything they could of military value, although the insurgents had secured more than 28,000 rounds of ammunition.

The remaining soldiers then hurried into four boats, hoping to get to Basey, 30 miles away. One boat, with 10 men, grounded short of its destination, however, and the insurgents killed the men, who were unable to flee. The insurgents also fired on the other boats from the jungle. Some of those who reached safety later succumbed to wounds. In the end, 48 soldiers died; only 26 survived.

U.S. authorities moved promptly to secure Samar. Sending Major Littleton W. T. Waller with a force of marines to the island, Army Brigadier General Jacob H. Smith ordered him to "kill and burn" and to take no prisoners. Waller was eventually tried for murder on Samar but acquitted. Smith too was court-martialed; he was convicted and forced to retire from the army. The harsh U.S. occupation policies on Samar eventually led to a Senate investigation into the U.S. presence in the Philippines.

Further reading: Gates, John M. *Schoolbooks and Krags: The United States in the Philippines, 1898–1902.* Westport, Conn.: Greenwood, 1973; Linn, Brian M. *The Philippine War, 1899–1902.* Lawrence: University of Kansas Press, 2000; Taylor, James O. *The Massacre of Balangiga, Being an Authentic Account by Several of the Few Survivors.* Joplin, Mo.: McCarn, 1931.

— Spencer C. Tucker

ballistic missiles *Missiles lacking aerodynamic surfaces to generate lift, the course of which is determined solely by gravity and wind resistance once propulsion is exhausted*

Predecessors of modern ballistic missiles first entered American military history in the form of Congreve rockets

Tomahawk cruise missile launched from the battleship *Wisconsin* during Operation Desert Storm   *(US Air Force)*

flying over FORT MCHENRY in September 1814. Although the United States made limited use of HALE ROCKETs during the MEXICAN-AMERICAN WAR and the CIVIL WAR, the ballistic missile remained little more than a novelty until Germany launched the V-2, the first modern ballistic missile, in September 1944. Armed with a conventional warhead, the V-2 remained more a terror weapon than a real military threat. The introduction of NUCLEAR WEAPONS in August 1945, however, promised to change that.

In the early years of the COLD WAR, the United States experimented with a bewildering array of missile programs, many stemming directly from captured German missile technology. The first American ballistic missile systems actually deployed to the field were short-range weapons designed for U.S. Army tactical use. Beginning in the mid-1950s, unguided "artillery rockets" such as the Honest John and guided missiles like the Corporal provided the capability to deliver nuclear weapons with reasonable accuracy to targets at 10–100 miles range. Successors to these early tactical nuclear weapons, such as the Little John, Sergeant, and Lance, continued in service well into the 1970s.

Higher priority, however, was given to the greater technical challenge of creating intermediate-range ballistic missiles (IRBMs) capable of attacking targets 1,000 or more miles away. The forerunner of these was the U.S. Army's Redstone, created in the early-to-middle 1950s by a development team that included German physicists and engineers, led by Wernher von Braun. The first operational U.S. IRBM was the Jupiter, a direct successor to the Redstone. It had a range of 1,500 miles and was deployed to bases in Italy and Turkey from 1958 to 1960. It was plagued by a variety of technical problems and was completely withdrawn from service by 1965. (The removal of the Jupiter missiles from Turkey was a component in the resolution of the 1962 CUBAN MISSILE CRISIS.) From 1959 to 1960 the

U.S. Air Force deployed to bases in Britain a more reliable IRBM of similar range, the Thor, but these missiles were also soon deactivated, the last in 1963.

By the late 1950s, developing an intercontinental ballistic missile (ICBM) had become the highest-priority U.S. military project. A practically indefensible means of delivering a nuclear warhead anywhere in the world in a matter of minutes had long been a goal, but fears of a MISSILE GAP elevated ICBM development to overriding national priority following the surprise Soviet ICBM test of August 1957 and the highly publicized confirmation of this success two months later in the form of the Sputnik satellite.

Early variants of the first U.S. ICBM, the Atlas, reached limited operational capability in September 1958, with full deployment of 12 squadrons (about 120 missiles total) in early 1963. A second, independent but related ICBM development project culminated in the deployment by 1963 of 63 Titan missiles and the first of their successors, the Titan II. Although all of these first-generation ICBMs (with the exception of about 60 Titan IIs) were removed from active service by 1965, they played an important military and psychological role during the cold war crises of the late 1950s and the early 1960s.

By 1963 the second generation of U.S. ICBMs, the Minuteman series, had already begun to enter service. These missiles were easier to maintain and less vulnerable to attack than first-generation ICBMs, in large part because of their use of solid fuels. The most important change within the second generation of ICBMs came in 1970, with the introduction of the Minuteman III and its three multiple independently targetable reentry vehicles (MIRVs). Critics contended that this new capability to strike accurately multiple targets added a dangerous new dimension to the nuclear arms race by making "silo-busting" a viable option, threatening to end reliance on the theory of mutual assured destruction (MAD). This new instability also was said to be increased by the new anti–ballistic-missile defense systems that both superpowers began fielding in the early 1970s as part of their continuing efforts at STRATEGIC DEFENSE. One potentially stabilizing factor was the introduction in 1960, largely through the efforts of Admiral Arleigh BURKE, of the first of the Polaris series submarine-launched ballistic missiles (SLBMs). Deployed for long periods at sea aboard nuclear-powered submarines, at least some of these missiles were almost certain to survive any surprise nuclear attack, thus providing a secure second-strike capability and enhancing deterrence. They also increased the bureaucratic stability of the postwar force structure by adding a component to the now-complete "nuclear triad" outside the control of the STRATEGIC AIR COMMAND. In 1971 Poseidon C3 missiles began to replace older Polaris SLBMs, adding MIRVs to the navy's arsenal as well.

The use of ballistic missiles in the space program also held great military significance. IRBMs and ICBMs like the Redstone, Atlas, and Titan were adapted for use in early space-exploration programs. For the ultimate psychological prize in the cold war space competition, the race to the moon, the new and massive Saturn series of missiles was developed. Adapted ICBMs and their successors also performed the unsung but critical task of placing into orbit satellites that fulfilled a variety of military missions relating to communications, early warning, and intelligence gathering.

In the 1980s, new generations of IRBMs, ICBMs, and SLBMs began to emerge, but most of these programs were curtailed or eliminated before completion due to arms control and the end of the cold war. Through advanced inertial navigation devices and other means, many of these systems were capable of delivering nuclear weapons with accuracies verging on those of conventional PRECISION-GUIDED MUNITIONS. Early U.S. IRBMs had been replaced in the 1960s by the mobile, more survivable, and easier-to-maintain Pershing missile. From 1983 to 1985, amid much controversy, the United States deployed its successor, the Pershing II, throughout Western Europe. This proved a major factor in producing the first successful cold war case of arms reduction, the 1987 Intermediate-Range Nuclear Forces (INF) Treaty; by 1991 the last American IRBMs had been destroyed (along with their Soviet counterparts). With respect to ICBMs, however, the Strategic Arms Limitation Talks (SALT) of the 1970s had produced only upper limits on their production, and into the 1980s the United States still deployed more than 1,000 ICBMs (almost all Minuteman II and IIIs). The new MX ICBM, first operational in 1986, was capable of delivering 10 highly accurate MIRVs, but budgetary constraints and a reduction in international tensions limited its deployment to 50 missiles. In the 1980s and 1990s the U.S. Navy's SLBM force converted to the advanced Trident series of missiles, carried on board new *Ohio*-class submarines.

In the 1990s and beyond, the United States and Russia drastically reduced their ballistic missile arsenals through a series of unilateral cuts and treaties, including a May 2002 agreement for a two-thirds reduction in deployed strategic nuclear warheads. As the world entered the 21st century, attention turned to attempts to prevent the further proliferation of ballistic missile technology to "rogue states" such as Iraq and North Korea.

See also SCHRIEVER, BERNARD A.

Further reading: MacKenzie, Donald A. *Inventing Accuracy: A Historical Sociology of Nuclear Missile Guidance.* Cambridge, Mass.: MIT Press, 1990; Neufeld, Jacob. *The Development of Ballistic Missiles in the United States Air Force, 1945–1960.* Washington, D.C.: Office of Air Force

History, 1990; Stumpf, David K. *Titan II: A History of a Cold War Missile Program.* Fayetteville: University of Arkansas Press, 2000.

— David Rezelman

Ballou, Charles C. (1862–1928) *U.S. Army general*
Born on 13 June 1862 at Orange Township, New York, Charles Clarendon Ballou was commissioned a second lieutenant of infantry on graduation from the U.S. Military Academy at WEST POINT in 1886. He served in the West and then was a professor of military science, tactics, and civil engineering at Florida State Agricultural College at Lake City, Florida.

Ballou attended the Infantry and Cavalry School at Fort Leavenworth from 1897 to 1898. Commissioned a temporary major during the 1898 SPANISH-AMERICAN WAR, he served with the 7th Illinois Volunteer Infantry, after which he reverted to the regular army rank of first lieutenant.

Assigned to the Philippines in 1899, Ballou was promoted to captain that March. As a member of the 15th Infantry Division, Ballou distinguished himself during the PHILIPPINE-AMERICAN WAR, fighting in the Battle of Zapote River (13 June 1899) and in other engagements. For his actions in the assault on Angeles on the island of Luzon on 16 August 1899, Ballou was awarded the Silver Star.

In spring 1900 Ballou was transferred to Fort Slocum, New York. During the next 15 years he held a variety of assignments, including four more tours in the Philippines. He was promoted to major in June 1909, lieutenant colonel in February 1915, and colonel in July 1916. After graduation from the Field Officers Course at Fort Leavenworth in April 1916, he joined the 24th Infantry Regiment (in which he had previously served) and participated in border patrol activities near Columbus, New Mexico. He accompanied his unit in the 1916 PUNITIVE EXPEDITION INTO MEXICO and then in September attended the Army War College.

In June 1917, after graduation from the war college and shortly after the United States entered World War I (April), Ballou took command of the Colored Officers Training Camp at Fort Des Moines, Iowa. Promoted to brevet brigadier general in September 1917, Ballou commanded the 163d Depot Brigade at Camp Dodge, Iowa.

In October 1917, Ballou took command of the 92d ("Buffalo") Division, the only division in the U.S. Army composed entirely of African Americans to fight during the war. Promoted brevet major general in November, Ballou took his division to France in June 1918 and commanded it in operations in the St. Die sector and in the early phases of the September–November MEUSE-ARGONNE OFFENSIVE as part of General Robert Lee BULLARD's Second

Army. Assigned to command VI Corps but retaining command of the 92d Division, Ballou participated in the Allied offensive on the Moselle River against the German fortress at Metz. Succeeded as commander of VI Corps, Ballou retained command of the 92d Division.

After the armistice, Ballou commanded the 89th Division in occupation duties in Germany until February 1919. He then reverted to the permanent rank of colonel and briefly commanded Camp Dodge, Iowa, before transferring to Camp Logan, Colorado. In August 1920, on the request of the governor of Colorado, Ballou restored order in Denver following two days of rioting there sparked by a tramway strike.

In October 1920, Ballou was assigned to Fort George Wright, Washington; from 1923 to 1926, he had charge of recruiting in New York. In 1925 Ballou vigorously refuted criticisms brought by his former commander, General BULLARD, about the 92d Division's battle performance.

Upon his retirement from the army in June 1926, Ballou moved to Spokane, Washington. He died there on 23 July 1928. Congress posthumously promoted him to major general.

See also AFRICAN AMERICANS IN THE MILITARY.

Further reading: Bullard, Robert Lee. *American Soldiers Also Fought.* New York: Longmans, Green, 1936; Coffman, Edward M. *The War to End All Wars: The American Military Experience in World War I.* New York: Oxford University Press, 1968.

— Nicholas Shallcross

Baltimore, attack on (12–14 September 1814)
After the British smashed American militia forces in the Battle of BLADENSBURG, Maryland, on 24 August 1814, they occupied WASHINGTON and burned public buildings and the navy yard there. Their next target was Baltimore, where many of the privateers utilized to attack British merchant shipping had been built.

On 12 September British troops under Major General Robert Ross landed on the western end of Patapsco Neck and marched toward Baltimore. Early the next morning the British began their bombardment of FORT MCHENRY, which guarded the entrance to Baltimore Harbor at the tip of Locust Point.

General Samuel Smith commanded at Baltimore. He had 15,000 men stretched from Fells Point across to Hamsted Hill, high ground northeast of the city. Smith had reinforced Fort McHenry, placing it under the command of Major George Armistead, and installed 60 large cannon there. He set up a string of lookouts near the tip of North Point and positioned guard boats between North Point and the city. Before the British arrived, Smith put the militia of

Baltimore, its county, and parts of Pennsylvania through rigorous training.

General Smith ordered Brigadier General John Stricker and his 3d Brigade to the western end of Patapsco Neck. Early on 12 September, Stricker learned that British troops were landing and placed his brigade on the narrow strip of land between Black River and Bear Creek and sent riflemen out to harass the advancing British. Two of Stricker's men shot and killed the British commander, General Ross, who was succeeded by Colonel Arthur Brooke. That evening, after delaying the British attacks, Stricker led his men back to the defensive positions on Hamsted Hill, reinforced with cannon that had been dragged there from ships in the harbor below.

On Tuesday, 13 September, as the Royal Navy ships began to bombard Fort McHenry, British troops attempted to outflank the fortifications on Hamsted Hill. The American defense held, however. Smith had positioned his troops so as to deliver a cross-fire upon any direct attack on Hamsted Hill from the flanks. The British saw that this maneuver would be too costly and made no further attempt to take the hill. That night, under cover of darkness, they withdrew.

Vice Admiral Sir Alexander Cochrane eventually realized that his bombardment of Fort McHenry was ineffectual. He feared to bring his fleet closer to the fort and its batteries; instead, he attempted a boat landing of 300 men on the far side of Fort McHenry, under the cover of darkness, to cripple the batteries guarding the harbor. The 20 barges he sent, commanded by Captain Charles Napier, were quickly halted by gunfire from Fort Babcock and forced to withdraw. Brooke never assaulted the city with his infantry, since the fleet could not secure the harbor. Cochrane and Brooke agreed that Baltimore was not worth the effort and ordered an end to operations. Withdrawing to Jamaica, the British reorganized for their eventual invasion of New Orleans at the end of the year.

See also WAR OF 1812, LAND OVERVIEW.

Further reading: Beirne, Francis F. *The War of 1812.* New York: Dutton, 1949; Scharf, Thomas. *The Chronicle of Baltimore.* Baltimore: Turnbull Brothers, 1874; Whitehorne, Joseph A. *The Battle for Baltimore: 1814.* Baltimore: Nautical & Aviation, 1997.

— D. Randall Beirne

Banks, Nathaniel P. (1816–1894) *Political leader and U.S. Army general*
Born on 30 January 1816 at Waltham, Massachusetts, the son of a textile mill foreman, Nathaniel Prentiss Banks began working in a factory as a bobbin boy at age 11. In his early 20s, after working as a carpenter and machinist, Banks studied law. He passed the bar in 1839 and rose swiftly in the local Democratic Party. An active campaigner and newspaper editor, Banks in 1843 received an appointment in the Boston Customs House. In 1848 he won election to the state legislature, and in 1851, after a coalition of Democrats and Free-Soil Whigs won control of the House, Banks was selected speaker.

Banks was elected to the U.S. House of Representatives in 1852 but broke with the Democratic administration two years later in opposition to the Kansas-Nebraska bill. Nevertheless Banks was selected Speaker of the House in late 1855, with the backing of both Republicans and members of the nativist Know Nothing party. Banks declined the presidential nomination of the Know Nothing Party in 1856, instead endorsing the Republican candidate and thereby enhancing his reputation as an opportunist. In 1857 Banks won the first of three consecutive one-year terms as Republican governor of Massachusetts, and in 1861 he accepted a position as a railroad executive. When the CIVIL WAR began that year, Banks volunteered his services to the LINCOLN administration and quickly became one of the highest-ranking "political generals" in the army.

As a major general of volunteers, Banks commanded federal forces in the Shenandoah Valley in 1861 and 1862. In August 1862, heavily outnumbered, he led his two divisions in a vigorous but unsuccessful attack on Confederate troops at CEDAR MOUNTAIN, Virginia. In December 1862 Lincoln transferred Banks to command of the Department of the Gulf, where his political skills were expected to assist in the reconstruction of Louisiana's state government. Banks led a troubled but ultimately successful campaign against PORT HUDSON from May to July 1863 and a nearly disastrous campaign up the Red River in spring 1864. General E. R. S. CANBY thereafter superseded Banks. Following the war, Banks resumed his political career. He served in Congress and as a U.S. marshal for many years before his death at Waltham on 1 September 1894.

See also CIVIL WAR, LAND OVERVIEW.

Further reading: Benedict, Michael Les. *A Compromise of Principle: Congressional Republicans and Reconstruction, 1863–1869.* New York: Norton, 1974; Hollandsworth, James G., Jr. *Pretense of Glory: The Life of General Nathaniel P. Banks.* Baton Rouge: Louisiana State University Press, 1998; Joseph, Alvin M., Jr. *The Civil War in the American West.* New York: Vintage Books, 1993.

— Michael Thomas Smith

Barney, Joshua (1759–1818) *U.S. naval officer and merchant seaman*
Born on 6 July 1759 in Baltimore County, Maryland, Joshua Barney became a merchant seaman at age 13 and at 15 received his first sea command. Barney served in the

Continental navy during the 1775–83 American Revolutionary War and eventually became the youngest captain of a Continental navy frigate. Barney was captured three times and paroled twice. His third capture resulted in a year in a British prison. Escaping and returning to America, Barney took command of the privateer *Hyder-Ally*, with which he defeated the British warship *General Monk*. After the British surrender, Barney brought the peace documents to Benjamin Franklin in Paris and was presented at the French court. Barney returned to the merchant service after the navy was disbanded.

When the U.S. Navy was established in 1794, Barney was offered command of one of the frigates constructed for service along the Barbary Coast. He refused when he discovered he would serve under an officer who had been junior to him during the Revolutionary War. Instead, he accepted an offer from the French to command a warship and a squadron. Barney returned to America in 1802 and reentered the merchant service.

At the outbreak of the War of 1812, Barney offered his services to President James Madison, who took no action on the request because of Barney's service with the French. Barney turned to privateering, commanding the schooner *Rossie*, and capturing several British ships. He also submitted to the War Department a plan to counter the British blockade of the Chesapeake Bay by constructing small gunboats that would be able to strike quickly at the British warships and then quickly retreat into the creeks lining the bay. President Madison approved the plan in August 1813 and commissioned Barney as commander of the Chesapeake Flotilla. The flotilla conducted a series of raids against British warships until it eventually was blockaded in the Patuxent River by the British.

In August 1814 British land and naval forces began a drive up the Patuxent River to attack Washington. Outnumbered and outgunned, Barney was ordered to move the flotilla upstream, destroy his vessels, and march his naval contingent toward Washington to aid in its defense. In the Battle of BLADENSBURG, British forces routed the Americans, although Barney and his naval contingent of flotillamen, marines, and naval cannon held their ground against the British advance, even counterattacking at one point, until all other American forces had retreated. Wounded in the thigh by a musket ball, Barney was taken prisoner. The British immediately paroled him for his heroic stand.

Barney was later honored by the city of Washington for his actions at Bladensburg. He returned to his home in Anne Arundel County, Maryland, where he died on 1 December 1818 from a fever related to the bullet that remained in his thigh.

See also AMERICAN REVOLUTIONARY WAR, NAVAL OVERVIEW; WAR OF 1812, NAVAL OVERVIEW.

Further reading: Footner, Hubert. *Sailor of Fortune: The Life and Adventures of Commodore Barney, USN*. Annapolis, Md.: Naval Institute Press, 1998; Norton, Louis Arthur. *Joshua Barney: Hero of the Revolution and 1812*. Annapolis, Md.: Naval Institute Press, 2000.

— Michael J. Manning

Barrel Roll, Operation (1964–1973) *Allied air campaign during the Vietnam War*

Operation Barrel Roll was carried out in northern Laos, primarily to support ground forces of the royal Laotian government and the CIA-trained Hmong (mountain people), irregular forces under General Vang Pao. The area of operations stretched from the Laotian capital of Vientiane on the border of Thailand north to the strategic Plain of Jars and then northeast to the Pathet Lao capital of Sam Neua, Sam Neua Province, which bordered North Vietnam.

In June 1964, in response to a communist Pathet Lao/North Vietnamese army spring offensive in the Plain of Jars, allied air forces, with approval from President Lyndon B. JOHNSON, commenced Operation Barrel Roll. The first attacks were on 9 June. Throughout its nine years, Barrel Roll operated under a strange set of rules of engagement, with all air assets controlled by the U.S. ambassador in Vientiane. No target could be struck without his permission. The last Barrel Roll sortie was flown on 17 April 1973.

In the end, allied aircraft dropped nearly 3 million tons of bombs on "neutral" Laos, three times the tonnage ever dropped on North Vietnam. Some 500,000 tons were expended in northern Laos—about 6 percent of all bombs dropped by the allies during the Second Indochina War. As with other Laotian air operations, such as STEEL TIGER and TIGER HOUND, the numbers and performances were impressive but ultimately fruitless.

See also VIETNAM WAR.

Further reading: Berger, Carl ed. *The United States Air Force in Southeast Asia, 1961–1973: An Illustrated Account*. Washington, D.C.: Office of U.S. Air Force History, 1984; Hamilton-Merritt, Jane. *Tragic Mountains: The Hmong, the Americans and the Secret Wars for Laos, 1942–1992*. Bloomington: University of Indiana Press, 1993; Momyer, Gen. William H. *Airpower in Three Wars*. Washington, D.C.: Office of U.S. Air Force History, 1978; Tilford, Earl H., Jr. *Crosswinds: The Air Force's Setup in Vietnam*. College Station: Texas A&M University Press, 1994.

— William Head

Barron, James (1768–1851) *U.S. Navy commodore and central figure in the Chesapeake-Leopard Affair*

Born on 15 September 1768 in Norfolk, Virginia, the son of the commodore of the Virginia navy, James Barron began training for a career at sea at age 12, serving as a midshipman during the American Revolutionary War. In 1798 he was commissioned a lieutenant in the newly established U.S. Navy. These were the formative years for the young navy, and Barron served with distinction.

During the 1798–1800 QUASI-WAR with France, he won praise for saving his ship, the frigate *United States*, during a gale. He also devised the navy's first signal code. During the 1801–1805 BARBARY WARS he served in the Mediterranean as captain of the frigate *President*.

Barron's career was permanently tarnished, however, by the CHESAPEAKE-LEOPARD AFFAIR of 22 June 1807. Appointed commodore of the Mediterranean Squadron, Barron was aboard the frigate *Chesapeake* (36 guns), headed for the Mediterranean, when his ship was stopped by HMS *Leopard* (56 guns). The captain of the *Leopard* demanded the right to search for deserters. Barron, though his ship was not ready to fight, refused to allow a British search party to board. He relented after several broadsides from the British ship, which killed a number of his crew. The British then mustered the *Chesapeake*'s crew and removed four as deserters.

Barron was court-martialed in a politically charged trial that divided the navy. He was found guilty and suspended for five years. Barron blamed two of the judges, Captains JOHN RODGERS and STEPHEN DECATUR. Unable to continue his naval career, Barron served as captain of a merchant ship, which was trapped in Denmark during the WAR OF 1812. When Barron returned home, Decatur attacked him publicly for having stayed abroad during the war and sought to block his return to active duty. On 22 March 1820, Barron killed Decatur in a duel at Bladensburg, Maryland. Barron survived a severe wound but was publicly condemned for killing Decatur, and though restored to the navy in his later years, he never saw sea service again.

Barron served as commandant of the Philadelphia and Norfolk Navy Yards. He is also credited with designing an ironclad steam ram for the U.S. Navy. Barron at least outlived his rivals. At the time of his death at Norfolk on 21 April 1851, he was the senior officer of the U.S. Navy.

See also NAVY, U.S.

Further reading: Latshaw, K. Michael. "Flawed Judgement: The Court Martial of Commodore James Barron." *The Virginia Magazine of History and Biography* 105, no. 4 (Autumn 1997): 377–408; Stevens, William Oliver. *An Affair of Honor: The Biography of Commodore James Barron, USN*. Norfolk, Va.: Norfolk County Historical Society, 1969; Tucker, Spencer C., and Frank T. Reuter. *Injured Honor: The Chesapeake-Leopard Affair of June 22, 1807*. Annapolis, Md.: Naval Institute Press, 1996.

— Rebecca A. Livingston

Barron, Samuel (1809–1888) *U.S. and Confederate naval officer*
Born on 28 November 1809 in Hampton, Virginia, Samuel Barron was the son of Commodore James BARRON (1768–1851), who commanded the ill-fated USS *Chesapeake* during the 22 June 1807 CHESAPEAKE-LEOPARD AFFAIR. Barron entered the navy in 1820 and served in various capacities. He was promoted to lieutenant in 1827, commander in 1847, and captain in 1855. He commanded a number of ships, including the *John Adams* and the steam frigate *Wabash*.

In April 1861 Barron resigned from the U.S. Navy, which recorded him as dismissed, having refused his resignation. Barron then accepted a commission as a captain in first the Virginia navy and then the Confederate States navy. He headed the Office of Orders and Detail until July 1861. He then convinced the Confederate secretary of the navy, Stephen MALLORY, to place him in charge of naval defenses in Virginia and North Carolina, only to be taken prisoner by the Union forces that seized Forts Hatteras and Clark in August. Exchanged the following year, Barron was named commander of all Confederate naval forces in Virginia waters.

In summer 1863, Barron traveled to England to oversee the completion of the two ironclad "Laird rams" ordered by the Confederate government. When these ships were seized by the British government, Barron transferred to Paris, serving there as commander of all Confederate naval forces in Europe until he resigned in February 1865. Barron spent his remaining years as a farmer, until he died in Essex County, Virginia, on 26 February 1888.

See also CIVIL WAR, NAVAL OVERVIEW.

Further reading: Spencer, Warren F. *The Confederate Navy in Europe*. University: University of Alabama Press, 1997; Still, William N., Jr., ed. *The Confederate Navy: The Ships, Men and Organization, 1861–65*. Annapolis, Md.: Naval Institute Press, 1996.

— Lance Janda

Barry, John (1745–1803) *Continental and U.S. Navy captain*
Born on 1 January 1745 in Tacumshane, Wexford County, Ireland, John Barry did not receive a formal education, apprenticing as a cabin boy on a merchant ship in 1755. In 1760 he immigrated to Philadelphia, where he steadily built a reputation as a sailor and shipmaster; he also garnered a small fortune.

When the American Revolutionary War began, men with Barry's experience at sea were in demand. In March 1776 Congress commissioned him and gave him command of the brig *Lexington*. Operating off the mid-Atlantic coast,

Captain John Barry receives his commission, the first in the U.S. Navy, from President George Washington, 22 February 1797. From a painting of Joseph Gurn, Barnes Collection, New York Historical Society.   *(Naval Historical Foundation)*

Barry defeated and captured the British sloop *Edward* in what was the first significant naval victory for the patriot cause. The propaganda value of this was immense, and Barry found himself one of the Continental navy's first heroes.

After several more captures, Barry took command of the frigate *Effingham,* still under construction. Barry's men and the ship's guns were formed into a battery that fought under General George WASHINGTON in the land battles of TRENTON and PRINCETON. The *Effingham* was destroyed when the British captured Philadelphia.

Barry then took command of the frigate *Raleigh.* Following a several-day engagement with two Royal Navy warships, Barry ran his battered ship aground to prevent capture. His reputation as a fighting sailor disarmed any critics, and in late 1780 he took command of the frigate *Alliance.* En route to France with diplomatic dispatches he took the British brig *Alert,* and during the return voyage he captured several British privateers. On 28 May Barry tangled with the brigs *Atalanta* and *Trepassey* off Newfoundland in a four-hour-long engagement that left Barry victorious but severely wounded. By war's end, Barry had cemented his position as one of the Continental navy's most capable commanders.

Barry reverted to the profitable merchant marine after the war, but when Congress established the U.S. Navy in 1794 he was ready to return to naval service. Commissioned captain, he ranked first on the naval list. Barry oversaw the building and fitting out of the frigate *United States,* taking command of it in 1798. He cruised in the West Indies during the QUASI-WAR WITH FRANCE. He also served as mentor to Stephen DECATUR and James BARRON, two rising stars in the next generation of naval officers.

Ill health forced Barry to serve in an advisory capacity ashore in his final years. Regarded as one of the founders of the U.S. Navy, he died at Philadelphia on 13 September 1803.

See also AMERICAN REVOLUTIONARY WAR, NAVAL OVERVIEW.

Further reading: Clark, William B. *Gallant John Barry, 1705–1803.* New York: Macmillan, 1938; Gurn, Joseph. *Commodore John Barry: Father of the American Navy.* New York: P. J. Kennedy, 1933.

— Michael S. Casey

Barton, Clarissa H. (Clara) (1821–1912) *Civil War nurse and founder of the American Red Cross*

Born on 25 December 1821 in North Oxford, Massachusetts, Clarissa Harlowe Barton was a shy child who exhibited compassion for the sick from a young age. Barton's concern for others contributed to her own lifelong battle with depression. She taught school as a young woman and in 1854 moved to Washington, D.C., where she worked as a copyist in the Patent Office. While in that position, Barton demanded and received pay equal to that of her male counterparts.

From the onset of the Civil War, Barton took an active role in aiding Union soldiers. She gathered and distributed supplies for troops stationed in the capital; former students of hers now serving in the 6th Massachusetts Regiment were among the first soldiers to benefit from her help. As the war progressed, Barton recognized the need for significant battlefield aid. The War Department originally blocked her efforts, but she persevered and finally received authorization to deliver medical supplies to the front.

Despite personal danger, Barton accompanied the Army of the Potomac for much of the war. She had no formal medical training, yet she attended the wounded, assisted in surgery, and in late 1864 supervised nurses for the Army of the James. Barton worked independently of the Sanitary Commission and of the superintendent of U.S. Army nurses, Dorothea DIX. Her compassion and commitment to the troops earned Barton the sobriquet "Angel of the Battlefield."

After the Civil War Barton led an effort to search for soldiers missing in action, and she toured the country from 1866 to 1868 speaking of her work during the war. Overcome by exhaustion and depression, Barton traveled to Switzerland in 1869 to recover. While there, she learned of the work of the International Red Cross (IRC), founded in 1863. During the 1870–71 Franco-Prussian War, Barton helped the IRC with relief distribution. Upon her return to the United States in 1873, Barton lobbied Congress for almost 10 years to ratify the Geneva Conventions, which it did in 1882.

Barton established the AMERICAN RED CROSS (ARC) in 1881 and presided over the organization until 1904. During her tenure, the mission of the ARC expanded from war relief to include assistance in natural disasters. Barton died at Glen Echo, Maryland, on 12 April 1912.

See also CIVIL WAR, LAND OVERVIEW.

Further reading: Oates, Stephen B. *A Woman of Valor: Clara Barton and the Civil War.* New York: Free Press, 1995; Pryor, Elizabeth Brown. *Clara Barton: Professional Angel.* Philadelphia: University of Pennsylvania, 1987.

— Tracy M. Shilcutt

Basey, march to (28 December 1901–28 February 1902) *Failed expedition against native revolutionaries ("Insurrectos") on the island of Samar during the Philippine-American War*

In November 1901, in reaction to the massacre of U.S. Army troops at BALANGIGA on 28 September, the commander of the 6th Separate Brigade, Brigadier General Jacob H. Smith, ordered Major Littleton W. T. Waller and his marine battalion at Lanang to "make the interior of Samar a howling wilderness." Major Waller promptly set out on an expedition across the island in search of "Insurrectos," although his official orders were to explore a possible telegraph route from Lanang to Basey.

Ignoring warnings from army officers not to make the march, Waller and his reconnaissance party left Lanang on 28 December 1901 with six officers, 50 marines, two Filipino scouts, and 33 porters. Waller insisted that the 50-mile march through the dense jungle would take only a few days, so his men carried only scant provisions.

Less than a day after leaving Lanang, Waller's party lost the trail and was forced to hack its way through the dense undergrowth, often marching three or four miles for every one gained in the intended direction. The intense tropical heat, heavy rains, mountainous terrain, leeches, and lack of rations all took their toll. On 2 January Waller, completely lost in the wilderness, decided to construct rafts and float back to Lanang on the nearby Soribao River. When the boats sank, Waller took two officers and 13 of his strongest men ahead of the main body to attempt to reach Basey.

Unable to catch up with Waller's advance party, the remainder eventually split, twice. Captain David D. Porter and four marines made it back to Lanang on 11 January. The main body, under Lieutenant Alexander Williams, wandered aimlessly through the jungle, leaving 10 men to die and one insane. His men, half-crazed with hunger and fatigue, believed the native porters were hoarding food and plotting against them. Williams killed one porter who had allegedly attempted to stab him.

Meanwhile, Waller, who arrived at Basey on 6 January, had immediately sent out a search party for Porter, whom he thought was a few hours behind him but was actually on the other side of the island. An army relief force rescued Williams and the remainder of the expedition on 18 January.

Among those serving in the Philippines, the failed march to Basey soon became an epic of bravery and leadership. In actuality, the expedition was doomed from its outset, fueled by Waller's bravado and poor planning.

See also PHILIPPINE AMERICAN WAR.

Further reading: Gates, John M. *Schoolbooks and Krags: The United States Army in the Philippines, 1898–1902.* Westport, Conn.: Greenwood, 1973; Linn, Brian M. *The Philippine War, 1899–1902.* Lawrence: University of Kansas Press, 2000. Schott, James L. *The Ordeal of Samar.* Indianapolis: Bobbs-Merrill, 1964.

— Bradford A. Wineman

Bataan, retreat to and siege of (7 December 1941–9 April 1942) *Early phase of World War II in the Pacific*

On 8 December 1941, Japan attacked the Philippine Islands, and months of heavy fighting began. When the Japanese attacked, defending forces numbered approximately 130,000 men, of whom 20,000 were Americans. Despite U.S. Army Air Corps resistance, the Japanese soon gained air superiority, and on 22 December the Japanese Fourteenth Army, under General Masaharu Homma came ashore on the main island of Luzon, where virtually all defenders were concentrated. While numerically inferior to the defenders, the invading force was well trained and equipped, and it enjoyed air superiority. The defenders also were cut off from resupply by sea. The first American tank-versus-tank battle took place, near Agoo.

Commander of U.S. forces in the Philippine Islands General Douglas MACARTHUR had planned to defeat the invaders on the beaches, but his forces were unable to prevent the Japanese from securing a strong foothold on the island. On 23 December MacArthur fell back on an earlier plan, ordering a general withdrawal into the Bataan Peninsula, where he hoped U.S. forces might hold out until reinforcements could be sent. MacArthur overestimated Japanese strength by almost two times.

The Japanese occupied Manila on 26 December. Meanwhile, the defenders withdrew under constant Japanese attack. This operation was costly to the Japanese, however. U.S. tanks employed in rear-guard actions did not stop the Japanese, but they did slow their momentum and allowed U.S. forces time to withdraw and fortify. The withdrawal was complicated and difficult, and American and

Filipino forces lost important supplies in the process, a key factor in their ultimate defeat.

On 31 December 10 U.S. tanks and supporting artillery ambushed Japanese armor, infantry, and artillery near Baliuag, destroying eight Japanese tanks with no loss to themselves. This briefly slowed the Japanese advance.

By 7 January 1942, the defenders were in fortified positions on the Bataan Peninsula. Both sides now settled in for a siege. The Filipino and U.S. presence on Bataan, as well as other positions across the island, denied the Japanese the use of Manila Bay throughout the siege.

The defenders, the "Battling Bastards of Bataan," defeated the initial thrusts so soundly that Japanese attacks ceased until mid-April. The defenders were, however, too weak to counterattack. They also had to feed more than 100,000 people, including civilians. This was many more than intended on fewer supplies than planned, and resupply was impossible. Malnutrition, dysentery, and malaria soon took their toll. Disease also affected the Japanese, whose command withdrew some units to the Dutch East Indies for recuperation.

In March, Washington ordered MacArthur to Australia. He left Major General Jonathan M. WAINWRIGHT in command. At the end of that month the Japanese threw more than 22,000 fresh troops, as well as additional aircraft and artillery, into the battle. By April the American and Filipino defenders were on short rations; they were also fighting malaria and had few medical supplies. Surviving on less than 1,000 calories a day, the majority fell ill.

At the beginning of April the Japanese attacked again, and the defenses disintegrated. On 9 April, with defeat inevitable and believing he was acting to spare lives, the U.S. commander on Bataan, Major General Edward P. KING, Jr., surrendered his forces, in the largest surrender in U.S. history. American and Filipino losses in the Bataan campaign came to some 20,000 men.

Though it was not appreciated at the time, the defenders had delayed the Japanese timetable. Tokyo had planned a 55-day operation; it lasted 148. The ambitious overall Japanese strategic plan and operations in China limited the size of forces that could be dedicated to the Philippines.

See also BATAAN DEATH MARCH; PHILIPPINES, LOSS OF.

Further reading: Caraccilo, Dominic J. *Surviving Bataan and Beyond.* Mechanicsburg, Pa.: Stockpile Books, 1999; Motron, Louis. *U.S. Army in World War II: The War in the Pacific: The Fall of the Philippines.* Washington, D.C.: Center of Military History, U.S. Army, 1953; Tenney, Lester I. *My Hitch in Hell.* Washington, D.C.: Brassey's, 1995.

— William Dwight Peveler

Bataan Death March   *One of the most notorious war crimes committed against American troops during World War II*

On 9 April 1942, Major General Edward P. KING, Jr., surrendered to the Japanese Fourteenth Army the 66,000 Filipino and 12,000 American troops constituting his Luzon Force on the Bataan Peninsula. King's capitulation came as a surprise to the Japanese commander, Lieutenant General Masaharu Homma, who thought Filipino-American resistance would continue for at least 10 more days. Furthermore, Homma's staff had anticipated snaring no more than 40,000 prisoners of war (POWs) and now had to deal with nearly twice that many.

Not only did the Japanese end up with more POWs than expected, but most of the Luzon Force entered captivity in poor physical condition. King's troops had begun the siege of Bataan in January 1942 on half-rations, and their meager allotment had been halved again by March. Three months of malnutrition and the strain of combat had left the Filipinos and Americans susceptible to such diseases as diarrhea, dysentery, beriberi, night blindness, and malaria.

Intent on capturing the fortified island of CORREGIDOR, less than three miles south of Bataan, General Homma did not devote much attention to his prisoners. He simply wanted to get them off Bataan and out of his way without delay. Fourteenth Army lacked motor transport and fuel; that meant most of the POWs had to be evacuated on foot. Depending on their point of capture, the feeble Filipinos and Americans had to walk distances 70–140 miles to a railroad station, where they boarded trains that would haul them to Camp O'Donnell, their first prison camp.

The situation was further complicated by the Japanese army's attitude toward POWs. Trained to fight to the death, the average Japanese soldier despised anyone, friend or foe, who permitted himself to fall into enemy hands alive. Also, many of Homma's veterans craved revenge for comrades slain in the preceding campaign.

Consequently, the Japanese guards detailed to handle the evacuation committed random atrocities against their helpless prisoners. They deliberately subjected POWs to long hours of exposure under a tropical sun. They also denied their charges water and food, even when such items were readily available. Japanese execution squads trailed after the columns, killing those Americans and Filipinos who grew weak and fell out.

An estimated 600 to 650 American soldiers and sailors died on the Bataan Death March; deaths among their Filipino allies ran as high as 5,000 to 10,000. In addition, another 1,600 Americans and 16,000 Filipinos, their health broken by their ordeal on Bataan, died during their first six or seven weeks at Camp O'Donnell.

In January 1944 the U.S. War Department released accounts of the Death March brought back by escaped prisoners. The news inflamed the American people to a fury that was not assuaged even by two atomic bombings and Japan's surrender. Tried by an American military commission for violating the rules of war, General Homma was executed by firing squad on 3 April 1946.

See also BATAAN, RETREAT TO AND SIEGE OF; PHILIPPINES, LOSS OF; WAR CRIMES; WORLD WAR II, U.S. INVOLVEMENT, PACIFIC.

Further reading: Daws, Gavan. *Prisoners of the Japanese: POWs of World War II in the Pacific.* New York: William Morrow, 1994; Falk, Stanley. *Bataan: The March of Death.* New York: Norton, 1962; Hubbard, Preston. *Apocalypse Undone: My Survival of Japanese Imprisonment during World War II.* Nashville, Tenn.: Vanderbilt University Press, 1990; Kerr, E. Bartlett. *Surrender & Survival: The Experience of American POWs in the Pacific, 1941–1945.* New York: Morrow, 1985; Knox, Donald. *Death March: The Survivors of Bataan.* New York: Harcourt Brace Jovanovich, 1981.

— Gregory J. W. Urwin

battleships *Term used first to describe the largest sailing warships, the ships of the line (or line-of-battle ship), those vessels capable of standing in the main battle line*
In the transitional period between sailing warships and steel steam-powered vessels, the term *battleship* went out of use, with the most powerful U.S. vessels being steam frigates and monitors. In the late 19th century the term became the designation for the most heavily gunned and best protected warships, which according to naval theorist Captain Alfred Thayer MAHAN were essential for projecting naval power.

The first U.S. battleships were the small *Texas* and *MAINE,* both commissioned in 1895. Although designated as battleships at the time, both are usually referred to as second-class battleships. The *Texas* displaced 6,315 tons and mounted a main battery of two 12-inch guns and a secondary battery of six six-inch, 12 6-pounders, six one-pounder, and four 37-mm guns. The *Maine* was fated to be blown up in Havana Harbor, an event that would be one of the principal causes of the 1898 SPANISH-AMERICAN WAR. The *Texas* was decommissioned and sunk for target practice in 1911.

The earliest first-class battleships authorized for the U.S. Navy were the *Indiana* (BB 1), *Massachusetts,* and *Oregon.* Each displaced 10,288 tons and had a speed of 16.7 knots and 18-inch armor. In keeping with the demands of the day, their armament consisted of long, medium, and short-range guns: four 13-inch, eight eight-inch, and four six-inch guns, as well as 20 6-pounder and six one-pounder rapid-fire guns, two Colt machine guns, and two 3-inch field guns.

The *Iowa,* the most recently designed of the battleships to participate in the war with Spain, was 1,200 tons larger than the *Indiana* class and mounted four 12-inch guns. By virtue of recent improvements in manufacture, the thickness of its armor was reduced to only 14 inches. The U.S. battleships saw action in the Spanish-American War in the Battle of SANTIAGO DE CUBA. Between 1900 and 1908 the United States commissioned an additional 21 battleships (BB 5 through 25): *Kearsarge, Kentucky, Illinois, Alabama, Wisconsin, Maine, Missouri, Ohio, Virginia, Nebraska, Georgia, New Jersey, Rhode Island, Connecticut, Louisiana, Vermont, Kansas, Minnesota, Mississippi, Idaho,* and *New Hampshire.* They went from 11,540 tons displacement and a main battery of four 13-inch guns in the *Kearsarge* to 13,000 tons and four 12-inch guns in the *Mississippi.*

The British began a new era of battleship design with HMS *Dreadnought,* commissioned in 1906. The first all-big-gun battleship, it mounted 10 12-inch guns and displaced 21,250 tons. The *Dreadnought* employed new steam turbine engines and, at 21 knots, was faster than any other battleship. Actually, the U.S. Congress was first to approve such ships, in March 1905, but the *South Carolina* (BB 26) and the *Michigan* were not completed until 1910, well after the British ship.

The two U.S. battleships introduced the superfiring (superimposed) main battery into battleship design. The second and third turrets were higher than the first and fourth and thus able to fire over them. This system became the international standard. Their main armament of eight 12-inch guns was less than that of the *Dreadnought,* they also mounted a secondary battery that included 22 three-inch guns. Relatively slow at 19 knots, the *South Carolina* class ships were nonetheless well designed.

The 20,000-ton ships of the *Delaware* class (*Delaware* and *South Dakota*) were laid down in 1907. They mounted 10 12-inch guns. In 1909 Congress authorized the *Utah* class (*Utah* and *Florida*). Completed a year later, these 21,800-ton ships mounted 10 12-inch and 16 five-inch guns. The *Arkansas* class (*Arkansas* and *Wyoming*) were considerably larger ships. Completed in 1911, they displaced 26,000 tons and mounted 12 12-inch and 21 five-inch guns.

The first superdreadnoughts were the *Texas*-class (*Texas* and *New York*) ships. They displaced 27,000 tons and were the first U.S. battleships to mount 14-inch guns. The *Texas* (BB 35), now a Texas state memorial, is the only surviving WORLD WAR I–era dreadnought.

The *Nevada*-class superdreadnoughts (*Nevada* and *Oklahoma*), completed in 1914, displaced 27,500 tons, were armed with 10 14-inch and 12 five-inch guns, and were capable of 21 knots. Their number-one and number-four turrets had three guns each; numbers two and three had two guns. They incorporated "all or nothing armor"—heavy armor protecting their vitals and little elsewhere.

This system was soon adopted by other naval powers. The *Nevada*s were powered by fuel oil instead of coal, allowing for a superior steaming radius and replenishment while underway.

The last U.S. battleships authorized prior to World War I were those of the *Pennsylvania* class (*Pennsylvania* and *Arizona*). They mounted 12 14-inch guns, three to each turret, as well as 22 five-inch guns. The United States laid down six other dreadnoughts of the *New Mexico* and *Tennessee* classes during the war. The powerful *Colorado*-class ships, authorized in 1917, were part of the U.S. Navy's "second to none" program. The *Colorado* (BB 45), commissioned in 1923, mounted 16-inch guns.

During World War I, U.S. battleships were dispatched to Scapa Flow. As the German navy did not attempt a fleet engagement after the U.S. entry, they did not see action in the war.

The Washington Naval Conference of 1921–22 (see WASHINGTON AND LONDON NAVAL AGREEMENTS) resulted in the scrapping of some U.S. capital ships and conversion of others. It also limited battleships to 16-inch guns, but it allowed some reconstruction to deal with antiaircraft and torpedo protection, limited to a maximum of 3,000 tons per ship. Existing ships could be replaced after 20 years.

In the 1930s all major naval powers assumed that battleships would continue to be the dominant vessels at sea. Congress authorized an overhaul of the U.S. fleet, in the 1934 Vinson-Trammel Act. This legislation provided funds to build new battleships and refurbish older warships.

In December 1937 the *North Carolina* (BB 55) was laid down. Commissioned in 1941, it represented a major step in U.S. battleship construction. The *North Carolina* and *Washington* displaced 35,000 tons and had main batteries of nine 16-inch guns. They had a maximum speed of 28 knots.

On 7 December 1941 the U.S. battleship fleet suffered a severe loss in the Japanese attack on PEARL HARBOR. At the time of the attack, the *Colorado* was refitting at Puget Sound. The three *New Mexico*s and two *New York*s were in the Atlantic, and the *Arkansas* was laid up. Of the battleships struck at Pearl Harbor, the *Pennsylvania* was hardly damaged, and the *Tennessee* and *Maryland* both soon returned to active duty. The *Nevada*, *West Virginia*, and *California* were rebuilt. The *Arizona* was a complete loss and was not raised, being left as a memorial. *Oklahoma* was raised but not rebuilt. In a real sense, Pearl Harbor marked the beginning of the end of the battleship era and the arrival of the aircraft carrier as the world's new capital ship.

The four ships of the South Dakota class were commissioned in 1942. They displaced 43,200 tons and mounted main batteries of nine 16-inch guns.

The epitome of U.S. battleship construction came with the four-ship IOWA-CLASS (BB 61–64), however. Authorized in 1938 and 1939 and launched in 1942–44, they were commissioned in 1943–44. The fastest battleships ever built at 33 knots, the *Iowa*s displaced 45,000 tons and mounted nine 16-inch guns. They had secondary batteries of 20 five-inch guns, along with, by late 1944, 80 40-mm and 50 20-mm antiaircraft guns.

During World War II, U.S. battleships saw little action against enemy ships, apart from actions at Casablanca, GUADALCANAL, and the Battle of LEYTE GULF. Their most important role was providing protection for aircraft carriers, the new titans of the sea, and conducting shore bombardment. The formal Japanese surrender ending the Pacific War was signed aboard the *Missouri* on 2 September 1945.

After World War II most of the battleships were decommissioned, and many were scrapped. The *Iowa*s remained in service and underwent upgrades, although only the *Missouri* was active by 1950. All four saw action during the KOREAN WAR, however, providing highly effective shore bombardment. The *Iowa*s fought in the VIETNAM WAR, and modification in the 1980s enabled them to fire guided missiles. The *Missouri* and *Wisconsin* took part in OPERATION DESERT STORM (the Persian Gulf War), firing cruise missiles and 16-inch guns at Iraqi targets.

Today no battleships remain in service. Their great size and operating costs, as well as the ability of other ship platforms to carry cruise missiles, preclude this. The *Missouri* is in Pearl Harbor as a museum ship; the *Wisconsin*, although still in reserve status, is a museum ship at Norfolk; the *New Jersey* is a museum ship at Camden, New Jersey; and the *Iowa* is at San Francisco, in reserve status and probably destined to become a museum ship in 2004.

See also MONITOR; NAVY, U.S.; SHIPS OF THE LINE.

Further reading: Friedman, Norman. *U.S. Battleships.* Annapolis, Md.: Naval Institute Press, 1985; Garzke, William H., and Robert O. Dulin, Jr. *Battleships.* Annapolis, Md.: Naval Institute Press, 1995; Harris, Brayton. *The Age of the Battleship: 1890–1922.* New York: Franklin Watts, 1965; Macintyre, Donald. *The Thunder of the Guns: A Century of Battleships.* New York: Norton, 1960; Padfield, Peter. *The Battleship Era.* New York: David McKay, 1972; Reilly, John C., Jr., and Robert L. Scheina. *American Battleships, 1886–1923: Predreadnought Design and Construction.* Annapolis, Md.: Naval Institute Press, 1980.

— Richard H. Donohue, Jr.

Bay of Pigs invasion (15–19 April 1961) *Abortive U.S.-backed invasion of Cuba, the failure of which contributed to the subsequent Cuban Missile Crisis*
On 1 January 1959, an indigenous revolutionary movement led by Fidel Castro seized power from Fulgencio Batista, a U.S. client who had been dictator of Cuba since 1933.

Although Castro initially declared that he was not a communist, he covertly sought Soviet aid and military protection; American economic pressure and boycotts gave him an excuse to move openly into the Soviet camp. In response, in March 1960 President Dwight D. EISENHOWER authorized the CENTRAL INTELLIGENCE AGENCY (CIA) to devise a scheme to train Cuban exiles based in Guatemala to invade the island and overthrow Castro, reserving to himself the right to decide whether or not this plan should ultimately be implemented. In early January 1961, shortly before leaving office, Eisenhower withdrew U.S. recognition from the Castro government.

Eisenhower's successor, John F. KENNEDY, who took office later that month, inherited this projected operation. Perhaps fearing that he might appear soft on communism, and despite lukewarm assessments from the Joint Chiefs of Staff and the misgivings of Secretary of State Dean Rusk, the president approved its implementation in March, while insisting on modifications that greatly jeopardized its chances of success.

Notwithstanding evidence that U.S. involvement in the training of Cuban exiles had become widely known throughout Latin America, Kennedy insisted, in an effort to maintain the deniability of any U.S. contribution to the operation, that no American troops or pilots participate. The invasion site was switched 100 miles west, from Trinidad on Cuba's southern coast (which offered defeated invaders potential escape into the neighboring Escambray Mountains, sanctuaries for a strong anti-Castro guerrilla movement) to the more vulnerable Bay of Pigs (Bahia de Cochinos), south of the city of Matanzas. Although Kennedy wished to include only liberal Cubans whose outlook was anti-Castro but also anti-Batista, the invasion force included many Batista supporters.

Initial air strikes against Cuba's air bases launched on 15 April 1961 by Cuban exile pilots flying surplus American B-26s inflicted damage but failed to destroy the entire Cuban air force. Alarmed by news reports exposing as untrue the deceptive American cover story given by U.S. ambassador Adlai Stevenson in the United Nations that defectors from Castro's military had flown these missions, Kennedy refused to authorize a scheduled second air strike, which had been expected to eliminate the remaining Cuban planes.

On 17 April 1961, 1,400 Cuban exiles, formed into Brigade 2506, participated in the invasion. Some dropped by air, others arrived by amphibious craft. Air attacks by Castro's forces slowed the invasion process, destroying one transport carrying vital supplies and ultimately forcing the invasion flotilla out to sea, while Cuban T-33 jets proved unexpectedly successful in downing the exiles' B-26s. Castro's rapid incarceration of 100–200,000 potential domestic opponents effectively precluded any internal uprising in support of the invasion.

Meanwhile, Cuban ground forces, tanks, and artillery rapidly played havoc with the invaders. A few escaped by small boats to U.S. naval vessels nearby, but 114 of the invaders were killed, and 1,113 were captured. Cuban losses were far greater, approximately 1,650 dead and 2,000 wounded. With Kennedy administration backing, 18 months later private American sources provided Cuba $62 million of food and medicine in exchange for the prisoners.

The Bay of Pigs represented a humiliating international failure, vindicating critics who characterized the United States as an overbearing, imperialist state that backed unpopular right-wing forces around the globe. Publicly, Kennedy took full responsibility for the operation; privately, he deeply resented what he perceived as CIA mismanagement. The following year he replaced both Allen W. Dulles, the CIA's near-legendary director, and Richard Bissell, the head of its Clandestine Service. From then on, the CIA placed greater emphasis on intelligence collection than on flamboyant but risky covert operations.

However, Kennedy's own reckless authorization and half-hearted implementation of this operation may have helped convince Soviet general secretary Nikita Khrushchev that he was a lightweight who lacked the resolve to confront the Soviet Union. Undoubtedly, the botched invasion and fear of a subsequent attempt impelled Castro to request Soviet protection, which brought Soviet missiles to Cuba. The presence of these weapons provoked the 1962 CUBAN MISSILE CRISIS. The Bay of Pigs also helped to precipitate at least four decades of intense Cuban–United States hostility, which remains in the early 21st century and whose ultimate resolution may well have to await Castro's death or retirement.

See also CONTAINMENT, DOCTRINE AND COURSE OF.

Further reading: Bissell, Richard M., Jr., with Jonathan E. Lewis and Francis Pudlo. *Reflections of a Cold Warrior: From Yalta to the Bay of Pigs.* New Haven, Conn.: Yale University Press, 1996; Blight, James, and Peter Kornbluh, eds. *Politics of Illusion: The Bay of Pigs Invasion Reexamined.* Boulder, Colo.: Lynne Rienner, 1998; Higgins, Trumbull. *The Perfect Failure: Kennedy, Eisenhower, and the CIA at the Bay of Pigs.* New York: Norton, 1987; Kornbluh, Peter, ed. *Bay of Pigs Declassified: The Secret CIA Report on the Invasion of Cuba.* New York: New Press, 1998; Paterson, Thomas G. *Contesting Castro: The United States and the Triumph of the Cuban Revolution.* New York: Oxford University Press, 1994.

— Priscilla Roberts

bazooka *Antitank weapon developed by the United States during World War II*
Operated by a two-man crew, the bazooka consisted of a rocket and five-foot launcher. Essentially a tube with a

shoulder stock, the bazooka had a hand grip containing a trigger assembly. When squeezed, the trigger sent an electric current that ignited the solid fuel in the rocket.

Successfully tested in May 1942, the bazooka (named for a long tubular musical instrument devised by comedian Bob Burns) soon was in full production, 5,000 being made in only 30 days. By the end of the war, 475,000 had been manufactured.

The 2.36-inch rocket had a shaped charge to concentrate the warhead explosion in a small area. It generated a superheated jet of gas with the bulk of its energy projected forward, burning a small hole through armor. Most of the damage was caused by the superheated jet of gas, which consumed oxygen, destroyed crew and equipment, and set fire to ammunition and fuel. In addition, molten droplets of armor were also propelled into the vehicle.

The 2.36-inch rocket proved successful against German tanks of World War II, but it was totally ineffective against Russian-built T-34/85s of the KOREAN WAR, as was discovered early in the Battle of OSAN. The 3.5-inch bazooka, introduced shortly thereafter, was, however, successful against the T-34. The chief drawbacks of the bazooka were its relatively short range and the slow speed of the rocket.

See also TANKS.

Further reading: Blair, Clay. *The Forgotten War. America in Korea, 1950–1953.* New York: Times Books, 1987; Gander, Terry. *Bazooka: Hand-Held Hollow-Charge Anti-Tank Weapons.* London: PRC, 1998.

— Spencer C. Tucker

Bear Paw Mountain, Battle of (30 September–5 October 1877) *Last engagement of the Nez Perce War* Forced from their homelands in northwest Oregon and central Idaho, the Nez Perce people embarked upon an epic bid for freedom, an attempt that became one of the most unique and compelling chapters of American military history. Led by White Bird, Looking Glass, JOSEPH, and his brother Ollokot, the Nez Perce proved capable of sustained campaigning and disciplined fighting that confounded their white adversaries. After a series of solid victories and desperate escapes—at WHITE BIRD CANYON, on the CLEARWATER RIVER, and at the BIG HOLE RIVER—the Nez Perce moved through Yellowstone National Park and turned northward toward Canada. North of the Yellowstone River, on 13 September 1877, they beat back an attack by the 7th Cavalry at CANYON CREEK and headed for the border, trailing a large army column commanded by Brigadier General Oliver O. HOWARD.

Meanwhile, Colonel Nelson A. MILES marched northwestward from Fort Keogh with five companies of infantry (most mounted on captured Indian ponies), six troops of cavalry, and a small complement of artillery. Miles was an ambitious and decidedly capable Indian fighter. He now raced to another opportunity (as Howard backed off), hoping to induce the Nez Perce to slow their pace.

As he had before a costly battle on the Big Hole River in August, Looking Glass now urged a halt for rest. The Nez Perce camped on Snake Creek near the Bear Paw Mountains in northern Montana—only 40 miles from the Canadian border. As at the Big Hole, the stop proved disastrous. On 30 September, Miles's column caught up.

Miles ordered a cavalry charge. Three troops of the 7th Cavalry headed for the camp, while three troops of the 2d Cavalry went after the pony herd. The 2d Cavalry troopers largely succeeded, but the 7th troopers ran into a wall of well-directed Nez Perce fire. Again, the Indians proved disciplined fighters, and they exacted a bloody toll. Concentrating on officers and sergeants, they killed one captain, one lieutenant, and all three first sergeants in the 7th Cavalry force and wounded the two other captains. In all, two officers and 21 enlisted men were killed, and four officers and 38 men were wounded—remarkably heavy casualties for the brief action. Wisely, Miles suspended the attack and settled in for a siege.

The Nez Perce had lost leaders too, including Ollokot, who had been very effective throughout the campaign. Despite their early success, the Nez Perce had lost most of their ponies and now suffered in a heavy snow. On 4 October Howard arrived, signaling the approach of still more soldiers. To Miles's relief, Howard declined to take command.

Nez Perce leaders argued over their course of action: Joseph wanted to negotiate, but White Bird and Looking Glass voted for escape. On 5 October Looking Glass was killed by a sharpshooter, after which Joseph met with Miles and Howard.

Miles promised Joseph that in the coming spring the Nez Perce would be returned to Idaho to live on their reservation. That afternoon Joseph surrendered to Miles, with the statement, "From where the sun now stands I will fight no more forever."

Some 400 hundred Nez Perce, including fewer than 100 warriors, surrendered with Joseph. Some 200 men, women, and children escaped with White Bird to Canada. Over Miles's strenuous objections, however, the government refused to allow the Nez Perce to return to Idaho. Sent to Kansas and then to Indian Territory, in 1885 Joseph and his people finally were allowed to move onto a reservation in Washington.

The Nez Perce bid for freedom made a legend of Joseph, and it remains one of the most-remembered events of the long struggle between white America and the Indians.

See also AMERICAN INDIAN WARS, OVERVIEW; INDIAN WARFARE; NEZ PERCE WAR.

Further reading: Beal, Merrill. *I Will Fight No More Forever: Chief Joseph and the Nez Perce War.* Seattle: University of Washington Press, 1963; Hampton, Bruce. *Children of Grace: The Nez Perce War of 1877.* New York: Henry Holt, 1994; Lavender, David. *Let Me Be Free: The Nez Perce Tragedy.* New York: HarperCollins, 1992; Miles, Nelson A. *Personal Observances and Recollections of General Nelson A. Miles.* Lincoln: University of Nebraska Press, 1992; Utley, Robert M. *Frontier Regulars: The United States Army and the Indian, 1866–1891.* New York: Macmillan, 1973.

— David Coffey and James Robbins Jewell

Beauregard, Pierre Gustave Toutant (1818–1893)
Confederate army general

Born on 28 May 1818 in St. Bernard Parish, Louisiana, to an influential family, Pierre Gustave Toutant Beauregard studied in New York, learning to speak English and developing an admiration of Napoleon Bonaparte. The young Creole graduated from the U.S. Military Academy at West Point in 1838. Commissioned a second lieutenant and posted to the 1st Artillery, he soon transferred to the engineers. Promoted to first lieutenant in 1839, he served on Major General Winfield SCOTT's staff during the MEXICAN-AMERICAN WAR, earning two brevets for gallantry. In 1853 he was promoted to captain and spent most of the next seven years on engineering projects in New Orleans.

On 23 January 1861 Beauregard, despite his support for secession, became superintendent at West Point. He was ordered to vacate the post two days later. He resigned his commission in February and offered his services to the Confederacy. Commissioned a brigadier general, he assumed command of Southern forces at Charleston. In April he directed the bombardment of FORT SUMTER that began the Civil War. An instant hero, he moved to the Virginia front, where he exercised tactical command during the First Battle of BULL RUN/MANASSAS. Promoted to full general in August, he ranked fifth, behind Samuel Cooper, Albert S. JOHNSTON, Robert E. LEE, and Joseph JOHNSTON.

Beauregard's open and heated criticism of the government's conduct of the war led to a serious rift with President Jefferson DAVIS that limited his usefulness for the remainder of the war. Transferred to the western theater as second in command to General Albert S. Johnston, Beauregard helped to direct the Confederate withdrawal from Tennessee and concentration at Corinth. During the April 1862 Battle of SHILOH, he assumed command after Johnston's death on the first day of fighting; he broke off the battle at dusk, and a reinforced Federal army forced him to retreat the following day. After yielding CORINTH, in June Beauregard took an unauthorized leave and was replaced by General Braxton BRAGG.

In August 1862 Beauregard returned to Charleston, as commander of the Department of South Carolina, Georgia, and Florida. Over the next several months he frustrated numerous Federal attempts to seize that port city. As the situation in the East grew critical, in April 1864 Beauregard was called to command the Department of North Carolina and Southern Virginia. He rendered some of his finest service in protecting the eastern approaches to Richmond and PETERSBURG. His heavily outnumbered force halted the Federal advance at Bermuda Hundred in May and stymied Lieutenant General Ulysses S. GRANT's advance on PETERSBURG in June, buying valuable time for Lee's Army of Northern Virginia.

Although he hoped for a major field command, Beauregard's relationship with Davis, which had only deteriorated, held him back. Instead, he became commander of the Military Division of the West, a largely administrative post with responsibility for all Confederate troops between the Appalachian Mountains and the Mississippi. He could do little to support General John B. HOOD's ill-fated Tennessee campaign or oppose Major General William T. SHERMAN'S MARCH TO THE SEA. In the final stages of the war he served with General Joseph E. JOHNSTON in the Carolinas, surrendering there with him in April.

Beauregard prospered after the war, working as a railroad executive and profiting from his involvement in the Louisiana Lottery. He also served as commissioner of public works in New Orleans and as adjutant general of Louisiana. He died at New Orleans on 20 February 1893.

See also CIVIL WAR, LAND OVERVIEW.

Further reading: Roman, Alfred. *The Military Operations of General Beauregard.* 2 vols. Reprint, New York: Da Capo, 1994; Williams T. Harry. *P. G. T. Beauregard: Napoleon in Gray.* Baton Rouge: Louisiana State University Press, 1955.

— Robert Beeks

Beecher Island, Battle of (17–25 September 1868)
Engagement between Plains Indians and a party of civilian frontiersmen employed as scouts under army officers

Hopes for peace on the southern plains fostered by the Medicine Lodge Treaty of 1867 crumbled when a fresh round of violence spread across Kansas, Colorado, Texas, and the Indian Territory during the summer of 1868. Reasons for the outbreak were many. The fragile nature of all Indian treaties—delays in promised inducements, the warriors' natural propensity to hunt and raid, and the unnatural restrictions imposed by the reservation system—contributed significantly. The massive influx of settlers along the emigrant trails and rivers of Kansas, coupled with the steady progress of the Kansas Pacific, which now approached the Colorado line, threatened the buffalo range and therefore the Indians' traditional way of life. During the summer of 1868, therefore, warriors struck at pillars of white encroachment—farms, ranches, and wagon trains—plundering stock herds and killing dozens of settlers and travelers.

Lieutenant General William T. SHERMAN, commander of the Military Division of the Missouri, and Major General Philip SHERIDAN, new head of the Department of the Missouri, which embraced Colorado, Kansas, and the Indian Territory, had been the Union's most accomplished practitioners of total war. They now brought that experience to bear on the southern plains. Sheridan planned a winter campaign, to strike the Indians when they were most vulnerable. In the meantime, he needed to stabilize the situation. To that end he concentrated troops along the rivers and trails of Kansas. He also authorized his aide, Major George Forsyth, to raise a company of 50 frontiersmen to guard the railroad as it approached Fort Wallace.

Forsyth organized his civilian force at Fort Hays and moved westward. In September 1868 the company followed a fresh trail up the Arikara Fork of the Republican River to a point near the Colorado-Kansas line. On 17 September some 700 warriors—Cheyenne dog soldiers, Oglala Sioux, and Arapaho—assailed Forsyth's camp. The major formed his men in a defensive perimeter on an island in the dry riverbed. His men, many Civil War veterans and all experienced frontiersmen, armed with repeating rifles, dug in and fought tenaciously, repulsing several frontal attacks by the vastly superior Indian forces. But the defenders lost most of their mounts and suffered heavy casualties. For the next seven days the attackers held Forsyth's men under siege.

Forsyth, wounded in both legs, sent out messengers to bring help, while he and his men grimly held on. On 25 September a relief column of 10th Cavalry BUFFALO SOLDIERS led by Captain Louis Carpenter arrived to raise the siege. Forsyth's command had suffered six killed, including Lieutenant Frederick Beecher, and 15 wounded in what became known as the Battle of Beecher Island.

That winter Sheridan launched an ambitious multi-pronged campaign that included Lieutenant Colonel George CUSTER's attack on Black Kettle's Cheyenne village on the Washita River. Successful, if not decisive, it confirmed Sheridan's belief in a total-war approach and established a model for future efforts in Texas and on the northern plains.

See also AMERICAN INDIAN WARS, OVERVIEW; INDIAN WARFARE; RED RIVER WAR; SIOUX WARS.

Further reading: Criqui, Orvel A. *Fifty Fearless Men: The Forsyth Scouts and Beecher Island.* Marceline, Mo.: Walsworth, 1993; Forsyth, George A. *Thrilling Days of Army Life.* Reprint, Lincoln: University of Nebraska Press, 1994; Monnett, John H. *The Battle of Beecher Island and the Indian War of 1867–1869.* Niwot: University Press of Colorado, 1992; Utley, Robert M. *Frontier Regulars: The United States Army and the Indian, 1866–1891.* New York: Macmillan, 1973; Werner, Fred H. *The Beecher Island Battle, September 17, 1868.* Greeley, Colo.: Werner, 1989.

— David Coffey

Belmont, Battle of (7 November 1861) *Early Civil War battle*

Both the Union and Confederacy hoped in the opening months of the war to secure Kentucky, especially the crucial river area in the western part of the state. Confederate positions at Columbus, in Kentucky, and Belmont, in Missouri, both on the Mississippi River, posed a threat to Union control of Kentucky, Missouri, and southern Illinois. Columbus, the "Confederate Gibraltar," was an especially strong position.

On 5 November 1861, U.S. Army Department of the West commander Major General John C. FRÉMONT ordered Brigadier General Ulysses S. GRANT to conduct a demonstration against Columbus to mask a Union effort in southeastern Missouri and to prevent Major General Leonidas POLK from sending reinforcements there from Columbus. Grant left Cairo, Illinois, the next day with 3,114 men and two artillery pieces in six transports escorted by the "timberclads" *Lexington* and *Tyler.* Knowing that Columbus was far too powerful for him to attack, Grant decided to assault Belmont.

On 7 November Grant landed 2,500 men three miles from Belmont to attack 2,700 Confederates. He ordered the two timberclads to engage Columbus as a diversion. At Belmont, Grant's men fought a four-hour battle, defeating the Confederates. The Union troops, however, stopped to loot the enemy camp, giving the Southerners time to regroup. Polk, meanwhile, had sent reinforcements across the river, protected by the lower batteries at Columbus. Grant now ordered his men to burn the Confederate camp, retreat to the river, and reembark on the transports. The outnumbered Union troops managed to cut their way through the Confederates and withdraw, protected by fire from the timberclads.

The battle was costly for both sides. Union casualties were 610, while the Confederates lost 642. Both sides claimed victory. The battle did not reflect well on Grant's generalship, but the Northern press celebrated the action, and President Abraham LINCOLN was delighted to find a general who would fight. The battle did little to influence events in the region, but the subsequent Confederate failure to launch an offensive in Missouri gave substance to Grant's claim of success.

See also CIVIL WAR, LAND OVERVIEW.

Further reading: Grant, Ulysses S. *Personal Memoirs of U. S. Grant.* Edited by E. B. Long. New York: Grosset & Dunlap, 1952; Hughes, Nathaniel C., Jr. *The Battle of Belmont: Grant Strikes South.* Chapel Hill: University of North Carolina Press, 1991; Simpson, Brooks D. *Ulysses S. Grant: Triumph over Adversity, 1822–1865.* New York: Houghton Mifflin, 2000.

—Thomas D. Veve and Spencer C. Tucker

Bennington, Battle of (16 August 1777) *American Revolutionary War battle*

After taking FORT TICONDEROGA on Lake Champlain in July 1777, British major general John Burgoyne moved south toward the Hudson River and his destination of Albany, New York. He made slow progress, however, because of the difficult terrain and a lack of wagons and draft animals. In late July Burgoyne planned an expedition eastward to alleviate these problems by procuring horses and provisions. He also sought to enlist Loyalists and disperse rebels who were gathering on his flank.

Lieutenant Colonel Friedrich Baum, a German officer who did not speak English, commanded the raid. His force, as large as 1,200 men, consisted of mercenary German infantry and dismounted dragoons, British riflemen, Canadians, Loyalists, and Indians, along with two small cannon. Baum departed on 11 August for Bennington, Vermont, where several hundred Americans supposedly guarded a large number of livestock. The Indians, however, raided ahead of the main column, alerting the countryside to Baum's approach.

Meanwhile, New Hampshire had raised a 1,500-man brigade under Brigadier General John STARK to resist Burgoyne. Stark marched to Manchester in early August and there conferred with Colonel Seth Warner and Brigadier General Benjamin LINCOLN. Refusing to place his troops under Continental army authority, Stark nonetheless agreed to harass Burgoyne's flank and counter his incursions into New England. He then headed for Bennington, where he arrived on 8 August.

On 14 August Baum was about four miles from Bennington when he ran into Stark's force. Baum requested reinforcement and then encamped along the Wallomsac River. Unwisely scattering his command, Baum deployed his dragoons and some British soldiers on a steep hill overlooking a bridge, where they constructed a redoubt. Several hundred Loyalists built a second redoubt on the other side of the river. Baum also placed smaller detachments in cabins on either side of the bridge, behind the hill redoubt to protect his baggage, and along the road over which he had advanced.

Stark observed Baum's deployment and requested aid from Warner, but he did not attack on 15 August because

of heavy rain. On the 16 August Stark, reinforced to 2,000 men, sent detachments of several hundred men each to encircle Baum's left and right flanks, while another 100 men demonstrated in his front. Another 200 soldiers attacked the Loyalist redoubt, leaving 1,200 men for a frontal assault. Baum detected the troops moving into his rear, but he believed that they were Loyalist reinforcements.

At 3 P.M. the flanking columns opened fire, signaling commencement of the assault. The Americans quickly overran the Loyalist position, scattering its defenders. Many of Baum's Indians and Canadians fled at the first fire, while other detachments were overwhelmed by the suddenness of the attack. The main fight took place on the hill, where troops from other parts of the field regrouped in the redoubt. Stark led his men up the slope toward the position, while others attacked from behind. Baum's men held off the Americans for two hours but ran low on ammunition; a wagon with extra cartridges exploded. As Stark's men closed in, Baum ordered his dragoons to use their swords to cut their way through the Americans, most of whom lacked bayonets. The dragoons made some progress but surrendered when Baum was mortally wounded. Stark's troops then scattered across the battlefield in search of prisoners and loot, but then a new threat appeared.

Lieutenant Colonel Heinrich Breymann's 642-man command had arrived on the field to reinforce Baum. Breymann steadily drove back the makeshift force that Stark managed to collect until American reinforcements arrived. Warner's regiment and some rangers, totaling 330 men, went into line with Stark's men, halting the advance. The two sides then fought until sunset when Breymann's troops also ran low on ammunition. Breymann, wounded in the leg, ordered a retreat, which became a rout as the Americans pursued.

Stark called off his men at darkness. He had secured an overwhelming victory. In the Battle of Bennington the British had 207 dead, about 700 captured (including 30 officers), and a large quantity of military supplies lost. Patriot losses had been 30 dead and 40 wounded. The victory at Bennington greatly reinvigorated the American effort against Burgoyne and helped set the stage for the decisive battles at SARATOGA.

See also AMERICAN REVOLUTIONARY WAR: LAND OVERVIEW; HUBBARDTON, BATTLE OF.

Further reading: Ketchum, Richard M. *Saratoga: Turning Point of America's Revolutionary War.* New York: Henry Holt, 1997; Parks, Joseph W. R. *The Battle of Bennington.* Old Bennington, Vt.: Bennington Museum, 1976; Ward, Christopher. *The War of the Revolution.* 2 vols. New York: Macmillan, 1952.

—Michael P. Gabriel

Bentonville, Battle of (19–21 March 1865) *Battle fought at the end of the Civil War near Bentonville, North Carolina*

The Confederates had little chance of winning any significant military advantage but were not yet ready to surrender. The Confederate Army of Tennessee had more or less ceased to exist after the dual fiascoes of FRANKLIN and NASHVILLE in November and December 1864. However, its remnants now gathered, along with other small Confederate units, under a new commander, General Joseph E. JOHNSTON, to contest the advance of Major General William T. SHERMAN's 60,000 Union troops through the Carolinas.

At Fayetteville, North Carolina, Sherman divided his forces into two columns, which moved north in parallel. Major General Oliver O. HOWARD's Army of the Tennessee, on the right, was to move toward Goldsborough and there join another Union force coming in from the Atlantic coast. On the left, Major General Henry SLOCUM's Army of Georgia (XIV and XX Corps) would advance toward Raleigh. The two columns were sufficiently separated so as not to be mutually supporting. Sherman did not anticipate any Confederate offensive operations against his forces.

On 16 March Slocum engaged Confederates near Averasborough and turned east toward Goldsborough as the Confederates retreated. General Johnston had some 21,000 men at his disposal, and he was determined to strike Slocum's troops before the Union armies could again combine.

Early on 19 March Slocum's leading units encountered Confederate cavalry near Bentonville. The Federals drove the cavalry back, but Johnston then attacked, and Slocum's troops soon found themselves fighting a defensive battle. Johnston mounted several desperate attacks, but these failed to break through. He then took up defensive positions.

There was little fighting on 20 March; Sherman brought up reinforcements, and Johnston merely held his ground. The next day, 21 March, however, with all his forces in place, Sherman attacked. Johnston was able to block a Union effort to outflank him, and that night he retreated toward Smithfield. He had fought a skillful battle but had had too few men to achieve success. Johnston now opened negotiations that led to the surrender of his forces on 26 April. Union casualties in the Battle of Bentonville were 1,645 men, while Confederate losses are said to have been 2,606.

See also CIVIL WAR, LAND OVERVIEW.

Further reading: Barrett, John G. *The Civil War in North Carolina.* Chapel Hill: University of North Carolina Press, 1963; ———. *Sherman's March through the Carolinas.* Chapel Hill: University of North Carolina Press, 1956; Bradley, Mark L. *Last Stand in the Carolinas: The Battle of Bentonville.* Campbell, Calif.: Savas Woodbury, 1996; Hughes, Nathaniel C. *Bentonville: The Final Battle of Sherman and Johnston.* Chapel Hill: University of North Carolina Press, 1996.

— Lawyn C. Edwards

Berkeley, Sir William (1606–1677) *Royal governor in 17th-century Virginia*

Born in 1606 in Somerset, England, and educated at Oxford, Berkeley had been knighted by Charles I in 1639 and appointed governor of Virginia in 1642. Despite the death of some 500 colonists during the Indian uprising (1644–45) led by Chief OPECHANCANOUGH, Berkeley won the admiration of colonists by organizing the militia, defeating Opechancanough in battle, and ultimately forcing tribes to move out of the Tidewater region beyond the fall line and into the Piedmont.

Berkeley sided with Charles I during the English Civil War, welcoming royalists who fled to Virginia after Charles's execution in 1649. When commissioners from the Rump Parliament arrived in Virginia in 1652 to demand adherence to the Commonwealth, Berkeley stepped down as governor and retired to his estates near present-day Williamsburg. In early 1660 a specially convened assembly elected him acting governor, a decision confirmed later in the year after Charles II was restored to the throne.

Berkeley's second period as governor was dominated by trade disputes, renewed Indian conflicts, and internal divisions, all of which contributed to BACON'S REBELLION. In 1661 Berkeley traveled to London in an unsuccessful effort to obtain relief from the Navigation Acts, which gave English merchants a monopoly on Virginian tobacco and placed export and import duties on colonial trade. The expansion of plantations into the Piedmont region beyond the fall line led to conflict with the Doeg in 1675. Although Berkeley authorized an expedition against the Doeg, the militia attacked the peaceful Susquehannah instead, causing the conflict to widen. By the end of January 1676, some 300 Virginians had been killed.

Berkeley's proposal for expensive fortifications along the fall line outraged frontiersmen, who believed that the forts, while protecting the Tidewater region from Indian attack, would leave settlers in the Piedmont defenseless. In addition, the construction costs would increase an already heavy tax burden. When settlers led by Nathaniel Bacon organized their own militia force to attack the Indians, Berkeley declared the settlers to be in a state of rebellion and attempted to raise a militia force against them. Berkeley was forced to flee Jamestown when Bacon seized and burned it in September, but Bacon's death in early October left his followers disorganized, allowing Berkeley to return and restore order. He would eventually have 23 of Bacon's cohorts executed. Berkeley left Jamestown in May 1677 for England, where he died in early July.

Further reading: Craven, Wesley Frank. *The Colonies in Transition, 1660–1713.* New American Nation Series. New York: Harper & Row, 1968; Pomfret, John E., with Floyd M. Shumway. *Founding the American Colonies, 1583–1660.* New York: Harper and Row, 1970; Powell, Phelan. *Sir William Berkeley: Governor of Virginia.* Philadelphia: Chelsea House, 2001.

— Justin D. Murphy

Berlin Blockade (June 1948–May 1949) *Early cold war crisis, demonstrating the Western powers' commitment to the Containment policy and their resolve to confront Soviet communism and prevent its further expansion*

From spring 1945, when World War II ended with the defeat of Germany, until 1948, growing COLD WAR tensions prevented the former allies from reaching agreement on the future government of Germany.

In May 1948 the three Western powers—the United States, the United Kingdom, and France (each of which, with the Soviet Union, had since 1945 occupied one sector of the German capital, Berlin, which lay deep within the Soviet occupation zone of Germany, soon to become the German Democratic Republic)—decided to merge their zones and introduce a new common currency there. They also announced that West Germany (comprising their respective zones of Germany) would definitely participate in the newly formulated Marshall Plan, a recovery program designed to facilitate Europe's postwar economic revival.

From late March 1948 on, the apprehensive Soviet Union began to tighten its grip on freight traffic into Berlin. On 24 June the Soviets dramatically cut off all land access, by rail, road, or water, to western Berlin. The Soviet objective was to force the three Western allies from Berlin, where the Soviets claimed that the four-power administration at an end and that the Allies no longer possessed any rights. This would have eliminated the Western bastion of Berlin, which not only possessed symbolic significance but also served as a conduit through which, between 1945 and 1952, 2 million East Germans migrated to the West, an embarrassing hemorrhage that deprived the East of many young, well-qualified workers.

Soviet obduracy met Western resolve. The military governor of the U.S. zone, Lieutenant General Lucius CLAY, presented President Harry S. TRUMAN with three options: do nothing, drive an armored column from West Germany to the city, or attempt an airlift. Truman was determined to keep U.S. forces in Berlin. He rejected the dangerous second choice, which ran the risk of armed clash with the Soviets, in favor of the third. Beginning on 26 June 1948, a massive American and British airlift began to ferry essential supplies into West Berlin and transport out its greatly reduced industrial exports to the West. A Western counterblockade of the Soviet zone in turn proved economically damaging, and each side progressively took incremental steps to tighten its control. In February 1949, for example, the West announced that in the future only German marks would be accepted as legal tender in Berlin, while the Soviets expropriated the homes, land, and businesses of East Berlin residents deemed to be bourgeois or capitalist in outlook.

The Soviets lifted the blockade in May 1949, but flights continued until September. Over the 15 months of the airlift, 275,000 flights transported 2,323,738 tons of food, fuel, machinery, and other supplies, at a cost of $224,000,000. Sixty fliers lost their lives in airplane crashes.

Early in the crisis, international tensions had continued to increase. By mid-July 1948 the Soviet army of occupation in East Germany had swelled to 40 divisions, whereas the Allies still had only eight divisions in their sectors. Both sides, however, demonstrated the practical caution that often characterized cold war crises. The Western powers

Fresh milk flown in during the Berlin airlift *(Library of Congress)*

continued to avoid any potential direct military confrontation with Soviet forces by eschewing attempts to resupply Berlin by road across Soviet-occupied territory, rejecting early recommendations from General Clay that armed supply convoys be sent over East German highways to Berlin. The Soviets likewise, despite strong protests and sporadic public announcements that they required the air corridors for their own military maneuvers, refrained from shooting down Western aircraft resupplying Berlin.

The Berlin blockade contributed to the Western decision to abandon hope of German reunification and to establish a separate state, the Federal Republic of Germany, comprising the former Western occupation sectors. With its foundation and that of the German Democratic Republic in 1949, the territorial borders of cold war Europe were clearly delineated, in many ways helping to stabilize a division that lasted until 1989. The first Berlin crisis also persuaded the United States to sign the 1949 Dunkerque Treaty, whereby it entered the NORTH ATLANTIC TREATY ORGANIZATION (NATO), concluding a permanent military alliance with most West European states, to which it extended a security guarantee. The blockade helped to persuade West Germans that their future lay in an alliance with the West. From then on the Western commitment to Berlin, over which from 1958 to 1962 a lengthy second crisis erupted, was viewed as a concrete demonstration of United States resolve to contain further Soviet advances, a policy to which ever since 1947 American officials had rhetorically pledged themselves.

See also CONTAINMENT, DOCTRINE AND COURSE OF; MILITARY AIR TRANSPORT SERVICE (MATS); VANDENBERG, HOYT S.

Further reading: Eisenberg, Carol. *Drawing the Line: The American Decision to Divide Germany, 1944–1949.* Cambridge, U.K.: Cambridge University Press, 1996; Haydock, Michael D. *City under Siege: The Berlin Blockade and Airlift, 1948–1949.* New York: Brassey's, 1999; Miller, Roger G. *To Save a City: The Berlin Airlift, 1948–1949.* College Station: Texas A&M University Press, 2000; Shlaim, Avi. *The United States and the Berlin Blockade, 1948–1949: A Study in Crisis Decision-Making.* Berkeley: University of California Press, 1983; Sutterlin, James S., and David Klein. *Berlin: From Symbol of Confrontation to Keystone of Stability.* New York: Praeger, 1989; Tusa, Ann, and John Tusa. *The Berlin Airlift.* New York: Hodder and Stoughton, 1988.

— Priscilla Roberts

Bickerdyke, Mary Ann Ball (1817–1901) *Civil War nurse*

Except that she was born on 19 July 1817 in Knox County, Ohio, Mary Ann Ball's early life is largely obscure. Recent research indicates that she received some medical training as a young woman. At age 30 she married Robert Bickerdyke. They had two sons before he died in 1858.

At the start of the Civil War Bickerdyke lived in Galesburg, Illinois, where she worked as a laundress and housekeeper. When members of her local church collected medical supplies and food for Union troops, Bickerdyke left her children with friends and delivered the supplies to Cairo, Illinois. Finding conditions there deplorable, she decided to remain in Cairo to nurse the wounded.

In the early days of the war Bickerdyke had no official authorization from the Federal government, yet she traveled with the Union troops in the western theater. Bickerdyke often worked in makeshift conditions, but she provided competent management. Soldiers referred to her affectionately as "Mother Bickerdyke," and Generals Ulysses S. GRANT and William T. SHERMAN praised her efforts.

Bickerdyke's official standing with the army changed following the Battle of SHILOH, when she became an agent for the Sanitary Commission. In this capacity Bickerdyke collected a salary and was able to utilize the commission's supplies.

Bickerdyke connected the occurrence of disease and death with poor nutrition and the filthiness of the camps. During her service with the Sanitary Commission she established laundries, improved the diet provided by kitchens, and supervised hospitals. She also was instrumental in aiding former prisoners of war from ANDERSONVILLE. She resigned from the Sanitary Commission in March 1866.

Following the war Bickerdyke helped families living in slum conditions in New York, worked as a pension attorney in California, and traveled the country securing benefits for veterans. She died at Bunker Hill, Kansas, on 8 November 1901.

See also AMERICAN RED CROSS; ARMY NURSE CORPS; BARTON, CLARISSA H.; CIVIL WAR, LAND OVERVIEW; DIX, DOROTHEA L.; WOMEN IN THE MILITARY.

Further reading: Baker, Nina Brown. *Cyclone in Calico: The Story of Mary Ann Bickerdyke.* Boston: Little, Brown, 1952; Kellogg, Florence Shaw. *Mother Bickerdyke, as I Knew Her.* Chicago: Unity, 1907; Osborne, Karen K. *Mother Bickerdyke, Civil War Mother to the Boys.* Milwaukee, Wisc.: Blue and Grey Chap Books, 1990.

— Tracy M. Shilcutt

Biddle, James (1783–1848) *U.S. Navy captain*

Born on 18 February 1783 at Philadelphia, James Biddle joined the navy in 1800, after graduating from the University of Pennsylvania. In 1802 he participated in the TRIPOLITAN WAR and was taken prisoner when the frigate *PHILADELPHIA* ran aground on 31 October 1803 and was captured. Released after 18 months of captivity, he subsequently commanded the Delaware flotilla, enforcing President Thomas JEFFERSON's embargo of 1807. After several years of conveying diplomatic dispatches to Paris, Biddle returned to the United States in time to participate in the War of 1812.

Biddle was first lieutenant on board the sloop *Wasp* under Captain Jacob Jones when it gained a signal victory over the British sloop *Frolic* on 18 October 1812. He distinguished himself by boarding the enemy ship and striking its flag. Both ships, severely damaged, were retaken by the British ship of the line *Poitiers* hours later. Exchanged and paroled in 1813, Biddle became master commandant of the sloop *Hornet*. He then ran the blockade of New London and sailed for the Dutch East Indies, where on 23 March 1815 he won his final naval engagement of the war, taking the brig *Penguin*. Biddle was promoted to post captain following a triumphant return to New York.

After the war Biddle enjoyed far-ranging naval service. In 1817 he commanded the sloop *Ontario* on a diplomatic mission to reclaim the Oregon Territory for the United States. In 1823, as commodore of the Mediterranean squadron, he concluded an important commercial treaty with the Ottoman Empire. The following year he ventured to Pensacola, Florida, with Lewis WARRINGTON to select a site for the new navy yard to be constructed there. In 1838 he gained appointment as governor of the Philadelphia Naval Asylum and there introduced the first course of instruction for midshipmen. Biddle also argued strenuously for the creation of a national naval academy.

After 1842 Biddle became closely associated with activities of the East India Squadron, and in 1845 he negotiated the first-ever U.S. treaty with China. He also attempted to open diplomatic relations with the Tokugawa shogunate in Japan but was rebuffed. His last command was of the Pacific Squadron off California during the initial stages of the MEXICAN-AMERICAN WAR in 1846. One of the most adept sailor-diplomats of his generation, Biddle died at Philadelphia on 1 October 1848.

See also NAVY, U.S.; WAR OF 1812, NAVAL OVERVIEW.

Further reading: Henson, Curtis T. *Commissioners and Commodores: The East India Squadron and American Diplomacy in China.* University: University of Alabama Press, 1982; Long, David F. *Sailor-Diplomat: A Biography of Commodore James Biddle, 1783–1848.* Boston: Northeastern University Press, 1983.

— John C. Fredriksen

Biddle, Nicholas (1750–1778) *Continental navy officer*
Born on 10 September 1750 at Philadelphia, Nicholas Biddle entered the merchant marine service at age 13. In

1770 he joined the British navy and served for three years on an Arctic expedition with the Royal Geographic Society under Captain Constantine John Phipps.

Returning to America in August 1775, Biddle took command of the *Franklin*, a riverboat fitted out by Pennsylvania to defend the Delaware River. In December Congress commissioned Biddle as one of five captains in the Continental navy. Biddle took command of the brig *Andrew Doria* (14 guns) and took part in the raid on New Providence Island in the Bahamas in February 1776.

Biddle then sailed the North Atlantic, capturing two British armed transports and several other vessels. In June 1776 he received command of the new frigate *Randolph* (32). In February 1777 Biddle set out for Martinique but was forced to put into Charleston, South Carolina, to make repairs.

On 12 February 1778 Biddle left Charleston for the West Indies with the *Randolph* and four ships of the South Carolina state navy: the ship-rigged *General Moultrie* (18) and brigs *Notre Dame* (16), *Polly* (14), and *Fair American* (14). On the evening of 7 March this small squadron encountered British ship of the line *Yarmouth* (64). Biddle did not hesitate to engage the far more powerful British ship. During the ensuing fight Biddle was wounded in the leg by a musket ball, but he had a chair brought on deck and had his wound dressed there, refusing to yield command. The *Randolph* fired more rapidly than the British ship and inflicted damage with its 12-pounders on the *Yarmouth*, but about 20 minutes into the fight the *Randolph* suddenly blew up. The four remaining American ships promptly scattered in the night.

On 12 March the *Yarmouth*, in the same vicinity, picked up four men in the water on a crude raft formed of debris. The other 311 crewmen of the *Randolph* had all perished. The cause of the explosion was never determined. James Fenimore Cooper wrote of Biddle, "For so short a career, scarcely any other had been so brilliant."

See also AMERICAN REVOLUTIONARY WAR, NAVAL OVERVIEW.

Further reading: Allen, Gardner W. *A Naval History of the American Revolution.* Reprint, New York: Russell and Russell, 1962; Cooper, J. Fenimore. *History of the Navy of the United States.* New York: Putnam, 1856; Miller, Nathan. *Sea of Glory: The Continental Navy Fights for Independence, 1775–1783.* New York: David McKay, 1974.

— Ryan M. Blake

Big Hole River, Battle of (9–10 August 1877) *Major engagement of Nez Perce War*
Following the June 1877 Battle of WHITE BIRD CANYON, the Nez Perce bands moved eastward into the Bitterroot

Mountains; a large army column led by Brigadier General Oliver O. HOWARD followed. After a major fight on the CLEARWATER RIVER, Nez Perce leaders opted to cross the Bitterroots and move onto the great buffalo range, where they hoped to find sanctuary among the Crow; if need be, they could press on and join SITTING BULL's people across the Canadian border. Some 800 men, women, and children climbed the difficult Lolo Trail into Montana and moved up the Bitterroot Valley. They crossed the Continental Divide on 6 August and descended into the Big Hole River Basin. Here, Chief Looking Glass insisted that they stop for much-needed rest. JOSEPH and other leaders protested, but Looking Glass held firm. The people erected lodges and began to enjoy their first real respite in almost a month.

Meanwhile, the army increased the pressure. At Missoula, Colonel John GIBBON, commander of the District of Montana, assembled a second pursuit force—six woefully depleted companies of his 7th Infantry, consisting of 15 officers and 146 enlisted men (later augmented by 45 volunteers). Gibbon loaded his foot soldiers in wagons and on 4 August followed the Nez Perce up the Bitterroot Valley.

Before dawn on 9 August Gibbon attacked the Big Hole camp. Concentrated rifle fire pelted the lodges, sending surprised men, women, and children scrambling for the nearby woods. Most of the Nez Perce casualties occurred during the opening volleys. Within 20 minutes Gibbon's men had control of the camp, but Looking Glass and White Bird rallied their warriors and directed a well-organized response from covered positions surrounding the village.

Gibbon, wounded in the thigh, was forced to withdraw to the wooded slope from which the attack had begun. Nez Perce warriors held the soldiers in place for most of two days while surviving family members gathered their belongings and resumed their now epic journey. During the night of 10 August the warriors disappeared, joining the others in flight. The following day Howard arrived with the lead elements of his column.

Two officers, 22 enlisted men, and six civilians had been killed; five officers, 30 enlisted men, and four civilians had been wounded. Gibbon's command inflicted much heavier casualties on the Nez Perce. The soldiers counted 89 bodies, many of whom were women and children; the Nez Perce had again thwarted the army, but they had paid a heavy price. As a result, Looking Glass, who had advocated the rest stop, lost much of his influence. The Nez Perce moved south and then east into Yellowstone National Park before turning northward toward Canada. They would fight two more large engagements and numerous smaller actions before being halted in October by a force under Colonel Nelson MILES just short of the border.

See also AMERICAN INDIAN WARS, OVERVIEW; CANYON CREEK, BATTLE OF; INDIAN WARFARE; NEZ PERCE WAR.

Further reading: Beal, Merril D. *"I Will Fight No More Forever": Chief Joseph and the Nez Perce War.* Seattle: University of Washington Press, 1963; Johnston, Terry C. *Lay the Mountains Low: The Flight of the Nez Perce from Idaho and the Battle of the Big Hole, August 9–10, 1877.* New York: St. Martin's Press, 2000; Lavender, David. *Let Me Be Free: The Nez Perce Tragedy.* New York: Harper-Collins, 1992.

— Todd Rodriguez

Billings, John Shaw (1838–1913) *Military surgeon, bibliographer, librarian, and leader in American medicine*

Born on 12 April 1838 in Cotton Township, Indiana, John Shaw Billings was the son of a small businessman and farmer. He gave up his part of his inheritance in return for his father's paying for his college education. Billings earned his B.A. from Miami University in 1857.

Billings put himself through medical school, graduating from the University Medical College of Ohio in 1860. He then became a lecturer of anatomy and student of surgery at the same institution. In July 1862 he signed on in the Union army as an assistant surgeon with the rank of first lieutenant. As surgeon and later medical inspector, he participated in the Battles of CHANCELLORSVILLE, GETTYSBURG, the WILDERNESS, SPOTSYLVANIA COURTHOUSE, COLD HARBOR, and the opening of the siege of PETERSBURG.

In December 1864 Billings was assigned to the surgeon general's office in recognition of his service; he would remain there until 1895. After the Civil War he wrote reports on army barracks and hospitals (1870). In 1875 his proposals for reform of the Marine Hospital Service led to notable improvements in the organization and discipline of this forerunner of the Public Health Service. Of great use to researchers was his *Index Catalogue* of 1880. Prior to that, in 1879, with Robert Fletcher, he had started the *Index Medicus*, a guide to contemporary medical literature. He also was instrumental in the building of Johns Hopkins Hospital, acting as medical adviser, providing sketches for the architect, and solving problems of ventilation and heating. He also helped to set up the New York Public Library, securing $5.2 million from Andrew Carnegie to build 65 branch libraries.

Billings retired from the army in 1895 with the rank of lieutenant colonel. He died at New York City on 11 March 1913.

See also CIVIL WAR, LAND OVERVIEW; MEDICINE, MILITARY.

Further reading: Billings, John D. *Selected Papers.* Chicago: National Library Association, 1965; Chapman, Carleton B. *Order out of Chaos: John Shaw Billings and*

America's Coming of Age. Boston: Boston Medical Library, 1994; Lyndenberg, Henry M. *John Shaw Billings.* Chicago: First Gregg, 1972.

— Alhaji S. Bnagura

Bismarck Sea, Battle of (2–3 March 1943) *World War II naval battle; the first example of land-based aircraft completely destroying a major naval force*

As General Douglas MACARTHUR's troops fought to expel the Japanese from New Guinea, it fell to the Army Air Forces to interdict Japanese resupply efforts. When Major General George C. KENNEY assumed command of the Fifth Air Force in August 1942, he found many of his units operating obsolescent aircraft and using ineffective tactics. Fifth Air Force quickly devised two important new techniques. First was the development of skip-bombing, in which medium bombers attacked Japanese ships from low altitude and literally "skipped" bombs into the sides of their targets. Second, crews installed additional forward-firing .50-caliber machine guns on medium bombers to sink small vessels and suppress antiaircraft fire.

In January 1943, Allied forces undertook a major offensive along the New Guinea coast. In response, the Japanese began to send convoys across the Bismarck Sea from their base at Rabaul, on New Britain Island. On the night of 28 February 1943, a large Japanese naval force of eight transports, seven destroyers, and the special service vessel *Nojima* left Rabaul carrying 6,900 troops of the 51st Division bound for Lae, New Guinea. Kenney knew of the Japanese activity through signal intelligence and reconnaissance flights. On 1 March an American B-24 reported first contact. The next day B-17s attacked the convoy, sinking a transport and damaging the *Nojima.* Two Japanese destroyers saved approximately 850 men and rushed ahead to Lae, returning to the convoy the next day.

On 3 March the largest Allied air force yet seen in the theater assembled to attack the Japanese when the convoy came within range of the medium bombers. At 10 A.M. B-17s bombed the convoy to disrupt its formation. Soon thereafter, Australian Beaufighters followed by heavily armed B-25s and A-20s attacked the convoy from low altitude, while P-38s engaged Japanese escort fighters. Out of 47 bombs dropped by the attackers, 28 reportedly found their targets. Allied aircrafts repeated their assault that afternoon. By the end of the day, all of the transports and three destroyers had been sunk. A fourth destroyer was heavily damaged and sunk by Allied aircraft the next day.

Over the next few days, aircraft and PT BOATS patrolled the area, strafing and bombing survivors. This action was taken to prevent any Japanese troops from reaching land, where they would pose a threat, since they refused to surrender. Additionally, the Allies sought retribution for

Japanese pilots who had machine-gunned an American crew parachuting from their stricken B-17. In all, the Japanese lost 12 vessels and more than 3,000 men. MacArthur later described the victory as "the decisive aerial engagement" in the Southwest Pacific theater.

See also AIRCRAFT, FIXED-WING; WORLD WAR II, U.S. INVOLVEMENT, PACIFIC.

Further reading: Craven, Wesley Frank, and James Lea Cate, eds *The Army Air Forces in World War II.* Vol. 4, *The Pacific: Guadalcanal to Saipan, August 1942 to July 1944.* Washington D.C.: Office of Air Force History, 1983; McAulay, Lex. *Battle of the Bismarck Sea.* New York: St. Martin's Press, 1991; Null, Gary. *The U.S. Army Air Forces in World War II. Weapon of Denial: Air Power and the Battle for New Guinea.* Washington, D.C.: Air Force History and Museum Programs, 1995.

— Rodney Madison

Black Hawk (Makataimesh-Ekiakiak) (1776–1838) *Chief of the Sauk and Fox tribes, who in 1832 led the last Indian war against the United States in the Old Northwest*

Born in Illinois in 1767, Black Hawk became a fierce opponent of white settlement. Rejecting the 1804 treaty by which other Sauk and Fox leaders had ceded 50 million acres of land in southern Wisconsin and northern Illinois, Black Hawk led the so-called British band of Sauk and Fox, which joined the British against the United States during the WAR OF 1812.

While his main tribal rival, Keokuk, led the majority of Sauk and Fox across the Mississippi as white settlement increased in the late 1820s, Black Hawk attempted to organize resistance. In 1831 he tried to enlist the Winnebago and Potawatomi as allies and traveled to Fort Malden (near Detroit) to seek aid from the British. Rumors of Black Hawk's actions prompted Illinois governor John Reynolds to dispatch militiamen toward Black Hawk's camp on Rock Island, forcing him and his band to cross the Mississippi in late June.

On 6 April 1832, however, Black Hawk led approximately 500 mounted warriors and 500 women and children back into Illinois in hopes of returning peacefully to their traditional lands, but Reynolds immediately dispatched 1,600 militiamen to stop this "invasion." On 14 May Black Hawk sent a truce party to Major Isaiah Stillman's camp near the juncture of Sycamore Creek and the Rock River. When Stillman's 300 militiamen seized three of his envoys and killed two, Black Hawk attacked and with just 40 warriors caused the militia to flee in panic.

Although "Stillman's Run" was an Indian victory, it ended any prospect of peace, as it led Reynolds to call for 2,000 more volunteers and the U.S. War Department to dispatch nine companies of regulars under brevet Major General Winfield SCOTT in late June. In the ensuing campaign, such future political and military figures as Abraham LINCOLN, Zachary TAYLOR, Jefferson DAVIS, Albert Sidney JOHNSTON, and Joseph E. JOHNSTON saw action.

Although some of Black Hawk's warriors, joined by renegade Potawatomi and Winnebago, killed more than 200 white settlers in the aftermath of Stillman's Run, Black Hawk recognized that the odds were insurmountable and attempted to retreat back to the Mississippi. After passing Lake Koshkonong and making his way through the Four Lakes region, Black Hawk was confronted on 21 July 1832 by Brigadier General James D. Henry's regulars near present-day Madison, Wisconsin. In the Battle of Wisconsin Heights, between 30 to 90 of his warriors were killed. His people dying of starvation, Black Hawk retreated to the juncture of the Bad Axe and Mississippi Rivers, where in the Battle of Bad Axe on 2 August some 150 warriors and 150 women and children perished as they attempted to cross the Mississippi. Black Hawk escaped, but only 150 of the original 1,000 members of his band remained. Captured on 25 August near the Wisconsin Dells, Black Hawk was held hostage to ensure that the Sauk and Fox complied with the terms of the Treaty of Fort Armstrong (21 September 1832), by which they ceded approximately one-fifth of present-day Iowa.

Taken to Washington and New York in 1833, Black Hawk created a popular sensation. He then returned to live in Keokuk's village on the Des Moines River, where he died on 3 October 1838. His corpse was disinterred by whites and put on display in Burlington, Iowa, until the museum housing it burned in 1855.

See also AMERICAN INDIAN WARS, OVERVIEW.

Further reading: Eby. Cecil D. *"That Disgraceful Affair": The Black Hawk War.* New York: Norton, 1973; Nichols, Roger L. *Black Hawk and the Warrior's Path.* Arlington Heights, Ill.: H. Davidson, 1992; Prucha, Francis Paul. *The Sword of the Republic: The United States Army on the Frontier, 1783–1846.* Bloomington: Indiana University Press, 1977.

— Justin D. Murphy

Bladensburg, Battle of (24 August 1814) *Decisive War of 1812 battle fought between the British forces advancing on Washington, D.C., and hastily organized U.S. forces attempting to depend the capital*

The British navy, supported by strong elements of the Royal Marines and the British army, controlled the waters of Chesapeake Bay in 1813 and 1814. They conducted a series of waterborne raids against coastal towns along the Chesapeake and its tributary rivers. Although American commanders knew a strong raid was imminent, the place to be attacked was unknown. Rear Admiral Sir George Cockburn wanted to strike directly at Washington. Other British commanders were considering attacks on Annapolis and Baltimore, which they believed would be easier from the land than by sea. British forces under Major General John Ross landed at Benedict, Maryland, on 19 and 20 August, forcing the destruction by the Americans of the small Chesapeake Flotilla, under the command of Commodore Joshua BARNEY.

Brigadier General William Winder, commander of the U.S. Tenth Military District, correctly believed that the cities of Baltimore, Washington, and Annapolis were all possible targets. However, neither Winder nor Secretary of War John ARMSTRONG made any concerted attempt to defend the capitol. Winder decided to spread his force of some 6,000 militia and 500 regulars to cover all three cities. The American force, although numerically superior to the British invasion force of 4,500 men, was no match for "Wellington's Invincibles."

The British were successful in misleading the Americans as to their actual objective. Winder realized that Washington was the true target only after learning on 24 August that the British were marching on Bladensburg. He gathered his forces on the west bank of the eastern branch of the Potomac River, opposite Bladensburg, and centered it on the road leading from the Bladensburg bridge to Washington. Winder was soon joined by Commodore Barney and his 500 flotillamen and 120 U.S. Marines from the Washington Navy Yard, who had brought two 18-pounder and three 12-pounder naval guns mounted on carriages. Unfortunately for Winder, Secretary of State James Monroe took it upon himself to rearrange some of the infantry lines.

The British force arrived at Bladensburg on the afternoon of 24 August and immediately struck the Americans' first line. The quickness of the British thrust and the use of Congreve rockets caused the American lines to melt away. Secretary Monroe's alterations of the troop deployments had created gaps in the lines. The retreat of the first line became a rout that affected the second line as well. Soon the entire army was in flight, in what became known as "the Bladensburg Races." Barney's artillerymen and the marines were the last to leave the field, after pouring a heavy fire into the British ranks. A wounded Barney was captured by the British as they overran the guns.

In less than three hours the battle was over. The Americans had suffered approximately 160 men killed, wounded, and captured. The British suffered 249 casualties. The rout left Washington open; it was taken by the British the following day.

See also MILITIA, ORGANIZATION AND ROLE OF; WAR OF 1812, LAND OVERVIEW; WASHINGTON, D.C., BURNING OF.

Further reading: Mahon, John K. *The War of 1812.* Gainesville: University of Florida Press, 1972; Norton,

Louis Arthur. *Joshua Barney: Hero of the Revolution and 1812.* Annapolis, Md.: Naval Institute Press, 2000; Pitch, Anthony S. *The Burning of Washington: The British Invasion of 1814.* Annapolis, Md.: Naval Institute Press, 1998.

— Michael J. Manning

Blakeley, Johnston (1781–1814) *U.S. naval officer during the War of 1812*

Born on 11 October 1781 in Seaford, County Down, Ireland, Johnston Blakeley came to the United States in 1783 with his parents, who settled in Wilmington, North Carolina. Blakeley briefly studied at the University of North Carolina but in February 1800, on the death of his father, left school and joined the navy as a midshipman. His early service was marked by long deployments and considerable action against the Barbary pirates.

Promoted to lieutenant in February 1807, Blakeley in 1811 received his first command, the schooner *Enterprise.* Promoted to master commandant in July 1813, he captured the British navy schooner *Fly* on 20 August 1813. After receiving command of the new ship-rigged sloop *Wasp* (22 guns), in May 1814 he managed to elude British blockaders and sailed from Portsmouth, New Hampshire, for the English Channel.

On 28 June Blakeley fell in with the British brig *Reindeer* (21), under Williams Manners. Their ferocious 19-minute battle left the British ship sinking and Manners dead. The British sustained 25 dead and 42 wounded. The *Wasp* lost only five killed and 21 wounded.

After the battle, Blakeley sailed for France to resupply and treat his wounded. On 27 August he returned to the English Channel and quickly captured two British ships. On 1 September he sighted a British convoy escorted by a 74-gun ship of the line. Taking advantage of his ship's speed, Blakeley cut out a British supply ship laden with military stores. Later that day, he spotted four vessels and sailed toward them; soon the *Wasp* engaged HMS *Avon* (18) in a fight that lasted nearly three hours. The battle left the British ship sinking. Blakeley's crew suffered two dead. He maneuvered to engage the next ship, but it fired, moved away, and went to the aid of the *Avon,* allowing the *Wasp* to escape.

Blakeley continued his raiding, and by October he had captured or destroyed a total of 14 merchant ships and two warships. Britain's commercial loss alone was estimated at £200,000, a staggering amount. The *Wasp* was last heard from on 19 October, when Blakeley sent a prize crew home on a captured British merchant ship. A Dutch ship reported seeing the *Wasp* heading south along the French coast; a heavily damaged British frigate later reported a night battle with an unidentified American ship that then disappeared. The fate of the *Wasp* is unknown.

Blakeley was certainly one of the most intrepid and successful of U.S. naval officers. Congress voted him a gold medal and posthumous promotion to captain to date from November 1814.

See also TRIPOLITAN WAR; WAR OF 1812, NAVAL OVERVIEW.

Further reading: Barnes, James. *Naval Actions of the War of 1812.* New York: Harper & Brothers, 1898; Duffy, Stephen W. H. *Captain Blakeley and the Wasp.* Annapolis, Md.: Naval Institute Press, 2001.

— Patrick R. Jennings

Bliss, Tasker H. (1853–1930) *U.S. Army general*

Born on 31 December 1853 at Lewisburg, Pennsylvania, one of 13 children, Tasker Howard Bliss graduated eighth in his class in 1875 from the U.S. Military Academy at WEST POINT. A linguist and dedicated scholar, Bliss won early recognition as a military theorist. Much of his career was spent teaching, including four years at West Point in the late 1870s and three more years at the Naval War College in Newport in the late 1880s. From 1903 to 1905 he was the founding president of the new Army War College, establishing its basic curriculum.

Tours in academe alternated with assignments that reflected the growth and modernization of the turn-of-the-century U.S. military. As military attaché to Spain in 1898, Bliss was present in Madrid when the United States declared war upon Spain. After the war he undertook assignments in America's new colonial possessions, serving with benevolent if firm paternalism as chief collector of customs in Cuba from 1899 to 1902 and as military governor of the Philippine Moro Province (1906–08). As a member of Secretary of War Elihu ROOT's general staff in the early 1900s and president of the Army War College, he played an integral part in early efforts to establish a professional U.S. Army with a general staff based upon the German model.

Promoted to major general in 1915, Bliss became assistant chief of staff of the army, serving under his West Point classmate Hugh L. SCOTT. Upon Scott's retirement, for three months in late 1917 Bliss was chief of staff in his own right. In April 1917 the United States entered the First World War, and Bliss bore much of the responsibility for the vast expansion of the U.S. armed forces consequent upon the decision to send the AMERICAN EXPEDITIONARY FORCE (AEF) to Western Europe.

In late 1917 Bliss was appointed the U.S. permanent military representative on the Supreme War Council, newly established to coordinate the Allied war effort. In this role, his moderation and common sense won general respect. In late 1918, immediately after Bliss retired, President Woodrow WILSON appointed him as one of the five

U.S. plenipotentiary peace commissioners at the Paris Peace Conference, although the president paid little heed to Bliss or most of his colleagues.

Bliss's wartime experience and his belief that modern methods of warfare, if unchecked, would destroy Western civilization made him a passionate supporter of disarmament, the League of Nations, and the World Court. He considered the peace terms imposed upon Germany overly harsh and supported their revision.

As governor of the Soldiers Home in Washington from 1920 to 1927, Bliss worked actively for internationalist causes, especially disarmament, and staunchly supported the newly created Council on Foreign Relations. He died on 9 November 1930 in Washington, D.C.

See also ARMY, U.S.; BAKER, NEWTON D.; EDUCATION, HIGHER MILITARY SCHOOLS; NATIONAL DEFENSE ACT; PARIS, PEACE SETTLEMENT OF; SPANISH-AMERICAN WAR.

Further reading: Palmer, Frederick. *Bliss, Peacemaker: The Life and Letters of General Tasker Howard Bliss.* Reprint, Freeport, N.Y.: Books for Libraries Press, 1970 [1934]. Thompson, Wayne Wray. "Governors of the Moro Province: Wood, Bliss, and Pershing in the Southern Philippines, 1903–1913." Unpublished doctoral dissertation, University of California at San Diego, 1975; Wainright, John D. "Root versus Bliss: The Shaping of the Army War College." *Parameters* 4, no. 1 (March 1974): 52–65.

— Priscilla Roberts

Bloody Ridge, Battle of (18 August–5 September 1951) *Sanguinary Korean War battle, so named by American soldiers because of their high casualties in taking this group of peaks*
The ridge was the highest part of the "Iron Triangle," located in the mountains of central Korea. Bloody Ridge was about 30 miles east of Kumhwa, the southeastern point of the Iron Triangle, and some five miles south of what became known as HEARTBREAK RIDGE.

From west to east, Bloody Ridge included Hills 983, 940, and 773. On 12 August 1951 the U.S. 2d Infantry Division, with attached Republic of Korea (ROK) units, was ordered to seize Bloody Ridge, then Heartbreak Ridge. Communist forces on Bloody Ridge were directing artillery fire onto the United Nations Command main supply route.

Bloody Ridge was defended by North Korean People's Army troops dug into well-built bunkers protected by thick minefields. The ROK 36th Regiment took most of the ridge on 23 August after five days of hard, often hand-to-hand fighting, but it lost Hill 983 and the ground between it and Hill 940 to a fierce North Korean counterattack.

On 30 August the U.S. 9th Infantry Regiment of the 2nd Division counterattacked, but by the end of the day Communist forces still controlled the ridge. Early on the 31 August the 9th captured Hill 773.

Heavy rain throughout the period of fighting on Bloody Ridge turned roads and trails into thick, deep mud. This impeded attacks and hampered the resupply of forward units and the evacuation of casualties. The combined efforts of rear-area personnel and Korean civilian porters were needed to bring forward supplies, which had to be carried up the steep, winding, rain-slick trails to the front.

UN aircraft, artillery, and tanks pounded the Communist troops, who remained protected in their bunkers until U.S. or ROK infantrymen approached. The Communist troops then moved out into firing positions and cut attackers down with automatic weapons and hand grenades. Mounting casualties eroded morale in the ROK 36th, and on 27 August some of its men broke and ran, panicking men of the nearby U.S. 9th Infantry.

Although attacks were now spread across the corps front in an attempt to reduce Communist resistance, by 3 September the 9th Infantry had failed to dislodge their enemy. On 4 and 5 September the 23d and 38th Regiments of the 2d Division executed a double envelopment of Bloody Ridge, while the 9th attacked the ridge itself. By 2 P.M. on the 4 September, the 9th had taken Hill 940. Communist troops fled to escape the trap, leaving behind more than 500 dead and a considerable amount of supplies. The broadening of the attack over the corps front, coupled with heavy losses, caused the North Koreans finally to yield Bloody Ridge.

UN casualties in the three weeks of fighting had exceeded 2,700 men, most from the 2d Division. There were 1,389 confirmed Communist dead and estimated enemy total casualties of 15,000. Much worse lay ahead for both sides on Heartbreak Ridge.

See also KOREAN WAR.

Further reading: Blair, Clay. *The Forgotten War: America in Korea, 1950–1953.* New York: Times Books, 1987; Hermes, Walter G. *Truce Tent and Fighting Front.* Washington, D.C.: Office of the Chief of Military History, 1966.

— Uzal W. Ent

Blue Jacket (Weh-yah-pih-erh-sehn-wah) (1740s/50s–1810) *Shawnee war chief in the Ohio Territory*
His early life is obscure, but Blue Jacket was probably born in the late 1740s or early 1750s. Although there is no known proof, legend has it that he was a young white man by the name of Marmaduke van Swearingen, taken, possibly voluntarily, by a war party in his teenage years. Whatever his origins, he grew into a very adept warrior and war chief for the tribes of the Ohio Territory.

Blue Jacket established himself as a warrior of some distinction on the frontier during the American Revolutionary War. He was a member of a sizable 1778 raiding party that attacked a salt-gathering party in northern Kentucky and took several white prisoners, including the already famous Daniel BOONE. Boone is supposed to have feigned friendliness to the Indian cause before escaping to warn the Kentucky settlements of the imminent attack by the hostiles who had captured him.

Blue Jacket himself was taken captive 10 years later but also escaped. He spent many years raiding settlements in the areas that became the states of Ohio and Kentucky, always displaying a ferocity that belied any possible blood ties to the whites. He was known to kill settlers with no warning or mercy, even after capture. (At the time this was not unusual behavior for either side.)

In the 1790s Indians from several tribes and bands joined under the leadership of the Miami war chief LITTLE TURTLE to execute well-planned and organized attacks against U.S. forces sent by President George WASHINGTON to tame and secure the Ohio Territory. Blue Jacket's abilities and military prowess earned him a position as a subchief in his Shawnee band. He participated in the defeat of forces led into the territory by Lieutenant Colonel Josiah HARMAR in 1790 and in the ambush and destruction of an even larger force under Arthur ST. CLAIR, territorial governor of Ohio. After these two campaigns, Little Turtle refused to fight any more and came close to advocating peace with the white men.

Although Blue Jacket was a fine warrior and respected subchief, he proved incapable of replacing Little Turtle as war chief, especially as the new American leader he was to face, Major General "Mad" Anthony WAYNE, had been selected for his aggressiveness and competence. In addition, Blue Jacket was to face a much better organized force, which had spent almost two years training for its fighting debut under Wayne. Abandoned by his British allies, faced with an enemy of skill and foresight, Blue Jacket and his forces were routed on 20 August 1794 in the Battle of FALLEN TIMBERS, on the Maumee River near present-day Toledo, Ohio. After the battle, Blue Jacket lost his leadership role and was not a player in the peace talks that led to the signing of the Treaty of Greenville. Blue Jacket lived out the remainder of his life in relative peace; he died in 1810.

See also AMERICAN INDIAN WARS, OVERVIEW; AMERICAN REVOLUTIONARY WAR, LAND OVERVIEW; INDIAN WARFARE.

Further reading: Eckert, Allan W. *Blue Jacket: War Chief of the Shawnees.* Dayton, Ohio: Landfall, 1969; Sugden John. *Blue Jacket: Warrior of the Shawnees.* Lincoln: University of Nebraska Press, 2000.

— Lawyn C. Edwards

Blue Licks, Battle of (19 August 1782) *Devastating rout of Kentucky militia by a multiethnic Indian army during the American Revolutionary War*

The Franco-American victory at YORKTOWN in 1781 had little effect on the chronic warfare on America's frontiers. Wyandot, Ottawa, Shawnee, Delaware, Miami, Mingo, and other Native peoples continued to fight against American settlers intruding on their hunting and agricultural grounds in Kentucky and the Ohio Valley.

With British and Loyalist support from Canada and Fort Detroit, the Indians frequently sent expeditions against fortified American settlements. In August 1782, loyalist officers William Caldwell, Simon Girty, and Alexander McKee, along with Butler's Rangers, accompanied a force of several hundred Indian warriors against Bryan's Station in Kentucky. Unable to capture the fort but suspecting that its Kentucky militia defenders would pursue them, the British and Indians feigned a retreat and conspicuously marked their route.

Daniel BOONE, John Todd, Stephen Trigg, and Hugh McGary, who commanded the 182 Kentucky militia, debated whether to pursue or to wait for reinforcements from Colonel Benjamin Logan. Members of a culture in which hesitation was equated with a lack of manhood and bravery, the Kentuckians decided to pursue. They easily followed the Indians' trail to the south bank of the Licking River opposite Lower Blue Licks, a salt spring. The officers held a council on the morning of 19 August.

Spotting a group of Indians on the river's north bank, Boone, who was intimately familiar with the area, saw an ambush in the making. He favored dividing the militia and flanking the enemy force by crossing upstream. Hugh McGary, smarting from accusations of timidity, impetuously urged an immediate attack on the Indians. The Kentuckians followed McGary, forded the river, formed into three columns, and advanced to the crest of a rocky ridge. Hidden in deep ravines in the woods, the Indians and British sounded their war cries, fired a devastating volley into the Kentuckians, and attacked the right column. Within 15 minutes they had surrounded, collapsed, and routed the entire force; brutal hand-to-hand fighting took place. The surviving militiamen fled back across the Licking.

The Kentuckians had lost 77 killed out of a total of 182 engaged, including Colonels Todd and Trigg. Daniel Boone managed to escape but lost his son Israel. In the panic that followed the disaster, many Kentucky colonists fled eastward across the mountains. Other Kentuckians later returned to the battlefields to bury the bloated corpses of their comrades.

When Britain and the United States signed a preliminary peace in November 1782, the Indian nations seemed to be winning the war on the frontier. In October and

November 1782, George Rogers CLARK organized an invasion of Ohio Indian towns. His forces failed to defeat the Shawnees or their allies but did destroy and burn Shawnee towns, crops, and possessions. Although called the last battle of the American Revolution, Blue Licks was in fact one of many battles that the French, British, Americans, and Indians fought between 1754 and 1814 for possession of the Ohio Valley and Great Lakes.

See also AMERICAN REVOLUTIONARY WAR, LAND OVERVIEW; AMERICAN INDIAN WARS, OVERVIEW; BLUE JACKET; BRANT, JOSEPH; DUNMORE'S WAR; FALLEN TIMBERS, BATTLE OF; HARMAR'S EXPEDITION; HARRISON, WILLIAM HENRY; INDIAN WARFARE; LITTLE TURTLE; PARIS, TREATY OF (30 NOVEMBER 1782); ST. CLAIR'S EXPEDITION; TECUMSEH; TENSKWATAWA; TIPPECANOE, BATTLE OF; VINCENNES, BATTLE OF; WAYNE, ANTHONY.

Further reading: Calloway, Colin G. *The American Revolution in Indian Country: Crisis and Diversity in Native American Communities.* Cambridge, U.K.: Cambridge University Press, 1995; Faragher, John Mack. *Daniel Boone: The Life and Legend of an American Pioneer.* New York: Henry Holt, 1992. Wilson, Samuel M. *Battle of the Blue Licks, August 19, 1782.* Lexington, Ky.: n.p., 1927.

— David L. Preston

Bong, Richard I. (1920–1945) *U.S. Air Force officer and America's ace of aces*
Born on 24 September 1920 at Superior, Wisconsin, Richard Ira Bong enrolled at Superior State Teachers College in 1938. There he received civil aeronautical training and earned his private pilot's license. In May 1941 Bong joined the Army Air Corps Aviation Cadet program, receiving his wings in January 1942.

While training in the P-38 "Lightning," Bong caught the attention of Brigadier General George C. KENNEY, soon to be commander of Fifth Air Force and General Douglas MACARTHUR's air commander in the Southwest Pacific. Kenney picked the second lieutenant to fly a P-38 under his command.

In September 1942, Bong reported to the 49th Fighter Group, stationed in New Guinea. While waiting for his unit's planes to arrive, Bong temporarily transferred to the 35th Fighter Group, operating out of Port Moresby, New Guinea. On 27 December, he shot down his first two Japanese planes, and on 8 January 1943 he became an ace (with his fifth kill). In February he returned to the 49th and by November had shot down 21 Japanese aircraft, this at a time when American pilots were facing some of Japan's best pilots.

In January 1944, on his return to the Fifth Air Force from leave in the United States, Bong joined the headquarters operations staff. Allowed to "freelance," over the next 10 weeks Bong shot down seven more Japanese aircraft, eclipsing Eddie RICKENBACKER's U.S. record of 26 victories on 12 April.

At the urging of the commander of the U.S. Army Air Forces, General Henry "Hap" ARNOLD, Kenney promoted Bong to major and sent him home on a public relations tour. In September 1944 Bong returned to the Fifth Air Force as a "gunnery instructor" for new pilots. Between 10 October and 16 December, he shot down 12 more Japanese planes. Kenney recommended Bong for the Medal of Honor, and General MacArthur presented the award to Bong on 12 December at Tacloben airfield.

In late December, Kenney, fearful that Bong might be shot down, sent him home. Bong by that time had 40 victories, 200 combat missions, and 500 combat hours. He then flew as a test pilot for the P-80 "Shooting Star," America's first jet fighter. On 6 August 1945, in a test flight, Bong's P-80 malfunctioned shortly after takeoff and crashed. Bong bailed out, but he was too low for his parachute to deploy fully and was killed.

See also AIRCRAFT, FIXED-WING; AIR FORCE, U.S.; WORLD WAR II, U.S. INVOLVEMENT, PACIFIC.

Further reading: Bong, Carl, and Mike O'Connor. *Ace of Aces: The Dick Bong Story.* Mesa, Ariz.: Champlin Fighter Museum Press, 1985. Kenney, General George C. *Dick Bong: Ace of Aces.* New York: Duell, Sloan, and Pearce, 1960; Sweeney, James B. *Famous Aviators of World War II.* New York: Franklin Watts, 1987.

— William Head

Bonhomme Richard*, USS, v. HMS *Serapis (23 September 1779) *Naval engagement of the American Revolutionary War, one of the most heralded in U.S. Navy annals*
Commanding the *Bonhomme Richard* (44 guns) and six smaller ships, Commodore John Paul JONES departed France on 14 August 1779 to raid British coastal cities and shipping in British waters. Several French privateers soon departed, leaving Jones with the *Bonhomme Richard;* the Continental navy frigate *Alliance* (36), with French captain Pierre Landais and an American crew; the French frigate *Pallas* (32); and French brig *Vengeance* (12). Following several captures, on 23 September they sighted a British convoy of 41 merchant ships off Flamborough Head, escorted by British frigate *Serapis* (44) and sloop *Countess of Scarborough* (20). Jones decided to attack. He closed with the *Serapis*, and the battle opened about 7:15 P.M. Captain Richard Pearson of the *Serapis* got off the first broadside. A sanguinary struggle ensued, with both ships holed on the first exchange of broadsides. The smaller ships

Engagement between the *Bonhomme Richard* and the *Serapis*, 23 September 1779   *(Naval Historical Foundation)*

on each side also fought; *Countess of Scarborough* struck to the *Pallas*. One of the unexplained aspects of the battle is that Captain Landais of the *Alliance* fired indiscriminately into both the *Bonhomme Richard* as well as the *Serapis*.

Jones soon recognized that he was outmatched. The *Serapis*, rated as a frigate, was actually a small two-decker. It carried a more powerful armament and boasted a copper-sheathed bottom, giving it greater speed and maneuverability. Then, early in the engagement, one—possibly two—of the *Bonhomme Richard*'s old 18-pounders blew up, possibly from being double-shotted, killing many of the crew and blowing out part of the ship's side. Jones ordered the other 18-pounders abandoned, leaving him only 12-pounders against British 18-pounders.

The two ships became entangled, and Jones had grapples thrown, lashing the vessels together. Both were soon flaming wrecks. At one point Pearson shouted to Jones asking if he wished to strike his colors. Jones replied, "No, I'll sink, but I'll be damned if I will strike!" That has come down in history as "I have not yet begun to fight!"

Sailors and French marines on the *Bonhomme Richard* killed most of the topside crew of the *Serapis* with small arms, while the cannon on both ships fired literally muzzle to muzzle. Finally, a crewman on the *Bonhomme Richard* succeeded in throwing a grenade down a hatch on the *Serapis*, detonating powder bags and killing at least 20 men. At 10:30 P.M., with his mainmast in danger of falling, Pearson struck.

The three-and-a-half-hour battle had cost Jones 150 casualties out of 322 men and Pearson approximately 130 out of 284. The *Bonhomme Richard* sank two days later from battle damage; Jones nursed the *Serapis* back to France as a prize.

The victory made Jones a hero in France and the United states. It also provided an example of leadership and bravery under fire that has been celebrated by the U.S. Navy ever since.

See also AMERICAN REVOLUTIONARY WAR, NAVAL OVERVIEW; DALE, RICHARD.

Further reading: Boudriot, Jean. *John Paul Jones and the* Bonhomme Richard. Translated by David H. Roberts. Annapolis, Md.: Naval Institute Press, 1987; Schaeper, Thomas J. *John Paul Jones and the Battle off Flamborough Head: A Reconsideration.* New York: Peter Lang, 1990; Walsh, John E. *Night on Fire: The First Complete Account of John Paul Jones's Greatest Battle.* New York: McGraw-Hill, 1978.

— Lance Janda and Spencer C. Tucker

Bonus Army (28 July 1932) *Dispersal of World War I veterans gathered in Washington, D.C., during the Great Depression to demand early payment of bonuses for wartime service*

From May to July 1932, as the Great Depression steadily intensified, between 12,000 and 20,000 unemployed World War I veterans converged on the nation's capital to lobby Congress to pass a bill mandating early payment of the adjusted compensation, or bonuses, for war service that under legislation passed in 1924 they were to receive in 1945. The previous year Congress had approved legislation allowing veterans to borrow sums up to a maximum of 50 percent of such compensation at favorable rates of interest, but many veterans still hoped to received early payment in full.

The protestors were led by Walter W. Waters, who for several weeks maintained near-military discipline and a pervasive patriotic atmosphere among his followers, expelling communist agitators. Although local police authorities provided some limited quarters, most protestors lived in flimsy shacks and hovels that they constructed around Washington, concentrated in a shantytown in the swampy Anacostia Flats section. Inevitably problems related to food, shelter, and sanitation arose, which the summer heat and humidity intensified.

In mid-June Congress, conscious that federal tax receipts were falling drastically, narrowly defeated the bonus bill. Lacking any other objective, for several weeks the disappointed veterans remained in Washington, making frequent appearances on the Capitol grounds. In late July the veterans were ordered to evacuate Washington. Most did so, but between 2,000 and 5,000 ignored the instructions and remained at the Anacostia camp. An initial police effort to remove them resulted in the deaths of two veterans and two police officers, whereupon the Washington municipal administration sought assistance from federal authorities. President Herbert Hoover and Secretary of War Patrick J. Hurley responded by ordering the Army Chief of Staff General Douglas MACARTHUR to disperse the protestors.

On 18 July 1932 MacArthur and his aide, Dwight D. EISENHOWER, accompanied four troops of cavalry, led by Brigadier General Perry L. Miles, to Anacostia. The troopers swept through the encampment with drawn sabers. They were followed by infantry with fixed bayonets, machine guns, tear gas, and tanks. The troops drove out the veterans and burned the shantytown to the ground. In the mêlée one veteran and a baby were killed, and more than 100 protestors, one soldier, and one policeman were wounded. To many, the use of military troops against largely unarmed former soldiers symbolized both the Hoover administration's inability to cope with the crisis presented by the Great Depression and its perceived absence of sympathy with the often desperate circumstances of average Americans.

By contrast, when a second Bonus Army assembled in Washington in May 1933, shortly after Franklin D. ROOSEVELT assumed power, its members were warmly welcomed by Eleanor, the new president's wife, and Louis Howe, his assistant. Congress still refused to pass bonus legislation, but under presidential urging it established various relief agencies, including the Civilian Conservation Corps, the programs of which provided work for many former veterans. In 1936 Congress passed a bill licensing early disbursement of almost $2.5. billion in veterans' benefits. At the end of World War II and subsequent wars Congress would prove far more generous with benefits to veterans, through the GI Bill of Rights.

Further reading: Lisio, Donald J. *The President and Protest: Hoover, MacArthur, and the Bonus Riot.* 2d ed. New York: Fordham University Press, 1994; Schlesinger, Arthur M., Jr. *The Crisis of the Old Order.* Boston: Houghton Mifflin, 1957. Waters, Walter W. *B.E.F.: The Whole Story of the Bonus Army.* New York: John Day, 1933.

— Priscilla Roberts

Boone, Daniel (1734–1820) *Frontiersman and militia officer*

Born on 2 November 1734 in Berks County, Pennsylvania, Daniel Boone moved with his family in 1750 to the Yadkin River on the North Carolina frontier. Boone's first military experience was in 1755 during the FRENCH AND INDIAN WAR, with British Major General Edward BRADDOCK's expedition to seize FORT DUQUESNE. Serving as a militia wagon driver and blacksmith, he escaped the debacle of the Battle of the MONONGAHELA.

In the autumn of 1767 Boone and a small party followed the Warrior's Path over the Appalachian Mountains through the Cumberland Gap into Kentucky. He then spent several years exploring. In 1773 Boone was leading a group of settlers to Kentucky when it came under Indian attack. Boone's eldest son, James, was among those killed; the settlers returned home.

In 1774 Boone served in DUNSMORE'S WAR. The next year he helped to build the Wilderness Road and later that year built Fort Boonesborough, where he moved his family. On 14 July 1776, Boone's daughter Jemima and two friends were kidnapped by Indians just outside Fort Boonesborough. Two days later Boone led a surprise attack that rescued the three young women unharmed.

On 7 February 1778, Boone himself was captured by a band of Shawnee Indians. They forced him to run the gauntlet, but his courage so impressed Chief Blackfish that he was adopted into the tribe as a Shawnee brave and Blackfish's son. Months later Boone learned that the British had incited an Indian attack on Boonesborough. He escaped and covered 160 miles through the wilderness in four days to warn of the attack.

In early September Chief Blackfish and more than 400 braves surrounded Boonesborough. Boone's leadership inspired the 60 men and boys to resist nine days of continuous attacks. Later Boone was acquitted in a court-martial of charges related to his relationship with the Shawnee.

In 1782, Kentucky militia pursued a band of Indians into the Blue Licks region against Boone's advice. The Battle of BLUE LICKS was a disaster and claimed the life of Boone's son Israel. In 1799, impoverished by lawsuits arising from defective land titles, Boone moved to Missouri at the invitation of the Spanish governor. He died in St. Charles County, Missouri, on 26 September 1820. In 1845 his and his wife's remains were moved to Frankfort, Kentucky.

See also AMERICAN INDIAN WARS, OVERVIEW; BLUE JACKET; BLUE LICKS, BATTLE OF.

Further reading: Bakeless, John E. *Daniel Boone.* New York: William Morris, 1939; Lafaro Michael. *The Life and Adventures of Daniel Boone.* Lexington: University of Kentucky Press, 1978.

— A. J. L. Waskey

Boston, siege of (19 April 1775–17 March 1776)

American Revolutionary War military operation
On 19 April 1775, fighting occurred between British troops and colonial militia in the Battles of LEXINGTON AND CONCORD, beginning the war. Militia from Massachusetts and other New England colonies then converged on Boston. From late May some 16,000 militia formed the "Army of Observation," so called in order that the colonies would not appear to be waging war against the Crown. This indifferently armed and poorly supplied force was loosely organized, but most commanders recognized the authority of Massachusetts major general of militia Artemeus Ward.

In May, the British commander and captain general of Massachusetts, Thomas Gage, received reinforcements, along with Major Generals William Howe, John Burgoyne, and Henry Clinton. Patriots in Boston asked Gage for permission to leave the city; he agreed, insisting only that they hand over their weapons. Some 9,000 to 10,000 Bostonians then departed the city.

Anxious to occupy the high ground around Boston and to demonstrate resolve, Gage decided to send troops to Charlestown on 18 June. This information became generally known, and Patriot forces entered Charlestown Neck on the night of 16 June and fortified both Bunker Hill and Breed's Hill. Gage ordered an attack against these positions on the afternoon of 17 June. In the resulting Battle of BUNKER HILL, British troops under Major General William Howe drove off the Patriot defenders but at the horrendous cost of 40 percent British casualties.

Two weeks later, General George WASHINGTON, appointed commander of the CONTINENTAL ARMY on 15 June, arrived at Boston to take command of patriot forces. An inventory revealed he had but 13,000 men, and whose enlistments would expire in December. Washington had to put together a new army. Lacking the resources to drive the British from the city or compel their surrender, he dispatched Major General Henry KNOX, his chief of artillery, to retrieve cannon from FORT TICONDEROGA, which the Patriots had taken in May. During the winter the Patriots moved some 55 guns on sledges through the snow to Boston.

On the nights of 2 and 3 March 1776, Washington surprised the British with an artillery bombardment. Then on the night of 4–5 March his troops occupied Dorchester Heights and began to emplace artillery there. With most of Boston within range of American artillery, Howe, who had replaced Gage as commander of British forces in October, realized his position was untenable. He considered an attack but, judging it too risky, decided to evacuate. The operation began on 7 March. Howe agreed not to set fire to Boston if Washington would not impede the British departure. On 17 March 1776, the Royal Navy completed the embarkation of 9,000 British troops and more than 1,000 Loyalists to Halifax, Nova Scotia. On 18 March Washington entered Boston. Two days later the rest of the army arrived, giving the Americans permanent control of the city. This ended the first phase of the war.

See also AMERICAN REVOLUTIONARY WAR, LAND OVERVIEW.

Further reading: Brooks, Victor. *The Boston Campaign: April 1775–March 1776.* Conshohocken, Pa.: Combined,

1999; Chidsey, Donald B. *The Siege of Boston: An On-the-Scene Account of the Beginning of the American Revolution.* New York: Crown, 1966; French, Allen. *The Siege of Boston.* New York: Macmillan, 1911.

— Julius A. Menzoff

Boston Massacre (5 March 1770) *Clash between the citizentry of Boston and British regulars that resulted in the death of five civilians*

Sometimes considered the first battle of the American Revolutionary War, the Boston Massacre resulted from passions aroused by the Parliament's passage of the Quartering Act of 1765, the Stamp Act of 1765, and the Townshend duties of 1767.

Prior to the FRENCH AND INDIAN WAR (1754–63), Britain maintained few regular troops in its American colonies, leaving them completely dependent on their own militia for defense. The war brought thousands of British regulars, and thereafter regular troops were garrisoned in the backcountry to prevent clashes between frontiersmen and settlers and the Indians.

These troops cost the Crown some £400,000 yearly, but London's attempts to have the colonies help pay this expense brought colonial opposition. In 1766 a plan was devised to move troops to the coast to reduce the expense of supplying them. London believed this would also increase their training and discipline. Further, it would make them available to keep unruly Americans in line; civil disorder over the Stamp Act seemed more pressing than the threat of Indian uprisings. The presence of these troops in Boston angered colonists, who saw them "moonlighting," taking jobs from Americans.

In March 1768, on the second anniversary of the repeal of the Stamp Act, a Boston mob marched on a custom commissioner's house, causing the captain general of Massachusetts, Thomas Gage, to order a regiment there. Before these troops arrived, a mob had run the customs officials out of town for the seizure of John Hancock's sloop *Liberty* for smuggling. In response, the British ordered additional troops to Boston. By November four regiments and part of a fifth were stationed in the city.

Despite the show of force, Bostonians found ways to harass customs officials and troops without breaking the law. Soldiers could not be called out to maintain order except at the request of civilian magistrates, who refused to do so. By the winter of 1769–70 the garrison in Boston had been reduced to two regiments, but many Bostonians were determined to drive the remainder out.

For several days leading up to 5 March, radical mobs attacked Loyalists. Soldiers and civilians also clashed, raising the level of resentment on both sides. Adding to the mob's bravado was the erroneous belief, encouraged by radical agitators, that the soldiers could not use force, even to defend themselves, unless requested by a civil magistrate.

On the evening of 5 March, various groups of citizens accosted soldiers. In one instance the lone sentry at the Boston Customs House, taunted by a crowd, retaliated by striking a civilian with his rifle butt. When the crowd grew to a threatening mob, throwing ice chunks and swinging clubs, a squad of seven regulars accompanied by an officer was dispatched, bayonets fixed, to rescue the sentry. Upon arrival, taunted by curses and threatened with bodily harm, the squad loaded its muskets and formed a line. The mob pressed in, daring the soldiers to fire, and someone in the crowd threw a club, striking and felling one of the soldiers. As he regained his footing the soldier discharged his weapon, sparking the others to fire as well. The crowd then dispersed. Eight civilians had been hit, including Michael Johnson (later identified as Crispus Attucks), thought to be a black man but probably part or full Natick Indian. Of the eight, five were wounded mortally.

The nine soldiers were tried for murder but were acquitted through the able defense of their attorney, John Adams, and a jury stacked with Loyalists, despite radical agitators like Samuel Adams. Under direct threat of violent uprising, the day following the massacre one regiment departed, and the second eventually withdrew to Castle Island, in Boston Harbor.

See also AMERICAN REVOLUTION, CAUSES OF.

Further reading: Jensen, Merrill. *The Founding of a Nation: A History of the American Revolution, 1763–1776.* New York: Oxford University Press, 1968; Shy, John. *A People Numerous and Armed: Reflections on the Military Struggle for American Independence.* New York: Oxford University Press, 1976; Zobel, Hiller B. *The Boston Massacre.* New York: Norton, 1970.

— Arthur T. Frame

Bouquet, Henry (1719–1765) *British army officer who excelled at wilderness warfare*

Born in 1719 at Rolle, Switzerland, Henry Bouquet continued the family practice of military service by joining as an ensign, at age 17, a Swiss mercenary regiment. Bouquet fought in the War of Austrian Succession and in 1748 became a lieutenant colonel of the Swiss Guards, who served the Dutch Prince of Orange. In 1756, during the FRENCH AND INDIAN WARS, when the British sought mercenary officers for service in North America after Major General Edward BRADDOCK's defeat in the Battle of the MONONGAHELA, Bouquet secured a commission as lieutenant colonel in the 60th Royal American Regiment (ROYAL AMERICANS).

Bouquet enjoyed service in America and liked the people and the environment. He studied Indian methods of warfare and trained his own unit in light infantry tactics, utilizing loose formations and aimed fire during skirmishes. Bouquet participated in several campaigns in which he proved a master at adapting conventional organization, training, and logistics to wilderness conditions. That knowledge proved invaluable during PONTIAC'S REBELLION in 1763.

In August 1763 Bouquet led an expedition of 600 men and a supply train through the western Pennsylvania wilderness to relieve besieged Fort Pitt. On 5 August the Indians ambushed the British column near BUSHY RUN. Although surprised, Bouquet's men held their ground then moved to a nearby hill, where they constructed a fortification with bags of flour intended for the garrison. When the Indians attacked the next day, Bouquet feigned a retreat, luring the Indians into an ambush. The ruse worked, and Bouquet achieved a costly but rare victory over the Native Americans.

In 1764 Bouquet led a successful expedition into Ohio to force the tribes to release white prisoners taken during the rebellion. In recognition of his achievements, in 1765 Bouquet was promoted to brigadier general and given command of southern British garrisons, with headquarters at Pensacola, Florida. But Bouquet soon contracted yellow fever and died there on 2 September 1765.

See also AMERICAN INDIAN WARS, OVERVIEW; INDIAN WARFARE.

Further reading: Peckham, Howard H. *Pontiac and the Indian Uprising*. Chicago: University of Chicago Press, 1961; Stevens, Sylvester K., Donald H. Kent, and Autumn L. Leonard, eds. *The Papers of Henry Bouquet*. 2 vols. Harrisburg: Pennsylvania Historical and Museum Commission, 1951–1972.

— Steven J. Rauch

Boxer Uprising (1900) *Antiforeign uprising in China, in the suppression of which U.S. forces participated*

In 1900 a xenophobic antiforeign uprising broke out in China, with the tacit complicity of conservative elements at the Manchu court, dominated by the elderly Empress Dowager Cixi. Among its triggers were China's defeat in the Sino-Japanese War of 1894–95; a subsequent scramble by the great powers for economic and political concessions from China, which appeared to prefigure the country's partition into spheres of influence; aggressive foreign missionary activity that seemed to threaten traditional family and social relations; and floods and famine in northern China. In reaction, during the late 1890s a secret society, the Righteous and Harmonious Band—whose members Westerners nicknamed "Boxers," because of a mistranslation of the final word as "fists"—appeared in Shandong Province. Demanding the expulsion of all foreigners and an end to growing external influences, the Boxers quickly gained strength and spread throughout northeastern China, attacking and often killing foreigners, including Western missionaries, businessmen, and diplomats, and their Chinese associates, in well-publicized episodes.

In the capital of Beijing (Peking), where the Boxer Uprising spread in summer 1900, U.S. minister Edwin Conger led the American community into refuge in the British legation, where many other foreign nationals likewise took shelter. They were besieged for 45 days. During the siege seven U.S. Marine guards were killed, and 14 Americans were wounded.

U.S. Secretary of State John Hay—who in 1899 had issued his first "Open Door" note, calling upon all external powers to safeguard China's political independence and refrain from carving out spheres of influence or arrogating to themselves special economic privileges within China—followed a bifurcated strategy of diplomatic persuasion and military pressure. In a second Open Door note, of 3 July 1900, Hay reiterated U.S. demands that foreign powers respect China's "territorial integrity," thereby enabling the United States to continue to represent itself as China's protector. Simultaneously, however, the United States transferred from the newly acquired Philippines a force of 2,500 troops, later increased to 5,000, as its contribution to an international relief force. The U.S. troops joined Russian, Japanese, British, and French contingents in an extraordinary effort to restore order in China and rescue the besieged nationals. This represented the first time since the YORKTOWN CAMPAIGN in the American Revolution that the United States had participated in a multinational operation.

The Chinese government declared war on the intervening powers, though some Chinese officials, including the governor of the major port city of Shanghai and its surrounding areas, refused to recognize this order and themselves suppressed the Boxers. Hay likewise refused to accept the declaration as valid, even when the dowager empress and court abandoned the capital and fled to the western city of Xian. On 14 July 1900, the international force reached and invaded the northern Chinese port of Tianjin, a Boxer stronghold. After various bloody encounters with Boxer supporters, many of whom erroneously believed that magical charms rendered them immune to foreign bullets, on 4 August the relief force moved toward Beijing, reaching the British Legation and lifting the siege on 14 August. Significant looting by the foreign troops, including the seizure and destruction of Chinese art treasures, accompanied the military action.

The Boxer Uprising helped convince foreign powers that, although unsettled, the Chinese situation was too complicated and the population insufficiently docile for partition, even as they successfully sought extraterritorial concessions in the treaty ports along China's coast. For three subsequent decades, therefore, they continued substantially to respect the Open Door principles Hay had enunciated. An international tribunal ordered China to pay the intervening powers an indemnity of $333 million in compensation for the losses their citizens had suffered and the expenses of the military relief mission. Some $42 million of this sum was awarded to the U.S. government, which accepted only $25 million, stating that this sufficed to cover all its relevant expenses. The remaining $17 million the United States, reaffirming its stance as China's firm but fair friend, returned to the Chinese government, which used the funds to finance the education of Chinese students in the United States. In subsequent years many of the beneficiaries, when they returned to their own country, helped to spread American influence within China itself.

See also CHAFFEE, ADNA R., JR.; SPANISH-AMERICAN WAR, CAUSES OF.

Further reading: Cohen, Paul A. *History in Three Keys: The Boxers as Event, Experience, and Myth.* New York:

Columbia University Press, 1998; Duiker, William J. *Cultures in Collision: The Boxer Rebellion.* San Rafael, Calif.: Presidio Press, 1978; Esherick, Joseph. *The Origins of the Boxer Uprising.* Berkeley: University of California Press, 1987; Preston, Diana. *The Boxer Rebellion: The Dramatic Story of China's War on Foreigners.* New York: Walker, 2000.

— Priscilla Roberts

Braddock, Edward (1694–1755) *British general*
Born in 1765 at Perthshire, Scotland, Edward Braddock followed his father into the Coldstream Guards in 1710. He served in Flanders during the War of Austrian Succession (1740–48) and at Gibraltar (1753) and came to be known as a politically reliable administrator and disciplinarian rather than as a strategist or tactician.

In November 1754, during the FRENCH AND INDIAN WAR (1754–63), Braddock assumed supreme command of British forces in North America. Arriving in Virginia in February 1755, Braddock ordered four offensives against the French, involving the capture of FORT DUQUESNE, FORT NIAGARA, Fort St. Frederic on Lake Champlain, and

The burial of Major General Edward Braddock *(Library of Congress)*

two forts in Nova Scotia. This ambitious plan, conceived in London, took little account of local conditions, such as difficult terrain, scarce forage, and inexperienced colonial troops. The most important error, however, concerned relations with the Indians, whom Braddock despised. His arrogant pronouncement that the Ohio Indians would be expelled from their lands after British victory led them to ally themselves with the French. Braddock also did not disguise his contempt for the English colonists, whom he regarded as entirely unsuited for military operations.

On 29 May Braddock set out for Fort Duquesne with two regiments of infantry (2,200 men) and George WASHINGTON as his aide-de-camp. Braddock chose a route from Virginia passing through dense woods and over mountains. On 9 July his advance force forded the Monongahela River, 10 miles from Fort Duquesne. In the Battle of the MONONGAHELA, French and Indian forces ambushed the British. Braddock rode about the British column to rally his men, having several horses shot from under him. He himself was finally shot in the back, whereupon his men retreated. Braddock died four days later, on 13 July, and was buried in an unmarked grave about a mile from FORT NECESSITY. Fort Duquesne did not fall to the British until 1758. Braddock's defeat in the Battle of Monongahela contributed to the false colonial belief that British tactics were not suited to American terrain or warfare.

Further reading: Anderson, Fred. *Crucible of War: The Seven Years' War and the Fate of Empire in British North America, 1754–1763.* New York: Knopf, 2000; Kopperman, Paul E. *Braddock at the Monongahela.* Pittsburgh: University of Pittsburgh Press, 1977; McCardell, Lee. *Ill-Starred General: Braddock of the Coldstream Guards.* New York: Stratford, 1958.

— James D. Perry

Bradley, Omar N. (1893–1981) *U.S. Army general, army chief of staff, and chairman of the Joint Chiefs of Staff*

Born on 12 February 1893 at Clark, Missouri, Omar Nelson Bradley graduated from the U.S. Military Academy at WEST POINT in 1915 and was commissioned in the infantry. To his great disappointment he spent World War I processing troops and did not see action in France. After the war he served in Hawaii and attended the Infantry Training School at Fort Benning, Georgia, and the General Staff School at Fort Leavenworth, Kansas. He then was an instructor at the Infantry School before graduating from the Army War College in Washington in 1934. Bradley, a natural teacher, spent 13 years of his first 23 in the army instructing—at South Dakota State College, West Point,

General Omar N. Bradley   *(Library of Congress)*

and Fort Benning. At the latter institution he impressed both his immediate superior, Major Joseph STILWELL, and assistant commandant Lieutenant Colonel George C. MARSHALL, who became army chief of staff in April 1939 and immediately requested Bradley's transfer to his personal staff.

In 1941 Marshall appointed Bradley as commandant of the Infantry School with the rank of brigadier general. Rising to major general in December 1941, Bradley took command of the 82d Division. In February 1943 Bradley was transferred to the North African theater, serving successively as aide to General Dwight D. EISENHOWER, assistant commander of II Corps under Lieutenant General George S. PATTON, Jr., and as commander of II Corps, in which capacity he remained at the successful completion of the North African campaign. Promoted to lieutenant general, in July 1943 he led II Corps in the invasion of SICILY. Appointed commander of U.S. ground forces for the forthcoming NORMANDY INVASION, Operation Overlord, in October 1943, Bradley landed in France in June 1944 and commanded Twelfth Army Group, eventually 1.3 million troops, the greatest American field command in history. It was the southern end of the sweep across France.

Calm and unassuming, Bradley became known as a "soldier's general." While his diplomatic skills had a certain emollient effect, he frequently differed with his colleague, Britain's Field Marshal Bernard C. Montgomery, who opposed Eisenhower's broad advance strategy and sought a quick knockout thrust toward Germany. Despite heavy initial American losses during the December 1944 Battle of the BULGE (Ardennes), Bradley's forces crossed the Rhine and entered Germany ahead of Montgomery, linking up with Soviet troops at the Elbe River in April 1945. Bradley had won promotion to full general the month before.

After the war Bradley headed the Veterans Administration. Appointed army chief of staff in February 1948, the following August he became the first chairman of the Joint Chiefs of Staff, and in September 1950 he won a fifth star. Controversy marked these years as U.S. defense spending expanded dramatically because of COLD WAR crises, especially the KOREAN WAR. Bradley advocated the development of the far more powerful hydrogen bomb and oversaw the implementation of the policy planning paper known as NSC-68, which recommended huge increases in American military budgets. Although Bradley supported U.S. intervention in Korea, after mainland China's late 1950 intervention in the war he opposed General Douglas MACARTHUR's efforts to extend the war to Chinese territory. He urged restraint upon the recalcitrant general and in spring 1951 supported Truman's recall of MacArthur. A firm believer in the idea that Europe and the new NATO alliance represented the first strategic priority, in 1951 Bradley famously characterized the Korean War's potential expansion into full-scale conflict with China or the Soviet Union as "the wrong war, in the wrong place, and with the wrong enemy."

In August 1953, after serving two two-year terms, Bradley retired. He strongly supported U.S. intervention in the Vietnam War and in March 1968 was one of very few senior advisers, or "wise men," to counsel President Lyndon B. JOHNSON to continue the conflict. Bradley died at Washington, D.C., on 8 April 1981.

See also CONTAINMENT, DOCTRINE AND COURSE OF; VIETNAM WAR, COURSE OF; WORLD WAR II, U.S. INVOLVEMENT, EUROPE.

Further reading: Bradley, Omar N. *A Soldier's Story.* New York: Henry Holt, 1951; Bradley, Omar N., and Clay Blair. *A General's Life.* New York: Simon and Schuster, 1983; Schnabel, James F., and Robert J. Watson. *History of the Joint Chiefs of Staff: The Joint Chiefs of Staff and National Policy.* Vol. 3, *The Korean War, 1950–1953.* Washington, D.C.: Joint Chiefs of Staff, 1998; Whiting, Charles. *Bradley.* New York: Ballantine Books, 1971.

— Priscilla Roberts

Bragg, Braxton (1817–1876) *Confederate army general*
Born on 22 March 1817 at Warrenton, North Carolina, Braxton Bragg graduated from the U.S. Military Academy at WEST POINT in 1837. Commissioned a second lieutenant in the 3d Artillery, he saw action in Florida during the SECOND SEMINOLE WAR, winning promotion to first lieutenant in 1838.

A skilled artillerist, Bragg won three brevets for gallantry and promotion to captain while serving under Major General Zachary TAYLOR during the MEXICAN-AMERICAN WAR. Hampered, however, by a quarrelsome personality and career frustrations, Bragg resigned his commission in 1856 to become a Louisiana sugar planter. With the secession crisis looming, Governor Thomas O. Moore of Louisiana tasked Bragg with organizing an army, and in January 1861 Bragg directed the capture of the Baton Rouge arsenal. Appointed major general in February, he assumed command of Louisiana state forces.

In March 1861 Bragg entered Confederate service as brigadier general and assumed command of forces at Pensacola. A gifted organizer, he drilled his soldiers into a disciplined small army. Promoted to major general and given command of the Department of Alabama and West Florida in September 1861, Bragg led his force to Corinth, Mississippi, the following spring. There he undertook the organization of General Albert Sidney JOHNSTON's army, leading a corps during the Battle of SHILOH, in which Johnston was killed. Promoted to full general shortly after the battle, in June 1862 Bragg replaced General P. G. T. BEAUREGARD as commander of the Confederacy's primary western army (later designated the Army of Tennessee) when Beauregard took an unauthorized leave of absence.

In September 1862 Bragg invaded Kentucky in conjunction with a thrust by Major General Edmund Kirby SMITH's forces from East Tennessee. Checked at PERRYVILLE, Tennessee, in October, he fell back to Murfreesboro, where he fought a bloody battle that closed 1862 and inaugurated 1863. In a subsequent campaign of maneuver, Union Major General William ROSECRANS forced Bragg from Tennessee.

Receiving reinforcements from Virginia in September 1863, Bragg's army routed but failed to destroy Rosecrans's forces in the Battle of CHICKAMAUGA. Bragg's chronic feuding with many of his top subordinates severely damaged the Army of Tennessee. Bragg besieged the Federals at CHATTANOOGA, but a new Union commander, Major General Ulysses S. GRANT, dealt Bragg a humiliating defeat, driving the Confederates from Lookout Mountain and Missionary Ridge.

Relieved of command in December 1863, Bragg became President Jefferson Davis's military advisor. In this capacity he rendered valuable service. As the war drew to a close, Bragg was ordered to North Carolina, where he failed to prevent the fall of FORT FISHER. He then served under General J. E. JOHNSTON in the final actions against Major General William T. SHERMAN's advancing Federal forces in North Carolina. Bragg fled with President Davis from Richmond on its evacuation and was captured in Georgia on 9 May 1865.

Bragg spent the last years of his life as a civil engineer in Alabama and on railroad projects in Texas. He died on 27 September 1876 at Galveston.

See also BENTONVILLE, BATTLE OF; CIVIL WAR, LAND OVERVIEW; HOOD, JOHN BELL.

Further reading: Connelly, Thomas L. *Autumn of Glory: The Army of Tennessee, 1862–1865.* Baton Rouge: Louisiana State University Press, 1971; McWhiney, Grady. *Braxton Bragg and Confederate Defeat.* Tuscaloosa: University of Alabama Press, 1991; Woodworth, Steven E. *Jefferson Davis and His Generals: The Failure of Confederate Command in the West.* Lawrence: University Press of Kansas, 1991.

— Roger W. Caraway

Brandy Station, Battle of (9 June 1863) *Civil War cavalry action*

To determine Confederate intentions following the Battle of CHANCELLORSVILLE, Major General Joseph HOOKER ordered his cavalry corps, under Brigadier General Alfred Pleasonton, to conduct a reconnaissance in force west of the Rappahannock River in Virginia, near a small town known as Brandy Station. Advancing on 8 June, Pleasonton had orders to disperse and destroy Confederate Major General Jeb STUART's cavalry, then thought to be organizing around Culpepper Courthouse in preparation for a raid northward. Stuart's cavalry had in fact been preoccupied by a series of marches in review.

On 9 June Pleasonton's 8,000 troopers, reinforced with 3,000 infantry, surprised Stuart's veteran 9,500 cavalrymen in one of the most bitter cavalry fights of the war. Pleasonton had divided his command into two bodies, hoping to double-envelop his adversary. Brigadier General John BUFORD's division crossed the Rappahannock at Beverly Ford northeast of Brandy Station, while Colonel Alfred Duffié and Brigadier General David Gregg's divisions crossed separately farther south, at Kelly's Ford.

Both fords were inadequately defended by Stuart, but Duffié's lead column became lost and thus was delayed. It then maneuvered too far west and consequently never reached Brandy Station. Duffié's error in turn delayed Gregg's move. In order to make up for lost time, Gregg left his infantry behind to secure the river ford. These mistakes cost the Federals any chance of complete success.

Despite these failings, Union forces might still have won the field but for a series of rallies led by Brigadier

Generals Wade HAMPTON and W. H. F. "Rooney" Lee, among others, that enabled Stuart to hold his ground. Stuart dealt first with Buford to the northeast of Brandy Station in the morning, then with Gregg to the south of town that afternoon. Duffié's division having failed to reach the battlefield, and with Confederate infantry threatening to join the fray, Pleasonton withdrew after a hard-fought, day-long encounter.

A tactical draw, Brandy Station is generally agreed upon as the battle that established a more confident and more effective Union cavalry. The Union cavalry had held its own against what most considered a superior opponent, at the expense of Stuart's reputation. On the other side, the Confederate cavalry had maintained the field despite its numerical inferiority and suffered fewer total casualties than the Union. Union casualties totaled 936, while the Confederates lost 523. The Federals had not crippled Stuart, nor had they identified Lee's true intentions, regardless of Pleasonton's later claims. Virtually no one credited Pleasonton for the solid Union performance, but Stuart found himself under heavy criticism for having been caught off guard.

General Robert E. LEE's second invasion of the north began after Brandy Station; Stuart screened Lee's main force as it moved toward Pennsylvania. Seeking redemption for Brandy Station, Stuart decided to raid behind the Union army, but he succeeded only in leaving Lee blind for nearly a week, thus robbing his commander of badly needed intelligence on Union troop locations.

See also CAVALRY; CIVIL WAR, LAND OVERVIEW.

Further reading: Downey, Fairfax. *Clash of Cavalry: The Battle of Brandy Station, June 9, 1863.* New York: David McKay, 1959; Longacre, Edward G. *Lincoln's Cavalrymen: A History of the Mounted Forces of the Army of the Potomac.* Mechanicsburg, Pa.: Stackpole Books, 2000; Starr, Stephen Z. *The Union Cavalry in the Civil War.* 3 vols. Baton Rouge: Louisiana State University Press, 1979–1985.

— Thomas D. Veve

Brandywine, Battle of (11 September 1777) *Closely fought American Revolutionary War battle*

Major General Sir William Howe left New York on 23 July 1777 with 13,000 British troops and landed at Head of Elk, Maryland, on 25 August, intending to march on and capture Philadelphia. The Continental army commander, General George WASHINGTON, determined to defend the seat of the revolutionary government and chose the Brandywine River, about halfway between Head of Elk and Philadelphia, as his line of defense. With 8,000 Continentals and 3,000 Pennsylvania militia, Washington hoped to hold the main road across the Brandywine, despite the difficulty of covering several other nearby crossing points as well.

With Washington's troops spread out in the wooded hills along the east side of the river, Howe divided his army into two divisions. Lieutenant General Wilhelm von Knyphausen's 5,000 troops were to feint against Washington's left and center (under Major General Nathaniel GREENE), while Howe took the remaining 8,000 troops on a long march to strike at Washington's right rear, via an unguarded ford.

Both British columns set out at dawn on 11 September. Knyphausen pushed an American covering force back across the river at Chadd's Ford but then pulled up short and commenced a cannonade. Washington, aware of Knyphausen's inactivity and later warned of Howe's approach by cavalry scouts, ordered his forces to wheel 90 degrees to cover Howe's presumed line of approach. He also began to prepare a strong counterstroke against Knyphausen's force. Unfortunately for Washington, a report arrived that led him to believe that Howe was in fact not approaching his rear. Washington therefore suspended the redeployment and called off his counterattack. Shortly thereafter, Howe's force suddenly appeared on Osborne's Hill. It was a critical moment, but Howe acted in a typically indecisive manner; he delayed, despite the fact that Continental troops under Major General John SULLIVAN were hurrying to complete the shift and reestablish a defensive line. Finally, at 4 P.M., Howe's troops, band and all, moved to the attack and exploited a gap in the hastily arranged American line. Washington previously had ordered Greene to send Brigadier General George Weedon's brigade to reinforce Sullivan, and its timely arrival prevented a rout (after a miracle march of four miles in 45 minutes). The British nevertheless succeeded in pushing the Americans off of Battle Hill after an hour and a half of intense fighting.

Meanwhile Knyphausen, who up to this point had merely maintained a light continuous pressure on Greene's position in the American center, responded to the sounds of Howe's attack by launching his own across the river. Greene's weakened division gave way and lost its artillery; Washington was forced to extricate his army and escape to the east.

Washington's force suffered more than 1,200 casualties, some 400 of whom were prisoners, while the British lost 577 killed and wounded. The defeat was not immediately disastrous, and several other actions would take place prior to Howe's occupation of Philadelphia, but the battle reflected poorly on Washington's generalship. His failure to scout the various crossing points properly had left Sullivan's right flank "in the air," and it was only through Howe's customary indecision and by dint of hard fighting that the Continentals did not suffer more severely. The Continental army's overall performance at Brandywine, however, served notice of the beginning of its transformation into a professional fighting force capable, at least some of the time and with increasing frequency, of trading fire with British regulars.

See also AMERICAN REVOLUTIONARY WAR, LAND OVERVIEW.

Further reading: Middlekauff, Robert. *The Glorious Cause: The American Revolution, 1763–1789.* New York: Oxford University Press, 1982; Smith, Samuel S. *The Battle of Brandywine.* Monmouth Beach, N.J.: Philip Freneau, 1976.

— Wayne E. Lee

Brant, Joseph (Thayendanegea) (1743–1807)
Mohawk leader

Born in 1743, probably in March, Joseph Thayendanegea gained an education and, in English eyes, a name from his stepfather Brant, the sachem of Fort Hunter. Joseph Brant began military service in the FRENCH AND INDIAN WAR, seeing action with British Major General James Abercromby, Colonels John Bradstreet and Sir William JOHNSON, and Major General Jeffrey Amherst. After briefly attending Reverend Eleazer Wheelock's school for Native Americans in Connecticut, Brant served Indian superintendents Sir William and Guy Johnson as messenger/envoy to the Iroquois and he fought for the British during PONIAC'S REBELLION.

With the outbreak of the AMERICAN REVOLUTIONARY WAR, Brant sided with the English, participating in Major General Sir William Howe's assault on New York and distinguishing himself in the Battle of LONG ISLAND. Unable to persuade the Iroquois to abandon their neutrality officially, Brant led individual warriors as well as Loyalists. Moving down the Mohawk River with Lieutenant Colonel Barry St. Leger to rendezvous with Major General John Burgoyne, Brant attacked Major General Nicholas HERKIMER's militia and Iroquois volunteers in the 6 August 1777 BATTLE OF ORISKANY, preventing them from reinforcing FORT STANWIX and shattering the Iroquois Confederacy.

In 1778 Brant was ordered to direct war parties along the frontier and gather supplies for Loyalist forces. Falsely blamed for every raid along the frontier, Brant had no part in the June 1777 "Wyoming Massacre," and he generally tried to prevent the killing of Loyalists, women, and children. However, too few to halt Major General John SULLIVAN's force at Newton, Brant and his fellow warriors and Loyalists avenged the destruction of Iroquoia by burning New York settlements. While on a mission to strengthen Iroquois relations with the Ohio nations and reignite their loyalty to the

British, in 1781 Brant attacked and captured Colonel Alexander Lochry's boats that were carrying supplies to Brigadier General George Rogers CLARK's forces on the Ohio River.

Angered at the 1783 peace settlement, Brant maintained that the British had betrayed the Native Americans by giving land they did not own to the United States. Never a chief, Brant's ability and his marriage to Mohawk headwoman Catherine Croghan made him a spokesman for his people. The governor general of Quebec, Frederick Haldimand, granted Brant's request for the Grand River Reserve in Ontario for the Mohawks, and Lord Sydney agreed to compensate the Six Nations for their losses. In the Grand Councils at Sandusky (1783) and Detroit (1786), Brant urged native unity in all negotiations with Americans and Europeans and a halt to expansion through Native control of water routes westward. Brant failed in his long diplomatic effort to negotiate peace between the northwestern nations and the United States because of British interference and declining Iroquois influence. Brant died near Brantford, Ontario, on 24 November 1807.

See also AMERICAN INDIAN WARS, OVERVIEW; AMERICAN REVOLUTIONARY WAR, LAND OVERVIEW.

Further reading: Chalmers, Harvey. *Joseph Brant, Mohawk.* East Lansing: Michigan State University Press, 1955; Graymont, Barbara. *The Iroquois in the American Revolution.* Syracuse, N.Y.: Syracuse University Press, 1972; Kelsay, Isabel Thompson. *Joseph Brant, 1743–1807: Man of Two Worlds.* Syracuse, N.Y.: Syracuse University Press, 1984.

— Michèle T. Butts

Breckinridge, John C. (1821–1875) *Confederate general and secretary of war*
Born on 16 January 1821 at Lexington, Kentucky, into a prominent family, John Cabell Breckinridge elected a career in law and politics. A militia major in the MEXICAN-AMERICAN WAR, he experienced a meteoric career, serving in the U.S. Congress and then, at age 35, as the youngest vice president in U.S. history, under President James Buchanan. Nominated in 1860 for the presidency by the breakaway Democrats of the Deep South, Breckinridge carried 11 slave states (although not Kentucky), despite his belief that slavery was a doomed institution.

Named to the U.S. Senate in March 1861, Breckinridge publicly denounced the outbreak of the Civil War as "unnatural" and "horrible." But fearing the Union military government of Kentucky, Breckinridge resigned his Senate seat in October 1861 and cast his lot with the Confederacy. Despite his slender military experience, he received a commission as brigadier general in November. Indicted as a traitor by the U.S. district court in Frankfort, he was formally expelled from the U.S. Senate in December 1861.

Breckinridge first saw action at SHILOH, where he commanded the Reserve Corps. His creditable performance in that battle led to his promotion to major general in April 1862. In August he failed in an attempt to retake Baton Rouge and then headed briefly the Department and Army of Middle Tennessee. Returning to the Army of Tennessee just in time for the Battle of STONES RIVER, Breckinridge quarreled with General Braxton BRAGG over that commander's misuse of Kentucky troops.

Breckinridge next joined General Joseph E. JOHNSTON for the VICKSBURG campaign and then led divisions at CHICKAMAUGA and Missionary Ridge. Ordered to the eastern theater, the Kentuckian saw frequent action on such fields as New Market, COLD HARBOR, and Monocacy. On 6 February 1865 Breckinridge was named the Confederacy's sixth and last secretary of war. As the South collapsed, he used his influence to avert a guerrilla war and to bring about an honorable surrender.

Still under indictment for treason, Breckinridge escaped to Cuba. He moved from there to Europe and finally to Canada, where he learned of his pardon. Returning to Kentucky in 1869, he spoke out against the Ku Klux Klan and for sectional healing. Exhausted by the war, he died on 17 May 1875 at Lexington.

Breckinridge must be judged one of the more successful "political" generals of the war on either side. Personally courageous and a quick study, he gave his all for a cause that he saw as doomed to failure.

See also CHATTANOOGA, BATTLE OF; CIVIL WAR, LAND OVERVIEW.

Further reading: Davis, William C. *Breckinridge: Statesman, Soldier, Symbol.* Baton Rouge: Louisiana State University Press, 1974; Heck, Frank H. *Proud Kentuckian: John C. Breckinridge.* Lexington: University Press of Kentucky, 1976.

— Malcolm Muir, Jr.

Brereton, Lewis H. (1890–1967) *U.S. Army Air Force general*
Born on 21 June 1890 at Pittsburgh, Pennsylvania, Lewis Hyde Brereton graduated from the U.S. Naval Academy at Annapolis in 1911. Within months of his graduation, he resigned his commission in the U.S. Navy and was commissioned in the U.S. Army Coast Artillery Corps. After a year's service he transferred, in September 1912, to the Aviation Section, U.S. Army Signal Corps, and qualified as a pilot in March 1913.

During World War I, Brereton commanded the 12th Aero Squadron and saw a significant amount of combat.

Upon his return to the United States in February 1919, he became the chief of the Operations Division in the office of the director of Air Service in Washington, D.C. In December 1919 he returned to France for duty as air attaché at the U.S. embassy in Paris. In August 1922 Brereton was assigned to Kelly Field, Texas, where he served successively as commanding officer of the 10th School Group and as assistant commandant of the Advanced Flying School.

In September 1924 Brereton became an instructor at the Air Corps Tactical School at Langley Field, Virginia, and in June of the following year became commanding officer of the 2d Bombardment Group, also at Langley Field. In June 1927, after graduating from the Command and General Staff School at Fort Leavenworth, Kansas, he was posted to Fort Sill, Oklahoma, where he became the commanding officer of the 88th Observation Squadron and an instructor at the Field Artillery School. Transferred to Panama in August 1931, Brereton commanded the 6th Composite Group. Promoted to lieutenant colonel in 1935, he was an instructor at the Command and General Staff school. Promoted to temporary brigadier general in 1940, Brereton commanded the 17th Bombardment Wing at Savannah, Georgia, and in 1941, as a major general, the Third Air Force at Tampa, Florida.

In November 1941 Brereton took command of the Far East Air Force in the Philippines Islands. Following the Japanese attack on PEARL HARBOR, Brereton wanted to strike Formosa, but General Douglas MACARTHUR refused permission, and as a consequence much of Brereton's force of modern P-40 fighters and B-17 bombers was destroyed on the ground. In January 1942 Brereton was reassigned as commander of the Fifth Air Force. After organizing and commanding the Tenth Air Force in India from March to June 1942, Brereton became the commander of the Middle East Air Force, later designated the Ninth Air Force. In October 1943 he took command of the Ninth Air Force in the European theater of operations (ETO). In August 1944, as a lieutenant general, he was assigned to command the First Allied Airborne Army and served in the ETO until the surrender of Germany in May 1945.

Brereton returned to the United States and in July 1945 resumed command of the Third Air Force at Tampa, Florida. In January 1946 he became the commander of the First Air Force at Mitchell Field, New York, but within a month he was reassigned to the office of the secretary of war. In July 1947, he was assigned to the Military Liaison Committee of the Atomic Energy Commission. He retired from the air force, to which he had transferred in 1947, as a lieutenant general in 1948. Brereton died in Washington, D.C., on 19 July 1967.

See also AIR FORCE, U.S.; ARMY AIR CORPS; STRATEGIC BOMBING; WORLD WAR II, U.S. INVOLVEMENT, EUROPE; WORLD WAR II, U.S. INVOLVEMENT, PACIFIC.

Further reading: Brereton, Lewis H. *Brereton Diaries.* New York: William Morrow, 1946; Crave, Wesley F., and James L. Cate. *Army Air Forces in World War II.* Chicago: University of Chicago Press, 1948.
—— Alexander M. Bielakowski

Brooke, John M. (1826–1906) *Confederate naval officer and ordnance designer*

Born on 18 December 1826 at Fort Brooke, the site of present-day Tampa, Florida, John Mercer Brooke entered the U.S. Navy in 1841 as a midshipman and graduated from the U.S. Naval Academy at Annapolis in 1847. Promoted to lieutenant in 1855, Brooke early showed an interest in science and invention, including deep-sea sounding leads that eventually made possible the laying of a transatlantic cable. Later he participated in and led exploring expeditions of the North Pacific and Japan.

Brooke resigned his commission on 20 April 1861, following the secession of Virginia. He was commissioned a lieutenant in the Virginia state navy three days later and entered the Confederate navy on 2 May. In June the Confederate secretary of the navy, Stephen MALLORY, transferred Brooke to the naval ordnance office. Here he supervised construction of the guns and armor for the ironclad CSS VIRGINIA. Brooke also was responsible for its slanting armor casemate, which became standard in other Confederate ironclads. Promoted to commander in September 1862, Brooke in March 1863 was named chief of the Bureau of Ordnance and Hydrography, a position he held until the end of the war.

Despite a lack of experience in this area, Brooke designed a variety of heavy guns for the Confederacy. These included eight-, nine-, 10-, and 11-inch smoothbores and 6.4-, seven-, and eight-inch rifled guns. His rifled guns were probably the finest in the war, on either side. These, and some smoothbores, were similar to the U.S. Parrott rifles in having their breech reinforced with wrought-iron bands. Some Brooke rifles had as many as three bands. The Brooke shell had a copper sabot featuring ratchets that expanded inside the cannon bore. The ratcheted copper sabot reduced vibrations that caused premature explosions.

After the war Brooke joined the Virginia Military Institute as a professor, teaching there from 1865 to 1899 and establishing its physics program. He died at Lexington, Virginia, on 14 December 1906.

See also NAVAL ORDNANCE.

Further reading: Brooke, George M., Jr. *John M. Brooke: Naval Scientist and Educator.* Charlottesville: University Press of Virginia, 1980; Olmstead, Edwin, Wayne Stark, and Spencer Tucker. *The Big Guns. Civil War Siege, Seacoast* *and Naval Cannon.* Alexandria Bay, N.Y.: Museum Restoration Service, 1997; Still, William N., ed. *The Confederate Navy: The Ships, Men and Organization, 1861–1865.* Annapolis, Md.: Naval Institute Press, 1997; Luraghi, Raimondo. *A History of the Confederate Navy.* Annapolis, Md.: Naval Institute Press, 1997.

— Colin P. Mahle

Brown, George S. (1918–1978) *U.S. Air Force general and chairman of the Joint Chiefs of Staff*

Born on 17 August 1918 in Montclair, New Jersey, George Scratchley Brown attended the University of Missouri for a year before receiving an appointment to the U.S. Military Academy at WEST POINT, where he graduated in 1941.

Brown attended flying school at Pine Bluff, Arkansas, and Kelly Field, Texas. During World War II he flew B-24s in the 344th and 329th Bombardment Squadrons (1941–42), the 93d Bombardment Group in Libya (1943–44), and the 2d Bombardment Division in England (1944–45), all with Eighth Air Force. Promoted to major in February 1943, Brown distinguished himself in the August 1943 air raid on PLOESTI, Romania. In September 1943 he was promoted to lieutenant colonel and in October 1944 to colonel.

In 1950 Brown took command of the 62d Troop Carrier Group, McChord Air Force Base, Washington, where he was involved in the airlift of men and supplies to Korea. In 1951 he made the transition to fighters, taking command of the 56th Fighter Interceptor Wing, Selfridge Air Force Base, Michigan. He then became director of operations for the Fifth Air Force in Korea (1952–53). In 1953 Brown took command of the 3525th Pilot Training Wing at Williams Air Force Base, Arizona, before attending the National War College during 1956–57.

Brown was then executive assistant to the chief of staff of the air force, General Thomas D. White. In 1959 he became military assistant to Secretary of Defense Thomas S. Gates, Jr., and later to Robert S. MCNAMARA. In June 1959 Brown was promoted to brigadier general.

Promoted to major general in 1963, Brown commanded the Eastern Transport Air Force at McGuire Air Force Base, New Jersey. In 1964 he took command of Joint Task Force Two, a weapon systems test unit at Sandia Air Force Base, New Mexico. Promoted to lieutenant general in 1966, Brown became assistant to Chairman of the Joint Chiefs of Staff General Earle WHEELER. Promoted a full general in 1968, Brown took command of Seventh Air Force. In 1970 he became commander of the Air Force Systems Command.

In 1973 Brown was named chairman of the Joint Chiefs of Staff, only the second air force officer to hold that position. His confirmation hearings led to discussion of Seventh Air Force's role in the secret bombing of Cambodia during the VIETNAM WAR. As chairman, Brown cut the staff by some 20 percent. Later he again came under fire for comments he had made about Jewish influence in banking and the press. George Brown died at Washington, D.C., on 5 December 1978 from cancer.

See also AIR FORCE, U.S.

Further reading: Edgar F. Puryear. *George S. Brown, General, U.S. Air Force: Destined for Stars.* Novato, Calif.: Presidio, 1983.

— Michael L. Butterfield

Brown, Jacob J. (1775–1828) *U.S. Army general, and its first to hold the title of general in chief*

Born on 9 May 1775 in Bucks County, Pennsylvania, Jacob Jennings Brown taught school for three years in New Jersey, surveyed land in Ohio, studied law, and briefly served as Alexander HAMILTON's military secretary in 1799 during the war scare caused by the QUASI-WAR with France. Brown then moved to upstate New York and became a successful businessman. His growing political influence led to his appointment as commander of the local militia regiment. In 1811 he was made a brigadier general of militia.

Charged with protecting part of the northern New York frontier when the War of 1812 began, Brown successfully

Major General Jacob Brown. An engraving by P. Maverick of a painting by J. Jarvis *(Naval Historical Foundation)*

defended Ogdenburg from a British attack on 4 October 1812. On 29 May 1813 Brown led a mixed force of regulars and militia in defending SACKETT'S HARBOR against a larger British force. In recognition of his services, Brown became a brigadier general in the regular army. He was a brigade commander in Major General James WILKINSON's disastrous campaign against Montreal that November and acquitted himself well.

On 24 January 1814, Brown was promoted to major general and given command of New York's western frontier. Assisted by able Brigadier Generals Winfield SCOTT and E. W. RIPLEY, Brown organized his troops, which were the best trained and led of this conflict. On the night of 2–3 July, Brown led his force across the Niagara River and took FORT ERIE without firing a shot. Moving north, Scott's brigade defeated the British in the Battle of CHIPPEWA River on 5 July. Deciding to remain in Canada despite the absence of naval support, Brown then fought a larger British force to a draw in the hard-fought Battle of LUNDY'S LANE on 25 July. Wounded in the battle, Brown was evacuated.

Brown's force then retreated back to FORT ERIE, which was successfully defended against a British assault on 15 August. After recovering from his wounds, Brown orchestrated a sortie on 17 September and surprised the British and caused them to abandon the siege. Brown then requested support to pursue the British, but his superior, Major General George IZARD, refused, and the army went into winter quarters after destroying Fort Erie. Brown replaced Izard in late 1814, but the war ended before he could begin a spring campaign in 1815.

After the war Brown was named commander of the Northern Division of the army. On 10 March 1821 he became general in chief of the army, holding that position until his death at Washington, D.C., on 24 February 1828.

See also WAR OF 1812, LAND OVERVIEW.

Further reading: Cruikshank, Ernest. *Documentary History of the Campaigns upon the Niagara Frontier in 1813 and 1814.* 9 vols. Welland, Ont.: Lundy's Lane Historical Society, n.d.; Mahon, John K. *The War of 1812.* Gainesville: University of Florida Press, 1972; Morris, John D. *Sword of the Border: Major General Jacob Jennings Brown, 1775–1828.* Kent, Ohio: Kent State University Press, 2000.
— J. W. Thacker

Browning, John M. (1855–1926) *Pioneering gunmaker and manufacturer*

Born on 23 January 1855 in Ogden, Utah, John Moses Browning learned gunsmithing at an early age in his father's gun shop. He and his brothers took over the business on their father's death in 1879. They utilized steam power to run tools and Browning's innovative techniques to connect foot-powered equipment to steam.

Designing firearms brought out Browning's inventive genius. In 1883 he patented his first breech-loading, single-shot rifle. Although the weapon sold well, Browning did not have resources for wider distribution or manufacture, so he sold to the Winchester Repeating Arms Company the manufacturing rights. This allowed Browning to focus more on new designs and less on production.

Browning continued to design guns for Winchester in his Ogden shop. Several went into mass production, but many were never available for public sale. The designs represented Browning's flair for experimentation, always based on practicality. His best-known guns from the Winchester period include the Winchester Model 1886 lever-action repeating rifle, the Model 1887 lever-action repeating shotgun, and the Model 1887 pump-action shotgun.

Browning's next design breakthrough involved an automatic shotgun, in which expanding gases of the fired shell were harnessed to reload the gun and ready it for the next shot. Although the test gun worked, Browning was unable to reach a satisfactory arrangement with Winchester for its production. Browning then turned to a new Belgian gun manufacturer, Fabrique National de Belgique. This firm mass-produced Browning's automatic shotguns, which became popular for hunting across Europe. Remington later produced the design in the United States.

Browning applied his gas-operation theory to the new concept of the MACHINE GUN. His gas-operated machine guns were purchased by both Colt and the U.S. government. The most famous of these included the Cold Model 1895 Peacemaker machine gun and the Browning automatic rifle (BAR).

Browning also experimented with and designed pistols. His innovations in automatic pistols included the enclosing slide and gas-operated mechanisms. Automatic pistols designed by Browning include the Colt M-1911 Government model .45 and the Fabrique National Browning P-35 Model 9 mm.

Browning died on 26 November 1926 at the Fabrique National factory, at Liège, Belgium. His weapons and designs greatly influenced gun making and warfare throughout the 20th century.

See also COLT, SAMUEL; GATLIN, RICHARD J.; MAXIM, HIRAM S.; SMALL ARMS PISTOLS; SMALL ARMS RIFLES; THOMPSON, JOHN T.

Further reading: Browning, John, and Curt Gentry. *John Moses Browning: American Gunmaker.* Garden City, N.J.: Doubleday, 1964; Ellis, John. *The Social History of the Machine Gun.* New York: Pantheon, 1975.
— William Thomas Allison

Buchanan, Franklin (1800–1874) *U.S. Navy captain and admiral of the Confederate States navy*

Born on 17 September 1800 at Auchentorlie, near Baltimore, Maryland, to a prominent physician and his wife, Franklin Buchanan attended local schools until he was 16, when he received a commission as a midshipman in the U.S. Navy. After serving with Oliver Hazard PERRY, he made cruises in the Mediterranean, China, and West Indies. Promoted to lieutenant in 1825 and to commander in 1841, he was appointed superintendent of the new U.S. Naval Academy at Annapolis, in 1845. He designed its curriculum and drafted its system of discipline.

During the MEXICAN-AMERICAN WAR Buchanan obtained command of a 20-gun sloop and helped capture VERACRUZ. He commanded the flagship during Matthew C. PERRY's expedition to Japan in 1853–54. Promoted to captain, he next commanded the Washington Navy Yard.

Believing that Maryland would secede from the Union when the Civil War began, Buchanan resigned his commission. When the state did not secede, he sought to regain the commission but was rebuffed by Secretary of the Navy Gideon WELLES. In August 1861, therefore, he

Captain Franklin Buchanan, CSS   *(Naval Historical Foundation)*

went to Richmond, Virginia, and offered his services to the Confederacy.

Granted the same grade he had enjoyed in the Union navy, Buchanan worked first on Virginia's coastal and river defenses and then as chief personnel detailer in the Navy Department, in which post he billeted persons on the basis of their ability rather than seniority. He also contributed to naval policy, compiled the Confederate navy's regulations, and advised Secretary of the Navy Stephen R. MALLORY.

On 24 February 1862, Mallory promoted Buchanan to flag officer (rear admiral) and placed him in charge of all Confederate ships on the James River. The principal warship in the aggressive Buchanan's command was the ironclad CSS *VIRGINIA*. With it, Buchanan planned to destroy Union blockading ships in Hampton Roads. On 8 March 1862 he sank the frigate *Cumberland.* He also forced the frigate *Congress* to surrender, but wounded in the thigh by a rifle bullet fired from the shore, he ordered the ship burned in reprisal. His wound, however, forced him to yield command to Lieutenant Catesby ap Roger JONES, and on the next day he was unable to participate in the pivotal battle of the *MONITOR* v. the *VIRGINIA.*

Confirmed by the Confederate Congress as an admiral on 21 August 1862, Buchanan was the highest-ranking naval officer in the South. New orders of September sent him to command forces in Mobile Bay, Alabama. When he finally obtained an ironclad ship, the *Tennessee,* in early 1864, he planned to destroy the blockading Union fleet. Instead, in the Battle of MOBILE BAY, Federal forces led by Admiral David G. FARRAGUT entered the bay, destroyed his small ships, and disabled the *Tennessee.* Wounded and captured in the fight, Buchanan was taken to a Northern prison and was not exchanged until February 1865. Returning after the war to his home state, he served for a year as president of the Maryland Agricultural College—later the University of Maryland. He died at his home in Talbot County, Maryland, on 11 May 1874.

See also CIVIL WAR, NAVAL OVERVIEW; IRONCLADS, CONFEDERATE, IN THE CIVIL WAR.

Further reading: Durkin, Joseph F. *Stephen R. Mallory: Confederate Navy Chief.* Chapel Hill: University of North Carolina Press, 1954; Lewis, Charles Lee. *Admiral Franklin Buchanan: Fearless Man of Action.* Baltimore: Norman, Remington, 1929; Luraghi, Raimondo. *A History of the Confederate Navy.* Trans. from the Italian by Paolo E. Coletta. Annapolis, Md.: Naval Institute Press, 1996; Symonds, Craig L. *Confederate Admiral: The Life and Wars of Franklin Buchanan.* Annapolis, Md.: Naval Institute Press, 1999.

— Paolo E. Coletta

Bucher, Lloyd (Mark) ("Pete") (1929–) *U.S. Navy commander*

Born on 1 September 1929 at Pocatello, Idaho, and orphaned as an infant, Lloyd Bucher moved between his adoptive family in Idaho and relatives in California until 1938 when he was placed in the St. Joseph's Children's Home in Culdesac, Idaho. He attended Boys Town near Omaha, Nebraska, from 1941 to 1945 but left to serve two years in the navy on the refrigerated stores ship USS *Zelima* (AF 49). He then returned to Boys Town, graduating in 1948. He later earned a degree in geology from the University of Nebraska.

In June 1953 Bucher was commissioned in the naval reserve and went on active duty. He served as a submarine officer in Submarine Flotilla 7 but in May 1967 took command of a surface ship, the *Pueblo,* a small 179-foot transport vessel transformed into a NATIONAL SECURITY AGENCY (NSA) vessel.

Promoted to commander in December 1967, Bucher took the *Pueblo* to sea. On 23 January 1968, the *Pueblo* was 15 miles off the North Korean coast when it was attacked by North Korean torpedo boats and MiG aircraft and was captured. It was the first U.S. naval ship taken at sea by a foreign power in more than 150 years.

The Koreans towed the *Pueblo* into port and took Bucher and his crew to Pyongyang. The captives were then interrogated, tortured, forced to read North Korean propaganda, and threatened with execution. Bucher also was forced to write letters in which he stated that the *Pueblo* was spying in North Korean waters and called on the U.S. government to apologize for the incident.

On 22 December 1969 Bucher and his men finally were released. Upon his return to the United States, Bucher was brought before a navy court of inquiry. He had been ordered to scuttle the *Pueblo* if threatened with capture and had not. His defense was that he had been too busy destroying top-secret documents. The court recommended that he and one other officer be court-martialed, a decision overruled by the secretary of the navy. Bucher never again received a ship command and retired from the navy in 1973.

See also COLD WAR; INTELLIGENCE; NAVY, U.S.

Further reading: Brandt, Ed, with crew members of the *Pueblo. The Last Voyage of the USS* Pueblo. New York: Norton, 1969; Bucher, Lloyd M. *Bucher: My Story.* New York: Doubleday, 1970. Liston, Robert A. *The* Pueblo Surrender: A Covert Action by the National Security Agency. New York, M. Evans, 1988; Murphy, Edward R., Jr., with Curt Gentry. *Second in Command.* New York: Holt Reinhart and Winston, 1971.

— James G. Sheldon

Buckner, Simon Bolivar (1823–1914) *Confederate general and politician*

Born on 1 April 1823 in Hard County, Kentucky, Simon Buckner graduated from the U.S. Military Academy at West Point in 1844. Earning two brevet promotions for gallantry during the MEXICAN-AMERICAN WAR, he resigned his commission in 1855 to manage family property in Chicago.

At the beginning of the Civil War, Buckner served as adjutant general of the Kentucky State Guard, responsible for ensuring the state's neutrality. He accepted a commission as brigadier general in the Confederate army in September 1861.

Ordered to reinforce FORT DONELSON, Tennessee, Buckner assumed command there when the fort had been lost, abandoned by the escaping Brigadier Generals John P. Floyd and Gideon PILLOW. On 16 February 1862 Buckner surrendered Donelson to Union forces under Brigadier General Ulysses S. GRANT. Exchanged in the summer and promoted to major general, Buckner led a division in General Braxton BRAGG's fall 1862 invasion of Kentucky and fought in the Battle of PERRYVILLE on 8 October 1862.

After a brief period fortifying Mobile, Alabama, Buckner commanded the Department of East Tennessee from May to August 1863. He commanded a division in the Battle of CHICKAMAUGA in September 1863. In September 1864 he received promotion to lieutenant general and served as chief of staff to General Edmund Kirby SMITH in the Trans-Mississippi theater.

Following the war Buckner lived in New Orleans for three years but eventually returned to Kentucky, where he became editor of the *Louisville Courier.* After a legal battle with members of his family, he recovered his property in Chicago and went into private business. Buckner entered politics as a Democrat and was governor of Kentucky from 1887 to 1891. In 1896 he ran unsuccessfully for the vice presidency with John M. Palmer, as a Gold Democrat, in opposition to the free-silver majority. Buckner died near Munfordville, Kentucky, on 8 January 1914.

See also CIVIL WAR, LAND OVERVIEW.

Further reading: Stickles, Arndt D. *Simon Bolivar Buckner: Borderland Knight.* Chapel Hill: University of North Carolina Press, 1940; Woodworth, Steven E. *Jefferson Davis and His Generals: The Failure of Confederate Command in the West.* Lawrence: Kansas University Press, 1990.

— Alexander Mendoza

Buckner, Simon Bolivar, Jr. (1886–1945) *U.S. Army general*

Born on 16 July 1886 at Munfordville, Kentucky, Simon Bolivar Buckner, Jr., was the son of Confederate Lieutenant

General Simon Bolivar BUCKNER. He attended Virginia Military Institute (1902–04) before entering the U.S. Military Academy at WEST POINT, graduating in 1908. He held numerous field assignments both in the United States and in the Philippines, including a stint with the Air Service. He was promoted to first lieutenant in 1914 and captain three years later.

Buckner's continuing military education and his recognized teaching ability kept him out of World War I and influenced his career during the interwar period. He taught infantry tactics at West Point (1919–23) and in 1924 completed the advanced infantry course at Fort Benning. In 1925 he attended the Command and General Staff School at Fort Leavenworth, remaining as an instructor until 1928. Buckner spent the next four years as a student and instructor at the Army War College. After a year as instructor of tactics at West Point, Buckner served as commandant of cadets (1933–36).

Promoted to major in 1920 and lieutenant colonel in 1932, Buckner was elevated to colonel in 1937. After serving with the 66th Infantry Regiment, he assumed command of Fort McClellan, Alabama, along with the 22d Infantry Regiment and District D, Civilian Conservation Corps. In 1939 he became chief of staff, 6th Division. In 1940 Buckner was selected to head the Alaskan Defense Command and was promoted to brigadier general shortly thereafter.

Buckner approached his new command with characteristic intensity. Exploiting concerns about Soviet aggression fostered by the Nazi-Soviet nonaggression pact, he brought Alaska to the attention of the Joint Chiefs. This threat never materialized, but the Japanese attack on Pearl Harbor focused new attention on Alaska. Promoted to major general (1941), he directed the buildup of Alaska's defenses and military usefulness, including construction of the Alcan Highway, which linked Alaska to the "lower 48" United States.

In June 1942 Japanese forces, in concert with operations at Midway, evaded U.S. Navy units and occupied the islands of Kiska and Attu in the Aleutian chain. Although this occupation posed little threat to the United States, the symbolic impact of Japanese troops on American soil demanded a response. In May 1943 Buckner's significantly enlarged command joined Rear Admiral Thomas KINKAID's naval forces in an effort to reclaim the islands. Bypassing Kiska, Buckner directed an amphibious assault on Attu on 11 May, taking the island after 18 days of bitter and costly fighting. Another amphibious landing on Kiska found that island evacuated. The Aleutians campaign proved valuable experience for Buckner, who earned promotion to lieutenant general.

In the summer of 1944 the popular Buckner assumed command of the newly created Tenth Army, which included Lieutenant General John H. Hodge's XXIV Corps

and Marine Major General Roy GEIGER's III Amphibious Corps. Tenth Army provided the ground troops for the April–June 1945 Battle of OKINAWA—one of the largest land-air-sea battles in history. Buckner's conservative yet costly advance brought criticism from the navy and the marines; the grinding offensive continued for most of three months.

Buckner, who habitually maintained close contact with the front, was killed by Japanese artillery fire on 18 June, becoming the highest-ranking American officer killed by enemy fire during the war. The conquest of Okinawa was completed three days later. In 1954 Buckner was promoted posthumously to full general.

See also IWO JIMA, BATTLE OF; STILWELL, JOSEPH.

Further reading: Feifer, George. *Tennozan: The Battle of Okinawa and the Atomic Bomb.* New York: Ticknor and Fields, 1992; Perret, Geoffrey. *There's a War to Be Won: The United States Army in World War II.* New York: Random House, 1991.

— David Coffey

Buell, Don Carlos (1818–1898) *U.S. Army general*
Born on 23 March 1818 in Washington County, Ohio, Don Carlos Buell was raised in Indiana. He graduated from the U.S. Military Academy at WEST POINT in 1841. Commissioned a second lieutenant and posted to the infantry, Buell served against the Seminole in Florida. Promoted to first lieutenant during the MEXICAN-AMERICAN WAR, he earned two brevets for gallantry and was seriously wounded in the Battle of CHURUBUSCO.

Buell held a series of staff positions until the outbreak of the Civil War. Promoted to lieutenant colonel in May 1861, he was adjutant general of the Department of the Pacific when appointed brigadier general of U.S. Volunteers in May 1861.

Initially, Buell commanded a division under Major General George B. MCCLELLAN and helped to organize the Army of the Potomac, but in November 1861 he assumed command of the Department and Army of the Ohio for a proposed strike into East Tennessee. Buell secured reluctant authorization to move on the Tennessee capital of Nashville, which his army took with little opposition shortly after the Union capture of FORT DONELSON. Promoted to major general of volunteers in March 1862, Buell moved to support Major General U.S. GRANT's army at Pittsburg Landing in southwest Tennessee. Buell's force arrived late on the first day of the Battle of SHILOH, and the next day the combined armies of Buell and Grant drove the Confederates from the field. During the campaign against CORINTH, Buell led the Army of the Ohio under the overall command of Major General Henry HALLECK.

Ordered in June 1862 to advance on Chattanooga, Buell was stymied by Confederate resistance. That fall his Army of the Ohio was forced to withdraw into Kentucky to oppose the Confederate invasion of that state. In October 1862 Buell turned back General Braxton BRAGG's Confederate army in the Battle of PERRYVILLE, but for failing to pursue the retreating Confederates aggressively he was relieved of his command. He remained without orders for more than a year, while a military commission reviewed his performance. Although the commission brought no charges, Buell was mustered out of the Volunteers in May 1864; a month later he resigned his regular colonel's commission. It was an unfortunate end to the military career of a man once considered among the Union's best generals. Buell possessed undeniable administrative talents and solid battlefield leadership skills. His ouster perhaps owed more to his close friendship with McClellan and the rise of Grant than to his actual performance.

Buell settled eventually in Kentucky, where he operated an iron works and coal mine. He died at his home near Paradise, Kentucky, on 19 November 1898.

See also CIVIL WAR; LAND OVERVIEW; SEMINOLE WAR, SECOND.

Further reading: Daniel, Larry J. *Shiloh: The Battle That Changed the War.* New York: Simon & Schuster, 1997; Engle, Stephen D. *Don Carlos Buell: Most Promising of All.* Chapel Hill: University of North Carolina Press, 1999; Reid, Richard J. *The Army That Buell Built.* Olaton, Ky.: R. J. Reid, 1994.

— David Coffey

Buena Vista, Battle of (22–23 February 1847) *Key battle in northern Mexico during the 1846–1848 Mexican-American War*

Following his capture of MONTERREY in September 1846, Major General Zachary TAYLOR began to expand his presence in northern Mexico. But because of the difficult terrain and Taylor's differences with Washington, President James K. Polk approved Major General Winfield SCOTT's plan to invade central Mexico and advance on the capital by way of a landing at VERACRUZ. Beginning in January 1847, much to Taylor's annoyance, Scott began to siphon off his forces. Taylor, consequently, concentrated the 4,500 men who remained to him around Saltillo.

Mexican dictator General Antonio López de Santa Anna, located at San Luis Potosí, some 250 miles to the south, learned of Taylor's weakness when a U.S. courier was killed and his dispatch bag captured. Santa Anna immediately decided to march north with his army of 20,000, expecting to drive Taylor's men back to the Rio Grande and then march south to meet Scott's drive on Mexico City.

Santa Anna set out in late January, but only about 15,000 of his men survived the forced march.

Taylor at first refused to believe that Santa Anna was marching against him. When he learned on 21 February that the Mexican general was nearby, he withdrew to the more easily defended Angostura Pass, near the Hacienda Buena Vista, some seven miles from Saltillo. (Mexican history records the battle by the name of the pass, U.S. history by that of the hacienda.) At Buena Vista Taylor ordered his second in command, Brigadier General John WOOL, to set up defensive positions. The difficult high ground would help nullify the superior numbers of Mexican cavalry.

Troops on both sides were in position by 22 February, and late that morning, Santa Anna, whose forces outnumbered Taylor's perhaps 15,000 to 4,700, confidently demanded a surrender, which Taylor rejected. That afternoon Mexican light infantry tried to climb the mountain on the U.S. right but was rebuffed. By nightfall, skirmishing there had died down.

The main battle began early the next morning. The Mexicans tried to push their way up the main road but were met and repulsed by fire from Captain John M. Washington's artillery battery in the pass. In midmorning Mexican forces on the U.S. left applied sufficient pressure to break one regiment. Soon the battle line collapsed. However, the Mexican infantry advance was dilatory. Mexican cavalry streamed around the American left and made for the hacienda. They were met by wagon guards and members of the U.S. commands that were driven back earlier, who successfully defended the hacienda.

Taylor remaining a bit to the rear, Wool exercised tactical control of the battle. With the assistance of reinforcements, Wool formed a new line that blocked the Mexican breakthrough. In the early afternoon U.S. troops counterattacked but were halted by Mexican reserves, who in turn pursued the Americans, capturing two guns. U.S. artillery, which played perhaps the leading role in the battle, rebuffed a second Mexican breakthrough. The Americans kept the guns in nearly constant motion, plugging gaps in the line until infantry reserves could solidify them.

By late afternoon, the battle was over. Santa Anna retired, leaving the field to the Americans. They expected to renew the fight the next day and were surprised to find that Santa Anna had departed with his men for Mexico City. Taylor did not pursue; his army had fought its last battle of the war.

U.S. casualties in the Battle of Buena Vista had been some 260 killed, 450 wounded, and 25 missing. Mexican losses were almost 600 killed, more than 1,000 wounded, and 1,900 missing. Although Santa Anna had suffered a serious defeat, he soon raised another army to meet the U.S. drive on the Mexican capital.

See also MEXICAN-AMERICAN WAR.

Further reading: Lavender, David. *Climax at Buena Vista: The American Campaigns in Northeastern Mexico, 1846–47.* Philadelphia: Lippincott, 1966; Nichols, Edward J. *Zach Taylor's Little Army.* Garden City, N.Y.: Doubleday, 1963; Winders, Richard Bruce. *Mr. Polk's Army: The American Military Experience in the Mexican War.* College Station: Texas A&M University Press, 1997.

— Lawyn C. Edwards

Buffalo, New York, burning of (29–30 December 1813) *Retaliatory British raid during the War of 1812*
On 10 December 1813, U.S. Brigadier General George McClure, lacking sufficient troops, decided to abandon FORT GEORGE in Canada. Before retreating to FORT NIAGARA, McClure burned nearby Newark and parts of QUEENSTON HEIGHTS to deprive the British of shelter, giving the villagers little time to save their possessions. British and Canadian forces advanced when they saw the flames, and the Americans retired across the Niagara River, leaving Fort George intact but the villages destroyed. McClure's wanton destruction infuriated British lieutenant general Sir Gordon Drummond. He ordered retaliation.

At 1:45 A.M. on 18 December, 562 British regulars surprised Fort Niagara's unprepared garrison, taking it with a bayonet assault. The British killed 65 Americans, captured 344, and took 27 cannon, 3,000 small arms, and tons of other supplies at a cost of only six dead and five wounded. Receiving a signal from the captured fort, Major General Phineas Riall then crossed the Niagara with 1,000 regulars and Indians. Riall sacked Lewiston, New York, and all the other American settlements along the river to within 10 miles of Buffalo, leaving them in ruins. Meanwhile, in response, New York militia major general Amos Hall gathered troops near Buffalo and Black Rock, several miles down stream. By 27 December Hall had gathered a motley force of 2,000 men, including 500 pro-U.S. Canadians.

Two days later, around midnight, Riall crossed the Niagara near Black Rock with 1,400 regulars, Canadian militia, and Indians. Hall dispatched 800 men to oppose them, but the U.S. forces broke and ran after the first volley. Near dawn, Hall advanced with the remainder of his command and met Riall, who attacked. After a sharp 30-minute fight, the American right flank collapsed, forcing Hall to retreat. He managed to rally 300 soldiers, who covered Buffalo's civilian population as it fled, but they could not stop the British from entering the town. Riall then burned Buffalo, leaving only four buildings standing. Before returning to Canada, he also destroyed five warships of Captain Oliver Hazard PERRY's Lake Erie squadron, which were docked nearby at Black Rock, and all the other structures in the area. The British lost 112 soldiers killed, wounded, or missing in the engagement, while the Americans

lost 30 dead, 40 wounded, and 69 captured. An undetermined number of American civilians were also killed.

On 22 January 1814, with the entire American side of the Niagara River in ruins from Lake Ontario to Lake Erie, the British announced a halt to their retaliatory attacks.

See also WAR OF 1812, LAND OVERVIEW.

Further reading: Elting, John R. *Amateurs, to Arms!: A Military History of the War of 1812.* Chapel Hill: Algonquin Books, 1991; Mahon, John K. *The War of 1812.* Gainesville: University of Florida Press, 1972; Quimby, Robert S. *The U.S. Army in the War of 1812: An Operational and Command Study.* East Lansing: Michigan State University Press, 1997.

— Michael P. Gabriel

Buffalo Soldiers *African-American soldiers of the regular U.S. Army serving on the western frontier*
African Americans fought as volunteers during the REVOLUTIONARY WAR, the WAR OF 1812, and, most notably, the CIVIL WAR. During the latter conflict approximately 180,000 blacks, mostly liberated slaves, fought for the Union in state organizations and in the federal volunteer establishment as U.S. Colored Troops. After the war, partly in recognition of this impressive wartime contribution and partly in observance of the pending citizenship and constitutional equality of black Americans, Congress, over heated opposition, authorized six African American regiments as part of the army's first major postwar reorganization.

On 28 July 1866 President Andrew Johnson signed the reorganization act into law. The new regular army featured two cavalry (9th and 10th) and four infantry regiments (38th, 39th, 40th, and 41st) composed of African-American soldiers and white officers. The inclusion of black regiments not only offered opportunities for hundreds of African-American men but created positions for some of the outstanding officers of the Civil War. Among the capable officers to find employment in the new black regiments were Colonels Benjamin GRIERSON (10th Cavalry), Edward Hatch (9th Cavalry), Nelson MILES (40th Infantry), and Ranald MACKENZIE (41st Infantry), as well as Lieutenant Colonels Wesley MERRITT (9th Cavalry) and William SHAFTER (41st Infantry).

Recruitment and training of the regiments presented numerous difficulties. Most recruits, being former slaves, were illiterate and had little grasp of military life. Black soldiers faced discrimination and even overt hatred from within the army and from the citizens they served, especially in former Confederate states such as Texas, where all the black regiments spent considerable time and rendered excellent service. They displayed a cheerfulness and a willingness to work that set them apart from white recruits. In

1869 the four infantry regiments were consolidated into the 24th and 25th Regiments; the 9th and 10th Cavalry Regiments remained intact. Still, African-American units continued to weather criticism and even efforts to abolish them by the army's top officers.

By the mid-1870s the black soldiers and their officers had largely silenced the critics. Compared to white regiments—often filled with the dregs of society, men who viewed military service as a last resort—the black regiments featured high reenlistment rates and little desertion, notable sobriety, and high esprit de corps. The army offered black men a career, one of the few opportunities for advancement available to them.

During the peak years of the AMERICAN INDIAN WARS (1874–86), the black regiments boasted a core of solid, proven veterans and a remarkable continuity of leadership (Hatch and Grierson commanded their regiments for 25 years). The one black officer to serve during the period, Henry FLIPPER, the first black to graduate from the U.S. Military Academy at West Point, apparently performed well before being forced out of the army on dubious charges.

The African-American regiments served in most of the major campaigns of the Indian wars (1866–91), participating in more than half of all actions fought in Texas, including the RED RIVER WAR, and in the SIOUX WARS. They also helped to restore order following the sad events at WOUNDED KNEE. Their finest service came during the APACHE WARS in the deserts of the Southwest, particularly in the Victorio campaign and along the Mexican border. The Buffalo Soldiers, as their Indian adversaries called them, displayed remarkable endurance on campaign and tenacity in battle.

Throughout, the black regiments served faithfully, despite prejudice and discrimination, poor equipment and horses, prolonged deployments in harsh climates, and routinely hostile postings. In so doing, they amassed service records equal to any regiment on the frontier. During the American Indian Wars, 14 Buffalo Soldiers won the Medal of Honor. The original African-American regiments existed well into the 20th century and continued to render fine service under difficult circumstances.

See also AFRICAN AMERICANS IN THE MILITARY.

Further reading: Fowler, Arlen. *Black Infantry in the West, 1869–1871.* Reprint, Norman: University of Oklahoma Press, 1996; Kenner, Charles L. *Buffalo Soldiers and Officers of the Ninth Cavalry, 1867–1898: Black & White Together.* Norman: University of Oklahoma Press, 1999; Leckie, William H. *The Buffalo Soldiers: A Narrative of the Negro Cavalry in the West.* Norman: University of Oklahoma Press, 1967.

— David Coffey

Buford, John (1826–1863) *U.S. Army general*
Born on 4 March 1826 at Versailles, Kentucky, John Buford graduated from the U.S. Military Academy at WEST POINT in 1848. His early postings were in the West, where he fought against the Sioux Indians.

At the start of the Civil War, Buford marched with his regiment from Kansas to Washington, D.C. When Major General John POPE was brought to Washington to command the capital's defenses, he was surprised to learn that the talented Buford was serving in a trivial post as an inspector. Thanks largely to Pope, Buford was appointed a brigadier general of volunteers in July 1862.

Buford soon proved himself one of the most talented and reliable cavalry officers in the army. As a dragoon officer in the West, Buford had learned to use cavalry as mounted infantry. Dismounted cavalry skirmishers, supported by artillery, could repel cavalry and force an enemy to deploy regular infantry. He also realized that the value of cavalry lay in scouting.

Buford employed these tactics effectively against dreaded Confederate cavalry commander Major General J. E. B. STUART prior to the Second Battle of BULL RUN/MANASSAS. At Thoroughfare Gap, unsupported by Pope, a vastly outnumbered Buford delayed Confederate lieutenant general James LONGSTREET's corps for six hours before withdrawing. He provided intelligence that would have prevented the subsequent Union defeat had it been acted upon. Buford was badly wounded while covering Pope's retreat after the battle. Buford's wounds kept him from ANTIETAM and FREDERICKSBURG. He returned for the Battle of CHANCELLORSVILLE, commanding a division of the Cavalry Corps, and covered the Union retreat.

Buford saw action at BRANDY STATION, then effectively masked the northward movement of the Army of the Potomac. Scouting in the GETTYSBURG area on 30 June, Buford's command clashed with lead elements of General Robert E. Lee's Army of Northern Virginia and then established a position on crucial ground northwest of town. Buford bought valuable time for Major General John REYNOLDS to bring up infantry reinforcements. Remounting his command, Buford marched to block Confederate lieutenant general Richard EWELL's corps along the Carlisle Road. By the time Ewell forced Buford aside, Major General Winfield Scott HANCOCK had arrived and solidified the Union positions. By delaying two Confederate corps, Buford had provided the Army of the Potomac's commander, Major General George MEADE, time to establish firm defensive positions.

Buford fought in small engagements following Lee's retreat and during the autumn of 1863. Prior to his death of typhoid fever at Washington, D.C., on 16 December 1863, Buford was promoted to major general of volunteers, to rank from 1 July 1863. His loss was a severe blow to the federal army.

See also CAVALRY; CIVIL WAR, LAND OVERVIEW.

Further reading: Longacre, Edward G. *The Cavalry at Gettysburg.* Teaneck, N.J.: Fairleigh Dickinson University Press, 1986; ———. *General John Buford.* Conshohocken, Pa.: Combined Books, 1995; ———. *Lincoln's Cavalrymen: A History of the Mounted Forces of the Army of the Potomac.* Mechanicsburg, Pa.: Stackpole Books, 2000; Phipps, Michael. *The Devil's to Pay: General John Buford, USA.* Gettysburg, Pa.: Farnsworth Military Impressions, 1995.

— Thomas D. Veve

Bulge, Battle of the (16 December 1944–16 January 1945) *Final World War II German offensive on the western front*

Planned at Adolf Hitler's instigation, the offensive, dubbed by the Germans *Wacht am Rhein* (Watch on the Rhine), was launched early on the morning of 16 December 1944, by Army Group B, consisting of three armies. A heavy artillery assault preceded the initial attacks, which were spearheaded by Sixth Panzer Army and were conducted on a broad front. The German goal was to capture the port of Antwerp and destroy the Allied armies in this sector of the front.

The Germans had prepared under tight security, including radio silence. This meant that ULTRA intercepts did not provide warning and the Germans were able to achieve surprise. Allied Supreme Commander General Dwight EISENHOWER had assessed the Ardennes as an unlikely avenue of enemy advance, given the difficult terrain, especially in winter, and so that sector was lightly held by mostly inexperienced troops.

Ranged along the front of some 75 miles from north to south were the U.S. 99th, 106th, 28th, and 4th Infantry Divisions. The 106th, recently arrived in Europe, had not yet seen combat action; the veteran 28th was recovering from severe losses of men and matériel suffered in recent heavy fighting.

The initial German attacks, supported by airborne assaults and special operations units, as well their largest air effort since the NORMANDY LANDING, met with mixed results. In the south, elements of the Fifth Panzer Army surrounded two regiments of the 106th Infantry Division in the Schnee Eifel and subsequently induced their surrender. A serious penetration of Allied lines, subsequently dubbed the "Bulge," was soon achieved in that sector. Allied units, committed to reinforce, scrambled to gain position. Meanwhile, foul weather kept Allied fighters and reconnaissance aircraft on the ground.

U.S. positions were established at St. Vith to the north and Bastogne in the south, the keys to the road network, essential for movement in the region's difficult terrain. The 7th Armored Division pushed elements into St. Vith, where they established a strongpoint and managed to hold until 22 December, significantly disrupting the German timetable. Although the desperate German offensive always lacked the potential to change the eventual outcome of the war, very serious fighting remained in store. For the Allies in the north, particularly, the first 10 days of the battle were marked by improvisation, shifting of forces, and desperate efforts by isolated forces to hold onto or extend their positions.

In a controversial decision (later much debated), on 20 December Eisenhower gave British field marshal Bernard Montgomery command of those elements of Lieutenant General Omar BRADLEY's 12th Army Group situated north of the Bulge, the rationale being that the German penetration had so disrupted communications as to preclude effective control by Bradley of these units.

Three days into the battle, Third Army to the south was directed to suspend its operations and move against the enemy penetration. In one of the most remarkable tactical and logistical feats of the war, Lieutenant General George S. PATTON, Jr., disengaged from the enemy elements of his forces then driving east, reoriented them northward, and within three days sent a three-division phalanx smashing into the southern flank of the German advance. The 4th Armored, 26th Infantry, and 80th Infantry Divisions, ranged west to east, drove some 100 miles north over icy roads in winter weather and on 22 December, just as Patton had promised, joined the battle. Eventually six infantry and three armored divisions were committed on the southern flank. Third Army's after-action report stated that during 17–23 December, 133,178 motor vehicles passed its traffic control points.

At Bastogne, the U.S. 101st Airborne Division and elements of the 9th and 10th Armored Divisions managed to establish a position but soon found themselves surrounded by advancing German columns. Resupplied by air and skillfully deploying their tanks from one crisis point to another, the Americans held until relieved on 26 December by the 4th Armored Division's 37th Tank Battalion, under Lieutenant Colonel Creighton ABRAMS. By then the German penetration had reached its deepest point, almost to the Meuse River, some 55 miles from the original battle lines.

Meanwhile, to the north, Major General Ernest Harmon's U.S. 2d Armored Division had launched a Christmas Day counterattack that essentially smashed the German 2d Panzer Division, the spearhead of the attack in that sector. These twin successes on opposite flanks of the bulge ended any prospect of further German advances. The stubborn defenses had bogged down the attackers,

After having been besieged there for 10 days, troops of the 101st Airborne Division leave Bastogne to drive the Germans from the surrounding area.   *(U.S. Army Military History Institute)*

clogging the roads on which their panzer units were advancing and disrupting logistical support for their operations. Also, the weather had cleared on 23 December, permitting aerial resupply at Bastogne and putting Allied fighter and bomber aircraft back into action.

Beginning on 26 December and continuing until mid-January, Allied forces launched coordinated counterattacks against German forces that, having been halted and logistically starved, decided to defend in place. Third Army built its forces relentlessly, especially in supporting artillery which, by the end of December, amounted to 88 battalions and more than 1,000 guns. These elements employed against German ground forces for the first time shells fitted with proximity fuses. These newly developed and then highly classified devices proved extremely effective. Much

hard fighting still lay ahead, and not until 8 January did Hitler concede failure and order his troops to withdraw. On 16 January, U.S. forces from south and north of the German salient met, eliminating the Bulge.

Of the 610,000 U.S. troops involved, 19,000 had been killed, about 50,000 wounded, and 21,382 made prisoners or missing. The effort had cost the Germans an estimated 120,000 casualties and considerable matériel lost. It delayed the inevitable for perhaps six weeks. Allied forces now resumed their advance on a broad front toward the Rhine and the German heartland.

See also WORLD WAR II, U.S. INVOLVEMENT, EUROPE.

Further reading: Blumenson, Martin, ed. *The Patton Papers: 1940–1945.* Rev. ed. Boston: Houghton Mifflin,

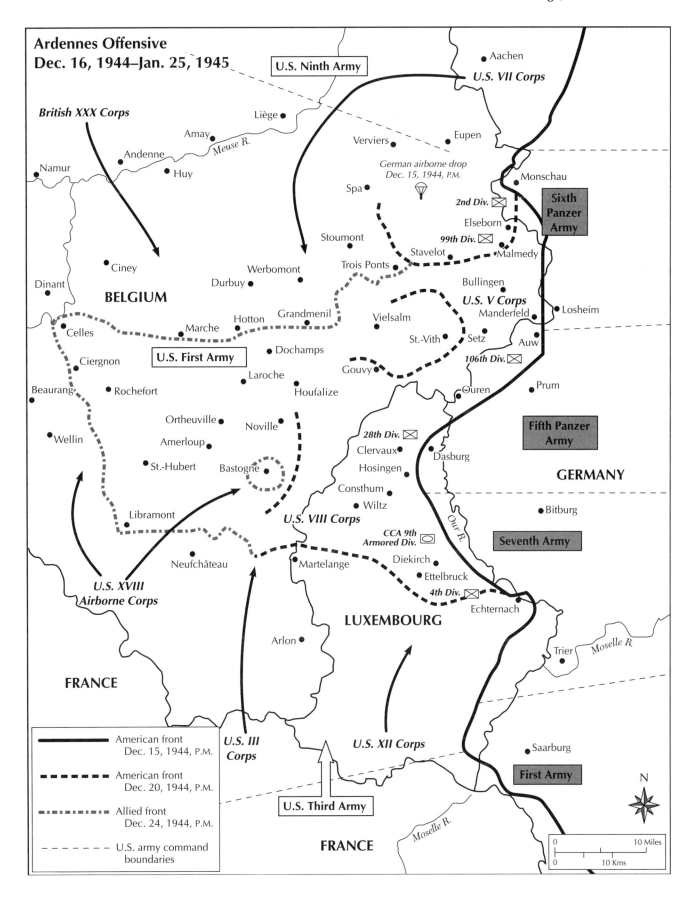

Ardennes Offensive
Dec. 16, 1944–Jan. 25, 1945

U.S. Ninth Army

U.S. VII Corps

Aachen

British XXX Corps

Liège

Amay

Andenne

Verviers

Eupen

Monschau

Namur

Huy

Meuse R.

German airborne drop
Dec. 15, 1944, P.M.

Spa

2nd Div.

Sixth
Panzer
Army

Elseborn

99th Div.

Ciney

Stoumont

Stavelot

Malmedy

Dinant

BELGIUM

Werbomont

Trois Ponts

Bullingen

Durbuy

Hotton

Grandmenil

Vielsalm

Manderfeld

U.S. V Corps

Losheim

Celles

Marche

Dochamps

St.-Vith

Setz

Auw

U.S. First Army

Ciergnon

Laroche

Gouvy

106th Div.

Beaurang

Rochefort

Houfalize

Ouren

Prum

Ortheuville

Noville

Wellin

Amerloup

28th Div.

Fifth Panzer Army

St.-Hubert

Bastogne

Clervaux

Dasburg

GERMANY

Hosingen

Libramont

Consthum

Wiltz

Bitburg

U.S. VIII Corps

CCA 9th
Armored Div.

Our R.

**U.S. XVIII
Airborne Corps**

Neufchâteau

Martelange

Diekirch

Seventh Army

Ettelbruck

4th Div.

Echternach

LUXEMBOURG

Arlon

Trier

Moselle R.

FRANCE

	American front Dec. 15, 1944, P.M.
	American front Dec. 20, 1944, P.M.
	Allied front Dec. 24, 1944, P.M.
	U.S. army command boundaries

**U.S. III
Corps**

U.S. XII Corps

Saarburg

First Army

N

U.S. Third Army

Moselle R.

FRANCE

0   10 Miles

0   10 Kms

1974; Cole, Hugh M. *U.S. Army in World War II, European Theater of Operations. The Ardennes: The Battle of the Bulge.* Washington, D.C.: Office of the Chief of Military History, Department of the Army, 1965; Forty, George. *The Reich's Last Gamble: The Ardennes Offensive, December 1944.* London: Cassell, 2000; Marshall, S. L. A. *Bastogne: The Story of the First Eight Days.* Washington, D.C.: Infantry Journal Press, 1946; Stamps, T. Dodson, and Vincent J. Esposito, eds. *A Military History of World War II with*

Atlas. Vol. 1, *Operations in the European Theaters.* West Point, N.Y.: U.S. Military Academy, 1953.

— Lewis Sorley

Bull Run/Manassas, First Battle of (21 July 1861)
First major battle of the Civil War

Brevet Lieutenant General Winfield SCOTT had warned that the newly assembled federal army was unprepared for

a battle, but the political leadership overrode his objections. The cabinet agreed with President Abraham LINCOLN's assessment that both sides were "green alike" and with his hope that a decisive victory would bring a quick end to the Southern rebellion. Toward this end, on 16 July 1861 Major General Irvin MCDOWELL ordered his approximately 32,000 troops (50 infantry regiments, 10 artillery battalions, and one cavalry battalion) to march from Arlington, Virginia, toward the key Confederate railroad junction at Manassas, Virginia. McDowell, a 42-year-old brevet major in the adjutant general's office when the war began, had occupied staff positions in the MEXICAN-AMERICAN WAR and had studied in France; he had never held a field command. His political connections, however, had secured the post.

McDowell's inexperience and overcaution, combined with the inexperience of his troops, resulted in costly delays that eliminated any hopes of catching the Confederates off guard. Indeed, it took the Federal army almost two and a half days to march 22 miles to Centreville. Another three days were wasted bringing up supplies and undertaking reconnaissance. As a result, Confederate brigadier general Joseph E. JOHNSTON gained the time needed to slip his 11,000-man army out of the Shenandoah Valley and bring it by rail to Manassas to reinforce Brigadier General Pierre Gustave Toutant BEAUREGARD. Had McDowell moved quickly, numbers alone might have given him the victory that Lincoln so desperately desired.

By the evening of 20 July Federal and Confederate forces had converged on Bull Run Creek, which ran in a northwest-to-southeast line on the outskirts of Manassas. McDowell and Beauregard, who had attended West Point together, both planned to launch attacks the next morning. McDowell called for the First Division, commanded by Brigadier General Daniel Tyler, to feint an attack against the stone bridge that crossed Bull Run along the center of the front, while the Second Division, under Colonel David Hunter, and the Third Division, under Colonel S. P. Heintzelman, would attempt to turn the Confederate left flank. One brigade of Colonel D. S. Miles's Fourth Division would launch a feint against Blackburn's Ford on the right, while the remainder of the division would be held in reserve. If all went according to plan, the First Division and Fourth Division could deliver the coup de grace after the Second and Third turned the Confederate flank.

Like McDowell, Beauregard planned a flanking attack against his opponent's left. Beauregard intended for his units to cross Bull Run then await orders to advance, but most of his commanders had misinterpreted his instructions to mean await orders to advance, period. Thus most of the Confederate army remained stationary. Otherwise, the Federal and Confederate armies might have launched simultaneous attacks on their rights and thus flip-flopped

their positions on the battlefield. By the time Beauregard realized his attack had not proceeded, McDowell's was under way.

Under the watchful gaze of federal congressmen and Washingtonian ladies, the battle quickly unfolded. By 9 A.M. Beauregard recognized that the main Northern force was attacking his left flank. He therefore ordered a brigade of Virginians commanded by Brigadier General Thomas J. JACKSON to reinforce his center at the stone bridge and brigades commanded by such future illustrious commanders as Richard S. EWELL, Jubal EARLY, and James LONGSTREET to reinforce his left. As the Federal divisions began to push back the Confederate left, Southern forces rallied around Jackson's Virginians, who were on the reverse slope of Henry Hill. Confederate colonel Barnard Bee shouted, "There is Jackson standing like a stone wall!"—an image that remained with Jackson and his brigade.

McDowell ordered Tyler's Second Division to cross the stone bridge and attack Jackson's position, but the attack was carried out piecemeal, one brigade at a time rather than all at once. This allowed Beauregard to insert fresh forces sent up by Johnston to reinforce Jackson and to extend his left flank. By 3:30 P.M., the two flanking Federal columns had turned inward toward Jackson and across the front of the Confederate left. At this point Beauregard launched a counterattack on the exposed Federal position. Federal troops, who had begun their maneuvers as early as 2 A.M., were by now exhausted in the hot sun.

As Confederate troops advanced, Federal forces panicked, ignoring McDowell's attempts to form a rallying line at Centreville. They fled all the way back to Washington in what observers called "the Great Skedaddle." Fortunately for the Federal army, the Southerners were almost as disorganized; overwhelmed with Federal prisoners, they failed to pursue and annihilate their opponents.

At a cost of 387 dead, 1,582 wounded, and eight missing, the Confederate army had inflicted heavy casualties on its larger Northern adversary (481 dead, 1,124 wounded, and more than 1,500 prisoners) and captured 28 artillery pieces, 37 caissons, 500,000 rounds of ammunition, 500 muskets, and nine battle flags. As the first in a series of early Confederate victories, the battle signaled to the North that the war would be prolonged and that far more time would be required to turn its "green" recruits into seasoned troops.

See also CIVIL WAR, LAND OVERVIEW.

Further reading: Davis, William C. *The First Battle of Manassas.* Conshohocken, Pa.: Eastern National Park and Monument Association, 1995; Foote, Shelby. *The Civil War: A Narrative.* Vol. 1, *Fort Sumter to Perryville.* New York: Vintage Books, 1986; Hennessy, John. *The First Battle of Manassas: An End to Innocence.* Lynchburg,

Va.: H. E. Howard, 1989; Wheeler, Richard. *A Rising Thunder: From Lincoln's Election to the Battle of Bull Run.* New York: HarperCollins, 1994.

— Justin D. Murphy

Bull Run/Manassas, Second Battle of (29–30

August 1862) *Confederate victory in the Civil War*
In the aftermath of the Battles of the SEVEN DAYS and Major General Thomas J. JACKSON's victory at CEDAR MOUNTAIN, Confederate general Robert E. LEE received reports that his Union counterpart, Major General George B. MCCLELLAN, was withdrawing from the peninsula between the James and York Rivers. Anxious to prevent the combining of McClellan's force with Major General John POPE's newly created Army of Virginia, a potential Federal force of 130,000 men, then at Culpepper, Lee dispatched 30,000 troops under Major General James LONGSTREET via rail on 13 August to link up with Jackson. He joined them himself on 15 August.

Although Lee hoped to cut off Pope before he could retreat across the Rappahannock, delays allowed Pope to withdraw. On 22 August Confederate cavalry under Major General J. E. B. STUART struck Pope's headquarters at Catlett's Station, seizing his dispatch case, the contents of which revealed that some of McClellan's forces would soon join Pope.

At this point Lee took a bold gamble. In the face of superior numbers, Lee divided his army in half on 24 August, ordering Jackson, with some 25,000 men, and Stuart's cavalry to advance around the Bull Run Mountains, through Thoroughfare Gap, and toward Manassas. This risked exposing one of the two Confederate elements before the other could provide support. Lee hoped, however, that he could force Pope into the open and converge upon him.

After marching some 56 miles in just two days, Jackson's forces arrived in Gainesville on 26 August, then swung south to Bristoe Station, where they severed the railroad supplying Pope, causing two trains to derail. During the morning of 27 August, Jackson's command looted the massive Federal supply base at Manassas, gorging themselves on federal provisions. When Major General Richard EWELL reported that Federal troops were marching up the Warrenton Turnpike, Jackson withdrew seven miles to woods near Stone Bridge.

The Second Battle of Bull Run/Manassas, 29 August 1862 *(Library of Congress)*

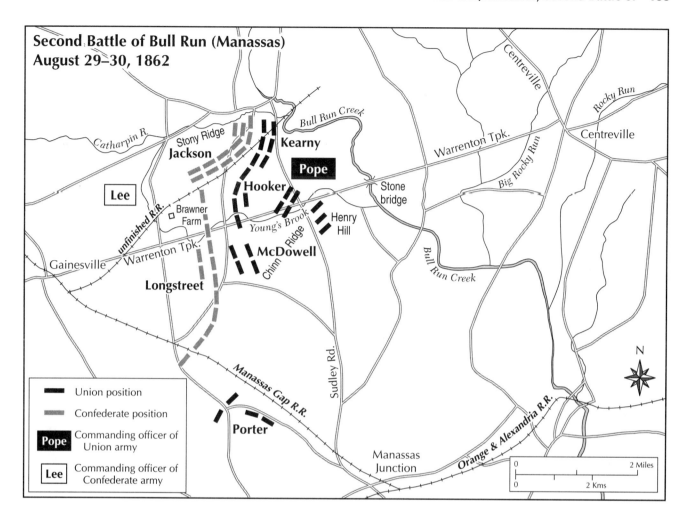

Second Battle of Bull Run (Manassas) August 29–30, 1862

Union position

Confederate position

Pope Commanding officer of Union army

Lee Commanding officer of Confederate army

In the meanwhile, Pope sought to bring his scattered forces from the Rappahannock to Warrenton Junction in hopes of defeating Jackson before Lee could reunite his army. Learning of Jackson's raid on Manassas, Pope ordered his commanders to march there. By the time Pope arrived at noon on 28 August, however, Jackson's forces were gone. Because Jackson's three subordinate commanders, Ewell and Brigadier Generals A. P. HILL and William Taliaferro, had taken different routes to Stone Bridge, Pope received conflicting reports of their whereabouts, leading him to order his tired troops to continue marching to Centreville.

Late in the evening of 28 August, as Brigadier General John GIBBON's Black Hat Brigade (2,100 raw troops from Wisconsin and Indiana) approached Stone Bridge, Jackson (after personally riding reconnaissance) ordered six of his brigades (6,200 men) to attack. Surprisingly, Gibbon's green troops, reinforced by two of Brigadier General Abner Doubleday's regiments, held their ground. By dusk, both sides had lost approximately 1,300 men. Confederate losses included Taliaferro, who was wounded three times, and Ewell, who lost a leg.

Now that Pope had finally discovered Jackson's whereabouts, he ordered all Federal forces to converge on Manassas and drafted plans for a two-prong attack. Major Generals Irwin MCDOWELL and Franz Sigel attacked with 30,000 men from the south and west to prevent Jackson from escaping through Thoroughfare Gap, while Major Generals Samuel Heintzelman, Fitz-John Porter, and Jesse Reno attacked with an additional 30,000 men from the East. This is exactly what Jackson wanted, because he knew that the main body either through Thoroughfare Gap or up the Warrenton Turnpike could outflank the Federal army.

Fixated on Jackson, Pope launched a series of piece-meal attacks on Jackson's position on 29 August, oblivious to the approach of Longstreet and Lee, who on the previous day had fought their way around and through Thoroughfare Gap, which had been defended by just one division under Brigadier General James B. Ricketts and by Brigadier General John Buford's cavalry. By 10:30 A.M., elements of Longstreet's corps began forming next to Jackson. Dismissing Porter's reports of Longstreet's arrival, Pope continued to attack Jackson, who repeatedly repulsed the attacks.

At dusk, Longstreet ordered Major General John Bell HOOD to carry out a reconnaissance in force of the Federal center. When Hood withdrew after engaging, Pope became convinced that Jackson was retreating. Regrouping his forces the next morning, Pope began his "pursuit" of Jackson at around 3 P.M., only to find that Jackson's forces were still entrenched in the woods above Stone Bridge. Pope then launched repeated assaults against Jackson, unknowingly marching troops across Longstreet's front. When Jackson appealed for assistance, Longstreet's artillery, which had been hidden in the woods, opened fire, followed by a full-scale assault, led by Hood's Texas Brigade, against Porter. The 5th New York ZOUAVES, which had entered the battle with 490 men, lost 223 wounded and 124 dead—the largest percentage killed in any Federal regiment in any engagement in the war.

Pope's army was thrown back, but divisions commanded by Major Generals George Sykes and John REYNOLDS held Henry Hill long enough to allow an orderly retreat to Centreville. Heavy rain later that evening thwarted any Confederate hopes of pursuit. Federal losses had totaled 1,724 killed, 8,372 wounded, and 5,958 missing and captured, while the Confederates had lost 1,481 killed, 7,627 wounded, and 89 missing.

In the immediate aftermath of the defeat, Lincoln transferred Pope's command to McClellan. Pope, who was relieved and sent to Minnesota, blamed Porter, who was court-martialed in a controversy that raged for years (Porter was vindicated by the army 20 years later). Lee, buoyed by this major Confederate victory, decided to take the war into the North, leading to the Battle of ANTIETAM/ SHARPSBURG.

See also CIVIL WAR, LAND OVERVIEW.

Further reading: Foote, Shelby. *The Civil War: A Narrative*. Vol. 1, *Fort Sumter to Perryville*. New York: Vintage Books, 1986; Hennessy, John J. *Return to Bull Run: The Battle and Campaign of Second Manassas*. Norman: University of Oklahoma Press, 1999; Sutherland, Daniel E. *The Emergence of Total War*. Fort Worth, Tex.: Ryan Place, 1996.

— Justin D. Murphy

Bullard, Robert L. (1861–1947) *U.S. Army general*
Born on 5 January 1861 in Russell County, Alabama, Robert Lee Bullard graduated from the U.S. Military Academy at West Point in 1885. As a junior officer, he served on frontier posts in New Mexico, Oklahoma, Texas, and Kansas before transferring to the Commissary Department. During the SPANISH-AMERICAN WAR he remained in the United States, commanding the African-American 3d Alabama Volunteer Infantry, a regiment that remained in the United States but that won general acclaim for its training and skills, in part due to Bullard's steadfastness in combating racist pressure. Bullard then served in the Philippines, effectively leading the 39th Volunteer Infantry Regiment in both conventional and guerrilla warfare on Luzon.

In 1901 Bullard was promoted to major. Before the American intervention in World War I, he saw extensive active service in Moro Province of Mindanao, the second Cuban intervention (1906–1909), and during the Mexican border crisis of 1915 and 1916, invariably winning high praise from superiors for his organizational skills and drive on field service. In April 1917 Bullard, now a brigadier general, commanded the 2d Brigade of the initial token AMERICAN EXPEDITIONARY FORCE (AEF) sent to France in World War I. Promoted to major general, that August Bullard took command of infantry specialist schools in France. In December 1917, the commander of the AEF, General John J. PERSHING, appointed him commander of 1st Division. Bullard led the division with distinction in the first independent American attack of the war, the May 1918 Battle of CANTIGNY. In July he took command of II Corps, participating in the AISNE-MARNE and MEUSE-ARGONNE offensives, which finally broke Germany's forces. Bullard was advanced to lieutenant general that October.

After the war Bullard returned to the United States to command the II Corps Area. He performed extensive public relations duties for the army, expounding the National Defense Act of 1920. Retiring in January 1925, for 17 years he chaired the National Security League, a preparedness lobby, speaking and writing prolifically on defense issues. Bullard died at New York City on 11 September 1947.

See also BAKER, NEWTON D.; LATIN AMERICA INTERVENTIONS, EARLY 20TH CENTURY; PHILIPPINE-AMERICAN WAR; SCOTT, HUGH L.; WORLD WAR I, U.S. INVOLVEMENT.

Further reading: Bullard, Robert L. *American Soldiers Also Fought*. New York: Longmans, Green, 1936; ———. *Personalities and Reminiscences of the War*. Garden City, N.Y.: Doubleday, Page, 1925; Coffman, Edward M. *The War to End All Wars: The American Military Experience in World War I*. New York: Oxford University Press, 1968; Millett, Allan. *The General: Robert L. Bullard and Officership in the United States Army, 1881–1925*. Westport, Conn.: Greenwood, 1975.

— Priscilla Roberts

Buna (1942–1943) *Major battle in the campaign for New Guinea during World War II*
Following their successful Philippine campaign during May and June 1942, the Japanese decided to expand their

perimeter in the central and southern Pacific. They planned to seize Port Moresby, the principal city of southern Papua, New Guinea.

In early July 1942, elements of the Japanese Eighteenth Army, under the command of Major General Tomitaro Horii, landed at Gona and Buna and attacked inland, driving Allied defenders back over the key pass through the Owen Stanley Mountains to within 30 miles of Port Moresby. At that point, partly under Allied pressure from the Australian 7th and U.S. 32d Divisions, and partly in compliance with instructions from the Japanese high command, Horii's forces fell stubbornly back over the mountains and established strong defensive positions in swampy regions around Buna and Gona. The Japanese put up a stiff defense, and the Allied counteroffensive bogged down. U.S. and Australian troops were wracked by disease, short of artillery ammunition and rations, and untrained in jungle warfare.

Lieutenant General Robert L. EICHELBERGER, placed in command by General Douglas MACARTHUR, rallied sagging Allied morale and took steps to rectify the logistical problems. The Australians, on the Allied left, took Gona on 9 December, but Buna was much more heavily fortified, and the Japanese strongly resisted U.S. attacks. The yard-by-yard fighting resulted in high casualties for both sides, but the American forces eventually advanced to within sight of the beach on the east side of Buna. A converging attack by U.S. and Australian forces finally overran the Japanese positions. Most Japanese resistance ceased by the end of January 1943. Some of the Japanese escaped by boat, but most died in the fighting.

Total Japanese casualties in the Buna-Gona operations had been more than 7,000 dead, an unknown number of wounded, and 350 wounded prisoners. The Australians lost 5,700 and the United States 2,783 killed and wounded. Both sides lost heavily from disease; about 60 percent of the 13,646 Americans were incapacitated.

This campaign had a significant impact on the remainder of the war in the Pacific. It demonstrated that Allied troops could defeat the hitherto seemingly invincible Japanese forces in jungle fighting. It also changed the direction of Allied strategy in the South West Pacific Area. MacArthur declared "No more Bunas!" Rather than attack Japanese strongholds directly, the Allies decided to "leapfrog" around them to cut their supply lines. Once that was accomplished, MacArthur moved to retake the Philippines.

See also LEAPFROGGING; WORLD WAR II, U.S. INVOLVEMENT, PACIFIC.

Further reading: Gailey, Harry A. *MacArthur Strikes Back: Decision at Buna; New Guinea, 1942–1943.* Novato, Calif.: Presidio Press, 2000; Mayo, Lida. *Bloody Buna.* Garden City, N.Y.: Doubleday, 1974.

— James H. Willbanks

Bunker Hill/Breed's Hill, Battle of (17 June 1775)

Important early land battle of the Revolutionary War
Following the clash of LEXINGTON AND CONCORD, Patriot militia forces closed in around Boston. The British commander and captain general of Massachusetts, Thomas Gage, recognized the vulnerability of his position should the Americans place artillery on the heights around the city and therefore the need to take Bunker Hill, Breed's Hill, and Dorchester Heights. Reinforcements of dragoons, infantrymen, and marines gave Gage 6,000 men by mid-June 1775. The Americans were largely inactive, but British morale was suffering. Gage was urged to do something by three recently arrived major generals, John Burgoyne, Henry Clinton, and William Howe.

Gage now laid plans to occupy the Charlestown Peninsula north of Boston, dominated by Breed's and Bunker Hills. But British preparations were an open secret, known throughout Boston by 14 June. On the night of 16 June Colonel William Prescott led men to occupy Bunker Hill, which was the highest ground and a good position as long as the adjacent land and narrow escape route across Charlestown Neck could be held. But the patriots also took up a position on Breed's Hill, which was closer to Boston but also lower and more vulnerable to a flanking attack. Fortunately for the colonials, the British failed to adopt the sounder plan of a landing on the narrow peninsula, outflanking the colonial positions. The British likely expected the colonials to flee in any case, or they wanted to teach them a lesson in a frontal assault with the bayonet.

The colonial arrival should have been met by an immediate British assault, but Gage did not order it until the next afternoon. The colonials used the delay to good effect in improving their positions, working in full view of the British to complete a redoubt on Breed's Hill. They also brought up six small cannon.

At 1 P.M. on 17 June, Howe led 1,500 British troops across the bay to Charleston Neck. They then began an assault, inadequately supported by a few British field guns and some naval gunfire. Some 2,500–4,000 colonial militia opposed the British. The Americans employed excellent fire discipline, waiting until the British were close and then shattering them with volleys of small arms fire. Twice the British were thrown back with heavy losses. The day was hot, 90 degrees, and the British were carrying 80-pound packs, which did not come off until the third and final assault. The uphill climb also prevented the British from charging with the bayonet while the militiamen were reloading.

Battle of Bunker Hill/Breed's Hill, 17 June 1775. Painting by John Trumbull   *(National Archives)*

Howe committed his 700-man reserve, and with the colonials largely out of powder, the British took Breed's Hill with the bayonet. The colonial militia retreated to Bunker Hill and thence to the mainland, suffering during the retreat most of their 140 killed and 271 wounded. The British lost 226 killed and 826 wounded.

The Battle of Bunker Hull had important effects. It convinced many patriots that a regular military establishment was unnecessary, thus adding to General George WASHINGTON's difficulties. (Appointed to command the CONTINENTAL ARMY on 15 June, he arrived at Boston two weeks after the battle.) The memory of the heavy casualties greatly affected Howe, who henceforth failed to press his victories. The battle also caused the British to employ mercenaries.

The British made no effect to take Dorchester Heights. Gage was recalled, and Howe took over in command. In March, when the colonials brought up cannon from Fort Ticondroga, Howe decided to evacuate Boston altogether.

See also BOSTON, SIEGE OF; AMERICAN REVOLUTIONARY WAR, LAND OVERVIEW.

Further reading: Brooks, Victor. *The Boston Campaign: April 1775–March 1776.* Conshohocken, Pa.: Combined, 1999; Chidsey, Donald B. *The Battle of Bunker Hill.* Garden City, N.Y.: Doubleday, 1961; Ward, Christopher. *The War of the Revolution.* Vol. 1. New York: Macmillan, 1952.

— Spencer C. Tucker

Burke, Arleigh A. ("31-Knot") (1901–1996) *U.S. Navy admiral and chief of naval operations*

Born on 19 October 1901 on a farm near Boulder, Colorado, Arleigh Albert Burke joined the U.S. Navy in 1919, graduating from the Naval Academy at Annapolis in 1923. One of a new generation of technically skilled ordnance officers, in 1931 Burke earned a degree in chemical engineering from the University of Michigan.

When the United States entered World War II in December 1941, Burke immediately applied for sea duty. He was not successful until 1943. In March Burke took command of Destroyer Division 43 in the South Pacific, leading it in support missions and earning a reputation as an excellent tactician and the nickname of "31-knot Burke." Promoted to captain, Burke then commanded Destroyer Squadron 23 ("the little beavers"), leading it to victory in the Battles of Empress Augusta Bay and Cape St. George. In these and 20 other engagements before February 1944, Burke's command sank one Japanese cruiser, nine destroyers, one submarine, and nine smaller vessels. It also severely damaged several other Japanese ships and downed some 30 aircraft, making him the war's most celebrated destroyer commander. Burke's success owed much to his readiness to introduce technological and tactical innovations. As chief of staff to Vice Admiral Marc A. MITSCHER, in 1944 and 1945 Burke coordinated naval striking force operations in the PHILIPPINE SEA, LEYTE GULF, IWO JIMA, and OKINAWA battles.

Holding high positions in the staff of the chief of naval operations in the late 1940s, Burke experienced high visibility in the "Admirals' Revolt," when the navy forcefully opposed nuclear strategic reliance on Air Force B-36 bombers and called for nuclear-armed aircraft carriers. This led the Truman administration to remove him temporarily from the flag officer selection list. Restored and promoted to rear admiral in 1950, he served in the Korean War and on the United Nations truce negotiating team.

In June 1955 President Dwight D. EISENHOWER, passing over 92 more senior admirals, appointed Burke as chief of naval operations, in which capacity he served an unprecedented three two-year terms. Burke attempted to appoint younger, vigorous officers and restore naval morale. He concentrated on promoting new technology, including nuclear-powered submarines and surface ships, guided missiles, and other innovations; he took particular pride in sponsoring the Polaris submarine nuclear deterrent program. He also focused on developing balanced naval forces that could fight limited wars. In 1961, refusing a fourth term from President John F. KENNEDY, Burke retired. He died on 1 January 1996 at the Bethesda Naval Hospital, Bethesda, Maryland.

See also DESTROYERS; NEW LOOK STRATEGY; SUBMARINES; U.S. NAVY.

Further reading: Jones, Ken, and Hubert Kelley, Jr. *Admiral Arleigh (31-Knot) Burke: The Story of a Fighting Sailor.* Philadelphia: Chilton Books, 1962; Potter, E. B. *Admiral Arleigh Burke.* New York: Random House, 1990; Rosenberg, David Alan. "Arleigh Albert Burke." In *The Chiefs of Naval Operations,* edited by Robert William Love, Jr. Annapolis, Md.: Naval Institute Press, 1980.

— Priscilla Roberts

Burnside, Ambrose E. (1824–1881) *U.S. Army general*
Born on 23 May 1824 at Liberty, Indiana, Ambrose Everett Burnside worked as a tailor until friends of his father, an Indiana legislator, secured him an appointment to the U.S. Military Academy at WEST POINT. He graduated in 1847 and was commissioned a second lieutenant of artillery. After garrison duty in Mexico and fighting against the Apache in the Southwest, he was promoted to first lieutenant in 1851.

Burnside resigned his commission in 1853, settling in Rhode Island to manufacture a breechloading rifle he had invented, but his company failed in 1857. Burnside became a major general in the Rhode Island militia and treasurer of the Illinois Central Railroad. On the outbreak of the Civil War, Burnside organized and became colonel of the 1st Rhode Island Infantry, a three-month regiment, which was among the first volunteer units to reach Washington at the start of the CIVIL WAR.

Burnside commanded a brigade in the First Battle of BULL RUN/MANASSAS, after which he was appointed brigadier general of U.S. Volunteers. In 1862 he commanded a successful amphibious operation along the North Carolina coast, capturing Roanoke Island and New Bern. Promoted to major general of volunteers, he was ordered to Virginia to support Major General George B. MCCLELLAN's Army of the Potomac. After McClellan's failure at Richmond, and again following Major General John POPE's defeat in the Second Battle of BULL RUN/MANASSAS, Burnside was offered but declined command of Army of the Potomac. In September 1862, in the Battle of ANTIETAM/SHARPSBURG, Maryland, his IX Corps's failure to cross,

Major General Ambrose Burnside   *(Library of Congress)*

after several attempts, Antietam Creek at what is now known as Burnside's Bridge cost the Federals the chance to rout General Robert E. LEE's Army of Northern Virginia.

Again offered command of the Army of the Potomac, Burnside reluctantly accepted. Prodded into action in December 1862, he ordered a series of disastrous attacks on the well-protected Confederate army at FREDERICKS-BURG. Relieved in January 1863, he assumed command of the Department of the Ohio. In this role he cracked down on "Copperhead" opposition and thwarted Confederate lieutenant general James Longstreet's attempt to capture Knoxville, Tennessee. In the spring of 1864 Burnside and his IX Corps returned to the East as an independent force under Lieutenant General U.S. GRANT until officially attached to the Army of the Potomac after the battles of THE WILDERNESS and SPOTSYLVANIA COURTHOUSE.

IX Corps fought throughout the 1864 overland campaign and at PETERSBURG, where in July one of Burnside's regiments constructed a tunnel that was packed with powder and exploded under Confederate lines. For his bungling of the ensuing Battle of the CRATER, Burnside was placed on leave and never recalled to duty. He resigned his commission in April 1865.

After the war Burnside enjoyed a successful career as a railroad executive and was three times elected governor of Rhode Island. Elected to U.S. Senate in 1874, he served until his death at Bristol, Rhode Island, on 13 September 1881.

See also CIVIL WAR, LAND OVERVIEW.

Further reading: Kinard, Jeff. *The Battle of the Crater.* Fort Worth, Tex.: Ryan Place, 1995; Marvel, William. *Burnside.* Chapel Hill: University of North Carolina Press, 1991.

— David Coffey

Burr, Aaron (1756–1836) *Colonel in the Continental army and prominent politician*

Born on 6 February 1756 at Newark, New Jersey, into a distinguished family, Aaron Burr was orphaned in his youth and raised by an uncle. He entered Princeton in 1769, graduating in 1772. Burr joined the Patriot cause in 1775. Upon their first meeting, Burr and the Continental army commander General George WASHINGTON took an immediate dislike to one another, as a result of which Burr was unassigned until Colonel Benedict ARNOLD organized an assault against Quebec. In the 1775–76 invasion of CANADA, Burr, now a captain, distinguished himself in the failed assault on the city. In the spring of 1776 he was appointed to Washington's staff but soon transferred to that of Major General Israel PUTNAM. In June 1777 Burr was promoted to lieutenant colonel and took command of a regiment. He spent the winter of 1777–78 at VALLEY FORGE, Pennsylvania, and participated in the Battle of MONMOUTH COURTHOUSE. In early 1779 Burr assumed command of the Westchester lines, the no-man's-land between the American and British positions in New York. His efficiency quickly earned the respect of his superiors, but his health deteriorated, and Burr resigned from the army on 10 March 1779.

Following the Revolutionary War, Burr became a successful lawyer and politician in New York, vying with Alexander HAMILTON for political supremacy in the state. During the 1790s Burr was New York's attorney general. He also served in the U.S. Senate from 1791 to 1797 and afterward in the state legislature. In the presidential election of 1800 Burr ran as a Republican for the vice presidency. He and Thomas JEFFERSON each received 73 electoral votes, sending the decision to the House of Representatives, where Hamilton used his influence to elect Jefferson. Burr was then vice president from 1801 to 1805. The Burr-Hamilton rivalry escalated until on 12 July 1804 they fought a duel ending in Hamilton's death.

Burr then began developing plans for the West, but their exact nature remains unclear. Apparently, he hoped to raise an army and seize the Louisiana Territory or Mexico. In late 1806 his co-conspirator, Major General James WILKINSON, betrayed him. Federal officers caught Burr trying to flee in February 1807, but Chief Justice John Marshall acquitted him of treason for lack of witnesses.

With few prospects and heavily in debt, Burr traveled to Europe. In 1812 he returned to the United States, where he practiced law in New York until his death there on 14 September 1836.

See also LOUISIANA PURCHASE; REVOLUTIONARY WAR, LAND OVERVIEW.

Further reading: Lomask, Milton. *Aaron Burr.* 2 vols. New York: Farrar, Strauss, Giroux, 1979–82; Parmet, Herbert S., and Marie B. Hecht. *Aaron Burr: Portrait of an Ambitious Man.* New York: Macmillan, 1967.

— Rodney Madison

Burrows, William (1785–1813) *U.S. Navy officer*

Born on 6 October 1785 at Kinderton, Pennsylvania, the son of the first Marine Corps commandant, William Burrows joined the navy as a midshipman in November 1799. In January 1800, he was assigned to the USS *Portsmouth* on a European cruise. Burrows was then granted a furlough to study navigation and French. He served on the CONSTITUTION throughout the TRIPOLITAN WAR, followed by service on the *President* and *Hornet*.

Bush, George H. W.

Frustrated by slow promotion, Burrows was granted a year-long furlough, which he spent aboard a merchant ship, the *Thomas Penrose,* on a cruise to the Far East. The ship was captured on its return voyage by the British following the outbreak of the WAR OF 1812.

Released, Burrows secured command of the sloop of war *Enterprise* (16 guns). On 6 September 1813, while searching for British privateers off Maine, Burrows intercepted the British brig-sloop *Boxer* (14). A savage fight ensued, and the *Boxer* finally surrendered, badly battered. The British ship had received a number of hull shots; several guns were dismounted, and its main top-mast was nearly separated. The *Enterprise* had also received some hull hits, and its mainmast and foremast were nearly shot away. In terms of casualties, most of which were from grape or canister shot, the British lost 21 and the Americans only 12.

Both captains were mortally wounded in the battle. Captain Samuel Blythe of the *Boxer* was cut in two by a cannonball, and Burrows was hit by canister in the thigh. Burrows remained on deck until the *Boxer* surrendered; he died later that day. When the *Enterprise* returned to Portland, Maine, on 7 September, the two captains were buried side by side, with full military honors.

The battle was the first American success at sea since the defeat of the frigate *Chesapeake* by HMS *Shannon* in June 1812. Since the two vessels in this engagement were of comparable tonnage and crew, the victory helped to restore U.S. Navy confidence.

See also CHESAPEAKE, USS, V. HMS *SHANNON;* WAR OF 1812, NAVAL OVERVIEW.

Further reading: Roosevelt, Theodore. *The Naval War of 1812.* New York: Putnam, 1882.

— Devon S. Miller

Burrows, William W. (1758–1805) *Marine Corps officer and first commandant*

Born on 16 January 1758 at Charleston, South Carolina, William Ward Burrows was educated in England. During the Revolutionary War he served with the South Carolina militia. He then moved to Philadelphia and became a lawyer and merchant.

Having funded in 1794 construction of six frigates, thereby establishing the U.S. Navy, Congress on 11 July 1798 passed legislation establishing a permanent Marine Corps. The next day President John Adams appointed Burrows as major commandant of the Marine Corps. He was the second commandant (the first was the commandant of the colonial marines during the American Revolutionary War) but the first of the permanent Marine Corps. The new law stipulated the rank of major.

Major Burrows was authorized to recruit 881 officers, noncommissioned officers, privates, and musicians to the corps. The first units were detachments for naval vessels assigned to protecting U.S. shipping in the QUASI-WAR with France. Burrows was soon busy bringing these units up to strength, coping with logistics problems, and defining the mission of the Marine Corps.

Promoted to lieutenant colonel in May 1800, in July Burrows moved his headquarters from Philadelphia to the new national capital of Washington. He continued to oversee the corps during the Quasi War and the subsequent TRIPOLITAN WAR.

In 1801 Burrows oversaw the building of the Marine Barracks at Washington, not far from the navy yard. Burrows established many traditions of the corps, such as the Marine Band, the use of "dress blues," and the stiff leather collar that was to provide the name "Leatherneck." Another tradition was that all marines would be trained as combatants, with aggressive martial spirit.

Health forced Burrows to resign his commission in March 1804. He died in Washington, D.C., on 6 March 1805 and in 1892 was reinterred in Arlington National Cemetery.

See also MARINE CORPS, U.S.

Further reading: Heinl, Robert Debs. *Soldiers of the Sea: The United States Marine Corps, 1775–1962.* 2d ed. Baltimore: Nautical & Aviation, 1991; Millet, Allan R. *Semper Fidelis: The History of the United States Marine Corps.* New York: Macmillan, 1980; Moskin, J. Robert. *The U.S. Marine Corps Story.* New York: McGraw-Hill, 1977.

— A. J. L. Waskey

Bush, George H. W. (1924–   ) *President of the United States*

George Herbert Walker Bush was born on 12 June 1924 at Milton, Massachusetts, the son of a future U.S. senator. In 1942, on his 18th birthday, Bush deferred entering Yale University to fight in World War II. He reported for duty in fall 1943 as the youngest pilot in the navy. He served on the light aircraft carrier USS *San Jacinto* in the Pacific theater and flew 58 combat missions. Shot down in September 1944 while flying a torpedo bomber, Bush was rescued by a submarine and returned to his ship.

After the war Bush left the service, graduated from Yale University with a B.A. degree in economics, and moved to Texas, where he amassed considerable wealth in the oil industry before switching to Republican politics. In 1966 he won election to the U.S. House of Representatives. He later served as ambassador to the United Nations (1971–73), chairman of the Republican National Committee (1973–74), head of the U.S. Liaison Office in Beijing (1974–75), director of the CENTRAL INTELLIGENCE AGENCY (CIA) (1976–77),

President George Herbert Walker Bush   *(Library of Congress)*

reflected his reluctance to sustain additional American casualties and his desire to prevent the breakup of Iraq, seen as a buffer against a resurgent Iran. Although Bush publicly stated that the Gulf War had finally "kicked the Vietnam syndrome," his cautious behavior in limiting the conflict suggested that the previous war's memories still resonated in his and other politicians' minds. In 1989 Bush deployed substantial American forces to oust and capture the Panamanian dictator General Manuel Noriega.

Despite record-high public approval ratings during the Gulf War, Bush later saw his popularity sag along with the economy. After losing the 1992 election to Bill Clinton, Bush retired to Houston, Texas, published his memoirs, diaries, and letters and commented occasionally on public affairs. In the 1990s, Bush's own defeat made even sweeter for him the political successes of his sons, George W. and John Ellis (Jeb), who won election as the governors of, respectively, Texas and Florida. In 2000 George W. Bush was elected president of the United States.

See also COLD WAR; DESERT SHIELD, OPERATION; GULF WAR, CAUSES OF; PANAMA INVASION; POWELL, COLIN; SCHWARZKOPF, NORMAN; VIETNAM WAR, COURSE OF.

Further reading: Bush, George, and Brent Scowcroft. *A World Transformed.* New York: Knopf, 1998; Hurst, Steven. *The Foreign Policy of the Bush Administration: In Search of a New World Order.* New York: Pinter, 1999; Hybel, Alex Roberto. *Power over Rationality: The Bush Administration and the Gulf Crisis.* Albany: State University of New York Press, 1993; Parmet, Herbert. *George Bush: The Life of a Lone Star Yankee.* New York: Scribner, 1997; Smith, Jean Edward. *George Bush's War.* New York: Hamilton Holt, 1992.

— Priscilla Roberts

and as vice president under Ronald Reagan (1981–88). Despite his lightweight image and often garbled syntax, in 1988 he won election as president of the United States.

Shortly after Bush became president the Soviet empire in Eastern Europe collapsed, followed in 1991 by the Soviet Union itself, developments for which he claimed more credit than he probably deserved. A devotee of the muscular internationalist tradition embodied by Henry L. STIMSON, whom the president and his father alike revered, Bush determined to resist and reverse Iraqi leader Saddam Hussein's 1990 invasion of oil-rich Kuwait and to preserve international access to Middle Eastern oil.

Bush created the coalition of Western and Arab states that provided the forces for the January–February 1991 United Nations OPERATION DESERT STORM, which expelled Iraqi forces from Kuwait. Many Allied leaders and Americans criticized Bush's decision to halt the war on 28 February, while Saddam still retained power, a decision that may have

Bushnell, David (1740–1824) *Inventor of mines and a submarine*
Born on 30 August 1740 at Pochaug (Saybrook), Connecticut, David Bushnell carried a very heavy burden. As the firstborn son, David received the largely unproductive family farm when his father died. He sold it to his brother Edgar and obtained tutoring for two years before graduating in 1775 from nearby Yale College. Solitary but not lonely, he loved to tinker with things mechanical. While at Yale he spoke of making gunpowder explode under water.

In January 1778, during the American Revolutionary War, Bushnell-designed mines were floated down the Delaware River (they sank no British ships). Bushnell also invented a primitive submarine. Named the *TURTLE* because it resembled one, it was powered by one man. Bushnell planned to use the *Turtle* to transport a mine and secure it to the hull of a British warship.

Bushnell was too frail to operate the *Turtle* himself, and his brother fell ill. Continental army sergeant Ezra Lee volunteered for the attempt. On 9 September 1776 Lee failed to place a mine against the hull of the British 64-gun ship *Eagle* in New York Harbor. However, later submarine inventors, such as Robert FULTON, learned much from Bushnell's work.

In 1779 the Continental army commander, General George WASHINGTON, organized companies of sappers and miners. Bushnell was made a captain-lieutenant, promoted to captain in 1781, and was stationed at WEST POINT in command of the Corps of Engineers on 4 June 1783. In November he was mustered out of the service. He may have lived in France for the next decade, reappearing in Georgia as a schoolteacher in 1799. With the aid of a home companion, another former soldier, he ran a private school. He then moved to Warrenton, Georgia, where he practiced medicine until his death in 1824.

See also AMERICAN REVOLUTIONARY WAR, NAVAL OVERVIEW; MINES, SEA; SUBMARINES.

Further reading: Allen, Gardner W. *A Naval History of the American Revolution.* 2 vols. Boston: Houghton Mifflin, 1913. Reprint, Williamstown, Mass.: Cornerhouse, 1970; Anderson, Frank. *Beginning of Modern Submarine Warfare under Captain Lieutenant David Bushnell.* Hamden, Conn.: Anchor Books, 1966; Hoyt, Edwin. *From the Turtle to the Nautilus: The Story of Submarines.* Boston: Little, Brown, 1963; Wagner, Frederick. *Submarine Fighter of the American Revolution: The Story of David Bushnell.* New York: Dodd, Mead, 1963.

— Paolo E. Coletta

Bushy Run, Battle of (4–6 August 1763) *British victory against Native Americans during Pontiac's Rebellion*
After the FRENCH AND INDIAN WAR, many Indians remained determined to resist British expansion along the western frontier. In May 1763 the Ottawa warrior PONTIAC organized a loose confederation of tribes west of the Allegheny Mountains to seize British outposts and drive the settlers from the land. Pontiac orchestrated nearly simultaneous attacks that captured nine British forts and killed almost 2,000 whites. He placed others, such as Fort Detroit and Fort PITT (present-day Pittsburgh), under siege. At Fort Pitt a mixed force of Delaware, Shawnee, Mingo, and Wyandot warriors besieged the garrison, prompting the British commander in chief, Major General Jeffrey, Lord Amherst, to organize a relief column led by Swiss-born mercenary officer, Colonel Henry BOUQUET. Bouquet's mission was to end the siege, reopen the lines of communication, and resupply the isolated garrison.

Bouquet's force consisted of 460 men from the 42d, 60th, and 77th Regiments, plus a detachment of rangers, along with Indian scouts. His column escorted more than 400 packhorses carrying foodstuffs and other supplies. Aware of this relief effort, the Indians planned to ambush the British near Bushy Run Creek, about 25 miles southeast of Fort Pitt.

During the hot afternoon of 5 August, Bouquet's advance guard moved through a quiet forest, expecting soon to complete the day's 17-mile march. Suddenly fire erupted from the brush, killing several soldiers; 400 Indians attacked the column. The Indians attempted to envelop Bouquet's force in a horseshoe-shaped trap, but the well-disciplined regulars stood firm. Bouquet ordered two light infantry companies to counterattack, firing platoon volleys and then charging with bayonets to drive off the Indians.

Bouquet organized a hasty defensive position on nearby Edge Hill, where he used bags of flour from the packhorses to form a circular barricade against the continued Indian assaults. His men suffered from dire thirst in the heat, and the lack of water added to the anguish of the wounded. Bouquet demonstrated his understanding of his enemy and the environment by devising a plan that concealed the location of two infantry companies on a secluded spur of the hill. When the Indians renewed their assault on 6 August, Bouquet led his entrenched forces in a feigned retreat, and the Indians pursued. Just as the Indians sensed victory, the concealed infantry fired a crushing volley, followed by a bayonet charge that devastated the Native Americans and caused them to flee.

In the battle Bouquet lost almost 50 men killed and about 60 wounded; Native American casualties are unknown. The British expedition then continued to Fort Pitt and relieved the garrison on 10 August. Bouquet had inflicted a rare defeat on the Indians in their own environment, with disciplined troops and tactics suited to wilderness warfare.

See also AMERICAN INDIAN WARS, OVERVIEW; INDIAN WARFARE; PONTIAC'S REBELLION.

Further reading: Anderson, Niles. *The Battle of Bushy Run.* Harrisburg: Pennsylvania Historical and Museum Commission, 1966; Bumberger, C. M. *The Battle of Bushy Run.* Jeannette, Pa.: Jeannette, 1928; Kopperman, Paul E. "The Captives Return: Bouquet's Victory." *Timeline* 7 (April/May 1990): 2–14.

— Steven J. Rauch

Butler, Benjamin F. (1818–1893) *Politician and U.S. Army general*
Born on 5 November 1818 at Deerfield, New Hampshire, Benjamin Franklin Butler grew up in Lowell, Massachusetts, where his widowed mother ran a boarding house. Graduated in 1838 from Waterbury (now Colby)

Major General Benjamin Butler   *(Library of Congress)*

College in Maine, he taught school in Lowell and studied law. In 1840 he began a successful practice in criminal law. As a Democrat, he was elected in 1853 to the Massachusetts legislature and in 1859 to the state senate. In the 1860 presidential race Butler championed Jefferson DAVIS's nomination and eventually supported southern Democrat John C. BRECKINRIDGE in the November election. Despite his backing of states' rights Democrats, Butler rallied to the Union once hostilities began.

Only days after the attack on FORT SUMTER, as brigadier general of Massachusetts Volunteers, Butler led the 8th Massachusetts Regiment to the relief of Washington and became the first man appointed major general of U.S. Volunteers by President Abraham LINCOLN. In June 1861, commanding the Department of Virginia, he was defeated in one of the Civil War's first engagements, at Big Bethel.

In the first of many controversial decisions, Butler ruled that slaves fleeing secessionist owners to Union lines were "contraband" and subject to seizure. That August he directed a successful amphibious campaign against the North Carolina coast.

In May 1862 Butler led occupation forces into NEW ORLEANS and became military governor of the area. There

he aroused much criticism and hatred. He ordered a man hanged for ripping down a U.S. flag and issued the infamous "Woman Order," stating that women who insulted or spat upon Union soldiers, a common practice, would be regarded as prostitutes. Charges both real and imagined clung to "Beast" Butler's administration of New Orleans. Even if many of the charges were unfounded, he and many of his associates apparently reaped considerable financial rewards during their stay in Louisiana. In December 1862 Lincoln pulled Butler out of New Orleans.

Butler remained inactive for most of 1863, during which time he courted favor among his new allies—the radical Republicans. Finally, in November 1863 he assumed command of the Department of Virginia and North Carolina and XVIII Army Corps. In April 1864 he was appointed to head the new Army of the James, consisting of X and XVIII Corps and a cavalry division. In May he moved his army up the James River and established a line across a bend on the south side of the James. Moving on Richmond, he was checked with heavy losses at Drewry's Bluff by a much smaller Confederate force commanded by General P. G. T. BEAUREGARD and withdrew into a Bermuda Hundred perimeter, where his force was isolated.

In December 1864 Butler failed miserably in an attempt to take FORT FISHER, guarding Wilmington, North Carolina—something accomplished with ease by Brigadier General Alfred TERRY weeks later. Butler was relieved in January 1865 and never held another command. He resigned his volunteer commission in November 1865 and resumed his political career as a Radical Republican.

Elected to five terms in the U.S. House of Representatives, Butler was prominent in the impeachment of President Andrew Johnson. In 1882 he was elected governor of Massachusetts and in 1884 was the Greenback Party's presidential nominee. Butler died at Washington, D.C., on 11 January 1893.

See also CIVIL WAR, LAND OVERVIEW.

Further reading: Hearn, Chester G. *When the Devil Came Down to Dixie: Ben Butler in New Orleans.* Baton Rouge: Louisiana State University Press, 1997; Sommers, Richard J. *Richmond Redeemed: The Siege at Petersburg.* Garden City, N.Y.: Doubleday, 1981.

— David Coffey

Butler, Smedley D. (1881–1940) *U.S. Marine Corps general and one of the most decorated of military personnel in U.S. history*

Born on 30 July 1881 at West Chester, Pennsylvania, Smedley Darlington Butler received a temporary commission in the marines at age 16 through the influence of his congressman father. He went to Cuba during the SPANISH-AMERICAN WAR but arrived too late for the fighting.

Reappointed as a lieutenant in the regular Marine Corps in 1899, Butler served in China during the BOXER UPRISING. On 21 June 1900, he and five other marines held off a force of several thousand Boxers during the relief of Tienstin. Since naval and marine officers were not eligible for the Medal of Honor until 1914, Butler received a brevet promotion, later confirmed by Congress. In 1921 the Marine Corps created its short-lived Brevet Medal to recognize those marine officers who had received brevet promotions for combat heroism. The now-obsolete medal ranked in order of precedence above the Navy Cross and just below the Medal of Honor.

Prominent in the Latin American interventions of the early 20th century, Butler led a marine battalion in the occupation of VERACRUZ in April 1914. He was awarded his first Medal of Honor for his leadership during the landings. He initially refused to accept the decoration, but the Navy Department ordered him to accept it and wear it. Butler received his second Medal of Honor the next year in Haiti for leading the attack on the Cacos stronghold of Fort Rivière. Butler's top sergeant during that action, the legendary Dan DALY, also received his second Medal of Honor in the action.

Butler served in France during World War I but, much to his disgust, did not see combat; as a brigadier general he commanded the replacement camp at Pontanezen, in Brest. In 1924 he was granted a two-year leave from the marines to serve as the director of public safety in Philadelphia. Returning to active duty, Butler spent most of the remainder of his career serving in foreign posts. In 1931 he got in trouble for making a speech critical of Benito Mussolini, then the leader of a friendly state. Butler was arrested and slated for court-martial, but he was allowed to retire as a major general in lieu of trial.

After retiring from the corps, Butler became an outspoken critic of U.S. military policy and a vigorous isolationist. He turned antiwar, but not antimilitary. In 1935 he published a book titled *War Is a Racket,* in which he characterized his own military career as little more than an effort to make the world safe for U.S. businesses. Butler died in Philadelphia on 21 June 1940. Two years later the U.S. Navy named a destroyer after him.

See also LATIN AMERICAN INTERVENTIONS, EARLY 20TH CENTURY; MARINE CORPS.

Further reading: Butler, Smedley D. *War Is a Racket.* New York: Round Table Press, 1935; Schmidt, Hans. *Maverick Marine.* Lexington: University Press of Kentucky, 1987.

— David T. Zabecki

Byrd, Richard E., Jr. (1888–1957) *U.S. Navy admiral and explorer*

Born on 25 October 1888 at Winchester, Virginia, Richard Evelyn Byrd, Jr., was a descendant of the famed Byrd family of colonial Virginia. He was the younger brother of Senator Harry F. Byrd, Sr., who dominated Virginia politics from the 1920s to the early 1960s. Educated at the Virginia Military Institute and the University of Virginia, Byrd was a 1912 graduate of the U.S. Naval Academy at Annapolis. An ankle injury from his Annapolis days denied Byrd his desired career as a seagoing officer, and prior to World War I he was relegated to desk jobs within the Navy Department.

In 1917, however, Byrd persuaded the navy to permit him to enroll in a flight training program at Pensacola, Florida. At war's end he was in charge of U.S. naval air forces in Canada. Byrd became a leading proponent of the role that airplanes could play in a 20th-century navy.

In 1923 Byrd became involved in an abortive plan to pilot an American dirigible over the North Pole and then took up an interest in the Arctic. Byrd retired from active duty in 1925 with the rank of lieutenant commander and began to plan privately financed flights in the Arctic region and to develop a transatlantic air route. Byrd's most famous exploit was a flight with Floyd Bennett to the North Pole and back on 9 May 1926—although some have claimed that the Byrd-Bennett plane never actually crossed the pole and thus does not deserve to be considered the first such flight.

In 1928 Byrd's attention turned to the South Pole. With financing from the National and American Geographical Societies, he and his party traveled to Antarctica, where in November 1929 Byrd, accompanied by three other aviators, flew to the South Pole and back. For his endeavor, Congress raised Byrd to the rank of rear admiral. Byrd's active exploration work in Antarctica continued until interrupted by World War II. (An expedition in 1934 nearly caused him his life by carbon monoxide poisoning.)

During the war Byrd was engaged in several clandestine missions in both the Pacific and European theaters. At war's end he resumed his leadership in activities in the Antarctic, not as an on-ground explorer but as an organizer and adviser for governmental endeavors there. Byrd died at Boston, Massachusetts, on 11 March 1957.

Further reading: Byrd, Richard Evelyn. *Alone.* New York: Putnam, 1938; ———. *Discovery: The Story of the Second Byrd Antarctic Expedition.* New York: Putnam, 1935; ———. *Little America: Aerial Exploration in the Antarctic: The Flight to the South Pole.* New York: Putnam, 1930; Rose, Lisle A. *Assault on Eternity: Richard E. Byrd and the Exploration of Antarctica, 1946–47.* Annapolis, Md.: Naval Institute Press, 1980.

— David W. Coffey

C

Cadoria, Sherian G. (1940–) *U.S. Army general*
Born on 26 January 1940 at Marksville, Louisiana, Sherian Grace Cadoria was heavily influenced by her mother and experiences of the segregated South. Cadoria's first contact with the military occurred in 1960, when she was a student at Southern University in Baton Rouge, Louisiana, and attended a WOMEN'S ARMY CORPS training session at Fort McClellan, Alabama.

On graduation from Southern University in 1961 with a B.S. in business education, Cadoria was commissioned in the army as a second lieutenant. Stationed at Fort McClellan, she was promoted in 1963 to first lieutenant. At Fort McClellan, Ku Klux Klan members often stood at the camp gate and taunted military African Americans.

In 1967 Cadoria was assigned to Vietnam as a protocol officer, overcoming opposition to her gender. She served 33 months in Vietnam. Intending to leave the army and enter a convent when she returned home, she changed her mind when the army selected her as the first African-American woman to attend the Command and General Staff College at Fort Leavenworth, Kansas. From 1971 to 1976 Cadoria served in various personnel slots, including an assignment with the deputy chief of staff for personnel. She then commanded the Military Police Student Battalion (1977–1978), was a division chief with the Physical Security Division of Seventh Army in Europe (1979–82), and then commanded a brigade in the 1st Region Criminal Investigation Command (1982–84).

Promoted in 1985 to brigadier general, Cadoria was the first black woman to achieve this rank. Cadoria then served as director for mobilization and operations and as director of human resources and personnel on the Joint Chiefs of Staff. She later held positions with the Law Enforcement Division and the Criminal Investigation Command. Cadoria retired from the military in 1990 and began a consulting business in Louisiana.

See also AFRICAN AMERICANS IN THE MILITARY; WOMEN IN THE MILITARY.

Further reading: Lanker, Brian. *I Dream a World: Portraits of Black Women Who Changed America.* New York: Stewart Tabori and Chang, 1999.

— Tracy M. Shilcutt

Calhoun, John C. (1782–1850) *U.S. senator, secretary of war, secretary of state, and vice president*
Born on 18 March 1782 in Abbeville, South Carolina, John Caldwell Calhoun was the son of one of the largest slave owners in the western portion of the state. He received an excellent classical education in local schools, which prepared him for his entry into the junior class at Yale College at age 20. He graduated in 1804, having earned recognition as one of the school's most outstanding students. Afterward he studied law for several years before opening his own practice in South Carolina. Having gained considerable local support for his condemnation of British attacks on American shipping, Calhoun won election to the South Carolina legislature in 1808 and to the U.S. House of Representatives two years later. There he emerged as one of the leading supporters of war with Great Britain.

In 1817 Calhoun resigned his seat in the House in order to accept the position of secretary of war in the incoming administration of James Monroe. The War Department was in disarray following its disastrous conduct of the WAR OF 1812, and several other leading politicians had declined the position. Calhoun accepted the challenge of reorganizing the nation's troubled military establishment and proved to be one of the most able secretaries of war in the nation's history. He created separate staff bureaus in Washington, improved coastal defenses, established important new forts in the West, created the position of commanding general of the army, and implemented congressionally ordered budget cuts without too greatly damaging the army's effectiveness.

After serving as secretary of war for eight years, Calhoun won election to the vice presidency in 1824 and reelection four years later. Although initially a supporter of President Andrew JACKSON, he soon fell out with the former general and resigned his position in December 1832 in order to accept election as senator from South Carolina. Calhoun emerged as a leading spokesman for the doctrine of nullification, which claimed that states had the right to nullify federal laws. A vigorous defender of slavery and opponent of the federal tariff, Calhoun, once a devoted nationalist, increasingly advocated the right of secession. With the exception of brief service as secretary of state in 1844 and 1845, during which he helped negotiate the annexation of Texas, Calhoun spent most of the last 20 years of his life in the Senate, where his forceful and logical debating style earned him considerable renown. He died at Washington, D.C., on 31 March 1850, shortly after an impassioned defense of slavery and states' rights during the debate over the Compromise of 1850.

Further reading: Bartlett, Irving H. *John C. Calhoun: A Biography.* New York: Norton, 1993; Niven, John. *John C. Calhoun and the Price of Union: A Biography.* Baton Rouge: Louisiana State University Press, 1988; Spiller, Roger J. "John C. Calhoun as Secretary of War, 1817–1825." Unpublished Ph.D. dissertation, Louisiana State University, 1977.

— Michael Thomas Smith

Calley, William L., Jr. (1943–) *U.S. Army lieutenant convicted of the murder of Vietnamese civilians in the March 1968 My Lai Massacre during the Vietnam War*
Born on 8 June 1943 in Miami, Florida, William Laws Calley was a mediocre student. Despite previous rejection for military service, he was drafted into the army in 1966. After brief enlisted service, Calley attended officer candidate school at Fort Benning, Georgia. He graduated 120th in his 156-man September 1967 class. Commissioned a second lieutenant, Calley was assigned to the 23d (Americal) Division. In Vietnam, Calley commanded the 1st Platoon of Charlie Company, 1st Battalion, 20th Infantry, 11th Infantry Brigade of the 23d Division.

On 16 March 1968 Calley led his platoon in a sweep through My Lai 4, a hamlet of Son My Village, in the Son Tinh district of Quang Ngai Province in northern South Vietnam. The operation was intended to eliminate some of the estimated 250 Viet Cong (VC) thought to be operating in the area. Prior sweeps had brought only light VC contact but a high rate of losses to snipers, mines, and booby traps.

Charlie Company found only women, children, and mostly old men, cooking breakfast. The soldiers of First Lieutenant Calley's platoon indiscriminately shot people as they ran from their huts, rounding up survivors to be executed at a nearby ditch.

The incident was brought to light a year later and investigated by an army board of inquiry. The subsequent Peers report produced a list of 30 people, mostly officers (including the division commander), who knew of the atrocities; however, only 14 were charged with crimes. All eventually had their charges dismissed or were acquitted by courts-martial, except Calley.

Found guilty, Calley was sentenced to life imprisonment. The verdict brought an outpouring of support for him. Supporters on the right wing were joined by some in the antiwar movement, who regarded the MY LAI MASSACRE as merely one example of everyday American military tactics. Undoubtedly, the widespread show of sympathy for Calley before, during, and after his trial influenced President Richard M. NIXON's handling of the case. Three days after Calley was sentenced to life imprisonment the White House announced that the president would personally review the case and that pending an appeal Calley could remain free. The Court of Military Appeals subsequently reduced Calley's sentence to 20 years; later the secretary of the army reduced it to 10. In November 1974 President Nixon granted Calley a parole. He had served three days in military jail. In effect, Nixon had pardoned him. Calley subsequently married and became a jeweler in Columbus, Georgia.

See also VIETNAM WAR; WAR CRIMES.

Further reading: Goldstein, Joseph, et al. *The My Lai Massacre and Its Cover-Up: Beyond the Reach of Law?* New York: Free Press, 1976; Greenshaw, Wayne. *The Making of a Hero: The Story of Lieut. William Calley, Jr.* Louisville, Ky.: Touchstone, 1971; Hersh, Seymour M. *My Lai 4: A Report on the Massacre and Its Aftermath.* New York: Random House, 1970; ———. *Cover-Up: The Army's Secret Investigation of the Massacre at My Lai 4.* New York: Random House, 1972; Peers, William R. *The My Lai Inquiry.* New York: Norton, 1979.

— Arthur T. Frame

Cambodian incursion (1 May–30 June 1970) *Brief U.S. military intervention during the Vietnam War into Cambodian territory, the culmination of attempts to eradicate People's Army of Vietnam (PAVN, otherwise North Vietnamese Army, NVA) guerrilla sanctuaries within Cambodia*
On 1 May 1970 forces of the United States and of the Army of the Republic of Vietnam (ARVN) began a series of military operations across the Vietnamese border in Cambodia, with the intention of denying that territory as a refuge to PAVN forces. From early 1969 onward the United States, under President Richard NIXON and his national security adviser Henry A. KISSINGER, had mounted an extensive

bombing campaign designed to eliminate PAVN bases within Cambodia, from which Communist forces had previously operated with impunity. These aerial measures proved largely unsuccessful and if anything drove Cambodian Khmer Rouge communists to the interior and increased their rural support.

Since 1967 top American generals had sought to wipe out North Vietnamese bases in Cambodia, a measure that Nixon believed would purchase time for his policy of "Vietnamization," the transfer of responsibility to ARVN forces. Nixon also perceived these operations as a means of signaling to North Vietnamese negotiators in ongoing peace talks his resolve and determination to adopt a hardline stance and to broaden the war if necessary. King Norodom Sihanouk of Cambodia, who professed neutrality in the conflict, had for many years maintained a careful balance between the United States and North Vietnam and would not permit U.S. ground forces to launch military operations on Cambodian soil. In March 1970, therefore, the CENTRAL INTELLIGENCE AGENCY supported a coup against the king, bringing to power General Lon Nol, his prime minister, and Prince Sirik Matak, his cousin. Almost immediately Sihanouk sought aid from the People's Republic of China, allying himself with the Khmer Rouge as their nominal leader. The addition of the popular Sihanouk enormously increased the Cambodian communists' prestige and enhanced their position among the population. Meanwhile, in March 1970 the ARVN began occasional limited operations within Cambodia, which continued sporadically until the 1973 Paris Peace Accords were signed.

On 1 May 1970, almost 12,000 American and 8,000 ARVN soldiers attacked a section of the Vietnamese-Cambodian border known as the Parrot's Beak. This area, they believed, contained the PAVN headquarters. Rather than offering battle, PAVN forces speedily retreated westward, abandoning to the invaders vast stocks of equipment and other supplies, including 23,000 weapons and 14 million pounds of rice. Wary of being drawn ever deeper into potential ambush in hostile and uncertain territory, American and South Vietnamese troops penetrated only 19 miles beyond the border, finally ending the operation and departing Cambodian territory on 30 June 1970. North Vietnamese and Viet Cong casualties were estimated at 11,000, while the joint U.S.-ARVN forces had lost 976 killed and 4,500 wounded.

Then and later, Nixon and Kissinger characterized the incursion as successful, claiming that it greatly disrupted enemy military capabilities, winning a year's breathing space in which to implement Vietnamization while allaying pressure on the new Cambodian government. Critics such as the journalist William Shawcross argued that the operation's military impact was limited and that it accelerated the political destabilization of Cambodia. The American bombing campaign had already set in motion this process and until 1973 continued to reinforce it, thereby facilitating the eventual Khmer Rouge takeover and the subsequent Cambodian genocide of the late 1970s.

Indisputably, the Cambodian incursion provoked fierce antiwar protests within the United States, a major reason why the Nixon administration quickly limited the incursion's geographical scope and withdrew American forces relatively expeditiously. Many Americans perceived the operation as an expansion and escalation of the war, one that entirely discredited Nixon's and Kissinger's claims that they were searching for peace in Vietnam. On 4 May 1970, National Guard troops fired on unarmed student demonstrators at Kent State University, Ohio, killing four and wounding nine, an episode that marked the beginning of a new level of violence in antiwar and civil rights protests. On 9 May more than 100,000 demonstrators protested in Washington against the Cambodian incursion, joined for the first time by many political moderates who had hitherto refrained from open opposition. Several administration officials resigned from the National Security Council in protest, while the Senate overturned the 1964 TONKIN GULF RESOLUTION that had authorized the president to respond to the Vietnam emergency as he thought appropriate. Not until 1973, however, did the Senate finally end the bombing of Cambodia.

See also BARREL ROLL, OPERATION; CONTAINMENT, DOCTRINE AND COURSE OF; PACIFISM/WAR RESISTANCE; VIETNAM WAR, COURSE OF.

Further reading: Chandler, David P. *The Tragedy of Cambodian History: Politics, War and Revolution since 1945.* New Haven, Conn.: Yale University Press, 1991; Nolan, Keith William. *Into Cambodia: Spring Campaign, Summer Offensive, 1970.* Novato, Calif.: Presidio Press, 1985; Shawcross, William. *Sideshow: Kissinger, Nixon and the Destruction of Cambodia.* New York: Simon & Schuster, 1979; Wells, Tom. *The War Within: America's Battle over Vietnam.* Berkeley: University of California Press, 1994.

— Priscilla Roberts

Camden, Battle of (16 August 1780) *Key American Revolutionary War battle*
Following the American surrender of Charleston in May 1780, Congress appointed Major General Horatio GATES, victor in the Battle of SARATOGA, to command the Southern Department. Gates arrived at Coxe's Mill, North Carolina, on 25 July to take command of Major General Johann de KALB's 1,200-man division of Delaware and Maryland Continentals, three artillery companies, and Colonel Charles Armand's 120-man "legion." Gates issued orders for an immediate movement on Camden, South Carolina.

This important British supply base was defended by only 700 men. The army set out on 27 July on a difficult two-week, 120-mile march on short rations. Gates was reinforced on the way by Virginia and North Carolina militia.

The British commander in the South, Lieutenant General Charles Cornwallis, believed that the only way to hold Georgia and South Carolina was to invade North Carolina, and Camden was to be the forward base for this invasion. He had placed in command there Lieutenant Colonel Lord Francis Rawdon.

Learning of Gates's approach, Rawdon sent word to Cornwallis at Charleston. As Cornwallis hurried north with reinforcements, Rawdon attempted to block Gates at Little Lynches Creek, 15 miles northeast of Camden, on 11 August. Withdrawing to Camden when Gates forded the river and attempted to outflank him, Rawdon ordered in reinforcements from British garrisons at Hanging Rock, Rocky Mount, and Ninety-Six.

On 14 August Gates reached Rugeley's Mill, about 10 miles north of Camden. There he was reinforced by 700 Virginia militia, but Gates detached 400 infantry and an artillery company to cooperate with South Carolina partisans against Camden's supply route. Gates now had 4,100 men, but the majority were militia.

Cornwallis arrived in the vicinity of Camden on 15 August. British total strength was now 2,239 men, including Tory militia. On the night of 15 August, both commanders decided to attack the other at daybreak. Gates advanced at 10 P.M. from Rugeley's Mill south toward Camden while Cornwallis moved at the same time from Camden toward Gates. Advanced units of the two armies encountered each other in the early morning darkness of 16 August. Both sides deployed for battle at daybreak.

Cornwallis deployed just north of Saunders Creek and Gates on high ground to the north. Gates was well aware of the common British practice of placing greater strength on the right wing, but he deployed American militia against British regulars while British provincials and militia faced American regulars.

Gates ordered the Virginia militia forward to attack the British right before it could deploy, but the order came too late; the militia panicked and fled the field without firing a shot. The British regulars then wheeled to their left to attack de Kalb's right flank, in conjunction with provincials and militia, who were already engaged. Dust and smoke from the battle prevented de Kalb from realizing that he was now fighting the entire British force alone, and he ordered a counterattack, which failed. Unhorsed and mortally wounded, de Kalb refused to order a retreat without orders from Gates, who had been swept from the field with the rout of the militia. British cavalry soon closed off the 2nd Maryland brigade's rear and ended the Battle of Camden.

Of his 4,000 men, only Gates and 700 reached Hillsboro, North Carolina. Gates had lost 250 killed and 800 wounded and 1,000 captured. British losses were just 68 men killed and 256 wounded. The Battle of Camden was one of the worst defeats ever inflicted on an American army. The Continental army commander, General George WASHINGTON, sent Major General Nathaniel GREENE south to replace Gates and rebuild the shattered army, while Cornwallis moved to invade North Carolina.

See also AMERICAN REVOLUTIONARY WAR, LAND OVERVIEW; CHARLESTON, SIEGE OF (1780); GREENE'S OPERATIONS.

Further reading: Buchanan, John. *The Road to Guilford Courthouse: The American Revolution in the Carolinas.* New York: Wiley, 1997; Morrill, Dan L. *Southern Campaigns of the American Revolution.* Mount Pleasant, S.C.: Nautical & Aviation, 1993.

— Benjamin L. Huggins

Canada, invasion of (1775–1776) *American Revolutionary War campaign*

Very early in the American Revolutionary War, the rebellious colonies sought to export their revolution to their northern neighbors in the British colony of Quebec, more commonly referred to as Canada. The traditional route to Canada was the Lake Champlain–Hudson River corridor, which the Americans moved quickly to seize in May 1775. A detachment of 200 militia under Colonel Benedict ARNOLD and Ethan ELLEN captured FORT TICONDEROGA at the southern tip of Lake Champlain on 10 May and then advanced down the lake to capture a smaller British post at CROWN POINT.

Following the capture of Fort Ticonderoga, the Continental Congress approved a plan for a major American invasion of Canada. The invasion called for a two-prong assault. Major General Philip SCHUYLER would push north out of New York along the Lake Champlain corridor, while Arnold crossed the Maine wilderness to strike at Quebec. Theoretically, the main British army, under Sir Guy Carleton at Montreal, would be split between the two American armies and easily crushed, leaving Canada under American control.

The main thrust of the invasion got under way at the end of August 1775. Reoccurring rheumatism and gout confined Schuyler to a sickbed and left prosecution of the invasion to his second in command, Brigadier General Richard MONTGOMERY. Montgomery proved an able commander, but his troops were raw recruits and few in number. Nonetheless, he pushed northward, instilling discipline in his army as he went, and easily captured a British garrison at Fort Chambly on 19 October. The Americans met with considerably less success at Fort St. Johns, a stone fort on the Richelieu River approximately 20 miles south of Montreal. After a month-long siege, the 600-man British garrison finally surrendered on 2 November when Montgomery bombarded the fort with heavy artillery captured at Chambly. Montgomery then took Montreal, the second-largest city in Canada, without a fight on 12 November. Carleton and his small British army narrowly evaded capture outside Montreal and managed to flee safely downriver to Quebec.

Arnold's prong of the invasion got under way on 6 September 1775. He led 1,050 volunteers—mostly New Englanders, along with several hundred Pennsylvanians and Daniel MORGAN's Virginia Riflemen—into the Maine wilderness along the Kennebec River. Arnold's expedition spent the majority of its time battling the elements; its provisions and supplies were exhausted only a few weeks into the journey. Desertion and starvation plagued the effort from that point, but nearly 700 Americans broke through the wilderness and reached Point Levis, across the St. Lawrence River from Quebec, on 9 November. Arnold's diminished command occupied the Plains of Abraham outside the main gate to Quebec a few days later and awaited Montgomery's arrival.

Montgomery met only sparse resistance on his drive toward Quebec, but daily desertions and illness gravely reduced his army. He reached the Plains of Abraham to rendezvous with Arnold during the first week of December with only 300 combat-ready troops. Together, their forces numbered barely 1,000 men, while Carleton had at least 1,200 men inside the walls of the city, although nearly half of these were undependable Canadian militia. Neither the Americans nor the British possessed the human resources necessary to conduct offensive operations, but the burden to act lay with Montgomery and Arnold. The Canadian winter already ravaged their small army, but an even greater dilemma became the approaching expiration of many of their troops' enlistments on 1 January 1776.

In a desperate assault, Montgomery and Arnold led 800 men against the city during a raging blizzard on New Year's Eve. Montgomery lost his life during the attack, Arnold was wounded, and a sizable portion of the American army was captured. Despite the disastrous outcome of the attack, Arnold managed to rally his troops and lay siege to the city of Quebec for the next several months. Blockaded by the ice-locked St. Lawrence River as much as by the Americans, Carleton was content to wait out the siege, hoping that relief would be sent.

He was rewarded for his perseverance in early May, when the spring thaw opened the St. Lawrence to the vanguard of 13,000 British and Hessian reinforcements. The American encampment, now under the command of Brigadier General David Wooster, degenerated into a mass of confusion and anarchy at the approach of the relief expedition and was surprised when Carleton led a sally from the city, which sent the disorganized force scrambling into retreat.

The Americans fell back down the St. Lawrence. Reinforced by more than 3,000 fresh troops at Sorel, located at the junction of the St. Lawrence and Richelieu Rivers, they regrouped and engaged the pursuing British army at TROIS RIVIÈRES, on 8 June, halfway between Quebec and Montreal. The result was another crushing defeat for the Americans, which combined with a successful British and Indian assault on an American post west of Montreal at the CEDARS to rout the Americans.

With Carleton's reinforced army approaching, the Americans at Sorel faced a crisis. Arnold, in command of a contingent of 300 Continental soldiers at Montreal, advocated withdrawing up the Richelieu River to defend Lake Champlain. Brigadier General John SULLIVAN, who had replaced Wooster, withdrew only a few miles south along the Richelieu to Chambly and then hesitated. On 9 June, while he waited, Arnold withdrew his forces to St. Johns, where he burned the naval yard and stripped the town of supplies, which he shipped down the lake to Fort Ticonderoga. A week later the British chased Sullivan out of Chambly and sent the dissipated American force limping into St. Johns, which they quickly abandoned to the advancing British, escaping south to Crown Point.

The American invasion of Canada was mercifully over, but the British were now poised to invade northern New York. Only the determined efforts of Arnold and his small fleet on Lake Champlain during the Battle of VALCOUR ISLAND that October prevented the British from investing Fort Ticonderoga. Arnold's actions on the lake delayed the decisive British push in the north until 1777, giving the Americans an invaluable year to regroup in preparation for their greatest success, at SARATOGA.

See also AMERICAN REVOLUTIONARY WAR, LAND OVERVIEW; CONTINENTAL ARMY; MILITIA, ORGANIZATION AND ROLE OF.

Further reading: Bird, Harrison. *Attack on Quebec: The American Invasion of Canada, 1775.* New York: Oxford University Press, 1968; Hatch, Robert McConnell. *Thrust for Canada: The American Attempt on Quebec in 1775–1776.* Boston: Houghton Mifflin, 1979; Lanctot, Gustave. *Canada and the American Revolution, 1774–1783.* Toronto: Clarke, Irwin, 1967; Stanley, George F. G. *Canada Invaded, 1775–1776.* Toronto: Hakkert, 1973.

— Daniel P. Barr

Canby, Edward R. S. (1817–1873) *U.S. Army general*
Born on 9 November 1817 at Piatt's Landing, Kentucky, Edward Richard Sprigg Canby graduated from the U.S.

Military Academy at West Point in 1839. Commissioned a second lieutenant of infantry, he fought in the Second SEMINOLE WAR in Florida and participated in the removal of the Creeks and Cherokees to Indian Territory. Promoted to first lieutenant in 1846 and then to captain, he won two brevets for bravery during the MEXICAN-AMERICAN WAR. He then held several staff assignments, gaining promotion to major in the 10th Infantry Regiment in 1855. He served on the frontier until the outbreak of the Civil War.

Promoted to colonel of the newly organized 19th Infantry Regiment in May 1861, Canby took command of the Department of New Mexico. Although defeated by Brigadier General Henry H. Sibley's forces at Valverde in January 1862, Canby succeeded in drawing the Confederates away from their supplies, which compelled Sibley's retreat to Texas and secured New Mexico for the Union.

In March Canby became a brigadier general of volunteers and moved to Washington as assistant adjutant general. In 1863 he briefly took command at New York in the wake of the draft riots there. Promoted to major general of volunteers in May 1864, Canby assumed command of the Military Division of West Mississippi, which embraced the Departments of Arkansas and the Gulf. Regrouping scattered Federal forces of the region, he commenced operations against Mobile in conjunction with the naval forces of Rear Admiral David G. FARRAGUT. The Federals gained control of MOBILE BAY in August 1864, but the city remained in Confederate hands until 12 April 1865, when Canby accepted its surrender. On 4 May Confederate lieutenant general Richard Taylor surrendered his Department of East Louisiana, Mississippi, and Alabama to Canby near Mobile, and on 26 May at New Orleans Canby accepted the surrender of the Confederate Trans-Mississippi Department from Lieutenant General Simon B. BUCKNER.

Breveted through major general in the regular and volunteer organizations, in 1866 Canby was promoted to brigadier general, U. S. Army. After Reconstruction duty in the South, he assumed command of the Department of the Columbia in 1870 and that of the Military Division of the Pacific in 1873. During peace talks with the Modocs in northern California, Canby was murdered by Modoc leader Captain Jack and two of his men on 11 April 1873. He thus became the only general officer (of substantive rank) to be killed by Indians in American history.

See also CIVIL WAR, LAND OVERVIEW; MODOC WAR.

Further reading: Frazier, Donald S. *Blood & Treasure: Confederate Empire in the Southwest.* College Station: Texas A&M University Press, 1985; Heyman, Max L. *Prudent Soldier: A Biography of Major General E. R. S. Canby.* Glendale, Calif.: Clark, 1959; Utley, Robert M. *Frontier Regulars: The United States Army and the Indian, 1866–1891.* New York: Macmillan, 1973.

— Roger W. Caraway

Cantigny, Battle of (28–31 May 1918) *World War I battle*

The small farming village of Cantigny in the Picardy region of France about 50 miles northwest of Paris was the scene of America's first significant battle of WORLD WAR I. In response to the German spring offensives of March 1918, the commander in chief of the Allied armies, General Ferdinand Foch, asked the AMERICAN EXPEDITIONARY FORCE (AEF) commander, General John J. PERSHING, to make his combat-ready divisions available to stem the tide. Pershing sent Major General Robert L. BULLARD's 1st Division to the Cantigny sector in early April with instructions to prepare to conduct offensive operations. Initially, the division would be under the control of the Fifth French Army, which was in reserve.

As the division moved toward the front, it passed to the command of the French VI Corps. It finished taking up positions on 26 April, and General Bullard assumed responsibility for the sector the following day. There were no finished trenches, only foxholes, and headquarters was in caves and cellars. The sides exchanged heavy artillery fire; during this period the division took an average of 60 casualties daily from German indirect fire. Brigadier General Charles P. SUMMERALL's division artillery fired as many as 30,000 shells a day.

During the night of 3–4 May, the 18th Infantry Regiment, quartered in the village of Villers-Tournelles, just west of Cantigny, was rendered ineffective by a bombardment of mustard gas and high-explosive shells. Nearly 900 men were incapacitated or killed. Major General Charles A. Vandenberg's French X Corps took over responsibility for the area from the VI Corps on 5 May.

Rehearsals on similar terrain in the rear, supported by the remainder of the division and French aircraft, tanks, and artillery, prepared the 28th Infantry Regiment to launch an assault on 28 May. A one-hour period of artillery registration followed by a preliminary bombardment of the same length preceded the attack, at 6:45 A.M. Much of the supporting French artillery was being withdrawn to meet an emergency in another sector even as the attack began. The enthusiastic American infantrymen swept through and beyond the village to the north and east with fewer than 75 casualties. Colonel Hanson E. Ely's 28th then awaited the expected German counterattacks and counterfire.

Soldiers of the German 82d Reserve Division, who had been pushed back, reacted violently to the repulse. Their commander had castigated them for losing the village; the result was repeated counterattacks and artillery fire that inflicted nearly 1,000 additional U.S. casualties in the next three days. It was an unforgiving battle initiation, but the Americans weathered it superbly.

General Bullard believed that the challenge of Cantigny had saved his division from the morale-sapping experience of trench-warfare training and the possibility of being forever employed under French or British command. General Vandenberg was effusive in his praise of the Americans, calling them the "men of Cantigny." General Pershing was pleased with the outcome and certain that questions about American leadership and organizational abilities had been answered.

See also WORLD WAR I, U.S. INVOLVEMENT.

Further reading: Bullard, Robert Lee. *Personalities and Reminiscences of the War.* Garden City, N.Y.: Doubleday, Page, 1925; Marshall, George C. *Memoirs of My Services in the World War 1917–1918.* Boston: Houghton Mifflin, 1976; Millett, Allan R., "Cantigny: 28–31 May 1918." In *America's First Battles, 1776–1965,* edited by Charles E. Heller and William A. Stofft. Lawrence: University Press of Kansas, 1986; Society of the First Division. *History of the First Division during the World War, 1917–1919.* Philadelphia: John C. Winston, 1922.

— John F. Votaw

Canyon Creek, Battle of (13 September 1877)

Battle during the Nez Perce War

Forced from their homelands in the Wallowa Valley of Oregon and along Idaho's Salmon River in June 1877, the Nez Perce fought major engagements with U.S. troops in WHITE BIRD CANYON and on the CLEARWATER RIVER before pressing eastward into the Bitterroot Mountains. Hoping to find sanctuary on the plains or in Canada, they moved into Montana Territory, eluding a large force commanded by Brigadier General Oliver O. HOWARD, in several converging columns, in their bid for freedom. After the August battle of the BIG HOLE RIVER, the Nez Perce turned south and then eastward, fighting a minor engagement at Camas Meadows before moving into Yellowstone National Park.

In early September the Nez Perce emerged from Yellowstone and skillfully eluded a trap set by Colonel Samuel Sturgis and six troops of the battered 7th Cavalry on the Clark Fork River. Turning northward, raiding parties struck white settlements along the Clark Fork. On 13 September they captured a stagecoach north of the Yellowstone River and were enjoying their catch when Sturgis and his troopers reappeared.

Nez Perce warriors fought a disciplined delaying action while their families moved into Canyon Creek, which led out of the Yellowstone Valley to the plains beyond. Sturgis did not order a charge. Instead, his troopers dismounted and engaged in a long-range exchange of rifle fire, which had no impact.

The Nez Perce warriors fell back into the canyon while sharpshooters held off the slowly advancing troopers and turned back a poorly executed cavalry charge. Finally, as more warriors broke off to join the withdrawal, only a handful of riflemen hidden in the canyon's recesses kept the soldiers at bay until one by one they too made their escapes.

For the 7th Cavalry, the engagement at Canyon Creek was yet another humiliation. Sturgis, who lost three men killed and another 11 wounded, was roundly criticized for his conduct. The Nez Perce had suffered only minor wounds and had proven once again their ability to fight and win a disciplined action against a large formation. The epic Nez Perce bid for freedom ended three weeks later at BEAR PAW MOUNTAIN, only some 30 miles from their destination of Canada.

See also AMERICAN INDIAN WARS, OVERVIEW; JOSEPH, CHIEF; MILES, NELSON A.; INDIAN WARFARE; NEZ PERCE WARS.

Further reading: Lavender, David. *Let Me Be Free: The Nez Perce Tragedy.* New York: HarperCollins, 1992; Beal, Merril D. *"I Will Fight No More Forever": Chief Joseph and the Nez Perce War.* Seattle: University of Washington Press, 1963.

— Todd Rodriguez

Carlson's Raiders *Elite World War II U.S. Marine Corps unit, created to provide fast, hard-hitting assault units that could inflict surprise strikes by landing from submarines, destroyers, air transports, or naval transports*

Lightly equipped amphibious hit-and-run raids, rather than sustained operations, were the Raiders' specialty. Although the Raiders existed for only two years as a separate Marine Corps organization, they made a significant contribution to the war in the Pacific.

The 1st Raider Battalion, formed at Quantico, Virginia, under Lieutenant Colonel Merritt A. Edson, was known as Edson's Raiders. The 2d Raider Battalion was organized on 16 February 1942 at Jacques Farm, near Camp Elliott, California, under Lieutenant Colonel Evans F. Carlson. As a result of his experiences in China, Carlson believed that guerrilla warfare was the wave of the future. His leadership was characterized by extraordinary personal courage, endurance, and unusual democratic discussion within the ranks. The unit's battle cry was "Gung Ho," Chinese for "work together" or "work in harmony." Ultimately four battalions were formed.

The Raiders' first test came when two companies landed from submarines off MAKIN ISLAND on 17 August 1942. The objectives of the operation were to secure intelligence, destroy supplies and installations, and draw Japanese attention from operations on GUADALCANAL. The operation went badly from the start when a weapon accidentally discharged and ruined any hope of surprise. The Raiders quickly engaged in a firefight with the Japanese; they were victorious by midmorning.

Believing there was still a sizable Japanese force on the island, Carlson decided to withdraw. Disaster struck when he and about 120 men missed the escape submarines and were stranded on shore. Following a council of war, they decided that anyone who wanted to escape to the submarines should do so, while the rest surrendered. However, at dawn the situation looked better. The surrender party returned, reporting no organized Japanese force left on the island; the Raiders evacuated on the night of 18 August 1942. Despite mistakes, they had wiped out the entire Japanese garrison of 160 men and destroyed its installations at a cost of 30 of their own men.

The landing on Makin by the 2d Raiders and another on Tulagi by the 1st Raiders were small operations, but they marked the first ground offensive against the Japanese in World War II by U.S. forces. They also dispelled the myth of Japanese military supremacy. On the other hand, the landings convinced the Japanese of the need to strengthen other island fortifications.

The 2d Ranger Battalion was then ordered to Guadalcanal. It landed at Aola Bay on 4 November 1942 to secure the beachhead for an army battalion and for Seabees who had been assigned to build an airfield. They encountered no opposition, but it became apparent that the swampy jungle was no place to put an airfield. The Raiders marched west and harassed the Japanese from the rear. Intense patrolling and scattered firefights characterized their operations. Their long patrol of 37 days behind Japanese lines was extremely successful from a tactical standpoint—the battalion killed 488 Japanese at a cost to itself of 16 dead and 18 wounded. On 15 December 1942 it withdrew to Espiritu Santo Island to recuperate.

On 15 March 1943 the Marine Corps created the 1st Raider Regiment and gave it control of all four Raider battalions. A week later, Lieutenant Colonel Alan Shapley took command of the 2d Raiders. Shapley, who thought the Makin raid had been a fiasco, had no interest in Gung Ho and wasted no time in turning the unit into a regular battalion. Carlson contracted malaria and soon was sent home. He returned to the war as an observer of the TARAWA landing and participated in the assaults on Kwajalein and Saipan.

By 1944 the tenor of the war had changed, and the Raiders no longer were needed. On 1 February 1944 the Raider battalions were incorporated into the reactivated 4th Marine Regiment, which distinguished itself in the assault operations of Guam and OKINAWA.

See also WORLD WAR II, U.S. INVOLVEMENT, PACIFIC.

Further reading: Blankford, Michael. *The Big Yankee: The Life of Carlson of the Raiders.* Boston: Little, Brown, 1947; Hoffman, Jon T. *From Makin to Bougainville: Marine Raiders in the Pacific War.* Washington, D.C.: Marine Corps Historical Center, 1995; Rosenquist, R. G., Martin J. Sexton, and Robert A. Buerlein. *Our Kind of War: Illustrated Saga of the U. S. Marine Raiders of World War II.* Richmond, Va.: American Historical Foundation, 1990.

— Lisa L. Beckenbaugh

Carson, Christopher (**"Kit"**) (1809–1868) *American frontiersman and soldier*

Born on 24 December 1809 in Madison County, Kentucky, Christopher "Kit" Carson had to leave school when he was nine, upon his father's death. Carson worked as an apprentice to a saddlemaker before leaving home at 15 to join a group of trappers and frontiersmen.

Carson reached Sante Fe in 1826 and for the next 16 years trapped and explored the area west of Taos, New Mexico, and northward. In 1842 he joined explorer John C. FRÉMONT, guiding his group to Oregon through the central portion of the Rocky Mountains and the Great Basin. Between 1842 and 1846 Carson guided three expeditions west, including Frémont's third expedition to California at the outbreak of the 1846–1848 MEXICAN-AMERICAN WAR.

When the California Battalion was organized in May 1846, Carson was appointed a 2d lieutenant. During Carson's California service, Frémont sent him to Washington, D.C., three times with dispatches. On his first trip, in September 1846, he encountered Brigadier General Stephen W. KEARNY in central New Mexico; Kearny ordered him to guide his forces back to California while others carried Frémont's dispatches to Washington. Kearny's force was defeated at San Pasqual on 6 December and besieged by Mexican forces at San Bernardo the next day; Carson escaped to bring a relief column.

Carson's army commission was voided by the U.S. Senate. Returning to New Mexico after the war, Carson raised sheep, which he sold in California for a handsome price during the gold rush of 1848–49. In 1853 Carson received an appointment as an Indian agent, a post he held until the CIVIL WAR.

Organizing a unit of New Mexico volunteer infantry that fought for the Union during the war, Carson focused on suppressing the Navajo Indians. When Carson destroyed their crops and livestock, the Navajo surrendered. He forced the surviving 8,000 Indians to walk from Arizona to Fort Sumner, New Mexico, where they lived in confinement until 1868.

In 1865 Carson moved to Colorado and resumed ranching. He died on 23 May 1868 at Fort Lyon.

See also AMERICAN INDIAN WARS, OVERVIEW.

Further reading: Gerson, Noel B. *Kit Carson: Folk Hero and Man.* Garden City, N.Y.: Doubleday, 1964; Roberts, David. *Kit Carson, John C. Fremont, and the Claiming of the American West.* New York: Simon & Schuster, 2000.

— Cynthia Clark Northrup

Carter, William G. H. (1851–1925) *U.S. Army general*
Born on 19 November 1851 at Nashville, Tennessee, William Giles Harding Carter was educated at the Kentucky Military Institute in Frankfort. At age 12, during the Civil War, he served with the Quartermaster Department of the Army of the Cumberland, and in 1864 and 1865 he was a mounted messenger, observing the Battle of NASHVILLE in December 1864.

After the war Carter moved to New York. He received an appointment to the U.S. Military Academy at WEST POINT and upon graduation in 1873 was commissioned in the 8th Infantry Regiment. He was promoted to first lieutenant in the 6th Cavalry Regiment in April 1879.

Carter distinguished himself during the August 1881 APACHE uprising, when, wounded and under fire, he and two other soldiers rescued wounded at Cibicu Creek. For this action he was awarded the Medal of Honor. He was promoted to captain in November 1889.

Carter became a cavalry instructor at Fort Leavenworth, Kansas, in 1893. Four years later he became assistant adjutant general in Washington, with the rank of major. He made lieutenant colonel in May 1898, and after the 1898 SPANISH-AMERICAN WAR Secretary of War Elihu ROOT selected him as an adviser. Carter influenced Root in creating what became the DICK ACT of 1903, the establishment of a general-staff system and the abolition of the post of commanding general in favor of a chief of staff. Carter also participated in the establishment of a hierarchial system of army schools, culminating in the new Army War College. He was promoted colonel in April 1902 and brigadier general three months later.

When the U.S. Army considered the establishment of horse-breeding farms in 1903, Carter went to England and France to study remount questions. He then commanded the Department of Visayas in the Philippine Islands (1904–06) and, after a brief time in the United States, commanded the Department of Luzon. Advanced to major general in November 1909, he served as assistant chief of staff of the army until 1911.

Sharply increasing tensions with Mexico prompted Secretary of War Henry L. STIMSON to order 50,000 troops to form a Maneuver Division on the border. Carter commanded this force at San Antonio, Texas, from March to August 1911. He instituted mandatory programs to improve hygiene, worked to improve march discipline, and tested new tactics. When the Maneuver Division was disbanded, Carter returned to Washington to work on resolving problems he had observed during the mobilization for World War I. After mobilizing another division at Galveston and Texas City, Texas, for the occupation of VERACRUZ in 1914, he was assigned to command in the Hawaiian Islands.

Carter retired from active duty in November 1915 but was recalled to active duty to assist in preparing legislation for the NATIONAL DEFENSE ACT (1916). Following U.S. entry into World War I, Carter commanded the Army's Central Department at Chicago from August 1917 to February 1918, then retired for a second time.

Carter wrote a number of books, including *From Yorktown to Santiago with the Sixth Cavalry* (1900), *The American Army* (1915), *Old Army Sketches* (1916), *Life and Services of Lieutenant General Chaffee* (1917), and *Horses of the World* (1923). His works on horses were for many years textbooks at West Point and in the U.S. Army. Carter died at Washington, D.C., on 24 May 1925.

See also WORLD WAR I, U.S. INVOLVEMENT.

Further reading: Bell, William G., ed. *Commanding Generals and Chiefs of Staff.* Washington, D.C.: U.S. Government Printing Office, 1983.

— Joseph W. Gunter

casualties in U.S. wars

Statistics regarding casualties in the major wars and conflicts waged by the United States are difficult to determine with absolute certainty. This is particularly true for the Civil War and generally true for wars fought prior to the 20th century. The figures below represent either generally agreed-upon totals or the best estimates available. Other works will almost certainly present conflicting figures, but such discrepancies should be small and inconsequential. Casualty figures exclude prisoners of war who survived and personnel listed as missing in action.

Further reading: U.S. Department of Defense. *Defense 94-Almanac,* no. 5 (September–October 1994); Millett, Allan R., and Peter Maslowski. *For the Common Defense:*

Number of Military Personnel Involved and Casualties Suffered in Major U.S. Wars and Conflicts, 1775–2001

	Total Serving	Battle Deaths	Other Deaths	Wounded	Total Casualties
American Revolution					
1775–1783	290,000 (estimated)	6,824	18,500 (estimated)	8,445	33,769
War of 1812					
1812–1815	286,730	2,260	17,500	4,505	24,265
Mexican War					
1846–1848	78,789	1,733	11,550	4,152	17,435
Civil War					
1861–1865					
Union	2,213,363	140,415	224,097	281,881	646,393
Confederate	600,000 to 1,500,000 (estimated)	74,524	59,297	unknown	133,821
Native American Wars					
1865–1898	106,000	919	unknown	1,025	1,944
Spanish-American War					
1898	307,420	385	2,061	1,622	4,068
Philippine–American War					
1899–1902	126,468	1,004	3,161	2,911	7,076
World War I					
1917–1918	4,743,826	53,513	63,114	204,002	320,629
World War II					
1941–1946	16,353,659	292,131	115,185	671,846	1,079,162
Korean War					
1950–1953	5,720,000	33,667	3,249	103,284	140,200
Vietnam War					
1964–1973	8,752,000	47,382	10,811	153,363	211,556
Persian Gulf					
1991	467,939	148	151	467	766

Notes: During the Civil War, an estimated 26,000 to 31,000 Confederates died in Union prisoner of war camps. Figures for World War I include personnel serving in northern Russia until August 1919 and in Siberia through April 1920; 4,120 servicemen were captured and 3,350 listed as missing in action (MIA) in World War I. World War II data carries through December 1946, when a presidential proclamation formally ended hostilities. Battle deaths and wounded include casualties suffered in October 1941; 130,201 service personnel were captured during World War II, while 30,314 were listed MIA. In Korea, 7,140 personnel were captured and 8,177 listed MIA, while during the Vietnam War, 826 became prisoners of war and 2,489 (as of September 1993) are still considered MIA.

A Military History of the United States of America. Rev. ed. New York: Free Press, 1994.

— Lance Janda

cavalry *Branch of military service, the members of which originally served and fought on horseback*
The term *horse* was often used to describe these units and essentially meant the same thing. By the 18th century, three distinct types of cavalry commands had developed based on mission, armament, and weight of horses: heavy cavalry, designed for shock effect; light cavalry, primarily used for reconnaissance, screening missions, and messenger service; and dragoons, infantry that traveled by horseback for speed and then dismounted to fight.

The U.S. Army's experience with cavalry was limited until the 1830s. It had its origins in a regiment of Connecticut "light horse" that joined the Continental army in August 1776. While mounted troops, essentially dragoons, served in both the American Revolutionary War and the

War of 1812, there was no real cavalry tradition in the United States such as existed in Europe, primarily as a consequence of the lack in the eastern forested regions of the United States of the open terrain needed for such forces to maneuver. Traditional American opposition to a large standing army and the fact that mounted troops were the most expensive forces to equip and maintain led to their total elimination.

As settlers moved west, first across and then onto the plains, however, they encountered horse-mounted Indians. Congress eventually recognized the need for mounted troops on the frontier. In 1832 Congress authorized the formation of a battalion of Mounted Rangers for defense of the frontier. After proving their worth, a year later the Rangers were expanded to become the First Regiment of U.S. Dragoons.

Although mounted forces gained permanence in the decade of the 1830s, throughout that period they operated on almost an ad hoc basis because there were no experienced cavalry officers in the army, no schools to train cavalrymen, and no manuals of cavalry tactics upon which to base training. Campaigning against the Indians emphasized the infantry side of the dragoon's function, for which the infantry tactics manual could be used. But infantry training was not sufficient to deal with some of the finest natural horsemen in the world; efforts were begun by 1835 to provide uniformity in the mounted service.

In 1835 a cavalry school was established at Carlisle Barracks, Pennsylvania, which eventually became the center of cavalry affairs for the army. In 1839, in order to provide a foundation for future cavalry officers, instruction in horsemanship was introduced at the U.S. Military Academy at West Point. Also in 1839, Secretary of War Joel Poinsett sent three lieutenants to France to attend the Royal School of Cavalry at Saumur and learn the theory and practice of the French system, considered by Poinsett to be the finest in Europe. Upon their return in 1840, the three, led by Lieutenant Philip KEARNY, were charged with writing a manual for the instruction of the mounted service. Based on the European model, this tactics manual was published in 1841. Twenty years later, in 1861, the manual was revised by Colonel Philip St. George Cooke of the 2d Dragoons.

In 1846, at the beginning of the MEXICAN-AMERICAN WAR, Congress authorized another mounted unit, the Regiment of Mounted Rifles, for the regular army. The two dragoon regiments and the Mounted Rifles served throughout the Mexican-American War and at war's end were not disbanded. Even with the addition of the Mounted Rifles, the territorial expansion brought by the Mexican-American War stretched mounted forces extremely thin trying to police the frontier. On Secretary of War Jefferson DAVIS's urging, in 1855 Congress authorized two additional mounted regiments, which were designated as cavalry.

The 1st and 2d Cavalry Regiments were organized like the existing horse regiments, but the general orders prescribing their organization made them a distinct and separate arm. Prior to the Civil War, then, the mounted force of the regular army consisted of dragoons, mounted riflemen, and cavalry. By August 1861, Congress organized all mounted troops into a single branch, the cavalry. The dragoon regiments were redesignated the 1st and 2d Cavalry; the mounted rifles became the 3d Cavalry; and the 1st and 2d Cavalry became the 4th and 5th.

At the beginning of the Civil War, elements of the horse units were widely scattered over the country, most in the West and Southwest. Before the war ended, 272 regiments, plus 45 separate battalions, and 78 separate companies saw service in the Union army; it is estimated that 137 regiments, 143 separate battalions, and 101 separate companies made up the Confederate cavalry.

After the Civil War, the cavalry was again reduced in size until difficulties with the western Indians forced Congress to expand the force, in the Army Reorganization Act of 1866. Throughout the period of the AMERICAN INDIAN WARS, cavalry units saw extensive combat and escort service in the West. They also were employed in constabulary duties in the South during Reconstruction.

During the 1898 SPANISH-AMERICAN WAR and the subsequent PHILIPPINE-AMERICAN WAR, most cavalry operations were dismounted because of logistical problems encountered in shipping and maintaining mounts. In 1916 seven regiments of cavalry crossed the border into Mexico as part of the PUNITIVE EXPEDITION INTO MEXICO under Major General John J. PERSHING.

In anticipation of U.S. involvement in World War I, Congress authorized the expansion of the cavalry to 25 regiments. During the war, however, only the 2d Cavalry deployed to France and only to run supply depots that handled remounts for horse transport units.

The arrival of the tank in World War I was the beginning of the end for the horse on the battlefield. Between the wars the army slowly began to mechanize, and by 1940 armored vehicles had all but replaced the horse. In March 1942 the War Department officially abolished the cavalry as a branch of service. However, the term *cavalry* reemerged concurrently with the arrival of HELICOPTERS used in surveillance, reconnaissance, and armed security roles. During the Vietnam War, units designated as air or armored cavalry filled all of the traditional roles of cavalry. Today, according to current army doctrine, cavalry employs its combined attributes of firepower, mobility, and shock effect as it provides security, reconnaissance, and surveillance.

See also BUFFALO SOLDIERS; BUFORD, JOHN; DRA-GOONS; CIVIL WAR, LAND OVERVIEW; FORREST, NATHAN B.; HELICOPTERS; INDIAN WARFARE; SHERIDAN, PHILIP; SPANISH-AMERICAN WAR, COURSE OF; STUART, J. E. B.; VIETNAM WAR, COURSE OF.

Further reading: Herr, John K., and Edward S. Wallace. *The Story of the U.S. Cavalry, 1775–1942.* Boston: Little, Brown, 1953; Starr, Stephen I. *The Union Cavalry in the Civil War.* 3 vols. Baton Rouge: Louisiana State University Press, 1979–1985; Stubbs, Mary L., and Stanley R. Connor. *Armor-Cavalry.* Part 1, *Regular Army and Army Reserve.* Washington, D.C.: Office of the Chief of Military History, U.S. Army, 1969; Utley, Robert M. *Frontiersmen in Blue: The United States Army and the Indian, 1848–1865;* Lincoln: University of Nebraska Press, 1967; ———. *Frontier Regulars: The United States Army and the Indian, 1865–1891.* New York: Macmillan, 1973.

— Arthur T. Frame

Cedar Falls, Operation (8–26 January 1967) *First multidivision U.S. operation of the Vietnam War*
The U.S. Army's corps-level II Field Force Vietnam mounted Operation Cedar Falls to eliminate Viet Cong (VC) strongholds in the Iron Triangle, a 60-square-mile area of jungle believed to contain Communist base camps and supply dumps. During this operation, about 16,000 U.S. troops from the 1st and 25th Infantry Divisions, 173d Airborne Brigade, and 11th Armored Cavalry Regiment joined 14,000 South Vietnamese. The offensive, the largest of the war to date, was designed to disrupt insurgent operations near Saigon in a well-fortified area that had provided a haven for the 165th and 272d VC regiments.

Cedar Falls was a classic "hammer and anvil" attack, the anvil being blocking positions along the Saigon River at the southwestern boundary of the Iron Triangle. The hammer consisted of ground and air assaults into the jungle north of the triangle in an attempt to push the Communist forces into the blocking forces. During the course of the operations, U.S. infantrymen discovered a massive tunnel complex, apparently a headquarters for guerrilla raids and terrorist attacks on Saigon.

One of the primary targets was the village of Ben Suc, which was the headquarters for four VC rear-service transport companies and had been under VC control since 1964. After an assault by 1st Battalion, 26th Infantry, 1st Infantry Division, under the command of Lieutenant Colonel Alexander M. HAIG, the village was secured; 5,987 civilians, 247 water buffalo, 225 oxen, 158 oxcarts, and 60 tons of rice were air-evacuated to resettlement areas. The village was then razed and abandoned.

The 18-day operation ended on 26 January 1967. Allied losses had been 83 killed and 345 wounded. Communist losses were estimated at 750 VC killed and 280 captured. Large quantities of arms and equipment were uncovered, including 23 mortars, 590 rifles, 60,000 rounds of ammunition, and 750 uniforms.

Cedar Falls was marked by several tactical innovations. One was the use of specially trained volunteers to explore the maze of tunnels. These "tunnel rats" uncovered underground hospitals, supply caches, and headquarters.

Another innovation was the use of "Rome plows" to clear away vegetation along roads in order to prevent Communist ambushes and to help construct landing zones for future operations. Rome plows (so named after their manufacturer, the Rome Caterpillar Company in Georgia) cleared four square miles of jungle during Cedar Falls.

Unfortunately for the United States, any gains made in the area during Cedar Falls were transitory because the VC moved back into the Iron Triangle as soon as the operation ended. In addition, Cedar Falls proved a public relations disaster. The forced evacuation of the 5,987 residents of Ben Suc and the subsequent destruction of the village was widely and critically reported and became a rallying event for the antiwar movement.

See also VIETNAM WAR.

Further reading: MacGarrigle, George L. *Taking the Offensive: October 1966 to October 1967.* United States Army in Vietnam series. Washington, D.C.: Center of Military History, U.S. Army, 1998; Rogers, Bernard William. *Cedar Falls–Junction City: A Turning Point.* United States Army in Vietnam. Washington, D.C.: U.S. Government Printing Office, 1974; Schell, Jonathan. *The Village of Ben Suc.* New York: Knopf, 1967.

— James H. Willbanks

Cedar Mountain, Battle of (9 August 1862) *Civil War battle*
In the aftermath of the Union defeat in the SEVEN DAYS' BATTLES, President Abraham LINCOLN and Secretary of War Edwin M. STANTON gave Major General John POPE the task of organizing the Army of Virginia, comprising federal corps stretching across Northern Virginia from the Shenandoah Valley to MANASSAS Junction. Pope's original objective was to threaten the Virginia Central Railroad in hopes of forcing General Robert E. LEE to transfer troops from Richmond, thereby allowing Major General George B. MCCLELLAN to resume his stalled Peninsula campaign. But in early August Pope's mission changed dramatically, when McClellan was ordered to evacuate the peninsula.

Although Pope had not completed the concentration of approximately 56,000 availables men (three corps, consisting of eight infantry divisions and two cavalry brigades) at his headquarters at Culpepper, Virginia, he decided to strike at Major General Thomas J. "Stonewall" JACKSON's corps before Lee could send him further reinforcements. Jackson's corps, recently reinforced by Major General A. P. HILL's division, was to the south at Gordonville.

On 8 August, therefore, Pope ordered Major General Nathaniel P. BANKS to march his corps of two divisions (approximately 8,000 men) south on the Culpeper Road. Although Pope probably intended for Banks simply to delay Jackson if encountered, on the morning of 9 August one of Pope's staff officers, Colonel Louis Marshall (Lee's nephew) conveyed to Banks a rather confusing verbal order that Banks interpreted to mean that he should attack.

Jackson, meanwhile, was marching up the Culpeper Road with approximately 24,000 soldiers in divisions commanded by Hill and Major Generals Charles S. Winder and Richard S. EWELL. On 7 August Jackson's corps had departed Gordonville and marched to Orange Court House, where it camped for the night. Jackson's failure to communicate to Hill a change of marching orders for 8 August led to confusion and delay. As a result, Confederate forces were strung out some seven miles when on 9 August Ewell's division encountered Banks approximately nine miles south of Culpepper.

After surveying the scene, Jackson instructed Ewell to place his batteries on the northern slope of nearby Cedar Mountain and to station Brigadier General Jubal EARLY's brigade in front of the Federal center, where he expected Banks to attack. Jackson then deployed the three brigades in Winder's division on Ewell's left, hoping they could turn Banks's flank. Jackson did not recognize, however, that two Federal brigades, under Brigadier Generals Samuel Crawford and George Gordon, were hidden in woods on Winder's left, thus leaving him vulnerable to attack.

Although he was greatly outnumbered, Banks was determined to attack, especially since he had interpreted Pope's instructions as requiring it. Federal and Confederate batteries exchanged fire with one another throughout the afternoon.

Just as Winder was mortally wounded by an artillery shell at about 4:30 P.M., a messenger from Ewell arrived to inform him that Crawford's and Gordon's brigades had been spotted on the extreme left. At 5 P.M., as Brigadier General William Taliaferro, who assumed command of the division, was attempting to reposition his forces, Crawford's brigade struck, routing Winder's three brigades, including the Stonewall Brigade. Informed that Union forces were turning his left flank, Jackson immediately galloped over, waving his sword (which had rusted stuck in its scabbard) to rally Winder's men.

While Jackson undoubtedly inspired his troops, it was the arrival of Hill's fresh division at about 5:30 that allowed the Confederates to turn defeat into victory. By 6:30 Crawford's exhausted brigade had been thrown back, having lost nearly 50 percent of its strength (the 28th New York Regiment had lost 17 of its 18 officers). With no additional forces at his disposal, Banks had to withdraw his corps, which had suffered 2,377 casualties compared to Jackson's 1,355.

During the next two days Federal and Confederate troops tended to their wounded under a truce, which Jackson violated by sending parties to gather muskets and ammunition from the battlefield. With other Federal forces converging toward him, Jackson ordered his soldiers to light campfires on the night of 11 August and withdrew across the Rapidan.

Although Cedar Mountain was not quite as great a victory as Jackson later claimed, it did force Pope to postpone an advance and allowed Lee time to transfer Major General James LONGSTREET's corps north to join Jackson, thereby setting the stage for the Second Battle of BULL RUN/MANASSAS.

See also CIVIL WAR, LAND OVERVIEW.

Further reading: Foote, Shelby. *The Civil War: A Narrative.* Vol. I, *Fort Sumter to Perryville.* New York: Vintage Books, 1986; Krick, Robert K. *Stonewall Jackson at Cedar Mountain.* Chapel Hill: University of North Carolina Press, 1990.

— Justin D. Murphy

Cedars, Battle of the (18–19 May 1776) *American Revolutionary War battle*

The Battle of the Cedars occurred in the wilderness approximately 40 miles southwest of Montreal during the later stages of the CONTINENTAL ARMY's failed invasion of CANADA. French-Canadian fur-trappers led by François de Lorimier, who was angry at the refusal of American major general David Wooster to reopen trade following the American capture of Montreal in November 1775, traveled to the British frontier posts along the Great Lakes in February 1776 and gathered support for an assault against the town. Fearing the possibility of an Indian attack, the Continental army sent a detachment under Colonel Timothy Bedel to erect a small fortification up the St. Lawrence River near rapids known as the Cedars.

A combined force of approximately 300 British regulars, Canadians, and Indians under Captain George Forster, the British post commander at Fort Oswegatchie, attacked the small American outpost at the Cedars on the morning of 18 May. The garrison of 390 Americans fell to the command of Major Isaac Butterfield when Bedel ignominiously fled the post upon learning of the impending attack. The Canadians and Indians surrounded the compound, and Forster called upon Butterfield to surrender.

Butterfield's refusal sparked a lengthy but largely futile fight, during which neither side suffered significant casualties. A small force of Canadian Loyalists arrived the following morning to reinforce Forster, who renewed his demand that Butterfield surrender. Forster's threats that the 200 Indians under his command might massacre the entire garrison if the Americans insisted on resistance convinced Butterfield to surrender, although the majority of his officers sharply disagreed with their commander's decision.

Shortly after Butterfield surrendered his garrison, a relief column of 150 Continentals under Major Henry Sherburne was ambushed by Forster's Indians a few miles east of the Cedars and defeated. Sherburne's column sustained heavy casualties in the hour-long fight, including upward of 28 dead that Sherburne claimed were tomahawked by Indians while trying to surrender.

Following Sherburne's defeat, Forster advanced his force (swelled by reinforcements to more than 500 men) to within a few miles of Montreal, but he encountered 500 Americans under Colonel Benedict ARNOLD firmly entrenched along the shoreline at Lachine. When a detachment of 400 Pennsylvania riflemen arrived to reinforce Arnold, Forster ordered a retreat. Arnold gave chase and cornered the British four miles from the Cedars. There a standoff ensued. Forster held 487 American prisoners of war and threatened to unleash the Indians against them if Arnold attacked. After some negotiation, an agreement was reached by which the British would release the American prisoners and then withdraw with their Indians allies to their frontier outposts. The American prisoners were released on 20 May 1776, but not before Arnold threatened to return and burn every Indian village he could find if the local tribes ever assisted the British in attacking the Americans again.

For their parts in the American surrender at the Cedars, Timothy Bedel was formally censured, while Isaac Butterfield was court-martialed and cashiered from the army.

See also AMERICAN REVOLUTIONARY WAR, LAND OVERVIEW.

Further reading: Hatch, Robert McConnell. *Thrust for Canada: The American Attempt on Quebec in 1775–1776.* Boston: Houghton Mifflin, 1979; Stanley, George F. G. *Canada Invaded, 1775–1776.* Toronto: Hakkery, 1973.

— Daniel P. Barr

Central Intelligence Agency (CIA) *Principal intelligence and counterintelligence agency of the U.S. government*

Formally created in 1947, the Central Intelligence Agency has its roots in the OFFICE OF STRATEGIC SERVICES (OSS), a World War II espionage organization established at the instigation of Colonel William J. ("Wild Bill") DONOVAN. The OSS was disbanded in October 1945, but the developing cold war soon persuaded President Harry S. TRUMAN to accept Donovan's recommendations that the country's greatly expanded postwar international role demanded a much-enhanced coordinated intelligence establishment as part of the growing defense bureaucracy.

A January 1946 presidential executive order created a Central Intelligence Group and a National Intelligence Authority, the personnel of which attempted to centralize postwar intelligence activities. These two bodies were disbanded when in 1947 Congress passed the National Security Act, which formally established the National Security Council (NSC) and, under it, the Central Intelligence Agency (CIA). The CIA's mandate included advising the NSC on intelligence activities and making recommendations as to their coordination; correlating, evaluating, and disseminating intelligence; and performing such intelligence functions and other activities as the NSC might assign.

As the cold war intensified, from December 1947 through 1948 the NSC promptly ordered an immediate and drastic expansion of CIA covert operations. In September 1948 it established the agency's Office of Policy Coordination to handle such activities, with overall guidance from the Departments of State and Defense. The OPC was largely responsible for such new CIA Cold War initiatives as Radio Free Europe and Radio Liberty, the Committee for Free Asia, the Asia Foundation, and assorted overseas youth, student, and labor programs. In the late 1940s it also provided effective assistance to noncommunist political forces in elections in Italy, France, and West Germany. The Central Intelligence Agency Act of 1949 exempted CIA activities from most accounting and procedural limitations on federal expenditures, enabling it to keep its budget secret.

The CIA's failure in June 1950 to predict North Korea's invasion of South Korea led its second director, General Walter Bedell SMITH, appointed the following October, to strengthen intelligence collection and analysis within the agency. He established the Office of National Estimates to provide coordinated intelligence analysis; the Office of Research and Reports to predict economic changes within the Soviet bloc; and the Directorate for Intelligence to furnish finished intelligence.

Allen Welsh Dulles, Smith's successor as director from 1953 to 1961 and the brother of President Dwight D. EISENHOWER's secretary of state, John Foster Dulles, was a lawyer and flamboyant former OSS operative who presided over what was perhaps the CIA's heyday. Apart from gathering and analyzing intelligence, the CIA launched a wide variety of sometimes spectacular clandestine operations, including the organization of successful pro-American coups in Iran and Costa Rica in 1953 and Guatemala in 1954 and less-effective covert activities in Indonesia, Tibet, and Cuba. These culminated in the disastrous American-backed BAY OF PIGS invasion of Cuba in March 1961, a humiliating failure that brought Dulles's resignation and reemphasis, under his successor, John A. McConeon, on intelligence gathering and analysis as opposed to covert operations. One consequence was that in the CUBAN MISSILE CRISIS of October 1962 American intelligence was far more accurate than during the Bay of Pigs. Even so, throughout the 1960s the CIA mounted extensive covert operations in Southeast Asia in support of U.S. intervention in Vietnam and also was responsible, at least partially, for numerous anti-China activities.

The VIETNAM WAR and the opposition that it aroused, together with the involvement of some former CIA operatives in the Watergate break-in of 1972 and the subsequent cover-up orchestrated by President Richard NIXON's White House, brought new congressional and public demands for CIA accountability. Throughout the 1970s and 1980s books scathingly critical of CIA activities were published regularly. In 1974, CIA director William E. Colby responded by providing Congress a detailed list of all illegal domestic and overseas CIA covert operations. The move was intended to clear the air, but Secretary of State Henry A. KISSINGER disagreed with it, and it led in November 1975 to Colby's replacement for a brief period by GEORGE H. W. BUSH. Admiral Stansfield Turner, who headed the CIA under President Jimmy Carter, made further efforts to rein in the CIA, announcing in August 1977 a plan to cut 800 positions, and firing almost 200 employees in the "Halloween Massacre" of 31 October 1977.

The Republican administration of Ronald Reagan, which took office in 1981, claiming that these measures had been gravely detrimental to the CIA, replaced Turner with William J. Casey, a long-time CIA operative. Casey's effectiveness was undercut by repeated clashes with the conservative Republican senator Barry Goldwater of Arizona and by his apparent personal implication in the 1986 Iran-contra scandal, whereby Reagan administration officials flouted congressional prohibitions against providing arms to Iran and support for Nicaraguan counterrevolutionaries. Casey's death from cancer in 1987 before testifying to a congressional investigative committee left the precise extent of CIA involvement unclear.

The end of the cold war in the late 1980s found the CIA seeking to ward off cutbacks by defining a new role for itself. Its failure to predict Iraq's invasion of Kuwait in 1990 brought new criticism, as did the fact that in May 1999 inaccurate information supplied by CIA analysts during the NATO intervention against Serbia led U.S. aircraft to bomb the Chinese embassy in Belgrade. Throughout the 1990s arguments were advanced that the new primacy of economics called for the CIA to devote more attention to economic espionage and analysis, and that the growing strength of the People's Republic of China demanded that the agency focus its effort on Asia. From its inception CIA activities have provoked controversy, a pattern that seems likely to continue well into the twenty-first century.

See also BUSH, GEORGE H. W.; DEFENSE INTELLIGENCE AGENCY; ESPIONAGE, AGAINST THE UNITED STATES, SURVEY OF; GULF WAR, CAUSES OF; INTELLIGENCE; NATIONAL INTELLIGENCE AGENCY; U-2 INCIDENT; VANDENBERG, HOYT S.

Further reading: Blum, William. *The CIA: A Forgotten History.* Atlantic Highlands, N.J.: Zed Books, 1986; Breckinridge, Scott D. *The CIA and the U.S. Intelligence System.* Boulder, Colo.: Westview Press, 1986; Darling, Arthur B. *The Central Intelligence Agency: An Instrument of Government, to 1950.* University Park: Pennsylvania State University Press, 1990; Laqueur, Walter. *A World of Secrets.* New York: Basic Books, 1985; Ranelagh, John. *The Agency: The Decline and Rise of the CIA.* London: Weidenfeld & Nicolson, 1986; Rudgers, David F. *Creating the Secret State: The Origins of the Central Intelligence Agency, 1943–1947.* Lawrence: University Press of Kansas, 2000.

— Priscilla Roberts

Cerro Gordo, Battle of (17–18 April 1847) *U.S. victory over a larger and better-situated Mexican force in the Mexican-American War*

Cerro Gordo was a town on the National Road between Veracruz and Mexico City. Before the town two hills rose alongside the road, La Atalaya and the larger El Telégrafo, which the Mexican army troop fortified to block the Americans from proceeding west. Brigade General Valentín Canalizo commanded some 2,000 national guardsmen, but in April 1847 General Antonio López de Santa Anna arrived with 12,000 troops and assumed command.

The U.S. commander, Major General Winfield SCOTT, was already planning to leave Veracruz because of the oncoming yellow fever season. Hearing of Santa Anna's efforts, Scott sent Brigadier General David E. Twiggs ahead with 2,600 men and some artillery. Scott ordered Twiggs not to attack until he arrived.

Before reaching Cerro Gordo with his 8,500-man army, Scott sent Lieutenant P. G. T. BEAUREGARD and Lieutenant Zealous B. Tower on a reconnaissance. The two found a mule path that would flank the Mexican left. Scott then sent Captain Robert E. LEE on a second mission; Lee discovered that the rough terrain to the right of the road was passable, contrary to earlier belief. This meant that U.S. forces could bypass the Mexican army unobserved.

At 8 A.M. on 17 April, Twiggs and his men attacked La Atalaya, which was held by only a small Mexican force and three artillery pieces. The Mexicans fled to El Telégrafo. Colonel William S. Harney's regiment pursued until repelled by Mexican artillery fire. During the remainder of the day, both armies reinforced, Twiggs on La Atalaya and Santa Anna on El Telégrafo.

The battle resumed early the next morning. Colonel Bennett Riley and the 2nd U.S. Infantry joined Brigadier General James Shield's brigade to the rear of El Telégrafo, on the Mexican left flank. Twiggs ordered his men to charge up the hill. The Americans faced artillery fire until they reached the Mexican troops, whom they fought hand to hand. The men of Mexican army then fled toward Cerro Gordo as Captain James B. Magruder turned their own guns on them. Shields's brigade then engaged Canalizo's artillery and 2,000 cavalry behind the Mexican camp. Shields was wounded by a bullet through his right lung, but his men forced Canalizo to retreat to the ravines leading to the nearby Río del Plan.

Brigadier General Gideon Pillow was to have attacked the Mexican right flank simultaneously with Riley's and Shields's attacks. However, he was late, and his troops were poorly organized. In less than five minutes, about 80 soldiers, including Pillow, were killed or wounded by Brigade General José María Jarero's forces, but the Mexican army was already in retreat, and Jarero was forced to surrender the bulk of his command.

U.S. casualties over the two-day battle had totaled 417, including 64 dead, but 1,100 Mexican soldiers had been killed or wounded and 3,036 captured as Scott's Army of Occupation pursued Santa Anna's army westward. On 19 April the Americans played "Yankee Doodle" in the streets of Jalapa.

See also MEXICAN-AMERICAN WAR.

Further reading: Bauer, K. Jack. *The Mexican War 1846–1848.* New York: Macmillan, 1974; Eisenhower, John S. D. *So Far from God: The U.S. War with Mexico, 1846–1848.* New York: Random House, 1989; Henry, Robert Selph. *The Story of the Mexican War.* Indianapolis, Ind.: Bobbs-Merrill, 1950; Singletary, Otis A. *The Mexican War.* Chicago: University of Chicago Press, 1960.

— Adrienne Caughfield

Chaffee, Adna R. (1842–1914) *U.S. Army general and chief of staff*
Born on 14 April 1842 at Orwell, Ohio, Adna Romanza Chaffee received only a minimal education at home before leaving his father's farm to enlist in U.S. Army soon after the outbreak of the Civil War. He joined the Sixth Cavalry as a private and remained with this regiment more than a

quarter of a century. He quickly won promotion to sergeant for his performance during the Peninsula campaign and at ANTIETAM. He was subsequently commissioned a 2nd lieutenant at the order of Secretary of War Edwin M. STANTON. During 1863 Chaffee suffered wounds at the Battle of BRANDY STATION and at GETTYSBURG. The next year he further distinguished himself in Philip H. SHERIDAN's operations in the SHENANDOAH VALLEY. In February 1865 he was promoted to 1st lieutenant.

Chaffee served as a quartermaster after the war before briefly resigning from the army in 1867 to find more lucrative employment elsewhere. Chaffee's commanding officer persuaded him to reenter the service a week later, and he was soon promoted to captain. He won a brevet promotion to major for his service in an engagement against Comanche at Paint Creek, Texas, in March 1868. He also participated in campaigns against the Cheyenne, Kiowa, and Apache, winning promotion to major in 1888 and lieutenant colonel in 1897.

Chaffee was made a brigadier general of U.S. Volunteers at the commencement of the SPANISH-AMERICAN WAR in 1898 and earned a promotion to major general of volunteers in July for his role in the Battle of EL CANEY. Chaffee next served as chief of staff to General Leonard WOOD during the occupation of Cuba. In July 1900 Chaffee assumed command of the American forces in the Chinese relief expedition, helping to relieve the foreign legations at Beijing (Peking) and to end the BOXER UPRISING.

Promoted to major general in the regular army in 1901, Chaffee took charge of American forces during the later stages of the PHILIPPINE-AMERICAN WAR. In 1904 he was promoted to lieutenant general and army chief of staff. He retired from the army in 1906 and died at Los Angeles on 1 November 1914.

See also AMERICAN INDIAN WARS, OVERVIEW; APACHE WARS.

Further reading: Barr, Ronald J. *The Progressive Army: US Army Command and Administration, 1870–1914.* New York: St. Martin's, 1998; Carter, William H. *The Life of Lieutenant General Chaffee.* Chicago: University of Chicago Press, 1917.

— Michael Thomas Smith

Chaffee, Adna R., Jr. (1884–1941) *U.S. Army general*
Born on 23 September 1884 at Junction City, Kansas, Adna Chaffee was the only son of Captain (later Lieutenant General) Adna R. CHAFFEE. The younger Chaffee graduated from the U.S. Military Academy at West Point in 1906 and was commissioned a second lieutenant of cavalry. His first assignment was in Cuba with the 15th Cavalry Regiment.

Chaffee attended the Mounted Service School, Fort Riley, Kansas (1907–09), and the French cavalry school at Saumur (1911–12). Later an instructor at the Mounted Service School, 1912–13, Chaffee served with the 7th Cavalry Regiment in the Philippines in 1914–15 and then as a cavalry instructor at West Point in 1916–17.

During World War I Chaffee attended the General Staff College at Langres, France, and was an instructor there in 1918. He participated as a staff officer with the 81st Division in the September 1918 SAINT-MIHIEL and September–November MEUSE-ARGONNE OFFENSIVES. Chaffee ended the war as a temporary colonel and a supporter of armored warfare.

After the war Chaffee served in III Corps on occupation duty in Germany, then was an instructor at the Line and Staff School at Fort Leavenworth, Kansas, in 1919–20. Reverting to permanent captain, he was promoted to major in 1920. He attended the Army War College (1924–25), then commanded a squadron of the 3d Cavalry at Fort Myer, Virginia. He was advanced to lieutenant colonel in 1929.

A fine horseman who competed in equestrian events internationally, Chaffee nonetheless was an early advocate of the tank and sought to convince the army of the need for a separate armor force. He was, in fact, the leading advocate of mechanized warfare in the United States between the wars. In 1934 Chaffee commanded the 1st Cavalry Regiment (Mechanized) and in maneuvers that year at Fort Riley, Kansas, demonstrated its potential. As chief of the Budget and Legislative Planning Branch of the War Department General Staff from 1934 to 1938, he worked to secure funds for armor development over the objections of more conservative superiors. Chaffee won promotion to brigadier general in November 1938 and commanded the 7th Mechanized Brigade, which he led in maneuvers at Plattsburgh, New York, in 1939 and in Louisiana in 1940. Chaffee now became an early exponent of combined-arms operations.

Made commander of the Armored Force in July 1940, Chaffee was promoted major general in October and organized I Armored Corps, of two divisions. His theories of armor warfare were vindicated by the September 1939 German invasion of Poland that began World War II. Chaffee died of cancer at Boston on 22 August 1941; he was succeeded by Major General Jacob DEVERS. In 1945 the army named its newest light tank, the M-24, in Chaffee's honor.

See also TANKS.

Further reading: Gillie, Mildred H. *Forging the Thunderbolt: A History of the Development of the Armored Force.* Harrisonburg, Pa.: Military Service Publishing, 1947; Johnson, David E. *Fast Tanks and Heavy Bombers:*

Innovations in the U.S. Army, 1917–1945. Ithaca, N.Y.: Cornell University Press, 1998.

— Spencer C. Tucker

Chamberlain, Joshua L. (1828–1914) *U.S. Army general, educator, and politician*

Born on 8 September 1828 at Brewer, Maine, Joshua Lawrence Chamberlain graduated from Bowdoin College in 1852 and from Bangor Theological Seminary in 1855. That year he joined the faculty of Bowdoin as a professor of religion. Later he taught rhetoric and modern languages, among other subjects.

Chamberlain volunteered for military service in 1862 and was appointed lieutenant colonel of the 20th Maine Infantry Regiment. He learned the military profession quickly and in 1863 was promoted to colonel. It was in command of the 20th Maine during the Battle of GETTYSBURG that he performed his greatest Civil War service, holding Little Round Top and then taking Big Round Top in the second day of fighting, 2 July 1863. Belatedly, in 1888, Chamberlain received the Medal of Honor for his actions that day.

Chamberlain continued with the Army of the Potomac and in August received command of a brigade, participating in the subsequent drive on Richmond. In June 1864 he was wounded at PETERSBURG while leading his brigade; Lieutenant General Ulysses S. GRANT promoted him on the field. Congress then confirmed him as brigadier general of volunteers. Leading a successful assault in the Battle of FIVE FORKS, he was again wounded. Chamberlain was breveted to major general of volunteers. When Grant finally cornered General Robert E. LEE's Army of Northern Virginia at APPOMATTOX COURTHOUSE, he gave Chamberlain the honor of receiving the formal Confederate surrender on 12 April 1865. In all, Chamberlain was wounded six times, cited for bravery four times, and took part in 24 major engagements.

One of the truly outstanding volunteer officers of the Civil War, Chamberlain left the army in June 1866. He returned to Bowdoin briefly before serving four consecutive terms as governor of Maine (1866–71). In 1876 he was elected president of Bowdoin, serving in that capacity until 1883. During this time he also taught mental and moral philosophy and, in the spirit of modernism, introduced science courses and deemphasized religion. Until 1885 he also lectured on political science and public law. When he retired from Bowdoin he had taught every subject in the curriculum except mathematics.

In 1900 Chamberlain was appointed U.S. surveyor of customs for the port of Portland, Maine, a post that he held the remainder of his life. He died at Portland on 24 February 1914, from the effects of his Civil War wounds.

See also CIVIL WAR, LAND OVERVIEW.

Further reading: Chamberlain, Joshua L. *The Passing of the Armies, an Account of the Final Campaign of the Army of the Potomac: Based upon Personal Reminiscence of the Fifth Army Corps.* Reprint, Lincoln: University of Nebraska Press, 1998; Nesbitt, Mark, ed. *Through Blood and Fire: Selected Civil War Papers of Major General Joshua Lawrence Chamberlain.* Mechanicsburg, Pa.: Stackpole Books, 1996; Trulock, Alice R. *In the Hands of Providence: Joshua Lawrence Chamberlain and the American Civil War.* Chapel Hill: University of North Carolina Press, 1992.

— Brian C. Melton

Champion's Hill, Battle of (16 May 1863) *Important Civil War battle, leading to the siege and capture of Vicksburg, Mississippi*

In May 1863 Major General Ulysses S. GRANT brilliantly turned the Confederate defenses of Vicksburg by landing his army below the town on the opposite (Louisiana) bank of the Mississippi River, crossing below Vicksburg to the Mississippi shore and striking boldly inland for Jackson and the rail line that tied Vicksburg to the rest of the Confederacy. His troops took Jackson on 14 May and then turned westward to approach Vicksburg from the rear.

Meanwhile, Confederate theater commander General Joseph E. JOHNSTON ordered the commander of the Vicksburg garrison, Lieutenant General John C. PEMBERTON, to move eastward from Vicksburg and strike Grant in the interior of Mississippi. Reluctantly, Pemberton complied, hesitantly feeling his way eastward.

A spy kept Grant well apprised of Confederate plans, and the Union general moved to intercept Pemberton's advance. The two armies collided on 16 May some 20 miles west of Jackson. Pemberton's Confederates took up a defensive position on a north-south ridge, anchored on the north by the higher ground of Champion's Hill. Federal forces advanced from the east on three separate routes—the Jackson Road on the Union right, the Middle Road in the center, and the Raymond Road on the Union left.

Federals on the latter two roads had orders to "advance cautiously," and they did little fighting in the early stages of the battle. But the Union column on the Jackson Road struck hard at the Confederate left, taking Champion's Hill by 1 P.M., along with the vital crossroads of the Jackson and Middle Roads behind it. It also threatened Pemberton's extreme left flank and his line of retreat via the bridge over Baker's Creek. Pemberton brought up reinforcements and counterattacked, retaking these key positions in ferocious fighting and temporarily relieving the threat to his flank.

Grant, however, had more troops available, and Pemberton was hampered by the stubborn insubordination of Major General W. W. Loring, who commanded his largest division and held the relatively quiet right end of the Confederate line. Loring repeatedly refused to obey Pemberton's orders to send reinforcements to the hard-pressed Confederate left. Grant brought up his own reinforcements on the Jackson Road, while the Union columns on the Middle and Raymond Roads finally began to advance in earnest against the Confederate center and right.

Pressed hard along its whole length, the Rebel line quickly collapsed. A rout ensued, with Pemberton's beaten army fleeing desperately toward the bridge over Baker's Creek. Loring's division, cut off from the bridge, abandoned the rest of Pemberton's army and left the battlefield via another route, finally joining General Johnston, east of Jackson.

Grant followed up next day, defeating Pemberton again at Big Black River Bridge, where the latter had attempted to hold a bridgehead in hope of being rejoined by Loring. The twice-beaten Confederate army fled to the fortifications of Vicksburg. The Battle of Champion's Hill had decided the maneuver portion of the campaign.

See also CIVIL WAR, LAND OVERVIEW; VICKSBURG, CAMPAIGN AND SIEGE OF.

Further reading: Arnold, James R. *Grant Wins the War: Decision at Vicksburg.* New York: Wiley, 1997; Bearss, Edwin C. *The Vicksburg Campaign.* 3 vols. Dayton, Ohio: Morningside, 1995; Winschel, Terrence J., ed. *Triumph and Defeat: The Vicksburg Campaign.* Campbell, Calif.: Savas, 1998; Winschel, Terrence J. *Vicksburg: Fall of the Confederate Gibraltar.* Abilene, Tex.: McWhiney Foundation Press, 1999.

— Steven E. Woodworth

Chancellorsville, Battle of (1–4 May 1863) *Civil War battle*

Following the Confederate victory at FREDERICKSBURG in December 1862, Major General Joseph HOOKER succeeded Major General Ambrose BURNSIDE as the commander of the Army of the Potomac. Although many of his senior subordinates regarded him as conniving, overly ambitious, and of low moral standards, Hooker restored morale. He also devised and began to carry out a sound strategic plan for the defeat of General Robert E. LEE's outnumbered Army of Northern Virginia, still holding its strong defensive position near Fredericksburg but weakened by the detachment of two divisions under Lieutenant General James LONGSTREET to gather supplies in southeastern Virginia. The defeat of Lee's army, President Abraham LINCOLN insisted, and not the capture of the Confederate capitol of Richmond, as Hooker would have preferred, was to be the operational goal of his forces.

The Battle of Chancellorsville, 1–4 May 1863. Lithograph by Currier & Ives   *(Library of Congress)*

Hooker initiated in late April 1863 a multipronged advance that at first succeeded in confusing, although not surprising, Lee, who had been expecting an advance by the Union forces. Hooker sent most of the Army of the Potomac's cavalry, under Major General George Stoneman, on a diversionary raid between Lee and his base of supplies in Richmond. Stoneman's cavalry inflicted only slight damage to the Virginia Central Railroad, which the Confederates quickly repaired. Hooker would be handicapped throughout the campaign by a lack of sound intelligence because of the absence of most of his cavalry.

Meanwhile, Hooker crossed the Rappahannock River with 75,000 men, the main body of his army, threatening Lee's rear. Major General John Sedgwick led 30,000 Federal troops in a simultaneous movement against Lee's front to the east at Fredericksburg, a movement that prevented the Confederates from initially detecting Hooker's crossing of the river. Hooker now expected Lee to withdraw from his position and retreat toward Richmond. Lee did not react as Hooker anticipated, however, thereby throwing the Federal commander off balance. Lee now seized the initiative and would not relinquish it for the balance of the campaign.

In response to Hooker's advance, Lee divided his heavily outnumbered 60,000-man army, leaving 10,000 men under Major General Jubal EARLY to block Sedgwick's forces while he led the bulk of the Army of Northern Virginia to confront Hooker. The surprised Hooker pulled back his advanced units and formed a defensive line in a heavily wooded area known as the Wilderness. He may have hoped to gain the advantage that fighting on the defensive often gave in Civil War battles, but Hooker would prove unable to capitalize on this tactical edge. Thanks to effective reconnaissance by his cavalry, under Major General J. E. B. STUART, Lee learned that Hooker's right flank was vulnerable to encirclement and attack. He then assigned Lieutenant General Thomas J. "Stonewall" JACKSON's corps to take advantage of this opportunity.

On 2 May, his movements largely shielded from federal observation by dense undergrowth, Jackson marched his 26,000 men into position. When the movement was reported to him, Hooker took it as evidence the Confederates were retreating. Major General Oliver O. HOWARD, whose corps held the exposed union right flank, was preparing for an attack from the west and was unconcerned. Thus Jackson's attack achieved surprise and routed the divisions on the extreme right of the federal line.

By nightfall, however, the Union line had been reestablished, despite heavy casualties in killed, wounded,

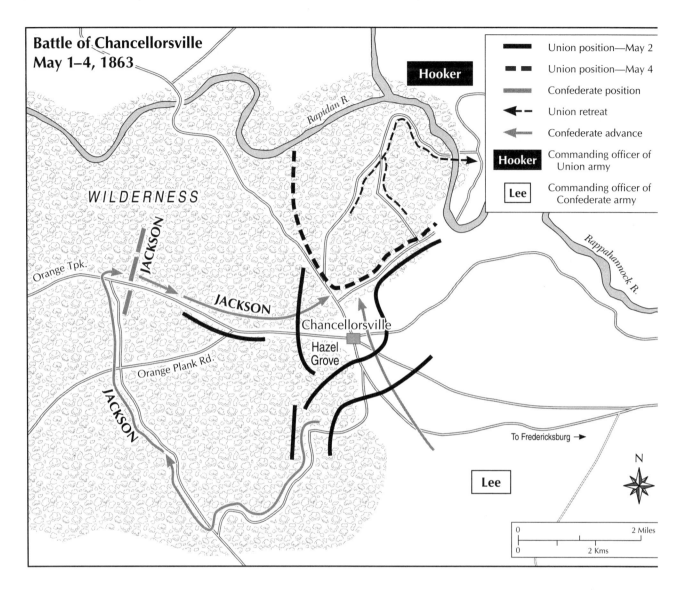

**Battle of Chancellorsville
May 1–4, 1863**

Union position—May 2
Union position—May 4
Confederate position
Union retreat
Confederate advance
Hooker Commanding officer of Union army
Lee Commanding officer of Confederate army

WILDERNESS

Rapidan R.

Rappahannock R.

Orange Tpk.

JACKSON

JACKSON

Orange Plank Rd.

JACKSON

Chancellorsville

Hazel Grove

To Fredericksburg →

Hooker

Lee

N

0   2 Miles
0   2 Kms

and captured, and the Confederate advance had been halted. The accidental wounding of Jackson and his senior division commander, Major General A. P. HILL, by Confederate troops that night robbed Lee's forces of the opportunity to continue to pursue their advantage.

The only advance of the night would be a misguided surprise attack by Major General Daniel Sickles's III Corps in an attempt to turn Jackson's right flank, which resulted in a number of casualties from friendly fire and did not achieve its objective.

Even worse, Hooker, fearing that his troops would be cut off, ordered Sickles to pull back from his exposed position at Hazel Grove, in the center of the Union line. By abandoning Hazel Grove, Hooker enabled the divided wings of Lee's army to reunite and allowed Confederate instead of Union artillery to move into this commanding position.

The next morning, 3 May, Stuart, temporarily assigned to the command of Jackson's Corps, followed up the Confederate advance of the previous day by continuing to attack the right of the Union line, while Lee directed the assault against the Federal left. In very heavy fighting, the Union forces held their ground. Hooker, who had been stunned when a Confederate cannonball struck a porch column against which he was leaning, did not exercise effective control over his forces and did not communicate effectively with Sedgwick.

Having put Hooker on the defensive, Lee now determined to crush the smaller Federal wing at Fredericksburg. Although Sedgwick had succeeded in seizing Early's position at Marye's Heights after repeated attacks on 3 May, Lee's advance caught the Federal commander by surprise. On 4 May, Lee drove Sedgwick back across the Rappahannock; Hooker remained in position, missing the opportunity to advance against Stuart's small force and rescue his subordinate from his desperate situation. Lee next intended to resume the offensive against Hooker's strong position, but Hooker robbed him of the opportunity by ordering a retreat across the Rappahannock on 6 May, despite the recommendation of a majority of his corps commanders that he stay and fight. Although Lee was disappointed by this development, he had nevertheless won what more than a few historians would judge to be the greatest of his many victories.

The Battle of Chancellorsville resulted in some 17,000 Federal and 13,000 Confederate casualties. The losses were, in proportion to men engaged, much higher for the South. Also, Jackson developed pneumonia and died on 10 May, depriving Lee of an experienced, capable lieutenant whose talents would be sorely missed in future campaigns. Hooker, having lost the confidence of his subordinates and the Lincoln administration, was relieved of his command the following month. The Confederate victory paved the way for Lee's subsequent June advance into Pennsylvania, which culminated in the Battle of GETTYSBURG.

Further reading: Furgurson, Ernest B. *Chancellorsville 1863: The Souls of the Brave.* New York: Knopf, 1992;

Sears, Stephen W. *Chancellorsville.* New York: Houghton Mifflin, 1996; Sutherland, Daniel E. *Fredericksburg & Chancellorsville: The Dare Mark Campaign.* Lincoln: University of Nebraska Press, 1998.

— Michael Thomas Smith

Changjin/Chosin Reservoir, Battle of and retreat from (27 November–11 December 1950) *Korean War campaign, one of the most masterly withdrawals against heavy odds in the history of warfare*

In the United Nations Command (UNC) drive to the Yalu River, Major General Oliver P. SMITH's First Marine Division of X Corps received the task of securing the Changjin (Chosin, on Japanese maps) reservoir in far northeast Korea. Smith was deeply concerned about flank security, especially the wide gap between his own forces and Eighth Army to the west. He slowed his advance and prepared a base at Hagaru-ri, steps that probably later saved his division from annihilation.

On 27 November 1950, Chinese forces massively counterattacked UNC forces throughout North Korea. Ultimately the Chinese fed 12 divisions of Ninth Army

U.S. forces withdraw southward following the massive Chinese intervention in the Korean War. Shown here is Weapons Company, in line with Headquarters and Service Company, 2d Battalion, 7th Marines on 27 November 1950. *(Naval Historical Center)*

Group (some 120,000 men) into the battle against the 1st Marine Division, elements of 7th Army Division, and other UNC forces (in all only about 22,000 men).

Despite the numerical imbalance in manpower, U.S. troops had a significant edge in firepower and maneuverability, and they enjoyed complete air superiority. By 28 November the Chinese had managed to cut off Smith's forces from the remainder of X Corps at several points around the reservoir. These were Yudam-ni and Sinhung-ni on the western and eastern sides of the reservoir, respectively; Hagaru-ri on the southern end; and Koto-ri, 10 miles southward.

In order to consolidate his dispersed and isolated forces and disengage from the Chinese, Smith had to execute an enormously complex and risky operation involving multiple breakouts through the lines of the numerically superior Chinese. Hagaru-ri was a crucial point of the operation. A road junction with a field hospital and a nearly completed airstrip, it was the main supply base, and it stood astride the only route to the UNC-held Hungnam perimeter on the coast. Hagaru-ri was held by a battalion-sized marine detachment and two artillery batteries.

At Koto-ri to the south, Smith formed a U.S.-British task force of 922 men and 141 vehicles, including 17 tanks, to relieve Hagaru-ri. On 29 November it drove northward but was ambushed and split by the Chinese at a location that came to be known as Hell Fire Valley. The force suffered heavy losses—321 men and 75 vehicles—but some 300 men managed to reach Hagaru-ri on the 30th.

The bulk of the marines, two regiments supported by 48 howitzers, were besieged at Yudam-ni, where they had repelled attacks by two Chinese divisions since 27 November. One other Chinese division had cut off the main marine supply line southward. In ferocious battles the marines broke through the Chinese lines, reaching Hagaru-ri on 4 December. Marine casualties came to almost 1,500 men.

The situation did not work out as well on the eastern side of the reservoir, where 2,500 men from two infantry battalions and one artillery battalion of the 7th Infantry Division were trapped around Sinhung-ri. On 29 November a company-sized relief force with tanks, formed by Brigadier General Henry J. Hodges at Hagaru-ri, failed to break through. Despite heroic American resistance, Chinese forces double-enveloped and defeated in detail U.S. forces around Sinhung-ri. Only 1,050 men had managed to reach Hagaru-ri across the reservoir ice by 30 November. U.S. losses were 300 killed, 1,150 missing, and 665 wounded or frostbitten.

From 1 to 4 December, UNC forces regrouped at Hagaru-ri. Some 9,965 men, including 9,800 U.S. troops (9,310 marines), and about 1,000 vehicles would attempt the 11-mile withdrawal to Koto-ri, where the Chinese surrounded another 4,000 U.S. troops. Utilizing the

Hagaru-ri airstrip, completed by 1 December, aircraft delivered more than 500 reinforcements, medical supplies, food, and ammunition. They also evacuated more than 4,000 wounded and sick. Air support was critical; air force and navy aircraft provided close air support and delivered some 100 tons of supplies per day before the breakout.

From 6 to 8 December U.S. and allied forces successfully drove south from Hagaru-ri behind a tank vanguard. The men had to repair blown bridges in order to reach Koto-ri. A major logistic feat involved the 7 December drop from C-119 aircraft near Koto-ri of prefabricated bridge sections to span a gorge. Reaching Koto-ri cost 616 UNC casualties, including 103 killed. On 8 December more than 14,000 UNC troops, 13,900 of them American, began the final drive to the coast.

A marine battalion located in Chinhung-ni, some eight miles south of Koto-ri, drove north; a task force from the Hungnam perimeter, drawn from the 3d Infantry Division, supported the advance of the Marines from Chinhung-ni. By 11 December Smith's men had fought their way to Hungnam, at a cost of an additional 75 men killed. On 15 December the 1st Marine Division was evacuated from Hungnam. By 24 December, in the HUNGNAM EVACUATION, the whole of X Corps and a number of Korean refugees had been extracted and the city's port facilities had been blown up.

Total U.S. casualties in the Changjin reservoir campaign came to more than 5,000 men. The 7th Infantry Division lost more than 2,000 men killed, missing, and wounded. First Marine Division losses from 27 November to 8 December were 523 dead, 186 missing in action, and 2,733 wounded. Additionally, more than 7,000 men were disabled by frostbite. Chinese combat losses are estimated at about 25,000 men, including 11,500 killed and 12,500 wounded. Frostbite may have claimed an additional 20,000 soldiers. The Changjin withdrawal remains one of the most masterly in the history of warfare and without parallel in U.S. military history.

See also CHINESE FIRST PHASE OFFENSIVE; KOREAN WAR.

Further reading: Appleman, Roy E. *East of Chosin: Entrapment and Breakout in Korea 1950.* College Station: Texas A&M University Press, 1987; ———. *Escaping the Trap: The U.S. X Corps in Northeast Korea, 1950.* College Station: Texas A&M University Press, 1990; Hopkins, William B. *One Bugle No Drums: The Marines at Chosin Reservoir.* Chapel Hill, N.C.: Algonquin Books, 1986; La Bree, Clifton. *The Gentle Warrior: General Oliver Prince Smith, USMC.* Kent, Ohio: Kent State University Press, 2001; Russ, Martin. *Breakout: The Chosin Reservoir Campaign, Korea 1950.* New York: Fromm International, 1999.

— Peter Rainow

chaplains *Service corps of the U.S. Army, Navy, and Air Force responsible for the religious and moral guidance of personnel and dependents*

Since each branch of the armed service has its own chaplain corps, the history of chaplains in the U.S. military is linked to the histories of the branches.

The chaplain corps was first established in 1775 during the American Revolutionary War when General George WASHINGTON asked the Continental Congress to approve chaplains to serve with the CONTINENTAL ARMY. On 29 July 1775 Congress approved the request and voted to pay chaplains. The state militias had their own chaplains, supported by the state governments.

Following the war, the ARMY was reduced significantly in size, and the number of chaplains reflected this. Chaplains again served with the army during the WAR OF 1812. Again, following the war the army was reduced in size, and the number of chaplains declined accordingly.

In 1818 the army chose to do away with chaplains and rely on civilian clergymen from communities close to military posts, or missionaries who accompanied expeditions to the West. It was a not until 1838 that the army again had a chaplain when one was appointed to serve at Fort Crawford, Wisconsin. Soon more than 30 chaplains were serving at frontier outposts. Most of them were clergymen from recognized denominations, including Episcopalians, Presbyterians, Baptists, and Methodists.

During the 1846–48 MEXICAN-AMERICAN WAR, Congress appointed chaplains to military units. Among new chaplains were two Roman Catholic priests appointed by the bishop of Baltimore. This was believed necessary because of the large number of recent Catholic immigrants among the soldiers. After the war the army reduced the number of chaplains to the 30 serving at frontier forts.

The immense number of men in the armed forces of the United States and Confederacy during the Civil War caused a great increase in the number of chaplains serving with both sides. Most state militias brought their chaplains with them, but legislation passed by the U.S. Congress on 3 August 1861 provided that a chaplain be appointed for every regiment in the Union army. At first Congress failed to regulate who could serve as a chaplain, but in July 1862 it passed legislation requiring chaplains to be regularly ordained by recognized denominations and appointed upon the recommendation of an authorized ecclesiastical body. During the Civil War, approximately 2,000 chaplains served in the Union army, including the first Jewish chaplains. The number of chaplains serving with Confederate forces is estimated at from 600 to 1,000.

Following the Civil War, chaplains continued to serve at frontier posts. The chaplaincy suffered from a lack of regulations, with a large number of chaplains being appointed through patronage. Immediately before the 1898 SPANISH-AMERICAN WAR, 34 chaplains ministered to soldiers at 80 garrisons in the United States. These chaplains accompanied troops to Cuba and the Philippines. Chaplains also served with U.S. troops occupying the Philippines after the war.

Secretary of War Elihu ROOT carried out reforms affecting the army chaplaincy. Chaplains could now be promoted, and *A Manual for U.S. Army Chaplains* was published (1898). Then in April 1909 a six-member Board of Chaplains met at Fort Leavenworth, Kansas, to recommend additional reforms. For the first time in its history, the army, rather than individual post commanders or the legislative and executive branches of government, addressed religious issues.

After U.S. entry into WORLD WAR I the number of chaplains dramatically increased, from 74 to 2,200, with 1,200 of them serving with American forces in Europe. A number of chaplains were wounded during the war, and many were decorated for valor.

Following the war, the National Defense Act of 1920 authorized appointment of a chief of chaplains, with the rank of colonel. Between the world wars, the number of military chaplains again decreased, in line with the reduction in the size of the military. At the lowest point in the interwar period, there were 135 chaplains on active duty and more than 1,000 in the reserves.

During WORLD WAR II the number of army chaplains increased from 125 in December 1941 to more than 8,000 by August 1945. Congress enacted legislation providing that the chief of chaplains be a major general. America's entry into the war mobilized members of the clergy. For example, more than half the ordained rabbis in the United States volunteered for service.

The number of army chaplains available at the beginning of the KOREAN WAR was about 700, a number reflecting in part the separation of the AIR FORCE as a separate service in 1947. Reservists were mobilized, and by the end of the war 1,600 chaplains ministered to soldiers in Korea. The number of chaplains serving in the VIETNAM WAR fluctuated with the number of troops in Southeast Asia, but in November 1970 there were more than 300 chaplains in South Vietnam. Two Roman Catholic chaplains, Charles Watters and Angelo Liteky, were awarded the Medal of Honor, the first chaplains so honored since the Civil War.

Chaplains also ministered to soldiers participating in the conflicts of the 1980s and 1990s. At the height of OPERATION DESERT STORM, some 560 army chaplains were serving in the Persian Gulf region.

The U.S. NAVY has had chaplains since the Revolutionary War. The Continental Congress authorized captains to hold Sunday services on board ships and that chaplains be paid. One chaplain was appointed in 1780, a second in 1781.

The navy was disbanded after the Revolutionary War; the first U.S. Navy chaplain was not appointed until 1798, with the separation of the Department of the Navy from the Department of War. The number of navy chaplains remained small over the next decade, never exceeding 12. Chaplains, who served on board only the larger ships, also worked to educate midshipmen and, often, illiterate sailors.

At the beginning of the Civil War, the navy had 24 chaplains. Only 36 served during the war. After the war, their number decreased, but navy chaplains were subject to more regulation and training than their colleagues on land. The first Roman Catholic navy chaplain was appointed in 1888. The number of chaplains did not increase during the Spanish-American War.

The post of chief of navy chaplains was created in 1917. The Marine Corps had depended on the navy for its chaplains, but in 1912 a navy chaplain was assigned exclusively to the marines.

As with the army, the number of chaplains increased dramatically during World War I. By the end of the conflict there were 203 chaplains in the navy, including 44 Roman Catholic priests and one rabbi. During World War II 2,811 chaplains, mostly reservists, served with the U.S. Navy.

The U.S. Air Force chaplaincy separated from the army in 1949, two years after the creation of the U.S. Air Force. Chaplains have served primarily at air bases. During World War II and immediately thereafter, chaplains serving with the Army Air Corps were trained at the Army Chaplains School, which had moved to Fort Slocum, New York, in 1951. In July 1953 a chaplain course for air force chaplains was established at Lackland Air Force Base in Texas.

In the 1990s the army and the navy commissioned the first Muslim chaplains, reflecting the religious diversity among service personnel. Today the military chaplaincy in the U.S. armed forces faces numerous challenges. There is a shortage of chaplains in every branch, leading some to call for a unified chaplain corps.

Further reading: Armstrong, Warren B. *For Courageous Fighting and Confident Dying: Union Chaplains in the Civil War.* Lawrence: University Press of Kansas, 1998; Brinsfield, John W. *Encouraging Faith, Supporting Soldiers: The United States Army Chaplaincy, 1975–1995.* Washington, D.C.: Office of the Chief of Chaplains, Department of the Army, 1997; Budd, Richard M. *Serving Two Masters: The Development of American Military Chaplaincy, 1860–1920.* Lincoln: University of Nebraska Press, 2001; Crosby, Donald F. *Battlefield Chaplains: Catholic Priests in World War II.* Lawrence: University

Press of Kansas, 1994; Groh, John E. *Facilitators of the Free Exercise of Religion: Air Force Chaplains, 1981–1990.* Washington, D.C.: Office of the Chief of Chaplains, U.S. Air Force, 1991; Moore, Withers M., Herbert L. Bergsma, and Timothy J. Demy. *Chaplains with U.S. Naval Units in Vietnam, 1954–1975.* Washington, D.C.: Office of the Chief of Chaplains, Department of the Navy, 1985; Slomovitz, Albert Isaac. *The Fighting Rabbis: Jewish Military Chaplains and American History.* New York: New York University Press, 1999.

— John David Rausch, Jr.

Chapultepec, Battle of (12–13 September 1847)
Final battle of the 1846–48 Mexican-American War, the culmination of the Major General Winfield Scott's march from Veracruz to Mexico City

Guarding the western approach to Mexico City, Chapultepec Castle rested on a 200-foot hill and housed the Mexican military academy. It was the "Halls of Montezuma," the ancient home site of Aztec kings. The Mexican position was heavily fortified. U.S. major general Winfield SCOTT could have bypassed the stronghold, but he did not wish to leave such a well-defended position in his rear.

Scott's plan was simple. After a lengthy artillery barrage, some 7,000 U.S. troops would storm the hill and the castle. The majority of his staff opposed the plan; only Lieutenant Pierre G. T. BEAUREGARD and Colonel Franklin Pierce supported it. Nonetheless, Scott perservered. Mexican general Antonio López de Santa Anna had about 7,000 troops to defend the approaches to Chapultepec, while General Nicolas Bravo commanded less than 800 soldiers, including some 80 cadets, behind the massive walls of Chapultepec Castle.

On the morning of 12 September U.S. artillery opened up on the hill and surrounding Mexican defensive positions. The barrage lasted 14 hours. Bravo requested reinforcements, but Santa Anna refused. During the bombardment the castle sustained serious damage, and Bravo's men suffered heavy casualties.

On the next morning, 13 September, a volunteer "forlorn hope," a party of 500 American soldiers from Brigadier Generals John A. Quitman's and David E. Twiggs's divisions, moved through the wooded area at the bottom of the hill toward the south and east walls of Chapultepec. Fighting was intense, as the Americans had to bring up scaling ladders while the Mexican defenders poured musket fire down upon them.

At the same time, Brigadier General Gideon PILLOW's division, with support from Brigadier General William J. WORTH's forces, attacked the western walls of the castle. Fighting along the causeways leading to the hill, Pillow's men faced fierce hand-to-hand fighting as they reached the walls. American deserters who had joined the Mexican San Patricio Battalion and had been recaptured and were now awaiting execution, could see the assault on Chapultepec.

Men from both attacking columns were able to scale the walls, attack the ramparts, and make their way into the compound. As the Americans poured into the castle, many Mexican defenders fled. A force of 400 Mexican sharpshooters, however, tried to fight its way into the compound to assist beleaguered comrades and save the position, but this effort was defeated. Many of the cadets, as young as 13, remained to defend their academy. Reportedly, six refused to surrender and gave their lives in defense of the castle. One, Juan Escutia, supposedly wrapped himself in the Mexican flag and jumped to his death from one of the ramparts. These cadets are remembered as the *Niños Héroes* (boy heroes) and are today honored in an annual ceremony.

The battle ended by 9:30 A.M., and Scott's men continued to fight their way into the city. By nightfall, exhausted and running low on ammunition, the Americans ceased fire. The fighting at Chapultepec had cost Santa Anna more than 1,800 men; the Americans had lost about 450.

On 14 September, city leaders surrendered the capital to Scott. Scott's campaign to take Mexico City had been successful. The Duke of Wellington commented, "His campaign is unsurpassed in military annals. He is the greatest living soldier."

See also MEXICAN-AMERICAN WAR; VERACRUZ.

Further reading: Eisenhower, John S. D. *So Far from God: The U.S. War with Mexico, 1846–1848.* Reprint, Norman: University of Oklahoma Press, 2000; Peter F. Stevens. *Rogues March: John Riley and the St. Patrick's Battalion.* New York: Brassey's, 1999.

— William Thomas Allison

Charleston, siege of (11 February–12 May 1780)

Pivotal military action during the Revolutionary War

Facing a stalemate in the northern theater of operations in the summer of 1778, the British commander in North America, Lieutenant General Sir Henry Clinton, secured the approval of the British government to shift the focus of the war to the South. This region was closer to British bases in the West Indies, and Clinton hoped that operations in the South would bring a large number of Loyalists into the British militia. His immediate goal was the capture of the city of Charleston and its garrison, commanded by Major General Benjamin LINCOLN.

The British expedition departed New York on 26 December 1779 with 8,700 men in 90 transports, protected by 10 warships. The British landed at Tybee Island near the occupied city of SAVANNAH on 30 January 1780. On 10 February, after assembling stores and artillery from British garrisons in Florida and the West Indies, Clinton moved his army by sea up the coast to Simmons Island. Completing his landing there by 12 February, Clinton then occupied James Island, across the Ashley River from Charleston, while Admiral Mariott Arbuthnot sailed the fleet around the islands to gain entry to Charleston Harbor.

To defend Charleston, Lincoln had a 3,600-man garrison, 2,000 of whom were militia, a line of strong fortifications, and a small flotilla. Lincoln's defensive line stretched for a mile and a half across the peninsula north of the city; marshes anchored both its river flanks. A moat or canal in front of the line connected the two marshes. Between the moat and the fortification line were two lines of abatis (defensive obstacles with sharpened stakes). The fortified line itself consisted of breastworks and redoubts mounting 66 guns and a masonry work in the center.

In late March the British began to attack these defenses, initiating the actual siege of Charleston. On 20 March Arbuthnot sent five frigates across the bar. On the morning of 29 March, Clinton surprised the Americans by crossing the Ashley River onto the Charleston Peninsula, 12 miles above the city. Lincoln made no effort to stop Clinton from moving south, and on 1 April the British began construction of their initial siege line 800 yards north of the American defense line. On 8 April, Arbuthnot sailed eight warships and six transports past Fort Moultrie into Charleston Harbor; one ship ran aground, and one ship was damaged. On 6 April the defenders were reinforced by the arrival of 750 Continental infantry, who managed to slip down the Cooper River on schooners past the British siege lines. On 10 April the British completed their first parallel trench, and Clinton and Arbuthnot demanded that Lincoln surrender. He refused.

The British then moved to isolate Charleston completely and move their siege lines closer to the American defenses. Clinton sent Lieutenant Colonel James Webster and 1,400 men to establish control east of the Cooper River; on 15 April Webster defeated an American force at Monck's Corner, 30 miles north of Charleston. Webster's men soon controlled the area east of the Cooper except for Fort Moultrie and a few American outposts along the river itself.

Clinton began his second parallel (closer to the defenses) upon Lincoln's refusal to surrender; on 18 April he received 2,566 reinforcements under Lieutenant Colonel Lord (Francis) Rawdon. A week later the British controlled all American posts with the exception of Fort Moultrie, and it surrendered when the British landed on SULLIVAN'S ISLAND on 7 May. On 19 April, meanwhile, Clinton had pushed trenches to within 250 yards of the American defensive perimeter. Despite American counter-battery fire, British artillery took a toll.

The final stage of the siege began on 21 April, when Lincoln, now convinced of inevitable defeat (though opposed in this view by Lieutenant Governor Christopher Gadsden), proposed surrender with the honors of war. Clinton rejected this and pressed on with the siege. The British repulsed a sortie by 200 Virginians and Carolinians on 24 April. On the night of 25 April the British opened their third parallel and the next day reached the canal, which they proceeded to drain, as well as the first abatis line. By 6 May the Americans had been reduced to a week's worth of supplies. On 8 May the British commenced a heavy artillery bombardment and sent a second summons to surrender, which Lincoln refused. By the night of 10–11 May the British forward line was within 30 yards of the American defenses, and in the morning the British began firing hot shot into Charleston itself. Gadsden then asked Lincoln to surrender. On 12 May 1780, Lincoln surrendered the city and its garrison.

American casualties in the siege were 89 killed, 138 wounded, and 2,571 Continental army soldiers captured. Another 1,000 militia were also taken. It was the greatest American defeat of the war. The British suffered only 76 killed and 189 wounded. After the capture of Charleston there was no organized opposition to the British in South Carolina, and Patriot morale plumeted throughout the southern states.

See also AMERICAN REVOLUTIONARY WAR, LAND OVERVIEW; CHARLESTON EXPEDITION.

Further reading: Buchanan, John. *The Road to Guilford Courthouse: The American Revolution in the Carolinas.* New York: Wiley, 1997; Lee, Henry. *The Revolutionary War Memoirs of General Henry Lee.* New York: Da Capo, 1998; Morrill, Dan L. *Southern Campaigns of the American Revolution.* Mount Pleasant, S.C.: Nautical & Aviation, 1993.

— Benjamin L. Huggins

Charleston, siege of (Civil War) (1861–1865) *One of the longest campaigns of the Civil War, lasting from mid-1861 until early 1865*

Leaders in Washington sought the capture of Charleston, the font of the rebellion, but did not realize the potential effects of a military reversal. The commander of the South Atlantic Blockading Squadron, Rear Admiral Samuel DU PONT, wanted a combined land-sea assault, but leaders in Washington believed only a naval assault was necessary and that if FORT SUMTER could be taken, Charleston would yield as well.

Throughout 1861, Confederate authorities at Charleston strengthened the city's three-tier defensive system: an outer layer on the Atlantic barrier islands, astride the harbor mouth; artillery batteries in the inner harbor; and land forts protecting the flanks. The Union attackers relied on ironclads; U.S. Secretary of the Navy Gideon WELLES believed

that monitors and the ironclad *New Ironsides* could smash their way into the harbor.

Charleston's defenses against attack from the sea consisted of Fort Johnson and Battery Glover on James Island, Fort Ripley and Castle Pinckney in the harbor itself, and the White Point Battery (Battery Ramsay) in Charleston. Forts Sumter and Moultrie, however, were the most powerful elements in Charleston's defenses.

On 31 January 1863 Confederates flag officer Duncan N. Ingraham sortied from Charleston with two ironclad rams to attack unarmored Union vessels off the harbor. A number of Union ships were damaged before the rams were chased back into the harbor. The Confederate commander in Charleston, Brigadier General P. G. T. BEAUREGARD, claimed erroneously that the blockade had been broken.

Under heavy pressure from Welles, Du Pont planned his attack. Never confident of the outcome, he planned to enter the harbor with seven monitors, the powerful *New Ironsides* (flying his flag), and the hybrid *Keokuk,* then shell Fort Sumter into submission. The defenders were well aware of Union intentions and prepared accordingly.

The battle occurred on 7 April 1863, the monitors taking terrific punishment. *Keokuk,* struck some 90 times, was the hardest hit and sank the next day. Because the monitors had few guns, the Union ships managed to get off only 139 rounds, while the Confederates fired 2,229 rounds in return. Du Pont now stated that Charleston could not be taken by naval attack alone. He also feared the capture of one of his ironclads, which the Confederates might use to threaten the Union blockade.

Du Pont's pessimism led to his relief and replacement by Rear Admiral Andrew H. FOOTE; however, Foote died in New York City before he could assume command. Rear Admiral John DAHLGREN replaced him. From his arrival in July until September, Dahlgren kept up a bombardment of the city's defenses.

On 10 July 1863 the navy landed 3,000 troops under Brigadier General Quincy Adams Gillmore on Morris Island. The Union troops then worked their way toward FORT WAGNER. The navy launched no fewer than 25 separate attacks to assist Gillmore's men in the capture of Fort Wagner. On 22 August Gillmore opened artillery fire on the city of Charleston, held to be an appropriate target because of its war industries. The principal weapon in the attack was a 200-pounder Parrott rifle known as the Swamp Angel, which before bursting sent three dozen shells into the waterfront district of the city, setting fire and causing panic.

On 23 August Dahlgren attempted a night attack against Sumter. He repeated this at closer range on 1 September. Both attacks were defeated. Fort Wagner, the principal object of Union land attacks, fell on 6 September, and its control by the Union greatly diminished the usefulness of Charleston as a haven for blockade runners.

On 7 September Dahlgren mounted a major monitor attack on Fort Sumter and on 8–9 September a night boat assault. Again, both failed. Dahlgren then requested additional monitors from Washington. Welles refused the request, in effect ending the campaign to run monitors into the harbor and shell Charleston into capitulation.

Charleston relied on technology, including spar torpedoes and the submarine *H. L. HUNLEY* to try, without success, to break the blockade. Charleston did not fall to the Union until February 1865, when Major General William T. SHERMAN's troops cut its lines of communications from the land side. Up to that point, Confederate blockade runners continued to slip in and out.

See also CIVIL WAR, NAVAL OVERVIEW.

Further reading: Burton, F. Milby. *The Siege of Charleston, 1861–1865.* Columbia: University of South Carolina Press, 1970; Coker, P. C., III. *Charleston's Maritime Heritage, 1670–1865.* Charleston, S.C.: CokerCraft Press, 1987; Wise, Stephen R. *Gate of Hell: Campaign for Charleston Harbor, 1863.* Columbia: University of South Carolina Press, 1994; Tucker, Spencer C. *A Short History of the Civil War at Sea.* Wilmington, Del.: Scholarly Resources, 2001.

— Alexander D. Haseley

Charleston expedition (June 1776) *Failed attempt by the British to capture Charleston, South Carolina, during the American Revolutionary War*

As their situation in Massachusetts became untenable late in 1775, the British cast about for ways to end the rebellion before it had properly begun. The now-exiled royal governors of North and South Carolina attested to a strong Loyalist presence in their respective jurisdictions and convinced the secretary of state for the colonies, William, Lord Dartmouth, that a few British regulars could bring the whole lower south back into the king's camp. In January 1776 Lieutenant General Henry Clinton departed from Boston with a small force to rendezvous at the mouth of the Cape Fear River in North Carolina with a combined army and fleet from Ireland under Major General Charles, Lord Cornwallis. Clinton reached the Cape Fear in March and met with the governors of North and South Carolina. He there learned of the defeat of a premature Loyalist uprising in North Carolina at MOORE'S CREEK BRIDGE. To compound his problems, the last elements of the fleet from Ireland did not arrive until the end of May. Searching for something effective to do in the short time remaining (Clinton was under orders to return north), Commodore Sir Peter Parker suggested capturing the unfinished Fort Sullivan in Charleston Harbor.

For their part, the rebels by this point had long anticipated a British descent on Charleston. South Carolina had increased its number of regular regiments (later to be transferred to Continental command) from 12 to 14, and South Carolina militia and two Continental regiments from North Carolina had poured into the city—6,500 by the day of the battle. Major General Charles LEE arrived on 4 June to assume overall command, although he played a negligible role in the actual battle. Finally, a network of defenses had been built in and around Charleston. Two islands, James and SULLIVAN's, straddled the entrance to the harbor. The rebels had captured Fort Johnson on James Island back in September 1775 and had half-completed Fort Sullivan on Sullivan's Island.

Clinton and Parker arrived on 7 June. After a reconaissance, Clinton decided to support Parker's direct naval attack on Fort Sullivan by landing his force on undefended Long Island, up the coast from Sullivan's Island. Clinton landed some 2,500 soldiers and seamen on the island on 16 June but soon found that the terrain prevented any serious support. Parker's naval force, delayed by weather, began its attack on 28 June. Two lines of ships opened fire on Fort Sullivan; fortunately for the Americans, when the second line of three ships tried to move into position to open an enfilading fire, all grounded on a shoal. The rebels' return fire was particularly accurate and effective, limited only by a shortage of powder. The exchange of fire continued until sunset, when the British ships slipped back out to sea, leaving the still-grounded *Actaeon* to be burned by its crew. Meanwhile Clinton's force on Long Island had been unable to divert the Americans; they would remain there for three more weeks before returning to New York.

The peculiar topography and construction of Fort Sullivan (shot-absorbing sand and palmetto logs) limited American casualties to 30 to 40 killed and wounded. The more exposed British suffered 225 casualties in addition to the loss of the *Actaeon*. More importantly, the British would not return to the southern theater for three years.

The rebel success at Charleston deserves more attention than it usually has received. The victory did not prevent the British from exercising the "southern option" in 1777 or 1778, but it helped stabilize colonials' control in the South. During the first six months of 1776 the southern rebels had struggled to consolidate their control and had been vulnerable to a determined British attack. Now, having forced Governor John Dunmore's scratch collection of Loyalist militia and British regulars out of Norfolk in January 1776, then defeated the Loyalists at Moore's Creek Bridge in February, and finally repulsing the British at Charleston in June, the colonials could point to a string of victories as validation of their regime. The proof came just in time, as the initial flush of enthusiasm for the rebellion (often known as the *rage militaire*) that had filled the ranks had begun to fade.

Further reading: Coker, P. C., III. *Charleston's Maritime Heritage, 1670–1865.* Charleston, S.C.: CokerCraft Press, 1987; Rankin, Hugh F. *The North Carolina Continentals.* Chapel Hill: University of North Carolina Press, 1971; Syrett, David. *The Royal Navy in American Waters, 1775–1783.* Brookfield, Vt.: Gower, 1989.

— Wayne E. Lee

Châteauguay, Battle of the (26 October 1813) *Land battle during the War of 1812, part of an American two-pronged attack against Montreal*

Victories against the British at York and FORT GEORGE failed to provide Americans with a decisive advantage. In the fall of 1813, Secretary of War John ARMSTRONG formulated a new strategy designed to sever British supply lines at Kingston. Armstrong replaced Major General Henry DEARBORN with Major General James WILKINSON and made him responsible for the logistical planning and execution of this new plan.

A meeting among Armstrong, Wilkinson, and Commodore Isaac CHAUNCEY resulted in a decision to combine land and naval forces in a two-pronged assault, with the American forces to join at the junction of the Châteauguay and St. Lawrence Rivers. Wilkinson would transport his forces by boat from Sacketts Harbor to the St. Lawrence. The second force, led by Major General Wade Hampton, would leave Plattsburg, New York, and follow the course of the Châteauguay until it reached the St. Lawrence. Personal animosity between Wilkinson and Hampton threatened to disrupt the execution of the plan, but Armstrong persuaded Hampton to cooperate.

Hampton left Plattsburg on 21 October 1813 with 4,000 regulars and 1,400 militiamen. When the army reached the border, the militia from New York refused to cross into Canada, arguing that they were required to defend their state but not to invade another country. On 25 October the remaining forces, which included wagons and heavy guns, halted at a point in the road barricaded by logs and debris. Some 1,700 Canadian militiamen and Indians manned the barricade.

Hampton ordered a portion of his force to move through the swampy woods beside the road and to attack the Canadians from the rear. On the sound of battle he would move the remainder of his troops forward. The flanking force, however, became lost and the next morning was easily halted by the Canadian militia. Major General George IZARD made one effort at a frontal assault of the barricade, but after two hours Hampton halted the fighting. The other column likewise retreated, and the entire force then withdrew back to U.S. soil. Casualties on both sides were slight.

Armstrong ordered Hampton to continue to Montreal, but Hampton refused, citing sickness. In March 1814 Hampton resigned his commission in protest over the conduct of the war.

See also WAR OF 1812, LAND OVERVIEW.

Further reading: Berton, Pierre. *The Invasion of Canada.* Boston: Little, Brown, 1980; Guitard, Michelle. *The Militia of the Battle of the Châteauguay.* Ottawa: Parks Canada, 1983.

— Cynthia Clark Northrup

Château-Thierry/Belleau Wood, Battles of (May–June, 1918) *World War I battles involving U.S. forces*

During the spring of 1918 Quartermaster General of the German army general Erich Ludendorff launched a series of major offensives on the western front. Utilizing veteran troops shifted from the eastern front, Ludendorff hoped to win the war before U.S. forces could make an impact. The Ludendorff offensives achieved the furthest German advances since 1914. In hope of drawing off Allied reserves prior to another blow in Flanders, in May Ludendorff

The Marines Take Belleau Wood (painting)   *(US Marine Corps)*

launched the Chemin des Dames offensive to secure high ground northeast of Paris. Startling German successes there led Ludendorff to continue the advance in the Aisne sector, between the cities of Soissons and Rheims.

On 31 May German troops reached the Marne River in the vicinity of Château-Thierry, less than 50 miles from Paris. The AMERICAN EXPEDITIONARY FORCES (AEF) commander, General John J. PERSHING, offered Allied general in chief Marshal Ferdinand Foch American help to stem the tide. Only the U.S. 2d and 3d Divisions were positioned to provide immediate assistance, however.

On 31 May the 3d Division's 7th Machine Gun Battalion arrived at the Marne to help the French hold the critical town of Château-Thierry, astride the main highway to Paris. The remainder of the division's infantry regiments arrived soon thereafter by rail, relieving the battered French units that had held the position. After days of stiff combat, the 3d Division's spirited defense earned it the nickname "Rock of the Marne." Throughout the month of June the division fought a number of actions around Château-Thierry, continuing to hold the south bank of the Marne.

On 1 June, the 2d Division, with its attached 3d Infantry Brigade and 4th Marine Brigade, began to move into defensive positions west of Château-Thierry. It also held against German attacks, and under French command the division counterattacked in a series of costly assaults through and around Belleau Wood. Belleau Wood was thought to be lightly defended, a mistake for which the Americans paid dearly. During three long weeks of fighting the 4th Marine Brigade fought a confused and bloody battle to seize the entire wood. Controversy continues over the strategic value of the area, but there is no question about the bravery of the marines. On 16 June the 7th Infantry Regiment of the 3d Division relieved the marines and continued the attacks for another week but still failed to displace the Germans. The marines returned to the cauldron on 22 June. Four days later, with additional French artillery support, the marines controlled Belleau Wood.

The battles around Château-Thierry and Belleau Wood not only helped to halt Ludendorff's offensive but initiated counterattacks that led to the general Allied counteroffensive, which would win the war by November 1918. The U.S. defense around Château-Thierry and subsequent counterattack in Belleau Wood signaled the beginning of the first real American influence on western front fighting.

See also CANTIGNY, BATTLE OF; HARBORD, JAMES G.; MARNE, SECOND BATTLE OF THE; VAUX, BATTLE OF; WORLD WAR I, U.S. INVOLVEMENT.

Further reading: Asprey, Robert B. *At Belleau Wood.* New York: Putnams, 1965; Rice, Earl. *The Battle of Belleau Wood.* San Diego: Lucent Books, 1996; Suskind, Richard.

The Battle of Belleau Wood: The Marines Stand Fast. London: Macmillan, 1969.

— Thomas D. Veve

Chattanooga, Battle of (23–25 November 1863)
Civil War Union victory that lifted the Confederate quasi-siege of Chattanooga and set the stage for the 1864 Atlanta campaign

After the Battle of CHICKAMAUGA, the Union army of Major General William S. ROSECRANS retreated into Chattanooga, an important rail and communications center in southeastern Tennessee, giving up outlying high ground on Missionary Ridge and Lookout Mountain. The latter, with adjoining Lookout Valley, commanded the Tennessee River gorge, the only practical Union supply line. Confederate troops under General Braxton BRAGG seized this high ground, forcing Rosecrans to supply his army by a miserable road over Walden's Ridge to the north. Starvation threatened.

Disgusted with Rosecrans, Union authorities sent Major General Ulysses S. GRANT to Chattanooga. Firing Rosecrans and replacing him with Major General George H. THOMAS as commander of the Army of the Cumberland, Grant quickly retook Lookout Valley and opened a viable supply line. Reinforced by Major General Joseph HOOKER and about 10,000 soldiers of the Army of the Potomac, and by Major General William T. SHERMAN with another 20,000 reinforcements from the Army of the Tennessee, Grant opened his attack on 23 November. He sent Thomas to capture Orchard Knob, a small hill between Chattanooga and Missionary Ridge near the center of the Confederate line, to be sure that Bragg's army was not reinforcing the Confederate effort against Union forces at Knoxville, Tennessee. Thomas's men easily brushed aside Confederate skirmishers and took the hill.

The next day, Grant directed Hooker to make a diversionary attack on the Confederate left at Lookout Mountain while Sherman took a position on the far north end of Missionary Ridge, beyond the Confederate right flank. Hooker's assault succeeded beyond expectations; the general got his troops on the flank of the thinly spread Confederate defenders and swept them off the towering and seemingly impregnable mountain. Sherman's operation seemed successful as well, and Grant anticipated that at dawn of 25 November Sherman would roll up the Confederate line along Missionary Ridge from the north while Hooker pressed on to threaten it on the south. Thomas would assault it in front when the time seemed ripe.

Morning brought disappointment. A burned bridge delayed Hooker's flank march, and Sherman discovered that appearances notwithstanding, Missionary Ridge was not continuous but rather a series of humps, each easily

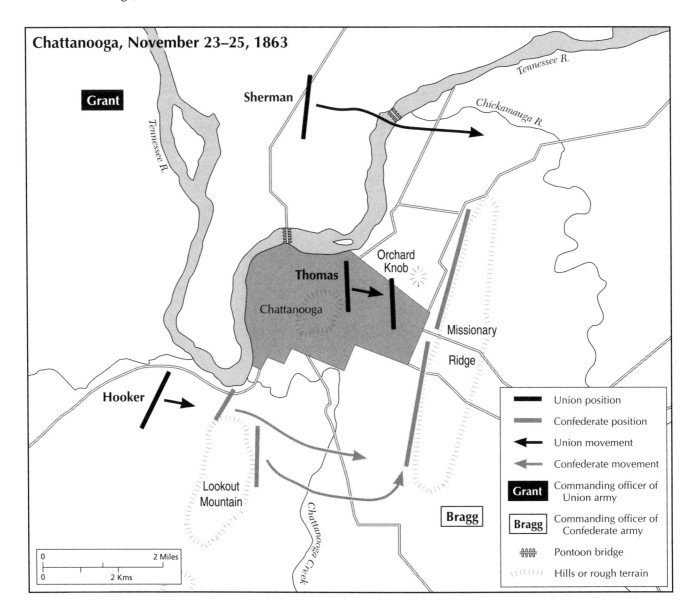

Chattanooga, November 23–25, 1863

defended against flank attack. Skillful Confederate defense combined with difficult terrain to stymie Sherman's attacks.

With daylight waning on a short November afternoon, Grant ordered Thomas to assault the Confederate center, first the line of rifle pits at the base of Missionary Ridge and later, perhaps, the crest itself. In one of the most dramatic spectacles of the war, Thomas arrayed 23,000 men in a massed assault that because of a confusion of orders halted only briefly at the rifle pits before charging up the ridge. Although steep, the ridge's terrain was favorable to attackers. This, coupled with poor Confederate defensive dispositions and the fierce determination of Thomas's troops to avenge their defeat at Chickamauga, produced a spectacular success. Even as Thomas's men stormed through the Confederate center, Hooker, having finally gained the

rebels' left flank, swept up the ridge, taking additional prisoners. As darkness closed the fighting, the Confederate army retreated in disorder. A few days later Bragg was relieved of command at his own request.

Federal casualties had totaled approximately 6,000, while the Confederates had lost more than 6,600, including some 4,000 captured and missing. The victory at Chattanooga completed Grant's meteoric rise; the following spring he was tapped to command all Federal forces.

See also ATLANTA CAMPAIGN; CIVIL WAR, LAND OVERVIEW.

Further reading: Cozzens, Peter. *The Shipwreck of Their Hopes: The Battles for Chattanooga.* Urbana: University of Illinois Press, 1994; McDonough, James Lee. *Chattanooga:*

A Death Grip on the Confederacy. Knoxville: University of Tennessee Press, 1984; Sword, Wiley. *Mountains Touched with Fire: Chattanooga Besieged, 1863.* New York: St. Martin's Press, 1995; Woodworth, Steven E. *Six Armies in Tennessee: The Chickamauga and Chattanooga Campaigns.* Lincoln: University of Nebraska Press, 1998.

— Steven E. Woodworth

Chauncey, Isaac (1772–1840) *U.S. Navy officer*
Born on 20 February 1772 at Fairfield County, Connecticut, Isaac Chauncey went to sea as a teenager and commanded a commercial vessel by age 19. In 1799 he received one of the senior lieutenancies in the reconstituted U.S. Navy. Promoted to post captain in 1806, he became superintendent of the New York Navy Yard, where he supervised construction of several naval vessels. Chauncey established a reputation as a fine naval administrator but had little combat experience when war with Great Britain began in 1812.

Appointed the Great Lakes commodore in the fall of 1812, Chauncey began a frantic effort to gain naval superiority on Lakes Erie and Ontario. Although ordered to emphasize Erie in his operations, Chauncey saw Lake Ontario as more critical and concentrated his forces at SACKETT'S HARBOR, New York, on its northeastern shore. The Lake Ontario campaign focused on a shipbuilding race; the U.S. Navy began with a 16-gun brig and had a 120-gun ship of the line under construction at war's end. Chauncey's administrative skill, combined with the shipbuilding experience of Henry Eckford on Lake Ontario and Noah Brown on Lake Erie, allowed the Americans to match British ship construction on Lake Ontario and surpass it on Lake Erie.

Early in his lake service Chauncey cooperated with the army in the 1813 attacks on YORK (Toronto) and FORT GEORGE, but an abortive 29 May British attack on Sackett's Harbor caused him to concentrate on the defense of that port. His unwillingness to support joint operations enthusiastically reduced U.S. military chances in the St. Lawrence Valley and on the Lake Ontario frontier in late 1813 and 1814.

In early 1813 Chauncey sent Master Commandant Oliver Hazard PERRY to Erie, Pennsylvania, to command on Lake Erie. Perry won the 11 September 1813 Battle of LAKE ERIE; Chauncey received the largest prize-money portion as the commodore. Chauncey never fought a conclusive engagement with the British on Lake Ontario. He caught his British opponent, Sir James Lucas Yeo, in the northwestern corner of the lake on 28 September 1813, but he refrained from delivering a decisive blow, and Yeo escaped. Thereafter the two commodores avoided direct combat when one side or the other was perceived to have a tactical advantage.

Chauncey spend most of his remaining 22 years in the navy as either commander of the New York Navy Yard or a member of the Board of Navy Commissioners in Washington, D.C., where he died on 27 January 1840.

See also WAR OF 1812, NAVAL OVERVIEW.

Further reading: Malcomson, Robert. *Lords of the Lake: The Naval War on Lake Ontario, 1812–1814.* Annapolis, Md.: Naval Institute Press, 1998; McKee, Christopher. *A Gentlemanly and Honorable Profession: The Creation of the U.S. Naval Officer Corps, 1794–1815.* Annapolis, Md.: Naval Institute Press, 1991; Skaggs, David Curtis, and Gerard T. Altoff. *A Signal Victory: The Lake Erie Campaign, 1812–1814.* Annapolis, Md.: Naval Institute Press, 1997.

— David Curtis Skaggs

chemical and biological warfare *Warfare using irritating, poisonous, or asphyxiating gases as chemical weapons or living organisms (or their toxic products) against humans, animals, or plants*
Early forms of chemical weapons were designed to attack enemies with flame or disable them with choking fumes. Thucydides in *The History of the Peloponnesian War* describes the use of fire weapons by the Boetians in 424 B.C. This early use of what would later become widely known as Greek fire was repeated throughout the sixth and seventh centuries by the Syrians. This highly flammable mixture of sulfur, naphtha, and quicklime burst into flame when combined with water. The mixture was used by the Byzantine navy against attacking Arab vessels in A.D. 673 and by Moslems in 1190 against European forces besieging Acre.

During the Middle Ages, combatants found that they could weaken their enemies by exposing them to deadly diseases. They practiced an early form of biological warfare by catapulting disease-ridden carcasses of men or animals into an enemy fortress or campsite. As simple a process as poisoning wells by dropping diseased bodies into them often spread illness or death among enemy soldiers who unwittingly drank the contaminated water. Not only were primitive chemical and biological weapons employed with lethal effect, but so too were various forms of irritating gasses. During the 1618–48 Thirty Years' War, quicklime, sulfur, coke, and other unrefined lachrymators (tearing agents) were used to render enemies less effective in battle.

European practices were later introduced to North America when British forces spread smallpox germs among hostile Indian tribes during PONTIAC'S REBELLION (1763–64) by presenting them with woolen blankets infected with smallpox. The practice of contaminating water supplies was followed during the American Civil War by retreating Confederate forces determined to deny clean drinking water to advancing Union forces.

Chemists continued to discover chemicals with lethal properties. Britain's Sir Humphrey Davy identified the toxin phosgene in 1811. Deadly biological agents such as the anthrax bacillus were discovered in the 1860s. However, the wartime use of chemical concoctions dropped out of favor during much of the Victorian period. When American inventor John Doughty suggested filling artillery shells with chlorine gas and firing them into Confederate forts, the Union War Department rejected his concept. In fact, the War Department published a general order in 1863 banning the use of any poisonous weapons of any sort.

Increasing concerns over the use of toxic gases and other forms of "inhumane" weapons, to include germ-laden articles or carcasses, led Western nations to convene conferences at The Hague in Belgium in 1899 and again in 1907. The conferees enacted prohibitions against the use of artillery shells filled with toxic gas and against various forms of biological or germ warfare. However, no mechanisms actually to regulate these strictures were in place when war broke out in Europe in 1914. World War I would see the extensive employment of poison gas, with the Germans initiating the use of chlorine gas on 22 April 1915. On that date they opened 5,700 cylinders of chlorine against French troops holding a section of the line around Ypres. The French forces suffered more than 15,000 casualties, 5,000 of whom died. Even the Germans were surprised by the impact of the gas attack.

Britain retaliated by attacking German positions with chlorine in September. A number of new lethal gases were developed by the belligerents to include phosgene, a choking agent and mustard gas, a blister agent. All sides rushed to provide their troops with protective masks designed to filter the harmful agents, thereby preventing the most serious types of gas injuries. The combatants developed improved means of delivering toxic gas, primarily by artillery or mortar shells. The British also developed the Livens projector, a metal tube four feet long buried in the ground and angled toward the enemy.

One study of chemical use in the Great War states that all sides used a total of 125,000 tons of toxic chemicals. Estimates of total gas casualties vary, but they numbered more than 1 million. Nearly 100,000 of those died.

Toxic chemicals were used in limited amounts during the period following World War I. In 1937, the Japanese were reported to be using gas against Chinese troops, and the Italians used mustard gas in Ethiopia. Two new and potentially devastating agents became available in the 1930s; both came from German laboratories. The nerve agent sarin was developed by German scientist Helmut Shrader, and Gerhard Schrader discovered a highly lethal organic phosphate compound he called tabun. A gas mask provided little defense against these agents; Odorless, tasteless, and colorless, even a drop of sarin or tabun absorbed through exposed skin could cause death. Advances also were made in aerial bombs and in artillery shell design as well as individual protective equipment and decontamination techniques. As World War II began, many of the combatants were equipped to engage in biochemical warfare.

In part because of a strong aversion to chemical weapons by the leaders of both sides, all combatants refrained from employing biological or chemical agents during World War II. They did, however, use flame weapons, especially air-dropped incendiaries, with great effect. The Germans firebombed English cities in 1940. The Allies retaliated by bombing German cities with incendiaries. Later the United States reduced large areas of Japanese cities to ruins. One series of firebombing raids carried out by American bombers against TOKYO in 1945 caused thousands of deaths and rendered more than 1 million Japanese homeless.

Changes in chemical and biological warfare research and development during the post–World War II years reflected the new bipolar balance of power that emerged. The United States and its noncommunist allies continued to maintain arsenals of weapons and to develop new procedures to deliver them. The Soviet Union made use of the information it had captured from Germany to enhance its weapons posture. It provided support to other communist governments as well as states that depended upon the USSR for weapons. The actions of these client states led to claims of chemical use by Egypt and Laos in the late 1960s and early 1970s. Iraq, with the help of Western governments, also developed a chemical weapons capacity and used both mustard and nerve gases fired by artillery against Iran and Kurdish tribesmen in the late 1980s. In that period the term *weapons of mass destruction*—nuclear, chemical, and biological—came into common usage around the world.

One of the greatest concerns of the forces allied against Iraq during OPERATION DESERT STORM was that the Iraqis would use chemical or biological weapons against coalition forces. That they did not is probably due as much to a lack of sufficient protective equipment for their own troops as to any fear of retaliation. A postwar search for Iraqi biochemical manufacturing sites and intact weapons was carried out by the United Nations Special Commission on Iraq (UNSCOM) for more than seven years before it was withdrawn from Iraq.

The tremendous threat posed by the use of biological weapons was demonstrated by a 1995 incident in which containers of liquefied sarin nerve agent were released by a Japanese extremist sect in the Tokyo subway system.

Twelve people died from the agent, and 5,000 required medical attention. This event caused governments around the world to take ever more seriously the threat posed by mass destruction weapons. The greatest danger appears to be an attack on a major population center.

Steps have been taken to limit the spread of weapons of mass destruction. They include the Biological and Toxic Weapons Convention (BTWC), which required its signatories to ban the development and use of biological warfare agents. The United States and the USSR signed this treaty in 1972. Their action subsequently led more than 140 other countries to sign the BTWC. The Chemical Weapons Convention (CWC) was concluded in 1997. Neither treaty provides complete safety from biochemical threats, however, as rogue states and terrorist groups do not feel constrained by the terms of either convention. As a result, nations worldwide must continue to seek effective protective measures as they live under the threat of a potential disaster.

See also NAPALM; WORLD WAR I, U.S. INVOLVEMENT; WORLD WAR II, U.S. INVOLVEMENT, EUROPE AND PACIFIC.

Further reading: Kleber, Brooks E., and Dale Birdsell. *The Chemical Warfare Service: Chemicals in Combat.* Washington, D.C.: U.S. Government Printing Office, 1990; Levy, Beth, and Brian Solomon, eds. *Chemical and Biological Warfare.* New York: H. W. Wilson, 1999; Norris, John, and William Fowler. *NBC: Nuclear, Biological and Chemical Warfare on the Modern Battlefield.* New York: Brassey's U.S., 1998.

— John W. Mountcastle

Chennault, Claire L. (1893–1958) *U.S. Army Air Forces general and air tactician*

Born on 6 September 1893 at Commerce, Texas, Claire Lee Chennault enlisted in the army in 1917. Because of his age and married status he had difficulty getting into pilot training. He finally graduated in August 1920. A maverick from the start, Chennault became an outspoken advocate of fighter aircraft during the period when the U.S. Army Air Corps was enamored of the bomber. While serving as an instructor at the Air Corps Tactical School in 1935, Chennault wrote *The Role of Defensive Pursuit,* an important but, at the time, controversial book. In 1937 the air corps removed him from flying status because of a serious hearing impairment. Chennault retired shortly thereafter as a captain.

In May 1937 Chennault accepted a position as aviation advisor to the Chinese Nationalist government of Chiang Kai-shek (Jiang Jieshi). When the Sino-Japanese War broke out that September, Chennault was appointed a colonel in the Chinese air force. Putting his theories to the test,

Chennault flew in air combat operations against the Japanese throughout 1938 and 1939.

In late 1940 supporters of China in the American government overcame the strong objections of the State, War, and Navy Departments to allow Chennault to recruit military pilots for service in China. The American Volunteer Group (AVG), popularly known as the Flying Tigers, consisted of roughly 100 American pilots flying semiobsolete P-40B fighters. Personally trained by Chennault on the basis of his theories, the AVG entered combat for the first time on 20 December 1941. During the next six months the AVG claimed 298 Japanese aircraft shot down (a figure subsequently revised downward to 100 kills, still an impressive feat), while losing only 12 planes and four pilots.

In April 1942 Chennault was recalled to active duty in the Army Air Corps as a colonel and quickly promoted to brigadier general. In July the AVG passed out of existence. Some of the pilots and ground crew volunteered to return to active duty in the newly formed China Air Task Force (CATF), a subordinate command of the U.S. Tenth Air Force in India. In March 1943 the CATF became the Fourteenth Air Force, with Chennault in command as a major general.

As "economy of force" organizations in a tertiary theater, the CATF and the Fourteenth Air Force always operated on a shoestring. Applying Chennault's theories, however, both organizations achieved combat effectiveness far out of proportion to their sizes and resources. By the end of the war the Fourteenth Air Force had accounted for about 2,600 Japanese aircraft and tons of supplies destroyed.

Stubborn and irascible, Chennault conducted a long-running and public feud with Lieutenant General Joseph STILWELL, American commander of the CHINA-BURMA-INDIA theater. Chennault was instrumental in Chiang Kai-shek's demand for Stilwell's recall. But Chennault himself was removed from command and retired for a second time a few months before the end of the war.

Following World War II, Chennault remained in China and assisted the Nationalist government in the civil war with the communists. He established there and operated an airline called Civil Air Transport (CAT). Chennault sold his interest in CAT in 1950, but he remained the chairman of its board until 1955. CAT became one of the Central Intelligence Agency's major resources in East Asia. Chennault died at New Orleans, Louisiana, on 27 July 1958. Just days before his death he received promotion to lieutenant general.

See also CHINA-BURMA-INDIA.

Further reading: Byrd, Martha. *Chennault: Giving Wings to the Tiger.* Tuscaloosa: University of Alabama Press, 1987; Chennault, Claire Lee. *Way of a Fighter.* New York: Putnam, 1949; Ford, Daniel. *Flying Tigers: Claire*

Chennault and the American Volunteer Group. Washington, D.C.: Smithsonian Institution Press, 1991; Samson, Jack. *Chennault.* New York: Doubleday, 1987.

— David T. Zabecki

Cherokee War (1759–1761) *War between Native Americans and whites on the South Carolina frontier during the French and Indian War*

In late 1758 a Cherokee war party, returning from unrewarding service in Brigadier General JOHN FORBES's expedition against FORT DUQUESNE, stole a few horses from frontier settlers. In a brief fight both Cherokee and whites suffered casualties. The fighting then intensified, with many deaths on both sides.

In November 1759 South Carolina governor William Henry Lyttelton declared war on the Cherokee nation. Two weeks later a delegation of moderate Cherokee chiefs arrived in Charleston seeking to negotiate with Lyttelton. When the chiefs refused to hand over individuals responsible for settler deaths, Lyttelton took them hostage. He then marched them under guard of 1,700 MILITIA and a few regulars to Fort Prince George, on the Keowee River. At Fort Prince George Lyttelton persuaded several chiefs to sign a treaty. He left 22 of the moderate chiefs in the fort as hostages and returned to Charleston after an outbreak of smallpox ended, claiming the matter concluded.

In February 1760 the fighting revived, and about 50 settlers were killed. On 14 February Cherokee warriors attacked Fort Prince George hoping to free the hostages; however, the garrison massacred them. In June, Colonel Archibald Montgomery marched on the Cherokee with 400 militia, approximately 50 Catwaba warriors, and 1,300 British regulars from the 1st and 77th Regiments of Foot.

Montgomery destroyed all Cherokee villages of the "Lower Towns" in the western South Carolina piedmont and killed more than 100 warriors. Montgomery then attacked the villages of the "Middle Towns" in the southern Appalachian Mountains. On 27 June 1760, at Echoe (near present-day Franklin, North Carolina), Montgomery won a pyrrhic victory, sustaining nearly 100 casualties while inflicting just 50. The next day Montgomery retired to Charleston.

In July the Cherokee attacked Fort Loudoun, built during 1756–57 at the confluence of the Little Tennessee and Tellico Rivers among the western Cherokee "Overhill Towns" to provide protection from the French. Invested and reduced to starvation by the Cherokee, the garrison surrendered on 8 August 1760. The next day the garrison set out under pledge of safe conduct for Fort Prince George, with a Cherokee escort. However, on 10 August, at Ballplay, where Cain Creek joins the Tellico River, a

Cherokee war party of 700 warriors attacked, in violation of the surrender agreement. More than 200 of the column were taken captive and held until the war's end. The garrison commander, Captain Paul Demere, 22 officers and enlisted men, and three women were slain in revenge for the Cherokee hostages killed at Fort Prince George.

In June 1761 a third expedition commanded by Lieutenant Colonel James Grant advanced against the Cherokee. On 10 June Grant, with 1,650 regulars and 600 provincials, fought a battle near the Cherokee town of Estatoe. Grant's troops suffered 12 killed and 52 wounded, while the Cherokees lost 30. Grant then burned all Indian crops and towns in the vicinity. With other tribes and famine threatening, the exhausted Cherokee sued for peace in August 1761.

See also AMERICAN INDIAN WARS, OVERVIEW; FRENCH AND INDIAN WARS.

Further reading: Hamer, Philip M. *Fort Loudon on the Little Tennessee.* Raleigh, N.C.: Edwards & Broughton, 1925; Hatley, Tom. *The Dividing Paths: Cherokees and South Carolinians through the Era of Revolution.* New York: Oxford University Press, 1993; Oliphant, John. *Peace and War on the Anglo-Cherokee Frontier, 1756–63.* Baton Rouge: Louisiana State University Press, 2001.

— A. J. L. Waskey

Chesapeake, First Battle of the (16 March 1781) *American Revolutionary War naval battle*

By the spring of 1781 the British had a significant military presence in the Chesapeake Bay area. Continental army commander General George WASHINGTON wanted to attack New York, which was also a base from which the British watched a French squadron at Newport, Rhode Island.

Washington supported a secondary effort to harass British forces in the Chesapeake Bay, however. This would include landing French troops to assist the marquis de LAFAYETTE in Virginia. Responding to Washington's appeal, on the evening of 8 March, French commodore Sochet des Touches sailed from Newport for the Chesapeake with eight ships of the line and three frigates, carrying 1,120 troops.

British vice admiral Marriott Arbuthnot learned of the French move and sailed in pursuit from Gardiner's Bay, Long Island. Arbuthnot also had eight ships of the line, but four frigates. As a result of recent coppering of the bottoms, the British ships reached Chesapeake Bay first.

The two fleets sighted one another about 40 miles off Cape Henry at about 6 A.M. on 16 March. Poor weather conditions—shifting winds, haze, and rain—led to a series of complex maneuvers in which each side tried to secure the weather gauge (that is, a windward position).

Superior seamanship ultimately gave the British the weather gauge. This meant, however, that the French were able to open their lowest gunports and thereby utilize their heaviest guns, as the British could not. The two lines of battle closed, and by 2:30 P.M. all the ships in the British van and center were engaged. The three leading ships took the heaviest punishment. Disabled by the French practice of firing high to create damage aloft, they were subjected to fire from the entire French line. The British practice of firing into the hull of an opponent produced greater personnel casualties, especially among the French troops aboard ship.

About 3 P.M. des Touches hauled off to the east. In the battle the British had lost 30 killed and 73 wounded; the French suffered 72 killed and 112 wounded.

Des Touches then returned with his squadron to Newport. Although he had displayed considerable tactical skill, he had failed to press his advantage. Had he persisted, the French might have controlled the Chesapeake. As it worked out, this inconclusive naval battle was a British strategic victory because des Touches had failed to land his troops.

See also REVOLUTIONARY WAR, NAVAL OVERVIEW.

Further reading: Dull, Jonathan R. *The French Navy and American Independence: A Study of Arms and Diplomacy, 1774–1787.* Princeton, N.J.: Princeton University Press, 1975; Gardiner, Robert, ed. *Navies and the American Revolution, 1775–1783.* Annapolis, Md.: Naval Institute Press, 1996; Tilley, John A. *The British Navy and the American Revolution.* Columbia: University of South Carolina Press, 1987.

— Cynthia Clark Northrup and Spencer C. Tucker

Chesapeake, Second Battle of the (5 September 1781) *Decisive naval engagement of the American Revolutionary War, also known as the Battle of the Capes*

The Continental Army commander, General George WASHINGTON, had hoped to attack New York in conjunction with units of the French fleet under Admiral François Joseph, comte de Grasse, which would be coming north from the West Indies during hurricane season. Washington then learned that de Grasse would be coming not to New York but to the Chesapeake Bay. He immediately sent the bulk of his forces south to join troops sent to Virginia earlier under

Second Battle of the Chesapeake (Battle of the Virginia Capes), 5 September 1781. Painting by V. Zveg   *(Naval Historical Foundation)*

the marquis de LAFAYETTE to contain British troops commanded by Brigadier General Benedict ARNOLD. Lieutenant General Charles, Earl Cornwallis had by then come up, and the British had established a base at YORKTOWN on the bay.

On 27 August, three days before de Grasse arrived in Chesapeake Bay, Admiral Alexander Hood stood into the bay with 14 ships of the line but, finding no French ships, made for New York, where he joined Admiral Thomas Graves, with five ships of the line. Graves, the senior admiral, took command. On 31 August the British sailed to intercept the French squadron under Admiral Jacques, comte de Barras, who had left Newport, Rhode Island, with eight ships of the line and transports.

De Grasse arrived in the bay on 30 August with 28 ships of the line. He offloaded his troops and sent his transports to help ferry Washington's men down the bay.

On 5 September 1781 a French frigate signaled the approach of the British. De Grasse, shorthanded with many men ashore, nonetheless immediately put to sea. The engagement that afternoon was indecisive, hampered by an inadequate British signaling system and the fact that Hood and Graves were personal rivals. The result was that only the vans actively engaged. The British sustained 336 casualties, the French 221. No ships were lost on either side.

Light winds impeded further engagement over the next several days, during which, however, de Barras slipped into the bay with a precious cargo of siege artillery. His fleet increased the French advantage to 36 ships of the line, to only 19 British. After a council of war, Graves decided to return to New York. The inconclusive engagement in the Chesapeake Bay was nonetheless one of the decisive naval battles in world history, as it cut off the British at Yorktown from the possibility of resupply and brought Cornwallis's surrender on 19 October of 8,000 men, one-quarter of British strength in North America. This defeat brought down the British government and led London to enter into negotiations to end the war.

See also AMERICAN REVOLUTIONARY WAR, LAND OVERVIEW; AMERICAN REVOLUTIONARY WAR, NAVAL OVERVIEW.

Further reading: Larrabee, Harold A. *Decision at the Chesapeake.* London: William Kimber, 1965; Lewis, Charles Lee. *Admiral de Grasse and American Independence.* Annapolis, Md.: U.S. Naval Institute, 1945.
— Cynthia Clark Northrup and Spencer C. Tucker

Chesapeake, USS, v. HMS *Shannon* (1 June 1813)
Frigate battle of the War of 1812, fought off Boston, Massachusetts

The *Shannon* patrolled off Boston, its crew hoping the American frigate would come out. The two ships were almost evenly matched in terms of size and ordnance. The *Chesapeake* was slightly larger than the *Shannon*, but the British ship mounted 52 guns and the American vessel 50. The chief difference was in their crews. Captain James LAWRENCE had just taken command of the frigate *Chesapeake*. First lieutenant Augustus C. Ludlow, and the acting third and fourth lieutenants and many of the crew were also new to the ship. Second Lieutenant George Budd was the only experienced officer with time on the ship.

The *Shannon* was probably the best-trained ship in gunnery in the Royal Navy. Captain Philip Vere Broke, who had been in command of the frigate for seven years, had been cruising American waters for the previous 18 months. He was anxious to avenge previous British ship losses, which had shocked British public opinion and the Royal Navy. Broke had regularly drilled his crew in gunnery and had instituted a number of procedural changes to improve both accuracy and speed of fire.

On 1 June Broke sent a challenge to Lawrence, promising an individual ship action. Lawrence needed no such urging; he had already ordered his ship out to engage the *Shannon*, flying a large banner proclaiming "Free Trade and Sailors' Rights." Lawrence was confident of victory, but his decision to fight with a new crew proved a foolish one.

The two ships joined at about 5:50 P.M. The sea was calm. Lawrence missed an opportunity to rake the British ship, either out of chivalry or overeagerness, and decided on a simple artillery duel at close quarters. Superior British shiphandling and gunnery decided the outcome. Devastating fire, especially from the *Shannon*'s carronades, cut the *Chesapeake*'s stays, causing it to drift helplessly toward its adversary. The *Shannon* was then able to rake the *Chesapeake* from stem to stern with both cannon and musket fire from the rigging and tops. Lawrence ordered a boarding party to form, but he and Ludlow were then mortally wounded. "Tell the men to fire faster and not give up the ship," Lawrence ordered. But Broke and about 50 British boarders leaped over to the American frigate. British losses were heavy, but the boarding party managed to overpower the *Chesapeake*'s crew. The battle had lasted only 15 minutes.

American losses were 62 dead and 58 wounded; the British lost 33 killed and 42 wounded. Lawrence subsequently died of his wounds; Broke was so severely injured that he never again saw active service. It was the bloodiest frigate engagement of the War of 1812. The *Chesapeake* was taken into the Royal Navy.

See also WAR OF 1812; NAVAL OVERVIEW.

Further reading: Padfield, Peter. *Broke and the* Shannon. London: Hodder & Stoughton, 1968; Pullen, Hugh F.

Engagement between USS *Chesapeake* and HMS *Shannon,* 1 June 1813   *(Naval Historical Foundation)*

Broke and the Shannon. Toronto: McClelland and Stewart, 1970; Tucker, Spencer C., and Frank Reuter. *Injured Honor: The* Chesapeake-Leopard *Affair of June 22, 1807.* Annapolis, Md.: Naval Institute Press, 1996.

— Uzal W. Ent

Chesapeake Bay campaign (February 1813–
September 1814) *British campaign to control Chesapeake Bay during the War of 1812*

The British navy, supported by various army units, entered the bay in February 1813. The operation was not so much a blockade as an occupation of the land and water areas. It succeeded in severely curtailing the activities of American privateers from the port of BALTIMORE, which British rear admiral Sir George Cockburn had described as "a nest of pirates." The privateers had disrupted British shipping throughout the Atlantic. American defenses were weak in the area, and the British were able to move about with little hindrance from U.S. naval or land forces. This campaign included the capture and burning of WASHINGTON, D.C., and the final British repulse from Baltimore.

Admiral Sir John Warren received orders in February 1813 to create a "flying army and squadron" to raid American ports and destroy naval stores, dockyards, ships, fortifications, and government facilities. London hoped that raids along the Chesapeake would divert critical forces from the Canadian frontier. The British committed to the effort some 80 warships supported by Royal Marines and British soldiers.

His second in command, Rear Admiral Cockburn, stepped up the first season's campaign by increasing the number and depth of his raids against the American coast. Only in the Battle of Craney Island, near Norfolk, were the Americans able to claim a small victory. British forces in ship's boats grounded on the ebbing tide and became easy targets for the Americans. The British retaliated by attacking and burning the town of Hampton. Small British raids continued throughout the winter of 1813–14.

In April 1814 Vice Admiral Sir Alexander Cochrane replaced Warren. Cochrane was accompanied by Royal Marines and elements of the British army under Major General Robert Ross. Again, the British strategy was to conduct a series of short, powerful incursions to devastate points on the American coast while diverting American troops from the Canadian theater of operations. The British believed that capturing Washington would put the U.S. government into turmoil and destroy American morale.

The first line of defense for the Americans was a small flotilla of gunboats commanded by Commodore Joshua BARNEY. Barney had submitted a plan to the War Department to construct small gunboats to strike quickly at the British warships and then retreat into the creeks that lined the bay. This new Chesapeake Flotilla conducted a series of raids against the British fleet, but it eventually was blockaded in the Patuxent River by British warships as the invasion force moved inland. Barney abandoned and burned his vessels and returned to Washington to assist in its defense.

Ross landed his men near Benedict, Maryland, on 19 August 1814. These troops were to march across the peninsula to Washington while a British naval force moved up the Potomac toward the same location. The naval force drove the small American garrison from Fort Warburton and quickly received the surrender of Alexandria, Virginia. On 24 August Ross's troops met hastily assembled U.S. forces under Brigadier General William Winder at BLADENSBURG, Maryland. Except for a staunch defense by Commodore Barney and his small contingent of U.S. Marines and flotillamen, the battle was a disaster for the Americans, whose quick retreat came to be known as the Bladensburg Races. The British then took Washington and destroyed numerous government buildings.

Flushed with success, the British force reembarked on their vessels and proceeded to their next target, the city of Baltimore. Ross landed his troops on North Point about 14 miles from Baltimore on 11 September to drive toward the city while the British fleet sailed into the Patapsco River to attack Baltimore from the water. The Maryland militia, which had performed so poorly in the Battle of Bladensburg, gave ground grudgingly at the Battle of North Point on 12 September. Ross was killed during this action. The British land advance was stopped by the defenses of Baltimore on 13 and 14 September. The Royal Navy's attempt to take the city was thwarted by the American coastal defenses centered on FORT MCHENRY; the attack was immortalized by Francis Scott Key's "The Star-Spangled Banner." The British then withdrew and reembarked, abandoning the Chesapeake to the Americans.

See also WAR OF 1812, NAVAL OVERVIEW.

Further reading: Elting, John R. *Amateurs to Arms: A Military History of the War of 1812.* New York: Da Capo, 1995; Pitch, Anthony S. *The Burning of Washington: The British Invasion of 1814.* Annapolis, Md.: Naval Institute Press, 1998.

— Michael J. Manning

***Chesapeake-Leopard* affair** (22 June 1807) *Naval incident in which the British ship* Leopard *halted and then fired into the U.S. Navy frigate* Chesapeake, *nearly leading to a U.S. declaration of war against Great Britain*

Royal Navy ships had operated in and around the Chesapeake Bay and off the Virginia shore patrolling for French warships that had entered the bay. The British ships frequently stopped in Hampton Roads for repairs and supplies, and a number of British sailors deserted, fleeing both brutal discipline and poor pay. Some of them joined U.S. Navy ships, including the new frigate *Chesapeake* (38 guns).

News of these events reached British naval commander in North America, Vice Admiral Sir George Berkeley at Halifax. He ordered British warships, including the *Leopard* (50), commanded by Captain Salisbury P. Humphreys, to stop the *Chesapeake* and search it for the deserters.

On 22 June the *Chesapeake* sailed from Hampton Roads bound for the Mediterranean under Commodore James BARRON. At midday it spotted the *Leopard* approaching with gunports open. The British ship stopped the American frigate; Humphreys, saying he had a dispatch for the American commander, sent a lieutenant on board the *Chesapeake.* The "dispatch" turned out to be Berkeley's demand to search for deserters. Barron refused this, denying the presence of any British deserters among his crew.

Barron had not expected any trouble and had not prepared his ship for combat. He tried to buy time so that his men could ready the ship's guns. Humphreys refused to allow Barron that opportunity and recalled his emissary. He then opened fire. The *Leopard* unleashed probably three broadsides at close range into the American ship, badly damaging it, before the *Chesapeake* was able to get off a single shot. Barron then struck his flag and surrendered.

The Americans had suffered three dead. Barron was among 18 wounded, one of whom died later of his wounds. There were no British casualties. Humphreys refused to accept Barron's surrender but sent men on board the *Chesapeake* to search for deserters. They mustered the crew, took off four of the men, and sailed away. One of those taken was subsequently tried and executed; another died in captivity. The *Chesapeake* then limped back to Norfolk.

The *Chesapeake-Leopard* affair created a crisis in U.S.-British relations. President Thomas JEFFERSON refused to yield to the clamor for war, however. Had he done so, there would have been a more united effort and probably a more satisfactory result than in the subsequent War of 1812. Barron was court-martialed and never held another command at sea. Ultimately the British admitted their mistake and returned the two surviving crewmen, who rejoined the *Chesapeake.*

See also WAR OF 1812, CAUSES; *PRESIDENT–LITTLE BELT ENCOUNTER.*

Further reading: Perkins, Bradford. *The Causes of the War of 1812: National Honor or National Interest?* New York: Holt, Rinehart and Winston, 1965; Tucker, Spencer C., and Frank T. Reuter. *Injured Honor: The* Chesapeake-Leopard *Affair, June 22, 1807.* Annapolis, Md.: Naval Institute Press, 1996.

— Richard H. Donohue, Jr.

Chickamauga Creek, Battle of (19–20 September 1863) *A costly and indecisive Civil War Confederate victory*

In midsummer 1863 Major General William S. ROSECRANS's Union Army of the Cumberland maneuvered General Braxton BRAGG's Confederate Army of Tennessee back to Chattanooga, Tennessee. Rosecrans then paused six weeks to secure his supply lines and plan his next advance. During this period Confederate authorities decided to send Bragg heavy reinforcements.

On 16 August Rosecrans launched his new offensive. Brilliantly concealing the true direction of his thrust, Rosecrans turned Bragg's left flank and crossed the Tennessee River and two formidable mountain ranges before the Confederate general could react. His communications threatened, Bragg had to fall back to La Fayette, Georgia, 28 miles south of Chattanooga.

Misinterpreting Bragg's movement as headlong retreat, Rosecrans pursued with his three corps widely spread out in order to take maximum advantage of the few gaps in Lookout Mountain, the last natural barrier between the Federals and Bragg's supply lines. Bragg, however, who had begun to receive his reinforcements, turned to pounce on Rosecrans's isolated columns. Three times in four days Bragg had opportunities to destroy portions of the Army of the Cumberland. Each time the Federals escaped because Bragg's subordinate generals refused to obey his orders. Dissension among generals had made the Army of Tennessee all but unusable.

Realizing his danger, Rosecrans hastily reunited his three corps on the west side of Chickamauga Creek, facing Bragg's army, which stood east of that stream. Bragg's last chance for decisive victory lay in turning Rosecrans's left and interposing his army between Rosecrans and Chattanooga. By the evening of 17 September Bragg's army was north of Rosecrans's left flank at Lee and Gordon's Mill. Bragg directed his troops to turn west, cross Chickamauga Creek, and seize the vital Chattanooga–La Fayette Road, cutting off Rosecrans's retreat. The creek crossings, however, were guarded by stubborn Union horse soldiers, who delayed the Confederates throughout most of 18 September.

That evening, as major elements of Bragg's army finally poured across the creek, Rosecrans, uncertain of the exact situation but believing that his left might be threatened, ordered Major General George H. THOMAS to march his corps through the night to the home of a farmer named Kelly, six miles farther north on the Chattanooga–La Fayette Road. Although in the darkness neither side knew it, Thomas was marching directly across Bragg's front.

At dawn, 19 September, Bragg, now possessing a numerical advantage of about 68,000 to Rosecrans's 62,000, prepared to launch an assault southwestward toward what he believed to be the Union left flank at Lee and Gordon's Mill. He was surprised when Confederate cavalry, screening his own right flank, collided with Thomas's infantry, igniting a rapidly growing fight.

Except for scattered fields of a few acres, the battlefield was open woodlands, with visibility of 100–200 yards. The location of enemy units was generally unknown to officers on both sides until the moment that close-range combat was joined. Throughout the day Bragg and Rosecrans fed troops into action as combat spread southward, roughly along the line of the Chattanooga–La Fayette Road. Each side experienced considerable confusion, and the advantage swung back and forth repeatedly.

At nightfall, Rosecrans still held the road and also retained access to Chattanooga via the inferior Dry Valley Road, farther west. Bragg, receiving overnight additional reinforcements, including Lieutenant General James LONGSTREET's corps from the Army of Northern Virginia, ordered a dawn (20 September) assault on the Union left, to be followed up along the whole line. Again, command dissension paralyzed the Army of Tennessee, delaying the assault until about 9:30 A.M., by which time the Union left had been entrenched and heavily reinforced.

The Federals slaughtered Bragg's initial assaults, but Rosecrans, suffering nervous exhaustion and sleep deprivation, sent to a division commander on his right center a garbled order that had the unintended effect of directing that officer to pull his command out of line. Just as the division commander obeyed, Longstreet launched his half of the Confederate assault, unwittingly exploiting the sudden Union vulnerability. Rosecrans's center and right collapsed and fled in disorder to Chattanooga on the Dry Valley Road. The Union left, along with remnants of the shattered center, rallied under Thomas's command and held off Confederate attacks until nightfall when, on orders from Rosecrans, it fell back toward Chattanooga.

Although the escape of the Union army to Chattanooga removed any possibility of decisive Confederate victory, Rosecrans nonetheless was a beaten man emotionally. He withdrew his army into Chattanooga, giving up important outlying positions and allowing Bragg to establish a quasi-siege of the city, lifted only with the Battle of CHATTANOOGA, 23–25 November, by which time Rosecrans had been relieved of command.

See also CIVIL WAR, LAND OVERVIEW.

Further reading: Cozzens, Peter. *This Terrible Sound: The Battle of Chickamauga.* Urbana: University of Illinois Press, 1992; Tucker, Glen. *Chickamauga: Bloody Battle in the West.* Indianapolis, Ind.: Bobbs-Merrill, 1961; Woodworth, Steven E. *Six Armies in Tennessee: The Chickamauga and Chattanooga Campaigns.* Lincoln: University of Nebraska Press, 1998.

— Steven E. Woodworth

China, U.S. military assistance to   (1937–1949)

The Nationalist (Guomindang, or Kuomintang) government of Generalissimo Chiang Kai-shek (Jiang Jieshi) came to power in 1928 and immediately began to build a professional military with Japanese, German, Italian, and Soviet assistance. In the early 1930s Chiang attempted to use military, economic, and diplomatic means to resist Japanese aggression and occupation of Chinese territory, but he suffered a series of defeats and setbacks. On 8 July 1937 Japanese and Chinese forces clashed at the Marco Polo Bridge on the outskirts of Beijing (Peking)—an event that marked the start of the Second Sino-Japanese War and, some argue, World War II.

In 1937 the Chiang government hired Claire CHEN-NAULT, a retired U.S. Army Air Corps captain, to advise the Chinese air force. Over the next few years Chennault worked to secure U.S. loans and build an air arm for the increasingly beseiged Chinese military. By 1939 Nationalist forces had retreated to the Chinese interior, and the Republic of China capital had moved to Chungking (Chongqing). With the signing of the Soviet-Japanese nonaggression pact in April 1939 and beginning of war in

The Curtiss P-40N Warhawk. The P-40 saw extensive service in World War II with the U.S. and Allied air forces in the Pacific. The N model was the last and most produced of the P-40 line. B models were flown by Claire Chennault's Flying Tigers.   *(San Diego Aerospace Museum)*

Europe in September, the Chinese turned increasingly to the U.S. government for loans and military assistance.

In December 1940 President Franklin Roosevelt approved military aid to China. Although Lend-Lease, passed by Congress in March 1941, was aimed primarily at assistance to Great Britain, Chinese requests for military aid were considered under this legislation. A fact-finding mission headed by presidential assistant Dr. Lauchlin Currie was sent to China to assess military needs. In March 1941 the Chinese requested 1,000 aircraft, equipment for 30 divisions, and assistance in keeping lines of communications with the Allies open. It was impossible to fulfill China's requests while still meeting British and U.S. military needs, but in mid-1941 the American Volunteer Group (AVG, the "Flying Tigers") began to receive P-40 aircraft, pilots, and support personnel. The Flying Tigers were organized in three squadrons and were trained with British assistance in Burma.

In July 1941 U.S. Army Chief of Staff General George C. MARSHALL approved the American Military Mission to China (AMMISCA). This team of officers, headed by Brigadier General John Magruder, arrived in China in September and October with a mandate to assist in training, procurement, transportation, and maintenance.

The 7 December 1941 Japanese attack on Pearl Harbor began a new phase of the military relationship between the United States and China. In March 1942, Lieutenant General Joseph W. STILWELL, selected by Marshall to head the U.S. military effort in China, arrived there after assessing the situation in Burma and India. Until replaced by General Albert C. WEDEMEYER in 1944, Stilwell devoted his energies to building and training a competent Chinese military and to clearing Japanese forces from key supply routes through Burma. In addition, with Chennault, now a major general and commander of the U.S. Fourteenth Air Force, Stilwell sought to build and maintain airfields to support air attacks against the Japanese home islands.

Until October 1944 the Japanese occupation of Burma and the difficulty of flying supplies "over the hump" severely curtailed the delivery of military supplies and equipment to China. By mid-1945, however, U.S. plans called for a force of 120 well-armed and equipped Chinese divisions, 80 of which were to have American liaison teams attached.

Toward the end of the war, U.S. policy was unclear with respect to the extent of American involvement in and military assistance for the looming Chinese civil war that would pit Chiang and the Nationalists against Mao Zedong (Mao Tse-tung) and the Communists. Although a U.S. State Department–supported military element, the "Dixie Mission," remained with Mao at Yenan, Washington clearly leaned toward the Kuomintang. Negotiations for a peaceful resolution, conducted from late 1944 through 1945, failed. President Roosevelt's special representative, Major General (later ambassador) Patrick J. Hurley, made it clear that U.S. military support would go to Chiang and the Nationalists when the war with Japan ended.

By August Chiang had negotiated a friendship pact with the Soviet Union, and U.S. support was virtually assured, despite the U.S.-brokered talks between the Chinese factions. After the Japanese surrender, both the Communists and the Nationalists hurried to move into Japanese-occupied areas. The Nationalists ordered the Japanese to resist any takeover by Communist forces. In addition, Washington began a major effort to support Chiang's military.

The U.S. Navy and Air Force transported more than 500,000 Nationalist troops into northeastern China and onto the island of Taiwan. In addition, more than 50,000 U.S. Marines occupied key eastern ports and cities, including Peking and Tientsin (Tianjin), until these could be turned over to the Nationalists. Massive amounts of U.S. military equipment, sufficient to equip nearly 40 additional divisions, and supplies continued to flow to the Nationalists as their forces battled the communists in north central and northeastern China.

In December 1945 President Harry S. TRUMAN sent General Marshall to China to secure a cease-fire and start peace talks. In mid-1946 Washington endeavored to implement an embargo against the Kuomintang as a bargaining chip; however, this was short lived, and even greater amounts of military armaments, trainers and advisers, civilian equipment, and humanitarian aid now flowed to the Nationalists. Meanwhile, battles for control of key areas of China continued until the end of the Marshall mission in January 1947.

Washington continued to attempt to mediate a peaceful settlement in China during the next two years, but Mao understood that the United States wanted Chiang to win. By early 1948, despite massive U.S. aid, the tide of the civil war had clearly turned against the Nationalists, and by the summer of 1949 Chiang had fled to Taiwan. That October the Communists established the People's Republic of China. The United States then suffered the consequences of having backed the losing side in the civil war.

See also CHINA-BURMA-INDIA THEATER; KOREAN WAR, U.S. INVOLVEMENT; WORLD WAR II, U.S. INVOLVEMENT, PACIFIC.

Further reading: Fairbank, John K., and Albert Feuerwerker, eds. *The Cambridge History of China.* Vol. 13, *Republican China, 1912–1949, Part 2.* Cambridge, U.K.: Cambridge University Press, 1986; Ford, Daniel. *Flying Tigers: Claire Chennault and the American Volunteer Group.* Washington, D.C.: Smithsonian Institute Press, 1991; Romanus, Charles F., and Riley Sunderland. *Stilwell's Command Problems.* Washington, D.C.: Center of Military History, 1985; ———. *Stilwell's Mission to China.* Washington, D.C.: Center of Military History, 1987;

———. *Time Runs Out in CBI.* Washington, D.C.: Center of Military History, 1990; Tuchman, Barbara W. *Stilwell and the American Experience in China, 1911–45.* New York: Macmillan, 1970.

— J. G. D. Babb

China-Burma-India theater (CBI) (1942–1945)

Important theater of action in World War II

In late December 1941 President Franklin D. ROOSEVELT and British prime minister Winston Churchill met at Washington, D.C., to discuss creation of an Allied theater of operations in India, Southeast Asia, and China and command relationships for it. During the next several months a vast, distinct operational area, known as the China-Burma-India (CBI) theater, stretching from Ceylon (Sri Lanka) to China, was interposed between the American-led commands in the Central and South Pacific and British-led command in the Middle East. The headquarters of the emerging CBI was split between the British in New Delhi and the Chinese and Americans in Chungking (Chongqing).

In February 1942, Lieutenant General Joseph STILWELL arrived in Chungking to consolidate the U.S. effort to advise, support, and supply the Chinese military so as to keep China in the war and to prepare bases in China for future operations against the Japanese. Critical to this mission was a united Allied effort to maintain lines of communication through India and Burma to China. Stilwell was appointed chief of staff to the supreme commander of the China theater, Generalissimo Chiang Kai-shek (Jiang Jieshi). In addition, Stilwell commanded U.S. Army troops in the theater.

Initially, Stilwell's senior commander in Burma and India was Field Marshal Sir Archibald Wavell. The acerbic "Vinegar Joe" Stilwell was forced to play the role of military and diplomatic middleman between Chiang and the several British commanders in India and Burma. In January 1942 the Japanese launched an offensive from Siam (Thailand) into Burma, seeking to capture Rangoon (Yangon) and cut the vital line of communication to China. British and Chinese forces deployed to resist them suffered from lack of unity of command, leading Chiang grudgingly to grant Stilwell greatly restricted operational command of Chinese forces in Burma. General Sir Harold Alexander commanded British forces in Burma, but Lieutenant General William Slim commanded the tactical ground forces engaging the Japanese.

By April 1942 the Japanese had captured Rangoon and were pushing north to drive British forces into India and defeat and expel the Chinese forces under Stilwell. Allied forces withdrew north, unable to halt the Japanese advance or to maintain a land supply route from India to China

across northern Burma. The Japanese kept up the advance, routing Allied forces and consolidating their control of Burma. Although overstretched, they were positioned for further operations into China and India.

Allied plans to rebuild their forces and retake Burma commenced immediately. Supplies to China now had to fly the long and dangerous route "over the hump" (the Himalayas). Air operations against the Japanese directed by Major General Claire CHENNAULT, former commander of the American Volunteer Group (the "Flying Tigers"), now nominally subordinate to Stilwell, took center stage, and air operations now received priority for scarce American supplies. Stilwell's mission to train Chinese ground forces in India and China became a secondary effort. The British, meanwhile, focused their attention in the Middle East and on minor operations against southern and central Burma. Shortages of critical war material, continued problems of unity of command, difficult terrain and climate, and touchy relations among the Allies restricted opportunities for decisive action against the Japanese.

In early 1943 British forces engaged the Japanese in the Arakan district of southern Burma. Brigadier General Orde Wingate, supported by U.S. air and logistics, began long-range brigade and battalion-sized insertions of special troops (known as Chindits) into central Burma to harass the Japanese and cut key lines of communications. U.S. units continued to prepare Chinese forces in India and China; they also began to build the Ledo Road, an attempt to reestablish a ground supply link from India to China. The establishment of a new headquarters, Southeast Asia Command under Admiral Lord (Louis) Mountbatten, with Stilwell as his deputy, further confused and complicated British, American, and Chinese command and support relationships in the region.

In late 1943 and early 1944 the British, Chinese, and, finally, a U.S. ground combat formation known as MERRILL'S MARAUDERS (the 5307th Composite Unit–Provisional) began the effort to retake Burma with a coordinated action against the Japanese in the north. By August 1944 the Allies, although nearly exhausted, had taken the key rail junction at Myitkyina. Slim's Fourteenth Army defeated Japanese attacks at Kohima and Imphal in India and began a British counteroffensive into central and southern Burma. However, the situation in China had deteriorated as the Japanese, stung by Chennault's air operations and their defeats in Burma, attacked to neutralize air bases in China. In addition, Operation Ichigo, designed to connect Japanese forces in China with those in Southeast Asia, was launched.

Stilwell, Chennault, and Chiang disagreed throughout the fall over how to respond to the Japanese offensive. In October, at Chiang's insistence, President Roosevelt relieved Stilwell, and shortly thereafter the CBI was split into two separate commands. Three generals took over Stilwell's responsibilities. Lieutenant General Albert WEDE-MEYER became chief of staff in China and commander of U.S. forces there; Lieutenant General Daniel SULTAN commanded U.S. forces in India and Burma; and Lieutenant General Raymond Wheeler became deputy commanding general of the Southeast Asia Command (SEAC).

In late 1944 the Japanese offensive ground to a halt short of Chungking and Kunming, and Allied forces, including the new U.S. "Mars Force," which had replaced Merrill's Marauders, retook the Burma Road closed by the Japanese in October 1942. In early 1945 American engineers completed the Ledo Road, and convoys began to roll into Kunming. By March General Slim, the brilliant Fourteenth Army commander, had crossed the Irawaddy River and retaken Mandalay, and by early May Rangoon was in British hands. The Japanese were on the defensive throughout CBI. A major offensive against the Japanese was being planned for July and August as the war in the Pacific ended.

See also CHINA, U.S. MILITARY ASSISTANCE TO; WORLD WAR II, U.S. INVOLVEMENT, PACIFIC.

Further reading: Romanus, Charles F., and Riley Sunderland. *Stilwell's Command Problems.* Washington, D.C.: Center of Military History, 1985; ———. *Stilwell's Mission to China.* Washington, D.C.: Center of Military History, 1987; ———. *Time Runs Out in CBI.* Washington, D.C.: Center of Military History, 1990; Slim, William J. *Defeat into Victory.* New York: D. McKay, 1961; Tuchman, Barbara W. *Stilwell and the American Experience in China: 1911–45.* New York: Macmillan, 1970.

— J. G. D. Babb

Chinese first phase offensive (15 October–
6 November 1950) *Initial Chinese military intervention in the Korean War*

Beginning on 15 October 1950, Chinese intervention marked a turning point in the KOREAN WAR and prevented the United Nations (UN) Command from defeating the Korean People's Army and Democratic Peoples' Republic of Korea (North Korea).

Through 26 October fierce fighting had occurred between Republic of Korea (ROK, or South Korea) army units and the Chinese People's Volunteer Army. The UN commander, General Douglas MACARTHUR, and his intelligence officers believed that China would avoid overt intervention. They were shocked to learn that UN troops were being engaged by well-trained Chinese forces.

Reacting to Chinese military attacks on ROK forces, Lieutenant General Walton H. WALKER ordered units of the 1st Cavalry Division to attack Chinese divisions at

Unsan. The ROK 6th Division had been to the northeast, while the ROK 1st Division was still holding its position around Unsan. On 1 November the U.S. 8th Cavalry Regiment replaced two regiments of the 1st ROK Division in the line. Hardly had units of the 8th Cavalry taken up defensive positions around Unsan when they were assaulted by two full Chinese divisions. Waves of Chinese infantry attacked, supported by heavy mortar fire. By midmorning on 2 November, little was left of the 8th Cavalry Regiment, the survivors of which retreated on foot in small groups to units of the U.S. 5th Cavalry sent to rescue them.

Other Allied units were quickly rushed to the Chongchon River to secure a bridgehead there with the 1st Cavalry Division. The three regiments of the U.S. 24th Division struggled to hold the bridgehead from Sinanju northeast to Kunu-ri. The 19th Infantry Regiment was almost overrun; the 21st Infantry went to its rescue on the north side of the Chongchon. Some members of the 19th were forced to swim to safety across the Chongchon. By 6 November these American units and remnants of ROK units were desperately holding the line of the Chongchon River. During this period columns of retreating ROK troops passed through UN lines.

UN units held on desperately along the Chongchon line, expected renewed attacks by the Chinese. Suddenly the Chinese disappeared. This pause—probably to reequip, resupply, and replenish losses from heavy UN artillery and air attacks—gave the U.S. Eighth Army a respite and convinced MacArthur that the Chinese were merely covering the North Korean withdrawal and that the UN offensive could soon resume.

See also CHANGJIN/CHOSIN RESERVOIR, BATTLE AND RETREAT FROM.

Further reading: Appleman, Roy. *Disaster in Korea: The Chinese Confront MacArthur.* College Station: Texas A&M University Press, 1989; ———. *South to the Naktong, North to the Yalu.* Washington, D.C.: Office of the Chief of Military History, 1961; Blair, Clay. *The Forgotten War: America in Korea 1950–1953.* New York: Times Books, 1987; Li, Xiaobing, Allan R. Millett, and Bin Yu. *Mao's Generals Remember Korea.* Lawrence: University Press of Kansas, 2001; Roe, Patrick C. *The Dragon Strikes: China and the Korean War, June–December 1950.* Novato, Calif.: Presidio, 2000.

— D. Randall Beirne

Chippewa, Battle of (5 July 1814) *Key land battle of the WAR OF 1812*

Despite Commodore Oliver Hazard PERRY's spectacular victory in the Battle of LAKE ERIE, the U.S. Army had accomplished little by the third year of the War of 1812.

The British had easily turned back several American attempts to invade Canada. In early 1814 Major General Jacob BROWN took command of the Niagara frontier and began a rigorous training program for his troops. Although the War Department listed them as regulars, the bulk of his men were, in reality, raw recruits.

On 3 July 1814 Brown led his force of 3,500 men in three brigades across the border into Canada and took FORT ERIE. As Brown advanced north, the British commander, Major General Phineas Riall, moved to block the American invasion. On the night of 4 July the Americans were camped at Street's Creek, almost a mile and a half from the British positions.

The next morning, with the Niagara River on their right and thick woods on their left, the Americans advanced toward Chippewa Creek. Brown ordered Brigadier General Peter Porter's brigade of Pennsylvania militia to clear the woods and cover his left. However, Porter's men broke and ran upon encountering a small force of British regulars. Upset but certainly not surprised, Brown ordered Brigadier General Winfield SCOTT forward, with Brigadier General Eleazar W. Ripley's brigade covering his left. Effective fire from U.S. artillery commanded by Major Nathan Towson, silenced British guns as Scott's brigade began to advance.

Riall, underestimating the Americans (Scott's men were wearing the gray uniforms of the New York militia, because of a shortage of regular army uniforms), ordered a hasty advance. As Scott led his men forward, he noticed gaps in the British lines between regiments. Scott made certain his own line was intact, moving up and down it to encourage his men.

When his force had advanced to about 80 yards from the British, Scott ordered a bayonet charge, personally leading the 11th Infantry Regiment into one of the gaps in the British line. At the same time, Major Thomas S. JESSUP's 25th Regiment struck Riall's right, while Major Henry LEAVENWORTH's 9th Regiment drove back Riall's left. The British line broke and fell back across the Chippewa River in confusion. Scott did not pursue. By the end of the day, both sides had returned to their original positions.

British losses in the battle had been 148 killed and 321 wounded, while the Americans had lost 60 killed and 235 wounded. The difference in the casualties was probably due to the U.S. practice of double-loading their weapons.

While the victory was not decisive, it was the first time in this war that a U.S. force had bested an equal force of British regulars in an open-field engagement. The cadets of the U.S. Military Academy at West Point were so impressed by Brown's victory in the battle that they adopted the grey uniforms worn by the Americans.

See also WAR OF 1812, LAND OVERVIEW.

Further reading: Barbuto, Richard V. *Niagara, 1814: America Invades Canada.* Lawrence: University Press of Kansas, 2000; Graves, Donald E. *Red Coats & Grey Jackets: The Battle of Chippewa, 5 July 1814.* Niagara Falls, N.Y.: Dundurn Press, 1974. Mahon, John K. *The War of 1812.* Gainesville: University of Florida Press, 1972; Morris, John D. *Sword of the Border: Major General Jacob Jennings Brown, 1775–1828.* Kent, Ohio: Kent State University Press, 2000.

— J. W. Thacker

Chongchon River, Battles of the (26–30 November 1950) *Key battles of the Korean War*

As the Chinese resumed their offensive in Korea by attacking along most of the front of the United Nations Command (UNC) Eighth Army on the night of 25–26 November, the Republic of Korea army (ROKA) II Corps and the U.S. IX Corps bore the brunt of the attack. The two American divisions of IX Corps, the 25th on the left and 2d on the right, had been progressing slowly toward the Yalu River when they first came in contact with the Chinese. They ran head-on into masses of attacking Chinese troops, who struck between their regiments.

Confusion set in as units became separated by the high mountains. The Chinese managed to infiltrate gaps between attacking units, get behind them, and set up roadblocks. In spite of this confusion and fearing a trap, men of the 25th Division were able to fall back to the Chongchon bridges at Anju. The heaviest blows by the Chinese People's Volunteer Army (CPVA) on American units in Eighth Army fell on the 2d Infantry Division. It caught the full brunt of three Chinese armies. Six Chinese divisions attacked the 2d Division directly, while six others poured through the ROKA II Corps and made a wide envelopment around the U.S. IX Corps. This resulted in one of the worst disasters incurred by any division-sized American unit in the war.

On 5 November the 2d Division was northeast of Kujang-dong, with the 9th Infantry Regiment on the left, the 38th Infantry on the right, and the 23d Infantry in reserve near Kunu-ri. The 9th Infantry was hit the hardest, on both flanks and in the rear. Two howitzer battalions, the 61st and 503d, were on the banks of the Chongchon River to give close support to the infantry. About 8 P.M., in bitter cold, some 1,000 Chinese soldiers, forded the river and swarmed over the American positions.

When the ROKA II Corps collapsed on the right flank of Eighth Army and allowed six Chinese divisions to make a wide envelopment, the 2d Division's escape route to Tockchon was blocked. Its only remaining route of withdrawal was along the Chongchon River to Kunu-ri and a key road junction, then south along the river to Anju. A secondary road, however, ran from Kunu-ri through a gap in the mountains to Sunchon.

The 2d Division's commander, Major General Lawrence Keiser, faced a major decision. The Chinese were reported to be blocking part of the mountain road to Sunchon, but the river route to Anju was longer and already congested with units of the fleeing 25th Division. He decided to move the 2d Division over the mountain road to Sunchon.

The division moved down the mountain road on 30 November, the infantry dispersed throughout the column between artillery, headquarters, and engineer units. Its lead elements had gone only about a mile when they ran into heavy fire from an entire Chinese division entrenched along both sides of the road for seven miles. The road became an avenue of death for the Americans.

The UNC air force did what it could. All day long its planes flew back and forth along the route and strafed suspected Chinese positions. Meanwhile, the division, burdened with heavy equipment, had great difficulty moving through the narrow mountain road to Sunchon.

The 23d Infantry Regiment formed the rear guard. As the day wore on and Chinese pressure increased, its commander, Colonel Paul L. Freeman, became concerned that his unit might be cut off. He believed that his best route of withdrawal was probably by way of the Chongchon River road to Anju. When he reported his belief that continuing over the mountain route would mean suicide for his unit, the assistant division commander, Major General Joseph S. Bradley, gave him permission to use the Anju road.

With the 23d Infantry no longer in the rear of the column, three field artillery and one engineer battalion became the division's rear guard. The Chinese now concentrated on these units, and casualty rates were high. Out of 977 men in the rear-guard units, only 266 would survive, and more than 95 percent of their equipment would be lost. These units suffered one of the highest casualty rates of any sizeable unit in the KOREAN WAR.

See also CHANGJIN/CHOSIN RESERVOIR, BATTLE AND RETREAT FROM; CHINESE FIRST PHASE OFFENSIVE.

Further reading: Appleman, Roy. *East of Chosin: Entrapment and Breakout in Korea, 1950.* College Station: Texas A&M University Press, 1987; ———. *Disaster in Korea: The Chinese Confront MacArthur.* College Station: Texas A&M University Press, 1989; ———. *South to the Naktong, North to the Yalu.* Washington, D.C.: Office of the Chief of Military History, 1961; Blair, Clay. *The Forgotten War: America in Korea, 1950–1953.* New York: Times Books, 1987.

— Daniel R. Beirne

Christie, John W. (1865–1944) *Engineer and inventor*
Born on 6 May 1865 at River Edge, New Jersey, the son of a farmer, J. Walter Christie was an engineering prodigy from childhood. At age 12 he used parts from a clock to build a motor for a toy boat that he had carved. Although his destroying the clock angered his father, his mother and his older sister were impressed with his ingenuity. Just four years later Christie traveled to New York City with money given to him by his sister in order to obtain employment as an apprentice machinist. He worked for the Delameter Iron Works, while at night attending the Cooper Union, a free school for workers, to learn drafting and engineering.

For 20 years Christie devoted his talents to maritime engineering, working for the likes of J. P. Morgan and the U.S. Navy, and he amassed a number of patents for his inventions. In 1901 he began to experiment with automobiles and was convinced that a front-wheel-drive system was the most efficient method, an idea since proved correct. In 1904 Christie's first automobile premiered at the New York Auto Show. During the next decade, he was a prominent auto racer and inventor, competing in many of the most prestigious races in the United States and Europe.

In 1915, during World War I, Christie became interested in producing vehicles for the armed forces. His first efforts involved a truck sent on the PUNITIVE EXPEDITION INTO MEXICO of 1916 and a mechanized 105-mm gun carriage. Although both were promising experiments, it was the TANK with which Christie was to become inexorably linked.

Christie's first tank, the Model 1919, which he referred to as a "steel steed," debuted at the Aberdeen Proving Grounds in November 1919. The first tank to have a rotating turret, it was an innovative design, years ahead of its time. However, conservative individuals in the U.S. Ordnance Department were not interested in designs that did not originate with them. Christie refused to quit, however, and he subsequently designed the first amphibious tank, which debuted in 1921. Unfortunately, despite its innovative nature, it failed to attack the interest of the army or the Marine Corps. In 1926, Christie perfected a half-track truck design, similar to those that would be used by the army during World War II. His half-track successfully completed a 1,000-mile test sponsored by the U.S. Army; however, the vehicle was returned without any orders.

In July 1928 Christie debuted a new tank design, the Model 1928, and in October the new design was tested by the army at the Aberdeen Proving Grounds. Despite its excellent performance during trials and the endorsement of the officer review board, the army ordered only seven Model 1928 tanks. For the next dozen years the U.S. Army failed to buy more tanks, and financial problems caused Christie to sell several to the United Kingdom and the Soviet Union. Germany offered him $1 million plus royalties on his patents to supervise the design and construction of tanks for their army, but he refused on the grounds that he believed the Nazis were the natural enemies of the United States.

Christie died at Falls Church, Virginia, on 11 January 1944, heartbroken, penniless, and facing eviction from his home, yet during World War II his designs were the basis for tanks used by the British and the Soviets to stem the German tide.

See also CHAFFEE, ADNA R., JR.; TANKS.

Further reading: Christie, J. Edward. *Steel Steeds Christie: A Memoir of J. Walter Christie.* Manhattan, Kans.: Sunflower University Press, 1985; Hofmann, George F., and Donn A. Starry, *Camp Colt to Desert Storm: The History of U.S. Armored Forces.* Lexington: University Press of Kentucky, 1999.

— Alexander M. Bielakowski

Church, Benjamin (1639–1718) *Colonial military leader*

Born in 1639 in the Plymouth colony, Benjamin Church moved with his family numerous times when he was a boy. His father sold one farm after another along the frontier in a restless quest for financial gain. Marrying in 1671, Benjamin Church continued this behavior with his own family to the great concern of the Puritan leaders of the colony, who scolded him for what they regarded as his irreligious, wordly ways.

Church's frontier upbringing gave him a great respect for the Indians; a number of prominent local Indians, especially the squaw sachem Awaskonks, became close friends. In early 1675 they warned him about upcoming attacks by KING PHILIP's warriors. Church warned the Plymouth authorities and tried to negotiate with the local Indians. When KING PHILIP'S WAR grew despite his efforts, Church was commissioned as a militia officer.

Involved in several small skirmishes, Church was soon appointed an aide and adviser to Governor Josiah Winslow, commander of the colonial army sent to attack the Narragansett tribe in December 1675. During the Battle of GREAT SWAMP, Church led a party of Plymouth soldiers. He advised against the burning of the fort and was proved correct when the militia, having done so anyway and now without shelter, was forced to march back to base with its wounded in a severe winter storm.

Church made a specialty of employing Indian tactics and Indian warriors to take the fight to the enemy; he was the forerunner of Robert ROGERS in this regard. Church even converted some Indians to his side on the battlefield. He was very successful in 1676, killing hostile Indians, destroying their villages and crops, and even capturing Philip's wife and son. Church finally tracked the elusive chief down in a swamp near Mount Hope, Rhode Island. On 12 August one of Church's Indian soldiers shot and killed King Philip. This, and Church's bold capture of

the last active war chief, Annawon, effectively ended the war.

Church later served in KING WILLIAM'S WAR and QUEEN ANNE'S WAR, in which, as a colonel, he led the assault on Port Royal in 1704. In the midst of a controversy over his treatment of French prisoners, Church retired in disgust and under suspicion in 1705. He died at Little Compton, Rhode Island, on 17 June 1718. His son, Thomas, published his diary as *Entertaining Passages Relating to King Philip's War;* it cemented Benjamin Church's place in colonial history as the first American hero of the frontier.

See also AMERICAN INDIAN WARS, OVERVIEW; INDIAN SCOUTS; INDIAN WARFARE.

Further reading: Church, Benjamin. *The History of King Philip's War.* Boston: John Kimball Wiggin, 1990; Leach, Douglas Edward. *Flintlock and Tomahawk: New England in King Philip's War.* Reprint, East Orleans, Mass.: Parnassus Imprints, 1992; Slotkin, Richard, and James K. Folsom. *So Dreadful a Judgment: Puritan Responses to King Philip's War, 1676–1677.* Middletown, Conn.: Wesleyan University Press, 1978.

— Kyle F. Zelner

Churubusco, Battle of (20 August 1847) *One of the pivotal battles of the Mexican-American War*

In the campaign for Mexico City on 19 August 1847, Major General Winfield SCOTT's forces routed Mexican troops under Division General Gabriel Valencia at Contreras. This gave Scott control of several key roads leading to and around Mexico City. The Mexicans then retreated northward to Churubusco.

In view of the momentum of his rapidly advancing forces, Scott opted for a frontal assault on the strong defensive positions held by the Mexicans at Churubusco. The single barrier to the American advance was the Churubusco River. Only one bridge crossed it, and a nearby convent provided excellent positions for Mexican defenses.

The army of General Antonia López de Santa Anna defended the bridge and convent with the so-called San Patricio Battalion, made up of foreigners and American deserters, many of the latter Irish Catholics immigrants who had come to believe that the United States was out to destroy Catholicism in Mexico. The battalion was led by Irish-American volunteer John Riley, formerly of the 5th U.S. Infantry Regiment. The San Patricios had seen action at MONTERREY, Satillo, and BUENA VISTA, each time receiving praise for their valor.

The American advance opened with artillery and then a rush across the bridge. Casualties were heavy on both sides. Wagons provided cover for the attackers, and the San

Patricios and Mexicans defending the convent began to run low on ammunition. Desperate appeals to General Santa Anna for resupply went unanswered until late in the battle. When ammunition did finally arrive, much of it was useless because it was of the wrong caliber. Reportedly the Mexicans attempted to raise a flag of surrender but were overruled by the San Patricios, who knew that surrender would mean their certain execution for desertion.

After three hours of fierce fighting, the convent fell to the Americans. Scott's army had been whittled down to slightly more than 8,000 effectives before the battle, but in the attack itself he lost fewer than 1,000 men. Mexican losses came to nearly 3,000 dead, wounded, or taken prisoner. Among the latter were eight generals and 72 San Patricios. The San Patricios were tried and convicted of desertion. After agonizing consideration, Scott signed the execution order, which was carried out on 13 September.

With the Mexican army near total defeat, Scott could have pushed for final victory. However, with his forces tired and hoping that the victory would convince government leaders in Mexico City to sue for peace, Scott halted his army just short of the gates of the Mexican capital. However, it would take yet another battle to capture the city.

See also MEXICAN-AMERICAN WAR.

Further reading: Eisenhower, John S. D. *So Far from God: The U.S. War with Mexico, 1846–1848.* Reprint, Norman: University of Oklahoma Press, 2000; Frazier, Donald S. *The United States and Mexico at War: Nineteenth-Century Expansionism and Conflict.* New York: Macmillan, 1998; Stevens, Peter F. *Rogues March: John Riley and the St. Patrick's Battalion.* New York: Brasseys, 1999.

— William Thomas Allison

civil affairs/military government *General policies governing occupied enemy territory during World War I and World War II*

Before the Geneva Convention in 1949, the rights of civilians in occupied territory remained questionable. World War I and World War II illustrated that civilians in occupied territories were unprotected. After World War I, America occupied part of the German Rhineland from 1917 until 1923. Likewise, after World War II, the U.S. occupied Japan and part of western Germany. The policies implemented reflected the need for a more detailed categorical set of rules.

Although in World War I the Americans had never intended to participate in an occupation of Germany, on 19 December 1918 they laid a foundation for a military government in the central zone of the Rhineland. Brigadier General H. A. Smith was given charge of civil affairs in the U.S. zone. He stipulated that all instructions regarding public matters would come from the officer in charge of civil affairs and that Third Army would act as an instrument of government. Both of these rules created confusion when the Americans withdrew from Germany because they did not tie the military government in with the established German government. The German public, although disgruntled by the presence of American troops, nonetheless praised them for reestablishing order.

There were problems with food and general unrest among a population under foreign occupation. The U.S. Senate's rejection of the 1919 Treaty of Versailles added additional difficulties. This led to communication problems and hostility between the Allied forces occupying Germany, as both Britain and France had endorsed the treaty. Many Americans believed that the Treaty of Versailles treated Germany too harshly, and this was apparent both in U.S. actions with its allies and its occupation policy toward Germany.

The Rhineland agreement, in which the Allies established a general occupation policy, excluded German law but did not bind the United States to the agreement because Washington had not ratified the Treaty of Versailles. Indeed, French and Belgian occupiers treated their territories in the Rhineland more harshly, and American commissioner Pierrepont Noyes experienced many difficulties in fulfilling the Rhineland agreement in a fair manner.

During World War II Washington began consideration of occupation policies long before it occupied Germany and Japan. U.S. goals included democratization, education, and punishment of people charged with WAR CRIMES. At first these goals were general. In the 14 August 1941 Atlantic Charter, President Franklin ROOSEVELT and British prime minister Winston Churchill spoke of ending Nazi tyranny and Japanese expansion. They also indicated that after the defeat of the Axis, more liberal governments would be installed. With the United States not yet in the war, they did not outline a policy.

In 1942, 43 countries, including the United States, Britain, China, and the Soviet Union, signed a United Nations Declaration that pledged to use all resources in an effort to crush the Axis powers. Each country also promised not to conclude a separate peace. This marked not only a basis for the future United Nations organization but a beginning in the formation of occupation policy.

Wartime conferences further influenced American occupation policy. During the October 1943 Moscow Conference, Secretary of State Cordell Hull met with foreign ministers Anthony Eden of Britain and Vyacheslav Molotov of the Soviet Union. They agreed that at the end of the war Germany's boundaries would be returned to those of 1937 and that individuals responsible for atrocities would be tried and punished. (The International

Military Tribunal, which met at Nuremberg from November 1945 to October 1946, fulfilled that goal.) At the November–December 1943 Teheran Conference, Roosevelt, Churchill, and Soviet premier Josef Stalin addressed the division of Germany, unconditional surrender, reparations, and the promise of the Soviet Union to enter the war against Japan after the defeat of Germany.

Still, by the end of the war Washington did not have in place a formal policy regarding U.S. occupation of enemy territories. The U.S. government had neglected to consider policies related to the care of civilians in occupied territories. Such basic concerns such as ensuring supplies of food and water had received scant attention. After the war the Americans did, however, devote considerable attention to education—furthering democratization. The United States put forth an extensive program to install Western-style democracy in both Germany and Japan.

U.S. military personnel were held responsible for the democratization of occupied territories, but occupation forces in Germany often lacked the skills necessary for many of the civil-affairs tasks expected of them. Very few, for instance, spoke German. Since communication with the German people proved necessary for a force required to displace Nazis and Nazi sympathizers from government, education, and business, this only exacerbated tension.

Furthermore, many of the rules governing military personnel, such as prohibitions against fraternization, which prohibited GIs from personally interacting with the Germans, actually caused more friction between the occupied and the occupiers. Nonetheless, military personnel continued their efforts to democratize Germany.

Goals for education in Germany underwent many changes from 1945 to 1949. Apart from simply getting schools running again, U.S. authorities worked to remove former Nazis from important positions of responsibility, such as teaching. By 1948 American influence had waned, with the beginning of the COLD WAR and the likelihood that a West German state would emerge. U.S. policy now merely emphasized German compliance with earlier measures.

U.S. authorities in Japan experienced different problems with education, resulting from cultural and religious differences. Still, the main goal of democratizing Japanese society remained.

By 1949 it has become evident that laws concerning the rights of an occupied territory and its citizens needed to be stated clearly. The 1949 Geneva Conference established the principle that civilian rights must remain intact, and it limited the power of occupying troops and officials. It also asserted rights of the civilian population regarding food, shelter, and medical needs.

In recent times there has been a switch from occupation, in the pursuit of narrow national interests, to *peace-keeping*, in order to prevent "ethnic cleansing" by one people against another, which might lead to a wider war. The most prominent examples of such operations have been the United Nations and NORTH ATLANTIC TREATY ORGANIZATION operations in Bosnia, Kosovo, and Macedonia. The United States entered into these operations reluctantly, yet its military has performed well. Clearly peacekeeping operations at the beginning of the 21st century present a new set of challenges beyond the occupation duties that arose in Germany, Japan, or Korea.

See also CLAY, LUCIUS D.; GERMANY, U.S. FORCES IN; MACARTHUR, DOUGLAS; PARIS PEACE SETTLEMENT; TRUMAN, HARRY S.; WILSON, WOODROW.

Further reading: Merritt, Richard L. *Democracy Imposed: U.S. Occupation Policy and the German Public, 1945–1949.* New Haven, Conn.: Yale University Press, 1995. Nelson, Keith L. *Victors Divided: America and the Allies in Germany, 1918–1923.* Berkeley: University of California Press, 1975; Ward, Robert E., and Sakamoto Yoshikazu, eds. *Democratizing Japan: The Allied Occupation.* Honolulu: University of Hawaii Press, 1987.
— Kristin L. Collins

Civil Air Patrol *Civilian auxiliary of the U.S. Army Forces (USAAF) from World War II to the present*
The Civil Air Patrol (CAP) was created on 1 December 1941 under the Office of Civilian Defense. Its first commander was Major General John F. Curry, a USAAF officer. The basic purpose of CAP was to organize for the war effort some of America's 25,000 private light aircraft into a unified national system. In 1942 the addition of a cadet program gave young people between the ages of 15 and 17 aviation and premilitary training. Significantly, the cadet program included both young men and women. By 1942 CAP had some 75,000 adult members in more than 1,000 units throughout the country.

CAP was a quasi-military organization from the start. Organized along military lines and partially staffed with active-duty officers, CAP members wore U.S. Army uniforms, with their own distinctive insignia. Both adults and cadets received training in general aviation and in many nonaviation military subjects. On 29 April 1943 the War Department assumed control of CAP and assigned the USAAF the responsibility for supervising and directing its operations. CAP remained a completely voluntary organization, however, and never came under the jurisdiction of U.S. military law.

CAP performed a wide array of military support tasks within the borders of the United States. Most CAP pilots flew their own planes. The only compensation they received was expenses, and quite often not even that. During the war CAP moved roughly 3.5 million pounds of mail and critical aviation spare parts; flew approximately 30,000 hours of dawn-to-dusk patrols along the southern borders; and flew 20,593 target-towing missions. This last task was particularly hazardous; 23 aircraft were lost, seven CAP members were killed, and five were seriously injured.

CAP's Coastal Patrol was its most significant contribution to the war effort. Between 5 March 1942 and 31 August 1943, CAP pilots and aircraft flew submarine-spotting missions along the 1,200-mile sea frontier from Halifax, Nova Scotia, to the Florida Keys. At that point in the war German U-boats were sinking merchantmen and tankers in American coastal waters at the rate of two or three a day. With the military spread very thin so early in the war, the CAP patrols provided hundreds of extra sets of eyes. Using radios donated by the major oil companies, CAP patrols summoned military aircraft to deal with any spotted U-boat. CAP planes also carried bombs with jury-rigged external racks.

During its 18 months of service, the Coastal Patrol flew 86,685 missions, for a total of 24 million miles. It reported 173 U-boat sightings, dropped bombs on 57 submarines, and actually sank two. Coastal Patrol pilots also summoned help for 91 vessels in distress and for 363 survivors of U-boat attacks. The cost was 90 CAP aircraft lost and 26 pilots and observers killed.

CAP flight crew members were awarded 825 Air Medals for wartime services. When the U.S. Air Force became a separate service in 1947, CAP became its official auxiliary. The CAP cadet program today has status equal to that of the high school Junior ROTC programs.

See also AIR FORCE, U.S.

Further reading: Glines, Carroll V. *Minutemen of the Air: The Valiant Exploits of the Civil Air Patrol in Peace and War.* New York: Random House, 1966; Keefer, Louis E. *From Maine to Mexico: With America's Private Pilots in the Fight against Nazi U-Boats.* Reston, Va.: COTU, Pub., 1997.

— David T. Zabecki

Civil War, causes of

Although several factors contributed to Southern secession, slavery was the dominant cause of the Civil War. Economic, social, and political factors all played significant roles in the onset of war, but the issue of whether slavery should be permitted in the western territories acquired during the 1846–48 MEXICAN-AMERICAN WAR proved to be the principal issue on the eve of war.

The secession of the Southern states in 1860–61 and the ensuing outbreak of hostilities culminated decades of friction between North and South arising from the fundamental differences between the Northern and Southern economies. The North's economy, which consisted of a growing manufacturing sector, major commercial interests, and small farms, was establishing itself as an industrial society (it had 85 percent of the nation's industry and 90 percent of its industrial output in 1860) and sought to prohibit the expansion of slavery into the western territories that would eventually become new states. Opponents of slavery opposed its expansion partly because they did not want to compete against slave labor. The South's economy, on the other hand, was for the most part agricultural and based on large plantations using slave labor to cultivate crops. Whereas the North wanted high tariffs to protect its industrial concerns from British competition, the South exported virtually its entire cotton output abroad and wanted low tariffs or none at all so as to be able to buy British goods at the cheapest possible prices. But increasingly slavery became the issue. Southerners feared not only that they would lose the federal government's protection of slavery in the new territories but that the North's stance would endanger the future of slavery in the South itself.

Northern and Southern social mores differed as much as their economies in the mid-19th century. Slavery again proved the primary cause of divergent attitudes, isolating the South from the North. Each region saw the other as a threat to its way of life, adding to the interregional hostility that had gripped both sections. As sectionalism intensified and violence in the territories grew, especially in Kansas and Missouri, the nation became increasingly divided. Political parties and churches split along regional lines.

The regions' political stance, masked by compromise since the 1820s, ultimately led to the rupture between the sections. The North wanted a strong central government that would protect its trading and financial interests, control the national currency, and fund internal improvements. The South, which was less dependent on the federal government, saw no need to strengthen it and feared that a stronger central government might interfere with the institution of slavery and further weaken state sovereignty.

The irrevocable break occurred in 1860 when Abraham LINCOLN, candidate of the Republican Party, which sought to end slavery in the territories, won the presidential election. Although Lincoln insisted that he had no intention to interfere with slavery where it existed, the Southern states feared Northern domination. Arguing that the Union was a voluntary compact entered into by sovereign states as long as it served their purposes, 11 southern states (South Carolina, Mississippi, Florida, Alabama, Georgia, Louisiana, Texas, Virginia, Arkansas, Tennessee, and North Carolina) seceded from the Union between December 1860 and May 1861 as a means of protecting their sovereignty, which included the right to preserve slavery. Lincoln insisted that the United States was a perpetual union and vowed to maintain it—a position that found precedent in the nullification crisis of the 1830s.

See also CIVIL WAR, LAND OVERVIEW; CIVIL WAR, NAVAL OVERVIEW; FORT SUMTER.

Further reading: Morrison, Michael A. *Slavery and the American West: The Eclipse of Manifest Destiny and the Coming of the Civil War.* Chapel Hill: University of North Carolina Press, 1997; Potter, David. *The Impending Crisis, 1848–1861.* New York: Harper and Row, 1976; Stampp, Kenneth. *The Causes of the Civil War.* Englewood Cliffs, N.J.: Prentice Hall, 1959.

— Alexander Mendoza

Civil War, land overview

Land campaigns of the Civil War were fought in three theaters: the eastern, from the Atlantic to the Appalachian Mountains; the western, from the Appalachian Mountains to the Mississippi River; and the trans-Mississippi, from the Mississippi River to the Pacific. The campaigns of the Civil War centered on three military objectives: to capture or threaten the enemy's capital; to protect one's own capital; and to destroy opposing armies in the field. To win, the Confederacy would have merely to stand on the defensive and preserve its independence. In order for the Union to win, it would have to conquer the South. Northern strategy followed the so-called ANACONDA PLAN, advanced by brevet Lieutenant General Winfield SCOTT, of squeezing the Confederacy by naval blockade and then bisecting it by powerful invading armies supported by naval forces on Southern rivers. Confederate strategy, given its far inferior manpower assets, was essentially defensive in nature.

Northern public opinion demanded a quick thrust against the South. As a result the principal Union army in the east, which became the Army of the Potomac, was committed before it was ready. The First Battle of BULL RUN/MANASSAS in July 1861 opened the war in the eastern

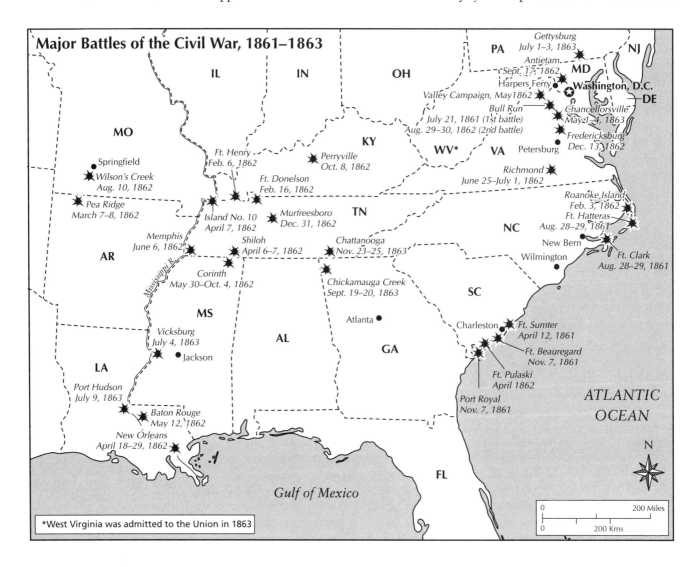

Major Battles of the Civil War, 1861–1863

*West Virginia was admitted to the Union in 1863

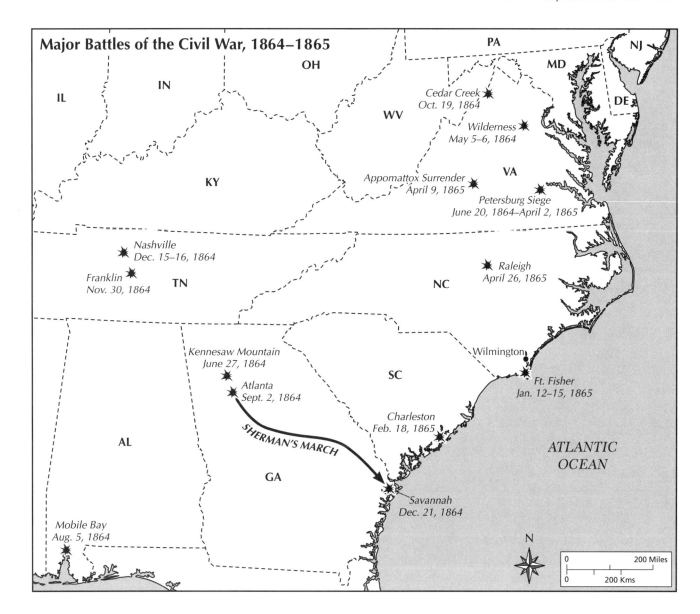

Major Battles of the Civil War, 1864–1865

theater. It was a relatively small engagement, fought with poorly trained volunteer militia, but it set the pattern for campaigns in this theater for the rest of the war.

In April 1862 Major General George B. MCCLELLAN's Army of the Potomac initiated a campaign to capture Richmond by advancing up the Virginia Peninsula. In the 31 May Battle of SEVEN PINES, the Confederates halted McClellan before Richmond. The Confederate commander, General Joseph E. JOHNSTON, was wounded, and President Jefferson DAVIS's military adviser, General Robert E. LEE, took over command of what would become the Army of Northern Virginia.

Lee had already impeded McClellan in March by reinforcing Major General Thomas J. "Stonewall" JACKSON's small army in the strategic SHENANDOAH VALLEY and

sending it against Union forces there. Jackson's brilliant use of terrain to mask his maneuvers and his speed in concentrating his forces against isolated federal units in six battles from March to June led U.S. president Abraham LINCOLN to withhold reinforcements from McClellan in order to protect the capital.

By June Lee had secretly moved Jackson's force to Richmond and attacked McClellan's slow-moving and badly positioned army at every opportunity between 27 June and 1 July, in what was called the Battles of the SEVEN DAYS. Although poorly coordinated and hampered by inexperienced leaders, Lee's offensive drove the Army of the Potomac away from the Confederate capital.

Lee then sought to seize the initiative, abandoning a defensive strategy, by striking north toward Washington.

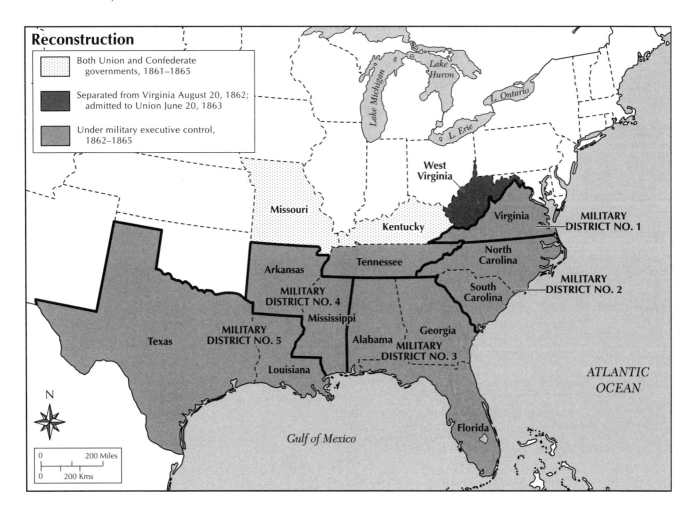

Reconstruction

Both Union and Confederate governments, 1861–1865

Separated from Virginia August 20, 1862; admitted to Union June 20, 1863

Under military executive control, 1862–1865

Lake Michigan

Lake Huron

L. Ontario

L. Erie

West Virginia

Missouri

Kentucky

Virginia

MILITARY DISTRICT NO. 1

Arkansas

Tennessee

North Carolina

MILITARY DISTRICT NO. 4

South Carolina

MILITARY DISTRICT NO. 2

Mississippi

Georgia

Texas

MILITARY DISTRICT NO. 5

Alabama

MILITARY DISTRICT NO. 3

ATLANTIC OCEAN

Louisiana

N

Florida

Gulf of Mexico

0   200 Miles

0   200 Kms

He employed Jackson's skill at maneuver to overcome the Army of Virginia under Major General John POPE in the Second Battle of BULL RUN/MANASSAS on 30 August. The battle was a brilliant success but did not achieve Lee's ultimate goal of destroying the Union army.

Lee hardly paused after this battle, moving immediately into neutral Maryland to seek a decisive battle with the Army of the Potomac. McClellan obtained a mislaid copy of Lee's orders and attempted to strike Lee's exposed and separated command, but he moved too slowly. Lee stood his ground on the banks of ANTIETAM Creek, at Sharpsburg, Maryland. On 17 September 1862, McClellan launched a series of uncoordinated attacks. The following day, McClellan hesitated to attack, claiming he was outnumbered, allowing the Army of Northern Virginia to escape.

In December 1862 new commander of the Army of the Potomac, Major General Ambrose E. BURNSIDE, sought to capture Richmond by an overland campaign. He was stopped at FREDERICKSBURG on the Rappahannock River, where Lee's army waited behind well-placed defenses. In the ensuing December battle Burnside's army suffered 12,000 casualties and accomplishing nothing.

In the spring of 1863 a new commander of the Army of the Potomac, Major General Joseph HOOKER, attempted another overland campaign against Richmond, intending to outflank Lee's army at Fredericksburg. His excellent plan went awry because of his own indecision in the tangled undergrowth area known as the Wilderness around CHANCELLORSVILLE. This was the most brilliantly conceived and executed battle Lee ever fought. Dividing his army several times, he defeated the Union army in detail and forced it back across the river. But he suffered the loss of his brilliant lieutenant, Jackson; wounded during the battle, "Stonewall" died a few days later.

Lee's victory led to the second invasion of the North. Lee headed for Pennsylvania, intending to threaten Washington and fight a decisive battle with the Army of the Potomac. The Army of the Potomac now had yet another commander, Major General George G. MEADE. As Meade and Lee sought each other out, advanced elements of both armies clashed at the small town of GETTYSBURG. It was a battle neither general intended to fight at that place or time, but after a three-day struggle over 1–3 July, Lee gave up the field. From that point on, the Union army held the initiative in the eastern theater.

In the spring of 1864, Meade's army, now directed for all intents and purposes by Lieutenant General Ulysses S. GRANT, commander in chief of all Union armies, initiated another overland attack. This time the objective was not Richmond but Lee's army. From May to June 1864, the two armies fought nearly continuously. Grant sought to capture the strategic road and rail center of PETERSBURG, but Lee got there first and Grant began siege operations. By April 1865 Grant's superiority in numbers and logistics overwhelmed the Confederates. Lee was forced to abandon Petersburg and, with it, Richmond. He attempted to link up with Joseph Johnston's army in North Carolina, but on 9 April Lee surrendered his army at APPOMATTOX Court House.

In the western theater, early in 1862 Union forces began offensive operations against General Albert Sidney JOHNSTON's thinly stretched Confederate forces. In February a joint land and naval expedition captured FORTS HENRY and DONELSON. These victories forced the Confederates to abandon Kentucky and most of Tennessee. Two Union armies, one under Major General Don Carlos BUELL and the other led by Major General Grant, advanced to attack Johnston in Corinth, Mississippi. Johnston counterattacked Grant's exposed army in the Battle of SHILOH, in southwestern Tennessee, on 6 April 1862, nearly destroying it. Johnston died on the field of battle, leaving command to General P. G. T. BEAUREGARD. That night Buell's army arrived and joined Grant's force to drive the Confederates from the field the next day.

Union inertia allowed the Confederacy to take the initiative in the summer of 1862. Major General Earl VAN DORN's army would open western Tennessee; General Braxton BRAGG and Major General Edmund Kirby SMITH were to control East Tennessee and invade Kentucky, an offensive meant to parallel Lee's invasion of Maryland. Bragg maneuvered Buell's army out of central Tennessee, but at PERRYVILLE, Kentucky, elements of the armies of Buell and Bragg fought to a standstill on 8 October 1862. Van Dorn's attack had failed, and Bragg decided to abandon the invasion, retreating into Tennessee.

Buell was replaced by Major General William S. ROSECRANS, who attacked Bragg's army at STONES RIVER/MURFREESBORO. From 31 December 1862 through 2 January 1863 the armies fought a bloody and indecisive battle. Bragg retreated, but Rosecran's Army of the Cumberland took no further action for six months.

Between March and May 1863 Grant's army attempted to capture the Confederate stronghold at VICKSBURG, which controlled the Mississippi River. Again,

with the cooperation of the navy, Grant landed forces below the city and initiated a campaign that led to a siege and the city's surrender in July. The Confederacy was now split in half.

In July Rosecrans forced Bragg out of the strategic rail center of Chattanooga, Tennessee, and advanced toward ATLANTA, the most important industrial center in the theater. Reinforced by Lieutenant General James LONGSTREET's corps from Lee's army, Bragg attacked from 19 to 20 September at CHICKAMAUGA Creek in northern Georgia. General George H. THOMAS directed a stubborn defense, allowing the rest of the army to retreat to Chattanooga. Bragg began a siege of CHATTANOOGA. But the Union army was reinforced from the eastern theater as well as from Major General William T. SHERMAN's Army of the Tennessee. Grant, the new commander of forces in the western theater, directed an attack to break the siege. Bragg's army was driven from its positions in disorder on 25 November 1863, opening the way for offensive Federal operations.

General Joseph E. Johnston then replaced Bragg. Grant took command of all Union armies, leaving SHERMAN to direct the western theater. As Grant began his campaign against Lee, Sherman moved on Atlanta and the Confederate army. Although Johnston fought a brilliant delaying action, President Davis replaced him with Lieutenant General John B. HOOD, who attacked Sherman's army outside ATLANTA to little effect. Besieged and outmaneuvered, Hood abandoned the city on 2 September 1864.

As part of Grant's plan, Sherman drove deep into the interior of the South between September 1864 and April 1865, marching through Georgia, South Carolina, and North Carolina, seeking to destroy civilian morale and arrive in the rear of Lee's army in Virginia. Hood invaded Tennessee but came to ruin in the Battles of FRANKLIN and NASHVILLE in November and December 1864. Sherman accepted Johnston's surrender on 26 April 1865 in North Carolina.

In the trans-Mississippi theater, both sides fought to control Missouri in 1861. Union forces gained full control of the state by defeating the Confederates at the Battle of PEA RIDGE in March 1862. In March Confederate forces invaded New Mexico, capturing Santa Fe before being forced to retreat back to Texas. Both Union and Confederate forces had to deal with uprisings of hostile Indian tribes.

Between March and April 1864 Major General Nathaniel BANKS led a joint army-navy expedition up the Red River toward Shreveport, headquarters of Lieutenant General Edmund Kirby SMITH. It was intended primarily to dissuade French emperor Napoleon III from intervention in Mexico, and to invade Texas. From September to October 1864 Major General Sterling Price invaded Missouri with the intent of capturing St. Louis but was forced to retreat into Indian Territory.

The overall Union victory resulted from three factors: a sound strategy, large-scale logistics support, and an excellent political-military team in Lincoln and Grant. Despite often brilliant campaigning and superb battlefield leadership, the Confederacy was overcome by President Davis's demands for an offensive strategy.

See also BENTONVILLE, BATTLE OF; BRANDY STATION, BATTLE OF; BRECKINRIDGE, JOHN C.; BUTLER, BENJAMIN F.; CASUALTIES IN U.S. WARS; CHAMPION'S HILL, BATTLE OF; CIVIL WAR, NAVAL OVERVIEW; COLD HARBOR, BATTLE OF; CRATER, BATTLE OF THE; EWELL, RICHARD S.; FIVE FORKS, BATTLE OF; FORREST, NATHAN BEDFORD; FORT FISHER, ATTACK ON; FORT SUMTER, ATTACK ON; FORT WAGNER, ASSAULT ON; HANCOCK, WINFIELD SCOTT; IUKA, BATTLE OF; JACKSON'S SHENANDOAH VALLEY CAMPAIGN; KENNESAW MOUNTAIN, BATTLE OF; MARCH TO THE SEA; MORGAN, JOHN HUNT; OVERLAND CAMPAIGN, 1864; SHERIDAN, PHILIP HENRY; SPOTSYLVANIA COURTHOUSE, BATTLE OF; STUART, JAMES EWELL; WHEELER, JOSEPH; WILDERNESS, BATTLE OF; WILLIAMSBURG, BATTLE OF.

Further reading: Freeman, Douglas Southall. *Lee's Lieutenants.* 3 vols. New York: Scribner, 1942–44; Hattaway, Herman, and Archer Jones. *How the North Won.* Urbana: University of Illinois Press, 1983; McPherson, James. *Battle Cry of Freedom.* New York: Oxford University Press, 1988; Weigley, Russell F. *A Great Civil War: A Military and Political History, 1861–65.* Bloomington: Indiana University Press, 2000.

— Keith D. Dickson

Civil War, naval overview

The Civil War occurred at a time of revolution in naval warfare, including the substitution of steam for sail and ironclad ships for those built of wood. It also saw the employment of shell guns, rifled ordnance, mines, and submarines.

The outbreak of war found the U.S. Navy in a poor state, its vessels badly scattered, with only 42 of its 92 ships in commission. Fortunately for the Federals, the secretary of the navy, Gideon WELLES, an honest and competent member of President Abraham LINCOLN's cabinet, took advantage of the North's industrial resources. Assisted by the able Assistant Secretary of the Navy Gustavus FOX, Welles took advantage of rapidly increased naval appropriations to build the navy to 671 ships—second in the world only to Great Britain—by December 1864, including 71 ironclads. Naval personnel went from 7,400 at the start of the conflict to more than 68,000 at war's end.

The federal navy focused first on establishing an effective blockade of nearly 4,000 miles of Confederate coastline. This was an important factor in the defeat of the South, even though the blockade did not become truly effective until late 1863. Union naval forces also helped to capture Confederate ports and inland fortifications. Although army-naval cooperation was not always satisfactory, generally this tandem worked well. In addition, especially on the western rivers, the Union navy provided important gunfire support to troops ashore, as in the Battle of SHILOH.

The Confederacy faced a more daunting challenge. Initially without a single ship at his command, Confederate secretary of the navy Stephen R. MALLORY dispatched agents to Europe to purchase warships for commerce raiding, attempted to refurbish captured or scuttled Federal vessels, and promoted the use of ironclad warships, which he first sought to buy in Europe and then had built at home. He also experimented with new methods of naval warfare, such as torpedoes, or mines, and supported the construction of "torpedo boats" (specially designed boats to carry spar torpedoes or mines) and submarines. Mallory's goals in commerce raiding were to drive up Union insurance costs, thereby diminishing support in the North for the war, and to divert Union warships from blockade duties.

President Lincoln ordered the blockade of the Confederate coastline almost immediately after the war began.

Many who served in the Civil War on land and sea were quite young. Note the Parrott rifled gun behind the young Union ship's boy in this picture. *(Library of Congress)*

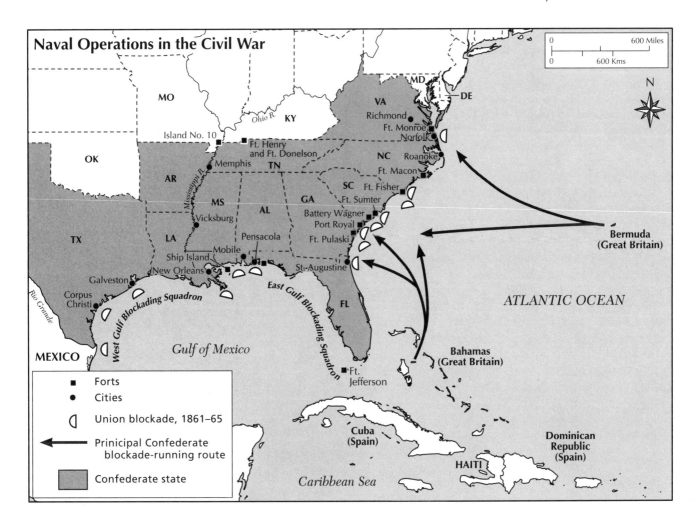

Naval Operations in the Civil War

In November 1861 a Federal flotilla under Flag Officer Samuel F. DU PONT captured Port Royal, South Carolina. In February and March 1862 the Union navy took Roanoke Island and New Bern, North Carolina. Fort Pulaski then fell, effectively closing Savannah to Confederate blockade runners. Despite Union efforts, the blockade proved ineffectual at the beginning of the war. Union ships were able to capture only one in 10 blockade runners during 1861–62. By the war's end, however, the number of ships attempting to run the blockade had fallen off sharply. A majority still got through, but the blockade at its height imposed great hardship on the Southern economy.

In the West, a Union flotilla under Flag Officer Andrew H. FOOTE captured FORT HENRY on the Tennessee River and played a role in the capture of FORT DONELSON on the Cumberland, both in February 1862. Foote then moved against ISLAND NO. 10, in the Mississippi.

On 9 March 1862, the first battle in naval history between ironclad warships occurred—MONITOR v. VIRGINIA. Technically a draw, the battle between the Union ironclad *Monitor* and the Confederate ram *Virginia* in effect ensured

continued Union control of Hampton Roads at the mouth of Chesapeake Bay.

In April 1862 Union naval forces in the Gulf of Mexico under Flag Officer David G. FARRAGUT ran past the Confederate forts at the mouth of the Mississippi and took New Orleans, the Confederacy's largest city. Vicksburg did not fall until 4 July 1863, but the Union navy had played a key role in splitting off the trans-Mississippi West from the remainder of the Confederacy. Pressured by Welles and Union public opinion, Du Pont mounted a monitor attack on Charleston, South Carolina, on 7 April 1863. It ended in perhaps the worst Union naval defeat of the war; the font of the rebellion remained in Confederate hands until near the end of the war. In August 1864 Farragut entered Mobile Bay, destroying several Confederate ships, including the powerful ironclad ram *Tennessee*. The Confederacy's last open Atlantic port, Wilmington, North Carolina, withstood a joint army-navy attack led by Rear Admiral David D. PORTER in December 1864. A month later, however, Porter, with a more powerful Union land force, bombarded FORT FISHER and forced its capitulation. On

17 February, Charleston finally fell to a combined Union naval/land attack. Galveston, Texas, was the only port in Confederate hands at war's end.

Because of its inferiority in conventional naval weapons, the Confederacy experimented with new weapons, including torpedoes (mines) and submarines. On 17 February 1864, the submarine *CSS HUNLEY* sank the Union steam sloop *Housatonic* in Charleston Harbor, a first in the annals of naval warfare. The *Hunley* sank shortly thereafter.

Confederate commerce raiders preyed on Union merchant ships. The most successful of these was the *ALABAMA,* commanded by Captain Raphael SEMMES. It took 66 Union merchant ships as well as the U.S. Navy warship *Hatteras.* On 19 June 1864 the Union steam sloop *KEARSARGE,* commanded by Captain John Winslow, sank the *Alabama* off Cherbourg, France. Another commerce raider, the *Shenandoah,* devastated the Union whaling fleet, continuing its depredations after the war's end. Such commerce raiding did not seriously disrupt Union trade, but it did drive up insurance rates and led many Northern shippers to change their vessels to foreign registry; a good many of these were permanently lost to the U.S. merchant marine.

Despite the best efforts and innovations of the Confederates, Southern manufacturing resources were too limited to allow a serious challenge to Northern naval dominance. As a consequence, U.S. naval forces were able to play a significant role in the defeat of the Confederacy.

See also FORT PULASKI; IRONCLADS, U.S., IN THE CIVIL WAR; IRONCLADS, CONFEDERATE, IN THE CIVIL WAR; WELLES, GIDEON.

Further reading: Anderson, Bern. *By Sea and by River: A Naval History of the Civil War.* New York: Knopf, 1962; Fowler, William M. *Under Two Flags: The American Navy in the Civil War.* New York: Norton, 1990; Luraghi, Raimondo. *The Southern Navy: The Confederate Navy and the American Civil War.* Annapolis, Md.: Naval Institute Press, 1995; Tucker, Spencer C. *A Short History of the Civil War at Sea.* Wilmington, Del.: Scholarly Resources, 2000.

— Alexander Mendoza

Clark, George Rogers (1752–1818) *Indian fighter, frontiersman, and militia leader*

Born on 19 November 1752 in Albemarle County, Virginia, George Rogers Clark was largely self-educated. In 1772 Clark began work as a surveyor on the Kentucky frontier. Growing white encroachment on Shawnee land increased tensions in the area, and in 1774 Clark joined others to invade Shawnee territory in what became DUNMORE'S WAR. Clark built a strong reputation as a soldier.

The Shawnee nation was defeated in 1774, but the onset of the American Revolution allowed the Shawnee to join the British and continue to fight white settlers. By June 1776 Kentucky leaders had decided to send Clark to Williamsburg to seek a more definite connection between Virginia and Kentucky. The mission was successful, and Clark left Williamsburg having achieved his diplomatic goals. He also had 500 pounds of gunpowder that had been provided by Virginia to be used to defend the frontier. Upon his return Clark found the frontier torn by increased Indian attacks. He also learned that Detroit's British lieutenant governor, Henry Hamilton, was operating with Indian allies out of Detroit and other outposts along the

George Rogers Clark's march against Vincennes across the Wabash through wilderness and flood. Copy of painting by Ezra Winter   *(National Archives)*

Mississippi and Ohio Rivers. Clark decided to raise a force to strike at the British and raid the Illinois country.

Securing a commission as lieutenant colonel in the Virginia Line (regular infantry) and official authorization for his project, Clark raised 175 men to raid the British fort at Kaskaskia on the Mississippi River. After an eight-day voyage Clark and his men surprised the garrison on 4 July 1778, occupying the fort and town without firing a shot. Clark offered the French inhabitants U.S. citizenship and opened diplomatic channels with the Spanish across the Mississippi, as well as with several Indian nations. After securing the Kaskaskia area, Clark dispatched men to Vincennes.

Learning of Clark's raid, Hamilton moved to Vincennes, arriving there on 17 December 1778. He quickly overwhelmed the Americans but elected to winter there before moving on to Kaskaskia. Clark learned of Hamilton's plans and decided to use the weather against him. Clark and his men took 17 days to cross the flooded lowlands, but on 23 February 1779 they surprised Vincennes. Two days later Hamilton surrendered, guaranteeing the area for American claims during peace negotiations.

After the war Clark served in a variety of territorial posts and watched his brother, William Jefferson CLARK, gain fame for his own explorations. Clark, who had funded many of his own military expeditions, was never repaid by Congress or Virginia. Clark died at Louisville, Kentucky, on 13 February 1818, bankrupt and living with his sister.

See also AMERICAN INDIAN WARS, OVERVIEW; AMERICAN REVOLUTIONARY WAR, LAND OVERVIEW.

Further reading: Harrison, Lowell H. *George Rogers Clark and the War in the West.* Lexington: University Press of Kentucky, 1976; Rankin, Hugh F. *George Rogers Clark and the Winning of the West.* Richmond: Virginia Independence Bicentennial Commission, 1976.

— Patrick R. Jennings

Clark, Mark W. (1896–1984) *U.S. Army general*
Born on 1 May 1896 at Madison Barracks, New York, Mark Wayne Clark graduated from the U.S. Military Academy at WEST POINT in 1917. He served as an infantry officer in World War I. Wounded, he recovered in time to fight in the 1918 SAINT-MIHIEL and MEUSE-ARGONNE offensives. Following the war, Clark held a succession of assignments. He graduated from the Command and General Staff School in 1935 and in 1937 from the Army War College, returning to the latter in 1940 as an instructor.

Promoted to brigadier general in August 1941 and major general in April 1942, Clark became chief of staff of Army Ground Forces in May and commanding general of II Corps in June. In October he led a covert mission to North Africa to meet with Vichy French leaders in an effort to prevent French resistance to the planned November Allied landings. Promoted to lieutenant general in November 1942, he commanded U.S. ground forces in North Africa. Beginning in September 1943 Clark led the U.S. Fifth Army during its protracted march up the Italian Peninsula. Here he played a controversial role at SALERNO; some blamed him for the fiasco of the ANZIO landing, and he also was accused of allowing German forces to escape in order to claim the honor of liberating Rome. In early December 1944 Clark assumed command of Fifteenth Army Group, consisting of all Allied forces in the Mediterranean theater. Promoted to full general in May 1945, at age 48 Clark was the youngest U.S. general to achieve that rank during the war.

After the end of the war in Europe, Clark commanded the Allied occupation of Austria. In 1949 he had charge of U.S. Army Field Forces, with headquarters at Fort Monroe, Virginia.

In May 1952 Clark replaced Lieutenant General Matthew B. RIDGWAY as the U.S. commander in chief Far East and United Nations Command (UNC), Korea. Clark arrived to find the KOREAN WAR in stalemate and armistice negotiations deadlocked over the issue of prisoner exchanges. While obedient to President Harry S. TRUMAN's desire to limit the Korean conflict, Clark agreed with former UNC commander General of the Army Douglas MACARTHUR that there was no substitute for victory. He also believed that the Chinese and North Koreans would agree to settle outstanding armistice issues only if he kept up military pressure. As ground actions held the potential for significant casualties, however, Clark used his air assets to cut Communist communications and supply lines and to destroy air fields, dams, and reservoirs. Like MacArthur, he chafed at restrictions that prevented him from ordering direct attacks on air fields and industry in Manchuria.

Clark hoped that General of the Army Dwight D. EISENHOWER's election as president in November 1952 would allow him to take the offensive. But a trip by Eisenhower to Korea made Clark realize that he, like Truman, was anxious to end the war through negotiations, a goal that was achieved in July 1953.

Clark retired from the army in October 1953. In his memoir *From the Danube to the Yalu* he made no secret of his disappointment over being "the only American commander to end a war short of victory." He also decried what he viewed as Communist sympathizers at home. President of The Citadel in Charleston, South Carolina, from 1954 to 1960, Clark sided with conservative causes and anticommunist political movements. Later, he publicly argued that the VIETNAM WAR was the natural outgrowth of compromise and "appeasement" in Korea. Clark died in Charleston on 17 April 1984.

See also ARMY, U.S.; SALERNO; TORCH, OPERATION; WORLD WAR II, U.S. INVOLVEMENT, EUROPE.

Further reading: Blumenson, Martin. *Mark Clark.* London: St. Martin's Press, 1984. Clark, Mark. *From the Danube to the Yalu.* New York: Harper, 1954.

— William Head

Clark, William (1770–1838) *U.S. soldier, explorer, territorial governor, and Indian superintendent*

Born on 1 August 1770 in Caroline County, Virginia, William Clark was the younger brother of American Revolutionary War hero George Rogers CLARK. He moved with his family to land presented to his brother for services rendered, in the area of the falls of the Ohio (Louisville) on the Kentucky frontier.

Commissioned a lieutenant in the LEGION OF THE UNITED STATES, William Clark served under Major General "Mad" Anthony WAYNE in the Battle of FALLEN TIMBERS (20 August 1794). Before he resigned his commission to return home and manage the family properties in 1796, Clark was the commander of the Chosen Rifle Company in the legion. It was while he commanded this unit that he encountered Ensign Meriwether LEWIS, who would later figure prominently in his life.

In 1803 Captain Lewis was personal secretary to President Thomas JEFFERSON and was designated commander of an exploration of the newly purchased Louisiana Territory. He recruited Clark's as co-commander of the expedition to the Pacific coast. Clark accepted, although the government never fulfilled Lewis's promise of equal official status. Clark served from late 1803 through September 1806 as the Corps of Discovery's co-commander, while officially a second lieutenant of artillery. Never once in their two-and-a-half-year journey did a rift develop between the two friends nor did any member of the corps question either's authority. Clark conducted the diplomatic relations with the native tribes through whose territory they passed, and he served in the difficult role of the expedition's cartographer. In a journey of over 8,000 miles, his distance estimate was off by less than 1 percent.

Upon his return to civilization in St. Louis, Clark was named Indian agent for the entire territory and appointed brigadier general in the territorial militia. After Lewis's death and the renaming of the territory, Clark became governor of the Missouri Territory in 1813. He served capably during the WAR OF 1812 as governor and commander in chief of territorial forces. Following the war, he became superintendent for Indian affairs because of his excellent relations with the native tribes. As the Indians were pushed out of the East into a newly designated Indian Territory in present-day Kansas and Oklahoma, his job became less important, although Clarke was responsible for putting down a number of small Indian insurrections.

Clark then became surveyor general of the states of Illinois, Missouri, and Arkansas, laying out the city of Paducah, Kentucky. He died on 1 September 1838 at St. Louis, Missouri.

See also LOUISIANA PURCHASE; PIKE, ZEBULON.

Further reading: Ambrose, Stephen E. *Undaunted Courage: Meriwether Lewis, Thomas Jefferson, and the Opening of the American West.* New York: Simon and Schuster, 1996; Steffen, Jerome O. *William Clark: Jeffersonian Man on the Frontier.* Norman: University of Oklahoma Press, 1977.

— Lawyn C. Edwards and Spencer C. Tucker

Clay, Lucius D. (1897–1978) *U.S. Army general and military governor of the U.S. occupation zone of Germany after World War II*

Born on 23 April 1897 at Marietta, Georgia, the son of a U.S. senator, Lucius DuBignon Clay graduated from the U.S. Military Academy at WEST POINT in 1918. Commissioned a second lieutenant in the Corps of Engineers, he was not promoted to captain until 1933. During the 1930s the New Deal's numerous construction projects gave Clay, who simultaneously spent four years as the congressional spokesman of the Corps of Engineers, scope to display his organizational talents with the Works Progress Administration and the Civilian Conservation Corps; later that decade he served as the army's chief engineer in the Philippines and Texas.

During World War II Clay initially undertook assignments with the Civil Aeronautics Authority, directing construction or enlargement of some 277 airfields for military use. In 1942 he became deputy chief for matériel and was promoted to major general. He subsequently rose to director of matériel, responsible for coordinating all logistical details of army war production and allocation. Following the June 1944 NORMANDY INVASION Clay rendered invaluable service by making the port of Cherbourg operational despite German destruction. Clay's administrative abilities won further recognition in 1944, when he was named deputy director of war mobilization and reconversion.

Appointed General Dwight D. EISENHOWER's deputy for civilian affairs in Germany in 1945, with responsibility for feeding and housing the population in the U.S. zone, in March 1947 Clay became military governor and theater commander in Germany, as a lieutenant general. He firmly opposed plans to "pastoralize" western Germany by destroying its heavy industry. He emphasized the need for timely restoration of civilian government in Germany and moved toward the establishment of a West German state.

In June 1948, when the Soviet Union initiated the BERLIN BLOCKADE, cutting off Western Allied–occupied West Berlin, Clay advocated dispatching an armed supply convoy through Soviet-occupied East Germany. His superiors in Washington rejected this forceful advice as overly confrontational but quickly endorsed Clay's plan to resupply Berlin by air for almost a year, evidence of U.S. commitment to the policy of CONTAINMENT of Soviet expansion, which Clay's stance quickly came to symbolize. In May 1949, a few days after the blockade ended, Clay left both the army and—to rapturous farewells—West Germany, where a civilian high commissioner replaced him. He retired as a full general.

In retirement Clay worked as chairman of Continental Can Company and as a senior partner with Lehman Brothers. Politically active, in 1952 he helped to persuade Eisenhower to seek the Republican presidential nomination. During the 1961 Berlin crisis President John F. KENNEDY dispatched him to the city as his personal representative, to demonstrate continuing American support. Clay died at Chatham, Massachusetts, on 16 April 1978.

See also CIVIL AFFAIRS/MILITARY GOVERNMENT; GERMANY, U.S. FORCES IN; MILITARY-INDUSTRIAL COMPLEX.

Further reading: Backer, John H. *Winds of History: The German Years of Lucius DuBignon Clay.* New York: Van Nostrand Reinhold, 1983; Clay, Lucius D. *Decision in Germany.* Garden City, N.Y.: Doubleday, 1950; Smith, Jean Edward. *Lucius D. Clay: An American Life* New York: Henry Holt, 1990; Smith, Jean Edward, ed. *The Papers of General Lucius D. Clay: Germany, 1945–1949.* 2 vols. Bloomington: Indiana University Press, 1974.

— Priscilla Roberts

Clearwater River, Battle of the (11–12 July 1877)
Second major engagement of the Nez Perce War
Following the June 1877 Battle of WHITE BIRD CANYON, Brigadier General Oliver O. HOWARD assembled a large force at Fort Lapwai. On 1 July a detachment sent to capture Looking Glass and his band instead fired on the village, sending more warriors and their families into the hostile camp. Over the next several days Nez Perce warriors wiped out a 12-man army scouting party and skirmished with another detachment on Cottonwood Creek. On 9 July a group of volunteers attempted to assail the Indians on the Clearwater River, only to be driven back and besieged. Meanwhile, Howard's large column of 400 troops and 100 volunteers moved in.

The 800 Nez Perce, of whom 200 were fighting men, established camp in a valley on the Clearwater River. Preoccupied with the volunteers, the Indians did not detect Howard's approach. On 11 July, from a bluff above the camp, Howard opened up with howitzers and Gatling guns but at too great a distance to inflict great damage. He then maneuvered onto the flats to attack the village, but the warriors took defensive positions that prompted him to form an elliptical line. Then he endeavored to use his howitzers and Gatling guns to drive the defenders from their positions. Long-range fire lasted until night, each side probing for weaknesses.

The next day, as Howard renewed the attack, the Nez Perce began to disengage. JOSEPH, the chief, prepared the women and children for escape while warriors tried to hold back the soldiers. It was almost too late. Howard, who received reinforcements and supplies that morning, pressed the attack. A cavalry charge drove the defenders from the protective ravines and back on the main camp. Howard moved his entire line forward and pounded the Indian camp with artillery fire as Nez Perce men, women, and children abandoned their belongings and fled. Howard failed to pursue the shaken Indians. Instead he occupied their camp, and his men picked over the abandoned lodges. In the fight on the Clearwater Howard had suffered 13 killed and 27 wounded. The Nez Perce later acknowledged four dead and six wounded, although Howard claimed to have killed 23.

The Nez Perce bands then moved eastward across the Bitterroot Mountains in search of freedom on the plains or in Canada. Howard might have claimed a victory, but the campaign continued until October and stretched over hundreds of miles.

See also AMERICAN INDIAN WARS, OVERVIEW; BEAR PAW MOUNTAIN, BATTLE OF; BIG HOLE RIVER, BATTLE OF THE; CANYON CREEK, BATTLE OF; INDIAN WARFARE; NEZ PERCE WAR.

Further reading: Beal, Merril D. *"I Will Fight No More Forever": Chief Joseph and the Nez Perce War.* Seattle: University of Washington Press, 1963; Lavender, David. *Let Me Be Free: The Nez Perce Tragedy.* New York: HarperCollins, 1992; Utley, Robert M. *Frontier Regulars: The United States Army and the Indian, 1866–1891.* New York: Macmillan, 1973.

— David Coffey

Cleburne, Patrick R. (1828–1864) *Confederate general*
Born on 17 March 1828 in County Cork, Ireland, Patrick Ronayne Cleburne was the son of a prominent physician. He apprenticed to a pharmacist, but his inability to pass

his apothecary exam led to a military career. He served three years in the British army before purchasing his discharge. In 1849 Cleburne emigrated to the United States, where he worked as a pharmacist in Cincinnati, Ohio. Moving to Helena, Arkansas, Cleburne co-owned a drugstore before becoming an attorney.

At the outbreak of the Civil War Cleburne quickly became colonel of the 1st Arkansas Infantry (later 15th Arkansas). After service in Kentucky, he was appointed brigadier general in the Confederate army. In April 1862 Cleburne led a brigade in the Battle of SHILOH. Fighting on the extreme Confederate left, his troops helped force the Federals back to the Tennessee River. His command suffered more casualties than any other Confederate brigade.

In the 1862 Kentucky campaign, Cleburne was twice wounded. In August at RICHMOND, commanding a division, he was shot in the face. In October, Cleburne was again wounded at PERRYVILLE, where his innovative leadership contributed to a Confederate tactical victory.

Because of his success in Kentucky, Cleburne was appointed major general in December 1862. He led a division at STONES RIVER, CHICKAMAUGA, and CHATTANOOGA and during the ATLANTA CAMPAIGN. After the Confederate retreat from Chattanooga, he was heralded for saving the Confederate Army of Tennessee with a determined stand at Ringgold Gap.

Realizing that the lack of manpower doomed the Southern cause, in January 1864 Cleburne advocated the enlistment of slaves in return for their freedom, a proposal he termed a "concession to common sense." In addition to swelling the ranks with new soldiers, Cleburne hoped the proposal would induce European powers to recognize the Confederacy. Received with scorn, this plan most likely prevented his promotion to lieutenant general and corps command.

On 30 November 1864, Cleburne's division spearheaded the attack against Union entrenchments in the Battle of FRANKLIN, Tennessee. Two horses were shot from under him, but he continued the charge on foot. His hat raised on his sword, Cleburne was killed 50 yards from the Federal works. A natural soldier, Cleburne was one of the finest division commanders of the war. Confederate president Jefferson DAVIS lauded him as the "Stonewall of the West."

See also CIVIL WAR, LAND OVERVIEW.

Further reading: Joslyn, Mauriel, ed. *A Meteor Shining Brightly: Essays on Major General Patrick R. Cleburne.* Milledgeville, Ga.: Terrell House, 1997; Symonds, Craig L. *Stonewall of the West: Patrick Cleburne and the Civil War.* Lawrence: University Press of Kansas, 1997.

— Stuart W. Sanders

coast defense

For most of its pre–World War II history, the United States largely dedicated its defensive efforts to the security of its shores against seaborne threats. Separated by oceans from the Old World and the powers most likely to pose such dangers, the United States constantly relied for the protection of its coasts on its naval and military technologies. Also, during its infancy most of the nation's population lived along the eastern seaboard, where its largest cities were located. This, together with a corresponding insularity regarding national defense, made coastal defense not only an important military activity but a central aspect of national defense policy, in which the United States was a leader.

From the 16th century, the various colonial powers in the New World erected forts to protect coastal settlements, harbors, and river entrances. These early defensive structures tended to reflect their diverse national origins in both architectural style and armament. Because of the variety of European matériel contributed during the American Revolutionary War, the United States was left at that war's end with a mixed assemblage of military architecture and technology.

The creation of a distinct American system of national defense began in March 1794, when Congress first provided for the fortification of several important seacoast locations between Canada and Florida, as well as for six frigates, the latter marking the establishment of the U.S. Navy. It was not yet clear where the principal coast-defense burden would lie, with forts or with ships. That uncertainty hinged in large part on the question of what the navy was to be—a force intended essentially for coastal defense or one that could oppose a major power on the high seas.

Soon faced with that question, President Thomas JEFFERSON opted for an economical and politically advantageous solution, which involved the production of inexpensive coastal gunboats in large numbers to accompany the modest group of new forts erected during the preceding decade. Although the War of 1812 revealed the JEFFERSONIAN GUNBOAT PROGRAM to have been a poor choice, militarily and economically, and despite the professional navy's abhorrence of such employment of its ships and forces, the idea of a naval coastal-defense function lingered in U.S. defensive strategy for another century. It emerged intermittently, for example, in the form of floating batteries at the end of the War of 1812 and in shallow-draft monitors during and after the Civil War; it persisted as late as 1900, when the first dozen or so of the modern battleships still bore the qualification "coast-line" in their official designations.

Only in the 1890s was the true emergence of the navy's primary (and modern) role advocated by the writings of Alfred Thayer MAHAN and nurtured by President Theodore

ROOSEVELT. The latter proclaimed that protection of the coasts required fortifications to leave the navy "footloose to search out and destroy the enemy's fleet . . . the only function that can justify the fleet's existence."

Coast-defense naval vessels continued to be projected for yet another decade, however, and (unsuccessful) proposals were made to shift shore-mounted coastal artillery from the army to the navy, as some European nations had done. But from this point on, the U.S. Navy grew in a new direction, becoming the nation's unencumbered instrument of power at sea. Yet to the very eve of U.S. entry into World War II the fleet continued to be identified popularly as the nation's "first line of defense," while the army's Coast Artillery Corps was often referred to as "the navy's goal-keeper."

Even the Army's Air Service and Air Corps, the predecessors of today's U.S. Air Force, pushed "coast defense" between the world wars as a nominal basis for heavy bomber procurement. Brigadier General William "Billy" MITCHELL's post–World War I test bombings of naval vessels were conducted to validate aerial bombardment (at least publicly) as a viable coast-defense technique. Some claim, inaccurately, that the B-17's popular designation of "Flying Fortress" derived from the plane's original intended employment as a coast-defense weapon. (Actually, the name was bestowed the day after the plane's first public rollout at the Boeing plant, by an exuberant Seattle newspaperman, awed by the bomber's bristling array of defensive machine guns. Only later was the coast-defense connotation of the name assumed for public discourse and procurement arguments before Congress.)

While naval and air power would appear to extend security far beyond that provided by the traditional coastal fortifications, the value of defense by such offshore mobile forces was in fact limited by a variety of limiting factors, such as the vagaries of weather, which seriously complicated the locating and targeting of hostile ships. Permanently sited defenses, in contrast, provided relatively reliable protection for a limited number of small areas, but these were the most significant coastal points—river entrances, naval bases, and seaports—where much of the nation's population resided.

In reality, true coast defense by a nation with such extensive shorelines was never a realistic possibility, despite the occasional claims of naval, air, or—within the army itself—mobile coast artillery enthusiasts. Like contemporary European generals, Americans understood the 18th-century military wisdom: "It is impossible to protect every point; all that can be done is to protect the most important positions," and Frederick the Great's dictum, "He who would defend everything defends nothing." The military professionals of the United States never had the resources or the narrowness of vision that produced Adolf Hitler's "Atlantic Wall." It was, on the whole, the public, Congress, and occasional presidents who have believed such a defense to be possible.

Well into the 20th century Americans possessed an aversion to large permanent military forces and sought safety by means perceived both by its own citizens and by other nations as patently nonaggressive. Seacoast fortification offered an economical mode of protection completely consistent with that tradition, which was perhaps best articulated only in the late 20th century as "nonprovocative" defense. It was this form of military investment (essentially deterrence) that, more than any other, typified the American defense orientation for the century and a half from the 1790s until World War II. The commitment to this type of defense at the end of the 19th century, when it peaked within the American military establishment, was later characterized as almost a substitute for military policy.

Thus, when embarking in 1794 on the small system of forts at a number of coastal locations between the Canadian border and Georgia's St. Marys River, the military planners understood that they were building a system not of coast defense but of harbor defense, the latter term not being officially adopted until the early 20th century. In any event, this initial effort produced a modest body of mainly earthwork defenses armed with a few smoothbore, cast-iron cannon that could project a defensive perimeter of nearly a mile. Within a decade or so these perishable works were modified into or replaced by more durable structures, some of masonry, that survive to the present.

After of the War of 1812 and the BURNING OF WASHINGTON the first effort to erect a permanent body of durable coastal forts was undertaken. Far larger than the works of the earlier efforts, these were impressive structures comparable to those of major European powers. Their armament was not appreciably advanced over that of 1800, but the guns were somewhat improved and certainly more numerous. In the largest works of this period, known as the American Third System, 200–300 cannon pointed out through or over brick or stone walls on up to four levels. Examples are Forts Monroe, Sumter, Paulaki, and Pickens.

The Civil War led to fundamental changes in both forts and artillery. The massive structures erected between 1815 and 1860, while still reasonably immune to gunfire from ships, proved during the war to be disastrously vulnerable to guns on land, whose more precise fire could be concentrated against masonry. More primitive types of fortification, such as low earthworks and sand revetments, proved much more useful and easily repairable than did high masonry walls.

Defense construction slowed after the war, and in the early 1870s it was suspended altogether for about 15 years. The same period, however, witnessed a remarkable surge in the development of artillery, particularly the heaviest types of guns, those meant for naval vessels and permanent fortifications. Included in the development were several innovations: the large-scale use of steel in guns, which allowed them to be lengthened significantly and rifled; the perfection of workable breech-loading; and the introduction of far more effective propellent powders. This combination represented in a short period the greatest advance in artillery between its invention in the 14th century and the appearance of nuclear projectiles in the mid-20th century.

By the late 1880s an entire new generation of essentially modern armament had been designed and tested and was ready for production. Based on this advanced weaponry, an enormous new program of harbor defense fortification was undertaken in the early 1890s. Within about 15 years it produced the most powerful and extensive coast artillery system in the world. Protected by low-profile concrete emplacements behind many feet of earth, hundreds of guns and rifled mortars of calibers between three and 12 inches, aimed by elaborate fire control systems and supported by shore-controlled harbor-entrance mines, protected more than two dozen coastal locations, from Portland, Maine, to Galveston, Texas, and from San Diego, California, to Puget Sound, Washington. Decades later, the American emphasis on this particular kind of protection was described as having grown virtually into an obsession.

The acquisition of territories in Hawaii, the Philippine Islands, and Panama at the turn of the century led to an additional increment of works between roughly 1908 and 1916. Far less grandiose than the preceding program, it introduced yet more powerful armaments, which reduced the number of weapons required at a given site. During World War I yet another modest generation of defenses was developed, not for reasons directly related to the war but mainly in response to technical improvements in naval weaponry. Not only had ships' gun ranges increased but also their firing angles; "plunging fire" had largely nullified the protective characteristics of most existing coast artillery emplacements. The new defenses, therefore, consisted of widely spaced, long-range guns.

In the 1920s and 1930s the threat of air attack against coastal defenses imposed further protective demands, which were met in the late 1930s by emplacement designs that included heavy overhead protection for, as well as increased spacing between, the new and extremely powerful guns of the last generation of American harbor defenses, constructed between 1937 and 1944. This little-known program was, in fact, quite extensive, comprising nearly two dozen twin-gun batteries of 16-inch naval guns with a 25-mile range, and hundreds of lesser weapons ranging in caliber from 90 mm to 12 inches.

The World War II armament was removed in the late 1940s, and the army's coast artillery branch was finally eliminated in 1950, ending a century and a half of an ancient form of security. Coastal defense became part of a much broader concept of "continental defense," based on the technology of the second half of the 20th century and its COLD WAR missiles, intercontinental bombers, and nuclear submarines. Only faint traces remain of what had once been the very essence of American security, the belief that the right technology in the right locations could forestall danger from abroad—a notion that still echoes occasionally in such proposals, for example, as the Star Wars missile defense shield of the 1980s or its more recent expression at the beginning of the 21st century.

See also AIRCRAFT; ARTILLERY; NAVAL ORDNANCE.

Further reading: Browning, Robert S., III. *Two If by Sea: The Development of American Coastal Defense Policy.* Westport, Conn.: Greenwood, 1983; Clary, David A. *Fortress America: The Corps of Engineers, Hampton Roads, and United States Coastal Defense.* Charlottesville: University Press of Virginia, 1990; Lewis, Emanuel Raymond. *Seacoast Fortifications of the United States: An Introductory History.* Washington, D.C.: Smithsonian Institution Press, 1970; Weigley, Russell F. *Towards an American Army.* New York: Columbia University Press, 1962.

— Emanuel Ray Lewis

Coast Guard, U.S. *U.S. armed service responsible for maritime law enforcement, marine safety and security, maritime search and rescue, and maintenance of aids to navigation*

The U.S. Coast Guard, formed with the combination of the Revenue Cutter Service and Life-Saving Service in 1915, has a unique national-security role, spanning military and civil spheres of activity. A military organization under the jurisdiction of the Department of Transportation and before 1 April 1967 the Treasury Department, the Coast Guard and its predecessors have fought in every American conflict since 1790.

Congress created the Revenue Cutter Service on 4 August 1790 at the behest of the secretary of the treasury, Alexander HAMILTON. He wanted a maritime service to help suppress smuggling and aid in the collection of customs revenues. From its creation, the Revenue Cutter Service was a multimission service. In addition to its customs responsibilities, the service cooperated with the Lighthouse Service, assisted mariners in distress, and regularly participated in naval operations. The Revenue Cutter Service was the nation's only naval establishment until the creation of the Navy Department (1798), and it played an important role in the building of the newly reestablished navy.

The Revenue Cutter Service saw extensive action in the 1798–1800 QUASI-WAR with France. Cruising in company with naval vessels, eight cutters helped patrol the

Coast Guardsmen on the deck of the U.S. Coast Guard cutter *Spencer* watch the explosion of depth charges against a German submarine trying to penetrate a convoy, 17 April 1943   *(National Archives)*

eastern seaboard of the young nation. Revenue cutters were credited with capturing 15 of the 39 French warships taken during the Quasi-War and with assisting with the capture of five others. The service emerged from the war with a fleet of 15 cutters and a firm place in the nation's growing naval establishment.

During the WAR OF 1812, nine cutters served with the navy and saw their greatest success in single-ship actions. Among highlights were the capture of the brig *William Blake* by the USRC *Gallatin* in 1812 and the capture of British privateer *Dart* by the cutter *Vigilant* near Block Island in October 1813. Even in defeat the revenue cutters fought bravely, as when the cutter *Surveyor* was taken by the much larger *Narcissus*, a British frigate, at the mouth of the York River in June 1813.

After the War of 1812 the Revenue Cutter Service continued to collect customs duties, but it expanded its operations in several areas. In cooperation with the navy, the service worked to eradicate piracy in American waters.

Regular winter cruising began in the 1830s to promote commerce by providing assistance to vessels in distress. In 1832 President Andrew JACKSON sent five cutters to Charleston, South Carolina, during the nullification crisis. The shallow-draft cutters and their cuttermen also proved to be valuable assets afloat and ashore in the Second SEMINOLE WAR.

The 1846–48 MEXICAN-AMERICAN WAR brought the Revenue Cutter Service more wartime service and expanded responsibility. During the conflict cutters fought alongside the navy, delivered supplies, carried dispatches, and escorted merchantmen, in addition to performed their normal duties. The cutters *Forward* and *McLane* participated in Commodore Matthew C. PERRY's Tabasco River expedition in autumn 1846. By war's end, heavy use had left half of the cutter fleet unserviceable, with only eight cutters ready for operations and six under construction. The war also added the long Pacific coast to the service's already immense responsibilities.

The Revenue Cutter Service performed both combat and support missions during the CIVIL WAR but on a much larger scale than in previous conflicts. The most remarkable of the service's vessels in the war was the auxiliary steam cutter *Harriet Lane.* It fired the war's first shot at sea near Fort Sumter in April 1861 and then took part in Commodore Silas Stringham's naval operations at Hatteras Inlet and served as Commander David D. PORTER's flagship in the Battle of NEW ORLEANS. A Confederate boarding party took it at Galveston on 1 January 1863. The cutter *Miami* carried President Abraham LINCOLN, Secretary of War Edwin M. STANTON, and Treasury Secretary Salmon P. Chase to Fortress Monroe and around Hampton Roads during the Peninsula campaign. The ironclad USRC *Naugatuck,* an experimental semisubmersible, fought with the Union flotilla in the York and James Rivers. Other cutters served as part of the Union blockading squadrons and fought against Confederate commerce raiders. The service's customs work was even more important during wartime, as the Morrill Tariff nearly tripled revenue collected by 1864.

In 1869 the Treasury Department joined the Revenue Cutter Service and the federally funded lifesaving stations of the Revenue Marine Bureau. Sumner I. Kimball, Revenue Marine chief from 1871 to 1878, modernized the administration of the two services and then served as superintendent of the newly named and independent U.S. Life-Saving Service from 1878 to 1915. During the 1870s and 1880s, the Revenue Cutter Service saw expanded operational responsibilities. After the purchase of Alaska in 1867, cutters served as the federal government's main presence in Alaska, upholding the law, providing humanitarian assistance, and exploring the vast new territory.

During the 1898 SPANISH-AMERICAN WAR, the Revenue Cutter Service cruised with the navy in the Atlantic and Pacific. The USRC *McCulloch* served with Commodore George DEWEY's squadron in the Battle of MANILA BAY. At Cardenas Bay, Cuba, the cutter *Hudson* towed the disabled torpedo boat USS *Winslow* from under the guns of Spanish shore batteries. In recognition for his intrepid leadership, the *Hudson*'s commanding officer, Lieutenant Frank H. Newcomb, received the only gold medal awarded by Congress during the war. Other cutters served in blockading fleets in both the Pacific and Caribbean and in a variety of other support roles.

An effort to disestablish the Revenue Cutter Service led to its combination with the Life-Saving Service and the creation of the Coast Guard in 1915. The newly created Coast Guard became one of the four armed forces of the United States, serving under the Treasury Department during peacetime and in the Navy Department during wartime or at the direction of the president. In April 1917

the United States declared war on Germany, and the service transferred to the navy.

During World War I the Coast Guard contributed large cutters to antisubmarine and escort efforts in the North Atlantic, assumed port safety and security missions, and assisted in training the expanding Navy while maintaining its own peacetime responsibilities. After the 1917 explosion of the ammunition-laden freighter *Mont Blanc* at Halifax, Nova Scotia, the Coast Guard assigned a captain of the port to New York, Philadelphia, Norfolk, and the Sault Ste. Marie. Coast Guardsmen ensured safe loading and unloading of explosives and implemented vessel traffic schemes to minimize the risk of collision in these critical ports. This established the Coast Guard as the lead federal agency in domestic marine safety and security.

In August 1918, Keeper John A. Midgett and Station Chicamacomico, North Carolina, saved 42 crewmen from the British tanker *Mirlo,* which a German U-boat had torpedoed in heavy seas near Cape Hatteras. Congress awarded Midgett and his crew the Gold Lifesaving Medal for their heroic efforts. The war ended on a tragic note for the Coast Guard when the cutter *Tampa* sank near Milford Haven, Wales, on 26 September 1918. She was escorting a convoy into Bristol Channel when struck by a U-boat torpedo. The loss of *Tampa*'s 115 crewmen was the U.S. Navy's greatest loss of life caused by enemy action in the war.

During the 1920s and early 1930s, restored to the Treasury Department, the Coast Guard played a prominent role in the fight against Prohibition-era smuggling. The late 1930s and early 1940s saw the expansion of the Coast Guard in terms of missions, ships, and personnel. The Lighthouse Service joined the Coast Guard on 1 July 1939, and the Bureau of Marine Inspection transferred to the service in 1942, strengthening the marine-safety mission. As World War II approached, the service began to prepare its 19,000 men and its cutter fleet for war. On 1 November 1941 President Franklin ROOSEVELT ordered the Coast Guard again transferred to the Navy Department.

During World War II the Coast Guard saw worldwide action, manning destroyers, transports, and auxiliary vessels as well as cutters and patrol boats. In September 1941, before the United States entered the war, the USCGC *Northland* seized a German weather station and its supporting trawler on the Greenland coast. The service sank 12 U-boats and rescued more than 1,000 Allied sailors on North Atlantic escort duty. The Coast Guard applied its small-boat-handling skills to manning landing ships and craft during all the major amphibious assaults of the war. It also trained others for this dangerous and difficult duty. In this role, Signalman First Class Douglas A. Munro led a group of landing craft in the evacuation of marines near Matanikau on GUADALCANAL in September 1942. For his actions, Munro posthumously earned the Medal of Honor. Sixty 83-foot Coast Guard patrol boats assigned to search and rescue during the NORMANDY INVASION rescued more than 1,500 soldiers whose landing craft had been destroyed on D day.

At home, Coast Guard captains of the port oversaw marine safety and security. Search-and-rescue stations and a wartime beach patrol conducted coastal surveillance for enemy submarines and espionage activity. Cutters, small boats, and aircraft played important roles in antisubmarine and rescue efforts in the western Atlantic. The Coast Guard rescued 1,500 sailors from vessels torpedoed along the U.S. Atlantic coast. As commandant of the Coast Guard, Admiral Russell R. Waesche piloted the service through the war and oversaw the enlistment of women and African Americans. Led by Captain Dorothy C. Stratton, the COAST GUARD WOMEN'S RESERVE, better known as the SPARs, played an important support role during the war. During the war more than 230,000 men and 10,000 women served in the Coast Guard. The skill and bravery of these Coast Guardsmen constituted the service's major contribution to victory.

After World War II the Coast Guard demobilized and refocused on its demanding peacetime missions. The COLD WAR, however, ensured that the military roles of the service would continue to be important. To guard against Soviet espionage, the service permanently implemented many port security measures taken during World War II. The service extended LORAN (long-range aid to navigation) coverage and established search and rescue detachments in the western Pacific to support the 1950–53 KOREAN WAR, although no big cutters took part in the action.

The Coast Guard had a greatly expanded role during the VIETNAM WAR. Twenty-six 82-foot cutters and 30 large cutters participated in Operation MARKET TIME. This joint navy–Coast Guard operation worked to stop coastal resupply of the People's Army of Vietnam and Vietcong units operating in South Vietnam. Based out of Da Nang, Vung Tau, and An Thoi, the 82-footers conducted tens of thousands of boardings and claimed the destruction of more than 2,000 vessels from 1965 to 1970. Both the 82-footers and larger cutters earned a solid reputation for their precise naval gunfire support to army and marine units operating close to the coast. The Republic of Vietnam took control of the last two 82-footers in August 1970 as a part of the Vietnamization program. The Coast Guard also took overseas its marine safety and security expertise, supervising the unloading of explosives in South Vietnamese ports and maintaining aids to navigation along Vietnam's extensive coastline.

During the 1980s the Coast Guard worked to define its role in U.S. defense plans. The service's deployable port-security units worked with the joint navy–Coast Guard harbor defense command to provide waterside security and limited shore-based protection in seaports of debarkation. These Coast Guard forces served in Saudi Arabia and Bahrain during OPERATIONS DESERT SHIELD and DESERT STORM and during OPERATION Uphold Democracy in Haiti in late 1994. Coast Guard law enforcement detachments also demonstrated their utility during the Persian Gulf War by boarding vessels to enforce United Nations economic sanctions against Iraq. These detachments served similarly in the Adriatic during late 1990s conflicts in the Balkans. Larger cutters continue to sail with the navy and to serve as representatives of U.S. interests in areas where the presence of a haze-gray warship would be objectionable. The Coast Guard also plays an important role in training the navies and coast guards of smaller nations around the globe.

See also NAVY, U.S.; CIVIL WAR, NAVAL OVERVIEW; WAR OF 1812, NAVAL OVERVIEW; WORLD WAR I, U.S. INVOLVEMENT; WORLD WAR II, U.S. INVOLVEMENT, EUROPE; WORLD WAR II, U.S. INVOLVEMENT, PACIFIC.

Further reading: Johnson, Robert Erwin. *Guardians of the Sea: History of the United States Coast Guard, 1915 to the Present.* Annapolis, Md.: Naval Institute Press, 1987; King, Irving H. *The Coast Guard under Sail: The U.S. Revenue Cutter Service, 1789–1865.* Annapolis, Md.: Naval Institute Press, 1989; Larzelere, Alex. *The Coast Guard at War: Vietnam, 1965–1975.* Annapolis, Md.: Naval Institute Press, 1997.

— Thomas J. Stuhlreyer

Coast Guard Women's Reserve (SPARs) *World War II Women's Reserve of the U.S. Coast Guard*

On 23 November 1942, Public Law 773 established the Coast Guard Women's Reserve. The nucleus came from the navy; Dorothy C. STRATTON, promoted to lieutenant commander, was its director. She was joined by 14 other officers and 153 enlisted women. Stratton named the women's reserve SPARs, from the COAST GUARD motto Semper Paratus (Always Ready).

The navy ties remained strong; the Coast Guard copied its uniform, substituting Coast Guard insignia. The navy initially trained all SPARs, but in 1943 the Coast Guard set up enlisted training at Palm Beach, Florida, in March and officers training at New London, Connecticut, in July.

Most enlisted SPARs served as yeomen, storekeepers, and pharmacist's mates, but by war's end they had entered other fields. They became parachute riggers, radiomen, air control operators, photographers, and gunner's mates, among other occupational specialties. The women officers often filled payroll and supply billets at major Coast Guard stations, including in Hawaii and Alaska.

The work of one group of SPARs was highly classified. As the German navy haunted the U.S. coastline and dimouts and blackouts became necessary, scientists developed LORAN (long-range aid to navigation), an electronic system that enabled planes and ships to fix their positions under all weather conditions without lighted aids. SPARs manned its monitoring stations. While most stations had only a few women, the Cape Cod LORAN station, at Chatham, Massachusetts, was staffed totally by SPARs.

By mid-1946 all SPARs had been discharged. A 1948 law that provided for women in the other armed forces did not apply to them; not until 1949 were women allowed back in the Coast Guard. About 200 former SPARs returned to serve during the KOREAN WAR.

See also WOMEN IN THE MILITARY.

Further reading: Johnson, Robert E. *Guardian of the Sea: History of the United States Coast Guard, 1915 to the Present.* Annapolis, Md.: Naval Institute Press, 1987; Thomson, Robin J. *The Coast Guard and the Women's Reserve in World War II.* Washington, D.C.: U.S. Coast Guard, 1992; Tilley, John A. *A History of Women in the Coast Guard.* Washington, D.C.: U.S. Coast Guard, 1996.

— Marie-Beth Hall

Cobra, Operation (25–31 July 1944) *American World War II offensive in Europe that led to the Allied breakout from the Normandy beachhead and the decisive defeat of German forces in France*

This successful American operation ended weeks of sluggish fighting and ushered in a mobile phase of the struggle in northwest Europe.

After the Allies gained a lodgment at NORMANDY on 6 June 1944, they struggled against determined German resistance and difficult terrain, especially numerous hedgerows, called *bocage,* that gave the German defenders ready-made defensive positions. British and Canadian forces on the Allied left flank fought to capture Caen, while the Americans clawed their way toward the port of Cherbourg. The Americans took Cherbourg on 27 June, but their renewed attacks thereafter progressed slowly in the bocage. British and Canadian pressure at Caen had drawn 14 German divisions (six of them panzer) to the Allied left flank. The Americans faced 11 divisions (two panzer), which had been sharply worn down by constant fighting.

The commander of the American First Army, Lieutenant General Omar N. BRADLEY, was the main architect of Cobra. Bradley planned to use Allied airpower to devastate a narrow sector of the German line just northwest of St. Lô. This "carpet bombing" was meant to annihilate the German defenders and provide a clear path for the American advance. Once through the German line, Bradley hoped, he would push forward mobile forces and exploit the attack around the German left flank.

Bradley assigned three corps to the offensive. The main American attack force, VII Corps, under Major General J. Lawton COLLINS, would make the initial penetration. On its right, Major General Troy H. MIDDLETON's VIII Corps was to exploit the advance by trapping German forces between the two American corps. Major General Charles H. Corlett's XIX Corps had the mission of protecting the American breakout from German counterattacks on the eastern flank.

The German defenders were tough veterans who had suffered heavily in the bocage. Field Marshal Hans Gunther von Kluge was the overall German commander in France, but he also assumed command of Army Group B when Field Marshal Erwin Rommel was wounded on 17 July. The German Seventh Army held the sector facing the brunt of the Cobra offensive.

Bradley wanted to launch Cobra on 21 July, but bad weather postponed the attack. On 24 July a sudden storm again delayed the offensive. Some aircraft could not be recalled, and a portion of their bombs hit American forces marshaled for the attack. The next day, the air bombardment began in earnest, but again some bombs fell on friendly forces, killing more Americans including, visiting Lieutenant General Lesley J. MCNAIR. Despite the miscues, Allied heavy bombers dropped 3,300 tons of high-explosive and fragmentation bombs, medium bombers added 137 tons of high explosives and 4,000 260-pound fragmentation bombs, and fighter bombers contributed 212 tons of bombs.

Initially, the air attack appeared to have achieved only limited results. On 25 July Collins's VII Corps found the Germans stunned but determined to resist. Despite tough going, Collins correctly judged that the German were vulnerable, and he committed two of his three mobile columns to the fight. On 26 July, one of these, the motorized 1st Infantry Division made steady, if not spectacular, progress. Similarly, the 2d Armored Division recorded mixed success. Then, on 27 July, the 2d Armored Division broke clear through the German lines at Saint Gilles.

The emerging success of the VII Corps undermined German resistance in front of the VIII Corps. Middleton accelerated his advance on the American right flank and was soon progressing faster than VII Corps. On 27 July Kluge transferred two panzer divisions to the Seventh Army area, but it was too late. On 28 and 29 July, with surprising suddenness, German resistance in front of the VII and VIII Corps collapsed. For several days the Germans attempted to avoid entrapment near Coutances, but tactical air support directed by Major General Elwood R. "Pete" QUESADA devastated the retreating Germans. The remnants of the German force veered to the east and were shattered by advancing VII and XIX Corps armor.

On 30 July the 6th Armored Division took Granville, and the 4th Armored Division took Avranches. The capture of the latter town separated the German left flank from the Gulf of St. Malo and paved the way for a rapid Allied advance through France.

Operation Cobra was one of the great Allied successes of World War II. Bolstered by General Bernard Montgomery's thrust on Caen, Bradley had provided the planning and inspiration for the breakout. Additionally, Collins had executed the attack with skill and verve, turning the concept of blitzkrieg back on its German originators.

See also BRERETON, LOUIS H.; PATTON, GEORGE S.

Further reading: Blumenson, Martin. *United States Army in World War II: European Theater of Operations: Breakout and Pursuit.* Washington, D.C.: Office of the Chief of Military History, 1961; Carafano, James J. *After D-Day: Operation Cobra and the Normandy Breakout.* Boulder, Colo.: Lynne Rienner, 2000; D'Este, Carlo. *Decision in Normandy.* London: William Collins Sons, 1983; Hasting, Max. *Overlord: D-Day and the Battle for Normandy 1944.* London: Michael Joseph, 1984; Weigley, Russell F. *Eisenhower's Lieutenants: The Campaigns of France and Germany, 1944–1945.* Bloomington: Indiana University Press, 1981.

— Curtis S. King

Cochise (ca. 1810–1874) *Chiricahua Apache chief*
Although he was one of America's most famous Native American leaders, little is known about Cochise prior to the 1860s. Estimates of his birthdate range from the 1790s to the 1830s, but it was likely around 1810 in the Chiricahua Mountains of southeastern Arizona. The Chiricahua frequently raided Mexican settlements of northern Sonora, but when much of the area became part of the United States, the Apache managed to accommodate most Anglo-American encroachment until 1861, by which time Cochise had emerged as chief of the Chiricahua.

In February 1861 Cochise responded to a request by U.S. Army lieutenant George Bascom for a meeting at Apache Pass. Bascom wrongly accused Cochise of kidnapping a boy during a raid on a local ranch. Cochise maintained his innocence, but Bascom announced that he would be held until the child was returned. Cochise escaped, but Bascom also had some of his relatives hostages, and violence soon erupted. Cochise captured several Mexicans and four Anglos, killing the Mexicans and offering the Anglos in return for his relatives held by Bascom. Bascom refused to trade without the boy, which led Cochise to torture and kill his captives. In retribution Bascom hanged

Cochise's brother and two nephews. This began an 11-year war between the Chiricahua and the United States.

Joined by Mangas Coloradas, a fellow Apache chief and father of his wife, Cochise and his followers struck ranches, mines, stages, and military patrols, killing dozens of people and devastating the area. In July 1862 they attacked Brigadier General James Carleton's sizable force at Apache Pass but were repulsed with artillery fire. In January 1863 the army captured Mangas Coloradas, who reportedly was killed trying to escape. Cochise only intensified his efforts. By the early 1870s casualties from Cochise's relentless campaigning reached into the hundreds; property damage and lost commerce brought further misery.

In 1872 the frustrated federal government sought peace. Cochise agreed to meet with Brigadier General Oliver O. HOWARD and Indian agent Thomas Jeffords, who arranged for the Apache to choose a new reservation in the Chiricahua Mountains. Cochise abided by the agreement and moved onto the reservation, where he remained until his death on 8 June 1874. He was buried secretly in the rocks of the forbidding mountains.

See also AMERICAN INDIAN WARS, OVERVIEW; APACHE WARS; GERONIMO; INDIAN WARFARE.

Further reading: Sweeney, Edwin R. *Cochise: Chiricahua Apache Chief.* Norman: University of Oklahoma Press, 1991; Utley, Robert M. *Frontier Regulars: The United States Army and the Indian, 1866–1891.* New York: Macmillan, 1973; Worcester, Donald E. *The Apaches: Eagles of the Southwest.* Norman: University of Oklahoma Press, 1979.

— Roger W. Caraway

Cochran, Jacqueline (1910–1980) *American aviator and business executive*
Born probably in 1910, at Pensacola, Florida, Jacqueline Cochran was orphaned young and brought up by foster parents, going to work at an early age. In 1932 she earned her pilot's license, entering her first air race in 1934. She married Floyd Odlum, a wealthy businessman in 1936. Two years later she became the first woman to win the Bendix Transcontinental Trophy Race.

When World War II began, Cochran was determined to do her part. In 1941 she flew a bomber across the Atlantic, after which she recruited 25 women pilots to fly for the British Air Transport Auxiliary, ferrying combat aircraft within the United Kingdom. Upon her return to the United States, she organized, with the aid of Army Air Forces general Henry H. ARNOLD, women pilots for a variety of flying jobs. This group merged with the Women's Auxiliary Ferrying Squadron to become the Women's Airforce Service Pilots, with Cochran as its leader. She was awarded the Distinguished Service Medal in 1945.

Cochran continued to fly after the war, becoming the first woman to break the sound barrier in 1953 and to launch from and land on an aircraft carrier in 1960. In 1964 she established a new world speed record, flying an F-104 at 1,429.2 mph. Cochran received more than 200 flying awards and trophies. In 1970 the U.S. Air Force awarded her the Legion of Merit. Appointed chair of the National Aeronautic Commission, she was enshrined in the Aviation Hall of Fame in 1971, the first living woman so honored. At the time of her death in India on 9 August 1980, Cochran held more speed, altitude, and distance records than any other pilot.

See also WOMEN AIRFORCE SERVICE PILOTS; WOMEN IN THE MILITARY.

Further reading: Cochran, Jacqueline, and Maryann Bucknum Brinley. *Jackie Cochran: An Autobiography.* New York: Bantam Books, 1987; Cochran, Jacqueline, with Floyd Odum. *The Stars at Noon.* New York: Arno, 1980; Holm, Jeanne M., ed. *In Defense of a Nation.* Washington, D.C.: Military Women's Press, 1998; Smith, Elizabeth S. *Coming Out Right: The Story of Jacqueline Cochran, the First Woman Aviator to Break the Sound Barrier.* New York: Walker, 1991.

— Marie-Beth Hall

Cold Harbor, Battle of (30 May–12 June 1864)
Civil War battle between Union forces under Lieutenant General Ulysses S. Grant and Confederate forces under General Robert E. Lee during the Overland Campaign in Virginia

Near the end of May, Ulysses S. GRANT found his move on Richmond blocked at the North Anna River. He ordered Major General George G. MEADE's Army of the Potomac to advance around Robert E. LEE's right flank.

Dead being reburied after the Battle of Cold Harbor   *(U.S. Army Military History Institute)*

Lee anticipated the Union move and positioned his forces in entrenchments on the Totopotomoy River on 29 May.

When the Union army paused, Lee saw an opportunity to hit the isolated Federal left flank. Lieutenant General Jubal A. EARLY's Confederate II Corps struck Major General Governeur K. WARREN's V Corps near Bethesda Church on 30 May, but the federals repulsed its attack.

Later that day Grant and Meade planned their next move—a shift farther to the south to take Cold Harbor, on Lee's right flank. Union cavalry under Major General Philip H. SHERIDAN was to seize Old Cold Harbor. Later, the Union VI Corps, supported by the newly arriving XVIII Corps, was to follow Sheridan and take New Cold Harbor, thus turning the Confederate flank.

Late on 31 May Sheridan's cavalry took Old Cold Harbor. For much of the next day he held the crossroads against Confederate attacks, until relieved by the VI Corps. However, confusion in the Union orders delayed the arrival of the XVIII Corps. Finally, on the evening of 1 June, both federal corps attacked. At heavy cost, they took the first line of the Confederate positions.

After the partial success of 1 June, Grant and Meade ordered Major General Winfield Scott HANCOCK's II Corps to make a night march to the Union left flank and join the VI and XVIII Corps in a morning attack on 2 June. Confusion over Hancock's route and the difficulties of moving at night delayed the II Corps and forced the Union leadership to postpone the attack. The delay allowed Lee time to transfer more troops to the threatened area and gave the Confederates time to improve their entrenchments.

Disadvantages not withstanding, an impatient Grant ordered the battle resumed. The Union attack on 3 June was a disaster. The only minor success came in the II Corps area, and even there the Confederates quickly retook their lost ground. The XVIII Corps attacked valiantly but was devastated before reaching the Confederate lines. The VI Corps barely advanced at all. The Federals suffered more than 6,000 casualties in their assaults.

After 3 June both sides continued to fortify their positions, and the battlefield took on the appearance of World War I trench lines. Grant used the next week to put in motion a new plan to cross the James River and approach Richmond from the south via PETERSBURG. The move began on 12 June, with the Union troops withdrawing in stages. By nightfall, only a rear guard faced the Confederates.

The assaults at Cold Harbor had been costly and bitter setbacks for the Army of the Potomac, and the battle left Lee's Army of Northern Virginia firmly astride Grant's path to Richmond. Nonetheless, Grant retained the initiative, and he developed a new plan to keep pressure on Lee's depleted forces. Cold Harbor provided further proof that Grant would continue at all costs.

See also CIVIL WAR, LAND OVERVIEW; OVERLAND CAMPAIGN; PETERSBURG, SIEGE OF.

Further reading: Baltz, Louis J. *The Battle of Cold Harbor, May 27–June 13, 1864.* Lynchburg, Va.: H. E. Howard, 1994; Furgurson, Ernest B. *Not War but Murder: Cold Harbor 1864.* New York: Knopf 2000; Maney, R. Wayne. *Marching to Cold Harbor: Victory and Failure, 1864.* Shippensburg, Pa.: White Mane, 1995; Trudeau, Noah Andre. *Bloody Roads South: The Wilderness to Cold Harbor, May–June 1864.* Boston: Little, Brown, 1989.
— Curtis S. King

cold war (1945–1990) *The global competition between the United States, the Soviet Union, and their respective allies that dominated international politics from 1945 to 1990*

Traditional definitions of military history need to be redefined when it comes to the cold war. It was fought not only by generals and soldiers but also by diplomats and spies, dissidents and refugees. Its symbolic end was announced not by a defeated general standing before a surrender document but by citizens standing on the Berlin Wall. Its end could just as easily have been announced by the explosion of thermonuclear warheads over Moscow and Washington. Although a third world war did not follow the second, before the end of the cold war each superpower had waged war on proxies of the other, and there had even been numerous (if often secret) direct Soviet-American military clashes. Millions also died cold war–related deaths at the hands of their own repressive internal regimes in such places as the Soviet Union, China, and Cambodia. The cold war may never have become as "hot" as it might have, but it was a very real war nonetheless, and not without bloodshed.

The roots of the cold war may be traced back at least as far as the November 1917 Bolshevik revolution in Russia. Marxist ideology predicted that the formation of a major communist state would be met with unremitting hostility from the capitalist powers, a belief seemingly borne out by the U.S. intervention in RUSSIA following World War I. The increasingly repressive nature of the government established by Vladimir I. Lenin and his successor, Joseph Stalin, did little to decrease the isolation of the Soviet Union, and it was not until 1933 that the U.S. government formally recognized the USSR. Mutual distrust between the Soviet Union and the Western democracies turned to outright animosity following the Nazi-Soviet Non-Aggression Pact of August 1939 and the subsequent Soviet invasions of Poland, Finland, and the Baltic Republics.

After the June 1941 German invasion of the Soviet Union, there was relatively close cooperation between the

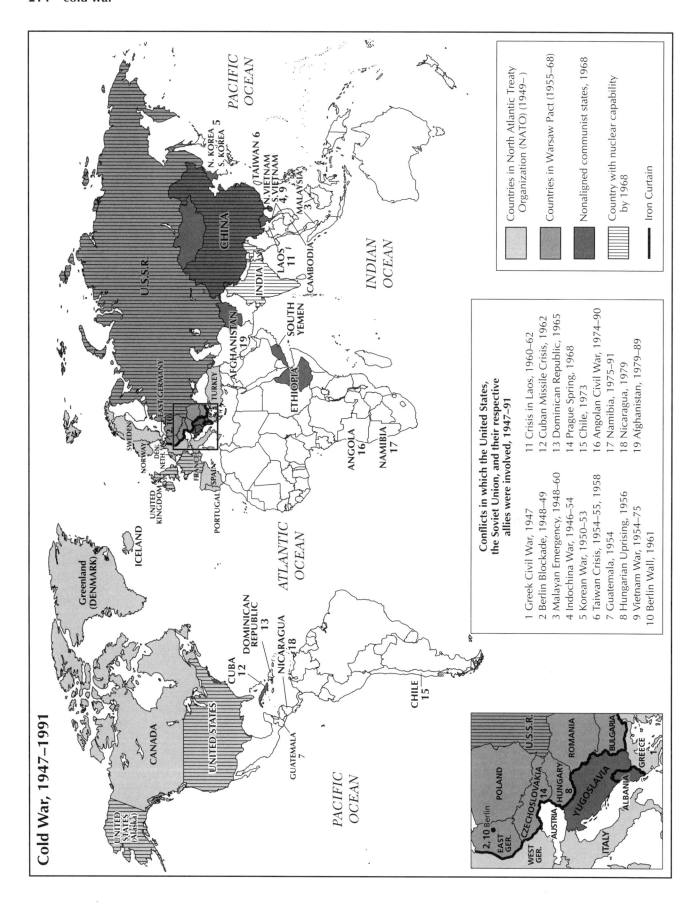

Cold War, 1947–1991

Countries in North Atlantic Treaty Organization (NATO) (1949–)

Countries in Warsaw Pact (1955–68)

Nonaligned communist states, 1968

Country with nuclear capability by 1968

Iron Curtain

Conflicts in which the United States, the Soviet Union, and their respective allies were involved, 1947–91

1 Greek Civil War, 1947
2 Berlin Blockade, 1948–49
3 Malayan Emergency, 1948–60
4 Indochina War, 1946–54
5 Korean War, 1950–53
6 Taiwan Crisis, 1954–55, 1958
7 Guatemala, 1954
8 Hungarian Uprising, 1956
9 Vietnam War, 1954–75
10 Berlin Wall, 1961
11 Crisis in Laos, 1960–62
12 Cuban Missile Crisis, 1962
13 Dominican Republic, 1965
14 Prague Spring, 1968
15 Chile, 1973
16 Angolan Civil War, 1974–90
17 Namibia, 1975–91
18 Nicaragua, 1979
19 Afghanistan, 1979–89

USSR and the other Allies for the balance of WORLD WAR II. Even during this period, however, mutual distrust remained a significant factor, especially regarding what the Soviets perceived as Western foot-dragging on the opening of a second front in France. Whether or not the U.S. decision to employ the ATOMIC BOMB over Hiroshima was intended in part to intimidate the Soviet Union, it was probably interpreted that way by Stalin.

At the end of the war, only two nations remained with the potential to fill the power vacuums left in Europe and Asia: the United States and the Soviet Union. Given this fact and the intense ideological differences between these two nations, some sort of postwar conflict seems in retrospect to have been likely, if not inevitable.

Contrary to the old saying that the United States always "wins the war and loses the peace," the settlement following World War II was very favorable to American interests. The Soviet Union may have lost 27 million people during the war, and another 5 million in an immediate postwar famine. U.S. deaths in the war came to 292,131. Not only was two-thirds of Germany controlled by the West, but both of the other two Axis Powers, Japan and Italy, were in American hands as well.

The Soviet Union initially showed a degree of restraint and allowed relatively free elections in several of the Eastern European nations, but by 1948, through a series of coups and political maneuvers, it had become clear that noncommunist governments would not be permitted in areas under Soviet control. Soviet threats against Turkey and the presence of a communist insurgency in Greece prompted the United States in March 1947 to issue the Truman Doctrine, promising aid and support to nations resisting "armed minorities" or "outside pressures." This policy of restraining perceived communist aggression by indirect means, dubbed "CONTAINMENT" by George F. Kennan, remained the basic American strategy throughout the cold war.

With the 1948 Marshall Plan Washington increased its already substantial financial aid to Western European nations, and the following year the United States committed itself to the military defense of Europe in the NORTH ATLANTIC TREATY ORGANIZATION (NATO). To supplement these foreign policy components of containment, the United States also reorganized and expanded its domestic national security bureaucracy. Through the 1947 National Security Act (and subsequent executive orders) the Joint Chiefs of Staff was officially recognized, and organizations such as the CENTRAL INTELLIGENCE AGENCY (CIA), the NATIONAL SECURITY AGENCY (NSA), and the National Security Council (NSC) were established.

These mechanisms for waging cold war were soon put to the test in a series of escalating crises that represented the darkest days of the cold war. In June 1948 the Soviet Union began the BERLIN BLOCKADE in an attempt to force the United States and its allies to evacuate the city, which had been under joint occupation deep inside the Soviet zone of Germany since the end of the war. In a public relations disaster for the Soviet Union, the city's population rallied around its Western "occupiers" as they sustained the city via an airlift; after 10 humiliating months the Soviet Union lifted its blockade.

Beginning in 1949 the cold war seemed to the West to take a dramatic turn for the worse, as communist forces under Mao Zedong triumphed in the Chinese civil war and the Soviet Union tested its first atomic bomb. When North Korea invaded South Korea in June 1950, the obvious analogy with divided Germany was alarming, to say the least. Direct Soviet-American military clashes had already taken place, with the first of the long history of Soviet attacks on American spy planes flying near (and sometimes within) Soviet airspace, and by late 1950 the bulk of the combat in the skies over North Korea was actually between American and Soviet pilots. General war appeared to many to be imminent. In accordance with a 1950 government study known as NSC-68, military spending by the United States tripled within the next year.

These foreign policy developments also combined with revelations about the tremendous success of Soviet ESPIONAGE AGAINST THE UNITED STATES to produce a period of domestic anticommunist hysteria, exemplified by congressional witch-hunts led by the likes of Senator Joseph McCarthy. By the early 1950s children in the United States were practicing seeking safety under their school desks during a nuclear attack, while their parents constructed backyard fallout shelters. The cold war now had a home front.

The KOREAN WAR did remain limited, however. It ended in an armistice during the slight relaxation of tensions that followed Stalin's death in March 1953. That year also saw a change of leadership in the United States, with the election of President Dwight D. EISENHOWER. His "NEW LOOK" military policy centered around reducing military spending on conventional forces by increasing reliance on NUCLEAR WEAPONS, PSYCHOLOGICAL WARFARE, and regional allies.

Containment was expanded into the developing world. The United States organized regional mutual defense organizations modeled on NATO, such as the Southeast Asia Treaty Organization (SEATO, 1954) and the Central [Asia] Treaty Organization (CENTO, 1959). Covert American interference in the Third World increased as well, including CIA involvement in coups in Iran (1953) and Guatemala (1954). This "hidden hand" approach contrasted sharply with the heavy-handed 1956 Soviet invasion of Hungary, which had predictable results with respect to world opinion. Soviet prestige took an unexpected upswing, however, following its first successful launch of an Earth satellite, *Sputnik,* in October 1957. This surprising Soviet advance in BALLISTIC MISSILE technology seemingly threatened to end U.S. dominance in the nuclear arms race, but American advances in technical INTELLIGENCE-collection capabilities, including the U-2 spy plane and the first reconnaissance satellites, showed by the early 1960s that if there was any "MISSILE GAP," it was in favor of the United States.

The late 1950s and early 1960s marked a second great period of danger in the cold war. In 1958 a new Soviet leader, Nikita Khrushchev, renewed pressure on the Western powers to leave Berlin, creating a prolonged international crisis that ended only three years later with the erection of what would become the greatest symbol of the cold war (and of Soviet skill in public relations), the Berlin Wall. The division of Germany, including Berlin, had finally become a settled matter, but only at the cost of the prolonged humiliation for the Warsaw Pact of having literally to fence in its own population to prevent its escape. President John F. KENNEDY took office in 1961, promising to replace the staid Eisenhower-era policy of "massive retaliation" with a strategy of "FLEXIBLE RESPONSE," thereby enabling him to, as he put it in his inaugural address, "support any friend" and "oppose any foe."

Kennedy's desire to "reinvigorate" the conduct of American foreign policy led to an increasing number of military and paramilitary entanglements around the world. The very first example of this new assertiveness, a CIA-supported invasion of Cuba at the BAY OF PIGS, begun under the previous administration, ended in disaster and furthered Khrushchev's determination to test the new American president. That test came the following year not in Berlin, where most had expected it, but with a secret Soviet attempt to place intermediate-range ballistic missiles in Cuba. Although the resulting CUBAN MISSILE CRISIS brought the world as close as it has ever come to nuclear war, in retrospect it may have been a blessing in disguise, as neither superpower would ever again show much stomach for nuclear "brinksmanship."

For this reason the 1962 Cuban missile crisis represents the turning point in the cold war. Within the next year the two superpowers took the first substantive steps toward reducing the threat of nuclear war, creating a direct "hot line" between their two capitals and finally signing a limited Nuclear Test Ban Treaty. The arms race continued throughout the 1960s, however, with Britain, France, and China all now members of the "nuclear club." By the 1970s, "mutually assured destruction" in an all-out nuclear war had become an obvious reality to both sides. The frequency and severity of direct crises between the superpowers lessened, replaced with a series of entanglements in peripheral areas. The most obvious and costly of these

poisonous interactions between the cold war and decolonization was the growing American military involvement in South Vietnam. Despite the presence of Soviet shipping in North Vietnamese harbors and Soviet military "technicians" in North Vietnam, maintaining and operating surface-to-air missile sites in direct action against American aircraft, U.S. policy makers consciously restrained their conduct in the VIETNAM WAR to avoid escalation with either the Soviet Union or China.

When areas of vital interest to either side were at stake—such as the unrest in Czechoslovakia in 1968 that resulted in a Soviet invasion of that country—caution between the superpowers prevented any crises of the scope and danger of those of the 1940s and 1950s. The greatest geopolitical shift of this period occurred in the late 1960s, with the violent Sino-Soviet split and the subsequent rapprochement between China and the United States, culminating in President Richard NIXON's 1972 visit to Beijing. The détente of this transitional era reduced Soviet-American tensions via arms control and other measures, and by the late 1970s the cold war seemed to have become, if not harmless, at least routine.

Progress on arms control and human rights within the Soviet Union remained slow, however. What remained of détente was shattered in 1979 by the Soviet invasion of Afghanistan. President Jimmy Carter announced that he had been wrong about the Soviet Union and proclaimed the need for greater "toughness," but in the 1980 presidential election, Ronald Reagan defeated him. Reagan took office calling for "rebuilding" of both the military and the pride of the United States. By 1983 the PROPAGANDA emanating from both sides was reaching a crescendo, with Reagan publicly referring to the Soviet Union as an "evil empire" and promising a dramatic new program to create a space-based defense against ballistic missiles, the Strategic Defense Initiative. Critics derided this as a *Star Wars* fantasy, but whether or not such a defense was technologically feasible, Reagan administration officials privately hoped it and other defense projects would spur the arms race to a level the Soviet economy could not match.

Other American foreign policy initiatives sought to ratchet up the economic and psychological pressure on the Soviet Union, such as by providing massive covert aid to the Mujahideen rebels in Afghanistan. The cold war in the developing world also intensified in places as disparate as Ethiopia, Angola, and Central America. In the latter especially, the United States provided military and economic aid to several extremely repressive right-wing regimes, all amid growing domestic fears of "another Vietnam." Soviet defectors reported that all of this provoked extreme anxiety at the highest levels of the Soviet leadership. In general, the early 1980s represented a renewal of the cold war to levels of tension unseen in two decades.

In the midst of this "second cold war" and a growing economic crisis in the Soviet Union, a leader of a new type took power in Moscow, Mikhail Gorbachev. Gorbachev embarked on an ambitious program to restructure the Soviet economy (*perestroika*) and accompanied it with an attempt to open Soviet society (*glasnost*). His purpose was to save a communist Soviet Union by reforming it; but instead the processes he unleashed spun out of his control and destroyed the Soviet Union. Gorbachev's "charm offensive" succeeded in convincing even such staunch cold warriors as Reagan and British prime minister Margaret Thatcher that the Soviet leader was sincere in his desire to end the cold war, but foreign policy successes could not prevent his domestic popularity from plummeting along with the Soviet economy.

Gorbachev informed the communist governments of Eastern Europe that the Soviet army would no longer use force to prop up their unpopular regimes, and in June 1989 free multiparty elections in Poland produced an unexpected victory for the anticommunist Solidarity movement. In November of that year an East German announcement that restrictions on travel to West Germany were to be lifted created an impromptu street party in Berlin, and within hours the world (private citizens and government policy makers alike) was watching in amazement as Germans from both sides of the wall literally danced on the physical remnants of the cold war. Within a year every communist government in Eastern Europe had fallen. Miraculously, the process was nearly bloodless.

Critics on the American right still worried that the abandonment of Eastern Europe might represent only a tactical withdrawal by the Soviet Union, but Gorbachev's rapid alignment with coalition powers against Iraq, a former Soviet client state, in 1990 demonstrated that the cold war had definitely ended. In a last-ditch effort to prevent most of the individual Soviet republics from proclaiming their independence, hard-liners in Moscow launched a coup against Gorbachev in August 1991; their failure ensured that the Soviet Union itself would not survive even as a formality. On Christmas Day, 1991, the Soviet flag was lowered over the Kremlin for the last time. The cold war crisis that had the potential to be the greatest of them all—the very dissolution of one of the two protagonists—proved instead to be almost anticlimactic.

The 1990s saw important but sporadic signs of increased openness with respect to historical records on the part of the American, Russian, and other governments around the world. Through the continuing efforts of such private organizations as the Cold War International History Project and the National Security Archive, historians continue today to learn much that is new about the cold war. Nevertheless, the cold war remains today the subject of intense historical controversy; the only thing that is certain

is that there are still many things historians do not know about it.

See also DEFENSE INTELLIGENCE AGENCY; GRENADA, INVASION OF; MILITARY-INDUSTRIAL COMPLEX; *PUEBLO*, USS; STRATEGIC AIR COMMAND; STRATEGIC DEFENSE; U-2 INCIDENT.

Further reading: Friedman, Norman. *The Fifty-Year War: Conflict and Strategy in the Cold War.* Annapolis, Md.: Naval Institute Press, 1999; Gaddis, John Lewis. *We Now Know: Rethinking Cold War History.* New York: Oxford University Press, 1997. LaFeber, Walter. *America, Russia, and the Cold War, 1945–1996.* 8th ed. New York: McGraw-Hill, 1997; McEnaney, Laura. *Civil Defense Begins at Home: Militarization Meets Everyday Life in the Fifties.* Princeton, N.J.: Princeton University Press, 2000; Miller, David. *The Cold War: A Military History.* New York: St. Martin's Press, 1998; Ross, Steven T. *American War Plans, 1945–1950: Strategies for Defeating the Soviet Union.* Portland, Ore.: Frank Cass, 1996; Schnabel, James F., and Robert J. Watson. *History of the Joint Chiefs of Staff. The Joint Chiefs of Staff and National Policy.* 7 vols. Washington, D.C.: Historical Division, Joint Chiefs of Staff, 1979–98; Zubok, Vladislav, and Constantine Pleshakov. *Inside the Kremlin's Cold War: From Stalin to Khrushchev.* Cambridge, Mass.: Harvard University Press, 1996.

— David Rezelman

Collins, J. Lawton (1896–1987) *U.S. Army general and diplomat*

Born on 1 May 1896 at New Orleans, Louisiana, Joseph Lawton Collins graduated from the U.S. Military Academy at WEST POINT in 1917 and was commissioned a second lieutenant. He missed combat in World War I but, promoted to captain, he served with occupation troops in Germany from 1919 to 1921. An instructor at West Point (1921–25) and Fort Benning (1925–31), he also served in the Philippines. Promoted major in 1932, he taught at the Army War College (1939–41).

After the U.S. entry into World War II, in 1942 Collins was promoted to first to brigadier general and then to major general. In December he commanded the U.S. Army's 25th Infantry Division on GUADALCANAL, relieving the 1st Marine Division there and clearing the island of Japanese. In January 1943 he led part of XIV Corps in driving the Japanese out of New Georgia.

In December 1943 Collins went to Britain to command VII Corps; he landed with it at Utah Beach in NORMANDY in June 1944. Known as an energetic and strong-willed commander, he drove his men hard to keep the Germans on the defensive, earning the nickname "Lightning Joe." His troops took Cherbourg on 24 June, closed the FALAISE Gap, crossed the Seine, and drove north into Belgium, where they captured Mons, Namur, and Liège. Collins participated in the counterattack and capture of Houfflalize during the December 1944–January 1945 Battle of the BULGE and crossed the Rhine at Remagen. Collins's troops drove through Germany, enveloped the Ruhr, and met the Soviet XXXVI Corps on the River Elbe.

Promoted to lieutenant general in April 1945, Collins was vice chief of staff of the army from 1947 to 1948. Advanced to full general in January 1948, Collins served as army chief of staff from 1949 to 1953. Following the de facto partition of Vietnam in 1954, Collins became prominently involved in the policy debate over U.S. support of Ngo Dinh Diem, the South Vietnamese premier, later president of the Republic of Vietnam. Collins initially urged that the United States withdraw support from Diem, whom Collins believed was incapable of leading South Vietnam. President Dwight D. EISENHOWER pledged to support Diem, however, and sent Collins to Vietnam as his personal representative, with the rank of ambassador, to aid the South Vietnamese government in establishing a military training program and agrarian reforms. When Diem refused to carry out these reforms, Collins again advised Eisenhower to withdraw U.S. support.

The State Department recommended a compromise, in which Diem would be retained as the titular head of state while real power would be in the hands of the Dai Viet party. Collins accepted this plan, but before it could be implemented Diem's forces crushed opposition religious sects that had plagued him. This, ironically, led to a reversal of U.S. policy to full support of Diem. Collins, who had come to symbolize American opposition to Diem, was soon replaced. He returned to Washington in 1955 and entered private business the next year. He died in Washington, D.C., on 12 September 1987.

See also OPERATION COBRA; VIETNAM WAR, COURSE OF; WORLD WAR II, U.S. INVOLVEMENT, EUROPE.

Further reading: Collins, J. Lawton. *Lightning Joe: An Autobiography.* Baton Rouge: Louisiana State University Press, 1979; Spector, Ronald H. *The U.S. Army in Vietnam: Advice and Support—The Early Years, 1941–1960.* Washington, D.C.: U.S. Army Center of Military History, 1983.

— James H. Willbanks

Colt, Samuel (1814–1862) *American arms inventor, developer, and manufacturer*
Born on 19 July 1814 near Hartford, Connecticut, Samuel Colt was the son of a successful manufacturer of cotton and woolen fabrics. When he was seven, his father's business slumped and his mother died. Colt then lived with relatives. He showed little interest in school, and his father put him to work in one of his dyeing and bleaching plants. Colt attended school only intermittently but did well enough to go a college preparatory school in Amherst, Massachusetts, at age 13. Here he again neglected his studies. His father sent him at 16 as a seaman on a merchantman to India. After a year at sea Colt returned to his father's plant. Soon he was out on his own, regaling people with talks on the marvels of chemistry and explosives.

At the same time Colt was working on the concept of a repeating pistol with a revolving cylinder, which he had first conceived while he was a seaman. In 1832 he applied for a patent. Colt built both a revolving pistol and a revolving rifle that he patented in England and France while abroad in 1835. He finally obtained his U.S. patent in 1836 and began manufacturing the revolver in Patterson, New Jersey.

Colt needed government contracts but could not interest the army or the navy in his pistol at the time, although he did sell some of the pistols to officers fighting in the SEMINOLE WAR in Florida. By 1842 had he lost his business and the patent rights to his revolver. He then went to work in New York, experimenting with explosives, this time on underwater electric mines. He also became involved in underwater telegraphy, helping lay the first cables from New York to Coney Island.

In the meantime, his revolvers were winning acclaim from soldiers in the 1836–42 Second SEMINOLE WAR and from buyers in the Republic of Texas. During the 1846–48 MEXICAN-AMERICAN WAR, on the urging of Major General Zachary TAYLOR, the army ordered thousands of pistols from Colt, and with these contracts he was able to buy back his patents and begin producing revolvers in one of Eli WHITNEY's plants until he could build his own in Hartford. Colt secured additional patents and even turned part of his factory over to building tools for other factories, which he then sold to Britain and Russia.

The U.S. Army subsequently adopted the Colt revolver as a standard weapon. Military contracts, along with civilian demand for the products of Colt's Patent Fire Arms Manufacturing Company, made Colt immensely wealthy. He died at Hartford, Connecticut, on 10 January 1862.

See also DRAGOONS; MEXICAN WAR, COURSE OF; MINES, NAVAL; SMALL ARMS, PISTOLS.

Further reading: Hosley, William N. *Colt: The Making of an American Legend.* Amherst: University of Massachusetts Press, 1996; Keating, Bern. *The Flamboyant Mr. Colt and His Deadly Six-Shooter.* New York: Doubleday, 1978.

— Arthur T. Frame

Conolly, Richard L. (1892–1962) *U.S. Navy admiral*
Born on 26 April 1892 at Waukegan, Illinois, Richard
Conolly graduated from the U.S. Naval Academy at
Annapolis in 1914. He served on destroyers in the Atlantic
and was awarded the Navy Cross during World War I for
helping to save a transport damaged in a German submarine attack. He earned an M.S. degree from Columbia
University in 1922 and was an instructor at Annapolis from
1925 to 1927. He then held destroyer commands and was
again an instructor at Annapolis (1936–39).

Conolly commanded Destroyer Squadron 7, then 6, in
the Pacific from 1939 to 1942 and the destroyer screen for
the TOKYO RAID in April 1942. He was next on the staff of
Chief of Naval Operations (CNO) and Commander in
Chief, U.S. Fleet Admiral Ernest KING (1942–43) and was
promoted to rear admiral in July 1942.

From March to October 1943 Conolly was with the
Amphibious Force Atlantic Fleet in command of landing
craft and naval bases in Northwest Africa. He participated
in the July 1943 invasion of SICILY and the September invasion of Italy. Transferred back to the Pacific theater, he participated in landings at Kwajalein, Wake, and Marcus
Islands. He commanded Group 3, Amphibious Force,
Pacific Fleet, during 1944 to 1945 and led the landings on
Guam in July 1944 and Lingayen in January 1945.

After the war Conolly was deputy chief of naval operations and naval representative to the 1946 Paris Peace
Conference. He commanded Twelfth Fleet (September
1946–January 1947) and then U.S. Naval Forces Eastern
Atlantic and Mediterranean (1947–50). His last assignment
was as the president of the U.S. Naval War College at
Newport, Rhode Island, from 1950 to 1953. He retired as
a full admiral in November 1953.

From 1953 to 1962 Conolly was president of Long
Island University. During his tenure the school grew from
2,000 to 10,000 students. Conolly and his wife were killed
in the crash of a commercial airliner on 1 March 1962 at
La Guardia Airport.

See also NAVY, U.S.; WORLD WAR II, U.S. INVOLVEMENT,
EUROPE; WORLD WAR II, U.S. INVOLVEMENT, PACIFIC.

Further reading: Morison, Samuel Eliot. *History of
United States Naval Operations in World War II.* Vols. 3, 8,
9, 12. Boston: Little, Brown, 1963.

— Matthew J. McKee

Constellation, USS *U.S. frigate and one of the first
  three U.S. Navy warships constructed*
Authorized by Congress in March 1794, *Constitution* was
designed by Joshua HUMPHREYs and built by D. Stodder
of Baltimore. *Constellation* was laid down in 1796,
launched in September 1797, and commissioned in the
spring of 1798. Rated at 36 guns, *Constellation* displaced
1,268 tons. Initially it mounted 28 24-pounders and 10 12-
pounders. This armament was found too heavy for its displacement, and in 1812 it was reduced to two 32-pounders,
24 18-pounders, and 18 32-pounder carronades.

On 9 February 1799, during the QUASI-WAR with
France, *Constellation* engaged the French frigate
L'Insurgente (40) in an action off Nevis in the West Indies.
Constellation had a much heavier armament, as the French
ship mounted only 18-pounders. *Constellation* outmaneuvered, overhauled, and raked the French vessel. By the
time *L'Insurgente* surrendered it had suffered 29 crewmen killed and 41 wounded, as opposed to *Constellation's*
two killed and three wounded.

On 2 February 1800 *Constellation* engaged the
French frigate *Vengeance* off Guadeloupe. The battle was
indecisive; both ships limped away from the fight, the
Constellation seeking refuge in Jamaica and the *Vengeance*
in Curaçao. *Vengeance* was more heavily armed; the weight
of shot of its broadside was 500 pounds, while *Constellation*
threw only 372 pounds. However, the French suffered 114
killed and wounded, while the Americans lost 14 killed and
25 wounded.

Constellation was in the Mediterranean during the
TRIPOLITAN WAR. Engaged in an action on 22 July 1802
with nine Tripolitan gunboats, it sank two. Laid up from
1805 to 1812, the *Constellation* was rebuilt between 1812
and 1815. In June 1815 it engaged the ship *Mashouda* (46)
and brig *Esledio off* Cape de Gatt, Spain. *Constellation*
then served off Brazil (1819–20), in the Pacific Squadron
(1820–22), and in the West Indies (1827). It returned to the
Mediterranean (1829–34) and served in the Gulf of Mexico
(1835–38) and the Far East (1841–43). It was then laid up.

Constellation was rebuilt entirely in 1855, although some
claim it to have remained the same vessel. Deployed to the
Mediterranean for most of the Civil War, the new *Constellation* joined Admiral David G. FARRAGUT's West Gulf Coast
Blockading Squadron in August 1864 at MOBILE BAY. Shortly
after the Civil War, the navy employed it and the frigate *Constitution* as training ships. In 1880 the *Constellation* delivered
supplies from the United States to Ireland during a famine
there. It was decommissioned on 16 June 1933. Beginning in
1954, the city of Baltimore rebuilt the *Constellation*. Today it
is a museum ship in Baltimore Harbor.

See also NAVY, U.S.; WAR OF 1812, NAVAL OVERVIEW.

Further reading: Chapelle, Howard I. *The Constellation
Question.* Washington, D.C.: Smithsonian Institution
Press, 1970; ———. *The History of The American Sailing
Navy: The Ships and Their Development.* New York:
Norton, 1949; Silverstone, Paul H. *The Sailing Navy,
1775–1854.* Annapolis, Md.: Naval Institute Press, 2001;
Williams, Glenn F. *USS Constellation: A Short History of*

the Last All-Sail Warship Built by the U.S. Navy. Virginia Beach, Va.: Dorning, 2000.

— Christopher J. Richman

Constitution, USS (1797) *U.S. Navy frigate and the oldest naval vessel in the world still afloat*

One of six FRIGATES authorized by Congress in 1794, the *Constitution* was designed by Joshua HUMPHREYS. Unusually large and powerful compared to its peers in the Royal Navy, it displaced 2,200 tons and measured 175 feet by 43 feet. Crewed by 450 men, the frigate was rated a 44-gun ship but was actually to be armed with up to 56 cannon. Constructed at Boston by Hartt's Shipyard, *Constitution* was launched in October 1797 and commissioned in July 1798. It made its first cruise the next summer during the QUASI-WAR with France, taking nine prizes in the Caribbean. In 1803, as flagship of the Mediterranean Squadron during the TRIPOLITAN WAR, it bombarded fortifications at Tripoli and captured five Barbary Coast craft. By 1809 it was flagship of the North Atlantic Squadron.

With the onset of hostilities against the British in the War of 1812, the frigate, under Captain Isaac HULL, ran (for the first of seven times) the blockade at Boston. After a narrow and celebrated escape, kedging away from a much more powerful British squadron, it defeated on 19 August the British frigate *Guerrière,* in which action the *Constitution* earned the nickname "Old Ironsides" for the stoutness of its wooden hull.

On 29 December 1812 the *Constitution* scored a second major success, under Captain William BAINBRIDGE, when it took the British frigate *Java* off Brazil. Its third such victory came on 16 February 1815, more than seven weeks after the signing of the Treaty of Ghent; handled with great skill by Captain Charles STEWART, the *Constitution* defeated and captured both the frigate *Cyane* and sloop *Levant.* Overall, Old Ironsides had made five war cruises to waters off South America, Europe, and Canada; it had defeated four British warships and had taken eight merchantmen. Thus, its final tally in three conflicts reached 26 naval and merchant vessels captured or destroyed.

After the war, the *Constitution* returned to the Mediterranean, frequently as the flagship of the U.S. squadron in those waters. In 1830 it was found to be unseaworthy and was slated for scrapping until a poem by Oliver Wendell Holmes elicited a public outcry. Following overhaul, it returned to service in 1835. During the next two decades it acted again as flagship on distant stations, at one point cruising to the South Pacific for two years.

In March 1844 *Constitution* began a circumnavigation of the globe, a voyage that took two years. Early in the next decade, it sailed on antislavery patrol. The beginning of the Civil War found it a training ship at Annapolis. Fearing its capture, the navy moved the *Constitution* to Newport, Rhode Island, where it served as a schoolship for U.S. Naval Academy midshipmen until 1865.

Refurbished once again in 1871, *Constitution* carried American exhibits to the Paris Exposition of 1877. Following training cruises, it was laid up in 1882 and deteriorated over the next decades. Facing demolition in 1905, *Constitution* was saved again by public opinion. In December 1917, it was renamed *Old Constitution* to free the name for a new battle cruiser. That ship was canceled, and in 1925 the frigate regained its original name.

Following a complete renovation with essential support coming from patriotic organizations and schoolchildren, the *Constitution* was recommissioned in July 1931 at Boston, its permanent station. As the nation's oldest commissioned warship, the *Constitution* has had 63 commanding officers. It goes "to sea" once a year on 4 July, when it is towed to Fort Warren for the annual "turnaround" cruise (to weather both sides of the hull evenly). In 1997 it set sail for the first time in 116 years for a brief cruise in Massachusetts Bay. As the only surviving frigate, it is a priceless relic of the great age of sail and a symbol of the early successes of the U.S. Navy.

See also NAVY, U.S.; TRIPOLITAN WAR; WAR OF 1812, NAVAL OVERVIEW.

Further reading: Chapelle, Howard I. *The History of the American Sailing Navy: The Ships and Their Development.* New York: Bonanza Books, 1949; Gilmer, Thomas C. *Old Ironsides: The Rise, Decline, and Resurrection of the USS* Constitution. Camden, Maine.: International Marine, 1993; Martin, Tyrone G. *A Most Fortunate Ship: A Narrative History of Old Ironsides.* Rev. ed. Annapolis, Md.: Naval Institute Press, 1997.

— Malcolm Muir, Jr., and Mary S. Rausch

Constitution of 1789

As delegates gathered in Philadelphia during the summer of 1787 to revise the ARTICLES OF CONFEDERATION, prominent among the problems to be addressed were those surrounding national security. There was great dissent as to how best to provide adequate federal power without also threatening personal liberty. The Founding Fathers collectively had great mistrust of standing armies, believing them to be instruments of monarchical power and tyranny. The American people placed great faith in the militia to protect national interests without menace, but, as many members of the Continental Congress had experienced during the American Revolutionary War, militia often proved undependable.

Through many compromises, the new constitution explicitly outlined the military authority of the national government. Article 1, section 8, granted Congress the ability to declare war, raise an army, maintain a navy, establish military regulations, call the militia into federal service, and regulate the militia in concordance with the states. Furthermore, section 10 prohibited the states from engaging in war independent of Congress. Article 2, section 2 made the president commander in chief of the armed forces, including militia called into federal service. Here the primary goal of the framers was to centralize war-making capabilities in the hands of the national government. To protect civil rights and prevent a military coup d'état, the executive, legislature, and states shared control of the military. Congress authorized the army, paid for it, and determined its structure and rules. The president commanded the troops. Should the national army still pose a threat, the state militias existed as a final check against a standing army. Federal control of the militia evoked the greatest debate as drafting progressed, leaving the exact relationship between the army and militia vague up through the early 20th century.

Antifederalists attacked the Constitution during the ratification process, giving notable attention to the military provisions. They argued that the new arrangement circumvented the authority of the states and would lead to tyranny. Nevertheless, the Constitution was ratified in 1789, with the understanding that a Bill of Rights would soon follow. Two of the amendments addressed military concerns. The SECOND AMENDMENT asserts the necessity of the militia and the right to bear arms, while the Third Amendment prohibits the quartering of troops in private homes during peacetime. Just as the Constitution itself was a triumph for the nationalists, the Bill of Rights satisfied the concerns of the antifederalists by enumerating specific limits on national authority.

The military provisions of the Constitution survived largely unchanged throughout the 19th century, as internal concerns predominated. As the frontier became more settled and industrialization demanded greater foreign markets, the need for a more vigorous military establishment arose. The 1898 SPANISH-AMERICAN WAR led to important reforms, based not only on the chaotic mobilization that had taken place but also on the new role of a military increasingly posted overseas. In 1903 Congress passed the DICK ACT, which replaced the MILITIA ACT OF 1792. It strengthened and clarified federal authority over the state militias, thereafter known as the National Guard. As the United States became more involved in international affairs throughout the 20th century, presidential authority increased as well. President Woodrow WILSON acquired broad wartime discretionary powers with the NATIONAL DEFENSE ACT OF 1916.

The COLD WAR after World War II militarized American society as nothing ever had before. The president assumed great authority independent of Congress. President Harry S. TRUMAN deployed troops to Korea in 1950 under the authority of the United Nations without a congressional declaration of war. The creation of the CENTRAL INTELLIGENCE AGENCY in 1947, answerable only to the president for more than two decades, constituted another source of unchecked executive power. Perhaps the greatest example of congressional carte blanche was the 1964 TONKIN GULF RESOLUTION, providing President Lyndon JOHNSON essentially unlimited authority to wage war in Southeast Asia. The quagmire there, however, led to the reassertion of congressional authority over military affairs. The War Powers Act of 1973 and CIA hearings demonstrated the effectiveness of the Founding Fathers' system of checks and balances. Perhaps there can be no better evaluation of the Constitution than to note that in more than 200 years the military has never posed a serious threat to civilian control of the U.S. government.

See also AMERICAN REVOLUTION, CAUSES OF; SHAYS'S REBELLION; WHISKEY REBELLION.

Further reading: Kohn, Richard H. *Eagle and Sword: The Federalists and the Creation of the Military Establishment in America, 1783–1802.* New York: Free Press, 1975; Kohn, Richard H., ed. *The United States Military under the Constitution of the United States, 1789–1989.* New York: New York University Press, 1991; Stuart, Reginald C. *War and American Thought: From the Revolution to the Monroe Doctrine.* Kent, Ohio: Kent State University Press, 1982.
— Rodney Madison

containment, doctrine and course of   *Fundamental controlling American cold war strategy, designed to prevent the further expansion of Soviet power after World War II*

Relations between the United States and the Soviet Union deteriorated in the months after WORLD WAR II. In February 1946 the administration of President Harry S. TRUMAN asked George F. Kennan, deputy chief of mission at the American embassy in Moscow and a Soviet expert, to explain the rationale behind Russian policies. In perhaps the seminal document of the cold war, Kennan replied with the 8,000-word "Long Telegram." He stated that Soviet antagonism toward the West arose from the need of Russian rulers to justify their oppressive domestic rule as being essential to combat the hostility of foreign powers and that therefore Western states could do little to alter Soviet policies. Instead, they must adopt policies of "long-term, patient but firm and vigilant containment," resisting attempts to expand Soviet influence while awaiting changes within the USSR that would alter the nature of Soviet government. Kennan's telegram, circulated throughout the higher echelons of American government, and his subsequent article "The Sources of Soviet Conduct," published in the influential quarterly *Foreign Affairs*, quickly became definitive documents of U.S. cold war strategy. From then

Limited Wars, Police Actions, and Peacekeeping Missions Involving the United States

until the early 1990s, the word *containment* described the underlying American policy toward the Soviet Union.

Kennan, who returned to Washington to head the newly created State Department Policy Planning Staff, charged with the long-range planning of foreign policy, soon deprecated the increasingly military emphasis of containment, subsequently claiming he had envisaged that the United States would rely primarily upon peaceful economic and cultural counterpressure to check Soviet expansion. In his March 1947 Truman Doctrine speech, the president publicly pledged to assist any country in which democracy was threatened either externally or internally by communism, simultaneously extending substantial economic and military aid to both Greece and Turkey. Some months later he announced the massive Marshall Plan, or European Recovery Program, to assist in the economic rebuilding of Europe.

Other civilian and military officials sought to expand American defense budgets substantially, considering that essential to meet increasing international commitments, including membership in the 1949 NORTH ATLANTIC TREATY ORGANIZATION security pact and to counter the recent Soviet acquisition of atomic weapons and the establishment of a communist state in mainland China. Various State and Defense Department representatives, led by

Paul H. Nitze, Kennan's successor on the Policy Planning Staff, argued that should war break out, the United States lacked the military resources even to meet its existing commitments. Implicitly, they endorsed the 1947 Truman Doctrine. Planning paper NSC-68, which they drafted and delivered to Truman in April 1950, demanded massive enhancements to U.S. conventional and nuclear military capabilities, including substantially augmented American troop contributions to NATO forces in Europe. "Without superior aggregate military strength, in being and readily mobilizable, a policy of 'containment' . . . is no more than a policy of bluff." NSC-68 advocated an increase in existing U.S. defense budget from $13.5 billion to between $18 and $50 billion, recommendations the economy-conscious Truman initially rejected.

The outbreak of the KOREAN WAR in June 1950 proved crucial to both the implementation of NSC-68 and the effective globalization of the COLD WAR, broadening its initial primarily European focus. U.S. defense spending for Europe and Asia soared, reaching $48 billion in fiscal 1951 and $61 billion the following year; after the armistice it remained far higher than before the conflict. In June 1950 the United States had 1,460,000 military personnel, of whom 280,000 were stationed abroad; four years later the totals were 3,555,000 and 963,000, respectively. The Mutual

Security Program, instituted in 1951, furnished military assistance to a wide array of American clients and allies.

By the late 1950s the United States had established numerous additional security pacts, including the Rio Pact, covering Latin America; the Central Treaty Organization (CENTO), in the Middle East; the Southeast Asian Treaty Organization (SEATO); the ANZUS defense pact with Australia and New Zealand; and bilateral treaties with South Korea, Japan, and the Republic of China, on Taiwan. Covert operations by the CENTRAL INTELLIGENCE AGENCY often ensured that new governments unsympathetic to the United States would be short-lived, as in Iran, Guatemala, and later Chile.

Despite rhetorical pronouncements in the 1950s by the administration of President Dwight D. EISENHOWER that the United States would "roll back" communism in Eastern Europe and elsewhere, in practice, after Chinese intervention prevented the "liberation" of North Korea in autumn 1950, U.S. strategy sought primarily to prevent further communist gains. This was particularly the case in countries experiencing decolonization and perceived as objects of U.S.-Soviet competition. In the late 1950s and early 1960s this outlook led successive American presidents to increase incrementally aid to the southern portion of Vietnam, where communists supported by the North threatened the existing regime. After 1975, the de facto defeat in the costly VIETNAM WAR, the greatest military setback in American history, led the United States to refrain from further large-scale interventions. Washington chose instead to rely upon surrogates, such as anti-Soviet guerrilla forces in Afghanistan during the 1980s. Exploiting the Sino-Soviet split, from the early 1970s onward American leaders differentiated between Chinese and Russian communism, using each big socialist power's distrust of the other to win concessions for the United States.

American strategy in the 1950s relied heavily on nuclear weapons as less costly than conventional forces, a policy termed the NEW LOOK STRATEGY. The potential it implied of launching nuclear war over relatively minor issues aroused heavy criticism. In the 1960s U.S. strategic thinking emphasized FLEXIBLE RESPONSE, enhancing both conventional and counterinsurgency capabilities. The expansion of American international commitments did not preclude efforts from the mid-1950s onward to reach an understanding with the Soviet Union that would prevent an accidental war or would place ceilings on ever more expensive and destructive nuclear weapons. These efforts culminated in the Strategic Arms Limitation Treaties of 1972 and 1979 and reflected the fundamentally cautious nature of American strategy.

Alarmed by what he perceived as the increasingly assertive nature of Soviet foreign policy in the 1970s, President Ronald REAGAN, elected in 1980, increased U.S.

defense budgets dramatically, adopted a firmly anti-Soviet posture, and announced the development of a new antimissile shield that would render the United States invulnerable to Soviet attack. By the late 1980s growing economic weakness led to the collapse of both the Soviet Union and its satellites, which many Americans interpreted as validating the premises of the containment strategy adopted more than 40 years earlier. In the opening years of the 21st century, no new strategic paradigm had attained similar intellectual dominance in the conceptualization of post–cold war U.S. policy.

See also BERLIN BLOCKADE; ESPIONAGE AGAINST THE UNITED STATES, SURVEY OF; NUCLEAR AND ATOMIC WEAPONS; KOREAN WAR, CAUSES; VIETNAM WAR, CAUSES.

Further reading: Borowski, Harry R. *A Hollow Threat: Strategic Air Power and Containment before Korea.* Westport, Conn.: Greenwood, 1982; Deibel, Terry L., and John Lewis Gaddis, eds. *Containment: Concept and Policy.* 2 vols. Washington, D.C.: National Defense University, 1986; Friedman, Norman. *The Fifty-Year War: Conflict and Strategy in the Cold War.* Annapolis, Md.: Naval Institute Press, 2000; Gaddis, John Lewis. *Strategies of Containment: A Critical Appraisal of Postwar American National Security Policy.* Oxford, U.K.: Oxford University Press, 1982; Kennan, George F. *Memoirs, 1925–1950.* Boston: Little, Brown, 1967; May, Ernest R., ed. *American Cold War Strategy: Interpreting NSC 68.* Boston: Bedford Books, 1993.

— Priscilla Roberts

Continental army *The regular patriot forces, more properly known as the Army of the United Colonies, of the American Revolutionary War*

In April 1775, in the aftermath of LEXINGTON AND CONCORD, the colonies were swept by a *rage militaire*. Patriots believed that because their cause was just, they certainly would be victorious. The skill of officers was held of little consequence, since the war would be short; virtue alone would triumph. Everyone should take their turn at the fighting, and the militia would bear the brunt of combat. This was, after all, the first army in modern history to be fighting for a political ideal.

During the war, militia forces almost invariably proved totally inadequate against regular British troops in pitched battle, often breaking and running at critical points. Militia did perform the useful functions of providing security and order, gathering intelligence, forcing noncommitted citizens to choose sides, and harassing supply lines when the British troops left their coastal enclaves and journeyed to the interior. But if the British army was to be defeated in the field, regular forces would have to accomplish it.

On 4 June 1775, the Continental Congress called for the formation of 10 rifle companies. This, the first regiment in the army, is generally regarded as the beginning of the U.S. Army. On 15 June 1775 Congress appointed George WASHINGTON as commander in chief of the Continental army, or the Army of the United Colonies, as it was officially designated. Washington had served with the British during the FRENCH AND INDIAN WAR, and he respected the British army as a fighting force. He tried to form the Continental army along similar lines, but the British army was a harsh and brutal service, recruited largely by impressment. What emerged was a cross between this model and the citizen army of the later French Revolution.

Washington himself was scarcely familiar with the forms and nuances of 18th-century warfare; there were others with greater military experience. He was selected largely for political reasons: he was a Virginian, and he was native-born. In the course of the war, Washington grew as a commander. Besides, he had far more important assets than military knowledge: an ability to learn from his mistakes, an innate sense of how to use his subordinates, and the priceless gifts of integrity and character. He became, by default, the "indispensable man."

Congress established a command structure for the army, but at times Congress simply sent orders to Washington's subordinates without consulting him. It also adopted a modified British military code, and it narrowed the difference in pay and privileges between officers and enlisted men. There was also a terrible problem with short-term enlistments. At first enlistments were only for one year, but by 1776 Washington's pleas had led Congress to authorize enlistments of three years or even for the duration of the war. There were few takers, and one-year enlistments continued to be the norm. Most Patriots thought everyone should take a turn, a view that was almost fatal to the American cause.

Congress requested the various states to raise specific numbers of troops. The states selected the colonels and officers of lower rank; Congress appointed the higher officers, with a quota system for each state rather than on the basis of ability. Congress also set up hospitals, quartermaster services, and a commissariat and appointed paymasters. Militias remained under the control of the individual states.

With 2.5 million people in 1775, America should have been able to raise an army of 100,000 men. This would have been difficult to feed and equip, but 35,000 men would have been sufficient to defeat the British. The Continental army, however, reached only 20,000 men at most. The army fluctuated wildly in size during the course of the war between this maximum and a low of only 5,000 men.

Congress set goals for troops and money on the basis of each state's wealth and population, but these quotas were seldom met. Logistics and finance remained difficult problems. At times Washington had trouble getting enough food to keep his troops alive, although much of this resulted from an inefficient quartermaster service and problems of transport.

After the encampment at VALLEY FORGE and advent of Friedrich von STEUBEN's training and simplified system of drill, the Continental army became an effective fighting force, able to compete on an equal basis, man-for-man, with the professional British army.

Victory in the war was largely attributable to the Continental army and the intervention of the French army and navy, but with the passage of time, the militia reclaimed the victory in the popular mind from the regular forces. At the end of the war, despite Washington's pleas, Congress virtually disbanded the army, reducing it to only 80 privates and the requisite number of officers (none above the rank of captain) to guard military stores at WEST POINT and Fort Pitt.

See also AMERICAN REVOLUTIONARY WAR, LAND OVERVIEW; ARMY, U.S.; CONWAY CABAL.

Further reading: Black, Jeremy. *War for America: The Fight for Independence, 1775–1783.* Stroud, U.K.: Alan Sutton, 1991; Carp, E. Wayne. *To Starve the Army at Pleasure: Continental Army Administration and American Political Culture, 1775–1783.* Chapel Hill: University of North Carolina Press, 1984; Martin, Joseph Plumb. *Private Yankee Doodle: Being a Narrative of Some of the Adventures, Dangers and Sufferings of a Revolutionary Soldier.* Edited by George F. Scheer. Boston: Little, Brown, 1962; Royster, Charles. *A Revolutionary People at War: The Continental Army and American Character, 1775–1783.* Chapel Hill: University of North Carolina Press, 1979; Wright, Robert K. *The Continental Army.* Washington, D.C.: U.S. Army Center of Military History, 1983.

— Spencer C. Tucker

convoy system, World Wars I and II *System devised by the Allies to secure shipping lanes and protect vessels from German commerce raiders, primarily submarines*

In both world wars the convoy system adapted to meet various challenges, but it usually consisted of large organized convoys sailing to and from key ports with escort forces made up of warships, and later aircraft, to combat commerce raiders. The success of the convoy system enabled the Allies to utilize their vast resources and industrial strength to emerge victorious in struggles that were essentially contests of attrition.

During World War I, the British implemented the convoy system in isolated situations, but they did not employ it generally until after the United States entered the war in

Allied convoy steaming south of Newfoundland, 28 July 1942

April 1917, and then only upon American insistence. Convoys demonstrated their usefulness early in the war with the safe transit of the large British convoys from Australia and New Zealand to the Middle East. From the outbreak of hostilities, troopships crossing the Atlantic from North America to Europe were also heavily escorted. Organized convoys were used to protect some short-haul trade routes, such as essential coal shipments crossing the English Channel to France. General transatlantic crossings were unprotected, as the conventional wisdom was that large convoys would be easily detected and would present too many targets to German U-boats. The British Admiralty also believed it had too few destroyers to both screen the Grand Fleet in the North Sea and protect merchantmen making transoceanic voyages.

The German revival of unrestricted submarine warfare in February 1917 brought a crisis that forced the reevaluation of merchant vessel protection; German submarines sank Allied and neutral vessels at a record pace of more than 2 million tons for April through June 1917. These sinkings pushed Britain perilously close to starvation and threatened the Allies with imminent collapse. Further analysis of the situation by the Admiralty showed that numerous individual sailings actually provided U-boats with a greater likelihood of success than would the mass sailing of an escorted convoy, the escort of which would also threaten attacking U-boats with destruction. America's entry into the war in April 1917 also brought new naval resources to assist in convoy duty and insistence that convoys be implemented. In May and June the first convoys sailed from Hampton Roads, New York, Halifax, and Gibraltar with British, American, and Canadian escorts.

The convoy system covered North Atlantic shipping lanes and the Mediterranean by the end of 1917. Although merchant vessel sinkings did not fall below 300,000 tons a month until the spring of 1918, the convoy system had reversed the deadly trend of mid-1917. British, American, and Canadian naval forces defeated the U-boats and made possible the buildup in Allied forces and resources necessary for final victory over the Central Powers in 1918.

The hard lessons of World War I were not lost on Allied naval staffs when World War II began in 1939. To the extent that resources allowed, the British implemented the convoy system immediately. At first British and Canadian forces carried the burden of fighting Hitler's U-boats alone. Increasingly, U.S. naval forces, implementing what President Franklin D. ROOSEVELT called measures "short of war," assisted the Royal Navy in protecting merchant shipping in the western areas of the Atlantic. In October 1941 *U-562* sank the U.S. destroyer *REUBEN JAMES,* killing 115 of its crew.

After U.S. entry into the war in December 1941, the scope of the convoy system and resources dedicated to it grew tremendously. Allied forces established a highly orchestrated, interlocking system of convoys from South America and the eastern seaboard of North America to Britain, the Arctic Ocean coast of Russia, and the Mediterranean to ensure that personnel and matériel reached combat fronts.

With more than 200 U-boats, directed by Admiral Karl Dönitz, Germany destroyed nearly 8 million tons of shipping in 1942. In spring 1943, U-boats and their wolfpack tactics seemed again to threaten Britain with defeat. However, naval forces becoming available in the Atlantic after Operation TORCH, the cracking of the U-boat code, and new techniques and technologies all turned the tide in the Allies' favor. Advances in sonar and radio direction finding, improved depth charges, and other new weapons helped Allied forces keep the upper hand. The use of escort carriers, which provided air cover even when convoys were out of range of shore-based aircraft, proved to be a major factor in defeating the U-boats. By war's end, the Allies had sunk 781 U-boats, with 32,000 men. Although Dönitz's U-boats sank 2,575 Allied and neutral vessels, totaling 14.5 million tons, during the war, the close cooperation of U.S., British, and Canadian forces had transported the personnel and matériel needed to defeat Nazi Germany in Europe.

See also ATLANTIC, BATTLE OF (WORLD WAR I); ATLANTIC, BATTLE OF (WORLD WAR II); DRUMBEAT, OPERATION; NAVY, U.S.

Further reading: Felknor, Bruce, ed. *The U.S. Merchant Marine at War, 1775–1945.* Annapolis, Md.: Naval Institute Press, 1999. Hogue, Arnold. *The Allied Convoy System, 1939–1945: Its Organization, Defence, and Operation.* Annapolis, Md.: Naval Institute Press, 2000; Halpern, Paul G. *A Naval History of World War I.* Annapolis, Md.: Naval Institute Press, 1994; Morison, Samuel Eliot. *The Two*

Ocean War: A Short History of the United States Navy in the Second World War. Boston: Little, Brown, 1963.
— Thomas J. Stuhlreyer

Conway cabal (September–December 1777) *Plot to remove George Washington as commander in chief of the Continental army*

Believing that WASHINGTON should have done more to prevent the British from capturing Philadelphia, disgruntled members of Congress, led by Richard Henry Lee and influenced by Thomas Mifflin, who had earlier served as Washington's quartermaster general, began to plot the replacement of Washington with Major General Horatio GATES, recent victor in the Battles of SARATOGA. While it is not entirely clear whether Gates was involved in the plot, his actions after Saratoga were suspicious. He sent his report on the battles directly to Congress rather than through Washington. In addition, Gates not only refused Washington reinforcements but also failed to release regiments that Washington had sent him earlier in the summer.

While Washington certainly had his share of critics after the disasters of 1777, Mifflin and Lee realized that Congress would never approve a resolution to strip Washington of his command. They therefore sought to provoke Washington's resignation by playing upon his antipathy for Brigadier General Thomas Conway, an Irish-born French officer serving in the Continental army who had openly criticized Washington for not promoting him to major general.

In late November 1777 Mifflin and Lee put their plan into motion by getting Congress to establish a Board of War. Although Washington had originated the idea, he had intended for the board to have only an advisory role over military training and supervision over supplies. Congress instead approved Mifflin's and Lee's proposal for a far more powerful board that would have overall supervision of military operations, with Gates as the presiding officer and Conway, who was to be promoted to major general, as inspector general. Congress had unwittingly aided Mifflin and Lee in bypassing Washington as commander in chief, a step that the two plotters now hoped would lead him to resign in protest.

Mifflin and Lee no sooner set their trap than Conway caused it to backfire. In October Conway had written Gates a cryptic letter in which he implicitly blamed Washington for the military failures of the Continental army and stated that he hoped Gates would succeed him. When Gates's inebriated aide Colonel James WILKINSON accidentally revealed the contents of Conway's letter, the plot began to unravel, especially after Conway wrote Washington two new letters that, in contrasting Washington's experience with that of European officers, insulted not only

Washington specifically but also American officers generally. Even Washington's critics were outraged. Gates wrote Washington to disavow Conway, and even Mifflin publicly announced his support for Washington to distance himself from Conway. After Brigadier General John Cadwallader seriously wounded Conway in a duel, Conway himself wrote Washington a letter of apology.

While the precise details of the Conway cabal are obscure, leading some historians to suggest that it was much ado about nothing, the outcome was significant in that it reaffirmed Washington's role as commander in chief of the Continental army.

See also AMERICAN REVOLUTIONARY WAR, LAND OVERVIEW.

Further reading: Alden, John Richard. *The American Revolution, 1775–1783*. New York: Harper & Row, 1954;

Flexner, James Thomas. *Washington: The Indispensable Man.* Boston: Little, Brown, 1969.

— Justin D. Murphy

Coral Sea, Battle of the (4–8 May 1942) *Important World War II naval battle, and the first fought in which the ships involved never made visual contact*
In March 1942 the Japanese initiated Operation Mo to capture Tulagi and Port Moresby, New Guinea. The commander in chief of the U.S. Pacific Fleet, Admiral Chester NIMITZ, knew through intelligence of an impending Japanese operation in the region. He directed Rear Admiral Aubrey Fitch to take the carrier *Lexington* and join Rear Admiral Frank J. FLETCHER's *Yorktown*, already in the Coral Sea.

In late April 1942 a Japanese fleet commanded by Vice Admiral Takeo Takagi sortied with two large carriers and a

Aircraft carrier USS *Lexington* burning during the Battle of the Coral Sea   *(Naval Historical Foundation)*

small one, plus troop transports and escorts. On 1 May the American carriers rendezvoused in the Coral Sea, forming Task Force 17 (TF 17), with Fletcher in overall command. He received word on 3 May that Japanese transports were disembarking troops at Tulagi. With Fitch busy refueling, Fletcher took the *Yorktown* north to attack. The next day U.S. planes destroyed a number of minor vessels and five floatplanes, severely reducing Japanese reconnaissance capabilities. After the attack, Fletcher returned to Fitch's position. On 6 May the Japanese discovered the oiler *Neosho* and destroyer *Sims*, which Fletcher thought he had sent out of harm's way. The Japanese sank both.

Responding to a mistaken reconnaissance report, on 7 May Fletcher launched 93 aircraft to attack vessels that did not exist. Fortunately, a B-17 pilot soon thereafter reported a Japanese carrier entering the Jormard Passage. American planes diverted and sank this ship, the light carrier *Shoho*. Takagi, lacking reliable reconnaissance, launched a late-afternoon strike without a clear idea of the U.S. fleet's whereabouts. American fighters intercepted and shot down nine of the Japanese planes, which failed to discover TF 17.

Early on 8 May both sides sent out reconnaissance planes. A U.S. pilot located the Japanese fleet shortly before the Japanese discovered the Americans. At 9:15 A.M. Fletcher launched 88 planes against the Japanese. At nearly the same time, Takagi launched 74 aircraft. U.S. dive-bombers damaged the carrier *Shokaku* with three strikes. Simultaneously, the Japanese reached TF 17, badly damaging the *Lexington* with two bombs and two torpedoes and hitting the *Yorktown* with one bomb. Damage control aboard the *Lexington* initially succeeded, but at 12:47 P.M. a ruptured gasoline tank exploded. The resulting blaze quickly grew out of control. By 5:00 P.M. Admiral Fitch ordered the ship abandoned. At 7:15 P.M. Fletcher ordered an escorting destroyer to finish off the carrier, marking the end of the battle.

Judged solely by tonnage, the Japanese had won another tactical victory over the U.S. fleet; however, it was a strategic defeat. With the loss of the *Shoho*, the withdrawal of the damaged *Shokaku*, and the depletion of aircrews, Takagi lacked the ability to continue Operation Mo. The invasion force bound for Port Moresby turned back. The Battle of the Coral Sea, therefore, signaled the first time that Allied forces halted a Japanese advance. It also strengthened the Japanese determination to locate and finish off the American carriers, leading to the most decisive battle of the Pacific War, MIDWAY.

See also AIRCRAFT CARRIERS; WORLD WAR II, U.S. INVOLVEMENT, PACIFIC.

Further reading: Hoyt, Edwin P. *Blue Skies and Blood: The Battle of the Coral Sea.* New York: S. Eriksson, 1975;

Potter, E. B. "The Battle of the Coral Sea." In *Great Naval Battles*, edited by Jack Sweetman. Annapolis, Md.: Naval Institute Press, 1998; Willmott, H. P. *The Barrier and the Javelin: Japanese and Allied Pacific Strategies, February to June 1942.* Annapolis, Md.: Naval Institute Press, 1983.

— Rodney Madison

Corbin, Margaret C. (1751–1800) *American Revolutionary War soldier (heroine)*

Born on 12 November 1751 in Franklin County, Pennsylvania, Margaret Cochran, known as Molly, was orphaned in 1756 and raised by her maternal uncle. She married John Corbin in 1772.

With the onset of the American Revolutionary War, John Corbin enlisted as an artilleryman with the 1st Company of the Pennsylvania Artillery. Molly Corbin accompanied her husband and was at his side in November 1776 when his unit fought Hessian mercenaries at FORT WASHINGTON, New York.

John Corbin was mortally wounded in the battle, and Molly Corbin took his place at the cannon. She continued to fire until grape shot severely wounded her in the left shoulder. This injury left her unable to use that arm.

Corbin's disability qualified her to enroll in the Invalid Regiment. Congress had created this regiment in 1777 for disabled soldiers who could not return to the field. She received an assignment to West Point, but her handicap left her unable to work or to care for herself. In 1779 Congress granted her half-pay pension and a suit of clothing each year or its monetary equivalent. She was the first woman in American service known to have received a military pension and benefits.

Records indicate that Corbin remarried but that she continued to use the name Mrs. Corbin. Her second husband also was an invalid, and so her circumstances remained bleak. The Invalid Regiment disbanded in 1783. It is unclear what became of her husband, but Corbin lived in the Highland Falls area of New York and continued to receive support from the federal government.

Corbin's story became confused with that of Mary MCCAULEY (Molly Pitcher) because records identified Corbin as "Captain Molly." Corbin died in 1800. In 1926 she was reburied at the U.S. Military Academy at West Point.

See also WOMEN IN THE MILITARY.

Further reading: Hall, Edward Hagaman. *Margaret Corbin: Heroine of the Battle of Fort Washington.* New York: American Scenic and Historical Preservation Society, 1932; Sherrow, Victoria. *Women and the Military.* Santa Barbara, Calif.: ABC-CLIO, 1996.

— Tracy M. Shilcutt

Corinth, Battle of (3–4 October 1862) *Civil War battle for control of western Tennessee and northern Mississippi*

Corinth, Mississippi, straddled the junction of two strategic southern transportation arteries, the Memphis-Charleston and Mobile-Ohio Railroads. Union forces captured the town on 30 May 1862 after a cautious 30-day, 22-mile march from Pittsburg Landing, Tennessee. Corinth subsequently became a major base for Union operations in northern Mississippi.

When Confederate general Braxton BRAGG left Mississippi for the 1862 invasion of Kentucky, he provided only vague instructions to his subordinates as to who would command northern Mississippi. Differences between the region's senior commanders, Major Generals Earl Van Dorn and Sterling Price, resulted in two independent commands. Price attempted to support Bragg's invasion of Kentucky by seizing IUKA, Mississippi, but was forced to evacuate it on 19 September. Price then agreed to Van Dorn's request to unite their commands.

Van Dorn, an impetuous and demanding leader, devised an attack on the Union position at Corinth. He hoped to drive Federal forces from western Tennessee and secure the safety of VICKSBURG. With a combined strength of 22,000 men, the Army of Mississippi moved north from Ripley, Mississippi, toward Bolivar, Tennessee. Building a bridge as if to cross the Tuscumbia River, Van Dorn instead wheeled right and advanced rapidly on Corinth from the northwest, which he mistakenly considered the weakest Union point. Van Dorn believed that Union forces, once defeated, would retreat to Jackson, Tennessee, and permit him to move north along Bragg's left flank to the Ohio River.

While Major General Ulysses S. GRANT left to visit his wife in St. Louis, Major General William S. ROSECRANS had command of the Union force of 23,000 men at Corinth. He improved the already formidable defensive works, which included five lunettes, or dug-in artillery batteries, on commanding ground around the town's northwest side, within a half-mile radius of the rail junction.

On 3 October Van Dorn's men arrived and launched a ferocious assault into the heart of these fortifications over difficult terrain and in extraordinarily hot weather. By nightfall they had pushed Rosecrans back two miles to Corinth's inner defensive positions.

The Confederates renewed their attack the following morning and achieved several breakthroughs, but well-directed Union fire from the lunettes broke up the attacks and erased the gains. With Union reinforcements approaching from his rear, Van Dorn retreated west toward Holly Springs, Mississippi. There his army received much-needed reinforcements from paroled FORT DONELSON prisoners and returning absentees. Exhausted Union troops attempted a pursuit but were unable to sustain it.

Union casualties for the battle of Corinth totaled approximately 2,500. The Confederates lost 5,000.

The campaign saw the Confederates effectively relinquish control of western Tennessee and northern Mississippi. Union forces subsequently shifted the focus of their operations to Vicksburg. Three days after Corinth, Bragg engaged Major General Don Carlos BUELL's troops in the Battle of PERRYVILLE. Although the battle was a stalemate, Bragg realized that he was outnumbered and fell back into middle Tennessee to protect CHATTANOOGA, since Van Dorn's defeat had left Bragg's army as the only substantial Confederate force between the Appalachians and the Mississippi River.

See also CIVIL WAR, LAND OVERVIEW.

Further reading: Cozzens, Peter. *The Darkest Days of the War: The Battles of Iuka and Corinth.* Chapel Hill: University of North Carolina Press, 1997; Engle, Stephen D. *Struggle for the Heartland: The Campaigns from Fort Henry to Corinth.* Lincoln: University of Nebraska Press, 2001; Hess, Earl. *Banners to the Breeze: The Kentucky Campaign, Corinth, and Stones River.* Lincoln: University of Nebraska Press, 2000.

— Derek W. Frisby

Corregidor, attack on and surrender of (9 April–6 May 1942) *World War II battle*

Corregidor is located at the mouth of Manila Bay on Luzon in the Philippine Islands. Situated two miles south of BATAAN Peninsula, Corregidor is 3.5 miles long and 1.5 miles across at its widest point. Also known as Fort Mills and nicknamed "the Rock," Corregidor was one of four islands, along with Forts Hughes, Drum, and Frank, guarding the entrance to Manila Bay.

After the fall of Bataan on 9 April 1942, Japanese general Masaharu Homma's Fourteenth Army focused its attention on the Rock. Although heavy artillery and aerial bombardment soon began in earnest, it took the Japanese some time to assemble the requisite number of landing craft and barges; 27 days elapsed between the fall of Bataan and the assault on Corregidor. Meanwhile, at least 37 Japanese artillery batteries fired against the island, while aircraft dropped some 1,700 bombs.

The island had some 11,000 defenders. Following General of the Army Douglas MACARTHUR's departure under orders for Australia, Army Major General Jonathan WAINWRIGHT had overall command of U.S. forces in the Philippines. On Corregidor, army major general George F. Moore commanded the artillery defenses, and Colonel Samuel L. Howard had charge of the 4th Marine Regiment, responsible for the beach defenses. The 4th Marines, nearly 800 men, had arrived at the end of December 1941 from

Shanghai, China. It was subsequently reinforced by Marines from Cavite Navy Yard and sailors from Mariveles. Following the fall of Bataan, officers and enlisted men from more than 50 different organizations were assigned to the regiment; by 29 April, the 4th Marines numbered 229 officers and 3,770 men. The regiment contained about 1,500 marines; the rest were a combination of personnel from the U.S. Navy and Army, Philippine Insular Navy, Philippine Army Air Corps, Philippine Scouts, Philippine Army, and the Constabulary.

The Japanese launched their invasion of the island at 11 P.M. on 5 May when a force of more than 2,400 men and some tanks came ashore between Infantry Point and Cavalry Point. U.S. forces counterattacked, but the tanks drove them back toward the Malinta Tunnel. By 11:30 A.M. on 6 May the Japanese were within 300 yards of the tunnel, which held some 1,000 wounded; Wainwright made the decision to surrender at noon. At midnight, Wainwright informed his officers in a broadcast message that he had surrendered all of the Philippines to the Japanese. The American surrender ended conventional warfare in the Philippines, although bands of Americans and Filipinos waged guerrilla warfare against the Japanese over the next three years.

See also BATAAN DEATH MARCH; FORT DRUM; PHILIPPINES, LOSS OF.

Further reading: Belote, James H., and William M. Belote. *Corregidor: The Saga of a Fortress.* New York: Berkley, 1984; Miller, J. Michael. *From Shanghai to Corregidor: Marines in the Defense of the Philippines.* Washington, D.C.: U.S. Government Printing Office, 1997; Morris, Eric. *Corregidor: The American Alamo of World War II.* New York: Cooper Square, 2000; Morton, Louis. *The United States Army in World War II: The War in the Pacific. The Fall of the Philippines.* Washington, D.C.: U.S. Government Printing Office, 1953.

— Trevor K. Plante

Cowpens, Battle of (17 January 1781) *Key Revolutionary War battle in the campaign for the Carolinas*

On 21 December 1780, Continental army major general Nathaniel GREENE, commander of the Southern Department, detached forces under Brigadier General Daniel MORGAN to harass the British. On 25 December Morgan

The Battle of Cowpens, 17 January 1781. Copy of print by S. H. Gimber *(National Archives)*

arrived at the Pacolet River in South Carolina. The British commander in the South, Lieutenant General Charles, Lord Cornwallis, received reports of Morgan's movements on 1 January 1781 and immediately dispatched Lieutenant Colonel Banastre Tarleton and his reinforced legion (a combined infantry and cavalry unit) to intercept Morgan. Tarleton had about 825 infantry and 300 dragoons.

On the morning of 16 January Tarleton surprised Morgan with a night crossing of the Pacolet River. Pursued by Tarleton all day, Morgan decided to halt that night at a meadow known as the Cowpens and fight there the next day.

The Cowpens is a meadow interspersed with trees. The terrain gradually rises for 400 yards to a military crest and then 300 yards more to a true crest some 70 feet high. A final crest is 600 yards farther back. The terrain then drops off for five miles to the Broad River.

Morgan had 300 Maryland and Delaware Continentals, 200 veteran Virginia riflemen, and 80 Continental dragoons under Lieutenant Colonel William Washington. About 500 militia had also joined him. On the morning of 17 January Morgan positioned his men in three lines. His forward line consisted of 150 picked Georgia and North Carolina militia riflemen concealed behind trees and in the tall grass in advance of the military crest. Morgan had ordered that on the British approach this line would fire twice and then fall back to the second line 150 yards back. Colonel Andrew PICKENS commanded the second line of 300 North Carolina and South Carolina militia. Morgan ordered them also to fire twice, concentrating on British officers and sergeants, then to fall back around the left flank of the third line, and reassemble in support of the main line, another 150 yards away. Morgan's final line formed about 150 yards in front of the true crest. At its center were the Continentals. The Virginia riflemen were posted on the left and right flanks. A Georgia militia company held the extreme right. Morgan placed his dragoons and a mounted Georgia infantry company a half-mile behind the main line as a reserve. By dawn, Morgan's men were in position.

Tarleton broke camp at 3 A.M. on 17 August and marched four hours to reach the Cowpens. On arrival, as Morgan anticipated, Tarleton immediately attacked, even before his infantry was fully formed. He placed his dragoons on the flanks and his legion cavalry in reserve. Morgan's men performed as ordered, firing and then withdrawing. Tarleton believed this latter meant the Americans were beaten, and he ordered his dragoons forward.

The British infantry and the American main line engaged in a heavy exchange of volleys lasting almost 30 minutes. The American flanking units, including the cavalry, then closed on the British line and forced its surrender. Tarleton ordered his only remaining reserve, his legion

horse, forward, but it rode off the battlefield. In the battle the British lost 100 killed and 829 captured (including 229 wounded), compared to American casualties of only 12 killed and 60 wounded.

This military masterpiece, often referred to as the "American Cannae," lifted Patriot morale, making it easier to recruit militia. It also deprived Cornwallis of his light infantry, which was a crucial factor in the upcoming campaign in North Carolina.

See also AMERICAN REVOLUTIONARY WAR, LAND OVERVIEW; GREENE'S OPERATIONS.

Further reading: Babits, Lawrence E. *A Devil of a Whipping: The Battle of Cowpens.* Chapel Hill: University of North Carolina Press, 1998; Buchanan, John. *The Road to Guilford Courthouse: The American Revolution in the Carolinas.* New York: Wiley, 1997; Edgar, Walter B. *Partisans and Redcoats: The American Revolution in the South Carolina Backcountry.* New York: Morrow, 2001; Fleming, Thomas J. *"Downright Fighting": The Story of Cowpens.* Washington, D.C.: U.S. Department of the Interior, 1988.

— Benjamin L. Huggins

Coxey's Army (1894) *An early example of laborers organizing peacefully to compel federal actions on their behalf*

In the wake of the Panic of 1893, Jacob Sechler Coxey (1854–1951), a Populist and former Greenbacker, recruited about 100 men and women from Ohio to join him in a march to Washington, D.C. There they would demand that Congress organize public work projects, primarily road-building, and authorize the printing of $500 million in currency to pay those hired to do the construction. Coxey himself was a well-to-do businessman in Massilion, Ohio, but his appeal was directed at those unable to find work as a consequence of the economic depression.

Departing on foot on Easter Sunday, 1894, Coxey's band proceeded through Pennsylvania to the nation's capital, joined by several hundred more followers along the way. Coxey's efforts to speak to a rally on the steps of the Capitol led to his arrest for trespassing and a 20-day jail sentence. Other members of his "army" were similarly arrested for trespassing on the Capitol lawn. Fifty of Coxey's Army were injured by police nightsticks and clubs. Returning to Ohio, Coxey ran for Congress as a Populist but was defeated.

The media attention that the trek of Coxey's Army attracted helped to publicize the issues of concern to these "petitioners in boots." It also further alarmed many already on edge about ongoing labor unrest, strikes, and anarchist activity. Notably, Coxey's campaign differed from earlier, somewhat similar, incidents, such as SHAYS'S REBELLION, in

Jacob S. Coxey (center, with glasses), 1914   *(Library of Congress)*

its peaceful intent. Although a near-total failure, Coxey's efforts served as an inspiration for such later marches on Washington, such as that of the Bonus Army in 1932.

Further reading: Hammond, Virgie L. *500 Rebels with a Cause: Coxey's Army Bound for Washington, D.C.* Quincy, Ill.: Mid-West Press, 1989; McMurry, Donald LeCrone. *Coxey's Army: A Study of the Industrial Army Movement of 1894.* New York: AMS Press, 1970; Schwantes, Carlos A. *Coxey's Army: An American Odyssey.* Lincoln: University of Nebraska Press, 1985.

— David W. Coffey

Craig, Malin (1875–1945) *U.S. Army general and chief of staff of the army*

Born on 5 August 1875 at St. Joseph, Missouri, Malin Craig entered the U.S. Military Academy at WEST POINT in 1894. The 1898 SPANISH-AMERICAN WAR caused his class to graduate one month early, and Craig was immediately

transferred to the cavalry. He took part in the Cuban campaign. Two years later he joined the relief expedition sent to China during the BOXER REBELLION and subsequently fought in the PHILIPPINE-AMERICAN WAR. He then attended the Infantry and Cavalry School, Army Staff College, and Army War College. These tours revealed Craig's substantial tactical and strategic abilities, which, with his administrative skills, brought teaching assignments at the Army War College and the General Service School, Fort Leavenworth.

When the United States entered World War I, Craig was serving in Washington under the chief of staff. He immediately sought overseas duty and in fall 1917 went to France with the AMERICAN EXPEDITIONARY FORCE (AEF), serving as chief of staff to the 41st Division and then I Corps. In 1918 he took part in the Second Battle of the MARNE and the SAINT-MIHIEL and MEUSE-ARGONNE Offensives, rising to brigadier general.

Between the wars Craig served as both director and commandant of the Army War College, assistant chief of staff for operations (G-3) of the Army General Staff, and chief of cavalry. In fall 1935 President Franklin D. ROOSEVELT unexpectedly selected the unassuming Craig to replace General Douglas MACARTHUR as army chief of staff, a position for which many others had lobbied fiercely. Facing threats of war in both Europe and Asia and greatly reduced military forces, the result of deep budgetary cuts in the 1920s and 1930s, Craig drastically reduced American mobilization plans to realistic and practicable levels. Immediately before and after American intervention in World War II, these plans provided an efficient and manageable blueprint for early American mobilization. Craig also instituted a major equipment purchasing program, upgraded American weaponry, reorganized the cavalry and infantry, and held the largest American peacetime military exercises to that date. Given that a persistent, bitter feud between Secretary of War Harry H. WOODRING and Under Secretary Louis JOHNSON tended to stymie all change within the War Department, Craig's quiet effectiveness in laying the foundation for his country's massive Second World War mobilization was the more remarkable.

Craig retired in August 1939 as a major general. Two years later he returned to active duty to head the War Department's Personnel Board, responsible for commissioning army officers. He held this post until shortly before his death at Washington, D.C., on 25 July 1945.

See also MARSHALL, GEORGE C.; WORLD WAR I, U.S. INVOLVEMENT.

Further reading: Bell, William. *Commanding Generals and Chiefs of Staff 1885–1983: Portraits and Biographical Sketches of the United States Army's Senior Officers.* Washington, D.C.: U.S. Army Center of Military History, 1999; McFarland, Keith D. *Harry H. Woodring: A Political Biography of FDR's Controversial Secretary of War.* Lawrence: University Press of Kansas, 1975; Pogue, Forrest C. *George C. Marshall: Education of a General, 1880–1939.* New York: Viking, 1963; Watson, Mark S. *Chief of Staff: Prewar Plans and Preparations.* Washington, D.C.: Historical Division, Department of the Army, 1950.

— Priscilla Roberts

Crater, Battle of the (Petersburg Mine Explosion)
30 July 1864 *Unsuccessful Union attempt to penetrate the Confederate defensive works and take Petersburg, Virginia*

Following a series of failed Federal assaults against PETERSBURG's formidable defenses, Federal troops constructed an opposing complex of trenches on the city's outskirts. A stalemate developed, and by the summer of 1864 the vital Confederate transportation hub was under siege. President Abraham LINCOLN, convinced that Petersburg was the key to capturing the Confederate capital of Richmond, put increasing pressure on his generals to reduce the city.

On 24 June Lieutenant Colonel Henry Pleasants, commander of the 48th Pennsylvania, a regiment composed of coal miners, submitted a radical plan to his superior, Major General Robert B. Potter. Pleasants targeted Elliott's Salient, a formidable Confederate emplacement opposite his own position. A mining engineer before the war, Pleasants proposed that his men excavate a tunnel between the trenches and detonate a large powder charge beneath the Confederate position. The resulting devastation and shock among the Confederates, Pleasants reasoned, would afford the Federal troops the opportunity to overwhelm the defenders.

Confident of the soundness of his scheme, Pleasants ordered his men to work before Potter could pass the proposal up the chain of command to his own superiors—IX Corps's commander, Major General Ambrose BURNSIDE, and, ultimately, Major General George G. MEADE, commanding the Army of the Potomac, and the Union army commander in chief, Lieutenant General Ulysses S. GRANT. By the time their grudging approval finally reached him, Pleasants's men had nearly completed their mine shaft.

The completed shaft, extending some 511 feet underground, held the distinction of being the longest military tunnel ever completed to that point. The wedge-shaped interior was approximately 4.5 feet in height, the same distance across the floor, and two feet across the ceiling. Pleasants' greatest achievement lay in the mine's ventilation system. He had instructed his troops to construct an eight-inch-square wooden duct that could be extended along the floor of the mine as the work progressed. He then ordered his men to construct, approximately 100 feet from the mine's mouth, a small fireplace and to drill a 22-foot exhaust shaft to the surface. By finally sealing the mouth of the mine with a burlap curtain, Pleasants created a flue effect that drew stale air out of the mine and fresh air in through the wooden duct.

Upon finally reaching the fort the miners excavated two powder magazines. On 28 July Pleasants reported the mine complete and charged with four tons of powder.

Unfortunately, the incompetence of Pleasants's superiors was more than a match for his considerable talents. Meade all but forgot the plan after approving it. By passing authority to the notoriously inept Burnside, the commander of the Army of the Potomac virtually assured a Federal disaster. Burnside initially proposed to lead the assault with two specially trained brigades of U.S. Colored Troops of Brigadier General Edward Ferrero's 4th Division. Citing political reasons, Meade and Grant overrode Burnside's plan and ordered him to lead the assault with a white unit. Too indecisive to choose a replacement division, Burnside ordered his remaining commanders to draw lots.

Leadership thus fell to Brigadier General James Ledlie, a reputed drunkard and coward, deemed by Grant "the worst commander in his corps."

Despite the confusion among his superiors, Pleasants detonated his mine at 4:44 A.M. on 30 July. The massive blast opened a 30-foot-deep crater some 60 feet across and nearly 200 feet wide, killing or wounding some 278 South Carolinians. The explosion, however, also stunned the Union attackers, poised only yards away.

Fifteen minutes elapsed between the blast and the Union assault, allowing the Confederates to regroup. By the time Federal troops reached the wrecked fort, Confederate troops had already begun to rally. Heavy fire from these troops as well as artillery fire from nearby batteries soon drove the attackers into the crater itself.

As the fighting intensified, Union leadership disintegrated. Both Ledlie and Ferrero abandoned their commands to seek the shelter of a surgeon's bombproof and medicinal rum supply. As more leaderless Federal troops crowded into the narrow front, Confederate brigadier general William Mahone organized a counterattack. Following some eight hours of hand-to-hand fighting, Federal officers finally surrendered to Mahone's men.

The Battle of the Crater was a humiliating defeat for the Union army. Of approximately 16,772 men engaged in the action, some 3,798 were killed, wounded, or missing. Of the 9,430 Confederates involved, 1,491 were casualties. While the Confederates congratulated themselves following the battle, the Union command searched for scapegoats, resulting in Burnside's ultimate resignation. Grant summed up the action as "the saddest affair I ever witnessed in the War."

See also CIVIL WAR, LAND OVERVIEW.

Further reading: Cavanaugh, Michael Arthur, and William Marvel. *The Battle of the Crater: "The Horrid Pit," June 25–August 6, 1864.* Lynchburg, Va.: H. E. Howard, 1989; Kinard, Jeff. *The Battle of the Crater.* Abilene, Tex.: McWhiney Foundation Press, 1995; Trudeau, Noah Andre. *The Last Citadel: Petersburg, Virginia, June 1864–April 1865.* Boston: Little, Brown, 1991.

— Jeff Kinard

Crazy Horse (Tashunca-uitco) (ca. 1842–1877)
Oglala Sioux chief and one of the most effective Native American war leaders

The birth date and early life of Crazy Horse are obscure. "Crazy Horse," or "Wild/Unbroken Horse," is the interpretation of his Indian name, Tashunca-uitco. A fearless fighter, he emerged as a leader of his people in their efforts to resist the encroachments of white America.

From 1865 to 1868 Crazy Horse participated in numerous actions in Wyoming, where he joined Oglala chief RED CLOUD in attacking emigrants and miners en route to the Montana gold fields, and later in challenging the establishment of military posts along the Bozeman Trail. He took part in the 1866 FETTERMAN DISASTER and the Hayfield and Wagon Box fights in 1867, which severely curtailed military activity in the region for some time.

Crazy Horse's marriage to a Cheyenne woman led to an alliance with the Northern Cheyenne, who thereafter formed the majority of his followers. Along with various Sioux tribes, the Cheyenne persistently defied treaties that confined them to reservations.

In 1874 gold was discovered in the Black Hills, an area considered sacred to the Indians of the northern plains and one set aside as a reservation in 1868. Miners soon invaded the reservation, and the Indians were ordered out. The army moved into the Powder River country to drive the "hostiles" onto less desirable portions of the reservation. Crazy Horse and other leaders resisted. On 17 June 1876 Crazy Horse's Cheyenne and Sioux force of 1,200 warriors attacked Brigadier General George CROOK's 1,300 soldiers and Indian auxiliaries in the Battle of the ROSEBUD RIVER. Crazy Horse's warriors stymied Crook's advance, inflicting heavy losses and forcing Crook to withdraw.

Crazy Horse then moved north to the LITTLE BIGHORN, where he joined Sioux Medicine Man SITTING BULL's large village. Here he and his warriors participated in the annihilation on 25 June of Lieutenant Colonel George A. CUSTER and much of his 7th Cavalry Regiment. Crazy Horse continued thereafter to fight against the troops of Colonel Nelson A. MILES, whose relentless campaign took its toll.

On 6 May 1877 Crazy Horse surrendered to General Crook at Fort Robinson, Nebraska, and settled at the Red Cloud Agency. On 5 September Crazy Horse was arrested for leaving the agency without proper authorization. Two days later, as he was taken into custody, he resisted and was mortally wounded, apparently bayoneted by one of his guards.

See also AMERICAN INDIAN WARS, OVERVIEW; INDIAN WARFARE; SIOUX WARS; TERRY, ALFRED H.

Further reading: Ambrose, Stephen E. *Crazy Horse and Custer: The Parallel Lives of Two American Warriors.* New York: Doubleday, 1975; McMurtry, Larry. *Crazy Horse.* New York: Penguin, 1999; Sajna, Mike. *Crazy Horse: The Life behind the Legend.* New York: Wiley, 2001.

— Robert Beeks

Creek War (1813–1814) *Internal tribal war that resulted in American intervention and victory*

Loosely united in a confederacy, the Creek tribes of Alabama and Georgia had become increasingly divided by the early 19th century. While most of the Upper Creek maintained traditional lifestyles, many Lower Creek had adopted white agricultural techniques and intermarried with whites. It was in this context that the Shawnee leader TECUMSEH, whose mother was Creek, visited the Creek nation in the fall of 1811 and spoke before the Creek Council. Although historians are divided on whether Tecumseh sought to incite war against the United States or simply to prevent further land cessions to whites, his visit increased tension between the Upper and Lower Creek. After a band of Upper Creek (Koasati) led by Little Warrior (Tuskeegee Tustunnuggee) traveled with Tecumseh on his return north, they became heavily influenced by the spiritual teachings of Tecumseh's brother TENSKWATAWA (known as the Shawnee Prophet) and upon their return spread his message to reject white culture among their Upper Creek brethren.

Civil war broke out in 1813 after the Creek Council, dominated by Lower Creek such as Big Warrior (Tustennuge Thlocco) and influenced by the federal Indian agent Benjamin Hawkins, ordered the execution of six Upper Creek (including Little Warrior) who had killed white settlers. In response to the executions, prowar Upper Creek known as the Red-Sticks (led by Menauway, Hopoie Tustanugga, Peter McQueen, and Hossa Yaholo) placed the council headquarters at Tuckabatchee under siege in June 1813, forcing Big Warrior and his followers to evacuate in July.

Meanwhile, a party of about 200 Red-Sticks led by McQueen went to Pensacola to obtain arms and on 27 July 1813 defeated a party of whites that confronted them at Burnt Corn Creek (approximately 80 miles north of Pensacola). At this juncture, William Weatherford (Red Eagle) became the principal war chief of the Creek. One month later, on 30 August 1813, Red-Stick warriors from 13 Upper Creek towns massacred as many as 500 men, women, and children (whites and mixed-bloods) at Fort Mims (approximately 35 miles north of Mobile on the Alabama River). The Fort Mims Massacre hastened American intervention, but it did not cause it. The federal government had already authorized Georgia and Tennessee (as well as the Mississippi Territory) to mobilize their militias against the Creek because of suspicions that the Creeks had allied with the British, against whom the United States was fighting in the WAR OF 1812.

American intervention decisively changed the nature of the Creek conflict. The Red-Sticks could mobilize at most 4,000 warriors and lacked access to military supplies; the white settlers in the surrounding states could not only mobilize more, better equipped militia but also could count upon the assistance of allied Cherokee and Choctaw. The Americans planned a three-pronged invasion of the Upper Creek territory: Brigadier General John Floyd would attack from Georgia with approximately 1,000 militiamen; Brigadier General Ferdinand L. Claiborne would attack from Mississippi with a mixed force of 1,000 regulars and militiamen and 135 Choctaw under Pushmataha; and, finally, Major General Andrew JACKSON and Brigadier General John Coffee would invade from Tennessee with 2,500 militiamen supported by about 600 Cherokee. In late November Floyd's Georgians burned two Red-Stick villages (Autosee and Tallassie), killing approximately 200 warriors, before withdrawing to the Chattahoochee River, where they built Fort Mitchell. Claiborne succeeded in burning the Red-Stick spiritual center of Ecunchate (near modern Benton, Alabama) in December, but he too withdrew after running short of supplies. The brunt of the fighting, therefore, fell to Jackson's Tennesseans.

After assembling his forces in Fayetteville in early October, Jackson moved south into Alabama, establishing Fort Deposit as a supply base on the Tennessee River and Fort Strother as an operations base on the Coosa River. On 3 November cavalry under Coffee attacked Tullushatchee, surrounding and killing more than 200 Red-Stick warriors. On 9 November Jackson attacked some 700 Red-Sticks at Talladega, killing approximately 300. On 18 November Cocke's forces also massacred some 60 Red-Stick warriors who attempted to surrender at Hillaubee. Despite these successes, Jackson withdrew to Fort Strother, where he not only faced low supplies but also had personally to put down a mutiny.

Jackson suffered defeats at Emuckfaw (22 January 1814), Enotachoplo (24 January), and Calibee Creek (27 January), but the arrival of reinforcements in February increased his army to 5,000 men, allowing him to resume the offensive. After marching to the Tallapoosa River, where Red-Stick forces had fortified themselves on a peninsula, Jackson won the Battle of HORSESHOE BEND/TOHOPEKA (27 March 1814), killing more than 900 Red-Stick warriors. Promoted to major general in the U.S. Army and commissioned to negotiate peace terms, Jackson forced the Creek to sign the Treaty of Fort Jackson, which stripped them of approximately two-thirds of their land (20 million acres) in Alabama and Georgia. Thus a major obstacle to white migration in the Old Southwest had been removed.

See also AMERICAN INDIAN WARS, OVERVIEW; DALE, RICHARD; INDIAN WARFARE.

Further reading: Griffith, Benjamin W. *McIntosh and Weatherford: Creek Indian Leaders.* Tuscaloosa: University of Alabama Press, 1998; Owsley, Frank L. *Struggle for the Gulf Borderlands: The Creek War and the Battle of New Orleans, 1812–1815.* Gainesville: University of Florida Press, 1981; Remini, Robert V. *Andrew Jackson and the Course of American Empire, 1767–1821.* New York:

Harper & Row, 1977; ———. *Andrew Jackson and His Indian Wars*. New York: Viking Penguin, 2001.

— Justin D. Murphy

Crook, George (1828–1890) *U.S. Army general*
Born on 8 September 1828 near Dayton, Ohio, George Crook graduated from the U.S. Military Academy at WEST POINT in 1852. Commissioned a second lieutenant and posted to the 4th Infantry Regiment, he served in California and Washington State.

A first lieutenant at the outbreak of the Civil War, Crook was promoted to captain in the 4th Infantry in May 1861. In September he entered the U.S. Volunteers as colonel of the 36th Ohio Infantry and saw much action in western (later West) Virginia.

Promoted to brigadier general of volunteers in September 1862, Crook commanded a brigade in the Army of the Potomac in the Battles of South Mountain and ANTIETAM/SHARPSBURG. In February 1863 he transferred to the western theater and commanded a cavalry division in the Army of the Cumberland in the September Battle of CHICKAMAUGA. In February 1864 Crook returned to West Virginia to command the Kanawha District and in May won the Battle of Cloyd's Mountain. That August he assumed command of the Army and Department of West Virginia. His force became the VIII Corps, Army of the Shenandoah, during Major General Philip SHERIDAN's fall campaign. Crook led his corps at Winchester, Fisher's Hill, and Cedar Creek, and he was promoted to major general of volunteers in October 1864.

In February 1865 Crook was captured by Confederate partisans at his headquarters in Cumberland, Maryland, and taken to Libby Prison in Richmond. Exchanged in March, he commanded a cavalry division (and briefly the Cavalry Corps) in the Army of the Potomac during the closing operations in Virginia. Breveted through major general in the regular army, he mustered out of the volunteers to resume his career as lieutenant colonel of the new 23d Infantry.

During the AMERICAN INDIAN WARS Crook quickly built a reputation as an active and innovative campaigner. He revolutionized the employment of INDIAN SCOUTS and auxiliaries, popularized the use of pack mules instead of burdensome wagon trains, and studied his Indian adversaries. A vigorous fighter, he was compassionate and respectful in victory. Crook insisted on honesty in negotiations and worked tirelessly for better treatment of the Indians.

Crook's methods paid off. He suppressed the Paiute in the Northwest and subdued the Apache in Arizona. In 1873 his success in the APACHE WARS brought him direct promotion from lieutenant colonel to brigadier general, a rare and controversial occurrence in the post–Civil War army. Commanding the Department of the Platte, Crook participated in the 1876 SIOUX WAR. On 17 June his column was turned back by CRAZY HORSE's warriors in the Battle of the ROSEBUD RIVER, which contributed indirectly to the disaster on the LITTLE BIGHORN days later. Crook played a major role in the subsequent campaign to conquer the Sioux and Cheyenne.

In 1882 Crook returned to Arizona in the wake of renewed Apache uprisings. During the next four years he campaigned relentlessly. He secured GERONIMO's surrender, only to have the dreaded warrior bolt once again. In 1886 Brigadier General Nelson A. MILES replaced Crook and eventually accepted Geronimo's surrender.

Promoted to major general in 1888, Crook assumed command of the Military Division of the Missouri, with headquarters in Chicago. Outraged at the government's treatment of loyal Indian scouts, he became a forceful advocate of Indian rights. Crook died in Chicago on 21 March 1890. Crook, Miles, and Brigadier General Ranald S. MACKENZIE were outstanding army field commanders of the Indian Wars.

See also INDIAN WARFARE; SHENANDOAH VALLEY CAMPAIGNS.

Further reading: Aleshire, Peter. *The Fox and the Whirlwind: General George Crook and Geronimo: A Paired Biography*. New York: Wiley, 2000. Crook, George. *General George Crook: His Autobiography*. Edited by Martin F. Schmitt. New ed. Norman: University of Oklahoma Press, 1960; Utley, Robert M. *Frontier Regulars: The United States Army and the Indian, 1866–1891*. New York: Macmillan, 1973.

—David Coffey

Crowder, Enoch H. (1859–1932) *U.S. Army general, judge advocate general of the army, and ambassador to Cuba*
Born on 11 April 1859 in Grundy County, Missouri, Enoch Herbert Crowder graduated from the U.S. Military Academy at West Point in 1881. He joined the 8th Cavalry Regiment but studied law in his spare time and by 1884 had won admission to the bar in Missouri, Texas, and federal courts. In 1895, following service in New Mexico, North Dakota, and Omaha, Nebraska, Crowder joined the Judge Advocate's Department, the army's legal branch, where he passed his remaining military career.

During the SPANISH-AMERICAN WAR Crowder went to the Philippines as a judge advocate, helping to negotiate the terms of Manila's surrender. He subsequently drafted a new Philippine criminal code. During 1900–1901, as secretary to the military governor, Major General Arthur

MACARTHUR, he supervised much of the islands' administration. Joining the army's new General Staff in 1903, during 1904–1905 Crowder observed the Russo-Japanese War from Manchuria. In 1906 when the United States, citing internal Cuban disorder, established a provisional government in Cuba under the 1901 Platt Amendment, Crowder functioned as that administration's legal adviser, supervising its Departments of State and Justice and drafting wide-ranging new statutes governing national, provincial, and local administration and the judicial, military, electoral, and fiscal systems.

Returning to the United States after supervising the 1908 Cuban elections, in 1911 Crowder became advocate general of the army, streamlining, rationalizing, and humanizing its penal and courts-martial system. After American intervention in World War I, Crowder drafted a conscription measure, the 1917 SELECTIVE SERVICE Act, under which the United States registered 24 million young men and inducted almost 3 million into the army. By allowing deferments for men with dependents or in vital occupations to be allocated by local draft boards—a loophole that could admit favoritism and discrimination—Crowder nonetheless made conscription more politically acceptable. His May 1918 "work or fight" policy, mandating the conscription of workers in occupations deemed nonessential for the war effort, eventually enhanced the government's ability to direct labor to occupations valuable to the war effort.

In 1919 Crowder revisited Cuba, still in turmoil, to draft a new and largely ineffective electoral code. Again returning to Cuba in 1921 as President Warren G. Harding's special envoy and residing on an American battleship moored in Havana harbor, Crowder forcefully exhorted Cuban president Alfredo Zayas to balance the budget, eradicate corruption, and implement constitutional and economic reforms. He blocked a badly needed loan from J. P. Morgan & Company until this took place. In 1922 Crowder's "moralization program" led to the replacement of Cuba's cabinet officials with his handpicked substitutes.

Retiring from the army in 1923, Crowder immediately became the first American ambassador to Cuba, enjoying a less fraught relationship with Zayas's successor, Gerardo Machado. From 1927 to 1931 he practiced law in Chicago. Crowder died in Washington, D.C., on 7 May 1932.

See also AMERICAN EXPEDITIONARY FORCE (AEF); BAKER, NEWTON D.; LATIN AMERICA INTERVENTIONS, EARLY 20TH-CENTURY; MARCH, PEYTON C.; PALMER, JOHN M.; ROOT, ELIHU; WORLD WAR, U.S. INVOLVEMENT.

Further reading: Chambers, John Witeclay, II. *To Raise an Army: The Draft Comes to Modern America.* New York: Free Press, 1987. Crowder, Enoch H. *The Spirit of Selective Service.* New York: Century, 1920; Lockmiller, David A.

Enoch H. Crowder: Soldier, Lawyer and Statesman. Columbia: University of Missouri Press, 1955; Perez, Louis A., Jr. *Cuba under the Platt Amendment, 1902–1934.* Pittsburgh, Pa.: University of Pittsburgh Press, 1986.

— Priscilla Roberts

Crown Point *Strategic peninsula that juts out into the southern narrows of Lake Champlain, dominating passing traffic*

The first recorded clash at Crown Point dates back to French explorer Samuel Champlain's expedition in 1609. His use of firearms on behalf of allied Indians in a battle with the Iroquois initiated a long period of enmity between them and the French. The French first fortified the position in 1731 as Fort Saint-Frédéric. Joint British and colonial expeditions failed to take it in 1755 and 1756. The decisive shift in British fortunes later in the FRENCH AND INDIAN WAR allowed Major General Sir Jeffrey Amherst to capture it without resistance in 1759. The French garrison having destroyed the fort at his approach, Amherst set about refortifying the area, although on a slightly different site. Amherst's fort was never completed, and in 1775 the British garrison consisted of a few cannon, served by nine enlisted men and 10 women and children. After the American Patriots' capture of FORT TICONDEROGA on 10 May 1775, Crown Point too fell to the rebel forces, without resistance. The Americans continued to hold the fort while using the Lake Champlain gateway to advance their invasion of CANADA, but it was reoccupied by the British after that expedition failed. The Americans in turn retook Crown Point until the approach of Major General John Burgoyne's forces in June 1777. The British again had to abandon it after Burgoyne's defeat at SARATOGA.

See also CROWN POINT, EXPEDITION AGAINST.

Further reading: Anderson, Fred. *Crucible of War: The Seven Years' War and the Fate of Empire in British North America, 1754–1766.* New York: Knopf, 2000; Ketchum, Richard M. *Saratoga: Turning Point in the America's Revolutionary War.* New York: Henry Holt, 1997.

— Wayne E. Lee

Crown Point, expedition against

(August–September 1755) *Unsuccessful British attempt during the French and Indian War to capture Fort Saint-Frédéric*

Built at CROWN POINT in 1734 by the French, Fort Saint-Frédéric controlled movement through the Champlain Valley and served as a staging point for French raids on the British colonies. To reduce this military threat and territorial challenge, the superintendent of northern Indian affairs, Sir William JOHNSON, led a force of provincials and Iroquois against the French outpost.

Johnson's expedition suffered delays from the outset. Competing for supplies, recruits, and Indian support with Massachusetts governor William SHIRLEY's expedition against FORT NIAGARA, Johnson spent months assembling his force and building the bateaux necessary to carry his army along the Lac Saint Sacrament–Lake Champlain waterway. En route he paused to build Fort Edward at the Great Carrying Place, cut a 16-mile portage road from Edward to Lac Saint Sacrament, and train his 3,500 provincials. By early September Johnson's army had reached only the southern tip of Lac Saint Sacrament.

Johnson's timidity and tardiness, as well as Major General Edward BRADDOCK's defeat at the Battle of the MONONGAHELA in August, allowed the French to reinforce Fort Saint Frédéric and attack the provincials' camp on 7 September. The resulting Battle of LAKE GEORGE was technically a British victory. However, casualties and demoralization among the troops, the wholesale desertion of the Mohawk, and new French entrenchments at Fort Carillon (TICONDEROGA) prompted Johnson to halt the expedition in late September after the construction of FORT WILLIAM HENRY on Lake George's southern shore.

See also FRENCH AND INDIAN WAR.

Further reading: Anderson, Fred. *Crucible of War: The Seven Years' War and the Fate of Empire in British North America, 1754–1766.* New York: Knopf, 2000; Jennings, Francis. *Empire of Fortune: Crowns, Colonies and Tribes in the Seven Years' War.* New York: Norton, 1988; Leach, Douglas E. *Arms for Empire: A Military History of the British in North America, 1607–1763.* New York: MacMillan, 1973; Starbuck, David R. *The Great Warpath: British Military Sites from Albany to Crown Point.* Hanover, N.H.: University Press of New England, 1999.

— David M. Corlett

cruisers *Fast, medium-sized warships equipped with moderate armament*

The cruiser ship-type dates to the Age of Fighting Sail in the 18th century. Ships known as FRIGATES often served on detached duty from a battle fleet to "cruise" in search of enemy ships and report any sightings to the main battle force. Frigates were also used to protect trade routes and raid enemy commerce.

In the mid-19th century, the advent of steam propulsion and iron armor produced the first modern cruisers for the missions previously given to frigates. The U.S. Navy took the early lead in their development in 1863 when it

USS *St. Louis* (CL 49), 1939   *(Naval Historical Foundation)*

laid down the *Wampanoag*, which many historians consider the first purpose-built cruiser. Other powers subsequently built similar cruisers to meet the traditional demands and address modern ones, such as the defense of capital ships against torpedo attack.

U.S. cruiser construction lagged significantly behind that of other world powers for nearly two decades after the Civil War. With the return of peace, much of the large U.S. Navy fleet was scrapped as unnecessary, and new ships were considered needless expenditures. In the 1880s, however, Congress came to see new ships as essential to protect U.S. interests in the Western Hemisphere. Indeed, the cruisers of the European powers and even some South American states were far more powerful than any belonging to the United States. In 1883 Congress authorized the construction of three steel-hulled cruisers: the *Atlanta*, the *Boston*, and the *Chicago*. These are generally regarded as the beginning of the modern U.S. steel navy.

By the end of the 19th century, cruisers comprised two types. The first was the armored cruiser, which displaced around 15,000 tons and was designed to operate with capital ships. The second, less powerful type was the protected cruiser, the armor of which was concentrated mostly on the decks to protect its machinery from plunging shellfire. Most naval powers built armored cruisers in the late 1880s and switched to protected cruisers in the 1890s.

The United States generally built armored cruisers, constructing 12 between 1890 and 1908. American naval officials believed that this type was more useful because it could be employed in a wider range of tasks, one of the most important being participation in engagements between battle fleets in war. Nevertheless, in late 1892 the U.S. Navy launched the 5,900-ton protected cruiser *Olympia*. This ship and the previously built cruisers formed the backbone of American naval forces during the 1898 SPANISH-AMERICAN WAR. By 1905 the experience gleaned from this conflict had led to the construction of an additional nine protected cruisers.

The U.S. cruiser force was rendered obsolete in 1908 when Great Britain launched a new type of all-big-gun armored cruiser known as the battle cruiser. The innovative design effectively stopped U.S. cruiser construction; naval officials now pursued battle cruiser designs. As a result, the U.S. cruiser force by the beginning of World War I in 1914 numbered only 37 ships, as opposed to 124 for Great Britain and 56 for Germany.

WORLD WAR I (1914–18) proved the importance of slightly smaller cruisers over that of the battle cruiser, which performed poorly at the 1916 Battle of Jutland. Cruisers carried out a variety of duties, including commerce raiding and protection, fleet reconnaissance, and engagements with forces of similar composition. Following the U.S. declaration of war against Germany in April 1917, U.S. Navy cruisers were largely devoted to escorting merchant and troop convoys across the Atlantic.

U.S. cruiser construction did not abate during the interwar years. All major maritime powers saw cruisers as essential for trade protection and fire support in amphibious operations. Cruisers also proliferated as part of a new naval arms race. The 1922 Washington Naval Conference placed restrictions on the number of battleships but set no such limitations on cruisers. The United States laid down 10 cruisers of the *Pensacola*, the *Northampton*, and the *Portland* classes between 1926 and 1930. All mounted eight-inch guns and had maximum displacements between 12,755 and 14,420 tons. Further arms agreements attempted to curtail this new arms race but were only partially successful. From 1934 to 1941, the U.S. built 19 cruisers of the *New Orleans*, the *Brooklyn*, and the *Atlanta* classes.

These ships served well in World War II, particularly in the Pacific theater. Cruisers formed the backbone of the U.S. surface fleet for the first year of the war following the December 1941 Japanese attack on PEARL HARBOR. Generally, the traditional reconnaissance role of cruisers was supplanted by that of protecting BATTLESHIPS and AIRCRAFT CARRIERS against air attack and providing shore bombardment. Cruisers were also used for commerce protection and in surface actions against forces of comparatively equal strength. During the course of the war, the United States built 33 cruisers of varying types. At the conclusion of the conflict, its 79 cruisers were second in number only to the 91-ship total of Great Britain.

The United States in the postwar years led the world in the construction of cruisers that incorporated a major technological innovation, missiles. In 1955 and 1956 the U.S. Navy reconstructed the World War II–era cruisers *Boston* and *Canberra* with a hybrid armament of guns and missiles. In the late 1950s and early 1960s all major maritime powers either converted or built cruisers with missiles as their main armament. Today's cruisers carry a combination of short and long-range missiles augmented by light defensive guns. They can attack aircraft, submarines, or surface ships; they are the most powerful surface warships in the world with the exception of aircraft carriers. In 2001 the U.S. Navy operated 27 *Ticonderoga*-class cruisers, making its force the largest in the world.

See also NAVY, U.S.; WASHINGTON AND LONDON NAVAL AGREEMENTS.

Further reading: Friedman, Norman. *U.S. Cruisers: An Illustrated Design History.* Annapolis, Md.: Naval Institute Press, 1984; George, James L. *History of Warships: From Ancient Times to the Twenty-first Century.* Annapolis, Md.:

Naval Institute Press, 1998; Howarth, Stephen. *To Shining Sea: A History of the United States Navy, 1775–1991.* New York: Random House, 1991; Musicant, Ivan. *Armored Cruisers: A Design and Operational History.* Annapolis, Md.: Naval Institute Press, 1985.

— Eric W. Osborne

Crysler's Farm, Battle of (11 November 1813)

Land battle on the Canadian frontier during the War of 1812

Major General William Henry HARRISON defeated the British in the October 1813 Battle of the THAMES, but other U.S. efforts in Canada that year failed. When Major General Henry DEARBORN's forces failed to secure the Niagara Peninsula, Secretary of War John ARMSTRONG settled on a move against Montreal. If U.S. forces could take that city, they could control the St. Lawrence River and cut off the chief British base at Kingston on Lake Ontario, the key to Upper Canada. Dearborn's replacement, Major General James WILKINSON, then traveled to SACKETT'S HARBOR to meet with U.S. Navy commodore Isaac CHAUNCEY and plan the campaign. They decided that while naval forces sealed off Kingston Harbor so that British naval vessels could not interfere, two land forces would advance on Montreal: Wilkinson's left, or western, wing of some 8,000 untrained regulars would move from Sackett's Harbor, while Major General Wade Hampton's right, or eastern, wing of 5,000 men departed the Lake Champlain area. This was not an effective arrangement, as Hampton and Wilkinson despised each other; cooperation between them was to be spotty at best.

Wilkinson's men departed Sackett's Harbor for the St. Lawrence in several hundred open bateaux and immediately ran into bad weather. High winds and sleet separated the boats and sank several dozen, with major loss of life. To make matters worse, Chauncey failed to prevent a number of British gunboats from following the Americans. At the same time, some 800 British regulars under Lieutenant Colonel Joseph Morrison shadowed the American advance along the Canadian shoreline.

Wilkinson managed to keep his force largely together until he approached the eight miles of the Long Sault Rapids in the St. Lawrence. Wilkinson put most of the men ashore to march around while the boats transited the rapids with lighter loads. Colonel Winfield SCOTT's brigade was to ward off any British attempt on the marchers or the boats as they traversed the rapids. Later Wilkinson sent Brigadier General Jacob BROWN's brigade with Scott's to the town of Cornwall, leaving only Brigadier General John Boyd's brigade near the boats. Wilkinson considered these 2,500 men sufficient to deal with Morrison's regulars and Canadian militiamen.

Wilkinson, his troops ashore and encamped for the night, learned that Morrison had established headquarters at John Crysler's farm nearby; he ordered Boyd, a commander with considerable military experience, to attack Morrison. Boyd moved out on the morning of 11 November. His troops attacked the British piecemeal, and the well-trained British regulars were able to shift their forces to defeat each thrust in turn. Boyd later sent in DRAGOONS, but superior British firepower prevented the horsemen from drawing close enough to fight with pistols and sabers.

Boyd then broke off the attack. Americans losses in the battle were 102 killed, 237 wounded, and more than 100 missing. The British lost 22 killed, 148 wounded, and nine missing. The Americans then crossed in their boats to the American side of the river. The next day Wilkinson learned that Hampton's force had been defeated in a battle at the CHÂTEAUGUAY River. He used this as a pretext for calling off the campaign and entering winter quarters.

Wilkinson blamed the failure to take Montreal on Hampton and his own subordinates, but in March 1814 Armstrong relieved Wilkinson, replacing him with Brown. Although Wilkinson was cleared in a court-martial he was cashiered from the army in 1815.

See also WAR OF 1812, LAND OVERVIEW.

Further reading: Graves, Donald E. *Field of Glory: The Battle of Crysler's Farm.* Toronto: Robin Brass Studio, 1999. Mahon, John K. *The War of 1812.* Gainesville: University Presses of Florida, 1972; Stanley, George F. G. *The War of 1812: Land Operations.* Toronto: Macmillan, 1983.

— Lawyn Edwards

Cuban missile crisis (October 1962) *Confrontation between the United States and the Soviet Union, the only time during the cold war that the two superpowers almost embarked on a full-scale nuclear war*

In October 1962, U-2 reconnaissance planes provided President John F. KENNEDY with photographic evidence that the Soviets had installed intermediate-range nuclear weapons on Cuba, little more than 100 miles from the American coast.

In 1958 an indigenous revolutionary movement led by Fidel Castro had seized power from Fulgencio Batista, dictator of Cuba since 1933 and a U.S. client. Although Castro initially declared that he was not a communist, from spring 1959 he covertly sought Soviet aid and military protection; American economic pressure and boycotts quickly gave him an excuse to move openly into the Soviet camp. In response, the CENTRAL INTELLIGENCE AGENCY planned to assist Cuban exiles in an attack on the island and an overthrow of Castro. Initiated under President Dwight D. EISENHOWER and inherited by Kennedy, the March 1961 BAY OF PIGS invasion attempt proved a humiliating fiasco for the United States. Kennedy and his advisers thereafter continued to devise plans, often both ingenious and far-fetched, to overthrow Castro, who sought further Soviet succor.

In mid-1961, as the Berlin crisis intensified, military hard-liners in the Kremlin, frustrated for several years, succeeded in obtaining 34 percent increases in spending on conventional forces. They may have been energized by both the Bay of Pigs and Kennedy's bellicose inauguration-day rhetoric that his country would "pay any price, bear any burden, meet any hardship, support any friend, oppose any foe to assure the survival and success of liberty."

The recent deployment of U.S. intermediate-range Jupiter missiles in Turkey, threatening Soviet territory, further angered the Soviet premier, Nikita Khrushchev. He also hoped to pressure the United States to make concessions on Berlin. In addition, Khrushchev apparently felt a romantic sense of solidarity with the new, revolutionary Cuban state, which reassured him and other old communists that their cause still possessed international vitality. He therefore offered Soviet nuclear missiles, under the control of Soviet technicians and troops, to Castro, who accepted.

When American officials discovered the presence of the missiles, the secret Executive Committee of top presidential advisers met to decide on a response. These advisers included the Joint Chiefs of Staff, Secretary of State Dean Rusk, Secretary of Defense Robert S. MCNAMARA, National Security Adviser McGeorge Bundy, and the president's brother, Attorney General Robert F. Kennedy.

However logical Khrushchev's behavior, politically it would have been almost impossible for any American president to accept the situation. In 1962 the Cuban missiles would have doubled or even trebled the number of Soviet warheads targeted on the United States. Eventually, Kennedy demanded that the Soviet Union remove the missiles, announcing a naval blockade, or "quarantine," around the island. A tense period followed as Washington waited to see whether the Soviets would attempt to force the blockade. After some hesitation, Khrushchev acquiesced, but he also secretly obtained an unpublicized pledge that the United States would likewise shortly remove the Jupiters from Turkey. The United States also promised not to mount another invasion of Cuba.

Recently released tapes of conversations among Kennedy and his advisers reveal that to avoid nuclear war, he was prepared to make even greater concessions to the Soviets. In that he parted company with some of his more hard-line advisers, such as General Curtis LEMAY. Showing considerable statesmanship, Kennedy deliberately refrained from emphasizing Khrushchev's humiliation. Still, recently opened documentary evidence reveals that the Cuban situation was even more critical than most involved then realized. American officials underestimated by a factor of four the number of Soviet troops on the island. They also failed to realize that 158 warheads, the use of which Castro urged should the United States invade, were already operational, and that 42 of these could have reached American territory. The potential for triggering a full-scale nuclear war almost certainly existed—retrospectively, chilling evidence of the dangers inherent in these weapons.

The Cuban missile crisis had a sobering impact on its protagonists. Humiliation at American hands impelled Soviet leaders to instigate an expensive major nuclear buildup to achieve parity with the United States, achieving this by 1970. The Soviet Union also built a powerful blue-water fleet.

Khrushchev's fall from power in 1964 was probably at least partly due to the missile crisis. On Kennedy it exerted a certain salutary maturing effect, leading the once brash young president to advocate disarmament strongly in the final months before his assassination in November 1963. His new stance impelled the Soviet leadership to establish a teletype "hot line" between Moscow and Washington to facilitate communications and ease tension during international crises. The two powers also finally reached agreement on a limited test-ban treaty, which had been stagnant for several years. Ratified in October 1963, it ended atmospheric testing of nuclear weapons. On no subsequent occasion did the two superpowers move so close to outright nuclear war.

See also COLD WAR; CONTAINMENT, DOCTRINE AND COURSE OF.

Further reading: Blight, James, and David Welch, eds. *Intelligence and the Cuban Missile Crisis.* London: Frank Cass, 1998; Fursenko, Aleksandr, and Timothy Naftali. *One Hell of a Gamble: Khrushchev, Castro, and Kennedy, 1958–1964.* New York: Norton, 1997; Gaddis, John Lewis. *We Now Know: Rethinking Cold War History.* New York: Oxford University Press, 1997; May, Ernest R., and Philip D. Zelikow, eds. *The Kennedy Tapes: Inside the White House during the Cuban Missile Crisis.* Cambridge, Mass.: Harvard University Press, 1997.

— Priscilla Roberts

Cunningham, Randall (Duke) (1941–) *U.S. Navy officer and congressman*
Born on 8 December 1941 at Los Angeles, California, Randall "Duke" Cunningham graduated from the University of Missouri in 1964 and earned a master's degree in education there the following year. For the next three years

Cunningham taught and coached in Hinsdale, Illinois, and San Diego.

In 1967 Cunningham joined the U.S. Navy. He completed pilot training the next year at the Miramar Naval Air Station, California. Assigned to Fighter Squadron 96, he served his first tour of duty during the VIETNAM WAR aboard the aircraft carrier *America* during 1969–70. Cunningham's second Vietnam tour was aboard the carrier *Constellation* in 1972, flying the F-4 Phantom. On 19 January 1972, Cunningham shot down a North Vietnamese MiG-21. He downed a MiG-19 on 8 May and three MiG-17s on 10 May. While returning to the carrier from the latter mission, his plane was hit by a surface-to-air missile. Both he and his radio-intercept officer were rescued by helicopter at the mouth of the Red River. With his five "kills," Cunningham was the only navy "ace" of the Vietnam War. He was also the first F-4 ace and the first ace to win all his victories with missiles. Cunningham flew 300 missions in Vietnam.

Cunningham was later assigned as an instructor to the navy's "Top Gun" school for advanced fighter pilots, at Miramar. He also served in Washington, D.C., and Japan before returning to Miramar in 1984, where he commanded the Adversary Squadron, which mimicked Soviet tactics and formations to enhance pilot combat skills. Many of his experiences were depicted in the film *Top Gun*. Cunningham retired from the navy in 1987 as a commander.

After retirement, Cunningham went into business in San Diego. He won election to the U.S. House of Representatives as a Republican in 1990.

See also AIRCRAFT, FIXED-WING.

Further reading: Cunningham, Randy. *Fox Two*. Mesa, Ariz.: Champlin Fighter Museum, 1984; Wilcox, Robert K. *Scream of Eagles: The Creation of Top Gun and the U.S. Air Victory in Vietnam*. New York: Wiley, 1990.

— John David Rausch, Jr.

Curtiss, Glenn H. (1878–1930) *Aeronautical engineer and aircraft designer; next to the Wright brothers, the most influential early American aviator*

Born on 21 May 1878 at Hammondsport, New York, Glenn Hammond Curtiss early experimented with bicycles, motorcycles, and flying devices. In 1901, after working at George Eastman's Kodak plant at Rochester, he established his own motorcycle manufacturing company, which led him into the development of aircraft engines. In 1907 he set a land speed record for motorcycles. His success with engines led to his involvement with the Aerial Experiment Association (AEA).

Curtiss designed the *June Bug*, AEA's third aircraft and first successful design. It won the Scientific American trophy in 1908. In 1909, in partnership with Augustus Herring,

Curtiss started America's first aircraft manufacturing company. Having established his credibility as an aircraft designer, in 1911 he began a flying school at San Diego to train pioneer army and navy pilots.

Also that year Curtiss developed the first amphibious aircraft, the A-1 Triad hydroplane, the world's first practical hydroplane and an important advance because of the lack of airfields at the time. This seaplane quickly caught the attention of the U.S. Navy. Soon Curtiss became known as the father of U.S. naval aviation.

During World War I, the Curtiss Aeroplane and Motor Company sold flying boats to both the United States and the Allies. It also developed the Curtiss JN-4 Jenny, which for years to come would be the training aircraft for virtually all U.S. and Canadian pilots.

In 1919 a U.S. Navy Curtiss NC-4 made a transatlantic flight. Ten years later his company merged with Wright Aeronautical. The Curtiss-Wright Company continued its development of aircraft. Curtiss had removed himself from active management of the company by 1921. He moved to Florida and made more money in five years in real estate than he had in all his years in aviation. He died at Hammondsport, New York, on 23 July 1930.

The Curtiss-Wright Company continued after his death. The company became famous for its air-cooled, radial engines. It also produced some 30,000 aircraft during World War II, including the P-40 Warhawk, the C-46 *Commando* transport, and the SB2C Helldiver.

See also AIRCRAFT, FIXED-WING.

Further reading: Bowers, Peter. *Curtiss Aircraft, 1907–1947*. Annapolis, Md.: Naval Institute Press, 1987; Eltscher, Lous R. and Edward M. Young. *Curtiss-Wright: Greatness and Decline*. New York: Twayne, 1998; Roseberry, Cecil R. *Glenn Curtiss: Pioneer of Flight*. Brooklyn, N.Y.: Brooklyn Publishing House, 1979.

— Matthew H. Burgess

Cushman, Robert E., Jr. (1914–1985) *U.S. Marine Corps general and commandant*

Born on 24 December 1914 in St. Paul, Minnesota, Robert Everton Cushman graduated from the U.S. Naval Academy at Annapolis in June 1935. Commissioned a second lieutenant in the Marine Corps, Cushman completed The Basic School at the Philadelphia Navy Yard and then served at Marine Corps Base, San Diego, California.

In 1936 Cushman served with the 4th Marines in China. He was then a platoon commander in the 2d Marine Brigade. In March 1938 he was assigned to the Brooklyn Navy Yard and then to the Norfolk Navy Yard. Promoted first lieutenant in August 1938, Cushman in April 1939 was assigned to the marine detachment at the New York

World's Fair. Later stationed at Marine Barracks, Quantico, Virginia, he was promoted captain in March 1941.

When the Japanese attacked PEARL HARBOR on 7 December 1941, Cushman was commanding the Marine detachment aboard the battleship *Pennsylvania*. In May 1942 he transferred to the 9th Marines in San Diego as a battalion executive officer. That same month he was promoted to major. His unit moved to Camp Pendleton, California, in September 1942 and left for the Pacific theater in January 1943. Promoted to lieutenant colonel in May 1943, Cushman took command of 2d Battalion, 9th Marines. For the next two years he led his battalion in combat on Bougainville, Guam, and IWO JIMA.

In May 1945 Cushman returned to the United States, where he attended various senior officer schools until June 1948, when he headed the Amphibious Warfare Branch, Office of Naval Research, in Washington, D.C. From October 1949 to May 1951 Cushman served at Headquarters, Marine Corps. In May 1950 he was promoted to colonel. From June 1951 to June 1953 Cushman was stationed in London. On returning to the United States, he was at Norfolk, Virginia, from 1953 to 1956 as a member of the faculty of the Armed Forces Staff College. In 1954 became director of the Plans and Operations Division.

In July 1956 Cushman took command of the 2d Marine Regiment, 2d Marine Division, at Camp Lejeune, North Carolina. From 1957 to 1961 he was Vice President Richard M. NIXON's national security adviser. Promoted to brigadier general in July 1958, in March 1961 Cushman was assistant division commander of the 3d Marine Division. Promoted to major general in August 1961, Cushman in September became the division commander. He returned to Marine Corps Headquarters in July 1962 as assistant chief of staff, G-2 (intelligence), and assistant chief of staff, G-3 (plans, operations, and training). From 1964 to 1967 Cushman commanded Camp Pendleton.

From 1967 to 1969 Cushman had charge of III Marine Amphibious Force in Vietnam, commanding 172,000 marines, the largest number ever by a marine officer in combat to that date. Responsible for operations in I Corps Tactical Zone (northern South Vietnam) Cushman clashed with U.S. senior commanders, including General William WESTMORELAND, over what Cushman regarded as mismanagement of marine assets, including marine aircraft wings.

Cushman left Vietnam in 1969, appointed by President Nixon as deputy director of the CENTRAL INTELLIGENCE AGENCY (CIA). In 1972 Cushman was appointed commandant of the Marine Corps. As commandant he sought to end voluntary racial segregation within the corps. Cushman retired in 1975 and died on 2 January 1985.

See also MARINE CORPS, U.S.; VIETNAM WAR, COURSE OF.

Further reading: Millett, Allan R. *Semper Fidelis: The History of the United States Marine Corps.* New York: Free Press, 1980; Moskin, J. Robert. *The U.S. Marine Corps Story.* New York: McGraw-Hill, 1982; Smith, Charles R. *U.S. Marines in Vietnam: High Mobility and Standown, 1969.* Washington, D.C.: History and Museums Division, Headquarters, U.S. Marine Corps, 1888.

— Brandon H. Turner

Custer, George Armstrong (1839–1876) *U.S. Army general, cavalry commander, and Indian fighter*

Born on 5 December 1839 at New Rumley, Ohio, George Armstrong Custer graduated last in his class from the U.S. Military Academy at WEST POINT in June 1861.

Second Lieutenant Custer saw action on 21 July 1861 at the First Battle of BULL RUN/MANASSAS. During the spring 1862 Peninsula campaign, he won a staff appointment from the commander of the Army of the Potomac, Major General George B. MCCLELLAN. After the latter's dismissal, Custer, now a first lieutenant, joined the staff of Major General Alfred Pleasonton, chief of the Army of the Potomac's Cavalry Corps.

Through Pleasonton's influence, Custer became a brigadier general of U.S. Volunteers on 28 June 1863, making him the youngest general in the army. Custer reported to the Michigan Cavalry Brigade in Brigadier General H. Judson Kilpatrick's 3d Cavalry Division. He helped to stop Confederate major general J. E. B. STUART from turning the Union right in the Battle of GETTYSBURG on 3 July 1863.

Major General Philip H. SHERIDAN relieved Pleasonton in March 1864, and Custer won his new commander's confidence at Yellow Tavern on 11 May 1864. There Custer carried out a charge that resulted in the death of Stuart.

Custer went along when Sheridan assumed command of the Army of the Shenandoah in August. After Custer turned the Confederate left during the Third Battle of Winchester on 19 September, he received command of the 3d Cavalry Division. He soon molded that unit into the best mounted division in the eastern theater and won promotion to major general of volunteers. Custer's military career peaked during the APPOMATTOX campaign. On 8 April 1865 he blocked the retreat route of General Robert E. LEE's Army of Northern Virginia at APPOMATTOX.

With the war's end Custer continued in the regular army as a lieutenant colonel of the 7th U.S. Cavalry on the Kansas frontier. His first campaign as an Indian fighter ended in 1867 in court-martial and suspension from rank and pay for a year. Returned to duty before his sentence expired, Custer destroyed a Cheyenne village on the

WASHITA RIVER on 27 November 1868. His other frontier exploits included a controversial scouting expedition into the Black Hills in 1874.

On 25 June 1876, as Custer commanded the spearhead of a major offensive into Sioux country, his scouts located a large Sioux and Cheyenne village along the LITTLE BIGHORN River. To prevent his enemy's escape, he divided the 7th Cavalry into three battalions and attacked. The Indians stood their ground, however, attacking and killing Custer and every man in the five companies under his immediate command. In the wake of Custer's demise, the army mounted a massive retaliation that largely ended Sioux and Cheyenne autonomy on the northern plains. Custer remains one of America's most famous soldiers.

See also AMERICAN INDIAN WARS, OVERVIEW; CAVALRY; CIVIL WAR, LAND OVERVIEW; CRAZY HORSE; CUSTER, THOMAS W.; INDIAN WARFARE; SIOUX WARS; SITTING BULL.

Further reading: Hutton, Paul A., ed. *The Custer Reader.* Lincoln: University of Nebraska Press, 1992; Urwin, Gregory J. W. *Custer Victorious: The Civil War Battles of General George Armstrong Custer.* Lincoln: University of Nebraska Press, 1990. Utley, Robert M. *Cavalier in Buckskin: George Armstrong Custer and the Western Military Frontier.* Norman: University of Oklahoma Press, 1988; Wert, Jeffry D. *Custer: The Controversial Life of George Armstrong Custer.* New York: Simon & Schuster, 1996.

— Gregory J. W. Urwin

Custer, Thomas W. (1845–1876) *U.S. Army officer*
Born on 15 March 1845 at New Rumley, Ohio, Thomas Ward Custer, even as a small boy, idolized his older brother George Armstrong CUSTER, six years his senior.

During the Civil War, Tom Custer enlisted as a private in Company H, 21st Ohio Volunteer Infantry, in September 1861. He saw action during the December 1862–January 1863 Battle of STONES RIVER. He then served as an escort for Generals James S. Negley, Ulysses S. GRANT, John M. Palmer, and George H. THOMAS.

Custer mustered out of the 21st Ohio as a corporal in October 1864 to accept a commission as a second lieutenant in the 6th Michigan Cavalry. This promotion was arranged by his brother George, who had risen to brigadier general in command of the Michigan Cavalry Brigade in Virginia. By the time Tom Custer reported to the eastern theater to join his brother's staff, the latter had assumed command of the 3d Cavalry Division, Army of the Shenandoah.

During the APPOMATTOX campaign the fearless young aide won two Medals of Honor for seizing two Confederate battle flags, the first American soldier to achieve this recognition. He captured his first enemy color at Namozine Church on 2 April 1865 and the second at Sayler's Creek four days later, suffering a painful facial wound in the process. He also was breveted lieutenant colonel for his gallantry.

In February 1866, Custer became a second lieutenant in the 1st U.S. Infantry. Before the year's end, he transferred as a first lieutenant to his brother's newly formed 7th Cavalry Regiment.

Tom Custer fought in the 27 November 1868 Battle of the WASHITA RIVER and participated in the arrest of the famous Sioux warrior Rain-in-the-Face in January 1875. Promoted to captain in December 1875, he entered the LITTLE BIGHORN campaign five months later as commander of Company C. Some authorities speculate that he served in a detached capacity as an aide to his brother in their final battle. The two brothers fell near each other on "Last Stand Hill," 25 June 1876.

See also AMERICAN INDIAN WARS; CRAZY HORSE; INDIAN WARFARE; SITTING BULL.

Further reading: Day, Carl. *Tom Custer: Ride to Glory.* Spokane, Wash.: Arthur H. Clark, 2001; Monaghan, Jay. *Custer: The Life of General George Armstrong Custer.* Boston: Little, Brown, 1959; Urwin, Gregory J. W. *Custer Victorious: The Civil War Battles of General George Armstrong Custer.* Lincoln: University of Nebraska Press, 1990; Wert, Jeffrey D. *Custer: The Controversial Life of George Armstrong Custer.* New York: Simon & Schuster, 1996.

— Gregory J. W. Urwin

D

Dahlgren, John A. B. (1809–1870) *U.S. Navy admiral and influential ordnance designer*

Born on 13 November 1809 at Philadelphia, Pennsylvania, the son of the Swedish consul, John Adolphus Bernard Dahlgren entered the U.S. Navy as a midshipman in 1826. After service in the South Atlantic and in the Mediterranean, he became a passed midshipman in 1832. Assigned to the coast survey, he developed vision problems. Promoted to lieutenant in 1837, he spent five years on recuperative leave. Returning to duty in 1842, he served aboard the frigate *Cumberland* until 1845. In 1847 he was assigned to ordnance duty at the Washington Navy Yard. This proved a fateful posting.

Dahlgren devoted his considerable talents to developing a new system of naval artillery. He produced new boat howitzers for the navy and new heavy guns, the most important of which were the nine- and 11-inch smoothbores bearing his name. These became the standard broadside and pivot guns of the Civil War.

Dahlgren earned promotion to commander in 1855. In April 1861, when Captain Franklin BUCHANAN resigned to enter Confederate service, Dahlgren became commander of the Washington Navy Yard. After working to secure the capital, in July 1862 he was named chief of the Ordnance Bureau, with the rank of captain. Promoted to rear admiral in February 1863, he parlayed his friendship with President Abraham LINCOLN into command of the South Atlantic Blockading Squadron in July. Dahlgren then led naval forces in operations against CHARLESTON and in Florida. In December 1864 he aided Union major general William T. SHERMAN in the capture of SAVANNAH. He was present at the occupation of Charleston in February 1865.

After the war Dahlgren commanded the South Pacific Squadron and in 1868 again assumed direction of the Ordnance Bureau. Relieved at his own request in 1870, he took command of the Washington Navy Yard. Dahlgren died at the yard on 12 July 1870. He was the author of many volumes on ordnance and naval doctrine. His son, federal colonel Ulric Dahlgren, was killed during an ill-advised cavalry raid on Richmond in 1864.

See also CIVIL WAR, NAVAL OVERVIEW; NAVAL ORDNANCE.

Further reading: Fowler, William M. *Under Two Flags: The American Navy in the Civil War.* New York: Norton, 1990; Schneller, Robert J. *A Quest for Glory: A Biography of Rear Admiral John A. Dahlgren.* Annapolis, Md.: Naval Institute Press, 1996; Tucker, Spencer C. *A Short History of the Civil War at Sea.* Wilmington, Del.: Scholarly Resources, 2001.

— David Coffey

Dak To, Battle of (1–22 November 1967) *One of the bloodiest and most sustained engagements of the Vietnam War, occurring near a U.S. Special Forces camp at Dak To, northwest of Pleiku in the Central Highlands*

From 1 to 9 November 1967, two battalions, one each from the 4th Infantry Division and 173d Airborne Brigade, engaged in savage fighting with three People's Army of Vietnam (PAVN, or North Vietnamese army, NVA) regiments near Hill 823.

On 11 November a major battle occurred on Hill 724 between the 66th PAVN Regiment and the 1st Battalion of the 173d, in which the Americans fought off a PAVN attack. Meanwhile, on Hill 223, Companies A, C, and D of the 1st Battalion of the 503d Infantry Regiment of the 173d were caught in a deadly ambush by well-camouflaged PAVN troops, who struck with mortar, rocket, and small-arms fire. The jungle canopy rendered U.S. tactical air support ineffective. Dropped off at a prepared landing zone 800 meters north of the ambush, C Company of the 4th Battalion of the 503d relieved the 1st Battalion.

Over 12 to 15 November units from the 1st and 2d Battalions of the 503d encountered PAVN troops in heavily fortified trenches and bunkers. On 15 November PAVN

245

Eleven-inch Dahlgren aft pivot gun on the USS *Kearsarge*   *(Naval Historical Foundation)*

rockets lit off ammunition dumps at Dak To Fire Support Base, destroying two aircraft but causing only minor personnel injuries.

On 19 November the 173d Airborne's commander, Brigadier General Leo H. Schweiter, ordered the 2d Battalion of the 503d to assault Hill 875. Companies C and D advanced on 174th PAVN Regiment defenders, only to be stopped by automatic-weapons fire and grenades. Some 200 meters to the rear, A Company was hit hard from behind, thanks to a tunnel complex connecting PAVN bunkers and trenches. The battalion then set up an emergency perimeter. Significantly adding to the casualties, late in the afternoon a U.S. Air Force aircraft mistakenly dropped a 500-pound bomb in the midst of C Company, killing 42 men and wounding another 45, many of them officers.

By 20 November the 2d Battalion had been without food or water for 50 hours. Its perimeter continually shrinking, the battalion fought off numerous PAVN attacks. That night three companies from the 4th Battalion reinforced the defenders and resumed the attack. Not until 22 November did the 4th Battalion secure the crest of Hill

875. These engagements are collectively known as the Battle of Dak To. In the fighting U.S. losses were 287 killed, 985 wounded, and 18 missing. The official count of Communist dead was 1,200. The PAVN had come close to destroying an American unit, but the three PAVN regiments involved were so badly mauled that they were unable to participate in the upcoming Communist TET OFFENSIVE.

See also GREEN BERETS; VIETNAM WAR.

Further reading: Murphy, Edward F. *Dak To*. Novato, Calif.: Presidio, 1993; Tucker, Spencer C. *Vietnam*. Lexington: University Press of Kentucky, 1999.

— Brian A. Cummings

Dale, Richard (1756–1826) *American naval officer of the American Revolutionary and Tripolitan Wars*
Born on 6 November 1756 in Norfolk County, Virginia, Richard Dale went to sea in 1768 and became chief mate of a merchant vessel by 1775.

In 1776 Dale became a lieutenant in the fledgling Virginia navy, was captured by the British, and served briefly on a British tender. When that ship was captured by the American warship *Lexington* in July 1776, Dale joined Captain John BARRY and the crew of the *Lexington* as a midshipman. Captured by the British again when HMS *Alert* defeated the *Lexington* in the English Channel in September 1777, Dale found himself imprisoned in Mill Prison, Plymouth. He escaped in 1779 and made his way to France, where he joined the crew of the *Bonhomme Richard* as first lieutenant to Captain John Paul JONES.

Dale fought conspicuously in the 23 September 1779 BONHOMME RICHARD-SERAPIS engagement, commanding the gun deck and leading the American boarding party in spite of serious wounds. He served with Jones again on cruises aboard ALLIANCE and *Ariel;* in August 1781, aboard the *Trumbell,* he was wounded while battling HMS *Iris.* Dale later served aboard and briefly commanded the privateer *Queen of France.*

After the war Dale commanded merchantmen in the East India and China trade for some 18 years. He returned briefly to the navy in 1794–95 and in 1798–99, during the QUASI-WAR with France, but he left the navy following a dispute over rank with Captain Thomas TRUXTUN. Dale returned to the navy a final time in 1801 when the United States was at war with Tripoli. He commanded the first U.S. squadron in the Mediterranean, defeating two Tripolitan vessels at Gibraltar and briefly blockading Tripoli before turning over command to Commodore Richard V. MORRIS.

Dale returned to the United States in spring 1802 and resigned from the navy in December as its third-highest-ranking officer. He lived quietly in Philadelphia until his death on 26 February 1826.

See also AMERICAN REVOLUTIONARY WAR, NAVAL OVERVIEW; TRIPOLITAN WAR.

Further reading: Chidsey, Donald B. *The Wars in Barbary: Arab Piracy and the Birth of the United States Navy.* New York: Crown, 1971; Strauss, W. Patrick, ed. *Stars and Spars: The American Navy in the Age of Sail.* Waltham, Mass.: Blaisdell, 1969.

— Lance Janda

Dale, Samuel (1772–1841) *Pioneer, Indian fighter, and politician*

Born sometime in 1772 in Rockbridge County, Virginia, Samuel Dale grew up along the Clinch River on Virginia's southwestern frontier. In 1783 his family moved to Greene County, Georgia, where Dale became a skilled woodsman, joining the likes of Daniel BOONE, Simon Kenton, and other pioneers who opened the Old Southwest to white settlers.

In 1792 both of Dale's parents died, leaving him to fend for his eight siblings. The family was plagued by debt. In 1793 Dale volunteered as a scout in Captain Jonas Fauche's company, which was later called into federal service. Dale distinguished himself against the Creek Indians along the Chattahoochee River and was entrusted with command of Fort Republic on the Appalachee River. In 1796 the company was disbanded, but thanks to pay for this service and tobacco produced by his siblings, Dale was able to pay off the family debts.

During the next 10 years Dale traded among the Creek and Cherokee, bartering merchandise for cattle and hogs, pelts, and hides, which he then sold. During this period a vigorous western migration began from Georgia and the Carolinas through Creek and Choctaw country to the newly organized Mississippi Territory. Dale operated wagon teams transporting settlers through Indian territory, returning with Indian goods and produce, which he sold in Savannah and Charleston. Around 1810 he moved to Clarke County, Georgia, later part of Alabama.

Dale played a major role in the 1813–14 CREEK WAR. In October 1811, during the annual meeting of the Creek Indians at Tuckabatchee, Dale heard TECUMSEH call on the Creek to join the Shawnee in halting the advance of white settlers. Dale informed an Indian agent, Colonel Benjamin Hawkins, of this, but Hawkins took no action. After fighting began in 1813, Dale became a militia captain. On 27 July 1813, in command of 50 men, he intercepted a supply train bound for the Indians. In the ensuing Battle of Burnt Corn Creek, Dale was seriously wounded by a musket ball that lodged against his spine.

On his recovery, Dale participated in one of the most celebrated actions of the war, the so-called Canoe Fight. On 13 November 1813, Dale, two associates, and one slave paddled out in the Alabama River in Monroe County to attack a large war canoe carrying nine Creek warriors. Dale himself leaped into the canoe and killed six of the warriors. Known to the Indians as Big Sam for his stature and impressive strength, Dale had killed many Indians in hand-to-hand combat, but nothing else contributed to his fame as did this fight.

Dale subsequently served as a courier for Major General Andrew JACKSON during the Battle of NEW ORLEANS and again fought with Jackson during the 1817–18 First SEMINOLE WAR. He then became active in both Alabama and Mississippi politics. Settling in Monroe County, Alabama, from 1817 to 1830 he was a member of the state general assembly. He also was a general in the state militia; an Alabama county was named after him. In 1818 he helped to pacify Indians who opposed the Fort Jackson Treaty. In 1831 he had charge of relocating the Choctaw Indians to the trans-Mississippi West; however, he was injured and unable to complete the mission.

When new lands opened in Mississippi following the Choctaw removal, Dale moved to what became Lauderdale County. In 1836 he was elected its first representative to the state legislature. He died on 23 May 1841 on his plantation near Daleville, Mississippi.

See also AMERICAN INDIAN WARS, OVERVIEW.

Further reading: Brewer, Willis. *Alabama, Her History, Resources, War Record, and Public Men from 1540 to 1872.* N.p., 1872. Reprint, Spartanburg, S.C.: Reprint, 1975; Claiborne, J. F. H. *Life and Times of General Sam Dale, the Mississippi Partisan.* New York: Harper and Brothers, 1860; Johnson, Harlon R. *Sam Dale and the Five Civilized Tribes.* Boaz, Ala.: H. R. Johnson, 1997.

— Justin V. Cole

Daly, Daniel J. (1873–1937) *Marine gunnery sergeant, one of the most decorated servicemen in U.S. military history*
Born on 11 November 1873 at Glen Cove, New York, Daniel Joseph Daly shunned publicity all his life and rarely talked about his military feats. He stood only five feet, six inches tall and weighed 130 pounds.

Daly enlisted in the U.S. Marine Corps at age 26 in January 1899. The following year he was assigned to the U.S. Legation Guard at Beijing (Peking), China, during the BOXER UPRISING. He earned his first Medal of Honor during the 56-day siege by the Boxers. Assigned to an exposed and isolated guard position on the Tartar Wall, Daly on the night of 14 August 1900 single-handedly repelled repeated attacks. By morning his position was surrounded with the bodies of more than 100 dead Boxers.

In 1915 Daly was assigned to the marine expedition to Haiti against nationalist insurgents known as Cacos. On 22 October he was the senior noncommissioned officer (NCO) on a 27-man patrol sent into the interior against Fort Rivière, a Cacos stronghold. The small force, commanded by Major Smedley D. BUTLER, was ambushed on the first day out as it crossed a river. Although none of the marines was hit, the patrol lost several pack animals in the river, including the mule carrying its only machine gun. That night the marines established a defensive perimeter in the jungle, surrounded by more than 400 Cacos.

After dark, Daly slipped out of the perimeter and made his way back to the river. The Cacos tried to ambush him along the way, but he killed several of them with his knife. Upon reaching the river, Daly began diving in the dark to recover the machine gun and ammunition from the dead mule, all the while under fire. After many dives, he shouldered the 200-pound load and returned through the jungle, killing several more Cacos on his way back. Later that day he helped lead the attack that resulted in the capture of the fort. He received his second Medal of Honor for this action.

Daly also served in the 4th Marine Brigade in World War I. Several of his actions in June 1918 resulted in a recommendation for a third Medal of Honor, but he received the Navy Cross and the Distinguished Service Cross instead. He is widely regarded as being the NCO who once urged his troops forward shouting, "Come on, you bastards, do you want to live forever!?"

Daly retired from the Marine Corps in 1919, one of the most decorated servicemen in U.S. history. He spent the rest of his life living quietly in New York City, working as a bank guard. He died on 27 April 1937. During World War II a U.S. Navy destroyer was named in his honor.

See also BOXER UPRISING; LATIN AMERICAN INTERVENTIONS, EARLY 20TH-CENTURY; MARINE CORPS, U.S.

Further reading: Butler, Smedley D. "The 'Fightingest' Man I Know." *American Magazine* 112 (September 1931): 34–35, 82, 84; Profit, Robert J., ed. *United States of America's Medal of Honor Recipients and Their Official Citations.* Columbia Heights, Mich.: Highland House II, 1997.

— David T. Zabecki

Danbury raid (25 April 1777) *British raid to destroy a large supply magazine in Connecticut during the American Revolutionary War*
In spring 1777, Major General Sir William Howe authorized raids on the New England coast to disrupt the American war effort and to divert patriot troops. On 25 April the royal governor of New York, William TRYON, and 1,800 British regulars and Loyalists landed east of Norwalk, Connecticut, and marched toward Danbury, 30 miles inland.

Meeting no resistance, the British reached the town the next day and drove off a small Continental garrison. The British then proceeded to burn much of Danbury and a large quantity of military provisions, including tons of food, 5,000 pairs of shoes, and 1,000 tents. The alarm had been sounded, however, and militia began to converge.

Its mission completed, Tryon's force marched toward the coast on 27 April, encountering CONTINENTAL ARMY and militia troops near Ridgefield. Brigadier Generals Benedict ARNOLD and Gold Silliman blocked the main road with approximately 500 soldiers behind a makeshift breastwork, while Major General David Wooster struck the British rear guard with 200 militiamen.

Wooster was mortally wounded in the attack, and his command was scattered. Tryon then opened the road by flanking the Americans in a sharp one-hour fight, during which Arnold was nearly killed. Tryon's exhausted command then encamped for the night before resuming the march at dawn.

Throughout the morning small bands of militia trailed the column, while others repeatedly sniped on it from behind trees, walls, and other cover. Meanwhile, Arnold gathered nearly 700 soldiers and three cannon at Saugatuck Bridge, several miles from the coast, to intercept Tryon. The British arrived there at 11 A.M., but a Loyalist guide showed them a way around the American position. Tryon then marched his command to Compo Hill, overlooking the landing site. Heavily reinforced by arriving militia, Arnold pursued with 3,000 to 4,000 men. A skirmish ensued, and Arnold tried to form his troops for an attack but with little success in the face of heavy fire. Tryon then launched a 400 man bayonet charge that dispersed the Americans. At sunset the British boarded waiting ships and set sail.

In the operation the raiders had killed 20 Americans, wounded 75 others, and destroyed a large amount of military supplies. Their own losses included 25 dead, 117 wounded, and 29 missing or captured. Following the raid, Congress promoted Arnold to major general in recognition of his service.

The Danbury raid demonstrated both the strengths and weaknesses of the militia system. The militia had been unable to prevent the destruction of Danbury yet the incident showed that thousands of troops could be mobilized at short notice.

See also AMERICAN REVOLUTIONARY WAR, LAND OVERVIEW.

Further reading: Kwasny, Mark V. *Washington's Partisan War, 1775–1783*. Kent, Ohio: Kent State University Press, 1996; Martin, James Kirby. *Benedict Arnold, Revolutionary Hero: An American Warrior Reconsidered.* New York: New York University Press, 1997; Nelson, David Paul. *William Tryon and the Course of Empire: A Life in British Imperial Service.* Chapel Hill: University of North Carolina Press, 1990; Ward, Christopher. *The War of the Revolution.* 2 vols. New York: Macmillan, 1952.

— Michael P. Gabriel

Daniels, Josephus (1862–1948) *U.S. secretary of the navy*

Born on 18 May 1862 at Washington, North Carolina, Josephus Daniels was a prominent North Carolina newspaper editor. Active in Democratic politics, he was a leading voice for progressive reform and an enthusiastic supporter of Woodrow WILSON, who won the presidential election of 1912.

Appointed secretary of the navy in 1913, Daniels immediately instituted a broad and controversial program of reforms to promote naval efficiency, including upgrades in naval education, its extension to enlisted men as well as officers, promotion based on both seagoing service and academic attainment, insistence on competitive bidding for naval contracts, and withholding of naval oil reserves from private exploitation. Withstanding naval pressure to establish a general-staff system, Daniels created the post of chief of naval operations and a secretary's advisory council of naval bureau chiefs. His measures reflected the progressive period's prevailing spirit of efficiency and systematization.

Daniels's innovations, especially the banning of alcohol from ships and his concern for enlisted men, offended many leading officers and the well-connected civilian Navy League. Daniels, a moderate naval interventionist, feared Germany might establish U-boat bases in the Caribbean. He won congressional support for building several new American battleships; he was prepared to defend the Panama Canal by force; he used the navy and the marines to occupy the Mexican city of VERACRUZ in 1914 and to restore order in Haiti and San Domingo in 1915; and he supported the 1917 U.S. acquisition of the Virgin Islands for naval bases.

When World War I began in 1914, Daniels's reluctance to endorse major increases in naval spending generated criticism that his supposed pacifist leanings had left the United States inadequately prepared for the European conflict. These charges were publicly repeated in 1920 by Admiral William S. SIMS, who had commanded U.S. wartime naval forces in Europe, although Congress failed to substantiate them. Daniels's initial distaste for pro-Allied policies and U.S. intervention in Europe also irked Franklin D. ROOSEVELT, his assistant secretary, whose occasional intemperance on the issue Daniels generously overlooked.

Although the last of Wilson's cabinet ministers to endorse intervention in World War I, Daniels ultimately presided over a major enhancement in U.S. naval forces and shipping, moving 2 million troops to Europe without loss of life and building a navy rivaling that of Britain, a program he unsuccessfully attempted to continue even after the November 1918 armistice.

After leaving office in 1921, Daniels remained a dedicated Wilsonian and a strong supporter of U.S. membership in the League of Nations. In 1933 Roosevelt appointed Daniels ambassador to Mexico, a position he held for 10 years, overcoming residual Mexican resentment over his involvement in the Veracruz incident to embody the best face of Roosevelt's Good Neighbor Diplomacy. He died at Raleigh, North Carolina, on 15 January 1948.

See also BAKER, NEWTON D.; LATIN AMERICA INTERVENTIONS, EARLY 20TH-CENTURY; NAVY, U.S.

Further reading: Coletta, Paolo E. "Josephus Daniels." In *American Secretaries of the Navy.* Vol. 2. Annapolis, Md.: Naval Institute Press, 1982; Cronon, David E., ed. *The Cabinet Diaries of Josephus Daniels, 1913–1921.* Lincoln: University of Nebraska Press, 1963; Daniels, Josephus. *The Wilson Era.* 2 vols. Chapel Hill: University of North Carolina

Press, 1944–46; Kilpatrick, Carroll, ed. *Roosevelt and Daniels: A Friendship in Politics.* Chapel Hill: University of North Carolina Press, 1952; Morrison, Joseph L. *Josephus Daniels: The Small-d Democrat.* Chapel Hill: University of North Carolina Press, 1966; Trask, David F. *Captains and Cabinets: Anglo-American Naval Relations, 1917–1918.* Columbia: University of Missouri Press, 1972.

— Priscilla Roberts

Darby, William (1775–1854) *Military surveyor and mapmaker*

Born on 14 August 1775 in Dauphin County, Pennsylvania, William Darby was the son of Irish immigrants. Though his family was unable to afford a formal education for him, Darby read widely and at age 18 began teaching school. After the death of his father in 1799 he went to Natchez, Mississippi, to farm cotton. Following a fire and heavy crop loss in 1804 he left that enterprise to become deputy surveyor for the United States until 1809.

From 1809 to 1814 Darby was chief surveyor for the Seventh Military District, working primarily in Louisiana. His knowledge of local geography and land conditions made him a key adviser to Major General Andrew JACKSON during the NEW ORLEANS CAMPAIGN in the closing stages of the War of 1812. Darby was also a student of social conditions and studied the immigration of freed slaves, the arrival of Jews, and the attraction of others to New Orleans. In *A Geographical Description of Louisiana,* he discussed issues arising from the diversity of the population. Darby also posited the theory of germ transmission through mosquito populations in the nearby swamps.

Darby's descriptions of the geopolitical aspects of Louisiana were very thorough and provided U.S. statesmen accurate information, especially in negotiations over making the Sabine River the boundary between the United States and Spanish Mexico and to determine the permanent western limit of the state of Louisiana. Darby's publisher, John Melish, used his statistical accounts and maps to compile the Melish Map of the United States, which was used as the basis for boundary delineation in the treaty of 1819 between the United States and Spain. Darby's role went largely unrecognized until August 1854, when Congress appropriated $1,500 as compensation to him.

In 1843 Darby moved to Washington, D.C., where he served as a government clerk, lectured, and wrote many books before his death on 9 October 1854.

See also WAR OF 1812.

Further reading: Darby, William. *View of the United States: Historical, Geographical and Statistical.* Philadelphia: H. S. Tanner, 1828.

— Ronald White, Jr.

Darby, William O. (1911–1945) *U.S. Army general and leader of the Rangers in World War II*

Born on 18 February 1911 at Fort Smith, Arkansas, William Orlando Darby graduated from the U.S. Military Academy at West Point in 1933 and was commissioned in the field artillery. Darby served with the 80th Field Artillery Regiment (1939–40) and was promoted to captain. He then commanded a battery in the 99th Field Artillery Regiment (1941–42). In June 1942 Brigadier General Lucian K. TRUSCOTT selected Darby, promoted to temporary major, to organize the Ranger training program in Achnacarry, Scotland, with assistance from British commandos. The Rangers were intended to be elite, small-unit troops for hit-and-run raids. Charismatic and an excellent trainer, Darby led by example.

Officially Darby commanded only the 1st Ranger Battalion, but actually he trained and led the 3d and 4th Battalions as well. These were collectively known throughout the war as Darby's Rangers. Promoted to colonel in December 1943, Darby officially took command of the three battalions. The Rangers first saw action in the raid against Dieppe, France, on 19 August 1942. They then fought in Operation TORCH, the invasion of North Africa, and the invasion of SICILY. After the 1st and 3d Battalions were destroyed in fighting at ANZIO, Darby took command of the 179th Infantry Regiment. He returned to the United States to serve in the Operations Division of the War Department General Staff in April 1944. Darby then became executive officer of the 10th Mountain Division in Italy, where he was killed by artillery fire on 30 April 1945, in the last days of the war. He won posthumous promotion to brigadier general.

See also WORLD WAR II, U.S. INVOLVEMENT, EUROPE.

Further reading: Darby, William O., and William H. Baumer. *We Led the Way: Darby's Rangers.* San Rafael, Calif.: Presidio, 1980; Hogan, David W. *Rangers or Elite Infantry? The Changing Role of U.S. Army Rangers from Dieppe to Grenada.* Wesport, Conn.: Greenwood, 1992; Ladd, James D. *Commandos and Rangers of World War II.* New York: David and Charles, 1989.

— Spencer C. Tucker

Davis, Benjamin O. (1880–1970) *U.S. Army general*

Born on 28 May 1880 at Washington, D.C., Benjamin Oliver Davis entered Howard University in 1897 but left the following year to serve as first lieutenant of U.S. Volunteers in the SPANISH-AMERICAN WAR.

Davis saw no action in the war, and in 1899 he mustered out of the volunteers, only to enlist as a private in the 9th cavalry. During service in the PHILIPPINE-AMERICAN WAR he rose through the ranks and was commissioned a 2d lieutenant in 1901. In 1905 Davis was promoted to 1st lieutenant and was assigned to Wilberforce University in Ohio as a professor of military tactics. After four years there, he served as military attaché in Monrovia, Liberia, from 1909 to 1912. Davis returned to Wilberforce in 1915 after serving three years in the American West with the 10th Cavalry. From 1917 to 1920 Davis served in the Philippines, where he was promoted to lieutenant colonel.

Upon returning to the United States, Davis taught at Tuskegee Institute in Alabama and Wilberforce. In 1930 he was promoted to colonel. In 1938 Davis assumed command of the 369th National Guard Infantry Regiment in Harlem, in New York City. He was promoted to brigadier general in October 1940, the first African-American general in the U.S. Army. The promotion occurred a month before the 1940 presidential election; many army officers believed that President Franklin ROOSEVELT had promoted Davis to gain the support of black voters.

Davis retired in June 1941, but he was recalled to active duty shortly thereafter and assigned to the office of the inspector general of the army. He worked during World War II to ease racial tension in the American military. Davis spent several tours of duty in the European theater as an adviser on race relations.

After the war Davis continued his work to end racial discrimination in the military. He retired again in July 1948, after 50 years of military service. He remained active on several national committees, including the American Battle Monuments Commission. Davis died on 26 November 1970 at Great Lakes Naval Hospital in Chicago. His son, Benjamin O. DAVIS, Jr., was to be the first African-American general in the U.S. Air Force.

See also AFRICAN AMERICANS IN THE MILITARY.

Further reading: Davis, Benjamin O., Jr. *Benjamin O. Davis, Jr. American.* Washington, D.C.: Smithsonian Institution Press, 1991; Fletcher, Marvin E. *America's First Black General: Benjamin O. Davis, Sr., 1880–1970.* Lawrence: University Press of Kansas, 1989; Lee, Ulysses. *The Employment of Negro Troops.* Washington, D.C.: Center of Military History, 1994.

— John David Rausch, Jr.

Davis, Benjamin O., Jr. (1912–) *U.S. Air Force general*

Born on 18 December 1912 at Washington, D.C., the son of Elnora and Benjamin O. DAVIS, the first African-American U.S. Army general, Benjamin Davis, Jr., attended Western Reserve University in Cleveland, later transferring to the University of Chicago.

Initially discouraged from attending the U.S. Military Academy at West Point because of discrimination, in 1932

Davis gained appointment there and endured four years of isolation. No one interacted with him unless issuing an order. Despite this treatment, Davis graduated from West Point, high in the class of 1936.

Davis applied for pilot training but was assigned to the infantry because the Army Air Corps was racially segregated. In July 1941, however, as a captain, he was one of the first cadets in a new pilot training program for African Americans at Tuskegee, Alabama, the result of political pressure to gain wider support for the military among African Americans. Davis completed training in March 1942.

The graduates of the Tuskegee program formed the core of the 99th Pursuit Squadron, commanded by Lieutenant Colonel Davis. In 1943 the squadron was sent to North Africa. After four months flying P-40s in the Mediterranean theater, Davis assumed command of the 332d Fighter Group, another all-black outfit. It flew in support of operations in Italy. In late 1944 Davis led the first Italy-based fighter group to escort bombers to Berlin. The 332d, flying P-51 Mustangs with distinctive red markings on their tails, downed three German jet fighters. Davis flew 60 combat missions and was promoted to colonel in March 1944.

After the war Davis commanded the racially troubled 477th Composite Group at Godman Field, Kentucky. He restored morale and then commanded Lockbourne Air Force Base, Ohio, achieving a degree of racial integration that was a model for the rest of the services. He attended the Air War College in 1949. During the KOREAN WAR he served in Washington as deputy chief of operations of the Fighter Branch in Air Force headquarters. In 1954 Davis was promoted to become the air force's first African-American brigadier general. Head of Twelfth Air Force in Germany from 1957 to 1959, in June 1959 he was promoted to major general. In 1965 he was advanced to lieutenant general, the first African American in any U.S. military service to reach that rank. He served as deputy commander in chief in the Middle East, southern Asia, and sub-Saharan Africa.

Davis retired in 1970 after commanding the Thirteenth Air Force during the VIETNAM WAR. In 1971 President Richard NIXON appointed him assistant secretary of transportation to establish a "sky marshals" program to combat skyjacking. Davis retired from government service in 1975. President Bill Clinton awarded Davis a fourth star on 9 December 1998. Davis died on 4 July 2002 in Washington, D.C.

See also AFRICAN AMERICANS IN THE MILITARY.

Further reading: Davis, Benjamin O., Jr. *Benjamin O. Davis, Jr. American.* Washington, D.C.: Smithsonian Institution Press, 1991; Dryden, Charles W. *A-Train: Memoirs of a Tuskegee Airman.* Tuscaloosa: University of Alabama

Press, 1997; Lee, Ulysses. *The Employment of Negro Troops.* Washington, D.C.: Center of Military History, 1994.

— John David Rausch, Jr.

Davis, Jefferson (1808–1889) *U.S. senator and secretary of war; president of the Confederate States of America*

Born on 3 June 1808 in Christian County, Kentucky, Jefferson Davis attended Transylvania University before entering the U.S. Military Academy at WEST POINT in 1824. He graduated in 1828. As a second lieutenant of infantry, Davis participated in the BLACK HAWK War. In 1833 he was promoted to 1st lieutenant in the dragoons, but he resigned his commission in 1835 and married the daughter of Colonel Zachary TAYLOR, against the latter's wishes. Shortly after settling in Mississippi, Davis's wife died of fever; he survived the same fever to become a successful planter.

In 1845 Davis won election as a Democrat to the U.S. House of Representatives, but the 1846 outbreak of the MEXICAN-AMERICAN WAR brought him back into the military. Elected colonel of the 1st Mississippi Volunteer Infantry (or 1st Mississippi Rifles), Davis served with distinction under Major General Taylor in northern Mexico and was wounded in the Battle of BUENA VISTA. Returning to the United States in 1847, Davis turned down promotion to brigadier general and was appointed by the Mississippi legislature to the U.S. Senate. Davis quickly emerged as a leading southern Democrat, noted for his interest in military affairs and new technology.

In 1853 President Franklin Pierce named Davis secretary of war. One of the more effective secretaries of war in U.S. history, Davis sponsored innovation and modernization. He ordered upgrades in small arms, artillery, and ordnance; he introduced new infantry tactics; and he advocated the construction of a transcontinental military railroad. He also was instrumental in establishing two new cavalry regiments for service on the frontier. Another innovation was the brief use of camels in the deserts of the Southwest.

Davis returned to the Senate in 1857, reassuming his role as defender of southern rights. Although devoted to the Union, he was unbending in his support of states' rights and slavery. He was largely responsible for the split in the Democratic Party in the election of 1860 that facilitated the election of Republican Abraham LINCOLN to the presidency.

Davis then advocated secession and the creation of a southern nation. He resigned from the Senate in January 1861 and returned to Mississippi, where he accepted command of state troops, with the rank of major general. In February Davis was elected president of the Confederate States of America, a position he accepted with trepidation.

Davis faced a daunting task that forced him to adopt policies contrary to his states' rights positions, such as a national military organization that wrested control from the states, as well as conscription, impressment, and taxation. Davis was not an effective commander in chief. His fierce loyalty to friends like Braxton BRAGG and Leonidas POLK proved costly, while his hostility, however justifiable, toward such officers as P. G. T. BEAUREGARD and Joseph E. JOHNSTON caused further damage.

Despite his fragile health, Davis was a hands-on executive and worked almost around the clock. His management of the war was often frustrated by an increasingly unresponsive Congress and states'-rights-minded governors. In other ways Davis exercised remarkable restraint, refusing to crack down on critics or nationalize essential industries.

After the fall of Richmond, Davis and members of his cabinet attempted to flee to the trans-Mississippi West. He was captured at Irwinville, Georgia, on 10 May 1965, and was imprisoned at Fort Monroe for two years. Released, he settled eventually at "Beauvoir," near Biloxi, Mississippi, where he wrote his memoirs and died on 5 December 1889.

See also CIVIL WAR, CAUSES OF; CIVIL WAR, LAND OVERVIEW; CIVIL WAR, NAVAL OVERVIEW; HOOD, JOHN B. JOHNSTON, ALBERT SIDNEY.

Further reading: Cooper, William J. *Jefferson Davis, American: A Biography.* New York: Knopf, 2000; Davis, Jefferson. *The Rise and Fall of the Confederate Government.* 2 vols. New York: Appleton, 1881; Davis, William C. *Jefferson Davis: The Man and His Hour, A Biography.* New York: HarperCollins, 1991; Woodworth, Steven E. *Jefferson Davis and His Generals: The Failure of Confederate Command in the West.* Lawrence: University Press of Kansas, 1990.

— Toby Thompson

Dean, William F. (1899–1981) *U.S. Army general*
Born on 1 August 1899 at Carlyle, Illinois, William Frishe Dean failed to gain admission to the U.S. Military Academy and graduated instead from the University of California at Berkeley in 1922. He obtained a reserve commission in 1921; two years later he secured a regular army commission.

Dean held a number of infantry regiment assignments; in Utah, Panama, and at the Presidio of San Francisco, California. He graduated from the Command and General Staff School in 1936, from the Army Industrial College in 1939, and from the Army War College in 1940. He then served on the War Department General Staff and became assistant to the secretary of the General Staff in January 1941. That same year he was promoted to lieutenant colonel.

In March 1942 Dean was reassigned to Headquarters, Army Ground Forces. Promoted to brigadier general in December 1942, in February 1944 he became assistant commander of the 44th Infantry Division, going with it to southern France in August 1944. He remained with the division throughout the remainder of the war, fighting in France and Germany. Named to command the division in December 1944, he was advanced to major general in March 1945.

In September 1945 Dean joined the faculty of the Army Command and General Staff School at Fort Leavenworth and became assistant commandant there the next June. In October 1947 he became military governor of South Korea. Following the creation of the Republic of Korea in August 1948, Dean took command of the 7th Infantry Division, taking it to Japan in January 1949. The following June he became chief of staff of the Eighth U.S. Army in Japan, and in October 1949 Dean assumed command of the 24th Infantry Division.

The 24th Division became the first U.S. division in South Korea following the North Korean invasion of 25 June 1950. Dean arrived in Korea on 3 July and assumed command of all U.S. forces there. Dean personally led his division in the bitter defense of Taejon on 19–20 July, on one occasion attacking a North Korean tank with only a hand grenade and pistol. (In February 1951 he was awarded the Medal of Honor.) Separated from his command in the confused withdrawal from Taejon City, Dean was betrayed by South Koreans and taken prisoner on 25 August 1950. The highest-ranking United Nations Command officer captured during the war, Dean demonstrated great courage in captivity; he was released after the armistice, in September 1953.

In December 1953 Dean became deputy commander of the Sixth U.S. Army at the Presidio. He retired from active duty in October 1955. Dean died at Berkeley, California, on 26 August 1981.

See also KOREAN WAR, COURSE OF; WORLD WAR II, U.S. INVOLVEMENT, EUROPE.

Further reading: Appleman, Roy E. *South to the Naktong, North to the Yalu.* Washington, D.C.: Office of the Chief of Military History, Department of the Army, 1961; Dean, William F., with William L. Worden. *General Dean's Story.* New York: Viking, 1954.

— Spencer C. Tucker

Dearborn, Henry (1751–1829) *U.S. Army general and secretary of war*
Born on 28 February 1751 at North Hampton, New Hampshire, Henry Dearborn apprenticed as a physician but abandoned medicine to fight in the American Revolu-

tionary War. Appointed a captain in the 1st New Hampshire Regiment by Colonel John STARK, he fought at BUNKER HILL under Stark's command. In September 1775 Dearborn commanded a company of New Hampshire volunteers in Colonel Benedict ARNOLD's expedition against QUEBEC. Dearborn was taken prisoner in the assault on Quebec City but was paroled in May 1776 and formally exchanged in March 1777.

Dearborn then received a commission as a major in Colonel Alexander Scammell's 3d New Hampshire Regiment. Commanding a light infantry force, he fought in the Battles of SARATOGA and won commendation by Major General Horatio GATES for his role at Bemis Heights; he was promoted to lieutenant colonel shortly thereafter. Dearborn spent part of the winter of 1777–78 at VALLEY FORGE and fought in the 1778 Battle of MONMOUTH COURT HOUSE, winning commendation from the Continental army commander, General George WASHINGTON.

During the spring and summer of 1779, Dearborn served under Major General John SULLIVAN in the campaign against the Indians of western New York and participated in a major victory over Tories and Indians on 29 August 1779 near Elmira, New York. In July 1781 Washington appointed Dearborn deputy quartermaster general of the Continental army. Dearborn subsequently participated in the YORKTOWN CAMPAIGN, leaving the service in June 1783.

After the Revolution Dearborn served in the Massachusetts militia, first as brigadier general (1787) and then as major general (1790). He also served as a selectman in Pittston. In 1789 President WASHINGTON appointed Dearborn U.S. marshal for the district of Maine, which post he held until 1793. From 1793 to 1797 Dearborn represented Massachusetts in Congress, identifying himself with the advocates of economy in military expenditures.

In 1801 President Thomas JEFFERSON appointed Dearborn secretary of war; he served capably in this post until 1809. Though paring down the military, Dearborn in 1803 ordered a barracks and stockade to be built at Chicago—FORT DEARBORN. He worked to introduce Eli Whitney's interchangeable-parts muskets and new gun carriages, to improve the militias, to create a light artillery, and to establish the U.S. Military Academy at WEST POINT.

From 1809 to 1812 Dearborn was collector of customs at Boston until the Senate approved him as senior major general of the army in January 1812—although he was then 61 and reluctant to accept the responsibility. Dearborn's plans for the invasion of Canada during the War of 1812 went awry; he became known as "Granny Dearborn" for his slowness of movement. Following the British victory in the Battle of Beaver Dams in July 1813, there were demands for Dearborn's removal from command. Replaced that same month by Major General James WILKINSON,

Dearborn took charge of the defenses of New York. He retired from the army in 1815.

In 1817 Dearborn was an unsuccessful Republican candidate for governor of Massachusetts. He served as minister to Portugal from 1822 to 1824. He died at Roxbury, Massachusetts, on 6 June 1829.

See also AMERICAN REVOLUTIONARY WAR, LAND OVERVIEW; WAR OF 1812, LAND OVERVIEW.

Further reading: Brown, Lloyd A., and Howard H. Peckham, eds. *Revolutionary War Journals of Henry Dearborn, 1775–1783.* Bowie, Md.: Heritage Books, 1994; Crackel, Theodore J. *Mr. Jefferson's Army: Political and Social Reform of the Military Establishment, 1801–1809.* New York: New York University Press, 1987; Erney, Richard A. *The Public Life of Henry Dearborn.* New York: Arno, 1979.

— A. J. L. Waskey

Decatur, Stephen (1779–1820) *U.S. Navy officer*
Born on 5 January 1779 at Sinepuxent, Maryland, Stephen Decatur came of seafaring stock; his father became rich as a trader and privateer during the AMERICAN REVOLUTIONARY WAR. During that war his mother took him and his siblings to Maryland's Eastern Shore when the British occupied Philadelphia. He attended an Episcopal school and for a year the University of Pennsylvania. Tired of studying, he obtained a commission as a midshipman in April 1798 during the QUASI-WAR with France.

Tall, athletic, and handsome, Decatur was promoted to acting lieutenant in May 1799. Following an argument with a mate of a merchant ship while Decatur was serving as a recruiter in Philadelphia, he shot the mate in a leg. After three more cruises he was promoted to lieutenant, serving thereafter first with Commodore Richard DALE and then (March 1801–July 1802) with Commodore Edward PREBLE in the TRIPOLITAN WAR.

In August 1802 Decatur was the first lieutenant of the *New York,* commanded by James BARRON. Toward the end of 1803 he served in the *Essex* (12 guns), earning undying fame when he led the party that burned the captured *Philadelphia.* Captain William BAINBRIDGE had run the *Philadelphia* onto an unmarked reef, and it had been seized by the Tripolitans and taken to Tripoli. Decatur secured Preble's permission to try to burn it. On the night of 16 February 1804 Decatur sailed a Tripolitan prize ketch, renamed the *Intrepid,* alongside the *Philadelphia.* He and 81 men cleared the frigate of Tripolitans and set it afire. On other occasions he acted so heroically that he was promoted to post captain. He continued his fine work in charge of gunboats obtained in Naples to fight Tripolitan ships. Decatur thus became the most striking figure of the war.

After commanding first the CONSTITUTION and then the *Congress,* Decatur returned to Norfolk and there met and married the mayor's daughter. During 1808 he served on a court-martial that suspended Captain James BARRON for his part in the 1807 CHESAPEAKE-LEOPARD AFFAIR. During the WAR OF 1812, while in command of the frigate UNITED STATES, he outfought the British frigate MACEDONIAN near Madeira on 8 October 1812 and gained the second of the three American frigate victories of the war. Seeking to escape from British blockaders off New York, however, he was outnumbered and outgunned and had to surrender the frigate *President.* Paroled, he returned to New London, Connecticut, in February 1815.

After the War of 1812 Decatur commanded a squadron against the dey of Algiers, who had mistreated Americans during the war, and he secured payments from Tunis, Tripoli, and Algeria. Upon his return, he was appointed to the new Board of Naval Commissioners.

Barron was angered that Decatur refused to allow his return to active service. On 22 March 1820 the two men fought a duel in Bladensburg, Maryland, near Washington. Barron received a leg wound, but Decatur was wounded mortally.

See also NAVY, U.S.

Further reading: Allen, Gardner. *Our Navy and the Barbary Corsairs.* Boston: Houghton Mifflin, 1905; Anthony, Irvin. *Decatur.* New York: Scribner, 1911; Chidsey, Donald E. *The Wars of America: Arab Piracy and the Birth of the U.S. Navy.* New York: Crown, 1971; Lewis, Charles Lee. *The Romantic Decatur.* Philadelphia: University of Pennsylvania Press, 1937.

— Paolo E. Coletta

Defense Intelligence Agency (DIA) *U.S. intelligence agency created in 1961 to consolidate all American military intelligence services*
The Defense Intelligence Agency was established under Secretary of Defense Robert S. MCNAMARA as part of a broader move to eliminate overlapping jurisdictions, duplication, and interservice rivalries within the U.S. military. It represented the culmination of efforts in this direction that had characterized the U.S. military since the unification of the armed services in 1947. These attempts to promote government centralization reached their peak in the administration of President John F. KENNEDY.

The immediate impetus for creating the Defense Intelligence Agency came from the Joint Study Group (JSG), established in 1959 by Secretary of Defense Thomas S. Gates. Beginning with the 1948 Hoover Commission on the Reorganization of Government, numerous Defense Department studies had focused on poor coordination among the different services' intelligence estimates, a situation that arose primarily from interservice rivalries and parochial interests. The Joint Chiefs of Staff had since 1945 possessed a small intelligence staff—the Joint Intelligence Group, created at the end of World War II—but it was too small to coordinate effectively the services' intelligence efforts. The divergence between the armed services' assessments in the late 1950s of whether or not a MISSILE GAP existed between the United States and the Soviet Union was a major factor in persuading Gates to move toward consolidation of military intelligence activities in one agency, a measure that the JSG recommended.

The DIA was established on 1 October 1961 in the next administration. Reporting to the secretary of defense through the Joint Chiefs of Staff, its mandate was to satisfy the intelligence needs of the secretary of defense, the Joint Chiefs of Staff, and the various services; to provide a single military viewpoint for national intelligence estimates; to provide military intelligence for other national purposes; to coordinate all Department of Defense intelligence collection; to manage the defense attaché system; and to provide intelligence support for the Joint Chiefs of Staff.

The DIA was handicapped by the fact that it did not recruit staff directly but relied upon officers detailed from services, which, particularly in its early history, often resented the agency's existence. Moreover, representatives of the individual services' intelligence units continued to attend meetings of the U.S. Intelligence Board and its successor, the National Foreign Intelligence Board. In the DIA's first decade, much energy was devoted to institutional consolidation, including the establishment in 1963 of a Defense Intelligence School, and to streamlining the production of intelligence material. Between 1968 and 1975 the DIA's human resources were reduced by 31 percent, as the U.S. government gradually reduced and then eliminated its commitment to the VIETNAM WAR. Although the DIA, having generally refrained from the extensive covert operations characteristic of the CENTRAL INTELLIGENCE AGENCY, emerged largely unscathed from the post-Vietnam congressional investigations of all American intelligence agencies, it found itself subject to greater congressional oversight.

By the 1980s, after several reorganizations and the appropriation of funding for a new building, the DIA had won acceptance as part of the broader intelligence community. Its intelligence, which relied heavily upon information technology and the international network of military attachés, was increasingly perceived as integral to the formulation of broad U.S. national security policy both in the long and short terms. Critics pointed to shortcomings in its analyses, such as the failure to predict the fall of the shah in Iran or the collapse of the Soviet empire. Defend-

ers argued that given the breadth of its clientele and mandate, and its reliance upon personnel seconded from the different services, the DIA's performance at least equaled that of the rival Central Intelligence Agency, to which it was often compared.

See also ESPIONAGE AGAINST THE UNITED STATES, SURVEY OF; INTELLIGENCE; NATIONAL SECURITY AGENCY.

Further reading: Corson, William R. *The Armies of Ignorance: The Rise of the American Intelligence Empire.* New York: Dial, 1977; Miller, Nathan. *Spying for America: The Hidden History of U.S. Intelligence.* New York: Paragon House, 1989; Ransom, Harry Howe. *The Intelligence Establishment.* Cambridge, Mass.: Harvard University Press, 1970; Richelson, Jeffrey. *A Century of Spies: Intelligence in the Twentieth Century.* New York: Oxford University Press, 1995; ———. *The U.S. Intelligence Community.* 4th ed. Boulder, Colo.: Westview, 1999.

— Priscilla Roberts

Demologos, **USS** (*Fulton*) *U.S. Navy steam battery*

In 1813, during the War of 1812, Robert FULTON submitted plans to President James Madison for a steam warship. Secretary of the Navy William Jones supported it, and Congress authorized construction in March 1814. Fulton oversaw its construction. Named *Demologos* ("Voice of the People"), it was launched in October 1814. After Fulton's death in February 1815 it was renamed the *Fulton,* subsequently *Fulton I.*

The *Fulton* was commissioned in June 1815, the first steam frigate in any navy in the world. However, it was in fact a floating battery for the defense of New York City and not a true frigate. It was a catamaran, its twin hulls protecting a centerline paddlewheel. Captain David PORTER took command of the *Demologos* while it was under construction. Fulton had wanted it propelled by steam alone, but Porter insisted on adding a twin-mast lateen sail rig. This change required bulwarks on the spar deck to protect men working the sails, adding significantly to its weight without enhancing fighting qualities.

Weighing 2,475 tons, 153 feet two inches in length and 56 feet in beam, *Fulton* was the largest war steamer in the world. It developed 120 horsepower and could make 4.8 knots under steam. Its 50-inch-thick outer bulwarks were considered shotproof. *Fulton* was rated at 30 guns, and there were plans to arm it with larger guns, but it carried long 32-pounders on its trial run.

Fulton did not see combat, and after the War of 1812 it became a receiving ship at the Brooklyn Navy Yard. It blew up there in June 1829, the result of careless handling of gunpowder in its magazine.

See also NAVY, U.S.

Further reading: Canney, Donald L. *The Old Steam Navy.* Vol. I, *Frigates, Sloops, and Gunboats, 1815–1885.* Annapolis, Md.: Naval Institute Press, 1990; Sliverstone, Paul H. *The Sailing Navy, 1775–1854.* Annapolis, Md.: Naval Institute Press, 2001.

— Spencer C. Tucker

Derna, capture of (27 April 1805) *Important action during the 1801–05 Tripolitan War*

On 31 October 1803, the U.S. frigate *Philadelphia* ran aground off the coast of Tripoli, and Captain William BAIN-BRIDGE and his crew were captured. The bashaw (pashar, or ruler) of Tripoli, Yusuf Karamanli, demanded a $200,000 ransom for their release. Yusef had seized the throne by murdering his eldest brother; his surviving older brother, Hamet, had fled to Egypt. William EATON, once a captain in the U.S. Army and now consul to Tunis, came up with a plan whereby the United States would help Hamet gain the throne of Tripoli in return for the release of U.S. prisoners and a favorable treaty.

Eaton assembled a polyglot force of some 400 men, including eight marines, a navy midshipman, a doctor, 25 artillerymen of mixed nationality, 38 Greeks, 70 Muslim troops under Hamet, and a number of camel drivers. The force set out from Marabout, Egypt, on 6 March 1805.

Despite difficulties from within the Muslim contingent, the strong-willed Eaton held the force together and in 50 days led it across 520 miles of forbidding and desolate desert to Derna, Tripoli's largest eastern city. Stopping at the seacoast, Eaton rendezvoused with the American warships *Argus* and *Hornet,* which landed supplies for the expedition. Eaton also arranged with Captain Isaac HULL of the *Argus* for a joint land and sea attack on Derna.

On 22 April Eaton learned that Hassan Bey, commander of Bashaw Yusuf's army, was en route to Derna from Tripoli with reinforcements and might arrive there ahead of him. Eaton pressed on and arrived first. Derna's defenses included a water battery of eight 9-pounders and a 10-inch howitzer at the palace across from the harbor's fort.

Eaton informed the governor of Derna, Mustapha, that "the legitimate sovereign" accompanied him. He demanded supplies in exchange for fair compensation and pledged in turn that Mustafa would remain governor. "My head or yours," Mustapha replied.

On 27 April the U.S. brig *Nautilus* arrived, along with the *Argus* and *Hornet.* These ships took up station to bombard Derna from the sea. The *Argus* also landed two carronades that Eaton had requested, but so much time was consumed in manhandling the first gun up an almost vertical cliff that Eaton decided to attack without the second.

The naval bombardment began at 2 P.M. on 27 April. It silenced the water battery within an hour. Meanwhile, Eaton attacked the city from two directions on land: Hamet struck from the south and southeast with a force of mounted Arabs, while marine lieutenant Presley O'Bannon led the main attack with the smaller Christian contingent and some lightly armed Arab infantry.

Hamet seized an old castle early on, securing the flank in case Hassan Bey should appear. Supported by the carronade, O'Bannon began his attack, but the carronade was put out of action when it was fired with the rammer still in the bore. The marines were undaunted, and Eaton ordered a charge that scattered the defenders. At 3:30 P.M. O'Bannon raised the American flag over Derna—the first time in history that it had been flown victoriously over a foreign land. The attackers suffered 14 casualties; one marine was killed, and two were wounded, one mortally. Eaton was among the wounded, his left wrist shattered by a musket ball.

When Hassan's army arrived, it was rebuffed. Yusuf then agreed to sign with the United States a peace treaty under which Hamet withdrew and the Americans departed Derna after paying $60,000 to ransom the crew of the *Philadelphia.* In recognition of O'Bannon's courage and leadership, Hamet presented him a Mameluke sword. It became the pattern for the sword still carried by marine officers on formal occasions. The words "to the shores of Tripoli" are enshrined in the Marine Hymn as a tribute to O'Bannon and his men.

See also DECATUR, STEPHEN; *PHILADELPHIA*, DESTRUCTION OF; PREBLE, EDWARD; TRIPOLITAN WAR.

Further reading: Chidsey, Donald Barr. *The Wars in Barbary.* New York: Crown, 1971; Irwin, Ray W. *Diplomatic Relations of the United States with the Barbary Powers, 1776–1816.* Chapel Hill: University of North Carolina Press, 1931; Millett, Allan R. *Semper Fidelis: The History of the United States Marine Corps.* New York: Macmillan, 1981; Nash, Howard P., Jr. *The Forgotten Wars.* New York: A.S. Barne, 1968; Tucker, Glenn. *Dawn Like Thunder.* Indianapolis: Bobbs-Merrill, 1963.

— Uzal W. Ent

Desert Shield, Operation (7 August 1990–17 January 1991) *Military operation mounted by an international coalition following the Iraqi invasion of Kuwait to deter further Iraqi aggression and, if necessary, defend Saudi Arabia*

The operation, originally known as Peninsula Shield, was the first phase of the Gulf War.

On 2 August 1990 six divisions of the elite Iraqi Republican Guard Corps invaded the independent nation of Kuwait. Having taking Kuwait, the Iraqi dictator, Saddam Hussein, controlled approximately 25 percent of the world's known oil supply. Additionally, Iraqi forces were on the Saudi border, within easy striking range of oil fields that represented another 28 percent of the world's known reserves. Even without moving his armies farther south, Saddam Hussein could apply tremendous political pressure on the Saudi government. This was a situation unacceptable to countries, especially in Europe, that ware highly dependent upon Middle Eastern oil. It was also unacceptable to the president of the United States, George II. W. BUSH. The day of the invasion, the United Nations Security Council voted 14–0 (Resolution 660) to demand Iraq's immediate and unconditional withdrawal from Kuwait.

Iraq refused to withdraw from Kuwait. Despite this, Saudi King Fahd was hesitant to ask for outside assistance—a move that would bring foreign troops into his very conservative Muslim state, home of the holy shrines at Mecca and Medina. Satellite photos of massing Iraqi troops and an accidental incursion by Iraqi forces into Saudi Arabia convinced King Fahd to allow non-Muslim forces into his country.

President Bush led diplomatic efforts to put together a formidable coalition that included Western and Islamic states. He and his advisers worked hard to keep Israel out of the conflict in order to secure the loyalty of the Arab states.

Operation Desert Shield then began. Its first goal was to deploy a credible military force capable of deterring the Iraqi military from entering Saudi Arabia. The closest American military assets were U.S. Navy ships stationed in the Persian Gulf. These original eight ships formed the nucleus around which the coalition's naval forces assembled. The U.S. naval presence would swell to 110 ships by the start of DESERT STORM, the active military phase of the Gulf War.

To establish a credible deterrent, more military might was needed. On 8 August elements of the U.S. Air Force's 1st Tactical Fighter Wing began to arrive in Saudi Arabia. Within three weeks the United States had approximately 400 combat and 200 support aircraft in the Gulf region.

Moving U.S. naval and air assets to Saudi Arabia was relatively easy compared to moving the necessary numbers of ground troops with their equipment into position, but years of military planning paid off in the first few weeks of Desert Shield. To speed up air deployment of U.S. Army and Marine units in case of such an incident, the U.S. military had prepositioned ships loaded with weapons, equipment, and supplies on the small Indian Ocean island of Diego Garcia. By mid-August the prepositioned ships were in Saudi ports as the first American ground units arrived by air. By the end of August the 7th Marine Expeditionary

Brigade and the U.S. Army 82d Airborne Division were in place. By the end of August the first phase of Desert Shield, providing sufficient forces to defend Saudi Arabia, had been completed.

Once the ability to defend Saudi Arabia was assured and it was obvious that Iraqi forces would not voluntarily depart Kuwait, the second phase of Desert Shield began. Thus was to create an offensive capability to drive the Iraqis out of Kuwait, should it be necessary. As diplomats attempted to resolve the crisis peacefully, efforts proceeded to increase the firepower available to coalition theater commanders. By January 1991 the United States, which contributed the largest element of coalition forces, had assembled a combined land-sea-air force with in excess of 500,000 personnel, 110 ships, 4,200 tanks and armored personnel carriers, 1,800 fixed wing-wing aircraft, and 1,700 helicopters. U.S. and coalition forces needed only to wait for the UN Security Council deadline of 15 January to see whether Saddam would leave Kuwait through a negotiated diplomatic settlement or an imposed military solution.

See also GULF WAR, CAUSES OF; POWELL, COLIN; SCHWARZKOPF, H. NORMAN.

Further reading: Atkinson, Rick. *Crusade: The Untold Story of the Persian Gulf War.* New York: Houghton Mifflin, 1993; Gordon, Michael R., and Bernard E. Trainor. *The Generals' War.* New York: Little, Brown, 1995; Scales, Robert H. *Certain Victory: The U.S. Army in the Gulf War.* Washington, D.C.: Brassey's, 1997.

— Craig T. Cobane

Desert Storm, Operation (17 January–28 February 1991) *Military operation to expel Iraqi forces from Kuwait, also known as the offensive portion of the Gulf War, or Persian Gulf War*

In response to Iraq's invasion of Kuwait on 2 August 1990, the United States and coalition members sent military forces to protect Saudi Arabia (Operation DESERT SHIELD). When sufficient assets were in place and it became apparent that Iraqi forces would not leave voluntarily, plans were developed for the liberation of Kuwait. Desert Storm, commanded by General H. Norman SCHWARZKOPF, began two days after the expiration of the United Nations Security Council deadline of 15 January 1991.

Desert Storm can be divided into two distinct phases, the air war and the ground war. The coalition strategy was to take advantage of its clear superiority in airpower. On 17 January the air war began when a flight of American Apache helicopters destroyed early-warning radar installations inside Iraq. This allowed American F-117 stealth fighter/bombers with laser-guided "smart bombs" to hit high-value targets, blinding Iraq's sophisticated air defense system and disrupt-

Fairchild A-10A Thunderbolt IIs, affectionately dubbed the "Warthog." This ground-support aircraft played a key role in Operation Desert Storm.   *(San Diego Aerospace Museum)*

ing communications. F-117s attacked even heavily defended targets in downtown Baghdad, without any losses. Just after the F-117 attack, the battleship *Wisconsin* launched Tomahawk cruise missiles against Iraqi targets. Within 24 hours the U.S. Navy fired 116 cruise missiles at targets in greater Baghdad. Only later did coalition airpower turn its attention to the Iraqi troops occupying Kuwait.

The absolute superiority of coalition airpower became clear in the first days of the war. Iraq possessed nearly 800 combat aircraft and an integrated air-defense system controlling more than 3,000 surface-to-air missiles. However, coalition forces were so dominant that Iraq was unable to win a single air-to-air engagement and in the first days lost 35 aircraft in air-to-air combat; by the end of the war coalition forces had destroyed more than 200 Iraqi aircraft. After the first week, Iraq ceased to challenge the coalition's con-

trol of the air. The only time the Iraqi air force reacted was when coalition forces began to use laser-guided bombs to destroy aircraft seeking shelter in hardened bunkers (nearly 600 bunkers were destroyed). Later, nearly 120 planes of the Iraqi air force flew to Iran, where they were immediately impounded as reparations from the Iran-Iraq War.

The only area means by which the Iraqis were able to strike back at the coalition was Scud surface-to-surface missiles. The Iraqis had a number of mobile Scud launchers that could quickly set up, launch their missiles, and then hide. During the course of the war, Iraq fired 46 Scuds against Saudi Arabia. The Iraqis also fired 40 Scuds against Israel in the vain hope of provoking an Israeli response that would fragment the coalition. In part because of the unsophisticated nature of the Scud and in part because of the U.S. Patriot missile defense system, the Scuds were more of an inconvenience than anything else. Concern that some Scuds might carry chemical or biological agents proved unfounded. The only strategic value of the Scuds was in taking coalition air assets away from the bombing campaign and send them on time-consuming and largely unsuccessful "Scud hunts."

The air war continued unabated for five weeks, with virtually no resistance from Iraq. More than 109,000 combat sorties were flown, some 40,000 of them against Iraqi ground forces, with the loss of only 38 coalition aircraft—the lowest loss rate per sortie of any air combat in history and less than the normal accident rate per sortie in combat training. By the end of the war coalition airplanes had dropped 88,500 tons of ordnance, of which 6,500 tons were precision-guided weapons.

Planning for the ground assault stressed the coalition advantages of mobility, technology, equipment, and training. Planning drew upon Air-Land Battle doctrine, a strategy developed for NATO troops to fight Soviet forces. The crux of combined-arms doctrine is to "look deep," 100 miles or more behind the front, stressing deception and maneuver. It seeks to combine speed, surprise, and mobility to protect one's own forces and keep an enemy off balance.

The plan for the ground assault used all elements of Air-Land doctrine to devastating effect. The plan was a large "left hook" that swung around Iraqi troops in Kuwait to hit the elite Republican Guard divisions from the west; Iraqi commanders were led to believe that the assault would be elsewhere.

Part of the deception was a threatened amphibious assault on Kuwait by U.S. Marines on ships in the Persian Gulf. To convince the Iraqis that the assault would occur, the U.S. Navy conducted two separate practice landings (Operations Camel Sand in October and Imminent Thunder in November). The finishing touch to the deception was delivered by the battleships *Wisconsin* and *Missouri*, which shelled the Kuwaiti coast just prior to the start of the ground assault.

With six divisions of Iraqi soldiers pinned down by the deception and Iraq's commanders blinded by the air war, coalition forces moved into position for the left hook. Three principal thrusts were planned. On the far left flank of the assault, the 82d and 101st Airborne Divisions, supported by a French Light Armored Division, moved several hundred miles to the west in order to swing around and cut off the Iraqis from support from the north or from any avenue of retreat.

The center of the assault, the "mailed fist," was mounted some 100 miles from the coast. It was made up of various heavily armored divisions from both the United States and Britain. This thrust was intended to drive deep, engaging and destroying the Republican Guard units. The third thrust occurred due south of Kuwait City, about 30 miles inland from the Persian Gulf. It comprised the Pan-Arab (Saudi, Kuwaiti, Egyptian, and Syrian) forces and the U.S. 1st Marine Expeditionary Force. Its job was to attack into Kuwait along a broad front and to liberate Kuwait City.

On 24 February the second, ground, phase of Desert Storm began. Almost immediately, beleaguered Iraqi troops surrendered en masse. Where they decided to fight, they died. The Gulf War was one of the most decisive military victories in history. The scale of the victory is indicated by estimates that coalition forces destroyed nearly 4,000 Iraqi tanks, more than 1,000 other armored vehicles, and nearly 3,000 artillery pieces. In contrast, the coalition suffered combat losses of four tanks, nine other armored vehicles, and one artillery weapon. Casualties were similarly lopsided, with up to 100,000 dead on the Iraqi side and less than 200 coalition fatalities, many of the latter to "friendly fire." The war was an almost textbook example of Air-Land Battle doctrine. The attack was so successful that President George H. W. BUSH called a ceasefire in less than 100 hours, allowing the Republican Guard to escape to Baghdad. Arguably, it was the first war in history decided by airpower. Certainly the Gulf War greatly enhanced the prestige of the U.S. military.

Some have argued out that the cease-fire was imposed too soon, probably chiefly to forestall the breakup of Iraq and the expansion of Iranian power in the region. In any case, much of Iraq's war machine escaped destruction. This equipment served not only to keep Iraqi dictator Saddam Hussein in power but to crush Kurdish and Shi'ite rebellions.

See also GULF WAR, CAUSES OF; POWELL, COLIN L.

Further reading: Atkinson, Rick. *Crusade: The Untold Story of the Persian Gulf War.* New York: Houghton Mifflin, 1993; Gordon, Michael R., and Bernard E. Trainor. *The Generals' War.* New York: Little, Brown, 1995; Scales, Robert H. *Certain Victory: The U.S. Army in the Gulf War.* Washington, D.C.: Brassey's, 1997. Watson, Bruce W., ed. *Military Lessons of the Gulf War.* London: Greenhill Books, 1991.

— Craig T. Cobane

De Seversky, Alexander P. (1894–1974) *Airpower advocate and aircraft designer*

Born on 7 June 1894 in Tbilisi, Republic of Georgia, Alexander Prokofieff De Seversky was the son of a wealthy Russian sportsman-pilot. He graduated from the Russian naval academy in 1914 and saw sea duty with the Russian navy in World War I, during the winter of 1914–15. He then transferred to the Imperial Naval Air Service. In July 1915, while on a bombing mission in the Gulf of Riga,

De Seversky was shot down, losing his right leg. During his recovery he inspected aircraft production. He returned to flying in the summer of 1916 and flew another 57 missions, downing 13 German aircraft and becoming chief of Russian naval fighter aviation in the Baltic.

In 1917 the Russian provisional government named De Seversky assistant naval attaché for air at its Washington embassy. After the Bolsheviks seized power in November 1917, de Seversky offered his expertise to the U.S. military, serving as a test pilot and consulting engineer.

After the war De Seversky remained in the United States. He became a citizen in 1927, whereupon he was commissioned a major in the Air Corps Specialists Reserve. He became a prominent aircraft designer, developing numerous significant technical improvements and innovations. In 1922 he formed the Seversky Aero Corporation, which produced the first automatic bombsight.

The company was reorganized and expanded in 1931 as the Seversky Aircraft Corporation. Its most successful aircraft was the P-35, predecessor of the P-47 Thunderbolt. In 1939 the company was reorganized as Republic.

Until his death De Seversky was a dedicated advocate of the strategic importance of airpower, working relentlessly to enhance U.S. aviation and eventually its missile and satellite capabilities. Between the wars he collaborated with Brigadier General William "Billy" MITCHELL on tests designed to prove the superiority of airpower over battleships, greatly facilitated by efforts De Seversky's close ties to the American military, flair for publicity, and continued record-breaking flying feats.

The Second World War and its aftermath won De Seversky's message a favorable hearing. Besides lobbying politicians and the military, he published numerous newspaper articles and three books on the indispensability of airpower in modern warfare, all urging that the U.S. Air Force should become the world's strongest. His book *Victory through Air Power* (1942) proved an immediate best-seller and subsequently was made into a movie. *Air Power: Key to Survival* (1950) and *America: Too Young to Die!* (1961) reiterated the same themes. De Seversky died at New York City on 24 August 1974.

See also AIR FORCE, U.S.; AIRCRAFT, FIXED-WING.

Further reading: De Seversky, Alexander P. *Victory through Air Power.* New York: Simon & Schuster, 1942; Leary, William M., ed. *Aviation's Golden Age: Portraits from the 1920s and 1930s.* Iowa City: University of Iowa Press, 1989; Warner, Edward. "Douhet, Mitchell, Seversky: Theories of Air Warfare." *Makers of Modern Strategy: Military Thought from Machiavelli to Hitler.* Edited by Edward Mead Earle, with Gordon Craig and Felix Gilbert. Princeton, N.J.: Princeton University Press, 1943.

— Priscilla Roberts

destroyers   *A relatively small, fast, lightly protected warship, armed initially with light guns and torpedoes*
U.S. interest in such a vessel began during the Civil War. Union and Confederate officers both envisioned attacking much stronger vessels with smaller warships armed with a mine connected to a large spar, what became known as a spar torpedo. In October 1864 Union navy lieutenant William B. Cushing utilized a 30-foot steam-powered launch to sink the Confederate ironclad *Albemarle* with a spar torpedo. The deficiencies of the weapon, however, precluded its widespread use. The proximity of the attacking craft to the target vessel ensured that the attacker would be caught in the blast of the weapon. Indeed, Cushing lost his craft in that fashion.

The development of the Whitehead self-propelled TORPEDO in 1868 made viable the idea of torpedo boats (TB) that could sink the most powerful warships afloat. The U.S. building program began in 1886 when Congress authorized construction of the first navy steel-hulled TB, which was laid down in 1888 and launched in 1890. This ship, the *Cushing*, was 140 feet long, displaced 116 tons, was armed with three torpedo tubes, and was capable of a maximum speed of 23 knots. The *Cushing* ushered in an experimental phase for TBs in the U.S. Navy in which 34 vessels of varying designs were produced.

The major maritime powers viewed the TB as a significant threat. Each nation sought to devise a method of defense for the BATTLESHIPS, the eventual answer being the 1882 British-developed torpedo boat destroyer (TBD), the forerunner of the modern destroyer. It was a larger TB, equipped with light guns and torpedoes, and designed to hunt down and destroy enemy torpedo boats.

Beginning in 1896, the United States followed the British lead with the construction of the four-ship *Farragut* class, generally regarded as the first U.S. Navy torpedo-boat destroyers. Production of TBDs was augmented at the insistence of Assistant Secretary of the Navy Theodore ROOSEVELT. He argued for a new class of ship to defend against enemy TB attacks and operate in support of larger warships outside American coastal waters, which the existing TBs could not because of their limited range. In May 1898 Congress called for the construction of 16 new torpedo-boat destroyers. The first of these was the five-ship *Bainbridge* class. The name ship, designated TBD 1, was laid down in August 1899 and commissioned in November 1902. The *Bainbridge* class ships were 250 feet in length and 24 feet in beam, with a displacement of 420 tons, were armed with two 3-inch guns and two 18-inch torpedo tubes, and were capable of 28 knots.

The *Bainbridge* class and similar designs in other navies suffered from unseaworthiness. In 1904 the British navy launched the first of its *River*-class torpedo boat destroyers, which are considered the first true, blue-water vessels of their type. From this point these vessels, known simply as destroyers, supplanted torpedo boats and assumed their role of attacking an enemy's fleet. They also served as escorts against the attacks of enemy destroyers.

The United States again followed the British lead with the launch in 1909 of the *Smith* class, its first oceangoing destroyers. In 1913 the U.S. Navy launched the first of eight ships of the *Cassin* class, the first destroyers to displace 1,000 tons. By August 1914 destroyers were the most numerous warships in the world's navies. The U.S. possessed about 50 destroyers of varying types, while Great Britain and Germany operated 221 and 90 respectively.

The destroyer proved its importance during World War I. These ships took part in numerous actions, but their primary mission was to safeguard the battle fleets. The rise of submarine warfare gave the destroyer the additional mission of hunting down enemy SUBMARINES. Destroyers became especially effective after the introduction of depth charges in December 1916 and hydrophones in 1917. Implementation of the CONVOY SYSTEM in May 1917 made destroyers vital to the Allied war effort. This fact was evident in the actions of the United States after its April 1917 declaration of war against Germany. By the end of August there were 35 U.S. destroyers involved in convoy duty. Congress also approved two new destroyer classes, totaling 273 warships. By the end of World War I the United States destroyer force was second only to that of Great Britain.

Destroyer construction continued unabated in the interwar years, as few restrictions were placed on their design and number during the naval disarmament talks of the period. Construction in the United States, however, stagnated, for numerous reasons. The overarching problem was the worldwide debate over the primary mission of the destroyer in an age of increasing technological innovation. Opinions varied between light gun support for amphibious operations and antisubmarine warfare, between destroyers as escorts and as minor surface combatants. U.S. officials were split between those who favored a few larger and more heavily armed ships and those who wanted large numbers of lighter, general-purpose vessels. Compounding the problem was the widely held belief that it was not necessary to construct new destroyers, as they could be quickly constructed in time of war, as in World War I.

The United States consequently relied almost entirely on its aging force of World War I–era destroyers. Construction and innovation, however, did not end entirely; the United States launched the first of the new eight-ship *Farragut* class in 1934. These were the first destroyers to mount dual-purpose five-inch guns—for both surface and antiaircraft defense. The collapse of the naval disarmament treaties in 1934 spurred an increase in the production of destroyers. By late 1939 the U.S. Navy had begun construction of the 95-ship *Benson/Gleaves* class.

The war at sea in World War II revealed that all the missions that had been debated for the destroyer were equally important. As the previous world war, they were also given a new task that arose from technological development. Their duties expanded to cover not only the protection of capital ships and convoys against surface and underwater attacks but also, especially in the Pacific theater, defense against air attack. The experience of World War II also revealed that the belief in the United States in the possibility of quick construction of destroyers in time of war was erroneous. The U.S. Navy force of 78 modern destroyers and 71 active World War I–era destroyers, although the second largest in the world, was insufficient to meet all the needs for this type of warship. Crash construction programs produced 392 new ships of varying classes during the war. The most successful was the 150-ship *Fletcher* class, considered by naval scholars as one of the best ever built. The *Fletchers* measured 376 feet in length by 40 in beam, displaced 2,325 tons, and were armed with five single-mount five-inch guns and 10 21-inch torpedo tubes. Their engines could drive them at a speed of 38 knots. By the end of World War II, the United States possessed the largest destroyer force in the world, and it continued to augment it in the immediate postwar years.

The dawn of the missile age after the war changed the weaponry of the destroyer but did not alter its role. The United States, as one of two superpowers, assumed the lead in destroyer design. From 1957 to 1961 the U.S. Navy launched the first purpose-built guided missile destroyers (DDG), the *Coontz* class. The Soviet Union countered with its first DDGs in 1958, followed by the United Kingdom in 1959 and the other major maritime powers in the 1960s.

The present-day destroyer is a large vessel capable of performing all the roles that have arisen since World War I, but its primary mission remains that of an escort. In the 1980s many naval experts believed that destroyer construction would abate as the major naval powers increasingly relied on cheaper, smaller vessels known as frigates. This assessment turned out to be false. In 2001 the United States operated 54 DDs and DDGs of varying types. An additional 58 destroyers were under construction or planned—26 of the improved *Arleigh Burke* class and 32 of the (later canceled) *Zumwalt* class.

See also NAVY, U.S.

Further reading: Friedman, Norman. *U.S. Destroyers: An Illustrated Design History.* Annapolis, Md.: Naval Institute Press, 1982; George, James L. *History of Warships: From Ancient Times to the Twenty-first Century.* Annapolis, Md.: Naval Institute Press, 1998; Hooten, E. R. *Destroyers, Frigates, and Corvettes: The World Market.* Coulsdon, Surrey, U.K.: Jane's Information Group, 1995;

Newcomb, Richard F. *U.S. Destroyers of the World Wars.* Paducah, Ky.: Turner, 1994.

— Eric W. Osborne

Detroit, surrender of (16 August 1812) *Major U.S. military failure during the War of 1812*

The surrender of Detroit was the culmination of a flawed U.S. plan to invade Canada during the summer of 1812. William HULL, governor of the Michigan Territory, reluctantly accepted the rank of brigadier general and command of the northwestern army of more than 2,000 men, predominantly militia. Hull believed it was impossible to invade Canada without control of the Great Lakes, which provided strategic and tactical advantages to the British. In June his army moved through 200 miles of Ohio wilderness, arriving at Detroit in early July.

Secretary of War William EUSTIS then ordered Hull to invade Canada. After some hesitation by militia units, the Americans crossed the Detroit River to Sandwich. However, instead of quickly advancing to engage the British at Fort Malden, Hull chose a deliberate approach, concerned about his vulnerable line of communication to Ohio. His apparent timidity and vacillation exacerbated the dissension of his militia officers.

In late July the British and Indians allied with them captured Fort MACKINAC at the confluence of Lakes Michigan and Huron, threatening Hull's water communications. Hull attempted to open communications to Ohio with two expeditions, both of which were ambushed by forces commanded by TECUMSEH. Hull then abandoned his operations in Canada and returned to Detroit. Concurrently, Major General Henry DEARBORN, commanding an invasion into Canada from New York, arranged an armistice with the British, inadvertently permitting British commander in Canada, Major General Isaac Brock, to move British reinforcements to Detroit for a counteroffensive. On 15 August Brock demanded Hull's surrender, but Hull refused, whereupon Brock ordered a bombardment of the fort that devastated the morale of the American troops and civilians inside.

On 16 August Brock moved 2,000 British and Indians to engage Hull. Hull's army had been reduced by illness and casualties, leaving about 800 effectives. Brock threatened to turn his Indians loose if Hull did not surrender. Hull's mental state has been much debated, but it perhaps reflected the cumulative stress of the campaign, lack of medical supplies and secure communications, fear of the Indians, and concern for the safety of civilians, including his own family. In any case he concluded that he must surrender.

This action shocked the Americans. In less than three months of war, an army and a strategic territory had been lost. Public opinion and President James Madison's admin-istration blamed Hull. Court-martialed, Hull defended his actions, but he was convicted of cowardice and neglect of duty and sentenced to be shot. Madison commuted the sentence in recognition of Hull's Revolutionary War record, but the stain upon his reputation has persisted. The Detroit campaign was a prime example of incompetent national political and military leadership during the War of 1812.

See also WAR OF 1812, LAND OVERVIEW.

Further reading: Antal, Sandy. *A Wampum Denied: Procter's War of 1812.* Ottawa: Carleton University Press, 1997; Quimby, Robert S. *The U.S. Army in the War of 1812: An Operational and Command Study.* East Lansing: Michigan State University Press, 1997.

— Steven J. Rauch

Devers, Jacob L. (1887–1979) *U.S. Army general*

Born on 8 September 1887 at York, Pennsylvania, Jacob Loucks Devers graduated from the U.S. Military Academy at West Point in 1909 and was commissioned in the field artillery. His early career included service in Hawaii, as an instructor at the military academy (1912–16), at the Field Artillery School at Fort Sill, and with occupation forces in Germany in 1919. Between the two world wars, Devers attended the Army War College and served on the staff with the War Department. He was serving in the Panama Canal Zone when he was promoted brigadier general in 1939.

Devers took command of the 9th Infantry Division at Fort Bragg, North Carolina, in 1940 and was promoted major general there. From 1941 through 1943 he commanded the Armored Force Training Center at Fort Knox, Kentucky. There he played a crucial role in the development of a large armor force, in combined arms doctrine, and in tank design and engine development. Following promotion to lieutenant general in September 1942, Devers received command of the European theater of operations, U.S. Army, in May 1943. This assignment gave him administrative command of the American troop buildup in the United Kingdom in preparation for the cross-channel NORMANDY INVASION. From this posting Devers moved to become commander of the North Africa theater and then deputy Supreme Allied Commander in the Mediterranean.

After the August 1944 Operation Anvil/Dragoon landings in southern France, Devers received the combat command he so much desired: Sixth Army Group, of 23 divisions, made up of Lieutenant General Alexander Patch's Seventh Army and Jean de Lattre de Tassigny's First French Army. He led his army group northward through France into Alsace and then eastward into Bavaria. Although Devers's army group pursued German forces northward with effectiveness, General Dwight D. EISENHOWER was critical of him for failing to reduce the Colmar pocket.

Notwithstanding, Devers was promoted to full general in March 1945. Sixth Army Group linked up with General Mark CLARK's Fifteenth Army Group in Austria in May 1945, just as the war in Europe ended.

Devers's last active military post was that of Chief, Army Ground Forces (June 1945–September 1949), supervising a rapidly shrinking American army. After his September 1949 retirement Devers served the United Nations as military adviser during the Indian-Pakistani dispute over Kashmir in the early 1950s. After a stint in private industry, Devers retired in Washington, D.C., where he died on 15 October 1979.

See also WORLD WAR II, U.S. INVOLVEMENT, EUROPE.

Further reading: Blumenson, Martin, and James L. Stokesbury. "Jake Devers." *Army* 23, no. 2 (February 1973): 26–31; Markey, Michael A. *Jake: The General from West York Avenue.* York, Pa.: Historical Society of York County, 1998; Weigley, Russell F. *Eisenhower's Lieutenants: The Campaign of France and Germany, 1944–1945.* Bloomington: Indiana University Press, 1990.

— Thomas D. Veve

Dewey, George (1837–1917) *U.S. Navy admiral and first president of the General Board*

Born on 26 December 1837 at Montpelier, Vermont, George Dewey graduated from the U.S. Naval Academy at Annapolis in 1858. He then spent three years on the frigate *Wabash,* flagship of the Mediterranean Squadron. During the Civil War he served under Flag Officer David G. FARRAGUT in the West Gulf Coast Blockading Squadron and became executive officer of the steam frigate *Mississippi.* After participating in the capture of NEW ORLEANS, he became executive officer of Farragut's flagship, the screw sloop *Monongahela.* He ended the war as a lieutenant commander aboard the screw sloop *Kearsarge* in European waters, having participated in four major campaigns.

Dewey's subsequent career included two lengthy stretches with the European Squadron, including three years commanding its flagship, the steam sloop *Pensacola.* He also completed a teaching assignment at Annapolis, tours of seven years apiece on the Lighthouse Board and as chief of Bureau of Equipment in Washington, and an appointment in 1895 to head the Board of Inspection and Survey. Well versed in Washington politics, Dewey supervised the implementation of innovative technology in the navy's new steel fleet.

Strongly supported by bellicose assistant secretary of the navy, Theodore ROOSEVELT, as the SPANISH-AMERICAN WAR approached Dewey lobbied successfully to command the Asiatic squadron. He took command in October 1897, promising assertive measures to prevent any Philippine-based Spanish naval threat against possible American

action in Cuba. Initially based in Hong Kong, when hostilities erupted in April 1898, the squadron swiftly moved to the Philippines. On 1 May Dewey, at dawn, attacked the Spanish fleet in the Battle of MANILA BAY. Within eight hours the Spanish fleet had been destroyed, losing seven ships and 370 men, while Dewey only suffered one fatality, the result of heat exhaustion. Within a week Congress made him the sole full admiral in the U.S. Navy. In July 1898 American troops arrived in substantial numbers, and the city of Manila surrendered in August.

The following May Dewey returned home to a hero's welcome. In 1900 he was appointed president of the new Navy General Board, thereby dominating naval planning as the United States became increasingly assertive internationally. He advocated an ambitious naval construction program, the acquisition of naval bases in the Pacific, and the aggressive projection of U.S. naval power overseas in support of the Monroe Doctrine and other American interests. In 1902 Dewey commanded training exercises deliberately designed to discourage an Anglo-Italian-German blockade of Venezuela, which had defaulted on its debts. He died at Washington, D.C., on 16 January 1917, one of the most famous naval officers in U.S. history.

See also TREATY OF PARIS (1898).

Admiral George Dewey   *(Library of Congress)*

Further reading: Dewey, George. *Autobiography of George Dewey: Admiral of the Navy.* New York: Scribner, 1913; Sargent, Nathan. *Admiral Dewey and the Manila Campaign.* Washington, D.C.: Naval Historical Foundation, 1947; Spector, Ronald. *Admiral of the New Empire: The Life and Career of George Dewey.* Baton Rouge: Louisiana State University Press, 1974; Williams, Vernon L. "George Dewey: Admiral of the Navy." *Admirals of the New Steel Navy: Makers of the American Naval Tradition, 1880–1930.* Edited by James C. Bradford. Annapolis, Md.: Naval Institute Press, 1990.

— Priscilla Roberts

Dick Act (1903) *Congressional act regulating the National Guard*

Named for its chief sponsor, Representative Charles W. Dick, a Republican from Ohio, the act addressed the problem of securing sufficient human resources for large-scale modern warfare. The Dick Act of 1903 repealed the MILITIA ACT OF 1792 and with it, in effect, the principle of universal military obligation. The legislation recognized two militias. The volunteer National Guard became the "organized Militia"—the first-line military reserve. The mass of adult males between ages 18 and 45 constituted the second militia.

The legislation exchanged greater federal control of the guard's organization and the subsidies paid for its training and maintenance. The more the guard trained, the more money it would receive. The National Guard was to be organized, trained, and equipped the same as the regular army. The federal government would provide the guard with weapons and equipment, and it would furnish regular army officers as instructors. The Dick Act allowed the army to impose minimum standards of weekly drill and field training. Washington also exerted a degree of control over officer competence by reserving the right to prepare them for equivalent commissions in any volunteer force that might be raised.

Washington could now call the guard into service for nine months rather than the previous three. But this could be done only to keep internal order or repel foreign invasion. For overseas use or major foreign wars, Washington could only ask for guardsmen to volunteer. The assumption was that in a true national emergency the guard would volunteer en masse and would thus arrive on the scene of action ready to fight.

In 1908 further legislation removed the time and geographic barriers to guard service, in return for assurance that guardsmen would go to war as National Guard units, not as individual replacements. But the provision that allowed the guard to serve overseas was declared unconstitutional in 1912.

The Dick Act of 1903, subsequent legislation concerning the guard, and the NATIONAL DEFENSE ACT OF 1916 were important steps in preparing the U.S. military for modern war.

Further reading: Colby, Elbridge. "Elihu Root and the National Guard." *Military Affairs* 23 (Spring 1959): 28–34; Derthick, Martha. *The National Guard in Politics.* Cambridge, Mass.: Harvard University Press, 1965; Millett, Allan R., and Peter Maslowski. *For the Common Defense: A Military History of the United States.* Rev. ed. New York: Free Press, 1994.

— Spencer C. Tucker

Dickman, Joseph T. (1857–1927) *U.S. Army general*

Born on 6 October 1857 at Dayton, Ohio, Joseph Theodore Dickman was commissioned in the cavalry on graduation from the U.S. Military Academy at WEST POINT in 1881 and was assigned to the 3d Cavalry Regiment. After seeing action in the APACHE WARS against GERONIMO, Dickman was an instructor at the Cavalry and Light Artillery School at Fort Riley, Kansas (1893–94). In 1894 his command was on duty in Chicago during the PULLMAN STRIKE.

At the start of the 1898 SPANISH-AMERICAN WAR, Dickman became acting adjutant general of the 3d Cavalry Division in Tampa, Florida. Promoted to captain in May 1898, he served on the staff of Major General Joseph WHEELER during the Santiago campaign. Promoted to major and sent to the Philippines in 1899, he was promoted to lieutenant colonel of volunteers and distinguished himself during the PHILIPPINE-AMERICAN WAR on the island of Panay.

Dickman was then chief of staff to Brigadier General Adna R. CHAFFEE, commander of the American contingent in the 1900 Peking (Beijing) relief expedition during the BOXER UPRISING in China. He took part in fighting at the Pa-ta-Chao temples near Peking in September 1900.

Dickman returned to the United States to become a member of the first Army General Staff in 1903. After graduating from the Army War College in Washington in 1905, he was attached to the 13th Cavalry Regiment at Fort Myer, Virginia, 1906–08. He spent the next three years as an inspector general in the Philippines and at Chicago, Illinois. He then visited France, Italy, Austria, Russia, Germany, and Britain while on a board to revise cavalry regulations. Promoted colonel in December 1914, Dickman commanded the 2d Cavalry Regiment at Fort Ethan Allen, Vermont, in 1915.

In July 1917, after the United States entered World War I, Dickman was promoted to brigadier general. He rose to temporary major general in August 1917 and took command of the 85th Infantry Division at Camp Custer, Michigan, organizing and training the division from August to October. In November 1917 he took over organization and training of the 3d Infantry Division at Camp Greene, North Carolina, and commanded the entire camp as well. In March 1918 he traveled to France in advance of his division; the 3d Division arrived the next month and went into battle at the end of May and early June.

Dickman's division fought in the July Battle of CHÂTEAU-THIERRY and held there despite devastating German attacks. His leadership so impressed the AMERICAN EXPEDITIONARY FORCE commander, General John J. PERSHING, that he gave Dickman command of IV Corps, comprising the 1st, 42d, and 89th Divisions. Dickman commanded it in the SAINT-MIHIEL OFFENSIVE of September 1918 and into the early stage of the MEUSE-ARGONNE OFFENSIVE. On 12 October he took command of I Corps. After the armistice, Dickman served on occupation duty in Germany, commanding Third Army around the Coblenz bridgehead over the Rhine until April 1919. He then wrote a report on lessons learned in the war and returned to the United States in July.

Dickman subsequently commanded the Southern Department and later VIII Corps until his retirement on 6 October 1921. He was advanced to major general on the retired list in August 1922. In retirement Dickman wrote extensively and translated numerous military works into English. He died at Washington, D.C., on 23 October 1928.

See also WORLD WAR I, U.S. INVOLVEMENT.

Further reading: Bullard, Robert L. *Fighting Generals.* Ann Arbor, Mich.: J. W. Edwards, 1944; Dickman, Joseph Theodore. *The Great Crusade.* New York: D. Appleton, 1927.

— Edwin Clarke

Dix, Dorothea L. (1802–1887) *Social reformer and Civil War superintendent of U.S. Army nurses*

Born on 4 April 1802 at Hamden, Maine, Dorothea Lynde Dix left home at age 12 to live with extended family in Boston. She began teaching at age 14 and worked as a teacher and writer until age 40, when she became an activist for prisoners and the mentally ill. Prior to the Civil War, Dix lobbied for and secured funding for state hospitals and asylums.

When the Civil War began, Dix traveled to Washington, D.C., where she offered her services to the War Department as coordinator for volunteer nurses. Although she had no prior nursing experience, Dix's reputation as a social worker secured her an official appointment. In June 1861 she began work as superintendent of U.S. Army nurses.

Dix approached her position with energy. She assisted hospitals with procuring supplies, and she appointed, trained, and supervised female army nurses. Nurses had to conform strictly to Dix's image of a caregiver. She required nurses to be at least 30, plain looking, and soberly dressed. Dix would not consider qualified women who differed with her religious convictions, and she dismissed nurses whom she had not appointed.

Dix's Civil War volunteer efforts proved frustrating both to her and to the army medical community. The army failed to define her role adequately, and Dix's rigid style of leadership and management alienated nursing staffs, hospital administrators, and surgeons alike. The conflict became so intense that in October 1863 Secretary of War Edwin STANTON reorganized the Medical Bureau and returned to the surgeon general the authority to appoint nurses. Although this order reduced her authority and wounded her pride, Dix continued as superintendent until the end of the war.

Dix remained in Washington for 18 months after the war to assist families in locating missing relatives and to help people caring for the sick and wounded soldiers. In 1866 she returned to her crusade on behalf of the mentally ill, but the negative impact of her Civil War experience and her advancing age limited her activities. Dix retired in 1881. She died at the Trenton, New Jersey, State Hospital, a hospital she helped to found, on 17 July 1887.

See also ARMY NURSE CORPS; BARTON, CLARISSA; BICKERDYKE, MAY ANN BALL; MEDICINE, MILITARY; NURSE CORPS.

Further reading: Marshall, Helen. *Dorothea Dix: Forgotten Samaritan.* Chapel Hill: University of North Carolina Press, 1937; Schlaifer, Charles, and Lucy Freeman. *Heart's Work: Civil War Heroine and Champion of the Mentally Ill, Dorothea Lynde Dix.* New York: Paragon House, 1991; Wilson, Dorothy Clarke. *Stranger and Traveler: The Story of Dorothea Dix, American Reformer.* Boston: Little, Brown, 1975.

— Tracy M. Shilcutt

Dogger Bank, Battle of the (5 August 1781) *Dutch-British naval battle off the Dogger Bank in the North Sea during the American Revolutionary War*

From 1780 to 1784 the Dutch Republic fought the so-called Fourth Anglo-Dutch War against Great Britain as an ally of the United States. The conflict was part of the wider struggle of the American Revolutionary War. The Dutch greatly assisted the United States by forcing the British to dissipate their naval assets. The British had imposed a blockade on the Dutch coast, but in July 1781 Rear Admiral Johann A. Zoutnam left the Texel with seven ships of the line, seven frigates, and one cutter to convoy a number of merchantmen to the Baltic. British vice admiral Sir Hyde Parker, with seven ships of the line and six frigates, was escorting a convoy of his own when he received the news. He immediately ordered his convoy to return home and moved to engage the Dutch.

From 8 to 11:30 A.M. on 5 August 1781, the two nearly equal squadrons fought a fierce close-range battle in two battle lines. Finally the Dutch ships withdrew and regained the Texel. Zoutnam lost only one ship, the *Hollandia,* which sank the next day. Dutch casualties were 142 dead and 403 wounded. The British had a number of ships heavily damaged but lost none. Their casualties came to 109 dead and 362 wounded.

Although both sides claimed victory and Parker had failed to destroy the opposing squadron, he had forced the Dutch convoy back to port. During the war the Dutch suffered heavy losses from British privateering and were unable to protect their overseas colonies effectively.

See also AMERICAN REVOLUTIONARY WAR, NAVAL OVERVIEW.

Further reading: Clowes, William L. *The Royal Navy. A History from the Earliest Times to 1900.* Vol. 3. London: Sampson Low, Marston, 1898; Edler, Friedrich. *The Dutch Republic and the American Revolution.* Baltimore: Johns Hopkins University Press, 1911.

— Max Plassmann

Dominican Republic, intervention in (1965) *The United States military intervention in the Dominican Republic to prevent communists from coming to power there*

During the U.S. interventions in the Caribbean in the first decades of the 20th century, U.S. Marines occupied the Dominican Republic from 1916 to 1924. During that occupation, the marines established a National Guard that was initially led by marine officers. After the withdrawal Dominican officers trained by the marines took command. One of these, Rafael Trujillo quickly rose to the top in the 1930s and took over not only the military but the government as well. Trujillo soon became a dictator and ruled the country with an iron hand for 30 years.

After World War II the anticommunist Trujillo became a staunch COLD WAR ally of Washington. By the late 1950s, however, the brutality of his regime became an embarrassment for the administration of President Dwight D. EISENHOWER. After Trujillo's agents attempted to assassinate opponents living in the United States as well as the democratically elected president of Venezuela, Washington turned against him. Both Presidents Eisenhower and John F. KENNEDY gave support to elements within the Domini-

can Republic trying to overthrow Trujillo. These opponents assassinated Trujillo in May 1961.

For the next four years the Dominican Republic lived on the edge of chaos as former Trujillo supporters, the military, and democratic elements vied for power. Several coup attempts (some successful) kept political life in turmoil. This situation came to a climax in the spring of 1965 when elements backing deposed democratic president Juan Bosch and led by reformist military officers started a revolution against the military-supported government.

U.S. President Lyndon JOHNSON, fearing that the Bosch supporters were influenced by communists, decided to intervene to prevent the country from becoming another Cuba. On 28 April 1965, with the embassy under fire from rebel troops, U.S. ambassador to the Dominican Republic. W. Tapley Bennett asked President Johnson to send in marines to safeguard American lives. That night Johnson announced to the nation that 450 marines had landed in Santo Domingo to protect American citizens in the Dominican Republic. He stressed that the United States would not become involved in the internal conflict. The next day the administration announced that 4,000 additional troops had landed for the same purpose of protecting Americans. On 30 April Johnson, fearing that a rebel victory would mean a communist government in Santo Domingo, announced to the nation that a full-scale intervention was under way. Eventually 23,000 U.S. soldiers and marines were inserted into the country.

The mission of U.S. forces was to keep the two sides apart and establish sufficient stability so that a provisional government could hold free elections. U.S. forces did engage in firefights with rebel soldiers, but overall casualties were light. Initially the United States acted unilaterally in the intervention, but by 29 April the administration had succeeded in getting five Latin American countries (four of which had dictatorial regimes) to send small contingents, and a Brazilian general was given command of the inter-American peacekeeping force. The Dominican intervention, however, was clearly a U.S.-dominated operation, one consistent with Washington's cold war foreign policy. Although most historians have argued that the administration overplayed the communist threat in Santo Domingo in 1965, it was evident from the beginning of the crisis that President Johnson was not going to risk another Cuba in the hemisphere, especially in a small country so close to the United States.

The U.S. intervention did pave the way for open elections in 1966, and for the remainder of the century the Dominican Republic enjoyed a period of relative peace under civilian, democratically elected governments.

See also: LATIN AMERICA INTERVENTIONS, EARLY 20TH CENTURY.

Further reading: Burke, Arleigh, ed. *Dominican Action—1965: Intervention or Cooperation?* Washington, D.C.: The Center for Strategic Studies, 1966; Gleijeses, Piero. *The Dominican Crisis: The 1965 Constitutionalist Revolt and American Intervention.* Baltimore, Md.: The Johns Hopkins University Press, 1978; Kurzman, Dan. *Santo Domingo: Revolt of the Damned.* New York: G. P. Putman's Sons, 1965; Lowenthal, Abraham. *The Dominican Intervention.* Cambridge, Mass.: Harvard University Press, 1972.

— Paul Coe Clark, Jr.

Doniphan, Alexander W. (1808–1887) *Lawyer, politician, and soldier*

Born on 9 July 1808 in Mason County, Kentucky, Alexander William Doniphan attended private school in Augusta and graduated from Augusta College in 1826. After reading law for two years, Doniphan was admitted to the bar in Kentucky and Ohio. In 1830 he moved to Lexington, Missouri, where he established a law practice with David Rice Atchison. Doniphan soon gained renown as a defense lawyer in murder trials, and over the next 30 years he was involved in almost every important case in northwest Missouri.

In 1833 Doniphan moved to Liberty, Missouri, and began a complicated legal involvement with the Mormon Church, assisting Mormons driven from Jackson County to regain their lost property or secure compensation for it. After his election to the state legislature in 1836, Doniphan helped create Caldwell County for Mormons and Daviess County for non-Mormon Missouri residents, but the Mormon population expanded into Daviess County, and hostilities resumed. Doniphan and Atchison then attempted to mediate between the Mormons and state authorities.

At this time Doniphan was a brigadier general in the state militia, commanding the 1st Brigade, which was now called up by Governor Lilburn W. Boggs to quell the Mormon disturbances. During the 1838 Mormon War Doniphan refused Boggs's order to kill Mormon leaders, believing it constituted murder. In ensuing trials, Doniphan won acquittal for Mormons who had not escaped the state.

An advocate of Manifest Destiny and a proslavery expansionist, Doniphan soon after the outbreak of the MEXICAN-AMERICAN WAR in 1846 organized the 1st Regiment of Missouri Mounted Volunteers, consisting of 10 companies. Enlisting as a private, he was elected the regiment's colonel and soon orchestrated what became known as Doniphan's Expedition.

Starting in Missouri in June 1846, Doniphan's force first linked up with then-Colonel Stephen W. KEARNY and his Army of the West at Fort Leavenworth. Kearny helped meld the regiment into an effective fighting force. Doniphan's men then marched to Bent's Fort, arriving there on 28 July. Both armies then marched to Santa Fe where, in the Battle of Canoncito on 18 August 1846, Kearny and Doniphan were victorious. Kearny then departed for California, leaving Doniphan in command at Santa Fe.

On Kearny's direction Doniphan served for some weeks as military governor of what was called New Mexico, drafting a constitution and code of laws, known as the Kearny Code, for the newly conquered region. He also secured a treaty with the Navajo, who had been harassing white settlers. Doniphan then yielded command to Colonel Sterling Price, who had arrived with a large force.

On 14 December Doniphan headed south with 800 men to join forces with Brigadier General John E. WOOL in Chihuahua. En route, on 25 December, Doniphan fought 1,200 Mexicans under Colonel Antonio Ponce de León at Brazito, 25 miles north of El Paso del Norte. Doniphan routed the Mexican force, losing only seven of his own men. Two days later the Americans occupied El Paso del Norte without resistance. Continuing south, Doniphan next encountered 4,200 Mexicans under Major General José Heredia at Sacramento, just north of Chihuahua City on 28 February 1847. Again victorious, Doniphan captured large amounts of supplies and sustained only one casualty, compared to 304 Mexican casualties. He then moved into Chihuahua City on 2 March.

With his men's terms of enlistment nearly expired, Doniphan marched his troops from Chihuahua to Saltillo where he joined Wool and Major General Zachary TAYLOR on 21 May, two weeks after the Battle of BUENA VISTA. From Saltillo, Doniphan marched his men to Matamoros, where they boarded ships, arriving back in Missouri in June 1847. During the expedition Doniphan and his men had marched 3,600 miles, much of it through difficult terrain, in 12 months.

Doniphan returned to Liberty and resumed the practice of law. In 1854 he was reelected to the Missouri state legislature and was appointed commissioner of public schools for Clay County. In 1855 he was the Whig candidate for the U.S. Senate but lost. Also in the 1850s, personal tragedy struck—Doniphan's two sons died in accidents and his wife's health sharply deteriorated.

In 1861, during the secession crisis, the legislature appointed Doniphan as a delegate to a peace conference at Washington. During his absence, he was elected to a state convention called by the legislature to decide the issue of secession. Doniphan, though a slave owner, opposed secession and favored neutrality. In June 1861 Governor Claiborne Jackson commissioned him as major general of the Missouri State Guard, but he relinquished the command after two weeks.

From 1863 to 1868 Doniphan was a commissioner of claims in St. Louis. He also established a legal practice there. After 1868 Doniphan moved to Richmond, Missouri, where he practiced law until 1875, when he retired to become president of Ray County Savings Bank. He died in Richmond on 8 August 1887. Given Doniphan's Mexican War success, historians have long speculated about the impact he might have had during the Civil War, had he chosen to participate.

Further reading: Dawson, James G. *Doniphan's Epic March. The 1st Missouri Volunteers in the Mexican War.* Lawrence: University Press of Kansas, 1999; Launius, Roger. *Alexander William Doniphan: Portrait of a Missouri Moderate.* Columbia: University of Missouri Press, 1997.

— Jason R. Maslow

Donovan, William J. ("Wild Bill") (1883–1959)
Founder of the Office of Strategic Services, the first U.S. foreign intelligence agency

Born on 1 January 1883 at Buffalo, New York, William Joseph Donovan attended Niagara University and Columbia University and Law School, subsequently practicing law in Buffalo. In 1911 Donovan joined the New York National Guard, rising quickly to captain and serving on the Mexican border during the 1916 crisis.

In July 1917, after the United States entered World War I, Donovan joined the AMERICAN EXPEDITIONARY FORCE, serving in the renowned 165th Regiment of the 42d ("Rainbow") Division. At this time Donovan, a notoriously demanding officer, won his enduring nickname, "Wild Bill." Distinguished service in France and exceptional leadership qualities made him the first American soldier to receive the Distinguished Service Medal, Distinguished Service Cross, and the Medal of Honor.

Between the wars Donovan practiced law, first in Buffalo and from 1929 in New York, where he founded the firm of Donovan, Leisure, Newton, Lumbard, and Irvine, specializing in corporate legal work. On several occasions he ran unsuccessfully for political office in New York State. From 1924 to 1929 he was assistant U.S. attorney general.

Donovan demonstrated great interest in international affairs, undertaking several missions as an overseas observer for the Rockefeller Foundation and both Republican and Democratic administrations. In the mid-1930s he reported on Italian and Spanish military conditions to President Franklin D. ROOSEVELT. In the late 1930s, when war began in Europe and Asia, Donovan accepted presidential assignments to investigate the situations in Asia, Europe, Latin America, and the Middle East. In March 1941 he publicly stated his conviction that Nazism threatened U.S. national security.

Donovan's travels and, especially, a close association with Sir William Stephenson, the head of British military intelligence, convinced him that the United States required an intelligence agency able to provide accurate information on foreign countries and, when appropriate, to mount counterespionage operations. His forceful representations to Roosevelt persuaded the president to establish in July 1941, under Donovan's leadership, the Office of Coordinator of Information, staffed by 250 experts. After PEARL HARBOR this became the OFFICE OF STRATEGIC SERVICES (OSS). It became known for its wide array of often unconventional academics, socialites, and other colorful figures recruited for a broad range of research, analysis, counterespionage, and propaganda activities around the globe. Donovan's uncompromising determination won it prominence but also attracted many bureaucratic enemies.

As the war ended, Donovan lobbied vigorously for a permanent, peacetime American intelligence agency modeled on the OSS. President Harry S. TRUMAN initially rejected these pleas, disbanding the OSS in late 1945. Within two years, however, the COLD WAR led him to establish the CENTRAL INTELLIGENCE AGENCY. It was staffed by many former OSS operatives, although Donovan's own hopes of heading it went unfulfilled. As a private citizen Donovan strenuously advocated relentless American opposition to international communism.

Appointed ambassador to Thailand in 1953, Donovan substantially expanded U.S. military and covert activities in that country as part of increasing American commitments in Southeast Asia. He resigned after only one year as ambassador. Donovan died at Washington, D.C., on 8 February 1959.

See also INTELLIGENCE.

Further reading: Cave Brown, Anthony. *The Last Hero: Wild Bill Donovan.* New York: Times Books, 1982; Dunlop, Richard. *Donovan, America's Master Spy.* Chicago: Rand McNally, 1982; Ford, Corey. *Donovan of OSS.* Boston: Little, Brown, 1970; Troy, Thomas F. *Wild Bill and Intrepid: Donovan, Stephenson, and the Origin of CIA.* New Haven, Conn.: Yale University Press, 1996.

— Priscilla Roberts

Doolittle, James H. (1896–1993) *Aeronautical engineer, test pilot, and Army Air Forces general*

Born on 14 December 1896 at Alameda, California, James Harold Doolittle earned his commission in the Army Air Service in March 1918. Early in the 1920s he made several pioneering flights. He was awarded the Distinguished Flying Cross for making the first flight across the United States in less than 24 hours.

Doolittle's abilities as a test pilot were complemented perfectly by a sharp scientific intelligence. In 1925 he earned from the Massachusetts Institute of Technology one of the first doctorates in aeronautical engineering awarded to an American. His remarkable pace of accomplishment continued during the next 15 years as he set a variety of aviation records. He initiated instrument flying and, as an executive with Shell Petroleum, pushed development of high-octane aviation fuels, thereby providing the United States with a distinct advantage in engine performance during World War II. The Mackay, Harmon, Bendix, and Thompson Trophies he received testify to some of his achievements.

In 1940 Doolittle returned to active duty. In early 1942, as a lieutenant colonel, he was selected to lead a hazardous raid against Japan. Overcoming the problems inherent in flying army medium bombers from an aircraft carrier "with the apparent certainty of being forced to land in enemy territory or to perish at sea" (in the words of his Medal of Honor citation), Doolittle struck a blow against Japan that salved American pride. The 18 April 1942 TOKYO RAID also pushed the Japanese to continued expansion, culminating in their defeat at MIDWAY. Doolittle received the Medal of Honor and promotion to brigadier general.

In September 1942 Doolittle assumed command of the Twelfth Air Force, which he led during Operation TORCH, the Allied invasion of North Africa in November. After briefly heading the Fifteenth Air Force in 1943, he took over the Eighth Air Force, flying from British bases. His promotion of aggressive fighter tactics paid dividends in the defeat of the Luftwaffe prior to the NORMANDY INVASION. Following the collapse of Germany, Doolittle moved to the Pacific theater.

With Japan's surrender, Doolittle returned to Shell, but he remained active in military aviation, serving on various government committees. His support was especially important in securing funding for the Air Force Scientific Advisory Board. Doolittle's promotion to the rank of full general by President Ronald Reagan in 1985 recognized the myriad accomplishments of this remarkable individual—rarely has a surname fitted an individual so poorly. Doolittle died on 27 September 1993 at Pebble Beach, California.

See also AIR FORCE, U.S.; STRATEGIC BOMBING, WORLD WAR II; WORLD WAR II, U.S. INVOLVEMENT, PACIFIC.

Further reading: Doolittle, James H., with Carroll V. Glines. *I Could Never Be So Lucky Again: An Autobiography by General James H. "Jimmy" Doolittle*. Atglen, Pa.: Schiffer, 1991; Glines, Carroll V. *Doolittle's Tokyo Raiders*. Salem, N.H.: Ayer, 1964; Thomas, Lowell, and Edward Jablonski. *Doolittle: A Biography*. Garden City, N.Y.: Doubleday, 1976.

— Malcolm Muir, Jr.

Douglas, Donald W. (1892–1981) *U.S. aircraft designer and founder of the Douglas Aircraft Company*

Born on 6 April 1892 in Brooklyn, New York, Donald Wills Douglas attended the U.S. Naval Academy at Annapolis from 1909 to 1912 but resigned to attend the Massachusetts Institute of Technology (MIT), graduating in 1914.

Douglas remained at MIT as an assistant professor in aeronautical engineering. He also began working at MIT alongside his former professor, Jerome Clarke Hunsaker, to design one of the first wind tunnels. In 1915 Douglas joined the Glen L. Martin Company as chief engineer.

Douglas remained with the Martin Company only briefly, but while with that company, in August 1917 he designed the first U.S. twin-engine bomber, the MB-2. The plane had a number of advanced features and remained in service with the U.S. Army for more than a decade.

Douglas left the Martin Company in 1920 to start his own aircraft firm. Backed by Dale Davis, Douglas formed the Davis-Douglas Company in Santa Monica, California. His first design was the Cloudster, intended to be the first plane to fly across the United States nonstop. The design was a failure, and shortly thereafter Davis sold his portion of the company to Douglas. The firm became the Douglas Company in 1921.

Douglas then built a new bomber for the U.S. Navy. This plane, designated the DT-1 and shaped like a long torpedo with wings, was highly successful. In 1922 the company built six more DT-1s and became financially stable.

In 1932 the army ordered seven Y1B-7 twin-engine bombers from Douglas. An all-metal, gull-wing monoplane, it had an open cockpit and retractable landing gear. In 1933 Douglas entered into a contract with Trans World Airlines for a new commercial aircraft, the DC-1. During its first flight it broke five world records and nine American records. The twin-engine DC-1 featured a completely streamlined metal frame and retractable landing gear. Its success led to the DC-2 (less then a year later) and the DC-3 in 1936. Douglas also designed a military version of the DC-3, known as the C-47. These planes saw extensive service both in civilian aviation and as troop and cargo transports during World War II. Some remained in commercial use into the 21st century.

Douglas retired in 1957, and his son took over as president of the company. In 1967, under financial duress, the Douglas Company merged with McDonnell Aircraft. McDonnell Douglas continued as a leader in aircraft manufacturing. Douglas remained active in the company even after his retirement. He died on 1 February 1981 at Palm Springs, California.

See also AIRCRAFT, FIXED-WING.

Further reading: Cunningham, Frank. *Sky Master: the Story of Donald Douglas and the Douglas Aircraft Company.* Philadelphia: Dorrance, 1943; Morrison, Wilber H. *Donald W. Douglas: A Heart with Wings.* Iowa City: Iowa State University Press, 1991.

— Jason M. Taylor

Dragoon, Operation (15 August 1944) *Successful Allied invasion of southern France during the later stages of World War II*

Invading France from the south had first become a possibility after the Anglo-American TORCH landing in northwest Africa in November 1942, but a southern France campaign did not become a reality until 21 months later. The main reason was that Dragoon, earlier codenamed Anvil, was always caught between Operation Overlord and operations in Italy, rather than being considered a major undertaking in its own right.

As a result, Anvil/Dragoon was an on-, off-, and on-again campaign. Allied leaders first discussed it as a viable option at Quebec in August 1943. At Teheran in November, with a push from Josef Stalin, they scheduled it to take place simultaneously with the NORMANDY INVASION farther north. But shortages in personnel and equipment (especially landing craft) forced General Dwight EISENHOWER, the Overlord commander, on 24 March 1944 to postpone Anvil in deference to Normandy and Italy. The Americans insisted on a southern France operation even after Overlord and beat back several British attempts to have it canceled. On 2 July the British reluctantly agreed to have Anvil—its codename changed to Dragoon for security reasons—go ahead on 15 August.

Although small by Overlord standards, Dragoon was still a major campaign, with 250,000 ground troops, mainly American and French, taking part. In addition, the Allies assembled an international armada of 2,250 ships and landing craft for the operation; 4,056 aircraft from bases in Italy, Sardinia, and Corsica and from carriers in the Mediterranean gave further support. Moreover, the French Resistance was counted upon to provide a helping hand. The U.S. Seventh Army commander, Lieutenant General Alexander M. PATCH, Jr., headed the Allied force. The VI Corps commander, Major General Lucian TRUSCOTT, Jr., led the ground units. Truscott had under him three experienced American infantry divisions—the 3d, 45th, and 36th—to spearhead the attack. Seven Free French divisions under General Jean de Lattre de Tassigny were to follow up, beginning on D+1. Admiral H. Kent HEWITT headed the naval Western Task Force, while Brigadier General Gordon P. Saville headed XII Tactical Air Command, made up of medium and strategic bombers.

The German opposition was meager in comparison. The Wehrmacht had eight and two-thirds, mostly second-rate, divisions in southern France, 210,000 troops in all. German naval and air support consisted of a mere 75 ships and 275 aircraft. About the only compensating factor was that General Johannes Blaskowitz, the overall commander, was an effective and resourceful leader. A few days before the assault, the Germans knew the date (15 August) and the approximate location (along the French Riviera) but there was little they could do about it. They were simply too outmatched to put up a stiff fight.

The invasion began to unfold on the night of 14–15 August with French, American, and Canadian special forces landing on the edges of the 45-mile assault area and eliminating German emplacements that might disrupt the attack. At 4 A.M. American and British airborne troops, who were to link up with the seaborne forces, started landing behind the invasion beaches. At 8 A.M., the tides not being a factor, American combat teams began to disembark at the three invasion beaches—Alpha, Delta, and Camel, centered on the St. Tropez Peninsula. The only stout opposition was at Camel, where enemy fire forced the 36th Division to land at an alternate beach. Nevertheless, by the end of the day all three divisions had secured their beachheads and had started moving into the interior. By 17 August they had advanced at least 20 miles inland from the coast and awaited further orders.

The Allies had already decided on two courses of action: liberate the ports of Toulon and Marseille, and pursue the already retreating Germans. The first task was assigned to the French, who succeeded in securing the ports much sooner than expected, by 29 August. As for the second task, the Allies, on 17 August knew through ULTRA intelligence that the Germans intended to withdraw the bulk of their forces north via the Rhône River corridor. The Americans responded by assembling an armored task force to move along a parallel highway to the east; at Grenoble it was to turn west to cut off the enemy. But the Germans, with the 11th Panzer Division guarding the rear, were able to hold open the escape route long enough for most of their troops to slip the American noose north of Montélimar and avoid capture.

Yet the Allies were able to take Lyon on 3 September, and they then made another attempt to trap German units before they could escape northeast to safety in eastern France. In this second instance, the Germans again managed to elude the fast-moving French and American formations and to reach a defense line west of Belfort. On 14 September the logistically stretched Allies, in the face of stiffening German opposition, ordered their forces to regroup. The French Riviera campaign was at an end.

The basic figures attest to an Allied victory of major proportions. At a cost of 13,203 casualties (7,491 Americans), the Allies had captured 79,000 prisoners. They had also flown 23,808 Dragoon-related sorties and dropped 14,030 tons of bombs. The navy reported only 13 ships lost and 47 damaged during the 30-day period.

At a higher level, Dragoon entailed a 400-mile advance, resulted in the liberation of virtually all of southern France, stepped up the introduction of French troops into combat, and opened up additional ports, which in 1945 assisted the Allies in carrying out their broad-front strategy. Therefore, despite the British assertion that Dragoon was unnecessary and that the resources diverted to it could have been utilized better elsewhere, especially in the Italian campaign, it is difficult to escape the conclusion that the French Riviera campaign did help the Allies defeat the Germans and in a timely manner.

See also WORLD WAR II, U.S. INVOLVEMENT, EUROPE.

Further reading: Clarke, Jeffrey J., and Robert Ross Smith. *The Riviera to the Rhine.* Washington, D.C.: U.S. Government Printing Office, 1993; Funk, Arthur L. *Hidden Ally: The French Resistance, Special Operations, and the Landings in Southern France, 1944.* Westport, Conn.: Greenwood, 1992; Jackson, Sir William G. F. *The Mediterranean and the Middle East.* Vol. VI, *Victory in the Mediterranean, Part 2.* London: H.M. Stationery Office, 1987; Wilt, Alan F. *The French Riviera Campaign of August 1944.* Carbondale: Southern Illinois University Press, 1981.

— Alan F. Wilt

dragoons   *A branch of horse-mounted military service*
Dragoons were trained as infantry but traveled by horseback, dismounting to fight. Mounted troops served with U.S. forces during and after the Revolution; however, there was no real cavalry tradition in America such as that which existed in Europe. In both the AMERICAN REVOLUTIONARY WAR and the WAR OF 1812, mounted forces played only a small role. After each of these conflicts, because of the U.S. aversion to large standing armies, mounted forces were eliminated, since they were the most expensive arm to equip and maintain.

As settlers moved west into newly acquired territories, the army needed mounted troops on the frontier to cope with the threat of the horse-mounted Indians of the Great Plains. In 1832 Congress authorized the formation of a battalion of Mounted Rangers for the frontier. Proving their worth, a year later the Rangers were expanded into the 1st Regiment of U.S. Dragoons. Many men who would later be famous served in this regiment, including Jefferson DAVIS and Stephen W. KEARNY. In 1836, responding to trouble with the Seminole Indians in Florida, Congress authorized the 2d Regiment of Dragoons. After the Second SEMINOLE WAR, in a cost-cutting measure, the 2d Regiment was

dismounted. It was remounted two years later when Congress recognized that one regiment of dragoons was insufficient to police the expanding frontier.

In 1846, with the onset of the MEXICAN-AMERICAN WAR, Congress authorized another mounted unit, the Regiment of Mounted Rifles, in the regular army. During the Mexican-American War the mounted regiments were broken up into companies and scattered among the major forces of Major Generals Winfield SCOTT and Zachary TAYLOR, often fighting as infantry. Their usual missions were reconnaissance and pursuit. The Mounted Rifles, like the two dragoon regiments, served throughout the war; and at the war's end it was not disbanded.

Dragoons were armed with carbines, sabers, and horse pistols. Mounted riflemen had Colt revolvers and percussion rifles but were not issued sabers. Riflemen could fire their weapons from horseback but were expected to do most of their fighting dismounted. Campaigning against Indians emphasized the infantry side of the dragoon's function, so the infantry tactics manual was used for that aspect of training.

Even with the addition of the Mounted Rifles, in view of the territory gained from the Mexican-American War, mounted forces were stretched thin trying to police the frontier. Thus, at the urging of Secretary of War Jefferson Davis, Congress in 1855 authorized two additional mounted regiments. Contrary to the secretary's recommendation, however, the General Orders prescribing their organization made them a distinct and separate arm of cavalry.

Between 1848 and 1860 these mounted regiments were engaged in a succession of campaigns and individual actions against Native Americans in the West. They also provided escort and protection for settler wagon trains, and they explored and surveyed Indian territory. When open warfare broke out between slavery and antislavery factions in Kansas Territory, the 2d Dragoons, along with some of the 1st Cavalry and some infantry companies, were dispatched to restore peace.

When the Civil War began in April 1861, there were still three distinctly named organizations of mounted forces in the U.S. Army. By August 1861 Congress had organized all mounted troops into a single branch, that of cavalry. For all intents and purposes, despite their similar organization and method of employment, the dragoon and mounted rifle regiments thus disappeared from American military structure. The 1st and 2d Dragoons became the 1st and 2d Cavalry respectively; the Mounted Rifles became the 3d Cavalry.

See also AMERICAN INDIAN WARS, OVERVIEW; CAVALRY; INDIAN WARFARE.

Further reading: Herr, John K., and Edward S. Wallace. *The Story of the U.S. Cavalry, 1775–1942.* Boston: Little,

Brown, 1953; Stubbs, Mary L., and Stanley R. Connor. *Armor-Cavalry.* Part I, *Regular Army and Army Reserve.* Washington, D.C.: Office of the Chief of Military History, U.S. Army, 1969; Utley, Robert M. *Frontiersmen in Blue: The U.S. Army and the Indian, 1848–1865.* Lincoln: University of Nebraska Press, 1981.

— Arthur T. Frame

Drumbeat, Operation (1942) *German World War II submarine offensive in American waters, January to July 1942*

Operation DRUMBEAT, ordered by Adolf Hitler on 12 December 1941, began in earnest on 12 January 1942, when *U-123* sank a British steamer east of Cape Cod. The German campaign was extemporized and was mounted with slender resources. No more than 14—and sometimes as few as five—submarines hunted off the eastern seaboard and in the Gulf of Mexico. Providing logistical support to the U-boats beginning in April were the first submarine tankers.

The German submarines found easy prey. American merchantmen sailed as in peacetime, singly and without escort. Radio discipline was neglected, and their unfettered chatter aided U-boat captains in locating targets. Navigational buoys remained lit, and coastal cities were slow to institute blackouts (in some cases for fear of adversely affecting the tourist season). The few patrolling American ships and aircraft usually followed a predictable pattern. Given these advantages, U-boats sank one ship daily in the second half of January; in February, that average doubled.

During the course of DRUMBEAT, Allied losses totaled 198 ships. Especially galling was the sinking of one-third of the U.S. tanker tonnage; the consequent fuel shortages curtailed Pacific Fleet operations. One prominent naval historian has compared the overall scale of disaster to what would have been the effect of the destruction by saboteurs of America's six largest ammunition plants. The army chief of staff, George C. MARSHALL, warned in June that the submarine losses threatened America's entire war effort.

The causes of this debacle were numerous. First, Admiral Ernest J. KING, commander in chief of the U.S. Fleet, maintained that a poorly escorted convoy was worse than no convoy at all, despite substantial evidence to the contrary. Second, King was loath to take advice from the British. Third, American naval leaders had assumed that escort craft could be built rapidly in an emergency. However, unanticipated priority given to landing craft and cargo vessels reduced the pace of escort construction. Fourth, intramural competition within the U.S. Navy for scarce escorts kept the coastal patrols shorthanded; most available destroyers operated in North Atlantic waters. Finally, strife between the navy and the Army Air Corps over control of coastal air defense—a perennial issue—was not resolved until Marshall in June ordered remedial measures.

Just as the causes of the disaster were many, so were the factors leading to its solution. In April, army pressure helped bring about the "bucket brigades," a partial CONVOY SYSTEM in which merchantmen, perforce only lightly escorted, moved exclusively by daylight on the eastern seaboard. This measure alone was sufficient to convince the Germans to shift their efforts to the Caribbean. In May and June coastal blackouts, increased numbers of escorts and aircraft, and a proper interlocking convoy system combined by July to cause the Germans to concentrate once more on the North Atlantic. In inflicting grievous damage to Allied resources, the Germans had lost only seven U-boats in American waters.

See also ATLANTIC, BATTLE OF THE (WORLD WAR II); WORLD WAR II, U.S. INVOLVEMENT, PACIFIC.

Further reading: Baer, George W. *One Hundred Years of Sea Power: The U.S. Navy, 1890–1990.* Stanford, Calif.: Stanford University Press, 1993; Cannon, Michael. *Operation Drumbeat: The Dramatic True Story of Germany's First U-boat Attacks along the American Coast in World War II.* New York: Harper, 1990; Hickam, Homer H. *Torpedo Junction: U-boat War off America's East Coast, 1942.* Annapolis, Md.: Naval Institute Press, 1989; Morison, Samuel Eliot. *History of United States Naval Operations in World War II.* Vol. 1, *The Battle of the Atlantic, September 1939–May 1943.* Boston: Little, Brown, 1962.

— Malcolm Muir, Jr.

Dunmore's War (Lord Dunmore's War) (1774) *War fought in 1774 between colonists of Virginia and Indian tribes living between the Ohio River and Great Lakes*

As the seaboard colonies expanded westward, the Ohio River Valley became hotly contested between the colonies of Pennsylvania and Virginia and the Indians. Control over the region first became an issue during the FRENCH AND INDIAN WAR (1754–63). Following that war, a British proclamation of 1763 in theory established complete Indian control of the region, ordering settlers not to venture past a line in the vicinity of the Appalachian Mountains. Despite this prohibition, colonists from Pennsylvania and Virginia continued to move west onto the Indian lands to establish farms.

The area became a major problem in the 1770s when both Virginia and Pennsylvania claimed that the contested area was within the land defined in their respective colonial charters. One of the key players in this struggle over the Ohio River territory was Virginia governor John MURRAY, fourth earl of Dunmore. The land-hungry Dunmore had become heavily involved in land speculation in the region, and he and other wealthy investors pressed for a fight with the Shawnee Indians in the valley. In 1773 he reasserted Virginia's claims to the region by proclaiming a new district, called West Augusta. Tensions with the Indians were exacerbated by the murder of a group of Indians by Daniel Greathouse during a drinking bout on Yellow Creek in April 1774.

With tensions rising and Indian attacks believed imminent, white settlers abandoned their farms in the Ohio Valley and headed back east across the Allegheny Mountains to safety. By July some 1,500 families had left the region. Dunmore now planned an invasion of Indian territory. In July he left Williamsburg for the frontier. In September he met at FORT PITT with representatives of the Delaware, Iroquois, and Wyandot Indians, indemnifying them for the deaths of their relatives and securing the neutrality of these tribes. In the process, Dunmore isolated the Shawnee. He saw their conquest as the key to Virginia's control south of the Ohio River in what is now West Virginia and Kentucky. Dunmore now mobilized the militia in Virginia's western counties against the Shawnee. These troops, largely from Augusta, Botetourt, and Fincastle Counties, were under the overall command of Colonel Andrew Lewis of Augusta County.

The militia mustered, beginning on 27 August, on the Greenbrier River in modern West Virginia. The only battle of the war took place at POINT PLEASANT at the juncture of the Kanawha and Ohio Rivers. Lewis and the main part of his force reached Point Pleasant on 6 October and there awaited supplies and reinforcements. They did little to fortify the position, confident that their strength of some 1,200 men would be sufficient to overawe the Indians. However, they knew almost nothing of the Indians. A force, mostly Shawnee, under Cornstalk, secretly crossed the Ohio on rafts and assembled nearby. Early on the morning of 10 October 1774, some 500 Indians suddenly struck. Lewis was determined to defend Point Pleasant, and although the Shawnee attackers put up a stiff fight, in the course of the day-long battle he ultimately forced them to retreat downriver. Some 70 Virginians had been killed or died of wounds; 77 others were seriously wounded but survived. Along with sick, these meant a casualty rate of some 15 percent. Indian losses were believed to have been no more than 50.

Later in October Dunmore negotiated with the Indians a peace settlement that confirmed Virginia's claims to the southern bank of the Ohio River, secured the return of white captives, and required the Indians to provide hostages to ensure their good behavior. Perhaps the greatest consequence of Dunmore's War, however, was upon the coming American Revolution. Dunmore misconstrued popular support for him and his victory as loyalty to the British crown during the events leading to the revolution.

See also AMERICAN INDIAN WARS, OVERVIEW; BOONE, DANIEL; CLARK, GEORGE ROGERS; INDIAN WARFARE.

Further reading: Kerby, Robert L. "The Other War in 1774, Dunmore's War." *West Virginia History* 36, no. 1 (1974): 1–16.

— Colin P. Mahle

Du Pont, Samuel F. (1803–1865) *U.S. Navy admiral*
Born on 27 September 1803 at Bergen Point, New Jersey, Samuel Francis Du Pont attended boarding school in Germantown, Pennsylvania, from 1812 to 1817. He received an appointment as midshipman in 1815 but did not begin his naval service until 1817 on the USS *Franklin* in the Mediterranean. He served on a number of ships in the Mediterranean, the West Indies, and along the coast of Brazil. From 1824 to 1826 he was sailing master of the *North Carolina.* Promoted lieutenant in April 1826, he served on a succession of ships in European waters and in the Gulf of Mexico. His first command was the *Grampus* in the Gulf of Mexico. He then commanded the *Warren* and the *Ohio* (1839–41), flagship of Commodore Isaac HULL in the Mediterranean.

Promoted to commander in January 1843, Du Pont took command of the *Perry*, but illness forced him to return home. In October 1845 he took command of the frigate *Congress*, flagship of Commodore Robert STOCKTON.

The *Congress* arrived off California just as the 1846–48 MEXICAN-AMERICAN WAR began. Shifting to the sloop of war *Cyane*, Du Pont captured San Diego in July 1846, and then La Paz, capital of Lower California. He went on to spike the guns of San Blas and destroy Mexican ships at Guaymas. In these operations Du Pont captured 30 Mexican ships and cleared the Gulf of California. He then participated in the occupation of Mazatlán, Mexico, in November 1847. Learning that American forces were besieged at San José de Guaymas, he led a landing party three miles inland and rescued the American force. Du Pont's men then continued to clear the region of Mexican troops.

Following the war Du Pont served on a board that called for a naval academy at Annapolis. In 1853 he submitted a report on defense matters and the importance of steam power. He also was a member of the 1855 Naval Efficiency Board, which culled deadwood from the officer corps of the navy. Promoted to captain in September 1855, in 1857 Du Pont took command of ship of the line *Minnesota,* sailing to China, Japan, India, and Arabia before returning to the United States. In December 1860 Du Pont assumed command of the Philadelphia Navy Yard.

Following the beginning of the Civil War, Du Pont headed the Blockade Board, helping to plan naval operations, specifically a blockade of the South and amphibious landings along its coast. In September 1861 he assumed command of the South Atlantic Blockading Squadron, the most important command in the navy and, with 75 ships, the largest by commanded any U.S. naval officer to that point. On 7 November 1861 Du Pont captured Port Royal, South Carolina, the first major victory of the war for the Union.

Promoted to rear admiral in July 1862, Du Pont took Tybee and FORT PULASKI. In March 1862 his forces took Cumberland Island, Amelia Island, and St. Mary's Island in Georgia; all the Georgia sounds; and Fernandina, Fort Clinch, Jacksonville, and St. Augustine in Florida. Du Pont then set up 14 blockade stations at these locations.

Secretary of the Navy Gideon WELLES ordered Du Pont to take CHARLESTON, South Carolina. Du Pont objected that this could not be done without landing troops at the same time. Welles ordered him to proceed regardless. Du Pont's 7 April 1863 attempt to take Charleston was repulsed, in perhaps the worst U.S. Navy defeat of the war. With Du Pont pessimistic about any future attempt, Welles relieved him in July. In the last engagement under his command, Du Pont's squadron took the Confederate ironclad *Atlanta*. For the remainder of his life Du Pont defended his actions at Charleston, denying responsibility for the failure.

Du Pont retired from the navy in 1863 to Louviers on the Brandywine River, near Wilmington, Delaware. He died at Philadelphia on 23 June 1865.

See also CIVIL WAR, NAVAL OVERVIEW; DAHLGREN, JOHN A.; FOOTE, ANDREW H.

Further reading: Burton, E. Milby. *The Siege of Charleston, 1861–1865.* Columbia: University of South Carolina Press, 1970; Du Pont, Henry A. *Rear Admiral Samuel Francis Du Pont, United States Navy: A Biography.* New York: National Americana Society, 1926.

— Frank Luis Trigueros

Dutch-Indian wars (1655–1664) *Colonial conflict between Dutch settlers and the Indians in New Netherlands*

The Dutch-Indian War, also known as the Peach War, began in August 1655 when a Dutch farmer killed a Delaware Indian woman for picking peaches in his orchard. The victim's family retaliated by ambushing and killing the farmer. This ended a decade of relative peace between the two sides. As word of the incident spread, other Delaware bands attacked and burned homes, killing several settlers at New Amsterdam. The Indians also took some 150 Dutch captive.

The governor of New Amsterdam, Peter STUYVESANT, called out the militia, which freed most of the captives and destroyed Indian villages. Dutch-Indian violence continued sporadically thereafter, draining both sides.

In October 1658 the Dutch sought assistance in a new conflict from the Susquehannock Indians, who agreed to intervene in the Esopus War, which had begun in September 1658 and was part of the ongoing struggle between the Dutch and the Esopus Indians, a Hudson River tribe. Although the Dutch were hardly friends of the Indians, the Dutch trade had become so important to the Indians that the Susquehannock united with their bitter enemies the Mohawk to pressure the Esopus tribe into concluding peace.

Despite these diplomatic efforts, in September 1659 the Esopus, aided by the Minisink, moved up the Hudson River to attack Wiltwyck (present-day Kingston, New York) and the surrounding area. Stuyvesant then called for a parlay, at which point a delegation of Esopus chiefs entered Wiltwyck to discuss peace. Dutch soldiers killed the chiefs as they slept following the first day of talks. In retaliation, the Indians took eight Dutch soldiers captive and burned them alive.

Sporadic warfare continued around Wiltwyck until 1660 when Stuyvesant instituted a new tactic of rounding up Indian children as hostages to extort "good behavior" from the various Delaware tribes. The weaker tribes along the Hudson offered little resistance and yielded up their children. The Esopus, recalling what had happened at the last meeting between the two groups, refused even to negotiate. Stuyvesant responded by selling his Esopus prisoners into slavery in the West Indies.

It was 1664 before the Esopus tribe finally yielded to the Dutch, and only after Stuyvesant called in his Mohawk allies against them. However, this was also the last year of Dutch rule in New Netherlands. On 4 October 1664, the English government officially took possession of the province, which they renamed New York.

Further reading: Jennings, Francis. *The Founders of America.* New York: Norton, 1993; Jennings, Francis, ed. *The History and Culture of Iroquois Diplomacy: An Interdisciplinary Guide to the Treaties of the Six Nations and Their League.* Syracuse, N.Y.: Syracuse University Press, 1985; Trelease, Allen W. *Indian Affairs in Colonial New York: The Seventeenth Century.* New York: Macmillan, 1960; Wright, Louis B. *The Colonial Civilization of North America.* London: Eyre & Spottiswoode, 1949.

— Adam T. Love

Eads, James B. (1820–1887) *Engineer and proponent of ironclad warships*

Born on 23 May 1820 at Lawrenceburg, Indiana, James Buchanan Eads had little formal education as a youth. Because of his father's unsuccessful business ventures, the family moved about a great deal, from Cincinnati, Ohio, to Louisville, Kentucky, and then finally to St. Louis, Missouri. While in St. Louis, Eads largely educated himself through extensive reading. He went to work in St. Louis as a dry goods merchant and then pursued the riverboat business.

In 1842 Eads established himself in the salvage business, taking advantage of frequent riverboat disasters. He designed a new type of salvage vessel, using it to recover iron and lead from wrecks for resale. His equipment was successful and made him a fortune. Eads also began the first glass industry in the West; it failed because of the MEXICAN-AMERICAN WAR. He then returned to the salvage business and built three powerful vessels, one of which was capable of pumping out and raising a sunken hull from the bottom of the river. Within a few years Eads was part owner of 10 salvage vessels.

With the start of the Civil War and the concurrent struggle for control of the Mississippi and other western rivers, Eads proposed to Washington that the U.S. Navy convert salvage vessels to warships for river fighting. Such vessels, reinforced with five-inch oak for protection against small-arms fire, became known as timberclads: the *Tyler,* the *Lexington,* and the *Conestoga.* Eads also suggested that Washington build ironclad steam-powered warships, and he secured the contract to construct them. With 4,000 men working around the clock, Eads completed these *Cairo,* or City, class gunboats in record time. The *Cairo, Carondelet, Cincinnati, Louisville, Mound City, Pittsburg,* and *St. Louis* (renamed the *Baron de Kalb*) played major roles in important western Civil War battles. Eads also converted the former *Submarine No. 7* into the powerful *Benton,* and he designed the four double-turreted *Milwaukee*-class monitors and two single-turret monitors,

the *Osage* and the *Neosho,* for work on western rivers. He also assisted with ironclad conversions *Choctaw* and *Lafayette.*

After the war Eads won a contract to bridge the Mississippi at St. Louis, and he constructed a triple-arch bridge over the Mississippi River at St. Louis from 1867 to 1874. The Eads, or St. Louis, Bridge was the largest bridge of any type built during this period in America and is regarded as an engineering landmark.

Eads also designed a navigation channel around the city of New Orleans. He was the first engineer honored by the Royal British Society of Arts with the Albert Medal, and he served as consultant on many different projects, from the Liverpool Docks to others in Toronto and in Veracruz and Tampico, Mexico. Eads died at Nassau, in the Bahamas, on 8 March 1887.

See also IRONCLADS, UNION; CIVIL WAR, LAND OVERVIEW; CIVIL WAR, NAVAL OVERVIEW.

Further reading: Milligan, John D. *Gunboats Down the Mississippi.* New York: Arno Press, 1980; Ormont, Arthur. *James Buchanan Eads: The Man Who Mastered the Mississippi.* Englewood Cliffs, N.J.: Prentice Hall, 1970; Tucker, Spencer C. *Andrew Foote: Civil War Admiral on Western Waters.* Annapolis, Md.: Naval Institute Press, 2000.
— Marshall J. Hardy

Eaker, Ira C. (1896–1987) *U.S. Air Force general*

Born on 13 April 1898 into a tenant farmer family at Field Creek, Texas, Ira Clarence Eaker graduated from Southeastern State Teachers College in Durant, Oklahoma, and joined the army. In early 1917 he was commissioned and assigned to Fort Bliss, Texas. He completed pilot training in 1918 and from 1919 to 1922 served in the Philippines.

From 1922 to 1924 Eaker commanded the 5th Aero Squadron at Mitchell Field, New York, and from 1924 to 1926 was in the Office of the Air Service. From December

1926 to May 1927 Eaker piloted one of several air corps planes on a goodwill tour of South America. During these years he became close friends with Majors Henry H. "Hap" ARNOLD and Carl A. "Tooey" SPAATZ. During the period 1–7 January 1929 the three men, with Eaker as chief pilot, flew the *Question Mark* in the first successful air corps aerial-refueling flight, establishing a new world flight endurance record. The next year, Eaker made the first transcontinental in-flight-refueled flight in history.

Eaker commanded the 34th and later the 17th Pursuit Squadrons at March Field, California. In 1933 he earned a degree in journalism from the University of Southern California. In 1936 he graduated from the Air Corps Tactical School at Maxwell Field, Alabama, and in 1937 from the Army Command and General Staff School at Fort Leavenworth, Kansas.

From 1937 to 1940 Eaker was assigned to the Office of the Chief of the Air Corps in Washington. From 1940 to 1942 as a colonel he commanded the 20th Pursuit Squadron at Hamilton Field, California. In 1936, 1941, and 1942, respectively, he and Arnold wrote *The Flying Game, Winged Warfare,* and *Army Flyer.*

Promoted to temporary brigadier general, Eaker in January 1942 took command of VIII Bomber Command in Great Britain, personally leading several B-17 missions, including the first U.S. heavy bomber strike against German-occupied Europe, the 17 August raid on Rouen, France. Promoted to temporary major general, in December he replaced Major General Spaatz as Eighth Air Force commander at a time when the B-17s were beginning deep-penetration raids into Germany against such high-value industrial targets as the ball-bearing plants in SCHWEINFURT and fighter factories at Regensburg. The Eighth Air Force suffered grievous, even debilitating, losses during these unescorted precision daylight raids, losses that did not lessen until the arrival of long-range fighter escorts for the bombers.

Late in 1943 Spaatz returned to Britain to take charge of General Dwight D. EISENHOWER's air operations in preparation for the upcoming cross-channel invasion of France. The negative publicity from the heavy losses of the daylight raids induced Spaatz, then commanding U.S. strategic air forces in Europe, reluctantly to replace Eaker with Major General James H. "Jimmy" DOOLITTLE. Eaker was promoted to temporary lieutenant general and in January 1944 was given command of Mediterranean Allied Air Forces, including the U.S. Twelfth and Fifteenth Air Forces, He led them with distinction, flying personally several shuttle-bombing raids from Italy to Russia in 1944.

On 30 April 1945 Eaker was named deputy commander of the U.S. Army Air Forces and chief of the Air Staff. In this position he played a key role in the formation of a separate U.S. Air Force in September 1947. He officially retired in August 1947, having planned the changeover

from the USAAF to the USAF. Arnold and Spaatz credited him with being the primary force in achieving independence for the air force. In June 1948 Eaker was promoted to lieutenant general on the retired list.

From 1947 to 1957 Eaker served as vice president of the Hughes Tool Company, part of the Hughes Aircraft Company. He later served as vice president of Douglas Aircraft Company. From 1962 to 1979 he wrote a column on airpower and military affairs that was syndicated in 180 newspapers. In October 1979, President Jimmy Carter awarded Eaker a special congressional gold medal for his contributions to aviation and national security. In 1985 he was officially promoted to four-star general on the retired list. Eaker died on 6 August 1987 at Andrews Air Force Base, Maryland.

See also AIR FORCE, U.S.; STRATEGIC BOMBING, WORLD WAR II.

Further reading: Copp, DeWitt S. *A Few Great Captains: The Men and Events That Shaped the Developments of U.S. Air Power.* Garden City, N.Y.: Doubleday, 1982; Mets, David R. *Master of Air Power: General Carl A. Spaatz.* Novato, Calif.: Presidio, 1988; Parton, James. *"Air Force Spoken Here": General Ira C. Eaker and the Command of the Air.* Bethesda, Md.: Adler and Adler, 1986.

— William Head

Early, Jubal A. ("Old Jube") (1816–1894)
Confederate army general

Born on 3 November 1816 near Rocky Mount, Virginia, Jubal Anderson Early graduated from the U.S. Military Academy at West Point in 1837. After service in the Second SEMINOLE WAR in Florida as a second lieutenant of artillery, he resigned his commission in 1838 to pursue a career in law. Early served one term in the Virginia legislature before taking up his law practice. He fought in the MEXICAN-AMERICAN WAR as a major in the 1st Virginia Regiment. As a delegate to the Virginia Convention of 1861, he voted against secession, but when his state left the Union, Early offered Virginia his services.

Commissioned a colonel in Virginia's state forces, Early soon entered Confederate service as colonel of the 24th Virginia Infantry. He led a brigade in the First Battle of BULL RUN/MANASSAS, and in August 1861 he was promoted to brigadier general. Wounded at Williamsburg in May 1862, he returned in time for the Battles of the SEVEN DAYS the following month. He led a brigade in Major General Thomas J. "Stonewall" JACKSON's corps in the Battles of Second BULL RUN/MANASSAS, ANTIETAM/SHARPSBURG, and FREDERICKSBURG. Although possessing a disagreeable personality and fiery disposition, Early was one of General Robert E. LEE's most capable subordinates.

Promoted to major general in April 1863, Early commanded a division in the Battles of CHANCELLORSVILLE and GETTYSBURG, and the WILDERNESS. He temporarily succeeded Lieutenant General A. P. HILL as III Corps commander and fought well at SPOTSYLVANIA in May 1864. Shortly thereafter he assumed command of Lieutenant General Richard EWELL's II Corps, with the rank of lieutenant general. Ordered with his corps to clear the Shenandoah Valley, he forced Major General David Hunter's Federal army from the valley and headed toward Washington, D.C. He won a battle at Monocacy, Maryland, but was turned away by the capital's defenses.

After cavalry from Early's command burned Chambersberg, Pennsylvania, the Federal army commander, Lieutenant General Ulysses S. GRANT, created a new army under Major General Philip SHERIDAN to deal with the new Confederate threat. Sheridan's superior force defeated Early's valley command at Winchester and Fishers Hill, and in October 1864 at Cedar Creek, where Early almost scored a stunning victory. What remained of II Corps rejoined Lee's army at Petersburg, while Early retained a small force in the valley until his final defeat at Waynesboro in March 1865.

Although he had occupied thousands of Federal troops for many months, Early received most of the blame for the devastation Sheridan brought to the valley. Relieved of command by Lee in late March 1865, only days before the surrender of Appomattox, Early fled to Mexico and then to Canada. In 1869 he returned to Virginia and the practice of law. In 1877 he became commissioner of the Louisiana lottery. He wrote and lectured on the war until his death at Lynchburg, Virginia, on 2 March 1894.

See also CIVIL WAR, LAND OVERVIEW; SHENANDOAH VALLEY CAMPAIGNS.

Further reading: Early, Jubal A. *War Memoirs.* Edited by Frank E. Vandiver. Bloomington, Ind.: Bobbs-Merrill, 1960; Freeman, Douglas Southall. *Lee's Lieutenants: A Study in Command.* 3 vols. New York: Scribner, 1942–44; Wert, Jeffry D. *From Winchester to Cedar Creek: The Shenandoah Campaign of 1864.* Carlisle, Pa.: South Mountain, 1987.

— Roger W. Caraway

Eaton, William (1764–1811) *U.S. diplomat and military adventurer*

Born on 23 February 1764 at Woodstock, Connecticut, William Eaton fought as a sergeant during the AMERICAN REVOLUTIONARY WAR. After the war he graduated from Dartmouth College in 1790 and rejoined the army to fight under Major General Anthony WAYNE in the Old Northwest (1792–95). Eaton then used the influence of his friend

Secretary of State Timothy Pickering to gain appointment as consul to the North African kingdom of Tunis in November 1798. Thus situated, he successfully renegotiated a commercial treaty that had previously been rejected by Congress.

Shortly thereafter, the United States encountered diplomatic and military difficulties with Tripoli, then ruled by Bey Yusuf Karamanli. When President Thomas JEFFERSON balked paying at higher tributes, the bey began to seize American shipping and to hold crews for ransom. Jefferson responded by dispatching naval squadrons to the Mediterranean in the 1801–1805 TRIPOLITAN WAR.

In 1803 Eaton suggested that Jefferson authorize him to foment a popular uprising against Karamanli by soliciting the aid of the bey's recently disposed brother, Hamet. Jefferson concurred, and Eaton then went to Egypt with the grandiose portfolio of "Naval Agent to the Barbary States."

Arriving in Egypt in 1804, Eaton solicited help from the former bey. Together they recruited a force of 60 Greek mercenaries, 60 Bedouin cavalry, and seven U.S. Marines under Lieutenant Presley O'Bannon. Marching 500 miles westward, they were joined by an additional 500 Arab cavalry. Eaton stormed the city of DERNA on 3 March 1805, with assistance from a small naval squadron under Lieutenant Isaac HULL. His force then defeated several attempts by Yusuf Karamali's followers to recapture the city. The bey was obliged to open negotiations with Tobias Lear, the American consul at Tunis.

Much to Eaton's disgust, a treaty was concluded with Karamali that recognized his throne, authorized the payment of gold for the return of hostages, and otherwise completely defeated the object of his quixotic expedition. He returned to the United States rather disillusioned. Furthermore, while Jefferson lauded his efforts and achievements, Congress refused to vote him a gold medal. Eaton then settled at Brimfield, Massachusetts, where he served one term in the state legislature. He died in Brimfield on 1 June 1811.

Further reading: Gerson, Noel B. *Barbary General: The Life of William Eaton.* Englewood Cliffs, N.J.: Prentice Hall, 1968; Wright, Louis B., and Julia Macleod. *The First Americans in North Africa: William Eaton's Struggle for a Vigorous Policy against the Barbary Pirates, 1799–1805.* Princeton, N.J.: Princeton University Press, 1945.

— John C. Fredriksen

education, higher military schools

Military educational institutions in the United States beyond the service academies have played a major role in the preparation of commanders and staff officers for modern warfare. Today, all of the military services have intermediate and senior service educational institutions.

Additionally, during and after World War II multiservice schools were established to educate officers on the complex command and staff issues of joint or combined operations.

The army established the first advanced school, the Artillery School of Practice, at Fort Monroe, Virginia, created by Secretary of War John C. CALHOUN in 1824. In 1827 an Infantry School of Practice was established at Jefferson Barracks, Missouri. Other advanced specialty schools followed, but there remained a need for further training. In 1881 the commanding general of the army, General William T. SHERMAN, established the School of Application for Infantry and Cavalry at Fort Leavenworth, Kansas. Over time the school's training and educational curriculum evolved and expanded. In 1901 Secretary of War Elihu ROOT organized a system of officer higher education, with the Army Service School at Fort Leavenworth as the core. Root also called for an Army War College that was finally established in 1903 at Fort McNair in Washington, D.C., where it remained until suspended in 1940. During World War II a joint Army-Navy College functioned at McNair that evolved after the war into the National Defense University.

Classes at Fort Leavenworth were suspended during the SPANISH-AMERICAN WAR and PHILIPPINE-AMERICAN WAR, but in 1902 a one-year course was reinstituted there to build on lessons from the recent combat experience. In 1907 the name of the institution was changed to the School of the Line, and a second-year program was added at the Army Staff College. The Fort Leavenworth schools were again closed from 1916 to 1919 but were reopened in 1920 to study the combat and staff experiences learned in World War I. In 1922 the Army War College assumed responsibility for the General Staff School, and the School of the Line at Fort Leavenworth became the Command and General Staff School. In 1940 the curriculum at Leavenworth was compressed, and new courses were developed to prepare the army for World War II.

In 1947, after a series of officer education reviews, the army schools were again reorganized. Fort Leavenworth became and remains home to the Command and General Staff College. In 1986, a second-year program, the School for Advanced Military Studies (SAMS), was established, with two-year Army War College fellows as the primary instructors. Thus the army intermediate and senior-level service schools continue to be divided between Fort Leavenworth and Carlisle Barracks; the other services' intermediate and senior courses are colocated.

The U.S. Navy also has a long and distinguished tradition of higher military education. In 1884 Secretary of the Navy William E. Chandler established the Naval War College at Newport, Rhode Island. The first president of the college, Stephen B. Luce, and his successor, Alfred Thayer MAHAN, personified the development of modern naval warfare theory and doctrine. Founded to study all aspects of warfare, the Naval War College maintained a broad and encompassing national security and naval warfare curriculum. Of particular note is the college's tradition of war-gaming operational plans and strategies.

The Naval War College suspended classes during World War I, but in 1919 the school reopened with a renewed charter based on the record of its graduates through the war years. It did not close during World War II, and Admiral Raymond A. SPRUANCE became president of the college in 1946. A two-year program was tried in the 1950s but was rejected. In the 1960s the college curriculum was split into two programs: the College of Naval Command and Staff provides a tailored course of study for mid-grade officers, and the College of Naval Warfare provides a curriculum for more senior officers. The college's research and war-gaming traditions not only continue but have been emphasized by the establishment of the Center for Naval Warfare Studies.

In addition to the Naval War College, the navy also operates the Naval Postgraduate School in Monterey, California. Originally established in 1909 as a school for marine engineering in Annapolis, Maryland, in 1912 the program was renamed the Postgraduate Department of the naval academy. In 1951 the school was moved to Monterey in facilities acquired by the navy during World War II. This higher-degree-granting institution has students from all branches of the service and several government agencies.

The U.S. Marine Corps established its Command and Staff College in the 1920s as the Field Officers' Course at Quantico, Virginia. The school was suspended at the beginning of World War II; however, from 1943 to 1946 shorter, specialized courses were established to support marine wartime missions. Since 1946 a course of one academic year has continued under several different names. From 1946 to 1964 the course was called the Senior School and, since 1964, the Command and Staff College.

Originally based on the army's curriculum at the Infantry School at Fort Benning, Georgia, and the Command and Staff College at Fort Leavenworth, the marine institution quickly added naval officers to its faculty. The marine school focused its unique curriculum on support to the maritime arm and, eventually, on amphibious warfare and the Fleet Marine Force mission. Today, Marine Corps University at Quantico houses the Command and Staff College, the Marine Corps War College, and the School of Advanced Warfighting.

The U.S. Air Force, established as part of the National Security Act of 1947, had a separate officer educational system prior to and during World War II. The Air Corps Tactical School had been in existence since 1931 at Maxwell Field in Montgomery, Alabama. This airfield and educational facilities had been the site of a flying school established by Orville WRIGHT in 1910.

In 1946 the Army Air Forces School moved from its World War II location in Orlando, Florida, back to Maxwell Field and was redesignated the Air University, with the mission of developing and educating the new air arm's future leaders. The Air University at Maxwell Air Force Base consists of the Officer Training School, the Squadron Officers' School, the Air Command and Staff College, and the Air War College. The air force also operates a higher-degree-granting institution at Wright-Patterson Air Force Base outside Columbus, Ohio, the Air Force Institute of Technology.

In addition to the higher-level schools developed by the individual services, after World War II the wartime Army-Navy Staff College was formally institutionalized. In 1946 the National War College was established at Fort McNair, at the former site of the Army War College. The National Defense University system was established in 1976. In 2001 it consisted of four separate colleges for senior military and selected government civilians. The National War College provides a senior-level course in national strategy and policy making. The Industrial College of the Armed Forces provides instruction in national-level resource management. The Information Resource Management College was established to provide instruction on the information resource component of national security strategy and power. The Joint Forces Staff College was established in 1946 as the Armed Forces Staff College in Norfolk, Virginia. This institution serves as both an intermediate and senior-level staff college, providing joint professional military education to selected service school graduates and offers specialty courses in joint warfare, as required by the Goldwater-Nichols Act (Defense Reorganization Act of 1986).

See also MILITARY ACADEMIES.

Further reading: Dastrup, Boyd L. *The U.S. Army Command and Staff College: A Centennial History.* Manhattan, Kans.: Sunflower, 1982; Nenninger, Timothy K. *The Leavenworth Schools and the Old Army: Education, Professionalism, and the Officer Corps of the United States Army, 1881–1918.* Westport, Conn.: Greenwood, 1978; Simons, William E., ed. *Professional Military Education in the United States: A Historical Dictionary.* Westport, Conn.: Greenwood, 2000.

— J. G. D. Babb

Eichelberger, Robert L. (1886–1961) *U.S. Army general*

Born on 9 March 1886 at Urbana, Ohio, Robert Lawrence Eichelberger attended Ohio State University for two years before entering the U.S. Military Academy at West Point in 1905. He graduated in 1909. His early infantry assignments

included several tours along the Mexican border before duty in Siberia in 1918 with the AMERICAN EXPEDITIONARY FORCE as a temporary major. During the interwar period, he caught the attention of the army chief of staff, General Douglas MACARTHUR. In 1938 his assignment to the Infantry School at Fort Benning was rapidly followed by a regimental command, promotion to brigadier general, and the superintendency of West Point.

In March 1942 Eichelberger, now a major general, assumed command of the 77th Infantry Division and in June of I Corps. He moved in August to the Southwest Pacific theater. In October 1942 Eichelberger won promotion to temporary lieutenant general. On 29 November, as MacArthur's attempts to take BUNA floundered, Eichelberger received the famous injunction from his superior, "I want you to take Buna, or not come back alive." Frequently on the front lines, Eichelberger galvanized his men. His skillful seizure of Japanese airstrips led to victory, but his very success brought publicity that threatened to put his commander in the shadow. Relegated therefore to rear-echelon training jobs, Eichelberger gave an outstanding performance in preparing green troops for jungle warfare.

In April 1944 Eichelberger was again in combat, as MacArthur launched an amphibious attack at Hollandia. Eichelberger's execution of the landing was rapid, throwing the Japanese off balance, and success was achieved at small cost. The army chief of staff, now General George C. MARSHALL, labeled the operation a model of its kind.

Eichelberger next proved his ability by energizing a stalled offensive at Biak in June. Elevated to command of the new Eighth Army on 9 September, Eichelberger slowly but effectively eradicated the Japanese on LEYTE. His later performance on Luzon and the islands of the central and southern Philippines garnered additional laurels. Altogether, Eichelberger's Eighth Army, nicknamed the "Amphibious Eighth," executed 52 landings, every one successful. Had he fought under a less vainglorious superior, Eichelberger would have won proper recognition as one of the top U.S. Army commanders in World War II.

On 30 August 1945 Eichelberger landed at Atsugi Air Field to begin the U.S. occupation of Japan. After the war, Eichelberger played a key role in the demilitarization and democratization of that country until his retirement at the end of 1948. Promoted to general on the retired list in 1954, Eichelberger died at Asheville, North Carolina, on 26 September 1961.

See also PHILIPPINES, RETAKING OF; WORLD WAR II, U.S. INVOLVEMENT, PACIFIC.

Further reading: Eichelberger, Robert. *Our Jungle Road to Tokyo.* New York: Viking, 1950; Luvaas, Jay, and John F. Shortal. "Robert L. Eichelberger: MacArthur's Fireman."

In William M. Leary, ed. *We Shall Return! MacArthur's Commanders and the Defeat of Japan.* Lexington: University Press of Kentucky, 1988; Shortal, John F. *Forged by Fire: General Robert L. Eichelberger and the Pacific War.* Columbia: University of South Carolina Press, 1987.
— Malcolm Muir, Jr.

Eisenhower, Dwight D. (1890–1969) *U.S. Army general and president of the United States*

Born on 14 October 1890 at Denison, Texas, Dwight David Eisenhower grew up in modest circumstances in Abilene, Kansas. He graduated from the U.S. Military Academy at WEST POINT in 1915. Various domestic assignments were followed in 1918 by a posting to the AMERICAN EXPEDITIONARY FORCE in France, but World War I ended before his arrival.

Promoted to major in 1920, Eisenhower held posts during the 1920s in the Panama Canal Zone and Paris. He graduated from the Command and General Staff School in 1926 and the Army War College in 1928. From 1930 to 1935 Eisenhower was assigned to the War Department in Washington. In 1936 he reluctantly accompanied General Douglas MACARTHUR, the outgoing army chief of staff, to the Philippines to train the commonwealth's army, but on the outbreak of World War II in Europe in 1939 Eisenhower insisted upon returning to the United States. During these years Eisenhower and MacArthur developed an enduring personal animosity.

President Dwight D. Eisenhower *(Library of Congress)*

As the United States began its defense buildup, Eisenhower initially served as chief of staff of the new Third Army as a temporary brigadier general. Transferred to the War Department in Washington after the Japanese attack on PEARL HARBOR, he held various increasingly responsible staff jobs. Working in the War Plans Division, he helped to elaborate the "Europe First" strategy. He was promoted major general in April 1942 and to lieutenant general in July. That summer he went to London as commander of American and Allied forces in Britain. In November 1942 he organized the North African campaign (Operation TORCH). Promoted to full general in February 1943, he directed the invasions of SICILY (July 1943) and Italy (September). In December 1943 President Franklin D. ROOSEVELT selected Eisenhower as supreme commander of the Allied forces scheduled to occupy Western Europe after the NORMANDY INVASION. He won promotion to general of the army (five-star rank) in December 1944. In spring 1945, victory in Europe made Eisenhower a national hero. By this time he apparently cherished hopes of translating his fame into a political career.

From 1945 to 1948 Eisenhower served as chief of staff of the army, then taking up the presidency of Columbia University, which he held until 1952. During this time he participated prominently in study groups at the Council on Foreign Relations and spent at least one or two days a week in Washington, informally chairing the Joint Chiefs of Staff during Admiral William D. LEAHY's illness. Eisenhower strongly endorsed President Harry S. TRUMAN's developing COLD WAR policies, including intervention in Korea in June 1950. Eisenhower's major focus, however, remained the European situation and the Soviet-American rivalry. On 1 January 1951, he took leave from Columbia to strengthen the infant NORTH ATLANTIC TREATY ORGANIZATION, which American officials feared the KOREAN WAR might jeopardize, by serving as supreme commander of its armed forces. He organized the NATO military headquarters in Paris.

In 1952 the Republican Party, desperate after five successive presidential defeats to choose a candidate who would be assured of victory, turned to Eisenhower. Internationalist Republicans, equally determined to ensure that their party's nominee would effectively endorse and continue the Truman administration's cold war policies, promoted his candidacy.

As president, Eisenhower fulfilled his campaign pledge to end the Korean War expeditiously, in part by threatening to employ nuclear weapons unless an armistice agreement was concluded. A fiscal conservative alarmed by rising defense budgets, he introduced the NEW LOOK STRATEGY of relying heavily on nuclear weapons rather than conventional forces. Within and outside the armed forces, critics such as General Maxwell D. TAYLOR, chairman of the Joint Chiefs of Staff, complained that this approach left the United States unprepared to fight limited wars. Eisenhower was appalled, however, by the destructive capabilities of nuclear weapons and became the first president to attempt, albeit rather unsuccessfully, to reach arms control agreements with the Soviet Union. His efforts began with his "open skies" proposal of 1955 and continued until he left office.

As president, Eisenhower was cautious in risking American troops in overseas interventions. He boasted that during his presidency no American soldier lost his life in combat duty. In 1954 he declined to commit American forces in Indochina to help avert French defeat at Dien Bien Phu. Eisenhower relied heavily instead on covert activities, authorizing the CENTRAL INTELLIGENCE AGENCY to back coups in both Iran and Guatemala in 1953 and to undertake numerous other secret operations. Somewhat ironically, in his farewell address of January 1961 Eisenhower warned that such cold war practices tended to undercut the democratic values that the United States claimed to defend.

In this speech Eisenhower also expressed his concern that high levels of defense spending had created a MILITARY-INDUSTRIAL COMPLEX with a vested interest in the continuation of international tensions. Eisenhower's anxieties were probably related to unfounded but well-publicized contemporary criticisms that his administration had allowed the Soviet Union to open a MISSILE GAP—to achieve nuclear superiority.

After leaving office Eisenhower backed American intervention in Indochina despite his own refusal to commit forces there. He specifically warned his successor, John F. KENNEDY, against abandoning the Republic of Vietnam. He died in Washington, D.C., on 28 March 1969.

See also CONTAINMENT, DOCTRINE AND COURSE OF; MARSHALL, GEORGE C.; NUCLEAR AND ATOMIC WEAPONS; U-2 INCIDENT; VIETNAM WAR, CAUSES OF U.S. INVOLVEMENT; WORLD WAR II, U.S. INVOLVEMENT, EUROPE.

Further reading: Ambrose, Stephen E. *Eisenhower.* 2 vols. New York: Simon & Schuster, 1983–84; Bowie, Robert R., and Richard H. Immerman. *Waging Peace: How Eisenhower Shaped an Enduring Cold War Strategy.* New York: Oxford University Press, 1998; Chandler, Alfred D., Jr., and Louis Galambos, eds. *The Papers of Dwight D. Eisenhower.* 17 vols. to date. Baltimore: Johns Hopkins Press, 1970– ; Perret, Geoffrey. *Eisenhower.* New York: Random House, 1999.

— Priscilla Roberts

El Caney, Battle of (1 July 1898) *Battle during the Spanish-American War, fought in conjunction with the Battle of San Juan Heights during the Cuban campaign*
El Caney occupied a strategic spot along the Santiago-Guantanamo road. U.S. forces under Brigadier General Henry LAWTON, seeking to invest Santiago, were one mile southeast of El Caney on the afternoon of 30 June 1898.

El Caney was defended by 650 Spanish troops under Brigadier General Joaquin Vara de Rey, who had fortified several blockhouses and the old village church of El Viso. Lawton's plan of attack called for three regiments under Brigadier General Adna CHAFFEE to take position several hundred yards from the old church on the east side of El Caney. Brigadier General William Ludlow's brigade would occupy the Santiago–El Caney road to the southwest and thus cut off the obvious route of a Spanish retreat. Colonel Evan Miles's two regiments would be held in reserve to the southeast of the village, while the other would support an American artillery battery a mile to the south. At daybreak on 1 July a barrage from the south battery would precede Ludlow's and Chaffee's advance into the village. Lawton predicted that the entire operation would take only two hours and that his force could then support the planned U.S. attack on the SAN JUAN HEIGHTS.

The south battery commenced fire at 6 A.M. on the 1st as planned but had little effect because the target was just beyond range. Spanish resistance did not crumble from the barrage as expected. Also, as the Spanish used Mauser rifles firing smokeless powder, pinpointing their sharpshooters was difficult. By 10 A.M. the American attack had stalled. Lawton then brought up his reserves. He now had more than 6,000 troops in the line.

The battle resumed an hour later. Furious Spanish fire met American attempts to advance upon the blockhouses and barbed-wire trenches around El Viso, and U.S. casualties mounted. At 1 P.M. Lawton received a frantic message from the V Corps commander, Major General William SHAFTER, to break off the El Caney attack and support the attack on the San Juan Heights. Lawton, having already ordered a final push on El Caney, refused to disengage.

With the south battery at last in range, U.S. artillery fire had effect on the Spanish positions. Chaffee's men finally took El Viso at 3 P.M. Spanish troops attempting to escape met other U.S. regiments on the main road. The last Spanish blockhouse fell after fierce resistance about 30 minutes later.

In the battle the Spanish lost 248 killed and more than 300 captured. El Caney cost the Americans 81 killed and 360 wounded. Combined with the losses at the San Juan Heights, on 1 July V Corps lost 10 percent of its effective fighting strength. However, U.S. forces could now be positioned to shell SANTIAGO, which facilitated the surrender of that city, along with 11,500 Spanish troops, on 16 July.

See also SPANISH-AMERICAN WAR.

Further reading: Cosmas, Graham A. *An Army for Empire: The United States Army in the Spanish-American War.* College Station: Texas A&M University Press, 1998; Musicant, Ivan. *Empire by Default: The Spanish-American War and the Dawn of the American Century.* New York: Henry Holt, 1998; Trask, David. F. *The War with Spain in 1898.* Lincoln: University of Nebraska Press, 1997.

— William Thomas Allison

electronic warfare *Techniques and technology used to confuse, disrupt, or damage sensors or communications equipment or to protect these systems from interference*

Electronic warfare methods serve both defensive and offensive functions in modern military operations. Defensive measures include the use of electromagnetic spectrum jamming to impair missile-tracking systems and other forms of active electronic guidance. When used effectively to disrupt surveillance and communications links between attacking force components, electronic countermeasures (ECM) introduce confusion and uncertainty into tactical situations and limit the ability of an enemy to respond to threats. Electronic counter-countermeasures (ECCM) technologies protect vital electromagnetic transmissions from disruption when operating in the vicinity of active ECM systems.

The earliest form of electronic warfare was radio-transmission jamming, first used in 1901 during the America's Cup yacht race, when the American Wireless Telephone and Telegraph Company disrupted radio reports sent by competing news services in order to "scoop" the victory. In 1902, the British navy jammed fleet radio signals during exercises in the Mediterranean, and in 1903 the U.S. Navy used similar techniques during war games off the Atlantic coast. Jamming methods were used by combatant forces during the 1904–05 Russo-Japanese War, when Russian radio operators used their transmitting equipment to impede fire-correction messages sent by Japanese picket boats during the bombardment of Port Arthur. More sophisticated forms of jamming were devised in the ensuing years as the use of radio by the world's military and naval forces became widespread.

Electronic warfare evolved quickly when radar (radio detecting and ranging) was introduced in the 1930s. Radar had direct application to the complexities of modern warfare, serving an important surveillance function. Robert Watson-Watt, an English engineer who helped to developed the first radar systems, devised effective radar countermeasures in 1938. British radio-interference systems that could impair or deceive radar receivers became available to the United States during World War II as a result of the LEND-LEASE agreements. Throughout the war, radar countermeasures played a key role in the success of U.S. and Allied military operations in the Atlantic and Pacific theaters.

The proliferation of military radio and radar systems and jamming methods created a requirement for ECCM to overcome the effects of deliberate signal interference generated by ECM systems. The earliest electronic counter-countermeasures methods were invented to overcome radio jamming. Before the introduction of radio-frequency discriminating technology, multiple signals garbled voice transmissions sent over common frequencies. This problem was addressed by preceding voice transmissions with audible tones of varying pitch, by which skilled radio operators could distinguish between overlapping signals and isolate specific messages. This simple solution was enough to overcome early jamming techniques, but as radio matured, more elaborate ECCM systems were developed. The problem of radar jamming was addressed in the late 1930s by using multiple-frequency emissions. ECCM protections were incorporated into the design of many systems used by stationary ground radar facilities during the war.

The introduction of radio and radar-guided missiles in the mid-1940s posed a new challenge to electronic warfare measures designed to protect military assets. The development of ground-based electronic warfare technology after World War II was guided by the need to thwart threats posed by a variety of increasingly accurate target-acquisition and fire-control systems. The introduction of accurate guided missiles in the 1950s and 1960s brought about a significant change in military operations with regard to the use of electronic warfare during combat.

Concerns about the vulnerability of stationary positions, transportation networks, and combat units susceptible to long-range guided-missile attack led to the development of ECM systems designed to confuse acquisition and tracking technologies, which after 1955 included low-light vision and infrared guidance instruments. Military ECM defenses evolved to include electromagnetic noise-generation emissions to blind surveillance radar systems; false-target-generation signals to fool enemy tracking equipment; chaff, consisting of strips of foil, to confuse guidance-radar instruments; and electronic decoys that generate powerful radar signals in order to attract missiles fitted with passive radar-homing systems.

Recent advances in materials science, metallurgy, microelectronics, and optics have raised the stakes for electronic warfare engineers. New ECM and ECCM systems had to contend with a host of new military technologies, including the application of "stealth" designs to missiles, laser guidance systems, highly accurate electro-optical tracking instruments, and digital computers capable of evaluating changing battlefield conditions, independent of human control.

Electronic warfare systems are costly but vital for the survivability of U.S. military forces. ECM and ECCM technologies are ongoing processes; as new sensors and guidance systems are introduced, countermeasures must be developed to address information-security and asset-protection issues.

See also INTELLIGENCE.

Further reading: Buderi, Robert. *The Invention That Changed the World: The Story of Radar from War to Peace.* New York: Touchstone, 1996; Price, Alfred. *The History of U.S. Electronic Warfare.* Vol. 1. Arlington, Va.: Association of Old Crows, 1984; ———. *Instruments of Darkness: The History of Electronic Warfare.* New York: Scribner, 1978.

— Shannon A. Brown

Ellyson, Theodore G. ("Spuds") (1885–1928) *U.S. Navy captain and first U.S. naval aviator*
Born on 27 February 1885 at Richmond, Virginia, Theodore Gordon Ellyson informed his parents in 1900 that he wished to enter the navy. He accordingly attended "Bobby" Werntz's preparatory school in Annapolis, Maryland, where his love of potatoes led his classmates to call him "Spuds." Nominated for the U.S. Naval Academy, he failed the academic tests but was admitted when a principal defaulted.

On graduation in 1910 Ellyson asked for submarine duty in order to learn about gasoline engines (which submarines then had), the kind used in aircraft. He then requested aviation duty. In November 1910, aircraft manufacturer Glen CURTISS offered the Navy Department flight training for one officer. In December the department sent Ellyson to Curtiss's camp at North Island, San Diego. There Curtiss taught him to fly, and Ellyson helped Curtiss prepare hydroplanes (prototypical seaplanes) for test flights.

In 1911 Ellyson became the first naval flight instructor at an aviation camp established across the Severn River from the Naval Academy. In June 1912 Ellyson piloted a hydroplane launched from a catapult built by fellow student Holden C. Richardson—and was dunked in the Severn. The introduction of improved catapults was later to be a milestone in naval aviation.

In 1913 Ellyson returned to sea, first in a battleship; then in command of a flotilla of 110-foot submarine chasers based at Plymouth, England, during World War I; then as captain of a troopship carrying 5,000 soldiers home. In January 1921 he returned to flying, as executive officer of the naval air station at Norfolk, Virginia. Later he commanded a destroyer. Beginning in 1924, he spent two years as the naval air attaché to Brazil.

Although Ellyson was not fully qualified for aircraft carrier command, Rear Admiral William A. MOFFETT, chief of the new Bureau of Aeronautics, had him assigned as commanding officer of the 18 twin-engine torpedo planes attached to the seaplane tender *Wright.* After observing air operations from the *Langley* (CV 1), Ellyson became the inspector of machinery and then executive officer of the 33,000-ton carrier *Lexington* (CV 2). Early on 28 February 1928, Ellyson and two pilots took off in an amphibian plane for Annapolis. They were never heard from again. Forty days later, Ellyson's body washed up on Willoughby Spit.

In addition to being the first U.S. naval aviator and naval air instructor, Ellyson was the first naval test pilot and the first to fly a plane off a catapult. He did much to improve early planes, and he inspired many younger men to take up aviation.

See also AIRCRAFT CARRIERS; U.S. NAVY.

Further reading: Arthur, Reginald Wright. *Contact! Careers of Naval Aviators Assigned Numbers 1 to 2000.* Washington, D.C.: Naval Aviation Register, U.S. Government Printing Office, 1967; Lord, Clifford L. "History of Naval Aviation." 6 vols. Manuscript. Washington, D.C.: Deputy Chief of Naval Operations (Air), 1938; Roseberry, Cecil R. *Glenn Curtiss: Pioneer of Flight.* Garden City, N.Y.: Doubleday, 1972; Turnbull, Archibald D., and Clifford L. Lord. *History of United States Naval Aviation.* New Haven, Conn.: Yale University Press, 1949; Van Deurs, George. *Anchors in the Sky: Spuds Ellyson, the First Naval Aviator.* San Rafael, Calif.: Presidio, 1979.

— Paolo E. Coletta

engineering, military *Profession dedicated to harnessing physical forces for the purpose of designing, constructing, and operating systems, processes, and devices for effective and efficient use in achieving military, and, in specific instances, nonmilitary national objectives*
Until the 18th century, engineering was essentially a craft in which cumulative experience was considered more important than formal learning. The exception was military engineering, the formal education for which dates back to the middle of the 17th century. During the 17th and 18th centuries, France led the world in military engineering.

The first U.S. school devoted to engineering was the U.S. Military Academy at West Point, New York, founded in 1802 at the urging of President Thomas JEFFERSON. His keen interest in science and engineering led not only to the establishment of WEST POINT, with an initial complement of seven officers and 10 cadets, but also to the provision of a formal course of study there in military strategy and engineering.

After the American Revolutionary War, COAST DEFENSE became a priority for the U.S. Army. Considerable money and effort were invested in erecting and manning a system of coastal fortifications. In 1794, when Congress voted to create a navy, it authorized construction of coastal fortifications and arsenals. It also allocated resources for the establishment of a corps of artillerists and engineers for the seaboard forts. By 1812, 24 forts, mainly of earth and brick, had been constructed along the Atlantic seaboard.

In 1803 the United States acquired 828,000 square miles of land in the LOUISIANA PURCHASE from France. This created a vast array of new assignments for U.S. military engineers. The Army Corps of Engineers was charged with exploring, surveying, and mapping the newly acquired territories. Topographical requirements led in 1816 to creation of the Topographical Engineers (which was integrated into the Corps of Engineers in 1863).

In the first years of Jefferson's administration (1801–09) there were 27 military posts. By 1817 the number had grown to 73, and by 1846 148 posts stretched from the Atlantic to the Rocky Mountains. Additionally, the War of 1812 demonstrated the need for new roads to connect the frontier with the rest of the country. All of this activity placed great demands on the Corps of Engineers.

In the first 10 years of its existence, the U.S. Military Academy, the only source of trained engineers in the United States, produced only 72 graduates. Faced with this shortage, in May 1812 Congress enlarged the Corps of Engineers and the military academy. Simultaneously, Congress created the Ordnance Department, to be responsible for testing of armaments and powder to be used by the army.

In 1824 the Rivers and Harbors Act gave the Corps of Engineers control of the nation's seaports and inland waterways, a responsibility it still has. Americans have traditionally been suspicious of standing armies, but the engineers were a positive influence—with their involvement in flood control and river navigation, for example. They also worked to provide relief supplies in natural disasters, such as hurricanes and floods. The construction of roads not only had military implications but also greatly assisted the growth of industry, trade, and western expansion. Thus army engineers played a pivotal role in building the new nation.

During the MEXICAN-AMERICAN WAR, topographical engineer officers served as scouts and facilitated army movements in all theaters of war. Other engineering duties included the construction of field fortifications and harbor defenses. A group of young West Point–trained engineers earned stellar reputations during the war, among them Joseph JOHNSTON, Robert E. LEE, George G. MEADE, and George B. MCCLELLAN, all of whom would command armies during the Civil War.

Engineers on both sides, especially the Union, played a vital role in the Civil War. Railroads were especially important in the rapid mass movement of men and supplies, and engineers assisted in their development. Combat engineering achieved great successes during the Civil War. New coastal and river fortifications were required. During the VICKSBURG CAMPAIGN (1862–63), Union engineers cut canals and manipulated rivers. The war also demanded elaborate fieldworks and fortifications, especially during its last year. Extensive entrenchments protected such cities as Richmond, PETERSBURG, and Atlanta; fortified lines connected strong points around Washington. The war witnessed widespread use of abatis, wire, and other obstructions. Pontoons also played a major role.

During the war Congress passed the Morrill Land Grant Act of 1862, by which the federal government gave to every state remaining in the Union huge tracts of federal land. The states were allowed to sell the land and use the proceeds to endow at least one college that would offer courses in agriculture and engineering. Another provision of the act required that military training be offered at each college, a program that ultimately became part of the RESERVE OFFICERS TRAINING CORPS (ROTC). A second Morrill Act in 1890 extended the program to 16 southern states. Naval engineering had been advanced with establishment of the Naval School in 1845 at Fort Severn, Annapolis, Maryland. It was renamed the U.S. Naval Academy in 1850.

The Industrial Revolution, which began in the late 18th century and gathered momentum in the 19th, brought improved manufacturing and metallurgical techniques, machinery capable of working at closer tolerances, and the introduction of interchangeability of parts and assembly-line techniques. This led to improvements not only in weapons but also in such things as the canning and refrigeration of food, which made feeding armies much easier. The invention of the steamship, telegraph, telephone, incandescent light, automobile, tank, and airplane changed warfare markedly by the end of World War I. Machines, not men, became the masters of the battlefield.

Combat engineers played important roles in the wars of the 20th century. In World War II in the Pacific theater, naval construction battalions, known as the Seabees, with the motto *Construmus, batuimus* (We build, we fight), were vital in the construction of airfields on Pacific islands for bombers that attacked the Japanese home islands. In the landings in Europe, combat engineers demolished Axis defensive positions, constructed bridges and harbor facilities, and opened supply corridors and routes of advance.

In June 1941 the Office of Scientific Research and Development (OSRD) was created to coordinate all government-sponsored scientific efforts, including work on atomic fission. To oversee this process and to ensure a sufficient level of security, a special army section was established within the Corps of Engineers, codenamed the Manhattan District. The MANHATTAN PROJECT expanded to include 125,000 personnel and consume nearly $2 billion. It produced the world's first ATOMIC BOMBS, which were employed against Japan in the waning days of the war in the Pacific.

Simultaneous with the nuclear age, military engineers were involved in new electronics developments. A U.S. Army team—including J. Presper Eckert, John W. Mauchly, Herman H. Goldstine, and John G. Brainerd—developed the first all-electronic, general-purpose computer, ENIAC (1943–45). During this time the ENIAC group formulated objectives basic to further development, such as stored programs, random-access memories, and conditional branching. In 1951 this team developed a commercially available line of computers.

The nuclear developments and information revolution led to the new fields of nuclear and computer engineering. Information and cyberspace developments would pave the way for information warfare in the closing decades of the century. Space exploration opened new vistas and a new engineering specialty, aerospace engineering. These specialized areas are taught at the service academies. Military engineering continues to evolve, and it remains of vital importance to the security of the United States.

See also ARMY, U.S.

Further reading: Fowle, Barry W. *Builders and Fighters: U.S. Army Engineers in World War II*. Fort Belvoir, Va.: Office of History, U.S. Army Corps of Engineers, 1992; Jacobs, James Ripley. *The Beginning of the U.S. Army, 1783–1812*. Princeton, N.J.: Princeton University Press, 1947; Jones, Vincent C. *Manhattan, the Army and the Atomic Bomb*. Washington, D.C.: Center of Military History, U.S. Army, 1985; Shallat, Todd A. *Structures in the Stream: Water, Science, and the Rise of the U.S. Corps of Engineers*. Austin: University of Texas Press, 1999; Thompson, Erwin N. *Pacific Ocean Engineers: History of the U.S. Army Corps of Engineers in the Pacific, 1905–1980*. Washington, D.C.: U.S. Government Printing Office, 1985.

— James B. McNabb

Enterprise, USS, v. HMS *Boxer* (5 September 1813)
Naval engagement of the War of 1812

On 5 September 1813 the British naval brig *Boxer* (14 guns) lay off Penguin Point, a few miles east of present-day Portland, Maine. Its commander, Captain Samuel Blyth, had put a hunting party ashore the day before. Early on 5 September the *Boxer's* crew sighted a vessel approaching, and Blyth immediately set sail to intercept the intruder. As the two ships closed, he ordered the British flag flown and a gun fired in challenge.

USS *Enterprise* v. HMS *Boxer,* off Pemmaquid, Maine, 5 September 1813. Lithograph   *(Navy Historical Foundation)*

The approaching ship, the USS *Enterprise* (16), was a converted sloop rigged as a brig, under Master Commandant William BURROWS. As the two ships neared and their crews cleared for action, the wind suddenly died. For the next six hours the two vessels drifted, each crew watching the other.

Late in the afternoon a slight breeze came up. A few minutes later Burrows fired a challenge and turned his vessel to meet the *Boxer* head on. Both crews displayed remarkable discipline as the warships came broadside to one another, firing only when instructed by their commanders.

The first broadsides hit with deadly effect. Captain Blyth was struck by an 18-pound shot and died instantly. Command passed to Lieutenant David McCreery. Moments later a British marine sharpshooter mortally wounded Burrows. Command of the *Enterprise* then fell to Lieutenant Edward McCall.

Fire from the *Enterprise* shattered the upperworks of the *Boxer,* leaving it unmanageable. McCall was then able to position his vessel off the stern off his opponent, masking most of the *Boxer's* guns, and rake the British ship for some 12 minutes. McCall then ordered a halt in the firing and heard the British crew calling to surrender. McCall then demanded to know why the *Boxer's* crew had not pulled down their colors, only to discover that the British had nailed them to the mast.

On board the *Enterprise,* Burrows lived long enough to receive the sword of his antagonist. In the fight the *Boxer* suffered 28 killed and 14 wounded, while the *Enterprise* sustained only Burrows killed and 13 wounded.

The *Enterprise* towed its prize into Portland. Both dead captains were brought ashore in a procession of barges rowed at minute strokes, past ships which dipped their flags in honor. The two crews, British and American, carried their leaders through the city to the same graveyard.

See also WAR OF 1812 AT SEA, OVERVIEW.

Further reading: Barnes, James. *Naval Actions of the War of 1812*. New York: Harper Brothers, 1904; Roosevelt, Theodore. *The Naval War of 1812*. Reprint, New York: Modern Library, 1999; U.S. Navy Department. *Dictionary of American Naval Fighting Ships: Historical Sketches*. Vol. 1(A). Washington, D.C.: U.S. Government Printing Office, 1998.

— Patrick R. Jennings

Ericsson, John (1803–1889) *Engineer and inventor*
Born on 31 July 1803 at Värmland, Sweden, John Ericsson was educated by his father and tutors before he and an older brother became cadets in the Corps of Mechanical Engineers. At the age of 13 he supervised 600 men who surveyed land for a canal across Sweden. When he was 17, he joined the Swedish army and served in the map division.

John Ericsson in 1862   *(Naval Historical Foundation)*

At 23 he moved to London, where he worked on the transmission of forced-air steam boilers that would permit a ship's engines to be placed below the waterline, where they were safer. Between 1826 and 1836 he registered 30 inventions, including pumping engines, cooling systems, steam fire engines, and a marine engine. In 1829 he won a competition with a locomotive that bettered the required speed of 10 miles per hour—by making 30.

Credited as coinventor of the screw propeller, Ericsson in 1837 proved that screw propulsion was superior to paddlewheels. He was then approached by U.S. Navy captain Robert F. Stockton to build a screw ship. Meanwhile, he married Amelia Byam. (Amelia refused to join him in America, remained childless, and died during the American Civil War.)

On Stockton's invitation, Ericsson moved to New York and was responsible for the steam engine and propeller for the U.S. Navy steam sloop *Princeton,* the first screw-propeller warship in any navy. During a cruise on the Potomac on 11 November 1844, a 12-inch iron gun burst on the *Princeton* when fired, killing two cabinet members and wounding others. Ericsson then sought to perfect a "caloric" ship, one that used solar power and hot air rather than steam to operate the engines. It proved too slow to be a warship and, after being raised from sinking during a storm, was fitted with a steam plant.

When Congress established a competition to design a shellproof ship, Ericsson provided plans later used in building the MONITOR. Only after the Civil War started, however, did the Lincoln administration order such a ship built. With its low freeboard, engines below the waterline, and two 11-inch guns in a revolving turret, it contained some 40 patentable innovations. Although its battle with the Confederate ram *Virginia* on 9 March 1862 was a draw, the *Monitor* proved the power of the ironclad ship. Ericsson went on to design other monitor classes for the U.S. Navy during the Civil War. After the war he helped develop the modern torpedo boat, which evolved into the DESTROYER.

A man of indomitable energy and vision, Ericsson was complex and unpredictable, a loner who had little patience and did not get along with those who worked with him, because of the pace set by his active mind. He died at New York City on 8 March 1889.

See also IRONCLADS, U.S., IN CIVIL WAR; MONITOR V. VIRGINIA.

Further reading: Church, William C. *The Life of John Ericsson.* 2 vols. New York: Scribner, 1890; Davis, William C. *Duel between the First Ironclads.* Garden City, N.Y.: Doubleday, 1975; Ericsson, John. "The Building of the Monitor." In Robert U. Johnson and Clarence C. Buel, eds. *Battles and Leaders of the Civil War.* Vol. 1. Reprint, New York: Castle Books, 1991.

— Paolo E. Coletta

espionage against the United States, survey of *The clandestine collection of intelligence on the United States*

Espionage has played an important role in most major American military conflicts, but it rarely, if ever, has been significant enough to change their outcomes.

Keeping secrets amid the divided loyalties of a civil war is next to impossible, and the American Revolutionary War proved no exception. Patriot organizations were plagued by "defectors in place," such as Benjamin Church, a member of the Boston Committee of Correspondence, and Joseph Galloway, a delegate to the Continental Congress. British spymasters in the colonies, such as Lieutenant General Henry Clinton's chief of INTELLIGENCE, Major John André, and his successor, Oliver De Lancey, supervised extensive spy networks and attempted to generate defections within the Patriot camp. The most famous of these operations, the planned betrayal of the fortifications at West Point by Major General Benedict ARNOLD, led to André's capture and execution. Perhaps most damaging, the secretary of the American delegation in France, Edward Bancroft, was a source for the British secret service, providing Britain information on virtually all American diplomatic activity in Europe from 1775 through to the 1783 TREATY OF PARIS, and beyond. Even after the end of the revolution, British intelligence operations within the United States continued to prosper well into the 19th century, exploiting the lingering loyalist sentiments of many Americans.

Keeping secrets proved little easier for the U.S. government during the Civil War. The most important source of information for the Confederacy was not clandestine at all; the Northern press arranged for numerous correspondents to travel with Union armies and report back to their newspapers what they saw on a daily basis, despite ineffective attempts at censorship by the Union army. In addition to their use of CAVALRY for reconnaissance, individual Confederate military commanders also frequently gathered tactical intelligence via an assortment of spies, scouts, and other operatives, such as the mysterious "Harrison," who provided warning of Union movements preceding the Battle of GETTYSBURG. Although the importance of clandestine civilian sources for the South has been exaggerated in popular literature on the war, in several cases such espionage did provide important information. Many of the most successful Confederate agents were women, such as Rose O'Neal Greenhow, a prominent member of Washington society. The Union counterintelligence efforts of Allan PINKERTON and others proved somewhat successful, however, and many high-level Confederate political spies ultimately were arrested, as was the case with Greenhow in 1862. The Confederacy also experimented with an early form of signals intelligence, by tapping Union telegraph communications, but it rarely was able to read encrypted messages.

Intelligence operations played a major role during World War I and its aftermath. German agents within the United States concentrated more on sabotage than espionage, and most of their networks were ultimately broken by the Secret Service, the Federal Bureau of Investigation (FBI), and other counterintelligence organizations. British intelligence officers operated within the United States with much more success, both working with American authorities to thwart German activities and conducting clandestine intelligence and PROPAGANDA operations of their own.

Far more damage was done to the United States during this period by fears of spies than by spies themselves, foreshadowing the communist "witch hunts" of the 1950s. During the war the FBI cooperated with the volunteer, semiofficial American Protective League, leading to numerous civil rights violations. Worse was the brief but intense period of officially sanctioned paranoia over the "Red Menace" in 1919–20, following the Bolshevik Revolution. It ultimately led to the arrest of thousands and deportation of hundreds, most simply for holding unpopular political beliefs.

The Axis powers had little espionage success against the United States during World War II. Through the use of double agent William Sebold, the FBI in June 1940 destroyed virtually the entire German intelligence network within the United States, arresting some 33 agents in all. Although there were some subsequent German attempts at sabotage and subversion within the United States and Latin America, these did not amount to much. Japanese espionage against the United States was also very limited, but this did not prevent antispy hysteria from again provoking large-scale civil rights abuses, most notably in the internment of more than 100,000 Japanese Americans in California to remote internment camps.

It was during the COLD WAR that espionage played its greatest role in American history. Disclosures from both sides following the end of the cold war revealed in detail the massive scope of Soviet intelligence successes within the United States and Britain, especially during the 1940s and 1950s. Probably the most important of these were the numerous "atomic spies" within the MANHATTAN PROJECT, whose collective efforts probably sped the first Soviet atomic test by at least a year. Penetrations of the Manhattan Project were so extensive that new Soviet sources within it were still being publicly revealed in the 1990s.

Almost as harmful to American security was the British "Cambridge spy ring." These five men and their associates, most committed communists recruited by

Soviet intelligence at Cambridge University in the 1930s, rose to important positions within the British government and in the process did extensive damage to both British and American national security. Harold "Kim" Philby, for example, was from 1944 through 1946 the top official in British intelligence, with the responsibility for *preventing* Soviet penetration of MI-6. From that vantage point he arranged for at least one Soviet would-be defector to be executed before he could unmask Philby as a traitor. In 1949 Philby was transferred to Washington and became the chief liaison officer between American and British intelligence. Before his recall to London in 1951 under a cloud of suspicion, he not only betrayed numerous British and American intelligence operations, but also befriended many top officials within the American intelligence community.

In the late 1940s there were several significant counterintelligence successes, some highly publicized and some tightly held secrets. One was the VENONA project, wherein some Soviet wartime communications were decrypted by predecessors of the NATIONAL SECURITY AGENCY. The resulting revelations about the genuine and massive scope of Soviet espionage within the United States were exploited by such demagogues as Senator Joseph McCarthy to create an atmosphere of almost hysterical anticommunism within the United States, during the "Second Red Scare" of the early 1950s.

Although the recruitment of human sources within the United States by Soviet intelligence and its Russian successors continued throughout the rest of the cold war and beyond, these betrayals were increasingly motivated less by ideology than by greed. Virtually no corner of the American national security bureaucracy has escaped penetration by foreign intelligence services. The list of "moles" uncovered within the U.S. government from the 1960s through the early 2000s is far too long to discuss in detail, but some of the most notable include John Walker (a U.S. Navy communications officer and Soviet source from the mid-1960s through 1985), Ronald Pelton (an employee of the NSA who provided extensive information to the Soviet Union in 1980), Jonathan Pollard (an Israeli source within U.S. naval intelligence from 1984 to 1985), Aldrich Ames (a high-level Soviet source within the CENTRAL INTELLIGENCE AGENCY [CIA] from 1985 to 1994), and Robert Hanssen (a high-level FBI counterintelligence officer and alleged Soviet source from 1985 to 2001).

The damage caused by such betrayals was often compounded by the internal counterintelligence investigations that followed, which sometimes, through the use of polygraph ("lie detector") tests and other questionable means, drove good people out of government service and damaged the morale of those who remained. Probably the most extreme example of the damage such "mole hunts" caused is the counterintelligence investigations of James Jesus Angleton, a hypersuspicious CIA officer and previous close friend of Kim Philby who in the 1960s possibly did more damage to the CIA than any actual mole could have accomplished. Finally, little is known about to what extent the Soviet Union was able to match American successes in the collection of intelligence via technical means, such as the interception of communications and the collection of imagery by satellites and spy aircraft.

In retrospect, large-scale national security programs appear historically to have manifested themselves in too many ways to have been kept secret for very long. Further, no matter how severely access to sensitive information is restricted, if the information is to be useful there will always be a large number of people with a "need to know," and any one of these can reveal the source. Even if enemy intelligence networks prove largely ineffectual, as in the two world wars, the openness of American society and the diligence of its press corps still make the general outlines of American military and political strategy difficult to conceal. The only prudent thing for policy makers to do, therefore, is to assume enemies and potential enemies know everything. Also, given the secrecy that continues to shroud world intelligence operations in the years after World War II, it is only prudent for historians to assume that there is still much that we do not know about the history of espionage.

See also DEFENSE INTELLIGENCE AGENCY; OFFICE OF STRATEGIC SERVICES.

Further reading: Andrew, Christopher. *For the President's Eyes Only: Secret Intelligence and the American Presidency from Washington to Bush.* New York: HarperCollins, 1995; Andrew, Christopher, and Oleg Gordievsky. *KGB: The Inside Story of Its Foreign Operations from Lenin to Gorbachev.* New York: HarperCollins, 1990; Andrew, Christopher, and Vasili Mitrokhin. *The Sword and the Shield: The Mitrokhin Archive and the Secret History of the KGB.* New York: Basic Books, 1999; O'Toole, G. J. A. *The Encyclopedia of American Espionage: From the Revolutionary War to the Present.* New York: Facts On File, 1988; ———. *Honorable Treachery: A History of U.S. Intelligence, Espionage, and Covert Action from the American Revolution to the CIA.* New York: Atlantic Monthly, 1991; Polmar, Norman, and Thomas B. Allen. *The Encyclopedia of Espionage.* New York: Gramercy Books, 1997; Richelson, Jeffrey T. *A Century of Spies: Intelligence in the Twentieth Century.* New York: Oxford University Press, 1995; Weinstein, Allen, and Alexander Vassiliev. *The Haunted Wood: Soviet Espionage in America—the Stalin Era.* New York: Random House, 1999.

— David Rezelman

Engagement between USS *Essex* and the HMS *Phoebe* and the *Cherub,* 28 March 1814, off Valparaiso, Chile   *(Naval Historical Foundation)*

Essex v. *Phoebe* and *Cherub* (28 March 1814) *An important naval battle in the War of 1812*

After more than a year at sea, Captain David PORTER, commanding the American frigate *Essex* and a small escort, the *Essex Junior,* arrived at Valparaiso on 3 February 1814 in search of British warships sent to find him. Five days later, Captain James Hillyar arrived with the British frigate *Phoebe* and the sloop *Cherub.* During the previous months Porter had devastated the British whaling fleet in the Pacific. Despite that accomplishment, Porter's quest for martial glory led him to seek out combat and risk destruction.

The two opposing captains agreed to respect Chilean neutrality; Porter, however, believed that applied to all of Chile's territorial waters, whereas Hillyar meant only the harbor itself. Failing to find an advantageous opportunity to attack, Porter decided after all to flee. On the afternoon of 28 March a storm provided the chance to escape to the windward of the British. As he dashed for open water, a squall tore away the *Essex*'s main topmast, severely hampering the ship's maneuverability. Porter put in at a small harbor a few miles from Valparaiso and dropped anchor, expecting Hillyar to continue to respect Chilean neutrality. Instead, the *Phoebe* and the *Cherub* assumed positions across the bow and the stern of the *Essex* and commenced firing. Porter had few options in the battle. Not only could the British outmaneuver him, but they enjoyed an immense advantage in firepower. While the *Essex* carried 46 guns, 40 of these were short-range carronades, whereas the *Phoebe* alone possessed 30 long guns able to reach the *Essex* from beyond the Americans' ability to respond. During the course of the battle, Porter brought three of his six long guns to bear by running them out stern funports, forcing the British briefly to draw off and make repairs. When he renewed battle, Hillyar assumed a position off the *Essex*'s starboard bow, where the Americans could not return fire.

Porter attempted to board the *Phoebe,* but the British simply sailed out of the way. With no means of attacking, Porter tried to beach the *Essex,* but a headwind pushed him away from shore. The *Essex Junior* took off some of the wounded but otherwise did not contribute. After two and a half hours Porter ordered the flag lowered, but it was another 10 minutes before Hillyar noticed and ceased fire. For the Americans it was a sanguinary fight. The *Essex* suffered 154 casualties, including 58 killed. The British sustained only 15 casualties. The *Essex* was severely damaged, but the British were able to repair it and sail it back to Europe. Hillyar then cartelled the *Essex Junior* and allowed it to take the surviving Americans home. Despite a letter of safe conduct, HMS *Saturn* seized the Americans off Sandy Hook, New Jersey. Porter and some of the crew escaped in a whaleboat the next day, landing on Long Island on 6 July 1814.

See also FARRAGUT, DAVID G.; PORTER, DAVID D.; WAR OF 1812 NAVAL OVERVIEW.

Further reading: Long, David F. *Nothing Too Daring: A Biography of Commodore David Porter.* Annapolis, Md.: Naval Institute Press, 1970; Turnbull, Archibald Douglas. *Commodore David Porter, 1780–1843.* New York: Century, 1929.

— Rodney Madison

Eustis, William (1753–1825) *U.S. secretary of war*
Born on 10 June 1753 at Cambridge, Massachusetts, William Eustis followed his father into medicine. He attended Harvard College until the outbreak of the American Revolutionary War on 19 April 1775. Eustis joined a militia company and was present during the Battle of BUNKER HILL on 17 June 1775. Thereafter he functioned as a regimental surgeon, acquitting himself well. He returned to private practice after the war, although he took briefly to the field during SHAYS'S REBELLION in 1786, when he marched with the troops. This last event made an indelible impression upon Eustis politically, for he thereafter became closely identified with the Republican Party.

Throughout the 1790s Eustis parleyed his political skills into a viable career. He served two terms in the U.S. House of Representatives, defeating such Federalist stalwarts as Josiah Quincy and John Quincy Adams. He himself was defeated in 1804, but his outspoken endorsement of Thomas JEFFERSON's national policies landed him the position of secretary of war in 1808. Jefferson's politically minded successor, James Madison, continued this appointment the following year.

As secretary, Eustis was well intentioned but lacked the merest scintilla of military administrative or planning skills. He simply implemented without foresight or direction whatever policies were foisted on the army by Congress or the president. Eustis oversaw expansion of the army in consequence of the 1807 CHESAPEAKE-LEOPARD AFFAIR, but otherwise his impact upon military affairs proved negligible until the declaration of war against Great Britain in June 1812.

After four years in office, Eustis had done little to prepare the army for armed conflict. Hence, at the commencement of the WAR OF 1812, U.S. forces were poorly trained and led, and incapable of coping with professional British forces in Canada. His greatest shortcoming was in failing to provide a strategic diversion to support Major General William HULL, whose army was forced to surrender at DETROIT in August 1812. Three months later, another embarrassing defeat at QUEENSTOWN HEIGHTS brought calls for his resignation. Eustis resigned from office on 3 December 1812 and returned to private life in Massachusetts.

Eustis eventually resurrected his political career and gained election as governor in 1823. He died at Boston on 6 February 1825.

See also WAR OF 1812, CAUSES; WAR OF 1812, LAND OVERVIEW; WAR OF 1812, NAVAL OVERVIEW.

Further reading: Crackel, Theodore J. *Mr. Jefferson's Army: Political and Social Reform of the Military Establishment, 1801–1807.* New York: New York University Press, 1987; Stagg, J. C. A. *Mr. Madison's War: Politics, Diplomacy, and Warfare in the Early American Republic, 1783–1830.* Princeton, N.J.: Princeton University Press, 1983.

— John C. Fredriksen

Eutaw Springs, Battle of (8 September 1781) *Last major battle in the South during the American Revolutionary War*
After the British lifted the American siege of Ninety Six in June 1781, they abandoned most of their inland posts in South Carolina and concentrated their forces around Charleston. Major General Nathanael GREENE likewise withdrew to the High Hills of Santee to rest his Continental troops.

In late August British Lieutenant Colonel Alexander Stuart marched from Charleston with 2,000 British and loyalist troops to protect the position at Orangeburg. Greene, with more than 2,000 men, marched to meet him. Stuart then fell back to Eutaw Springs to protect his communications with Charleston.

Greene advanced on the British camp early in the morning of 8 September and surprised a British foraging party. The American cavalry attacked, taking 40 prisoners. The remainder escaped and warned Stuart, who took position astride the Charleston road. Greene formed his troops with North and South Carolina militia in the first line; Virginia, North Carolina, and Maryland Continentals in the second line; and cavalry and Delaware Continentals in reserve.

The Americans attacked after an exchange of artillery fire. The South Carolina militia advanced steadily on the right and left, but a British bayonet charge drove back the North Carolinians in the center and also forced the South Carolinians to retreat. Greene sent forward the North Carolina Continentals to restore his line. British volleys checked the advance, and Stuart ordered a bayonet charge by his left and center. Greene responded with a countercharge by his Virginia and Maryland Continentals. Other troops flanked the British left, and Stuart's men broke, except for Major John Majoribanks's battalion on the right.

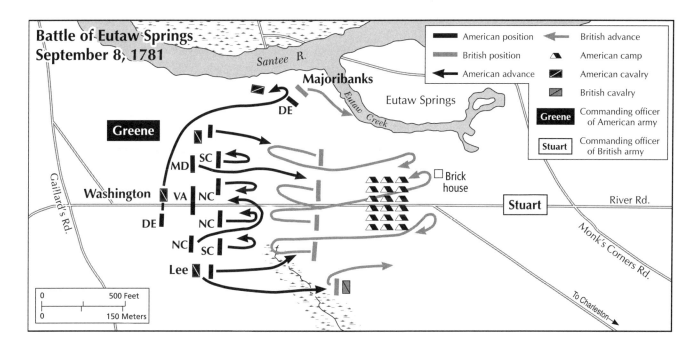

Battle of Eutaw Springs
September 8, 1781

	American position		British advance
British position		American camp
	American advance		American cavalry
			British cavalry
Greene	Commanding officer of American army
Stuart	Commanding officer of British army

Majoribanks repulsed several American attacks, while New York Loyalists occupying a two-story brick house poured a heavy fire into the Americans. These efforts enabled Stuart to form a new line, to which Majoribanks withdrew.

The British had fallen back beyond their encampment, and many American troops left their ranks to plunder. They found the abandoned rum particularly appealing. Continued fire from the brick house added to the Americans' confusion. Majoribanks then attacked the American left, while British cavalry attacked the right. When a cavalry counterattack failed to check the British, Greene saw the danger of his position and ordered a withdrawal. Majoribanks was killed in the final British assault, which drove the American rear guard from the field and captured Greene's artillery.

British losses had been nearly 700 men, including more than 250 captured, American casualties between 500 and 700. Although the British had won a tactical victory, they gave up their efforts to hold territory outside Charleston, leaving Greene in control of the rest of the state. He kept the British confined to Charleston until they evacuated the city in December 1782.

See also AMERICAN REVOLUTIONARY WAR, LAND OVERVIEW; GREENE'S OPERATIONS.

Further reading: Lumpkin, Henry. *From Savannah to Yorktown: The American Revolution in the South.* Columbia: University of South Carolina Press, 1981.

— Jim Piecuch

Evans, Robley D. (1846–1912) *U.S. Navy admiral*
Born on 18 August 1846 at Floyd Court House, Virginia, Robley Dunglison Evans moved to Washington, D.C. His father died when he was 10, and Evans was raised there by an uncle. He then moved to Utah. While traveling West at age 13, he was wounded in a fight with Indians. Evans graduated from the U.S. Naval Academy at Annapolis, in 1863 and was assigned to the steam frigate *Powhatan* in the West Indies Squadron.

During 1864–65, Evans served in the North Atlantic Blockading Squadron, and on 15 January 1864 he took part in the second attack on FORT FISHER, in North Carolina, commanding marines in the amphibious assault. Wounded four times, he was invalided out of the service but appealed the decision and was reinstated.

In 1866 Evans was promoted to lieutenant. From 1867 to 1869 he had charge of ordnance at the Washington Navy Yard and in 1868 was promoted to lieutenant commander. He served a tour at the Naval Academy during 1871–72. From 1873 to 1876 he was on the *Shenandoah* and then the *Congress,* on European station. In 1876 Evans perfected a long-distance signal lamp that was to be long used in naval service. From 1877 to 1881 he commanded the training ship *Saratoga.* Promoted to commander in July 1878, he was a lighthouse inspector during 1881–82. In 1886–87 he was the chief steel inspector for the navy, with the task of determining the quality of construction materials for the new fleet.

In August 1891 Evans took command of the gunboat *Yorktown* off Chile, skillfully handling a crisis with that nation. The next year he was in charge of a naval force in the Bering Sea charged with ending unlawful sealing. On that station he took a British supply ship and other sealing vessels that had entered U.S. waters.

Having been promoted to captain in 1893, Evans was assigned to command the battleship *Indiana* in 1894. In 1896 he served on the Lighthouse Board. During the 1898 SPANISH-AMERICAN WAR he commanded the battleship *Iowa* and took a leading role in the Battle of SANTIAGO BAY, 3 July 1898, earning the nickname of "Fighting Bob." Promoted to rear admiral in February 1901, Evans in 1902 took command of the Asiatic Fleet, improving the quality of its subcaliber gunnery and inventing a loading machine for naval guns.

In 1907 President Theodore ROOSEVELT selected Evans to command the Great White Fleet. Halfway through its around-the-world cruise, Evans succumbed to illness and was replaced by Rear Admiral Charles S. Sperry. Evans retired from the navy in August 1908 and wrote two volumes of memoirs. He died at Washington, D.C., on 3 January 1912.

See also CIVIL WAR, NAVAL OVERVIEW.

Further reading: Evans, Robley D. *A Sailor's Log, Recollections of Forty Years of Naval Life.* New York: D. Appleton, 1901; ———. *An Admiral's Log; Being Continued Recollections of Naval Life.* New York: D. Appleton, 1910; Falk, Edwin A. *Fighting Bob Evans.* New York: J. Cope and H. Smith, 1931. Hart, Robert A. *The Great White Fleet: Its Voyage around the World, 1907–1909.* Boston: Little, Brown, 1965.

— Benjamin J. Kaler

Ewell, Richard S. (1817–1872) *Confederate army general*

Born on 18 February 1817 at Georgetown, in the District of Columbia, Richard Stoddert Ewell graduated from the U.S. Military Academy at WEST POINT in 1840. Commissioned a second lieutenant in the 1st Dragoons, Ewell served mostly on the western frontier. He was promoted to first lieutenant in 1845 and served with distinction during the MEXICAN-AMERICAN WAR, earning a brevet for gallantry at Contreras and CHURUBUSCO. Promoted to captain in 1849, Ewell was on duty in the Southwest for the next 10 years. When Virginia seceded from the Union in April 1861, he resigned his U.S. commission and was appointed lieutenant colonel of cavalry in the Confederate service.

Wounded in June 1861 at Fairfax Courthouse, Virginia, Ewell was promoted to brigadier general that same month. He commanded a brigade in the First Battle of BULL RUN/MANASSAS. Promoted to major general in January 1862, he led a division under Major General Thomas J. "Stonewall" JACKSON in the Shenandoah Valley, participating in Confederate victories at Winchester and Cross Keys, Virginia. Ewell fought during the Battles of the SEVEN DAYS around Richmond and in the Second Battle of BULL RUN/MANASSAS, in which he lost a leg.

Following a long recovery, in May 1863 Ewell was promoted to lieutenant general and named to command the fallen "Stonewall" Jackson's old corps in the Army of Northern Virginia. After defeating a sizable Federal force at Winchester in June, Ewell's corps spearheaded General Robert E. LEE's invasion of Pennsylvania. During the first day's fighting at GETTYSBURG, Ewell's corps fought well, but it failed to capture the high ground at Cemetery Hill. The general's performance over the next two days was lackluster at best; he appeared unable to exercise the initiative that Lee expected of his corps commanders or to respond effectively to Lee's discretionary orders.

Ewell performed solidly enough in the WILDERNESS in May 1864, but his line was pierced at SPOTSYLVANIA. The strain of command and weakening health rendered Ewell ineffective, and in June Lee relieved him of corps command. Placed in charge of the Richmond defenses, he rendered valuable service. When the Confederates were forced to evacuate Richmond in April 1865, Ewell led a ragtag corps of soldiers, sailors, clerks, and convalescents toward APPOMATTOX. Forced to surrender at Sayler's Creek, he was imprisoned until July at Fort Warren in Boston.

After the war Ewell managed his wife's plantation in Maury County, Tennessee. He died there on 25 January 1872.

See also JACKSON'S SHENANDOAH VALLEY CAMPAIGN; PETERSBURG, SIEGE OF.

Further reading: Freeman, Douglas Southall. *Lee's Lieutenants: A Study in Command.* 3 vols. New York: Scribner, 1942–44; Gallagher, Gary W. *Lee and His Generals in War and Memory.* Baton Rouge: Louisiana State University Press, 1998; Pfanz, Donald C. *Richard S. Ewell: A Soldier's Life.* Chapel Hill: University of North Carolina Press, 1998.

— Roger W. Caraway

Falaise-Argentan pocket (13–19 August 1944)

World War II European theater battle and the culmination of the Allied breakout following the June 1944 Normandy invasion

Within the Falaise-Argentan pocket were 100,000 Germans in two armies, under the commander of Army Group B, Field Marshal Hans Günther von Kluge. They were surrounded by British, U.S., Canadian, and Polish troops.

The situation had begun to develop on 7 August, when the Seventh Panzer Army, backed by the Fifth Panzer Army and the Erenbach Panzer Group, launched an offensive in the wake of the Allies' Operation COBRA. Their immediate objective was the French town of Avranches. The German advance, which was halted at Mortain on 9 August, created a dangerous salient, the base of which extended roughly from Falaise in the north to Argentan in the south. Adolf Hitler ordered von Kluge to have his men press forward. However, the American First Army launched a massive counterattack against Mortain, while the First Canadian Army (with the support of Polish troops) threatened the German right flank by advancing towards Falaise from the north.

U.S. lieutenant general Omar BRADLEY, commander of Twelfth Army Group, saw an opportunity to encircle the Seventh Panzer spearhead, by linking British and U.S. forces with the Canadians and Poles along an arc from Falaise to Mortain. Lieutenant General George S. PATTON, Jr., whose U.S. Third Army was operating south of the salient, proposed to push his forces toward Argentan and link with the Canadians coming from Falaise. Patton's plan offered the possibility of encircling the entire Seventh Panzer Army.

On 11 August German forces were told to abandon Mortain; they began to retreat toward the Orne River. This order had arrived too late, however, for by then British field marshal Bernard Montgomery had issued orders for a new plan to encircle the German forces. It called for Lieutenant General Henry D. G. Crerar's Canadian First Army (Canadians and Poles) to capture Falaise and for Patton's forces to capture Alençon. The two forces would then press toward Argentan, closing the 35-mile gap separating them. In the meantime, the American First Army would keep the pressure on the Germans from Mortain and Vires. The plan also called for Lieutenant General Miles C. Dempsey's Second British Army to drive on Falaise and Argentan from the northwest.

As Allied ground forces began to carry out Montgomery's plan, unchallenged Allied fighter-bombers pressed attacks on the retreating Germans. The volume of the aerial attack increased as the gap between the Allied forces began to close, and the densely packed columns of German vehicles provided perfect targets for the bombs, rockets, and cannon fire from the Typhoons, Spitfires, and P-47 Thunderbolts. In addition to the air attacks, the Germans took artillery fire from Allied guns on three sides of the pocket. Disabled vehicles clogged the roads, and many still running had to be abandoned.

Patton advanced on Alençon and subsequently on Argentan, which was secured without much difficulty on 14 August. The Canadians and Poles, however, faced fierce opposition and advanced very slowly toward Falaise. With Argentan secured by the Americans, the neck of the pocket had narrowed to about 20 miles. Patton sought to continue, but Bradley ordered him to halt his advance on Falaise. Apparently, Bradley feared that Patton's troops would be overrun by the German divisions desperately attempting to escape encirclement. Bradley was also concerned about Canadian and American troops clashing with each other by mistake as they closed the gap.

The decision to halt Patton's advance to the north gave rise to much subsequent debate, for the delay in closing the gap allowed a significant portion of the German forces to escape. Falaise fell to the Canadians on 16 August, and Patton was finally allowed to proceed north; Crerar was ordered to move south toward Trun and then to Chambois, where his forces would link with Dempsey's army moving in from the west. The Canadians captured Trun and St-Lambert on 18 August, and the next day the Poles reached Chambois. A few narrow corridors were left open, but these became killing grounds; there the Germans sustained their heaviest losses in men and equipment. The Falaise gap was closed on 21 August; fierce attempts by the II SS Panzer Division to reopen it from the outside were futile.

It is estimated that 10,000 Germans were killed and 50,000 were captured inside the Falaise pocket. However, because of the hesitation of Allied generals Dwight D. EISENHOWER, Montgomery, and Bradley to commit resources quickly, and the courage and discipline of the Germans, approximately 100,000 Germans escaped encirclement and were able to participate thereafter in the defense of Germany. Had the gap been closed earlier, the war might have ended in 1944.

See also NORMANDY INVASION; WORLD WAR II, U.S. INVOLVEMENT, EUROPE.

Further reading: Blumenson, Martin. *The Battle of the Generals: The Untold Story of the Falaise Pocket.* New York: Morrow, Williams, 1993; Breuer, William. *Death of a Nazi Army.* New York: Madison Books, 1990; McKee, Alexander. *Caen: Anvil of Victory.* St. Martin's Press, 1984.
— Gilmar E. Visoni

Fallen Timbers, Battle of (20 August 1794)

Climactic engagement in the U.S. campaign against the Indians in the Old Northwest, 1786–94

After the American Revolution, most American Indians and Canadians sought to stop American settlement north of the Ohio River in accordance with the Treaty of Fort Stanwix of 1768. Canadian authorities retained Fort NIAGARA, Detroit, and Fort MACKINAC inside U.S. territory; their Indian Department agents supported resistance to the Americans. Meanwhile, U.S. settlers moved into this vast area and claimed Indian lands.

The Algonquin-speaking peoples of the Old Northwest now united under the leadership of Miami and Shawnee chiefs LITTLE TURTLE and BLUE JACKET. The Indians concentrated their multitribal villages along the Maumee and upper Wabash Valleys and began raiding white settlements along the Ohio River. By 1790, under Little Turtle's nominal leadership, the most formidable Indian confederacy in U.S. history had been formed. It included Miami, Shawnee, Wyandot, Delaware, Ottawa, Chippewa, Mingo, Sac, Fox, and Potawatomi, with ties to the militant Cherokee and Creek in the South.

Urged on by British Indian agents Alexander McKee, Simon Girty, and Matthew Elliott, and supported by British arms and ammunition, the Maumee-Wabash confederacy in 1790 routed an American expedition of regulars and militia being led by Brigadier General Josiah HARMAR against the largest Miami settlement, Kekionga (modern Fort Wayne, Indiana). The next fall, Major General Arthur ST. CLAIR led a second, ill-equipped and ill-trained, U.S. force, which Little Turtle's warriors forces routed in the Battle of the Wabash (near modern Fort Recovery, Ohio) on 4 November 1791.

After these defeats Congress reconstituted the army into the LEGION OF THE UNITED STATES. President George WASHINGTON selected Anthony WAYNE to command it, as a major general. Wayne rigorously trained and disciplined his troops during the next two years and in the summer of 1794 began a deliberate march northward.

The confederacy had reached its peak in 1792 and had since slowly disintegrated; intertribal rivalries and a lack of logistical support for the Indians of the upper lakes caused many to remain at home. Little Turtle correctly suspected

The Battle of the Fallen Timbers, 20 August 1794 *(Library of Congress)*

that the British would not support the confederacy militarily, even though they had built Fort Miamis at the Maumee River rapids (near modern Maumee, Ohio). Also, the Indian leadership was in disarray; Little Turtle and Blue Jacket appeared to have lost control of the confederacy's military forces.

The remaining Indians confronted Wayne's Legion and Kentucky cavalry about two miles west of Fort Miamis on a site of wind-blown, fallen trees. Wayne's well-disciplined infantry and cavalry forces attacked the outnumbered Native American center and both flanks at once, inflicting a severe defeat. The legion lost 33 dead and 140 wounded. The Indians' casualties had been light, but the British had failed to support them in the battle or offer refuge inside their post after the American victory; the disillusioned Native Americans had to concede U.S. control of lands north of the Ohio in the Treaty of Greenville in 1795. Concurrently, the Americans negotiated Jay's Treaty, which forced the British to evacuate their posts inside U.S. boundaries.

British betrayal had divided the Native Americans. The victory for the regular army helped to justify its continuation in a republic that placed great emphasis on the virtues of the militia.

See also AMERICAN INDIAN WARS, OVERVIEW; HARMAR'S EXPEDITION; INDIAN WARFARE; ST. CLAIR'S EXPEDITION.

Further reading: Carter, Harvey Lewis. *The Life and Times of Little Turtle: First Sagamore of the Wabash.* Urbana: University of Illinois Press, 1987; Dowd, Gregory Evans. *A Spirited Resistance: The North American Indian Struggle for Unity, 1745–1815.* Baltimore: Johns Hopkins University Press, 1992; Nelson, Larry L. *A Man of Distinction among Them: Alexander McKee and British-Indian Affairs along the Ohio Country Frontier, 1754–1799.* Kent, Ohio: Kent State University Press, 1999; Nelson, Paul David. *Anthony Wayne: Soldier of the Early Republic.* Bloomington: Indiana University Press, 1985. Palmer, David R. *1794: America, Its Army, and the Birth of the Nation.* Novato, Calif.: Presidio, 1994; Sugden, John. *Blue Jacket: Warrior of the Shawnees.* Lincoln: University of Nebraska Press, 2000.

— David Curtis Skaggs

Farragut, David G. (1801–1870) *U.S. Navy admiral*
Born on 5 July 1801 at Campbell's Station, Tennessee, David Glasgow Farragut became the ward of Captain David Porter after his own family moved to New Orleans. At nine Farragut entered the navy as a midshipman, and in 1811 he joined Porter aboard the frigate *Essex.* While serving in the Pacific during the WAR OF 1812 he was appointed prizemaster of a captured British warship. He was

Midshipman David G. Farragut (right). Artist unknown *(Naval Historical Foundation)*

captured during the sanguinary engagement of the ESSEX V. PHOEBE AND CHERUB in Valparaiso Harbor in March 1814. Exchanged in 1814, Farragut spent the next five years in the Mediterranean. An acting lieutenant in 1821, he engaged in pirate suppression in the Gulf of Mexico, gaining his first command, the *Ferret.* He was promoted to lieutenant in 1825.

Appointed commander in 1841, Farragut soon took command of the sloop *Decatur.* In 1847 he assumed command of the sloop *Saratoga* but was not meaningfully engaged during the MEXICAN-AMERICAN WAR. Promoted to captain in 1855, he was awaiting orders at his home in Norfolk, Virginia, at the outbreak of the Civil War.

Despite Virginia's secession, Farragut remained loyal to the Union and moved his family to New York. As a Southerner he was viewed with suspicion in some quarters and was not called to duty until September 1861. In January 1862 Farragut took command of the West Gulf Blockading Squadron, with which he moved on New Orleans.

In April Farragut ran his squadron past Forts Jackson and St. Phillip and captured NEW ORLEANS without resistance in one of the most decisive actions of the war. Promoted to rear admiral in July 1862, Farragut moved up the Mississippi River to Vicksburg before returning to operations along the Gulf coast. In March 1863 he attacked PORT HUDSON, again forcing his way up the Mississippi.

Arriving on leave in New York, Farragut received a hero's welcome. When he returned to the Gulf in 1864, he began operations against Mobile. In the Battle of MOBILE BAY on 5 August Farragut's fleet of monitors and wooden warships ran past Forts Morgan and Gaines to engage the Confederate ram *Tennessee* and win control of Mobile Bay. Farragut again returned to New York on leave, where grateful citizens presented him with $50,000 to purchase a home. Promoted to the newly created rank of vice admiral in December 1864, Farragut led naval forces on the James River. In April 1865 he was among the first Federal officers to enter Richmond.

In 1866 Farragut became the first full admiral in U.S. history. He commanded the European Squadron until 1868. Still on active duty in his 60th year of service, Farragut died on 14 August 1870 at Portsmouth, New Hampshire.

See also BUCHANAN, FRANKLIN; CIVIL WAR, NAVAL OVERVIEW; VICKSBURG CAMPAIGN.

Further reading: Hearn, Chester G. *Admiral David Glasgow Farragut: The Civil War Years.* Annapolis, Md.: Naval Institute Press, 1998; Hoehling, A. A. *Damn the Torpedoes! Naval Incidents of the Civil War.* New York: Gramercy Books, 1989.

— Roger W. Caraway

Fetterman disaster (21 December 1866) *Sioux attack on U.S. troops in the Powder River country of Dakota Territory (present-day northeastern Wyoming)*
A year after the Civil War, the regular army was struggling to reassume its place on the frontier just as it was called upon to protect a wave of postwar westward expansion. Emigrants packed the main western trails, while construction of the transcontinental railroad across the northern plains threatened the buffalo range and exacerbated an already volatile relationship with the Indians, especially the Teton (Lakota) Sioux. The Bozeman Trail, running from Fort Laramie through the Powder River country and along the Bighorn Mountains to the gold fields of Montana, posed the most immediate challenge to the Sioux.

In June 1866 the 2d Battalion of Colonel Henry B. Carrington's 18th Infantry Regiment moved up the Bozeman to establish a line of posts, reactivating Fort Reno on the Powder River. In July Carrington established Fort Phil Kearny on Piney Creek at the base of the Bighorn Moun-

tains. In August, a detachment established Fort C. F. Smith 90 miles to the northwest. The Sioux vowed to drive out the invaders.

Attacks by RED CLOUD's Oglala Sioux began in July and continued into the winter as soldiers worked on the new forts. Carrington, assured that valid peace agreements existed, was unprepared to deal with the Sioux threat. Fort Phil Kearny became the focus of Indian activity; by November Carrington had been reinforced, but his command of almost 400 officers and men was poorly armed and inexperienced. Open dissension among his officers further weakened the command. Still, pressure mounted for punitive action.

On 6 December Miniconjou and Oglala warriors attacked a wagon train carrying wood to Fort Phil Kearny, attempting to lure the soldiers into a trap. Carrington ordered a relief operation. The relieving force, under Captain William Fetterman, rescued the wood train and pursued the Indians, but the Indians turned on the soldiers along Lodge Trail Ridge, killing Lieutenant Horatio Bingham and a sergeant. Carrington, leading a converging column, was engaged in Reno Valley and failed to support the main effort. Encouraged, Sioux leaders on 19 December again attempted to lure the soldiers into a trap but Captain James Powell refused to take the bait.

On 21 December 1,500–2,000 Sioux and Cheyenne warriors mounted another effort. A decoy led by Oglala warrior CRAZY HORSE struck the wood train. Carrington ordered Fetterman to relieve the train but not to pursue the Indians over Lodge Trail Ridge. Fetterman disregarded his orders and followed the decoy over the ridge with a mixed force of infantry and cavalry and two civilians (81 men in all). The cavalry charged into the ravine where the Bozeman Trail descended from Lodge Trail Ridge; the waiting warriors struck. The fight broke down into three separate circles, but in less than an hour Fetterman and his entire command were wiped out. A second relief column found the bodies of Fetterman and his men, stripped and mutilated. Indian casualties remain unknown but were not significant.

The army rushed reinforcements to the area and established Fort Fetterman in 1867, but relentless Indian pressure forced the government to abandon Forts C. F. Smith, Phil Kearny, and Reno in 1868. That year Red Cloud signed the Fort Laramie Treaty, which brought relative, if temporary, peace.

See also AMERICAN INDIAN WARS, OVERVIEW; INDIAN WARFARE; POWDER RIVER EXPEDITION; SIOUX WARS.

Further reading: Brown, Dee. *Fort Phil Kearny: An American Saga.* New York: Putnam, 1962; Utley, Robert M. *Frontier Regulars: The United States Army and the Indian, 1866–1891.* New York: Macmillan, 1973.

— Jon B. Rhiddlehoover, Jr.

Fiske, Bradley A. (1854–1942) *U.S. Navy admiral,*
inventor, reformer, and philosopher of seapower
Born on 13 June 1854 at Lyons, New York, Bradley Allen
Allen Fiske graduated from the U.S. Naval Academy at
Annapolis in 1874. He could not look at an object or procedure without desiring to improve it. In time he became
the navy's greatest inventor. He also sought to institute progressive organizational reforms and improve graduate education for officers.

Granted a year's leave in the 1880s to study electric-
ity, Fiske wrote a textbook on the subject. As a mere lieutenant, he improved ships by electrifying their turret-turning
and ash-and-shell-hoisting gear and their steering and
engine-order telegraph mechanisms and by fitting tele-
phones. He created fire control equipment and improved
telescopes, and he invented the stadimeter, a hand-held
instrument that measures distance to an object of known
height.

As the navigator of the gunboat *Petrel* in the Battle of
MANILA BAY on 1 May 1898, Fiske used his stadimeter in
the first display of modern fire control methods. He commanded a monitor during the 1899–1902 PHILIPPINE-
AMERICAN WAR. Promoted to captain in 1912 and to rear
admiral in 1913, he served on the General Board and as
second in command of the Atlantic Fleet.

In 1913 Fiske was billeted as aide for operations to
Secretary of the Navy Josephus DANIELS. The two men
soon clashed. Fiske wanted to increase the number of ships
and personnel, create a naval general staff, and prepare
the navy for war; Daniels would not oblige. Fiske patented
a torpedo plane in 1912, believing that only aircraft could
attack fleets lying in defended harbors; Daniels refused to
develop the torpedo plane until it was too late for use during World War I (the type was to be vindicated during
World War II).

Fiske, meanwhile, went around Daniels to obtain
congressional legislation that created the office of chief of
naval operations (CNO). He was constantly irritated by
changes Daniels made, such as increasing the use of civilian instructors at the Naval Academy, his treatment of
enlisted men as members of his family, and his racism—
African Americans were allowed only to be messmen.
Fiske supported Daniels's decision to promote officers
on the basis of merit rather than seniority but disagreed
with his interference in the economic, moral, and social
aspects of the navy and objected to his neglect of
preparedness.

Daniels readily accepted Fiske's resignation in April
1915 and sent him to serve his final year at the Naval War
College in Newport, Rhode Island. Fiske retired from the
navy in June 1916. He lived his last years in New York City,
continuing his work as president of the U.S. Naval Institute
from 1912 to 1923. He wrote six books and 65 articles,
many on naval tactics and strategy. Fiske died in New York
on 6 April 1942.

See also NAVY, U.S.; SIMS, WILLIAM S.

Further reading: Coletta, Paolo E. *Admiral Bradley*
Allen Fiske and the American Navy. Lawrence: Regents
Press of Kansas, 1979; Daniels, Josephus. *The Wilson Era:*
Years of Peace, 1910–1917. Chapel Hill: University of
North Carolina Press, 1944; Fiske, Bradley A. *From Mid-*
shipman to Rear-Admiral. New York: Century, 1919.
— Paolo E. Coletta

Five Forks, Battle of (30 March–1 April 1865) *Civil*
War battle between elements of Lieutenant General
Ulysses S. Grant's Union forces and General
Robert E. Lee's Confederate army southwest
of Petersburg, Virginia
In this engagement a Federal force under the command of
Major General Philip H. SHERIDAN crushed Confederate
units sent by LEE to protect his right flank and thereby
forced Lee to abandon PETERSBURG.

In late March 1865 Ulysses S. GRANT set in motion
plans to break Lee's right flank. Grant's objective was the
crossroads of Five Forks, a point from which his troops
could move north and cut the Southside Railroad. Grant
sent Sheridan's cavalry toward Five Forks, while Major
General Gouverneur K. WARREN's V Corps advanced on
Sheridan's right to provide infantry support. Lee sent a
combined force under Major General George E. PICKETT
to block Sheridan's move and drive the Federals back to
Dinwiddie Courthouse.

On 29 March Sheridan's cavalry arrived at Dinwiddie.
That same day, Warren's infantry drove Major General
Bushrod Johnson's two Confederate divisions back to
White Oak Road. Heavy rains on 30 March delayed Union
operations, but Sheridan convinced Grant to continue the
offensive the next day.

Sheridan's cavalry moved north from Dinwiddie on 31
March, but it ran into Pickett's troops advancing south
of Five Forks. The Union cavalry, fighting mostly dismounted, managed to hold off Pickett, and the Confederates pulled back on 1 April. While Sheridan held at
Dinwiddie, Warren's V Corps drove Johnson's Confederates from their entrenchments on White Oak Road, effectively isolating Pickett's troops at Five Forks.

The Union forces were in a good position to destroy
Pickett's force on 1 April. Grant transferred the V Corps to
Sheridan's control for this goal. However, a series of confusing orders delayed the movement of the V Corps.
Although the delays were not Warren's fault, Sheridan
now looked unfavorably on the recently attached V Corps
commander.

The Union attack finally began at 4 P.M. on 1 April. The plan was simple. Sheridan's dismounted cavalry was to pressure Pickett's front while Warren's corps struck the Confederates left flank, which formed a right angle at Five Forks.

The already precarious Southern position was worsened by command mistakes. After his repulse on 31 March, Pickett positioned his force at Five Forks, but he seemed to discount the possibility of a Union attack on 1 April. He and several other leaders decided to enjoy a shad bake near their headquarters, and they failed to let their subordinates know their location.

As the struggle began, Union cavalry pinned the center of the Southern lines, but the bulk of Warren's corps missed the Confederate flank. Warren attempted to retrieve his errant units, while Sheridan and Brigadier General Joshua CHAMBERLAIN directed V Corps units into contact. Toward the evening two V Corps divisions smashed into the Confederate flank and routed the Southerners. Union cavalry joined in the attack and completed the victory. Belatedly, Pickett received news of the disaster and tried to rally his men, but it was too late to change the tide of events.

The battle was a complete Union victory. The Southerners had lost 4,000 prisoners, and their flank had been broken. In a sad footnote to the battle, Sheridan relieved Warren of command on the evening of 1 April. Sheridan deserves much credit for the Union victory, but he was probably too harsh on Warren, whose actions at Five Forks, while not spectacular, were competent. Lee's army now evacuated Petersburg in a vain attempt to reach much-needed supplies. The race to Appomottax was on.

See also CIVIL WAR, LAND OVERVIEW; CUSTER, GEORGE ARMSTRONG; MACKENZIE, RANALD S.

Further reading: Bearss, Ed, and Chris Calkins. *Battle of Five Forks.* Lynchburg, Va.: H. E. Howard, 1985; Freeman, Douglas Southall. *Gettysburg to Appomattox.* Vol. 3 of *Lee's Lieutenants: A Study in Command.* New York: Scribner, 1944; Hendrickson, Robert. *The Road to Appomattox.* New York: Wiley, 1998.

— Curtis S. King

Flaming Dart, Operation (February 1965) *Vietnam War air strikes, signaling a sustained bombing campaign against North Vietnam*

The U.S. ambassador to the Republic of Vietnam, General Maxwell TAYLOR, had for months proposed bombing North Vietnam. On 1 December 1964 the National Security Council recommended to President Lyndon JOHNSON an air interdiction campaign against the Ho Chi Minh Trail complex in Laos and the bombing of North Vietnamese targets. Johnson authorized the secret bombing of Laos, codenamed OPERATION BARREL ROLL, but he decided to delay the bombing of North Vietnam. He did not, however, rule out reprisal air strikes executed jointly by South Vietnamese and U.S. flyers.

In the early morning of 7 February 1965 Vietcong forces attacked the U.S. base at Camp Holloway and nearby Pleiku airfield in the Central Highlands of South Vietnam. The attacks killed eight U.S. service personnel, wounded 126, and destroyed or damaged 25 aircraft. It has been suggested, but never proven, that the North Vietnamese leadership ordered these attacks at this time to force from the United States a military response that would compel Soviet premier Alexei Kosygin, then visiting Hanoi, into extending greater aid.

Following the Pleiku attack, President Johnson decided on a reprisal strike to demonstrate U.S. resolve and convince the North Vietnamese that Communist forces could not launch attacks in South Vietnam without paying a heavy price. He discounted any effect on Soviet policy.

In Operation Flaming Dart, on the afternoon of 7 February, 49 A-4 Skyhawks and F-8 Crusaders aircraft from the Seventh Fleet carriers USS *Coral Sea* and *Hancock* struck barracks and staging areas at Dong Hoi, 40 miles north of the 17th parallel. At the same time Air Vice Marshal Nguyen Cao Ky led 24 South Vietnamese aircraft north, striking an unauthorized target in the Vinhlinh area—in order, he said, to avoid collisions with U.S. aircraft.

When the Viet Cong on 10 February attacked Qui Nhon, 75 miles east of Pleiku, killing 23 Americans, Johnson ordered a second series of air strikes, codenamed Flaming Dart II. Some 100 U.S. and South Vietnamese aircraft bombed the barracks and staging area at Chan Hoa and Chaple, north of the Demilitarized Zone. Three U.S. Navy aircraft were shot down; one pilot was rescued.

The sustained bombing of the North, Operation ROLLING THUNDER, scheduled to begin on 20 February, instead began on 2 March; Kosygin, who had in fact been applying pressure on the North Vietnamese leadership to avoid direct attacks on the Americans, was furious. Within two weeks Soviet surface-to-air missiles arrived in North Vietnam.

See also VIETNAM WAR.

Further reading: Clodfelter, Mark. *The Limits of Air Power: The American Bombing of North Vietnam.* New York: Free Press, 1989; Gaiduk, Ilya V. *The Soviet Union and the Vietnam War.* Chicago: Ivan R. Dee, 1996; Johnson, Lyndon Baines. *The Vantage Point: Perspectives of the Presidency, 1963–1969.* New York: Holt, Rinehart and Winston, 1971; McNamara, Robert S., with Brian VanDeMark. *In Retrospect: The Tragedy and Lessons of Vietnam.* New York: Times Books, 1995.

— Spencer C. Tucker

Fletcher, Frank Jack (1885–1973) *U.S. Navy admiral*
Born on 29 April 1885 at Marshalltown, Iowa, son of
Admiral Frank Friday Fletcher, Frank Jack Fletcher grad-
uated from the U.S. Naval Academy at Annapolis in 1906
and was commissioned an ensign in 1908. Fletcher won the
Medal of Honor for supervising the evacuation of 350
refugees from a steamer while under fire during the 1914
U.S. occupation of VERACRUZ. During World War I he
earned a Navy Cross for his command of the destroyer
Benham on antisubmarine patrol.

After the war Fletcher transferred to the Asiatic Fleet
and began a long association with the Pacific. He saw action
in the suppression of an uprising in the Philippines in 1924.
In 1930 he graduated from the Naval War College and was
promoted to captain. He graduated from the Army War
College in 1931.

After service as aide to Secretary of the Navy Claude
A. Swanson from 1933 to 1936, Fletcher served in the
Bureau of Personnel. In 1939 he was promoted to rear
admiral. At the time of the 7 December 1941 Japanese
attack on PEARL HARBOR, Fletcher was off Hawaii in command of Cruiser Division 6.

Vice Admiral Frank Jack Fletcher   *(Naval Historical
Foundation)*

Fletcher's credentials gave him prominence in the early
weeks of the Pacific War, but he soon drew criticism for
indecisiveness. Fletcher was also not an aviation officer,
and some doubted his skill in deploying carriers; however,
his defenders today claim that he acted with prudence.

Directed to relieve the marine garrison on WAKE
ISLAND, Fletcher proceded with caution, unwilling to risk
his only carrier, the *Saratoga.* He turned back when the
island fell before his arrival.

In January 1942 Fletcher formed Task Force 17,
centered on the carrier *Yorktown,* and the next month
conducted raids on the Marshall and Gilbert Islands. Promoted to vice admiral, he commanded U.S. forces during
the May Battle of the CORAL SEA, the first battle in naval
history fought entirely by airpower; during that battle the
Lexington was lost. He next commanded a three-carrier
force under Rear Admiral Raymond SPRUANCE in the June
Battle of MIDWAY; he helped to orchestrate the U.S. victory
but was criticized for abandoning the carrier *Yorktown.* As
commander of Task Force 6 with his flag in the *Saratoga,*
he oversaw the U.S. landings on GUADALCANAL but then
made a controversial decision to withdraw his carriers after
the U.S. defeat in the August Battle of SAVO ISLAND. In
December 1943 Fletcher was removed from carrier service
and assumed command of forces in the North Pacific, conducting raids and air strikes against the Kurile Islands.
After the war he oversaw the occupation of the northern
Japanese islands of Hokkaido and northern Honshu.
Fletcher then chaired the Navy's General Board. He
retired as a full admiral in May 1947 and died at Bethesda,
Maryland, on 25 April 1973.

See also WORLD WAR II, U.S. INVOLVEMENT; PACIFIC.

Further reading: Hoyt, Edwin P. *Blue Skies and Blood:
The Battle of the Coral Sea.* New York: Berkley, 1975;
Morison, Samuel Eliot. *The Two Ocean War: A Short His-
tory of the United States Navy in the Second World War.*
Boston: Little, Brown, 1963; Regan, Stephen D. *In Bitter
Tempest: The Biography of Admiral Frank Jack Fletcher.*
Ames: Iowa State University Press, 1994; Spector, Ronald
H. *Eagle against the Sun: The American War with Japan.*
New York: Vintage Books, 1985.

— John T. McNay and Spencer C. Tucker

flexible response *Military strategy, described by
        General Maxwell Taylor, pertaining to the
        development of both nuclear and conventional forces,
        subsequently adopted by President John F. Kennedy*
The term *flexible response* was popularized in TAYLOR's *The
Uncertain Trumpet,* published in 1959. A scathing critique
of President Dwight D. EISENHOWER's NEW LOOK policy,
the book discussed the internal military debates that had

raged within the Eisenhower administration and proposed a new security program that would enable the United States to compete with the Soviet Union at a time of approaching nuclear parity.

Taylor was particularly incensed about inequities in spending that had developed under Eisenhower's tenure. The army's share of total military spending had declined precipitously during the 1950s as Eisenhower shifted resources to the nuclear deterrent forces in the air force, and later the navy. Flexible response called for a new distribution of spending that would maintain and modestly expand the existing U.S. nuclear arsenal. Beyond this, however, flexible response depended upon conventional military forces that would be used in instances and in places where nuclear weapons might not produce a decisive military victory.

By supporting a substantial increase in military spending, flexible response implicitly rejected the economic principles that were the foundation of the New Look strategy. Eisenhower had argued that the U.S. economy could not sustain a level of military spending in excess of 10 percent of the gross national product; the New Look sought to achieve and maintain a stable deterrent to the Soviet Union without bankrupting the United States. By contrast, Taylor argued that the U.S. economy could easily sustain higher defense expenditures, and he specifically called for additional taxes to help pay for these increases.

Flexible response was put into practice beginning in early 1961, under President John F. KENNEDY and his Secretary of Defense, Robert S. MCNAMARA. Believing that relative nuclear parity between the two superpowers had given cover to Soviet premier Nikita Khrushchev's "wars of national liberation," Kennedy expanded conventional forces and also encouraged unconventional and counterinsurgency military forces, including army special forces and navy Sea-Air-Land (SEAL) teams.

Forces created under the guise of flexible response did not play a decisive role during the Kennedy administration, but a newly expanded army was increasingly deployed in Southeast Asia in the late stages of Kennedy's term. Flexible response was given its greatest practical test during Lyndon Baines JOHNSON's tenure as president. Constrained in the use of nuclear weapons by Soviet and Chinese threats, Johnson and Taylor prosecuted a conventional war in Vietnam, using the very forces and weapons that had been constructed for flexible response. Aircraft designed to drop nuclear weapons rained conventional bombs on Vietnam, and naval forces patrolled the waters of the South China Sea.

Flexible response was never formally abandoned as military policy, but the fallout from the Vietnam debacle prompted future presidents to attempt to constrain military spending.

See also CONTAINMENT, DOCTRINE AND COURSE; VIETNAM WAR, CAUSES OF U.S. INVOLVEMENT.

Further reading: Gaddis, John Lewis. *Strategies of Containment: A Critical Appraisal of Postwar American National Security Policy.* New York: Oxford University Press, 1982; Taylor, Maxwell. *The Uncertain Trumpet.* New York: Harper, 1959.

— Christopher A. Preble

Flipper, Henry O. (1856–1882) *Army lieutenant; the first African-American graduate of the U.S. Military Academy at West Point*

Born into slavery on 21 March 1856 at Thomasville, Georgia, Henry Osian Flipper beginning in 1866 attended a school run by the American Missionary Association. From 1869 to 1872 he attended Atlanta University. His light skin color, educational background, and financial stability all earned him appointment to the U.S. Military Academy. He entered WEST POINT in 1873 but was ostracized by his white classmates throughout his entire cadetship. White cadets spoke to him in nonduty settings on only two occasions.

Commissioned a second lieutenant on his graduation in June 1877, Flipper reported to the African-American 10th Cavalry Regiment at Fort Sill, Indian Territory (Oklahoma), in December 1878. In fall 1879 the 10th moved to Fort Elliot in the Texas Panhandle, with Flipper as post adjutant. In winter 1880 the 10th moved again, to Fort Concho near San Angelo, Texas, and then in the spring to Fort Davis in West Texas. Flipper participated in the Victorio campaign, a 1,200-mile chase of the Apache chief and his band.

Although an efficient officer, Flipper was again ostracized by his white fellow officers at Fort Davis because of his open friendship with a white woman who refused to marry another officer. The officer blamed Flipper. In August 1881 Flipper was arrested by Colonel William SHAFTER on charges of embezzling nearly $4,000 in commissary funds. Court-martialed, he was acquitted of embezzlement but convicted of conduct unbecoming an officer, and in June 1882 he was dismissed from the military.

For the next 40 years Flipper pursued a career as a civil and mining engineer and surveyor. He also served as chief engineer for the Altar Land and Colonization Company, 1890–92, and he became editor of the Nogales (Arizona) *Herald* in 1899. From 1893 to 1901 Flipper was special agent to the Court of Private Land Claims in the Department of Justice. He then joined the Balvanera Mining Company of Mexico as chief engineer, resident engineer, and chief legal adviser. Flipper repeatedly tried to get his court-martial overturned and secure reinstatement in the army. He died on 3 May 1940 in Atlanta, Georgia.

In 1976 Georgia schoolteacher Ray MacColl forced the army to reopen the case against Flipper. Its investigation concluded that Flipper was innocent. The army issued him an honorable discharge, dated 30 June 1882.

See also AFRICAN AMERICANS IN THE MILITARY; BUFFALO SOLDIERS.

Further reading: Black, Lowell D., and Sarah H. Black. *An Officer and a Gentleman: The Military Career of Lieutenant Henry O. Flipper.* Dayton, Ohio: Lora, 1985; Harris, Theodore D., ed. *Black Frontiersman: The Memoirs of Henry O. Flipper, First Black Graduate of West Point.* Fort Worth: Texas Christian University Press, 1997; Leckie, William H. *The Buffalo Soldiers: A Narrative of the Negro Cavalry in the West.* Norman: University of Oklahoma Press, 1967; Pappas, George S. *To the Point: The United States Military Academy, 1802–1902.* Westport, Conn.: Praeger, 1993.

— John J. Stewart

Florida, CSS   *Confederate commerce raider*

The steam corvette *Florida* was built at Liverpool, England. It was patterned after a Royal Navy dispatch boat but lengthened to provide more stowage space. It displaced about 700 tons and had one screw propeller. The ship was 191 feet in length and 27 feet three inches in beam. It could make 9.5 knots under steam and 12 under sail.

In January 1862 the U.S. consul at Liverpool uncovered information as to the true identity of a ship supposedly under construction for Italy, the *Oreto.* Confederate naval agent James D. Bulloch was able to get the ship to sea for Nassau on 22 March before it could be seized. Bulloch then sent out a cargo ship with its guns, ammunition, and provisions.

At Nassau, Captain John N. Maffitt took command. Some 75 miles from Nassau, at Green Key, the raider was armed and outfitted. It mounted two seven-inch and six six-inch rifled guns and a 12-pounder howitzer.

CSS *Florida* at Brest, France   *(Naval Historical Foundation)*

On 17 August the *Florida* officially went into service. With much of his crew down with yellow fever, Maffitt put into Cardenas, Cuba, for medical help. Five men died, including Maffitt's stepson, and were buried at sea; Maffitt himself was at one point near death. The *Florida* then put into Havana, where Maffitt engaged a pilot who knew the entrance to Mobile.

Keeping close to the Cuban coast, the *Florida* managed to avoid Union warships searching for it. Maffitt then made a desperate dash across the Caribbean. On 4 September, with only a skeleton crew, the *Florida* arrived off Mobile Bay and, flying a British flag, ran past Commander George Preble's squadron of three U.S. Navy ships. Although damaged by Union fire, the *Florida* reached safety in the bay.

Maffitt completed repairs to the *Florida* between October 1862 and January 1863. On 17 January, under cover of a storm, the *Florida* eluded a dozen Union Navy blockaders and escaped into the Gulf. The commerce raider then cruised the North Atlantic, taking 22 merchantmen—including two barks, the *Coquette* and *Lapwing,* which Maffitt used as tenders. The *Coquette,* taken on 6 May 1863, was renamed the *Clarence.* It in turn took six prizes before it was deliberately burned at sea on 12 June; the crew transferred to one of its prizes and a faster ship, the *Tacony,* sometimes known as the *Florida No. 2.* The new raider took 15 prizes before its crew burned it on 15 June and transferred to yet another prize, the *Archer.*

From August 1863 to February 1864 the *Florida* was laid up for repairs at Brest, France. On its second cruise it operated principally off South America, taking another 11 Union merchantmen. In two years of operations the *Florida* captured 33 Union merchant ships and caused an estimated $4,051,000 in damages. Its construction and support probably cost $400,000.

On 7 October the *Florida* was in the Brazilian port of Bahia to recoal. In that neutral port it was attacked by USS *Wachusett,* which towed it out to sea. Sent to the United States under a prize crew, *Florida* was anchored at Newport News, Virginia, where on 28 November it sank after being struck by the army transport *Alliance.*

See also CIVIL WAR, NAVAL OVERVIEW.

Further reading: Hearn, Chester G. *Gray Raiders of the Sea: How Eight Confederate Raiders Destroyed the Union's High Seas Commerce.* Baton Rouge: Louisiana State University Press, 1996; Owsley, Frank L., Jr. *The C.S.S. Florida: Her Building and Operations.* Tuscaloosa: University of Alabama Press, 1987; Shingleton, Royce. *High Seas Confederate: The Life and Times of John Newland Maffitt.* Columbia: University of South Carolina Press, 1994; Tucker, Spencer C. *A Short History of the Civil War at Sea.* Wilmington, Del.: Scholarly Resources, 2001.

— Spencer C. Tucker

Foote, Andrew H. (1806–1863) *U.S. Navy admiral*

Born on 20 June 1863 at New Haven, Connecticut, Andrew Foote briefly attended the U.S. Military Academy at WEST POINT in 1822 but resigned to accept an appointment as an acting midshipman in the navy. Foote first served in the West Indies, then in the Pacific. A religious conversion in 1827 during another Caribbean cruise led to lifelong interests in furthering Christianity and in reform. Following cruises in the Mediterranean and around the world from 1837 to 1841, Foote was executive officer at the Philadelphia Naval Asylum, a home for convalescing and disabled sailors and school for midshipmen. In 1843 he became first lieutenant of the frigate *Cumberland,* making it the first temperance ship in the navy.

From 1849 to 1851 Foote commanded the brig *Perry* in suppression of the African slave trade and took two slavers. On his return to the United States, Foote published *Africa and the American Flag* about his experiences. After five years ashore, a period that included service on the 1855 board that culled "deadwood" officers from the navy, he returned to sea as commander of the sloop *Portsmouth* in the Asia Squadron. To avenge firing by Chinese on U.S. vessels, in November 1856 Foote led a force ashore to destroy four Chinese forts guarding the river approach to Canton.

On the outbreak of the Civil War, Foote commanded the Brooklyn Navy Yard. In August 1861 Secretary of the Navy Gideon WELLES named this capable administrator to command the Union flotilla in the western theater. Foote brought Union gunboats to completion, equipped and manned them, and trained their crews.

Foote got along well with his army counterpart, Brigadier General Ulysses S. GRANT. Foote was an aggressive commander, and his flotilla took the leading role in the 6 February Union attack on FORT HENRY on the Tennessee River, securing its surrender before Grant's troops could come up. His ironclads were, however, rebuffed in the subsequent Union attack on FORT DONELSON on the Cumberland, and he himself was slightly wounded in the leg.

Foote's flotilla then participated in attacks against New Madrid and ISLAND NO. 10. After repeated pleas from Major General John POPE, Foote sent two ironclads past the Confederate forts to cut off Island No. 10 and operate in conjunction with Pope's Army of the Mississippi. The Confederates surrendered, and the flotilla and Union troops moved farther down the Mississippi to attack Fort Pillow. Foote was now exhausted and virtually immobile, his leg wound having failed to heal, and in early May he left the flotilla to recuperate.

In July 1862 Foote returned to active duty to head the Bureau of Equipment and Recruiting in Washington. One of the first Union naval officers promoted to the new rank of rear admiral, Foote was unhappy ashore. When Welles relieved Rear Admiral Samuel DU PONT as commander of the South Atlantic Blockading Squadron, Foote agreed to assume that post, though he had not sought it. He was preparing to go to Charleston when he was struck down by Bright's disease, dying in New York City on 26 June 1863.

See also CIVIL WAR, LAND OVERVIEW; CIVIL WAR, NAVAL OVERVIEW; DAHLGREN, JOHN A.; FARRAGUT, DAVID G.

Further reading: Milligan, John D. "Andrew Foote: Zealous Reformer, Administrator, Warrior." In *Captains of the Old Steam Navy. Makers of the American Naval Tradition, 1840–1880.* Edited by James C. Bradford. Annapolis, Md.: Naval Institute Press, 1986; Tucker, Spencer C. *Andrew Foote: Civil War Admiral on Western Waters.* Annapolis, Md.: Naval Institute Press, 1999.

— Spencer C. Tucker

Forbes, John (1707–1759) *British general who captured Fort Duquesne in 1758 during the 1754–63 French and Indian War*

Born on 5 September 1707 in Edinburg, Scotland, John Forbes was the son of a British army officer. Trained as a surgeon, he gave up this profession and purchased a cornetcy in July 1735 in the Second Royal North British Dragoons, the Scots Greys. He saw action in the 1740–48 War of the Austrian Succession, at Fontenoy and Laffeldt, and he helped suppress the Highland Scots at Culloden in 1746.

During this period Forbes rose steadily in rank, being promoted to captain in 1744, major a year later, and lieutenant colonel in 1750. Many of his assignments were staff positions; he served as aide-de-camp to Sir John Ligonier in 1747 and as quartermaster general to the Duke of Cumberland the following year.

In February 1757 Forbes received the colonelcy of the 17th Regiment of Foot and went to Halifax, Nova Scotia, that summer as adjutant general to Lieutenant General John Campbell, earl of Loudon. Promoted to brigadier general in December, Forbes received command of the FORT DUQUESNE expedition in March 1758. He spent the next three months in Philadelphia, assembling and provisioning a force of 7,000 men, most of whom were colonials, including Colonel George WASHINGTON.

Rather than using the road that General Edward BRADDOCK had constructed from Virginia three years earlier in his failed attempt against Duquesne, Forbes opted to cut a new one through Pennsylvania over the Appalachian Mountains. This more direct route allowed him periodically to erect blockhouses, where he could stockpile provisions and give permanence to the advance.

Leaving Carlisle in June, Forbes's army moved steadily west; the general, now terminally ill, had to be transported by litter. Advancing through Shippensburg, Bedford, and Ligonier, Forbes was one day's march from Duquesne when on 24 November the French blew up the fort and abandoned it. He occupied the site the next day and named it FORT PITT.

Forbes returned in January 1759 to Philadelphia, where he died on 11 March.

See also BOUQUET, HENRY; FRENCH AND INDIAN WAR.

Further reading: Anderson, Fred. *Crucible of War: The Seven Years' War and the Fate of Empire in British North America, 1754–1766.* New York: Knopf, 2000; James, Alfred Procter, ed. *Writings of General John Forbes Relating to his Service in North America.* Menasha, Wisc.: Collegiate Press, 1938; Nester, William R. *The First Global War: Britain, France, and the Fate of North America, 1756–1775.* Westport, Conn.: Praeger, 2000.

— Michael P. Gabriel

Forrest, Nathan Bedford (1821–1877) *Confederate general and cavalry leader*

Born on 13 July 1821 at Chapel Hill, Bedford County, Tennessee, Nathan Forrest entered military service in June 1861, enlisting as a private in the 7th Tennessee Cavalry at Memphis. That same month he was commissioned a lieutenant colonel of cavalry and was authorized to raise a battalion of mounted rangers. Successful in real estate and the slave trade prior to the war, Forrest equipped the battalion himself.

In February 1862 Forrest fought in defense of FORT DONELSON, Tennessee. Refusing to surrender his command, he led it out of the fort at night just prior to its capitulation. He then fought in the April 1862 Battle of SHILOH and was wounded. On his recovery, he led a cavalry regiment in independent operations in middle Tennessee during July–October 1862. Beginning with this campaign and for the remainder of the war, Forrest acted as an independent raider throughout western and middle Tennessee and the northern portion of Mississippi, Alabama, and Georgia, attacking Union garrisons and destroying supply and communications lines and depots. A daring raid on Murfreesboro, Tennessee, in July 1862 brought Forrest promotion to brigadier general.

Forrest often induced Union commanders to surrender their units by threatening to put entire commands to the sword. Forrest's tenacity and ruthlessness were such that the mere mention of his presence was often sufficient to force a capitulation. This was exemplified in his pursuit of Federal forces under Colonel Abel D. Streight.

Dispatched from Eastport, Mississippi, on 21 April 1863 with some 2,500 infantry mounted on mules, Streight had orders to ride across Alabama and into northern Georgia to disrupt Confederate lines of communication and destroy war supplies. General Braxton BRAGG sent Forrest to Decatur, Alabama, to halt this raid. Forrest pursued Streight for more than a week, cornering him near Rome, Georgia, on 3 May. Streight had almost 1,700 troops and Forrest less than 500, but Forrest bluffed Streight into surrendering his entire command.

Forrest performed less spectacularly when supporting major armies in large campaigns. Following Bragg's refusal to pursue Union forces after the Battle of CHICKAMAUGA, Forrest confronted him. The Confederate president, Jefferson DAVIS, granted Forrest's request for a transfer and allowed him to raise another command in western Tennessee. This brought him promotion to major general in December 1863.

Forrest raised and outfitted a new command at the expense of the Federal army, and soon he was again conducting raids. Forrest became the object of Northern propaganda following his capture of FORT PILLOW, Tennessee, on 12 April 1864, where he reportedly ordered the deaths of Federal African-American troops who had surrendered or been taken prisoner during the battle. However, battle reports and testimony from officers and men in Forrest's unit claimed that they had been killed in action. Two months later, on 12 June, Forrest defeated Union brigadier general S. D. Sturgis at Brice's Crossroads, Mississippi.

Forrest continued operations in Tennessee and Alabama, commanding the cavalry during General John B. HOOD's invasion of Tennessee in late 1864. Promoted to lieutenant general in 1865, he remained a problem for Federal authorities until his surrender at Gainesville, Alabama, on 5 May 1865.

Forrest had changed cavalry tactics forever, by using it as mounted infantry. Forrest often pushed his artillery to the front of an infantry or cavalry advance, sometimes making it the lead element. Once he gained the initiative, he refused to let go.

Following the war Forrest was influential in the rise of the Ku Klux Klan in the South and served as its first leader. He dissolved the Klan in 1869 after being summoned to Congress to testify in proceedings that accused the Klan of violent actions against African Americans across the South. (The Klan was to reemerge in 1915.) Forrest died in Memphis, Tennessee, on 29 October 1877.

See also AMERICAN CIVIL WAR, LAND OVERVIEW; SHILOH, BATTLE OF.

Further reading: Lytle, Andrew Nelson. *Bedford Forrest and His Critter Company.* Nashville: J. S. Saunders, 1993; Wyeth, John Allen. *That Devil Forrest.* New York: Harper and Row, 1959.

— John W. Downs

Forrestal, James V. (1892–1949) *Secretary of the navy and first secretary of defense*

Born on 15 February 1892 at Matteawan, New York, James Vincent Forrestal attended Dartmouth College and Princeton University, although he withdrew from the latter without graduating. In 1916 Forrestal joined the prestigious New York brokerage house of Dillon Read as a bond salesman. During World War I he served as a naval aviator, resigning in late 1918 to return to Dillon Read. There he remained throughout the 1920s and 1930s, becoming a partner and then president and a prominent and wealthy Wall Street figure.

In June 1940 Forrestal, like many other pro-Allied New York financiers and lawyers, joined the government bureaucracy, which was preparing the United States to enter the European war and to aid France and Britain against Germany. After six weeks as personal assistant to President Franklin D. ROOSEVELT, in August 1940 Forrestal became the first undersecretary of the navy, working under Frank KNOX, one of several pro-Allied Republicans whom the Roosevelt administration recruited to ensure bipartisan support for the war effort.

Forrestal's primary responsibility was procurement, a function the vast wartime expansion of the American military had made fundamental to success. From early 1942 he headed the newly created Office of Procurement and Material. Working closely with his counterpart in the War Department, Undersecretary Robert P. PATTERSON, Forrestal introduced streamlined and systematic contracting and purchasing procedures that greatly facilitated the navy's expansion from 1,099 vessels and 160,997 men in 1940 to 50,759 vessels and 3.4 million men five years later.

When Knox died suddenly in 1944, Forrestal succeeded him as secretary. Despite his expressed wish to return to private life in 1945, Forrestal remained at this post until 1947. Even before the war ended, he had strongly supported the creation of a U.S. military establishment capable of responding swiftly to any international challenge.

In the administration of President Harry S. TRUMAN, Forrestal quickly became one of the staunchest advocates of firm resistance to Soviet expansion. Convinced of the dangers of international communism, in 1946 he publicized throughout the government bureaucracy the views of George F. KENNAN, views that developed into the overarching American COLD WAR strategy known as CONTAINMENT. In 1947, still secretary of the navy, Forrestal supported American aid to Greece and Turkey, as well as the Marshall Plan for Western European economic recovery. As secretary of defense he was a dedicated advocate of the NATO security alliance between the United States and Western European countries, the revival of Germany and Japan as defense partners of the United States, and

substantial permanent increases in American military budgets and commitments.

Although Forrestal had opposed unification of the armed services, in September 1947 Truman appointed him as the first secretary of defense, in which capacity he sought to hold the balance between the three armed services. Constant interservice infighting, public criticism by influential newspaper columnists, and differences with Truman over substantial permanent increases in American military budgets (which he supported but Truman opposed) gradually wore Forrestal down. His behavior, especially his pronounced fear of communist agents, became increasingly paranoid and irrational, and in March 1949 Truman dismissed him. Admitted to Bethesda Naval Hospital for treatment for depression, on 22 May 1949 Forrestal committed suicide, jumping from a high window.

See also LOVETT, ROBERT A.; STIMSON, HENRY L.

Further reading: Albion, Robert Greenhalgh, and Robert Howe Connery, with the collaboration of Jennie Barnes Pope. *Forrestal and the Navy.* New York: Columbia University Press, 1962; Dorwart, Jeffrey M. *Eberstadt and Forrestal: A National Security Partnership, 1909–1949.* College Station: Texas A&M University Press, 1991; Hoopes, Townsend, and Douglas Brinkley. *Driven Patriot: The Life and Times of James Forrestal.* New York: Knopf, 1992; Millis, Walter, ed., with the collaboration of E. S. Duffield. *The Forrestal Diaries.* New York: Viking, 1951.

— Priscilla Roberts

Forsyth, Benjamin (1760–1814) *U.S. Army officer*

Born in 1760 in Stokes County, North Carolina, Benjamin Forsyth joined the U.S. Army in 1800 as a second lieutenant. He resigned shortly after to pursue politics, serving several terms in the state legislature. However, following the British firing on the U.S. frigate *Chesapeake* in 1807, Forsyth rejoined the army as a captain in the newly created Regiment of RIFLEMEN. This green-coated elite unit was armed with special weapons and was trained as sharpshooters.

When the War of 1812 against Great Britain commenced in June 1812, Forsyth's company became the first regular unit deployed in northern New York. From his base at SACKETT'S HARBOR, he quickly acquired a reputation as the war's foremost raider. On 21 September 1812, Forsyth's command surprised the town of Gananoque, Ontario, capturing 80 prisoners and a large amount of supplies. The following month he relocated his command to Ogdensburg, New York, astride the vital St. Lawrence River. On 6 February 1813 Forsyth successfully stormed the village of Elizabethville, taking 52 prisoners and winning promotion to lieutenant colonel.

The British considered Forsyth's advanced position a direct threat to their tenuous lines of communication, and on 22 February 1813 a force of 600 British and Canadians under Colonel George MacDonnell attacked Ogdensburg and drove the Americans out. The marksmen fought exceptionally well, inflicting 60 casualties for the loss of 20, but Forsyth was denied reinforcements by nervous superiors. He sullenly retraced his steps back to Sackett's Harbor.

In the spring of 1813 Forsyth's rifle company was chosen as the spearhead of an amphibious attack upon YORK (Toronto), Upper Canada, which was seized on 15 April 1813. The following month Forsyth fought with distinction during the capture of FORT GEORGE, and he served well during the subsequent abortive Montreal offensive. Throughout the spring and summer of 1814, Forsyth's men were stationed at PLATTSBURGH, New York, from where they conducted several successful forays against British light troops and Indians.

Forsyth's luck ran out in a heavy skirmish with superior forces on 22 June 1814. Rather than retreat as ordered and lure the British into a trap, he recklessly exposed himself to enemy fire and was killed.

Forsyth's dash, skill at ambush, and overall excellence as a light infantry leader were exemplary. He was one of few bright aspects of an otherwise dismal period of U.S. Army history. Forsyth County, North Carolina, is named in his honor.

See also CHESAPEAKE-LEOPARD AFFAIR.

Further reading: Fredriksen, John C. *Green Coats and Glory: The United States Regiment of Riflemen, 1808–1821.* Youngstown, N.Y.: Old Fort Niagara Association, 2000; Lemmon, Sarah. *Frustrated Patriots: North Carolina and the War of 1812.* Raleigh: North Carolina State Department of History and Archives, 1973.

— John C. Fredriksen

Fort Beauséjour, capture of (June 1755) *British effort during the 1754–63 French and Indian War to take French Fort Beauséjour on the west bank of the Missaquash River in French Canada*

Built in 1751 in response to the British erection of Fort Lawrence on the east bank of the Missaquash, in present-day New Brunswick, Beauséjour was a pentagonal, palisaded structure. The French used the fort as a center of activities to convince Acadians to migrate to this area away from British control and to control the Indians of the region. Captain Louis du Pont Duchambon de Vergor commanded a force of some 150 French officers and soldiers. He could also rely on local Indians and some 1,500 Acadians from surrounding villages, but he did not expect an attack, and the garrison was not prepared.

In 1754 Governor Charles Lawrence of Nova Scotia and Governor William SHIRLEY of Massachusetts conceived a plan to take Fort Beauséjour and drive the French back to the St. Lawrence River, securing the rich farmland of the area. London agreed to provide naval and military support. Ultimately the British force numbered some 2,250 men, 2,000 of them provincials and the remainder British regulars. British colonel Robert Monckton and American major general John Winslow had command.

On 2 June the invasion force set out from Boston, sailing to Halifax and then on to Fort Lawrence. The expedition arrived at Fort Beauséjour on 4 June and began siege operations. During the next several days the British worked their way closer to the French fort; on 14 June they opened fire on Beauséjour with mortars. On 16 June a British shell exploded in a casemate, killing six French officers. The next day the French surrendered. The British took some 450 prisoners, a third of whom were the French regulars. The British then renamed the post Fort Cumberland, for the duke of Cumberland.

This small battle removed French support for the Acadians and their Indian allies in this region. It also led directly to the now-infamous destruction of key French villages and removal of Acadian farm families. In October, in one of the first forced deportations of a civilian population as a security risk in modern history, the British forcibly removed the Acadians and shipped them to England and the mainland colonies.

See also FRENCH AND INDIAN WAR.

Further reading: Anderson, Fred. *Crucible of War: The Seven Years' War and the Fate of Empire in British North American, 1754–1766.* New York: Knopf, 2000; Ferling, John. *Struggle for a Continent: The Wars of Early America.* Arlington Heights, Ill.: Harlan Davidson, 1993; Frégault, Guy. *Canada: The War of the Conquest.* Translated by Margaret M. Cameron. Toronto: Oxford University Press, 1969.

— J. G. D. Babb and Spencer C. Tucker

Fort Dearborn, massacre at (15 August 1812) *Site of U.S. defeat and massacre in the early months of the War of 1812*

Fort Dearborn was an isolated post built in 1803 on the bank of the Chicago River and Lake Michigan under the direction of Captain John Whistler. Named after Secretary of War Henry DEARBORN, it served as a trading post for Great Lakes merchants. The fort had two blockhouses and a 12-foot-tall stockade that surrounded a barracks, hospital, magazine, and officer's and commandants quarters.

Captain Nathan Heald commanded the fort, which was garrisoned by a company of the 1st U.S. Infantry Regiment and some militia. Several soldiers' families added to the population, which totaled about 100 people. After the fall of FORT MACKINAC on 25 July, Brigadier General William HULL, commander of the Northwestern Army in DETROIT, anticipating further British and Indian attacks, ordered Heald to evacuate Fort Dearborn quickly and move to Fort Wayne, Indiana.

Emboldened by the British victory at Mackinac, the Potawatomi Indians had already begun to make threatening gestures. To ensure their goodwill, Heald offered them surplus public clothing and nonmilitary goods in return for their promise not to interfere with his movement. Heald destroyed all excess whiskey and small arms, which struck the Indians as a sign of mistrust. On 14 August William WELLS, Indian agent at Fort Wayne, arrived with some Miami Indians to reinforce the fort and provide an escort for the march.

The long-delayed march, now widely known to the Indians, began on 15 August. The column was less than two miles from the fort along the shore of Lake Michigan when more than 400 Potawatomi warriors ambushed it. Heald ordered his soldiers to counterattack to keep the Indians off the beach, and a fierce firefight ensued. Some Indians managed to make their way to the baggage train, where they quickly killed several women and children. A few civilians, including Heald's wife, made their way to safety with the help of friendly Indians.

The Indians demanded that Heald surrender, and he complied but only upon receiving assurance that there would be no further slaughter. The promise meant nothing, particularly for those already wounded. In the end 53 whites, including soldiers and dependents, were killed. Others were taken prisoner and ultimately ransomed. Fort Dearborn was burned, yet another lost strategic position in a series of U.S. defeats that included Mackinac and Detroit. All of Michigan had been surrendered, and the entire northwest frontier lay in the hands of the British and their Indian allies, as it would until 1813.

See also INDIAN WARFARE; WAR OF 1812, LAND OVERVIEW.

Further reading: Kinzie, John. "John Kinzie's Narrative of the Fort Dearborn Massacre." *Journal of the Illinois State Historical Society* 48 (Winter 1953): 343–62; Musham, H. A. "Where Did the Battle of Chicago Take Place?" *Journal of the Illinois State Historical Society* 36 (March 1943): 21–40; Quimby, Robert S. *The U.S. Army in the War of 1812: An Operational and Command Study.* East Lansing: Michigan State University Press, 1997.

— Steven J. Rauch

Fort Donelson, Battle of (12–16 February 1862)
Important Confederate fort on the Cumberland River in Tennessee captured by Federal forces during the Civil War

After Kentucky failed to join the Confederacy in 1861, the Confederate theater commander, General Albert Sidney JOHNSTON, established a line centered on FORT HENRY, on the Tennessee River, and on Fort Donelson, nearby on the Cumberland. They were designed to block Federal forces attempting to invade Tennessee by water. On 6 February 1862, Federal naval forces, including ironclad gunboats, under Flag Officer Andrew Hull FOOTE took the surrender of FORT HENRY. Foote then repositioned his squadron to the Cumberland, while troops under Brigadier General Ulysses S. GRANT prepared to move east by land against Fort Donelson. Heavy rains delayed this movement, but on 12 February Union land elements neared Donelson.

In order to buy time for the garrisons that were withdrawing from Bowling Green, Kentucky, and Columbus, Missouri, General Johnston reinforced Donelson, which now came under the command of Brigadier General John B. Floyd, assisted by Brigadier Generals Gideon J. PILLOW and Simon B. BUCKNER.

On the 14th, while Grant built up his forces to contain the Confederates at Donelson by land, Foote attacked the fort's well-positioned river defenses. The latter were on high ground, and their plunging shot struck the sloping sides of the Union gunboats damagingly at right angles. The gunboats got the worst of the exchange, and Foote himself was wounded.

On the night of 14 February, Floyd called a council of war. He and his subordinates held out little hope for a successful defense and concluded they would try the next day to break out and retreat to Nashville. The Confederates struck early on 15 February, while Grant was away conferring with Foote. The attack proved surprisingly successful, rolling up the Union right flank and opening up an escape route toward Clarksville. However, Floyd vacillated, and Pillow became convinced that he could defeat the entire Union force rather than merely hold open an escape corridor. Meanwhile, Grant arrived and rallied the Union forces. Concluding that the Confederates must have weakened their right flank, he ordered Brigadier General Charles F. Smith to assault there. The attack carried into Fort Donelson itself, rendering the Confederate situation hopeless.

That night the three Confederate generals again conferred. Floyd and Pillow, unwilling to go into captivity, escaped across the Cumberland with some 3,000 troops. The cavalry commander, Lieutenant Colonel Nathan B. FORREST, also refused to surrender and managed to slip out with a number of cavalrymen across flooded ground near the river.

On the morning of 16 February, Buckner asked for terms. Grant responded by saying that he would only accept only unconditional surrender, and Buckner had no choice but to comply. Grant secured more than 14,000 prisoners and some 57 guns as well as a considerable amount of supplies. This first major Union victory of the war opened up much of central Tennessee to Federal forces. Had the troops lost to the Confederacy at Donelson been available to him later at SHILOH, in early April, Johnston might have defeated Grant, and the war might have taken a different turn.

See also CIVIL WAR, LAND OVERVIEW.

Further reading: Cooling, Benjamin F. *Forts Henry and Donelson: The Key to the Confederate Heartland.* Knoxville: University of Tennessee Press, 1987; Tucker, Spencer C. *Andrew Foote: Civil War Admiral on Western Waters.* Annapolis, Md.: Naval Institute Press, 2000; ———. *Unconditional Surrender. The Capture of Forts Henry and Donelson.* Abilene, Tex.: McWhiney Foundation Press, 2001.

— John W. Mountcastle

Fort Drum   *A coastal defense structure constructed in 1913 as a major unit in the Manila Harbor defenses* Fort Drum included powerful fortifications on CORREGIDOR Island and other batteries on Carabao and Caballo Islands. Its unique warshiplike shape was dictated by the shape of the narrow island, which was cut down to below water level to provide a foundation for the fortification. The structure, 350 feet by 144 feet, was built entirely of poured concrete, with walls no less than 20 feet thick and a deck 18 feet thick. Fort Drum's dreadnoughtlike appearance soon earned it the nickname of "the Army's concrete battleship."

Fort Drum was armed with four Model 1909 14-inch naval rifles in two armored turrets, mounted in a superfiring configuration. Secondary armament consisted of four six-inch rifles in two double-decked armored casements. The fort's armament was fired only once (after its initial trials), in 1923, before it was placed in caretaker status, where it remained until the Japanese invasion of the Philippines in December 1941.

The first Japanese bombardment knocked out the fort's ventilator, and temperatures soon soared to and remained at about 100 degrees Fahrenheit. Water was strictly rationed, and the defenders also were put on half-rations. The fort's main weakness lay in its supply of fuel oil, which powered all of its machinery.

Nonetheless, Fort Drum remained a formidable fighting unit from 6 February 1942 when its heavy guns opened fire until the American capitulation on 5 May. Its main battery devastated a Japanese tank park and on one occasion killed no fewer than 3,000 Japanese troops massing for the final assault on Corregidor Island. For months its guns were the heaviest weapons engaging America's enemies on any front. Yet the fort itself remained basically unscathed, despite its bombardment by Japanese 240-mm howitzers, throwing 400-pound shells. It seemed to shake off the pounding. Aside from tossing large chunks of concrete into the air, the Japanese bombardment only slightly injured one man.

Fort Drum also harassed the Japanese final assault on Corregidor, but with the fall of that headquarters and main fortified island, it was ordered to surrender. Some of the garrison were reluctant to do so and considered fighting to the end. But low fuel supplies meant that the guns could have only been turned by hand, a process that would take hours for each shot. So the garrison did its best to make the fort unusable to the Japanese.

The great guns of the fort were never used against Americans, but Fort Drum had to be retaken by the returning Americans in early April 1945. The Japanese garrison rejected a surrender-or-die ultimatum and was burned alive or blown to pieces by a hellish mixture of fuel oil and napalm pumped into the fort and then ignited. None survived.

Fort Drum survives to this day, derelict and battered, but as imperishable as the pyramids of Egypt.

See also BATAAN, RETREAT TO AND SIEGE OF; PHILIPPINES, LOSS OF; PHILIPPINES, RETAKING OF; WAINWRIGHT, JONATHAN M.

Further reading: Belote, J. H., and W. H. Belote. *Corregidor, Saga of a Fortress.* New York: Harper, 1967; Kingman, J. J. "The Genesis of Fort Drum, Manila Bay." *Military Engineer* (April 1945); Sandler, Stanley. "Fort Drum." *Military History Quarterly* 12, no. 2 (Winter 2000).

— Stanley Sandler

Fort Duquesne, expedition of 1755   (June–July 1755)   *Disastrous attempt during the French and Indian War by British forces to capture Fort Duquesne* Fort Duquesne was the key French post in the Ohio country, and an attempt to seize it was part of Britain's 1755 campaign to evict the French from British-claimed territory in North America.

Seeking to secure the Ohio territory and hamper British expansion, in 1754 France had constructed Fort Duquesne at the confluence of the Ohio, Monongahela, and Allegheny Rivers. The French presence in British-claimed territory, coupled with their defeat of Lieutenant Colonel George WASHINGTON's forces at FORT NECESSITY in July 1754, spurred the British ministry to devise a scheme to reassert British sovereignty over the region and check French territorial aspirations. While other forces attacked FORT NIAGARA, CROWN POINT, and FORT

BEAUSÉJOUR, Major General Edward BRADDOCK would lead an army of regulars and provincials to take Fort Duquesne and other French posts in the Ohio.

Accompanied by the 44th and 48th Regiments of Foot, Braddock arrived in Virginia in spring 1755. He intended immediately to embark on his campaign. Instead, he encountered vicious political squabbles between colonial assemblies and their governors and between key governors. He also had great difficulty in manning, arming, and supplying four disparate expeditions. Only after threats and the intercession of Benjamin Franklin were the colonials forthcoming with material support. However, colonial intrigue and Braddock's low opinion of Indians left him with fewer than 10 Indian auxiliaries—a fatal omission.

Braddock's army of 2,200 men departed Fort Cumberland, Maryland, in early June 1755. Besides the two regiments from Ireland, three independent companies of regulars, 600 provincials, and numerous pioneers and artillerymen marched with Braddock, along with a lengthy column of wagons and siege artillery. One hundred twenty miles of harsh landscape lay between the army and its objective. Washington's force had cut a nominal road for part of the route in 1754, but pioneers had to widen and grade it to accommodate the wagons and artillery. Progress was therefore slow, and after a week the army had advanced only 35 miles. Accordingly, Braddock formed a "flying column" of 1,400 troops and pressed ahead of the main body.

On 9 July the flying column crossed the Monongahela River, 10 miles from Duquesne. Realizing that he could not withstand a siege, the French commander, Captain de Contrecoeur, sent 250 French regulars and militia and more than 600 Indians to ambush the English. In the resulting Battle of the MONONGAHELA, the British left two-thirds of their number lying dead and wounded. Braddock was among those killed. The survivors rendezvoused with the second division two days later. Colonel Thomas Dunbar, Braddock's successor, panicked; he ordered all supplies destroyed and marched his regulars into winter quarters at Philadelphia.

Suffering only 23 dead and 16 wounded, the French and Indian force had inflicted a stunning defeat on the British. The French ensured their dominance of the Ohio for another three years and secured the loyalty of the Ohio Indians. Furthermore, the shock of defeat and the subsequent border raids caused a full-scale flight of English settlers from the Pennsylvania/Virginia backcountry. Finally, Governor William SHIRLEY assumed the mantle of commander in chief, and his cautious leadership guaranteed little action for the remainder of 1755.

See also FRENCH AND INDIAN WAR.

Further reading: Anderson, Fred. *Crucible of War: The Seven Years' War and the Fate of Empire in British North America, 1754–1766.* New York: Knopf, 2000.

Hamilton, Charles, ed. *Braddock's Defeat: The Journal of Captain Robert Chomley's Batman; The Journal of a British Officer; Halkett's Orderly Book.* Norman: University of Oklahoma Press, 1959; Kopperman, Paul E. *Braddock at the Monongahela.* Pittsburgh: University of Pittsburgh Press, 1977; Pargellis, Stanley. "Braddock's Defeat." *American Historical Review* 61 (October 1935–July 1936): 253–69.

— David M. Corlett

Fort Duquesne, expedition of 1758 (July–November 1758) *Campaign of the French and Indian War*

In 1758 the war that would come to be known in Europe as the Seven Years' War (1756–63) and in America as the FRENCH AND INDIAN WAR (1754–63) remained inconclusive. British prime minister William Pitt believed that Britain's future depended upon the preservation and growth of the empire. He sought to preserve the colonies and break French power in America.

English disasters in America between 1755 and 1757 encouraged Pitt to develop a new strategic concept to achieve his major objective—the conquest of Canada. His grand strategy was to attack Canada in a two-pronged effort, with Quebec as the final objective. The plan called for an attack from the east by way of Nova Scotia and one from the south by way of the British colonies and the Ohio River. The latter, along the western frontier to the Ohio River, would undermine the French position and prevent its garrisons there from rushing north to defend the St. Lawrence Valley. Fort Duquesne was the principal objective of the southern offensive. Pitt chose as commander for this operation Brigadier General John FORBES.

Forbes assembled his force in Philadelphia around a strong nucleus of 1,600 regulars, centered on the Highland Regiment. Swiss colonel Henry BOUQUET commanded four companies of ROYAL AMERICANS. Pennsylvania provided 2,700 men, while Virginia contributed Colonel George WASHINGTON and 2,600 men. Forbes had a low opinion of the colonial contingents, styling them a collection of "broken innkeepers, horse jockeys and Indian traders—a gathering from the scum of the worst of people."

The Indians were a problem. Their unpredictability tempted Forbes to reject their assistance, but he desperately needed them as scouts. He knew what the absence of these auxiliary warriors had meant to Major General Edward BRADDOCK three years earlier. To forge an alliance of the eastern Indian tribes and keep the western tribes from providing support to the French, Forbes sent out a Moravian missionary, Christian Post, with an invitation to the eastern Indians to meet with the western Indians at a conference at Easton, Pennsylvania.

Forbes also had to determine the most effective route to his objective. He would need to construct a new road through the wilderness for heavy supply wagons, and Virginia and Pennsylvania each wanted the road on its land. Forbes initially intended to use Braddock's previous route, by way of Fort Cumberland, Maryland. Later he was persuaded to alter this plan and proceed west across the Pennsylvania mountains.

The final stages of the campaign favored the British. Influenced by a treaty negotiated at Easton as well as approaching British military strength, most of the Ohio Valley Indians moved away from Fort Duquesne. During the march Forbes's troops were well deployed to guard against any repetition of the disaster that had befallen Braddock three years earlier on the MONONGAHELA River.

On 25 November the three British brigades emerged from the forests at the confluence of the Allegheny and Monongahela Rivers, where Fort Duquesne had stood. There remained only a cluster of blackened chimney stacks and charred ruins. The French had destroyed Duquesne, dumped its cannon in the river, and departed. For the first time since May 1754, the Ohio River was controlled by the British. Forbes promptly renamed the ruins FORT PITT and commenced reconstruction.

Further reading: Bouquet, Henry. *The Papers of Henry Bouquet.* Vol. 2, *The Forbes Expedition.* Edited by Sylvester K. Stevens, Donald H. Kent, and Autumn L. Leanard. Harrisburg: Pennsylvania Historical and Museum Commission, 1951; Leach, Douglas E. *Arms for Empire: The Military History of the British Colonies in North America, 1607–1763.* New York: Macmillan, 1973; Parkman, Francis. *Montcalm and Wolfe.* Vol. 2. Boston: Little, Brown, 1899.

— D. Randall Beirne

Fort Erie (1812–1814) *Key Canadian fort during the War of 1812*
Located at the point where the Niagara River enters Lake Erie, Fort Erie guarded one of the major invasion routes from the United States into Upper Canada. The fort was never strongly held; at any given time only a few hundred British soldiers formed its garrison.

Constructed across the Niagara River from Black Rock and Buffalo, New York, Fort Erie was never considered a major objective of invading U.S. forces. On 9 October 1812, U.S. forces led by Navy Lieutenant Jesse D. Elliott surprised the British at Fort Erie and seized two vessels, the *Detroit* and *Caledonia,* from under its guns. In the fight that followed, the *Detroit* was burned.

In May 1813 elements of Major General Henry DEARBORN's army, led by Colonel Winfield SCOTT and Master Commandant Oliver Hazard PERRY, landed near FORT GEORGE, forcing the British to evacuate Fort Erie. After PERRY's victory in the Battle of LAKE ERIE, U.S. forces advancing into Canada occupied Fort Erie without a fight. However, after the subsequent U.S. Army retreat across the Niagara River that fall, British forces reoccupied Fort Erie.

The following year, the Left Division, under Major General Jacob BROWN, took Fort Erie on 3 July 1814, after the British fired a few shots for honor's sake. Brown continued his advance and defeated the British in the battles of CHIPPEWA and LUNDY'S LANE but withdrew to the fort at the end of July. Ordering his men to enlarge and strengthen the fort, Brown, who had been severely wounded, on 4 August turned over command to Major General Edmund P. GAINES.

Gaines transformed Fort Erie into a fortified camp 800 yards long, protected by ditches and earthworks and 18 guns. Unable to mount a long siege, the British commander, Lieutenant General Sir Gordon Drummond, ordered an assault on the fort on 14 August, but he was repulsed with heavy losses. When GAINES was wounded on 28 August, BROWN retook command and broke the siege with a sortie on 17 September. The British withdrew four days later when Brigadier General George IZARD advanced in relief.

Izard advanced north to the Chippewa River but, unwilling to attack the remaining British forces under Drummond, returned to Fort Erie on 19 October. U.S. forces blew up Fort Erie on 5 November 1814, then returned to Buffalo to go into winter quarters.

See also REGIMENT OF RIFLEMEN; WAR OF 1812, LAND OVERVIEW.

Further reading: Barton, Pierce. *Flames across the Border.* Toronto: Penguin, 1980; Hickey, Donald R. *The War of 1812: A Forgotten Conflict.* Urbana: University of Illinois Press, 1989. Mahon, John K. *The War of 1812.* Gainesville: University of Florida Press, 1972; Morris, John D. *Sword of the Border: Major General Jacob Jennings Brown, 1775–1828.* Kent, Ohio: Kent State University Press, 2000.

— J. W. Thacker

Fort Fisher, attack on (13–15 January 1865) *Union assault during the Civil War*
In late December 1864 a Federal expedition under Major General Benjamin F. BUTLER failed in its effort to drive Confederate forces from Fort Fisher and close the key blockade-running port of Wilmington, North Carolina. By this point in the war, General Robert E. LEE's Confederate Army of Northern Virginia largely depended on supplies brought in through Wilmington; thus the capture of Fort Fisher took on special strategic significance.

The Union assault on Fort Fisher, 15 January 1865. Painting by Lewis Prang   *(Library of Congress)*

Following Butler's subsequent relief from command, Brigadier General Alfred H. TERRY, a former Connecticut attorney with considerable experience in combined operations, took charge of the land forces involved in the effort. Terry's command numbered 8,000 men—essentially the same troops involved in Butler's December debacle, with the addition of two brigades of African-American soldiers intended to offset expected Confederate reinforcements. Terry and his men sailed from Virginia on 4 January 1865, their destination sealed orders that the commander was not to open until at sea. The army contingent of the assault force rendezvoused off Beaufort, North Carolina, with a powerful naval squadron led by Rear Admiral David Dixon PORTER and arrived at Fort Fisher on 12 January, having been delayed by bad weather.

The small Confederate garrison, commanded by Colonel William Lamb, soon received reinforcements led by Major General William H. C. Whiting, but it still numbered less than 2,000 men. Two days of intense bombardment by Porter's fleet killed and wounded several hundred troops of the garrison and silenced most of the defending

artillery. The naval guns fired more than 1.6 million pounds of shells during this prolonged engagement, more than had ever been fired at a single target in history. Meanwhile, Terry's men landed unopposed and established a beachhead. Once ashore, they fortified their position in anticipation of the arrival of Confederate reinforcements from Major General Robert Hoke's veteran division, north of the fort. The department commander, General Braxton BRAGG, failed to give the necessary orders, however, and Hoke's men did not move to reinforce the besieged Fort Fisher garrison.

On 15 January, beginning at about 3 P.M., Federal forces launched a full-scale assault on the fort. Covered by a renewed naval bombardment and the fire of army sharpshooters, 4,000 troops, many of whom had to wade through waist-deep swamp water to reach their target, stormed the fort from the west. This force consisted of three brigades, commanded respectively by Colonels Galusha Pennypacker, Newton M. Curtis, and Louis Bell. Terry's remaining men guarded their lines against the possible arrival of Hoke's division. At the same time, a force of

2,000 volunteer sailors and marines led by Commander K. R. Breese attacked Fort Fisher from the northeast. These troops, armed largely with only swords and pistols and unused to combat on land, were repulsed with heavy losses before reaching the walls of the fort.

The army forces, however, breached the fort's defenses, aided by the diversion of the garrison's attention by the bombardment and the unsuccessful attack by Breese's men. Axe-wielding soldiers literally hacked their way into the fort. Once inside, the Federals engaged in hand-to-hand combat. The Confederates had constructed extensive earthworks within the outer wall of the fort, and the attackers therefore had to drive the defenders from a series of tenaciously held positions. Both Colonel Lamb and General Whiting were wounded severely during this engagement; Whiting subsequently died of his wounds. Among the attackers, Colonel Bell was killed, and Curtis and Pennypacker were both wounded. A Federal brigade under Colonel Joseph C. Abbott reinforced the attacking forces at about 9 P.M.

The fighting raged within Fort Fisher for nearly seven hours, ending at about 10 P.M. with the surrender of the Confederate survivors. The defenders had suffered about 500 casualties, not including prisoners; Union losses totaled nearly 1,500—a figure that rose unexpectedly with the accidental explosion of 13,000 pounds of gunpowder on 16 January, resulting in more than 100 casualties.

Fort Fisher's capture closed a crucial port, reduced the already meager flow of supplies to Lee's army, and opened Wilmington and the interior of North Carolina to Federal invasion.

See also AFRICAN AMERICANS IN THE MILITARY; CIVIL WAR, NAVAL OVERVIEW.

Further reading: Gregg, Rod. *Confederate Goliath: The Battle of Fort Fisher.* New York: Harper and Row, 1991; Robinson, Charles M., III. *Hurricane of Fire: The Union Assault on Fort Fisher.* Annapolis, Md.: Naval Institute Press, 1998.

— Michael Thomas Smith

Fort Frontenac, destruction of (27 August 1758)

Key French fortification on Lake Ontario, destroyed by the British during the French and Indian War
Strategically located where the Cataraqui River enters Lake Ontario and Lake Ontario empties into the St. Lawrence River, Fort Frontenac secured the line of communication between Quebec and all of the French western forts.

Supervising the supply of FORT OSWEGO in 1755, British lieutenant colonel John Bradstreet recognized Fort Frontenac's strategic importance. For the next three years he continually advised his superiors to attack and destroy the fortress. By 1758, the commander of British forces in

North America, Lieutenant General John Campbell, earl of Loudon, had agreed to Bradstreet's proposal. At a meeting in Hartford, Connecticut, with British colonial governors on 23–24 February, Loudown outlined an ambitious strategy of attacks on LOUISBOURG, Fort Carillon (TICONDEROGA), Fort Frontenac, and FORT DUQUESNE.

Major General James Abercrombie (Abercomby), who replaced Loudon in March 1758, initially canceled the attack on Fort Frontenac in order to concentrate his forces on Fort Carillon. After Abercrombie lost the Battle of TICONDEROGA (8 July 1858), Bradstreet convinced him to authorize the Fort Frontenac expedition, at least nominally under Brigadier General John Stanwix; Bradstreet was second in command and effectively in charge.

With 5,400 militia and 200 regulars, Bradstreet moved quickly, in hopes of catching the French off guard. Setting out on 13 July from Schenectady, Bradstreet reached the portage between the Mohawk River and Wood Creek in mid-August. He left part of his force to begin construction of a fort there (the future FORT STANWIX) and proceeded with the remaining 3,100. On 21 August he arrived at the site of Fort Oswego, which had been destroyed in August 1756. During the next four days, Bradstreet's force traveled by bateaux to Fort Frontenac.

On 26 August Bradstreet landed his siege guns and moved them to within 150 yards of the fort. Bradstreet expected heavy resistance, but Major Pierre-Jacques Payen de Noyan surrendered on the morning of 27 August, just a few hours after Bradstreet commenced firing. Noyan's superiors had stripped Fort Frontenac of its garrison in order to reinforce Fort Carillon, leaving him only 110 soldiers, a force capable of manning just 12 of the fort's 60 guns. In addition to the fort and its massive amount of supplies, Bradstreet captured all nine of the French sloops on Lake Ontario.

Fearing that French reinforcements could arrive at any time, Bradstreet transferred such supplies as he could to two of the sloops, then destroyed the fort and everything else before departing on 28 August. To keep from being slowed down by prisoners, Bradstreet allowed Noyan to evacuate his men and their families to Montreal on condition that he secure the release of a similar number of British prisoners. The destruction of Fort Frontenac not only deprived the French of irreplaceable supplies but greatly weakened their hold on all their western forts.

See also FRENCH AND INDIAN WAR.

Further reading: Anderson, Fred. *Crucible of War: The Seven Years' War and the Fate of Empire in British North America, 1754–1766.* New York: Knopf, 2000; Eccles, W. J. *France in America.* Rev. ed. Markham, Ont.: Fitzhenry & Whiteside, 1990.

— Justin D. Murphy

Fort George, capture of (27 May 1813) *War of 1812*
U.S. amphibious assault against a British fort
in Canada
In May 1813, Major General Henry DEARBORN, ably assisted by Colonel Winfield SCOTT, massed 4,700 American troops near FORT NIAGARA. Dearborn planned to capture Fort George, near the mouth of the Niagara River, and drive the British from the Niagara Peninsula.

On 25 May American artillery pounded Fort George to divert its garrison from the real attack. At 4 A.M. on the 27th, Dearborn's troops embarked on Commodore Isaac CHAUNCEY's Lake Ontario fleet, sailed west, and landed behind the fort. Scott led the initial 800-man assault, assisted by sharpshooters under Captain Benjamin FORSYTH. British brigadier general John Vincent and 1,300 regulars and militia met the attack on the shore. Superior American numbers and heavy naval gunfire soon overwhelmed the defenders, who retreated, abandoning Fort George. Scott, injured when one of the fort's magazines exploded, pursued the British for five miles but was then ordered to halt by Dearborn. Consequently the Americans failed to capture the main body, which was to fight again at STONY CREEK in June.

In the battle the British lost 108 killed, 163 wounded, and 115 captured. An additional 507 Canadian militia were captured and paroled. The Americans sustained 39 killed and 111 wounded.

See also PERRY, OLIVER HAZARD; WAR OF 1812, LAND OVERVIEW; WAR OF 1812, NAVAL OVERVIEW.

Further reading: Johnson, Timothy D. *Winfield Scott: The Quest for Military Glory.* Lawrence: University of Kansas Press, 1998; Quimby, Robert S. *The U.S. Army in the War of 1812; An Operational and Command Study.* East Lansing: Michigan State University Press, 1997.
— Michael P. Gabriel

Fort Henry, attack on (6 February 1862)
Confederate fort on the Tennessee River captured
by Federal naval forces
The Confederate defenders of Tennessee established Fort Henry on the Tennessee River in 1861 as a means of blocking Union movement southward along the river from Kentucky into Tennessee.

On 1 February 1862, Brigadier General Ulysses S. GRANT and Flag Officer Andrew H. FOOTE began a campaign to capture Fort Henry. The troops moved southward on the Tennessee River in transports protected by Foote's

Flag Officer Andrew H. Foote's gunboats attacking Fort Henry, 6 February 1862   *(Library of Congress)*

gunboats. Grant's tactical plan was to ensure that all routes of withdrawal of Confederate troops from Fort Henry were sealed by his troops when the Union ships began their attack on the fort.

The Union plan might have succeeded in killing or capturing a large percentage of the original Confederate garrison of some 2,000 men had the Rebels attempted to hold Fort Henry or had the Union columns moved more swiftly. However, Confederate brigadier general Lloyd Tilghman determined that Henry could not be held against the 17,000-man Union force and gunboats; he directed that it be evacuated. The troops from Forts Henry and a nearby earthwork named Fort Heiman retreated eastward to FORT DONELSON, a larger and better-sited Confederate fort about 12 miles away on the Cumberland River.

Having seen his troops safely on their way to Donelson, Tilghman held Fort Henry with only a skeleton force of 70 men, most of them artillerymen, and awaited the Union attack. The Union naval assault began at 11:45 A.M. on 6 February. Although Fort Henry had been built on such low ground that some of the gun positions occasionally were flooded, the small garrison held out for two hours, firing as rapidly as it could at the approaching Union naval forces. Despite losing two of their most effective cannon to accidental explosions, the defenders succeeded in hitting the Union gunboats and damaging one of them. The gunboat *Essex* had a number of crewmen scalded when a Confederate shot pierced its boiler, releasing clouds of steam.

Finally, with most of his guns disabled, Tilghman surrendered Fort Henry to Commodore Foote. It shortly before 2 P.M., and the Union troops had yet to arrive because recent heavy rains had made the roads muddy. The seizure of Fort Henry opened the Tennessee River to Union traffic to Muscle Shoals, Alabama, and also provided a base for the subsequent Union attack upon FORT DONELSON.

See also CIVIL WAR, LAND OVERVIEW.

Further reading: Cooling, Benjamin F. *Forts Henry and Donelson: The Key to the Confederate Heartland.* Knoxville: University of Tennessee Press, 1987; Tucker, Spencer C. *Andrew Foote: Civil War Admiral on Western Waters.* Annapolis, Md.: Naval Institute Press, 2000; ———. *Unconditional Surrender. The Capture of Forts Henry and Donelson.* Abilene, Tex.: McWhiney Foundation Press, 2001.

— Matthew B. Brady and John W. Mountcastle

Fort Lee (20 November 1776) *Revolutionary War fort*
After the British withdrawal from Boston in March 1776, General George WASHINGTON moved to defend New York City and the Hudson River Valley. The British comman-

der, Major General William Howe, planned to seize the city and the Hudson River, separating New England from the remainder of the colonies.

To meet the British threat, Washington ordered fortifications constructed around New York City and along the Hudson. To protect the river, two forts were constructed on either side, and ships were sunk in the channel. FORT WASHINGTON was located on the water's edge in upper Manhattan, above Harlem Heights; Fort Constitution was erected across the Hudson, atop the New Jersey palisades. Construction on Fort Constitution began in July 1776. Located on high cliffs, it covered some 10 acres of land; its garrison varied from several hundred men to 2,000. By November, Major General Nathanael GREENE was in command of the fort, its name having been changed to honor Major General Charles LEE.

On 12 July 1776, Admiral Richard Howe sent two British warships up the Hudson River. The Continentals suddenly discovered that their guns at Fort Lee were too high to strike targets close to shore; work was begun on a supplementary battery at the ferry landing below the fort. Manned by 150 men, it mounted several pieces. Still, British ships could move on the river largely at will. Meanwhile, British troops steadily pushed the American troops out of the New York City area in a series of battles, including LONG ISLAND, HARLEM HEIGHTS, KIP'S BAY, and WHITE PLAINS.

On 16 November, utilizing naval forces to isolate it, the British captured Fort Washington, its large garrison, and its guns. General Washington observed the British operation from Fort Lee. With the fall of Fort Washington, Fort Lee no longer had any strategic value, and Washington ordered its evacuation and removal of its vital supplies.

General Howe did not give the Continental army the time it needed to complete the evacuation. On the night of 19–20 November he sent Major General Charles, Lord Cornwallis and 5,000 men across the Hudson to capture Fort Lee. They landed, with several pieces of field artillery, some six miles north of the fort.

Warned early on the morning of 20 November of the British advance, Greene quickly marched his 2,000 men out of the fort. The British advance guard spotted the Americans passing over the New Bridge to Newark. Cornwallis chose not to pursue the Americans; he was after the fort and its supplies. The Americans continued on to Brunswick.

At Fort Lee the British captured 300 tents, 1,000 barrels of flour, 50 cannon, and 12 drunken soldiers who had broken into the fort's liquor stores before the British arrived. Another 150 Americans were captured in the surrounding woods. Altogether, with the capture of Forts Washington and Lee the British secured 400,000 rounds of small-arms ammunition, nearly 100 cannon, some 3,000 prisoners, and a large fraction of the Continental army's supplies in New York and New Jersey. Greene had managed to bring off the gunpowder from Fort Lee; other than that, it was a complete disaster.

Washington and Greene continued their retreat across New Jersey to Pennsylvania. The British army kept Fort Lee until 1779. The fort was then turned over to Loyalist forces, who strengthened the works and continued in garrison there until after 1781.

See also REVOLUTIONARY WAR, LAND OVERVIEW.

Further reading: Judd, Jacob. *Fort Lee on the Palisades: The Battle for the Hudson.* Tarrytown, N.Y.: Sleepy Hollow Restorations, 1963; Ward, Christopher. *The War of the Revolution.* 2 vols. New York: Macmillan, 1952.

— A. J. L. Waskey and Spencer C. Tucker

Fort Mackinac, capture of (17 July 1812) *First U.S. post captured during the War of 1812*

Established by the British on Mackinac Island in the straits between Lakes Huron and Michigan, Fort Mackinac occupied a high bluff overlooking a small commercial harbor and stood in the shadow of a large hill. The fort supported the fur trade and served as a symbol of political power in the eyes of the Indians. The United States gained control of Mackinac in 1796. In 1812, Lieutenant Porter Hanks commanded the fort with 61 men and several 9-pounder cannon.

Upon notification of war between the United States and Britain, the British commander in Canada, Major General Isaac Brock, saw Mackinac as a strategic site that had to be taken quickly. The nearest British post was on St. Joseph Island, where Captain Charles Roberts commanded a company of about 30 men. Roberts, a veteran of India and Ceylon, gathered his regulars; more than 200 Canadian fur traders from the Northwest Company; 113 Menominee, Sioux, and Winnebago Indians directed by Robert Dickson of the Southwest Company; and 280 Objibwa and Ottawa warriors commanded a British Indian agent, John Askin, Jr. On 16 July this mixed force of more than 600 men, armed with a variety of weapons, embarked on the Northwest Company schooner *Caledonia*, 10 bateaux, and 70 canoes for their objective, 40 miles away.

At about 3 A.M. on 17 July, the British force landed and moved two 6-pounder cannon to a position on the hill overlooking Fort Mackinac. Hanks had not received word that Britain and the United States were at war, but he had sent scouts to monitor Indian movements. At dawn Hanks discovered the landing and learned war had been declared. Hanks observed the overwhelming strength against him and concluded that British artillery was aimed at his highly vulnerable position. In order to save lives in what was a

foregone conclusion, Hanks surrendered the fort. Roberts allowed Hanks the honors of war, and the Americans were sent to Detroit on parole.

The capture of Fort Mackinac provided the British both strategic and morale advantages. As word spread of the British victory, many Indian tribes, vacillating about their roles in the war, decided to oppose the Americans. The event also greatly affected Brigadier General William HULL, military commander at Detroit, who saw British operations accelerate while his own became paralyzed. Mackinac precipitated a domino effect of defeats that summer, including the massacre at FORT DEARBORN and the surrender of DETROIT.

The United States tried but failed to recover Mackinac Island in August 1814. The fort was returned to U.S. control in February 1815 by the Treaty of GHENT.

See also WAR OF 1812, LAND OVERVIEW.

Further reading: Antal, Sandy. *A Wampum Denied: Procter's War of 1812.* Ottawa: Carleton University Press, 1997; May, George S. *Historic Guidebook: Fort Mackinac.* Michigan: Mackinac Island State Park Commission, 1962; Quimby, Robert S. *The U.S. Army in the War of 1812: An Operational and Command Study.* East Lansing: Michigan State University Press, 1997.

— Steven J. Rauch

Fort McHenry, attack on (13–14 September 1814) *Battle of the War of 1812*

Following their capture and burning of WASHINGTON (24–26 August 1814), 4,500 British troops commanded by Major General Robert Ross pressed their offensive against the nearby city of BALTIMORE in early September 1814. When Ross was killed by a sniper during the march to Baltimore at the Battle of North Point, Colonel Arthur Brooke assumed command of the British force. Brooke coordinated a combined land-sea attack on the city.

Baltimore was defended by approximately 15,000 troops, mostly militia, commanded by Major General Samuel Smith, a former senator who led Maryland state forces. The key to the American defense of the harbor was Fort McHenry, manned by 1,000 troops led by Major George Armistead of the regular army. Located at the tip of Locust Point, it guarded the entrance to Baltimore Harbor. Fort McHenry mounted 57 guns.

Upon learning of the British invasion, Smith mobilized Baltimore's citizens to build defenses around the city and strengthen the batteries along the harbor approaches at the smaller installations of Fort Babcock, Fort Covington, and Lazaretto Point.

The naval battle began before dawn on 13 September, as British vice admiral Alexander Cochrane moved his lighter warships and bomb and rocket ships (16 vessels in all) through the outer harbor shoals. Since the entrance to the harbor had been blocked by merchant vessels sunk by the defenders, Cochrane began his bombardment of Fort McHenry at a range of two miles. At this distance the British fleet was beyond the range of American cannon in the fort and gunboats but was too far out to inflict serious damage.

During the next 24 hours, the British fired more than 1,500 rounds, of which more than 400 hit their targets. American casualties were slight; the barrage killed only four and wounded 20 of the fort's defenders and disabled only one gun emplacement. Luck favored the Americans; the fort's powder magazine took a direct hit, but the shell failed to explode.

Because the British could not secure the harbor, they decided to make only a cursory attempt against Baltimore and then depart. This rebuff provided the Americans a morale boost following their humiliation at Washington. It also inspired observer Francis Scott Key, who was aboard a British warship (attempting to secure the release of a prisoner) during the bombardment of Fort McHenry, to pen "The Star-Spangled Banner," which eventually became the U.S. national anthem.

See also WAR OF 1812, LAND OVERVIEW.

Further reading: Muller, Charles G. *The Darkest Day: The Washington-Baltimore Campaign.* Philadelphia: J. B. Lippincott, 1963; Sheads, Scott S. *The Rockets' Red Glare: The Maritime Defense of Baltimore in 1814.* Centerville, Md.: Tidewater, 1986; Whitemore, Joseph A. *The Battle for Baltimore, 1814.* Baltimore: Nautical & Aviation, 1997.

— Bradford A. Wineman

Fort Meigs (1813) *War of 1812 fortification established by Major General William Henry Harrison in February 1813*

Fort Meigs served as a base of operations for the defense of northern Ohio from British attack following the January 1813 U.S. defeat at Frenchtown. Captain Eleazer D. Wood directed construction of the fort on a bluff overlooking the Maumee River. The eight-acre stockaded structure had seven blockhouses, five artillery batteries, powder magazines, and traverses across its length to shield the garrison from artillery fire.

Throughout the spring William Henry HARRISON amassed troops until by the end of April he had almost 1,100 men to defend the fort. The British, commanded by Brigadier General Henry Procter, and Indians under the Shawnee leader TECUMSEH prepared to attack Fort Meigs with more than 2,000 men. In late April the British prepared artillery positions on the opposite side of the Maumee, while the Indians encircled Fort Meigs on land to prevent reinforcements from joining the garrison.

Procter began to bombard the fort on 1 May. He continued for four days, doing little damage to the structure or to the well-protected Americans. On 3 May the British established an artillery battery east of the fort, providing a crossfire. On 4 May Harrison learned that Brigadier General Green Clay would soon arrive with 1,200 Kentucky militia. Harrison ordered Clay to send 800 men to attack the British artillery positions. The force, commanded by Lieutenant Colonel William Dudley, routed the British gun crews and spiked 11 of their cannon. The Americans then chased the British toward their main camp in the woods where the Americans met an Indian counterattack that surrounded and killed most of them. Simultaneously an American detachment attacked the British battery below the fort, captured it, and spiked the guns. Although half of the militia were casualties, Harrison had been reinforced, and Procter was unable to sustain the siege. On 9 May the British fired a last salvo, boarded their boats, and returned to their base at Amherstburg, Upper Canada.

Tecumseh insisted on another attack in late July and developed a plan to trick the garrison by staging a mock battle against simulated American reinforcements, hoping to ambush the Americans as they emerged Fort Meigs to assist their supposed friends. Clay, who now commanded the fort, became aware of the enemy presence. When the Indians began their mock battle Clay's men urged him to assist, but he resolutely refused to allow any unit to leave the fort. Thus the Americans defeated Tecumseh's ruse, and Fort Meigs remained in U.S. hands. It continued to be manned by militia until the end of the war. A reconstructed fort now stands at the site.

See also FORT STEPHENSON; WAR OF 1812, LAND OVERVIEW.

Further reading: Antal, Sandy. *A Wampum Denied: Procter's War of 1812.* Ottawa: Carleton University Press, 1997; Nelson, Larry. *Men of Patriotism, Courage, and Enterprise! Fort Meigs in the War of 1812.* Canton, Ohio: Daring Books, 1985; Quimby, Robert S. *The U.S. Army in the War of 1812: An Operational and Command Study.* East Lansing: Michigan State University Press, 1997.

— Steven J. Rauch

Fort Necessity campaign (February–July 1754) *First military campaign of the 1754–56 FRENCH AND INDIAN WAR*

Attempting to establish Virginia's claims to the Ohio River Valley before the French did so, in February 1754 Governor Robert Dinwiddie commissioned George WASHINGTON a lieutenant colonel of Virginia militia with orders to build a fort where the Monongahela and Allegheny Rivers join to form the Ohio River (modern Pittsburgh). As Washington collected supplies at Wills Creek, Captain William Trent, assisted by Seneca chief Tanaghrisson, began construction of a fort at the site on 17 February. On 17 April, however, Captain Claude-Pierre Pécaudy, seigneur de Contrecoeur, arrived from Fort LeBoeuf with 500 French troops and demanded that the Virginians evacuate. On the following day, Ensign Edward Ward, left in charge by Trent who had gone back for supplies, agreed to Contrecoeur's demands, much to the chagrin of Tanaghrisson. Once the Virginians departed, the French began construction of FORT DUQUESNE.

Learning of Ward's surrender on 10 April, the inexperienced Washington, rather than wait at Wills Creek for reinforcements, immediately ordered his small contingent of 160 soldiers to march some 80 miles to Red Stone Fort, an Ohio Company fortified storehouse approximately 40 miles from Fort Duquesne. Cutting trees as they marched in order to make way for future supply wagons, Washington's force advanced a mere two to three miles per day, losing all chance of surprise.

Learning of Washington's approach, Contrecoeur dispatched Ensign Joseph Coulon de Villiers de Jumonville and an escort of 35 men to meet Washington and warn him to withdraw. On 24 May Washington arrived at Great Meadows (approximately halfway between Wills Creek and Red Stone Fort). Notified of Jumonville's location by Tanaghrisson, Washington and the Seneca chief attacked Jumonville's greatly outnumbered party on the morning of 28 May. After a few volleys had been fired, Jumonville, who had been wounded, asked for a parley with Washington. However, he was murdered by Tanaghrisson. Seneca warriors then massacred 13 wounded French soldiers. One Frenchman managed to avoid capture, but 21 others were taken prisoner. Washington's report to Dinwiddie made these events appear as a brief skirmish in which Jumonville had been killed, Contrecoeur considered it an ambush and violation of the rules of war.

Following the confrontation with Jumonville, Washington returned to Great Meadows and on 2 June began construction of a 50-foot-diameter, seven-foot-high circular palisade, which he named Fort Necessity. By mid-June Washington had been reinforced by 200 Virginians and a South Carolina company of 100 British regulars under Captain James Mackay—who refused to place his force directly under militia (i.e., Washington's) command. Again displaying his inexperience, Washington chose to advance, taking 300 Virginians to Red Stone Fort, only to be forced to return to Fort Necessity after learning that Contrecoeur had been reinforced by some 1,000 men under the command of Jumonville's older brother, Captain Louis Coulon de Villiers, who had immediately demanded the right to

attack Washington and avenge his brother's death. His request was granted.

On 1 July Washington's exhausted men arrived back at Fort Necessity, where they were invested by a force of some 600 French regulars and 100 Shawnee, Delaware, and Mingo warriors on 3 July. By the end of the day nearly one-third of Washington's men were dead or wounded. Villiers, whose men were running low on ammunition, offered Washington the chance to surrender, which he accepted on 4 July. The French paroled and released the Americans and then destroyed Fort Necessity.

Further reading: Anderson, Fred. *Crucible of War: The Seven Years' War and the Fate of Empire in British North America, 1754–1766.* New York: Knopf, 2000; Eccles, W. J. *France in America.* Revised ed. Markham, Ont.: Fitzhenry & Whiteside, 1990.

— Justin D. Murphy

Fort Niagara, expedition against (1755)

(August–September 1755) *Abortive British attempt during the French and Indian War to seize a strategic French fortification at the head of Lake Ontario*

Shortly after his arrival in Virginia as the new British commander, Major General Edward BRADDOCK convened a conference of colonial governors at Alexandria and outlined four major military expeditions for 1755. Braddock would march on FORT DUQUESNE; Major General William JOHNSON was to lead a joint colonial-Mohawk force against Fort St. Frédéric (CROWN POINT); Massachusetts governor William SHIRLEY would lead the 50th and 51st Regiments from Albany and march on Fort Niagara; and a New England militia force would strike French positions in Acadia. Shirley and the other governors tried to convince Braddock that their colonies were incapable of providing the human resources and provisions needed for four simultaneous campaigns, but Braddock ignored their advice and demanded action.

From the outset Shirley faced numerous difficulties in fulfilling Braddock's unrealistic expectations. It took several weeks for the 50th and 51st Regiments, which had been deactivated at the end of KING GEORGE'S WAR, to be restored to full strength. New York lieutenant governor James DeLancey, angered that Shirley had contracted with a rival mercantile firm headed by Lewis Morris III and Peter Van Burgh Livingston, not only failed to cooperate but even refused to allow Shirley to use New York cannon. Likewise, Johnson, angered when Shirley detached Massachusetts units from his Crown Point expedition, used his connections with the Mohawk to ensure that they would not cooperate with Shirley, thereby depriving him of much-needed scouts. DeLancey and Johnson later conspired to have Shirley stripped of his command. All of these factors created delays that shortened the window of opportunity to a strike at Fort Niagara.

By the time Shirley reached the portage between the Mohawk River and Wood Creek in early August, the military situation in the colonies had deteriorated. Braddock's army had been destroyed in the Battle of the MONONGAHELA, which not only impacted Shirley's military situation but also left him emotionally devastated—his son, William Jr., had been killed in the battle. Shirley also learned that British vice admiral Edward Boscawen, who had been dispatched to the mouth of the St. Lawrence River, had failed to prevent more than 2,500 French regulars from reaching Quebec safely, thereby allowing Baron Jean-Armand de Dieskau to reinforce French positions. When Shirley arrived in early September at FORT OSWEGO, intending to use it as an operational base for his attack on Fort Niagara, he found the fortifications in such poor condition that he had no choice but to suspend his expedition so that Fort Oswego could be repaired. Shirley planned to resume the offensive the following year, but he was sacked as commander and recalled to London, a victim of Braddock's unrealistic plans and his own colonial political rivals.

See also FORT NIAGARA, EXPEDITION AGAINST (1759); FRENCH AND INDIAN WAR.

Further reading: Anderson, Fred. *Crucible of War: The Seven Years' War and the Fate of Empire in British North America, 1754–1766.* New York: Knopf, 2000; Dunnigan, Brian L. *Siege—1759: The Campaign against Niagara.* Youngstown, N.Y.: Old Fort Niagara Association, 1996; Simmons, R. C. *The American Colonies: From Settlement to Independence.* New York: Norton, 1976.
— Justin D. Murphy

Fort Niagara, expedition against (1759) (June–July 1759) *Successful British campaign during the 1754–63 French and Indian War that severed contact between French forces in Quebec and the western forts*

Encouraged by the success against FORT FRONTENAC in 1758, British prime minister William Pitt decided on a three-pronged invasion of Canada in 1759. Major General Jeffery Amherst was to assault Fort Carillon (TICONDEROGA) and Fort St. Frédéric (CROWN POINT); Major General James Wolfe and Rear Admiral Charles Saunders were to launch an amphibious assault on Quebec; and Brigadier General John Prideaux was dispatched with 2,000 British regulars to seize Fort Niagara.

At the end of May, Prideaux left Schenectady and headed up the Mohawk River, arriving on 27 June at FORT OSWEGO, where he was joined by Sir William JOHNSON and approximately 1,000 Iroquois warriors. Although the Mohawk and a few Oneida had joined in previous British operations, all six nations of the Iroquois Confederacy, including the French-leaning Seneca, had decided at Onondaga to join the Fort Niagara expedition in hopes of securing control over the upper Ohio Valley. On 30 June, leaving approximately 1,000 men behind to rebuild the fortifications at Oswego, Prideaux and his Anglo-Iroquois force set out for Fort Niagara.

Although Fort Niagara's able commander, Captain Pierre de Pouchot, had made great improvements to his fortifications, he had not expected a British attack and thus had sent 2,500 of his 3,000 men to Fort Machault to aid Captain François-Marie Le Marchand de Lignery in an expedition into the Ohio Valley. The arrival of British and Iroquois forces on 6 July, therefore, caught Pouchot off guard. With just 500 French troops and 100 Niagara Seneca, Pouchot was ill prepared to withstand a siege, especially after Seneca chief Kaendaé decided to leave on 14 July rather than fight his fellow tribesmen. Prideaux, who had refrained from firing while Kaendaé and the Seneca were in Fort Niagara, began to bombard the fortress as soon as they departed.

Prideaux was accidentally killed when he stepped in front of one of his own mortars, but the Anglo-Iroquois force, taken over by Johnson, continued to rain shells into the fort. By 23 July Pouchot's hopes for survival depended on Lignery, who was approaching Fort Niagara with a relief party of about 1,600 French regulars, Canadian militia, and Indians. Unfortunately for the French, Lignery's Indian allies deserted after being warned by Iroquois emissaries that they would be greatly outnumbered. Despite this defection, Lignery attempted to charge Johnson's position at La Belle Famille with about 600 men on the morning of 24 July. Johnson's well-entrenched British and Iroquois forces fired volley after volley into the French attackers, killing and capturing more than half of them. The remaining French forces fled. Viewing the debacle through a telescope, Pouchot realized that all hope was lost, and on 25 July he surrendered. He and his men were transported back to New York, where they were imprisoned.

The seizure of Fort Niagara was immensely significant because it not only effectively isolated French forces in the West but threatened Montreal. As a result, the French commander in Canada, Major General Louis-Joseph, marquis de Montcalm-Gozon de Saint-Véran, detached a portion of his forces defending Quebec to reinforce Montreal. This turn of events contributed greatly to Wolfe's subsequent capture of Quebec, which in turn all but ensured British victory in the FRENCH AND INDIAN WAR.

See also FORT NIAGARA, EXPEDITION AGAINST (1755).

Further reading: Anderson, Fred. *Crucible of War: The Seven Years' War and the Fate of Empire in British North America, 1754–1766.* New York: Knopf, 2000; Simmons,

R. C. *The American Colonies: From Settlement to Independence.* New York: Norton, 1976.

— Justin D. Murphy

Fort Niagara in the War of 1812   *Site of numerous engagements during the War of 1812*

Strategically located at the west end of Lake Ontario, where the Niagara River drains out of the lake, and ceded by the British to the United States in 1796, Fort Niagara consisted of a central stone "castle" surrounded by a wooden palisade, earthworks, and five detached batteries.

On 13 October 1812, during the War of 1812, Fort Niagara engaged in an artillery duel with FORT GEORGE on the opposite side of the Niagara River. Fort George, on higher ground, swiftly silenced Niagara's batteries and drove its garrison from the fort, but because of the Battle of QUEENSTOWN HEIGHTS that same day, the British were not able to capitalize on this success.

The Americans then strengthened Fort Niagara and mounted a battery on the roof of the castle to compensate for the height disadvantage. On 21 November 1812 Niagara withstood a second artillery duel, this time with Fort George and British warships. On 27 May 1813 Fort Niagara's guns and a naval force led by Master Commandant Oliver Hazard PERRY supported troops led by Colonel Winfield SCOTT who assaulted and captured Fort George.

Weakly garrisoned by New York militia units commanded by Captain Nathaniel Leonard, the fort was taken by the the British on 18 December 1813 in a night bayonet assault that resulted in 65 Americans killed, 15 wounded, and 350 captured.

Fort Niagara remained in British hands until the end of the war. It was returned to U.S. control on 22 May 1815.

See also WAR OF 1812, LAND OVERVIEW.

Further reading: Babcock, Lewis L. *The War of 1812 on the Niagara Frontier.* Buffalo, N.Y.: Historical Society, 1927; Berton, Pierre. *The Invasion of Canada, 1812–1813.* Boston: Little, Brown, 1980; Bowler, R. Arthur. *War along the Niagara: Essays on the War of 1812 and Its Legacy.* Youngstown, N.Y.: Old Fort Niagara Association, 1991.

— John E. Foley

Fort Oswego   *Fortification at the mouth of the Oswego River on Lake Ontario from 1727 to 1946, originally constructed as a result of the struggle between France and Britain for North America*

In 1727 New York governor William Burnet ordered the construction of a blockhouse on Lake Ontario in response to French construction of FORT NIAGARA. Burnet hoped to capture the lucrative fur trade, attract the loyalty of the Iroquois and the western Indians, and check French expansion. Unfortunately, the fort was poorly sited, dominated by two nearby hills. The original blockhouse and outworks eventually grew to include outposts on these hills.

Fort Oswego's active role in military affairs began as the staging point for proposed British expeditions against Fort Niagara in 1755 and FORT FRONTENAC in 1756. Suffering from infrequent resupply, all-too-frequent raiding, and pitifully poor construction, the fort fell in 1756 to a French force under Major General Louis-Joseph, marquis de Montcalm-Gozon de Saint-Véran. In 1758 the British rebuilt Oswego's outpost known as Fort Ontario in preparation for the 1759 assault on Montreal and Quebec.

At the onset of the American Revolutionary War, the British abandoned the fort; the Americans destroyed it in 1778. In 1782 the British rebuilt the post and held it until 1796. During the War of 1812 the British attacked and burned the post for the third time to deter American commerce on Lake Ontario.

The United States reoccupied Fort Oswego in 1838 and maintained the post until 1901. A modern fort, built on adjacent property, served as a "safe haven" for victims of the Holocaust during World War II.

See also AMERICAN REVOLUTION, LAND OVERVIEW; OSWEGO, BATTLE OF; WAR OF 1812, LAND OVERVIEW.

Further reading: Anderson, Fred. *The Crucible of War: The Seven Years' War and the Fate of Empire in British North America, 1754–1766.* New York: Knopf, 2000; Cooper, Johnson Gaylord. *Oswego in the French-English Struggle in North America 1720–1760.* Book copy of microfilm. Ann Arbor, MI: University Microfilms, 1961.

— David M. Corlett

Fort Pillow, Battle of   (12 April 1864) *Civil War battle*

Named for Confederate Brigadier General Gideon PILLOW and located 40 miles north of Memphis on the Mississippi River, Fort Pillow was situated on a bluff overlooking the river. Surrounded by a dirt parapet about eight feet high that formed a 125-foot semicircle and by two outer defensive lines, the fort occupied the site of two older forts.

Fort Pillow was occupied by Union troops in 1862. On 12 April 1864, Major Lionel F. Booth had command of its garrison of 262 African-American troops of the 11th U.S. Colored Troops and Battery F of the 4th U.S. Colored Light Artillery, as well as 295 white troops from the 13th Tennessee Cavalry.

At 5 A.M. on 12 April Fort Pillow came under attack by 1,500 Confederates under Brigadier General James R. Chalmers of Major General Nathan Bedford FORREST's cavalry corps. When Major Booth was killed by sniper fire, Major William Bradford took command. By 8 A.M. the

Confederates had occupied the outer works; the Union defenders could not bring their six artillery pieces to bear on the attackers.

At 3:30 P.M. Forrest sent forward a flag of truce, demanding immediate surrender. Bradford asked for an hour to consider, but with Union reinforcements coming up by water, Forrest gave him only 20 minutes. Bradford rejected Forrest's terms, whereupon the Confederates charged and quickly overwhelmed the Union garrison.

In the battle the Confederates lost 14 killed and 86 wounded, while the Federals suffered 231 killed, 100 wounded, and 236 captured. Only 58 African-American troops were taken alive. Union officers later claimed that a massacre had occurred—that their troops had been shot down deliberately as they tried to surrender and that the Confederates had bayoneted the wounded. The Confederates replied that the majority of Union killed had died trying to escape capture by running down the river bluff and jumping in the river to swim to the Federal gunboat *New Era*.

While the battle was not significant from a military standpoint, the high casualty rate among Union soldiers at Fort Pillow, particularly the African Americans, made it a special case. The Committee on the Conduct of the War investigated, gathering testimony from some of the Union wounded left behind when Forrest's men abandoned the post on the night of 12 April. Controversy over the battle remains, but Southern antipathy toward African-American troops is well documented.

See also CIVIL WAR, LAND OVERVIEW.

Further reading: Fuchs, Richard L. *An Unerring Fire: The Massacre at Fort Pillow.* Rutherford, N.J.: Farleigh Dickinson University Press, 1994; Tap, Bruce. *Over Lincoln's Shoulder: The Committee on the Conduct of the War.* Lawrence: University Press of Kansas, 1998.

— Bruce Tap

Fort Pitt *British fort at the confluence of the Allegheny, Monongahela, and Ohio Rivers from 1759 to 1772*
During the FRENCH AND INDIAN WAR the French, the British, and various Ohio Indian tribes struggled for control of the Ohio Valley, especially the strategic junction of the Allegheny, Monongahela, and Ohio Rivers. New France established a military presence among the Ohio Indians by constructing FORT DUQUESNE in 1753.

Three years after Major General Edward BRADDOCK's disastrous defeat in the Battle of the MONONGAHELA in 1755, Brigadier General John FORBES's army finally captured Fort Duquesne on 25 November 1758. Forbes renamed the post after the British prime minister, William Pitt. Much to the dismay of the Shawnee and the

Delaware, the British also built the temporary Fort Mercer in 1759, later replacing it with a larger structure.

The pentagonal Fort Pitt, designed by Captain Harry Gordon, was comparable in size and design to the British fort at CROWN POINT; it covered nearly 18 acres of land. The British garrisoned Fort Pitt from 1759 to 1772, and it played an important role in their attempts to extend imperial authority over former French possessions. The Ohio Indians unsuccessfully besieged the fort during PONTIAC'S REBELLION (1763–64), and Colonel Henry BOUQUET launched his punitive 1764 expedition from there.

Fort Pitt was also a military community, consisting of soldiers, traders, artisans, farmers, laundresses, and Indians. On the eve of the American Revolutionary War in 1772, the British army abandoned Fort Pitt (because of shaky finances and the need to maintain order on the seaboard), an act that angered many western Pennsylvania settlers.

See also BUSHY RUN, BATTLE OF; DUNMORE'S WAR (1774); FRENCH AMERICA.

Further reading: Hunter, William A. *Forts on the Pennsylvania Frontier, 1753–1758.* Harrisburg: Pennsylvania Historical and Museum Commission, 1960; McConnell, Michael N. *A Country Between: The Upper Ohio Valley and Its Peoples, 1724–1774.* Lincoln: University of Nebraska Press, 1992; Stotz, Charles Morse. *Outposts of the War for Empire: The French and English in Western Pennsylvania—Their Armies, Their Forts, Their People, 1749–1764.* Pittsburgh: University of Pittsburgh Press/Historical Society of Western Pennsylvania, 1985; Waddell, Louis M., and Bruce D. Bomberger. *The French and Indian War in Pennsylvania, 1753–1763: Fortification and Struggle during the War for Empire.* Harrisburg: Pennsylvania Historical and Museum Commission, 1996.

— David L. Preston

Fort Pulaski *One of 30 forts built as part of the third system of coastal fortifications following the War of 1812*
Fort Pulaski was meant to defend the port of Savannah, Georgia. Army Corps of Engineers officials chose as its site Cockspur Island at the mouth of the Savannah River just east of Tybee Island. A French engineer, Simon Bernard, designed the fort, named for an American Revolutionary War hero, Count Casimir PULASKI, killed at the 1779 Battle of Savannah.

Construction of the pentagon-shaped masonry fort took place from 1829 to 1847 at a cost of $1 million and more than 25 million bricks. With its double-layer, 18-foot walls, the fort seemed impregnable. Workers also built a moat around the fort, seven feet deep and 32 to 48 feet wide. An earth-covered room stored ammunition and supplies, and the fort had a 200,000-gallon freshwater cistern.

Planned for 150 guns, the fort had only 20 32-pounder naval guns between 1840 and 1861. Confederate troops occupied Pulaski in January 1861, completed its gun emplacements, and mounted 48 cannon. Major, later Colonel, Charles H. Olmstead commanded a 384-man garrison. General Robert E. LEE, who had helped supervise its initial construction, was certain that its walls could not be breached.

In February 1862 a Union force under Captain Quincy A. Gillmore began emplacing on Tybee Island siege batteries of heavy mortars and large rifled guns. At dawn on 10 April Gillmore demanded the fort's surrender. Olmstead, confident the fort could withstand the Union fire, refused. At 8:15 A.M. on 10 April, Union batteries began an intense shelling of one portion of the main wall. In five hours shells from Union rifled guns cut a breach, and by nightfall the fort's magazine had been exposed. The next morning Union shells were hitting the magazine. With no hope of reinforcements and afraid that the fort might be blown up and defenders killed in an explosion of their own magazine, Olmstead surrendered at 2 P.M. Only one man on each side had died in the shelling.

The taking of Fort Pulaski remains a primary example of the effect of rifled cannon fire on brick and stone coastal forts. The bombardment rendered all such coastal forts obsolete. By comparison, sand forts, such as Fort WAGNER, could withstand the new rifled guns.

In 1864 Fort Pulaski became a prison for 600 Southern officers. In 1879 the army abandoned it, except for a brief period during the 1898 SPANISH-AMERICAN WAR. In 1924, after years of lobbying by veterans and historic groups, Congress declared Fort Pulaski a national monument. Restoration work occurred during the 1930s, and follow-up projects were completed in 1942. Fort Pulaski is today a popular tourist attraction.

See also ARTILLERY, LAND; CIVIL WAR, LAND OVERVIEW; COAST DEFENSE.

Further reading: Gillmore, Quincy A. "Siege and Reduction of Fort Pulaski." Official Report No. 8. New York: D. Van Nostrand, 1862. Reprint, Gettysburg, Pa.: Thomas, 1988; Lattimore, Ralston B. *Fort Pulaski.* Historical Handbook Series no. 18. Washington, D.C.: National Park Service, 1954; Schiller, Herbert M. *Fort Pulaski and the Defense of Savannah.* Civil War Series. Washington, D.C.: Eastern National Press, 1977.

— Brian Head

Fort Stanwix (July–August 1777) *Successfully defended objective of a British offensive during the American Revolutionary War*
In 1777 the British conceived a plan to seize the Lake Champlain–Hudson River line with a three-pronged attack

from Oswego (on Lake Ontario), Montreal, and New York City. The primary goal of the Oswego-based expedition was the seizure of Fort Stanwix (present-day Rome, New York), which dominated the Mohawk Valley's approach to Albany. Lieutenant Colonel Barry St. Leger arrived at Oswego on 25 July and immediately began to march down the Mohawk with about 2,000 men, of which only 340 were regulars. As many as 1,000 were Indians, and the remainder were Tory and Canadian militia. St. Leger was unaware that the fort was strongly held and had been much repaired by 550 New York Continental troops under Colonel Peter Gansevoort. The fort was further reinforced by 200 men, arriving fortuitously just before St. Leger did on 2 August. St. Leger lacked heavy artillery, and the Americans dismissed his call for surrender. He settled in for a siege.

St. Leger lacked enough troops to invest the fort fully, so he kept his regulars concentrated and strung out his militia and Indian troops in light encircling screens. Except for the sniping, his preparations made little impression on the American defenses. When he learned on the 5th that an American relief column of New York militia was on its way, he determined to intercept and ambush it. In a battle at ORISKANY on the 6th he turned away the rebel militia.

Unfortunately for St. Leger, the American garrison had learned of the militia's approach and took advantage of the departure of part of his force to sally out and loot the empty Indian and Tory camps (most of the regulars had remained at Stanwix). When St. Leger returned he sent an ultimatum to the garrison, warning that he would be unable to control the "savages" when the fort eventually fell. The American defenders refused to surrender and reviled St. Leger for making such threats.

St. Leger's troubles were just beginning. General Philip SCHUYLER, with the main American force on the Hudson, decided to dispatch a relief column of 800 Continentals under Major General Benedict ARNOLD. Arnold began moving toward Stanwix on August 10, reaching Fort Dayton (about halfway) on 21 August. St. Leger had continued to build approach works toward the fort but now found his army crumbling around him, apparently taken in by a ruse. From Arnold's column had come one Hon Yost Schuyler, a supposed "half-wit" Tory, apparently held in awe by the Indians. Arnold had offered him a reprieve from a death sentence if he went into St. Leger's Indians' camp and spread exaggerated rumors of the strength of Arnold's relief force. The stories took hold among the Indians, who were already disappointed at the lack of plunder and prisoners from Oriskany, demoralized by the looting of their camp outside Stanwix, and discouraged by the generally slow progress of the siege. They deserted en masse, and St. Leger was forced to give up the siege, retreat to Lake Ontario, and return to Montreal. The army of Major General John BURGOYNE was thus denied badly needed reinforcements, contributing to his defeat in the Battles of SARATOGA two months later.

See also BRANT, JOSEPH.

Further reading: Mintz, Max. *Seeds of Empire: The American Revolutionary Conquest of the Iroquois.* New York: New York University Press, 1999; Ward, Christopher. *The War of the Revolution.* New York: Macmillan, 1952.

— Wayne E. Lee

Fort Stephenson (1813) *War of 1812 American fort*
Established in June 1812 on the Sandusky River near modern Fremont, Ohio, this small, rectangular stockade fort was designed to guard a point critical to Major General William Henry HARRISON's operations in Ohio. Major George Croghan commanded at Fort Stephenson with two companies of troops and one 6-pounder naval cannon, known affectionately as "Old Betsy."

On 1 August 1813 Croghan and his men found themselves facing a large force of Native Americans under Shawnee leader TECUMSEH and regular British troops commanded by Major General Henry Procter. Procter demanded surrender of the post, but Croghan refused. On 2 August the British fired more than 500 cannonballs at the fort but caused little damage. Procter then ordered more than 100 men to assault the small fort. This British attack was quickly repulsed by grapeshot from Old Betsy.

Croghan's defense of Fort Stephenson induced the British to retreat back to Canada, never again to threaten Ohio territory. The British sustained more than 90 casualties, while the Americans lost one killed and seven wounded. Croghan became a national hero for his actions, the epitome of the defiance and determination of U.S. forces during the War of 1812.

See also WAR OF 1812, LAND OVERVIEW.

Further reading: Bowlus, Bruce. "A 'Signal Victory': The Battle for Fort Stephenson, August 1–2, 1813." *Northwest Ohio Quarterly* 63 (Summer/Autumn 1991): 43–57; Quimby, Robert S. *The U.S. Army in the War of 1812: An Operational and Command Study.* East Lansing, Mich.: Michigan State University Press, 1997.

— Steven J. Rauch

Fort Sumter, attack on (12 April 1861) *Opening action of the Civil War*
Fort Sumter, a pentagonal brick fort, protected the mouth of the harbor at Charleston, South Carolina, from foreign attack. With five-foot thick walls and room for 650 soldiers and 146 guns, the fort was incomplete in 1861. Major Robert ANDERSON commanded its garrison of 84 officers and men.

The Fort Sumter crisis began in December 1860 when Anderson evacuated Fort Moultrie at Charleston and concentrated his men at Sumter. In January 1861 South Carolina artillery fired on the Union supply ship *Star of the West,* which was attempting to resupply Sumter. It turned back. In his inaugural address of 4 March 1861, President Abraham LINCOLN outlined his intent to hold, occupy, and possess all Federal property within the seceded states that now composed the Confederacy. The main items of Federal property in question were Fort Sumter and Fort Pickens, in Pensacola Harbor, Florida. The following day Lincoln received distressing news from Anderson that his provisions would last for only four to six weeks.

While Lincoln pondered his next move, Brigadier General P. G. T. BEAUREGARD, commanding Confederate forces at Charleston received orders from Confederate president Jefferson DAVIS to prevent any reinforcement of Fort Sumter.

Although the U.S. Army's commanding general, brevet Lieutenant General Winfield SCOTT, had advised him to abandon both forts to prevent war, Lincoln had been exploring the possibility of a relief expedition to Sumter. On 8 April Lincoln notified South Carolina governor Francis W. Pickens that he intended to resupply the fort with food only. No arms or ammunition or additional troops would be offloaded, unless the resupply ships were attacked.

On 9 April (the day before the relief expedition was to sail), Davis decided that Lincoln's announcement was a provocation and sent word to Beauregard to demand the evacuation of the fort. If refused, Davis instructed, Beauregard was to take military action. On the morning of 11 April, three representatives of the Confederate government met with Major Anderson and demanded the evacuation of the fort. Anderson declined, but he did reveal that his garrison would be out of food in a few days. This information was provided to Beauregard, who returned a messenger to the fort around midnight on the 12th, asking for clarification as to when the garrison would be obliged to surrender. Anderson answered that the fort would be surrendered 15 April if nothing happened to change his situation. His answer was deemed insufficient, and Anderson was notified that Sumter would be fired upon. At 4:30 A.M. a Confederate mortar shell exploded directly over Sumter, the signal for the other Confederate guns to begin the bombardment.

With thousands of spectators watching, Confederates guns exchanged fire with the few guns at Sumter that were actually mounted and functioning. After 33 hours of spectacular cannonading, Anderson surrendered. With Beauregard's permission, Anderson then began a 100-gun salute to the American flag. The gun firing the 50th shot exploded, killing one soldier outright and mortally wounding another. These were the only Union casualties of the siege, apart from one horse that had been killed in the shelling. Anderson and his small garrison left the fort, departing aboard one of the Federal relief ships that had arrived and had been loitering outside the harbor since the 12th. The Civil War had begun.

See also CIVIL WAR, CAUSES OF.

Further reading: Current, Richard N. *Lincoln and the First Shot.* Philadelphia; Lippincott, 1963; Hendrickson, Robert. *Sumter, The First Day of the Civil War.* Chelsea, Mich.: Scarborough House, 1990; Klein, Maury. *Days of Defiance: Sumter, Secession, and the Coming of the Civil War.* New York: Knopf, 1997; Stampp, Kenneth M. *And the War Came: The North and the Secession Crisis, 1860–1861.* Baton Rouge: Louisiana State University Press, 1950.

— Keith D. Dickson

Fort Ticonderoga, Battle of (8 July 1758) *Battle between French and British forces in the struggle for control of upper New York during the 1754–63 French and Indian War*

Originally built by France as Fort Carillon in 1755, Fort Ticonderoga controlled Lake George and Lake Champlain, the critical waterway approaches to French Canada. In 1757 Major General Louis-Joseph de Montcalm-Gozon de Saint-Véran staged a successful assault against the British FORT WILLIAM HENRY, resulting in Prime Minister William Pitt's resolve to capture Ticonderoga.

On 6 July 1758 the British commander in chief in North America, Major General James Abercrombie (Abercronby), led 6,300 British regular and 9,000 American provincial troops against Ticonderoga. The fort was defended by 3,500 veteran French regulars and marines.

Abercrombie, a political appointee, relied upon subordinates, particularly his second in command, acting Brigadier George Augustus, Viscount Howe, for operational

Ethan Allen captures Fort Ticonderoga, 10 May 1775. Copy of engraving after Alonzo Cappel   *(National Archives)*

leadership and tactical advice. Unfortunately, Howe was killed on 6 July in a French ambush.

On 8 July, without a pre-assault artillery barrage, Abercrombie sent four columns against the abatis barricades and entrenchments that protected the landward approaches to the fort. His men suffered heavy casualties from French musketry. An attempted amphibious flanking maneuver also failed. A late-afternoon attack by the 42d Royal Highland Regiment (the Black Watch) on the French right resulted in a momentary breakthrough, but the French repulsed the Scots. Further British assaults late in the afternoon on the French center and left also failed, precipitating a retreat.

British casualties approached 2,000 men, while Montcalm lost less than 400. The failure to take Fort Ticonderoga, though, spurred a British operation the next year, staged on the St. Lawrence River, that led to the capture of QUEBEC and eventually that of New France.

See also FRENCH AND INDIAN WAR.

Further reading: Bird, Harrison. *Battle for a Continent.* New York: Oxford University Press, 1965; Hamilton, Edward Pierce. *Fort Ticonderoga: Key to a Continent.* Boston: Little, Brown, 1964; Leach, Douglas Edward. *The Northern Colonial Frontier, 1607–1763.* New York: Holt, Rinehart and Winston, 1966; Parkman, Francis. *Montcalm and Wolfe.* Boston: Little, Brown, 1892.
— Stanley D. M. Carpenter

Fort Ticonderoga, campaign (June–July 1759)

Successful British campaign during the French and Indian War to capture Fort Carillon (renamed by the British Ticonderoga) on Lake Champlain as part of a three-pronged 1759 campaign against New France

In summer 1759, the commander of British forces in North America, Major General Sir Jeffery Amherst, led an invasion of New France by way of the Hudson River–Lake Champlain waterway, intent on capturing Forts Ticonderoga and St. Frédéric (CROWN POINT) before proceeding down the St. Lawrence River. At the same time the British mounted offensives against FORT NIAGARA and QUEBEC.

Amherst's attack on Ticonderoga suffered serious delays from its inception, the result of circumstance and the general's cautious nature. The Ticonderoga and Niagara expeditions shared Albany as their staging point and therefore competed for stores; flooded rivers hampered the transportation of supplies and soldiers; provincials balked at joining the campaign until offered lucrative bonuses; and the bulk of these recruits, the critical source of manual labor for the expected sieges, did not arrive until well into June. To compound these problems, Amherst insisted upon absolute security before he moved, spending much time improving roads, building way stations along his route, constructing FORT GEORGE to replace FORT WILLIAM HENRY, and stockpiling supplies.

Amherst's army left Fort George on 21 July. Nearly 600 bateaux and whaleboats transported his 10,000 troops: seven battalions of regulars, nine battalions of New England provincials, and nine companies of Rangers. This force landed south of Ticonderoga on 22 July, briefly skirmished with French soldiers, and halted for the night. Amherst proceeded with great caution, determined to avoid Major General James Abercrombie's bloody debacle of 1758.

Amherst's prudence allowed the bulk of the French defenders to slip away. Under orders from Quebec, Colonel François Charles de Bourlamaque withdrew from Fort Carillon at the first sign of Amherst's army, leaving 400 men to hold as long as possible before destroying the fort and retreating.

On the morning of 23 July Amherst's soldiers occupied the fort's abandoned outer trenches and began a methodical siege, positioning batteries and digging ever closer to the walls. The French defenders offered a spirited defense, keeping the British soldiers under fire for four days. Then, under cover of darkness on the 26th, the French garrison spiked their cannon, set a fuse to the magazine, and withdrew to the north, leaving behind a burning and partially destroyed fortress. The following day Amherst became master of the "Key to the Continent," having lost fewer than 50 men in the effort.

Bourlamaque's soldiers continued their strategic retreat northward, destroying Fort St. Frédéric before occupying defensive positions on Île-aux-Noix on the Richelieu River. Guarded as ever and lacking intelligence of acting Major General James Wolfe's assault on Quebec, Amherst proceeded at a snail's pace, initiating repairs on both forts and constructing ships to combat French warships on the lake. Amherst secured Lake Champlain, but he never proceeded much north of Crown Point, nor did he begin his attack down the St. Lawrence, thus possibly delaying the conquest of New France by a year.

See also FRENCH AND INDIAN WAR.

Further reading: Anderson, Fred. *Crucible of War: The Seven Years' War and the Fate of Empire in British North America, 1754–1766.* New York: Knopf, 2000; Gipson, Lawrence Henry. *The Great War for the Empire: The Victorious Years.* Vol. 7, *The British Empire before the American Revolution.* New York: Knopf, 1949; Hamilton, Edward P. *Fort Ticonderoga: Key to a Continent.* Boston: Little, Brown, 1964.
— David M. Corlett

Fort Ticonderoga in the American Revolution (10 May 1775 and 5 July 1777) *Strategic fort overlooking the base of Lake Champlain, captured by the rebels early in the American Revolutionary War and then recaptured by the British in 1777*

Word of the clashes at LEXINGTON AND CONCORD set in motion parallel rebel plans to capture Fort Ticonderoga on the western shore of the southern end of Lake Champlain. The primary motivation was its stockpile of munitions, especially the artillery. These efforts coalesced on 7 May 1775 into a gathering of some 200 volunteers and militia from the "New Hampshire Grants" (later Vermont), Connecticut, and Massachusetts at Castleton, New York, where the majority Green Mountain Boys of Vermont elected their leader, Ethan ALLEN, as the overall expedition commander. Meanwhile, Benedict ARNOLD, after seeking official approval from the Massachusetts Committee of Safety to raise troops for such an expedition, learned of the other plans already in motion. He joined Allen's group, with a commission as a colonel of militia but no troops, on 9 May. After the men threatened to go home if he took command, Arnold arrived at an understanding with Allen, creating a sort of joint command.

Before dawn on 10 May the small force was waiting for their planned boats on the eastern shore of the lake, about a two-mile paddle from the fort. Only two boats arrived. These were not the ones expected and had room for only 83 men. Trusting to surprise, they crossed despite a series of squalls, landed, and rushed through the ruined southern walls of the fort. Allen hurried to the officers' quarters to demand the British surrender. Captain William Delaplace, although previously warned of the possibility of a rebel attack, at that time had only one other officer and 48 men as the garrison. Roused from his bed, he quickly agreed to give up.

Allen then dispatched a small group to take CROWN POINT, which it did on 12 May, bringing the total matériel haul to 78 guns, six mortars, three howitzers, and a great store of cannonballs and other munitions. This artillery train proved crucial to General George WASHINGTON's siege of BOSTON.

In 1777 the British leadership conceived a plan to seize the Champlain-Hudson line with a three-pronged attack from Oswego, Montreal, and New York City. The first obstacle to confront Major General John Burgoyne's Montreal-based offensive was the rebuilt American fortifications at Ticonderoga. Despite the new and extensive defensive works and the political value placed on holding Ticonderoga, there were insufficient American troops (2,500) to defend what was in reality a vulnerable position. Burgoyne advanced with 7,000 regulars and 2,500 militia and Indians, arriving outside of Ticonderoga in early July.

The British operated on both sides of the lake, seeking to cut off any American retreat while bringing up guns to lay siege. The key for the British turned out to be the building of a road to the top of Mount Defiance, from which artillery could fire down into the main fort and threaten the bridge of boats that represented the American route of retreat. Major General Arthur ST. CLAIR, witnessing the British preparations, decided that his position was untenable and, under a cannonade and the cover of darkness, pulled out toward Skenesboro on 5 July.

See also SARATOGA, CAMPAIGN AND BATTLES OF; FORT STANWIX; HUBBARDTON, BATTLE OF.

Further reading: Ketchum, Richard M. *Saratoga: Turning Point in the America's Revolutionary War.* New York: Henry Holt, 1997.

— Wayne E. Lee

Fort Wagner, assault on (18 July 1863) *Civil War engagement and a Union blunder transformed into a moral victory by the redemptive bravery of the 54th Massachusetts Volunteer Infantry, the first black regiment raised by a Northern state east of the Mississippi.*

In the summer of 1863 Brigadier General Quincy A. Gillmore, commander of the Union Department of the South, launched siege operations against CHARLESTON, South Carolina, with 11,750 troops. Gillmore first planned to seize Morris Island on the southeast side of Charleston Harbor. Cummings Point at the northern tip of Morris Island sat 1,390 yards from FORT SUMTER, which guarded the harbor's mouth. With heavy rifled artillery on Cummings Point, Gillmore hoped to neutralize Sumter. Rear Admiral John A. DAHLGREN's Union warships would then enter the harbor and force Charleston's surrender.

Union infantrymen landed on lower Morris Island on 10 July 1863 and quickly occupied it, with the exception of Fort Wagner, 1,200 yards south of Cummings Point. The fort measured 630 feet from east to west and 275 feet from north to south. Its thick sand walls stood 30 feet high. Two bastions flanked the south wall, which sat behind a wide moat, and a bombproof shelter inside the southeast bastion had room for 900 men. The fort mounted 10 heavy guns and one seacoast mortar.

The Federals were restricted as to the axis of their attack. They could approach the fort only along a narrow beach bounded by the Atlantic Ocean and a marshy creek. Gillmore tried to rush Wagner with three regiments early on 11 July, but the Confederate garrison repulsed the attack with 339 Federal casualties.

Gillmore decided to subject Fort Wagner to thorough artillery preparation before storming it again. Between 12 and 16 July Union engineers emplaced 41 guns and siege mortars within range of the Rebel works. In the meantime, the Confederates reinforced Wagner and increased its armament to 11 guns and one mortar aiming south, two guns facing seaward, and two field pieces covering the beach.

At 9 A.M. on 18 July Gillmore's batteries opened fire. Eleven Union warships joined in the bombardment, making it the most intensive of the war. Incredibly, the 9,000 shells that struck Fort Wagner left the 1,620-man garrison virtually unscathed.

Gillmore chose Brigadier General Truman Seymour's 6,000-man infantry division to overrun Fort Wagner. With the acquiescence of Colonel Robert Gould SHAW, the 54th Massachusetts, the Union army's model black regiment, headed the assault column.

The assault commenced at 7:45 P.M. Assuming that Gillmore's bombardment had either killed or dislodged the fort's defenders, Seymour fed his division into the assault piecemeal. His first two brigades encountered deadly cannon and rifle fire as they closed on Wagner. Fragments from 54th Massachusetts and other Northern units penetrated the fort at two points, but the Confederates contained these lodgments. Before Seymour's third brigade could enter the bloodbath, Gillmore canceled the assault.

The defeat cost Gillmore 1,515 casualties. A shell fragment prostrated Seymour, and two of his brigade commanders suffered fatal wounds. The 54th Massachusetts reported 272 losses, including Shaw, who had died in the attack. Thus was more any other attacking regiment, but the 54th's courage justified the Union army's recruitment of black soldiers. Wagner's defenders suffered only 222 casualties.

See also AFRICAN AMERICANS IN THE MILITARY; CIVIL WAR, NAVAL OVERVIEW.

Further reading: Duncan, Russell, ed. *Blue-Eyed Child of Fortune: The Civil War Letters of Colonel Robert Gould Shaw.* Athens: University of Georgia Press, 1992; Emilio, Luis E. *A Brave Black Regiment: The History of the Fifty-fourth Regiment of Massachusetts Volunteer Infantry, 1863–1865.* New York: Da Capo, 1995; Wise, Stephen R. *Gate of Hell: Campaign for Charleston Harbor, 1863.* Columbia: University of South Carolina Press, 1994; Yacovone, Donald, ed. *A Voice of Thunder: The Civil War Letters of George E. Stephens.* Urbana: University of Illinois Press, 1997.

— Gregory J. W. Urwin

Fort Washington (16–20 November 1776) *Fort on the northern neck of Manhattan Island, captured by the British during the War of the American Revolution in the campaign for New York City*
When the British moved to outflank General George WASHINGTON's position on HARLEM HEIGHTS by landing on the the Bronx Peninsula, Washington was forced to abandon the heights. He marched across Kings Bridge to the mainland, clashing with Major General William Howe's force at WHITE PLAINS. Washington did not entirely abandon Manhattan Island, however. He left behind 1,200 men under Colonel Robert Magaw to hold Fort Washington, with 1,600 more in other nearby smaller positions.

The fort dominated the northern end of the island, perched on a hill a mile long, 230 feet high, and with nearly vertical cliffs fronting both the Hudson and East Rivers. The fort was not well constructed, however, and lacked most of the amenities and features required of an 18th-century strongpoint. The decision to hold it arose from its role, in combination with its twin FORT LEE across the Hudson in New Jersey, in blocking naval movement up the Hudson. Congress had advocated closing the river here, and in fact a British effort to run the gauntlet on 27 October had failed.

After Washington was forced to retreat from White Plains, Howe, rather than pursue, turned south to capture the bypassed Fort Washington. Howe was in position by 15 November and on that day demanded the fort's surrender. Magaw declined, and the next day Howe attacked from the north, east, and south. Washington had arrived at Fort Lee and on the day of the attack crossed over to Fort Washington. Unable to provide any assistance, he quickly returned to New Jersey. The Americans put up a strong resistance but finally were forced to surrender at 3 P.M. Washington thus suffered the loss of another 2,800 men and much matériel, while the 8,000 British attackers had lost 458 killed and wounded. The battle was a serious blow to the American cause.

See also FORT LEE; PRINCETON, BATTLE OF; TRENTON, BATTLE OF.

Further reading: Middlekauff, Robert. *The Glorious Cause: The American Revolution, 1763–1789.* New York: Oxford University Press, 1982.

— Wayne E. Lee

Fort William Henry (August 1757) *British fortress on Lake George captured by the French during the French and Indian War*
Constructed in the fall of 1755, Fort William Henry (named after the dukes of Cumberland and Gloucester) was intended to defend upper New York and serve as a base for attacking the French at Fort Carillon (TICONDEROGA) and Fort St. Frédéric (CROWN POINT).

In early 1757 the French commander in chief in Canada, Major General Louis-Joseph, the marquis de Montcalm-Gozon de Saint-Véran, launched plans to destroy Fort William Henry. After a French and Indian raiding party burned outlying buildings in mid-March, Lieutenant Colonel George Monro brought five companies of the 35th Regiment of Foot to relieve Captain William Eyre. With subsequent reinforcements, Monro would have just 2,500 men (including militia) to defend his position.

Indian attacks throughout the spring and summer of 1757 disrupted supply lines from Fort Edward and prevented reconnaissance, allowing Montcalm to depart Fort Carillion unnoticed at the end of July with a force of approximately 6,000 regulars and militia, and 2,000 Indians from 33 different tribes. When the British awoke on 3 August 1757, they were startled to discover 250 French bateaux and 150 Indian canoes bringing some 4,000 men and siege guns toward them and to find that an advance force of 2,500 French regulars, Canadians, and Indians had moved behind them. Monro rejected Montcalm's initial demand that he surrender, but on 7 August he received word that Fort Edward's commander, Major General Daniel Webb, had declined to come to his aid until he himself received reinforcements. With Montcalm's batteries pounding his own position, Monro had no choice but to surrender, which he did on 9 August.

Although Montcalm generously granted safe passage for the entire garrison, the members of which were allowed to retain their small arms and personal possessions on the condition that they remain noncombatants for the next 18 months, Montcalm's Indian allies refused to abide by the terms. On the evening of 9 August they massacred some 60 wounded British soldiers who had remained behind, and on 10 August they attacked Monro's retreating column, killing as many as 185 soldiers and civilians and taking approximately 400 captives. Montcalm condemned this Indian action and even paid ransoms for some 200 captives, who were returned by the end of August. Because many of the other captives suffered from smallpox, the western tribes would soon pay for their actions.

The capture of Fort William Henry wounded British pride, but it was not decisive. Lacking provisions and having lost his Indian allies, Montcalm had to be content with destroying the fort before returning to Fort Carillan.

See also QUEBEC, CAMPAIGN OF (1759).

Further reading: Anderson, Fred. *Crucible of War: The Seven Years' War and the Fate of Empire in British North America, 1754–1766.* New York: Knopf, 2000; Barck, Oscar Theodore, Jr., and Hugh Talmage Lefler. *Colonial America.* 2d ed. New York: Macmillan, 1968.

— Justin D. Murphy

Foulois, Benjamin D. (1879–1967) *U.S. Army Air Corps general and leading advocate of military airpower during the years between the world wars*

Born on 9 December 1879 at Washington, Connecticut, Benjamin Delahauf Foulois enlisted in the army during the SPANISH-AMERICAN WAR. He quickly rose to first sergeant and then received a commission directly from the ranks. In 1908 Foulois became one of the first officers detailed to the new Aeronautical Division of the Signal Corps. In 1909 he flew as Orville Wright's passenger during the army's final acceptance test of the Wright Flyer.

Foulois served for a time as the chief of the Air Service of the AMERICAN EXPEDITIONARY FORCE (AEF) in France during World War I. During the 1920s he held various air and ground assignments. In 1931 Foulois became chief of the U.S. Army Air Corps, with the rank of major general. His four years in office were marked by controversy and almost constant battling with the War Department and the Army General Staff. In 1934 he testified before the House Military Affairs Committee that the army was incapable of managing and developing the nation's air assets.

Foulios retired in 1935 under a cloud. His constant agitation for an independent air force, however, forced the army to reorganize its air arm under a General Headquarters (GHQ) Air Force, which became the organizational model for the Army Air Forces in World War II. For the first time, all of the army's air assets came under a single commander, Major General Frank M. ANDREWS.

Foulois played no direct role in World War II, but the influence of his earlier contributions was great. When he took office in 1931, the speed, range, and payload of the U.S. bomber force were little different from what they had been in World War I. By the time he left office, the Army Air Corps was already starting to purchase the B-17 bomber. Foulois died in Ventnor City, New Jersey, on 25 April 1967.

See also AIR FORCE, U.S.

Further reading: Foulois, Benjamin D., and Carroll V. Glines. *From the Wright Brothers to the Astronauts: The Memoirs of Major General Benjamin D. Foulois.* New York: McGraw-Hill, 1968; McClendon, R. Earl. *The Question of Autonomy for the U.S. Air Arm.* Maxwell Air Force Base, Ala.: Air University, 1950.

— David T. Zabecki

Fox, Gustavus V. (1821–1883) *Assistant secretary of the U.S. Navy during the Civil War*

Born on 13 June 1821 at Saugus, Massachusetts, Gustavus Vasa Fox spent his formative years in Massachusetts. He attended Phillips Academy in Andover before entering the navy as a midshipman in 1838. After being stationed in the Mediterranean and off Africa, Fox saw service in troop-transport duty during the MEXICAN-AMERICAN WAR and was promoted to lieutenant in 1852. In 1856 he resigned his commission to enter private business, becoming an agent for Bay State Mills in Lawrence, Massachusetts.

During the secession crisis preceding the Civil War, Fox went to Washington to propose a plan to relieve the Federal garrison at FORT SUMTER, but President James Buchanan rejected his proposal to send steamships past the Charleston Harbor batteries at night. Following his inauguration in March 1861, President Abraham LINCOLN approved the plan and sent Fox to Charleston in an attempt to seek an arrangement that would allow the resupply of Sumter. Fox did not arrive in Charleston until 12 April, too late to do anything except transport Federal troops north after the surrender of Fort Sumter on the 13th.

Despite the failure of Fox's expedition, Lincoln was pleased with his efforts and offered him a ship command. Fox turned down the opportunity in order to serve instead as chief clerk in the Navy Department. In July 1861 Congress authorized the position of assistant secretary of the navy, to which post Lincoln appointed Fox.

Fox made significant contributions to the Union's war effort. An early advocate of ironclads, he persuaded Secretary of the Navy Gideon WELLES to employ the *MONITOR*. He also urged appointment of Flag Officer David G. FARRAGUT to command the 1862 expedition against NEW ORLEANS. Fox's political ability, honesty, and knowledge of naval affairs made him indispensable to the Union cause.

Fox resigned his post in May 1866 and was appointed to be an emissary to Russia. Following this mission, he returned to private business, serving as an agent for the Middlesex Company in Lowell, Massachusetts. Fox died in New York City on 29 October 1883. His papers, published after his death, are a valuable source of information on the Civil War at sea.

See also CIVIL WAR, NAVAL OVERVIEW; IRONCLADS, U.S., IN CIVIL WAR.

Further reading: Fowler, William M. *Under Two Flags: The American Navy in the Civil War.* New York: Norton, 1990; Fox, Gustavus Vasa. *Confidential Correspondence of Gustavus Vasa Fox, Assistant Secretary of the Navy, 1861–1865.* Edited by Robert Means Thompson and Richard Wainwright. Freeport, N.Y.: Books for Libraries Press, 1972.

— Alexander Mendoza

France and the American Revolution

As an absolute monarchy and a colonial power, France was not motivated to support the American colonies in their struggle for independence from Great Britain by sympathy for their cause. Rather, it was a calculated strategy to maintain France's standing as a great power and secure revenge for the humiliating losses of the Seven Years' War (FRENCH AND INDIAN WAR, 1754–63). King Louis XVI's foreign minister, Charles Gravier, comte de Vergennes, oversaw a global strategy that included an alliance with Spain and direct challenges to British interests in the Caribbean, the Mediterranean, and India. In pursuit of its larger goal, France was willing to abandon its hopes of regaining New France (Canada) in favor of striking a blow at British control of North America.

As early as September 1775 French agents were in America to assess the status of the rebellion. In March 1776 France opened unofficial contacts with American representatives and provided loans. During 1776 and 1777 a substantial amount of covert French military supplies, channeled by HORTALEZ AND COMPANY, sustained the Continental army. American PRIVATEERS raiding the English coastline received covert assistance in French ports. France played a waiting game in the first years of the war, seeking to sustain the Americans enough to keep British land and naval forces occupied in a debilitating war of attrition.

In October 1777 the Americans forced the surrender of a British army at SARATOGA, greatly aided by French weapons. King Louis XVI then authorized treaty negotiations with American representatives in France, and on 6 February 1778 a Treaty of Commerce and Alliance was signed. Soon thereafter French warships were escorting American merchant ships across the Atlantic.

Initial French efforts to support the Americans directly met with failure. In 1778 Vice Admiral Charles Hector, Comte d'Estaing, arrived with a squadron and 4,000 troops to assist American forces. Reluctant to commit his force against New York, he instead joined an American effort to capture NEWPORT, Rhode Island. But d'Estaing then abandoned the Americans, moving to Boston to refit after a storm. Hostility between French sailors and Americans brought confrontations in Boston that led to the death of a French officer. Nonetheless, in October 1779 d'Estaing provided ships and troops to support Major General Benjamin LINCOLN's effort to capture British-held SAVANNAH, Georgia. He left the Americans after a disastrous assault on the British defenses failed to capture the city.

In 1779 Marie-Joseph Paul Yves Roch Gilbert du Motier, the marquis de LAFAYETTE, a French nobleman on the staff of the Continental army commander, General George WASHINGTON, returned to France to help American representatives convince King Louis XVI to send French troops to America. But the poor condition of American forces in 1779 and 1780, as well as British successes in the American South, worried Vergennes. In July 1779 a squadron of 17 French warships ships reached Newport escorting transports carrying Lieutenant General Jean-Baptiste Donatien de Vimeur, comte de Rochambeau, and 12 battalions of French regulars (4,000 men). Although small, the force was self-sufficient and included engineers, logistics, and administrative support (including several million livres in gold). Rochambeau's instructions were to keep

328 Franklin, Battle of

the French force together, serve only under Washington, and resist any American plan to attack Canada. In the short term, the French troops and French money were intended to prevent the American army, which had been neither paid nor supplied for months, from disintegrating altogether.

On 21 May 1781 Washington and Rochambeau met at Wethersfield, Connecticut, to discuss strategy. Initial planning centered on a joint French-American attack against the British in New York City. In August Admiral François Joseph Paul, comte de Grasse, sent word that he would sail for North America on 13 August with 25–29 ships of the line, 3,200 soldiers, and 1.2 million livres for Rochambeau's army. He would be coming not to New York but to Chesapeake Bay.

Washington immediately saw the possibility of a strategic concentration of force against the base of Major General Charles, Lord Cornwallis at YORKTOWN. Within a week of receiving word from de Grasse, Washington and Rochambeau were moving the bulk of their combined force south to Virginia to meet him.

Their combined arms sealed Cornwallis's fate. On 5 September 1781, in the Battle of the CHESAPEAKE (Capes), de Grasse drove off a British naval force. Meanwhile a French squadron from Newport arrived, transporting all-important siege artillery and supplies. Formal siege operations then began at Yorktown, and Cornwallis surrendered on 19 October. A small number of French troops remained in America until the end of the war, but the vast majority embarked for the West Indies in December 1782.

French intervention had proved decisive. France had spent an estimated 40 million livres to support the Americans in their war for independence. Even though France was fighting Britain around the globe, after it entered the war it was able to supply to North American operations 63 ships with 22,000 officers and sailors. France also sent 12,000 troops to North America, including some of the best regiments in its army. Of these, 2,112 died in battle.

But this revival of French naval power and the expenses of the war exhausted the national finances. To raise new revenue, the crown attempted to tax the nobles, an act that resulted in the French Revolution of 1789. France received few tangible rewards for its efforts in America.

See also AMERICAN REVOLUTIONARY WAR, LAND OVERVIEW; AMERICAN REVOLUTIONARY WAR, NAVAL OVERVIEW; PARIS, TREATY OF (1782); SPAIN IN THE AMERICAN REVOLUTION.

Further reading: Dull, Jonathan R. *The French Navy and American Independence. A Study of Arms and Diplomacy, 1774–1787.* Princeton, N.J.: Princeton University Press, 1975; Kennet, Lee. *The French Forces in America,* *1780–1783.* Westport, Conn.: Greenwood, 1977; Rice, Howard C., and Anne S. K. Brown. *The American Campaigns of Rochambeau's Army.* 2 vols. Princeton, N.J.: Princeton University Press, 1972; Ross, Maurice. *Louis XVI, America's Forgotten Founding Father: With a Survey of the Franco-American Alliance of the Revolutionary Period.* New York: Vantage, 1976.

— Keith D. Dickson

Franklin, Battle of (30 November 1864) *One of the most intense battles of the Civil War*
In July 1864 General John Bell HOOD assumed command of the Confederate Army of Tennessee, relieving General Joseph E. JOHNSTON, who had withdrawn to the outskirts of ATLANTA. Hood launched a series of desperate attacks before yielding the city to the Federal army of Major General William T. SHERMAN in September. Sherman soon began his MARCH TO THE SEA, cutting a wide swath of destruction through Georgia. Hood attempted to draw Sherman out of the Deep South by threatening Federal communications in northern Georgia, swinging his army into Alabama before turning northward into Tennessee and its Union-held capital of Nashville. Sherman refused to take the bait but did dispatch a large portion of his force, under Major General George THOMAS, to deal with Hood.

After turning a Federal position at Columbia but failing to trap Major General John M. SCHOFIELD's force at Spring Hill, Hood's army arrived on 30 November before Franklin, where Schofield had moved into prepared works. Hood perceived an opportunity to crush the Federals and ordered an attack, not waiting for his force to concentrate (Lieutenant General S. D. Lee's corps and most of the army's artillery had not come up). The infantry corps of Major General Benjamin F. Cheatham and Lieutenant General Alexander P. STEWART, with flank support from Major General Nathan Bedford FORREST's cavalry, would have to attack more than two miles of fairly open ground on a broad front without artillery preparation to strike the well-protected Federal position, which covered the town and the vital crossings of the Harpeth River.

The attack came at about 3:30 P.M. Exploiting a flawed Federal deployment, the ferocious Confederate assault briefly pierced the Union center before reserves sealed the breach. In some of the most desperate fighting of the war, Hood's men pounded away at the Union center, held by the divisions of Brigadier Generals Thomas Ruger and Jacob Cox. The carnage mounted as Confederate infantry doggedly pressed the Federal entrenchments. Meanwhile, cavalry attacks against both flanks were turned back. Hood finally suspended the effort at 9 P.M., but fighting lasted until almost midnight. Later that night Schofield withdrew across the Harpeth, leaving Hood the field.

Of some 27,000 Confederates engaged, 6,250 were casualties. The losses were particularly heavy among Hood's generals: one was captured, six were badly wounded, and six were killed or mortally wounded, including Major General Patrick CLEBURNE, one of the most talented division commanders in the Confederate army. Schofield's casualties amounted to 2,300 of about 28,000 engaged. The bloody Battle of Franklin virtually crippled Hood's army, but the young, one-legged general pushed on nonetheless to NASHVILLE, where Thomas on 15–16 December delivered the coup de grace to Hood in one of the most decisive victories of the war.

Hood retreated into Mississippi, where in January 1865 he was relieved of command. Remnants of the Army of Tennessee were shipped to Mobile or to North Carolina to serve again under Johnston.

See also CIVIL WAR, LAND OVERVIEW.

Further reading: Bailey, Anne J. *The Chessboard of War: Sherman and Hood in the Autumn Campaigns of 1864.* Lincoln: University of Nebraska Press, 2000; Cox, Jacob D. *Sherman's March to the Sea, Hood's Tennessee Campaign, and the Carolina Campaign of 1865.* Reprint, New York: Da Capo, 1994; Sword, Wiley. *The Confederacy's Last Hurrah: Spring Hill, Franklin, and Nashville.* New York: HarperCollins, 1992.

— Colin P. Mahle and David Coffey

Frederick, Robert T. (1907–1970) *U.S. Army general*
Born on 14 March 1907 at San Francisco, California, Robert Tryon Frederick graduated from the United States Military Academy at WEST POINT and was commissioned a second lieutenant of coast artillery in June 1928. Throughout the late 1920s and early 1930s, Frederick served in coast artillery assignments at various locations in the United States and the Canal Zone.

After assignments with the Civilian Conservation Corps, a stint as a general's aide, and a year of study at the Coast Artillery School at Fort Monroe, Frederick attended the Command and General Staff School at Fort Leavenworth. In 1939 he was assigned to Hawaii as a battery commander with the 64th Coast Artillery.

In August 1941 Frederick was assigned to the War Plans Directorate of the War Department. While serving there he was promoted to colonel and selected to command the 1st Special Service Force (1st SSF), a combined U.S. and Canadian special operations brigade. At Fort William Henry Harrison, Montana, Frederick trained the 1st SSF in winter and mountain warfare. He continued the brigade's training at Camp Bradford, Virginia, and Camp Ethan Allen, Vermont. On 15 July 1943, Frederick led the brigade in its assault on Kiska Island in the ALEUTIANS CAMPAIGN, only to find it deserted by Japanese forces.

After returning to the United States in September, Frederick received orders to move the 1st SSF to the Mediterranean theater. It arrived at Naples, Italy, in December 1943 and went into the line at Santa Maria. In Italy Frederick led the 1st SSF through several significant engagements, including the attacks on Monte la Difensa, Monte Sammucro, and Monte Vischiataro. He was promoted to brigadier general in January 1944. On 2 February Frederick led the brigade onto the ANZIO beachhead, where it fought for the next three months. The 1st SSF fought so effectively that the Germans called it the Devil's Brigade.

In July 1944 Frederick was appointed commander of the 1st Airborne Task Force for Operation DRAGOON, the invasion of southern France. On 15 August 1944, two weeks after Frederick's promotion to major general, the task force jumped into France near Le Muy-Le Luc and blocked German access to the invasion beaches. Over the next three months, Frederick pushed the task force through Cannes and Nice to the Franco-Italian border.

In December 1944 Frederick assumed command of the 45th (Thunderbird) Division near the Maginot Line in eastern France. From there, he led the division through the rest of its campaigns in the war, ending at Munich, Germany, in May 1945. Frederick was wounded in combat eight times, more than any other American general of World War II.

After the war, Frederick held several key assignments, including command U.S. Troops, Vienna, Austria (1948); of the 4th Infantry Division (1949–50); and of the 6th Infantry Division (1950–51). Frederick retired from the army in 1952. He died at Stanford, California, on 29 November 1970.

See also AIRBORNE FORCES; WORLD WAR II, U.S. INVOLVEMENT, EUROPE; WORLD WAR II, U.S. INVOLVEMENT, PACIFIC.

Further reading: Adleman, Robert H., and George Adleman. *The Devil's Brigade.* Philadelphia: Chilton Books, 1966; Ross, Robert T. *The Supercommandos: First Special Service Force, 1942–1945: An Illustrated History.* Atglen, Pa.: Schiffer, 2000; Whitlock, Flint. *Rock of Anzio: From Sicily to Dachau, History of the 45th Infantry Division.* Boulder, Colo.: Westview, 1968.

— Steven E. Clay

Fredericksburg, Battle of (13 December 1862) *Civil War battle*
On 7 November 1862 Major General Ambrose BURNSIDE replaced Major General George B. MCCLELLAN as commander of the Federal Army of the Potomac. Uncertain of his own abilities but determined to utilize the army that

Battle of Fredericksburg, Virginia, 13 December 1862. Lithograph by Currier & Ives   *(Library of Congress)*

MCCLELLAN had been so hesitant to employ, Burnside almost caught General Robert E. LEE's Army of Northern Virginia off guard.

Feinting an advance toward Warrenton, Virginia, on 15 November Burnside moved rapidly southeast to Falmouth on the Rappahannock River across from the town of Fredericksburg. For several days Burnside had the Confederates confused as to his whereabouts. If he had crossed the river quickly, Burnside could have positioned his force between Lee's army and the Confederate capital of Richmond.

The pontoons needed to make the river crossing had not been assigned high priority, and they were unready when Burnside arrived at Falmouth on 19 November. Burnside chose to wait, losing his advantage, as the pontoons did not arrive until 30 November. By that time, Lee had ascertained Burnside's objective and had taken position at Fredericksburg. Lee also ordered Lieutenant General Thomas J. "Stonewall" JACKSONS's II Corps up from its position in the Shenandoah Valley.

Burnside, undaunted, was determined to cross the river and engage Lee. Union army engineers worked to complete the pontoon bridges under constant harassment by Confederate snipers. This fire took such a toll that

Burnside finally resorted to a preliminary assault by boat. These troops dislodged the Confederates and secured the riverbank.

On 13 December Burnside's force of 121,000 men crossed the river on five pontoon bridges. Facing the Army of the Potomac were 74,000 Confederates, spread out to the south and west of the town of Fredericksburg. At Marye's Heights, a steep incline west of the town, Lieutenant General James LONGSTREET's I Corps had fortified an already strong position behind a stone wall. Jackson's corps was on the Confederate right, behind a railroad embankment south of town in the vicinity of Prospect Hill.

Burnside's army consisted of three "grand divisions" (groups of divisions) commanded by Major Generals William B. Franklin, Joseph HOOKER, and Edwin V. Sumner. Franklin, with 50,000 men, was to attack the Confederate right, while Sumner would assault Marye's Heights. Hooker's grand division was to assist whichever Union force achieved a breakthrough.

The Union attack began on 13 December. Franklin's divisions hit Jackson's portion of the line. Two, those commanded by Brigadier General John GIBBON and Major General George G. MEADE, broke through for a short period of time, only to be halted when Franklin failed to

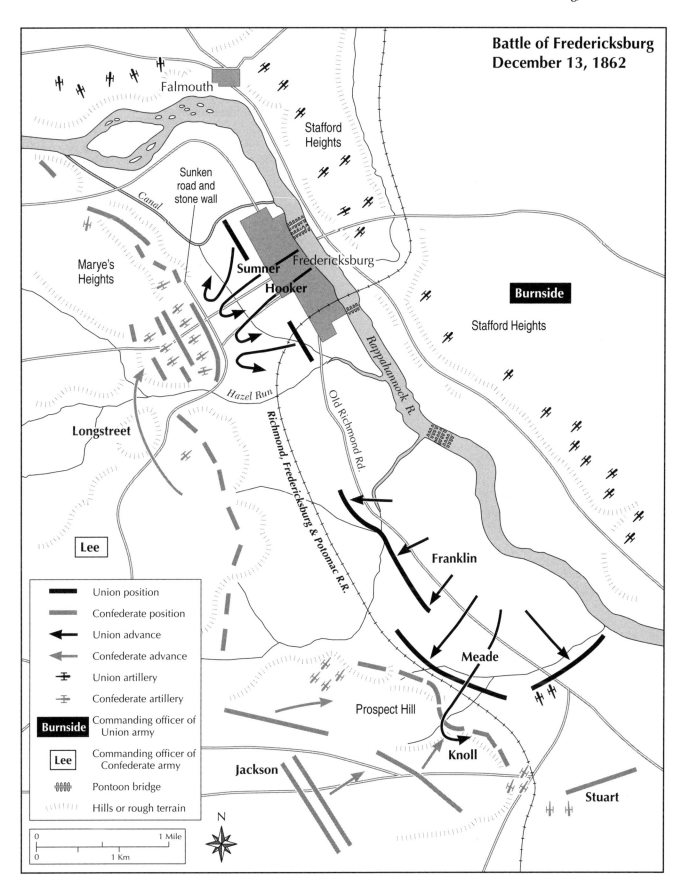

**Battle of Fredericksburg
December 13, 1862**

Falmouth

Stafford
Heights

Canal

Sunken
road and
stone wall

Marye's
Heights

Sumner

Fredericksburg

Hooker

Burnside

Stafford Heights

Rappahannock R.

Hazel Run

Longstreet

Richmond, Fredericksburg & Potomac R.R.

Old Richmond Rd.

Lee

Franklin

Union position

Confederate position

Union advance

Confederate advance

Union artillery

Confederate artillery

Burnside Commanding officer of
Union army

Lee Commanding officer of
Confederate army

Pontoon bridge

Hills or rough terrain

Meade

Prospect Hill

Jackson

Knoll

Stuart

0   1 Mile

N

0   1 Km

reinforce. Had Franklin done so or renewed the attack, the outcome of the battle might have been different.

On the Union right, Sumner and Hooker launched a series of futile attacks against Longstreet's position on Marye's Heights. Despite superior numbers, each Federal attack was repulsed with heavy casualties from well-organized Confederate artillery and rifle fire. The bulk of rebel firepower was provided by Brigadier General Thomas R. Cobb's Georgians, who lined up behind a four-foot-high stone wall along a road paralleling the crest of Marye's Heights. Again and again Union assaults by Sumner and then Hooker's men were turned back, the front rank of Longstreet's men would fire and stepped back from the wall to reload while a second and third rank took their turns. None of the advancing troops reached the wall. On the approach of darkness, Burnside halted the attacks. Nearly overcome with grief, Burnside nonetheless planned to renew the attack the next day, leading it in person, but was talked out of it by his senior commanders. He then withdrew his army across the river to Falmouth. In January, a second attempt to turn Lee's position was foiled by bad weather.

Fredericksburg was one of the most demoralizing Union defeats of the war. It was also Lee's most lopsided victory. Union casualties were 12,653 dead, wounded, and missing compared to only 5,309 for the Confederates. President Abraham LINCOLN replaced Burnside with Hooker, who in turn met defeat the next spring at CHANCELLORSVILLE. The battle also brought a profound crisis of confidence in the North and charges and countercharges against the Lincoln administration.

See also CIVIL WAR, LAND OVERVIEW.

Further reading: Brooks, Victor. *The Fredericksburg Campaign: October 1862–January 1863.* Conshohocken, Pa.: Combined, 2000; Gallagher, Gary W., ed. *The Fredericksburg Campaign: Decision on the Rappahannock.* Chapel Hill: University of North Carolina Press, 1991; Marvel, William. *Burnside.* Chapel Hill: University of North Carolina Press, 1991.

— Bruce Tap

Frémont, John C. (1813–1890) *Explorer and U.S. Army general*

Born on 21 January 1813 at Savannah, Georgia, John Charles Frémont was the illegitimate son of a Virginia woman and an itinerant Frenchmen. Frémont studied at the College of Charleston from 1829 to 1831 but did not graduate. In 1833 he received an appointment as a math instructor on a naval vessel, a position he retained for two years. He then served on several western survey projects and in 1838 was commissioned a second lieutenant in the Army Corps of Topographical Engineers. After serving as a subordinate to the explorer and scientist Joseph Nicolett on several expeditions, Frémont in 1842 headed his own expedition, a four-month survey of the Oregon Trail. Assisted by the skills of his guide, the legendary mountain man Christopher "Kit" CARSON, and his wife Jesse Benton Frémont, who contributed her literary talents to the preparation of his report of the expedition, Frémont won acclaim for this mission. His growing reputation was enhanced by subsequent western expeditions in 1843–44 and 1846.

Upon the outbreak of the MEXICAN-AMERICAN WAR in 1846, Frémont played a leading role in the American occupation of California. A conflict between Frémont and General Stephen KEARNY, however, resulted in Frémont's court-martial, conviction, and dismissal from the army. President James K. Polk suspended the sentence, but Frémont resigned.

Frémont led another western expedition in late 1848, an attempt to cross the Rocky Mountains in winter, which resulted in disaster and the death of 10 of his men. He briefly served as senator from California from 1850 to 1851 and received the presidential nomination of the Republican Party in 1856. Although Frémont was widely popular, due to his heroic image and antislavery views, he lost decisively.

In May 1861, at the outbreak of the Civil War, Frémont was appointed a major general of U.S. Volunteers and assigned to command the Federal Department of the West. He proved unequal to the task and was removed in November 1861. In 1862, after a brief assignment in the Shenandoah Valley as commander of the newly formed Mountain Department, Frémont resigned. In 1864 he briefly considered, but ultimately rejected, another run for the presidency. After the war he served as governor of the Arizona Territory (1878–81) and pursued a variety of unsuccessful business ventures. Frémont died in New York City on 13 July 1890.

See also JACKSON'S SHENANDOAH VALLEY CAMPAIGN.

Further reading: Nevins, Allan. *Frémont: The West's Greatest Adventurer.* 2 vols. New York: Harper and Brothers, 1928; Rolle, Andrew. *John Charles Frémont: Character as Destiny.* Norman: University of Oklahoma Press, 1991.

— Michael Thomas Smith

French America

New France and the Indian nations of eastern North America's interior, not the British colonies, were the dominant military powers for most of the 17th and 18th centuries. The French empire in North America was a network of forts, trading posts, missions, and small settlements stretching from the Gulf of St. Lawrence to the Great

Lakes and down the Mississippi River to Louisiana; by the 1750s the French had also fortified the lower Lake Champlain Valley and the upper Ohio Valley.

The French enjoyed the most harmonious (if occasionally discordant) relations with Indian peoples of all the various European colonizers. New France's military power was largely dependent upon its many fur-trading alliances with Indian nations, Catholic missionary influence among the Indians, and the parish-based militia from the St. Lawrence Valley settlements. Much of New France's history was marked by chronic warfare—first with the Five Nations (Iroquois) and then with the British colonies—over control of North America and its resources.

After preliminary explorations and failed colonization ventures in the 16th century, the French planted a permanent colony (Quebec) in North America along the St. Lawrence River in 1608 under Samuel de Champlain. The local Huron, Algonquin, and Montagnais formed trading and military alliances with the French, who soon found themselves embroiled in conflict with their allies' traditional enemies, the Five Nations. Champlain's use of firearms against an Iroquois war party in 1609 at Lake Champlain symbolize the clash of European and Indian military practices; it also marked the beginning of New France's nearly 100-year-long struggle with the Five Nations.

The French sought to expand their influence among the far-western Indians through the fur trade. The Five Nations sought territorial security and waged "mourning wars" against other native peoples to replace kin lost to epidemic diseases and combat. The French and their allies were never able to conquer the Five Nations, but they inflicted tremendous casualties. After the peace of 1701 at Montreal, the embattled Five Nations coexisted with the French and pledged neutrality in any future Anglo-French wars—a policy that lasted until the 1750s.

In the largely indecisive Anglo-French imperial wars that occurred from 1689 to 1748 (KING WILLIAM'S WAR, QUEEN ANNE'S WAR, and KING GEORGE'S WAR), the French and their Indian allies held the more populous British colonies at bay. With few economic incentives (excepting the fur trade), New France never attracted large numbers of colonists. Consequently, by the 1750s the white population of the British colonies was about 20 times that of New France. But the French held many advantages that gave their military power considerable longevity. New France and allied Indian nations were commercially and militarily interdependent and wished to preserve their lands from English encroachment. The French had greater mobility on crucial interior waterways, such as the St. Lawrence River, the Great Lakes, and the Mississippi. New France's governor-general more effectively mobilized the colony and coordinated military offensives than the disunited British colonies could. French-Canadian officers were skilled in diplomacy with their Indian allies, and French-Canadian militia were highly adapted to fighting in the woods. As a result, joint war parties of Indian warriors and Canadians frequently devastated the vulnerable British frontiers in New England, New York, Pennsylvania, and Virginia.

During the FRENCH AND INDIAN WAR, under Governor-General Pierre Rigaud de Vaudreuil's direction, the French and their native allies initially inflicted catastrophic defeats upon British armies and destroyed British settlements on the frontier. Franco-Indian victories at MONONGAHELA, OSWEGO, and FORT WILLIAM HENRY stymied British advances. But in 1758 and 1759, the British regrouped, capturing the French fortresses of LOUISBOURG, FRONTENAC, DUQUESNE, CROWN POINT, and NIAGARA, thereby interrupting supply of and communication with far-western Indian and French forces. Combined with British naval mastery on the Atlantic, these victories put the French on the defensive in North America. Major General James Wolfe's victory in the Battle of the PLAINS OF ABRAHAM in 1759, however, did not end French resistance; not until three British armies encircled MONTREAL in 1760 did the French capitulate. The Treaty of PARIS (1763) ended the Seven Years' War and ceded New France to Great Britain.

The French were again a military presence in North America during the American Revolutionary War. American PRIVATEERS, which often called in French ports, precipitated a diplomatic crisis between Britain and France by 1777. After the American victory at SARATOGA, France declared war on Britain and allied with the United States. The French navy and army were crucial components in the British defeat at YORKTOWN in 1781, which helped to secure American independence.

See also CANADA, INVASION OF; CHESAPEAKE, FIRST AND SECOND BATTLES OF; CROWN POINT, EXPEDITION AGAINST, FORT PITT; FORT TICONDEROGA, BATTLE OF; FORT TICONDEROGA, CAMPAIGN; FRANCE AND THE AMERICAN REVOLUTION; JOHNSON, SIR WILLIAM; LAKE GEORGE, BATTLE OF; LAFAYETTE, MARQUIS DE; LOUISIANA PURCHASE; TROIS RIVIÈRES, BATTLE OF.

Further reading: Eccles, W. J. *Essays on New France.* New York: Oxford University Press, 1987; ———. *The Canadian Frontier, 1534–1760.* Rev. ed. Albuquerque: University of New Mexico Press, 1992; Greer, Allan. *The People of New France.* Toronto: University of Toronto Press, 1997; White, Richard. *The Middle Ground: Indians, Empires, and Republics in the Great Lakes Region, 1640–1815.* Cambridge, UK: Cambridge University Press, 1991.

— David L. Preston

French and Indian War (1754–1763) *A war for American empire fought between France and Britain, their respective colonies, and American Indian tribes*
The war began in a struggle for control of the vast lands of the trans-Appalachian region, especially the Ohio River Valley. To exclude English settlers from lands they claimed, the French established a series of forts across this area. The British built forts at Oswego, on Lake Ontario, and at Halifax, Nova Socita.

In 1750 British and French representatives met in Paris in an effort to resolve territorial differences, but they made little progress. In response in 1752 France sent Ange de Menneville, the marquis de Duquesne, to New France with orders to secure the Ohio Valley and drive the British from that area. The following year Duquesne sent soldiers to western Pennsylvania to construct additional forts. At the same time the governor of Virginia, Robert Dinwiddie, was granting land to British citizens under the charter of the Ohio Company.

On learning of the French activities, Dinwiddie dispatched Major George WASHINGTON to demand that the French leave the region. Not surprisingly, the mission was a failure, but on his return Washington surveyed a point of land at the confluence of the Ohio and Monongahela Rivers and recommended that a fort be built there. The British started construction on Fort Prince George in 1754 but were soon forced to surrender it to the French, who completed the fort under the name of FORT DUQUESNE.

In the meantime Major Washington was sent out with a small force of militia. On learning of events at Fort Prince George, Washington set up camp at Great Meadow. There Washington received reports that the French intended to attack his small outpost; he launched a preemptive strike with 40 men and 10 Indians against the French camp. This raid produced nothing more than a skirmish, and Washington moved back to Great Meadow and built FORT NECESSITY. A few weeks later the French attacked this position, forcing Washington to surrender and leave the area. The French now controlled the entire region west of the Allegheny Mountains.

In response, the British sent out reinforcements under Major General Edward BRADDOCK, who received

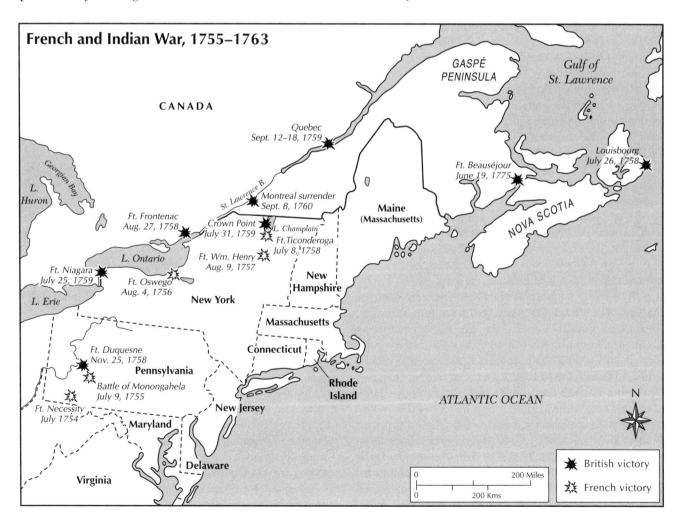

French and Indian War, 1755–1763

GASPÉ PENINSULA

Gulf of St. Lawrence

CANADA

Quebec
Sept. 12–18, 1759

Louisbourg
July 26, 1758

L. Huron

Georgian Bay

St. Lawrence R.

Ft. Beauséjour
June 19, 1775

Montreal surrender
Sept. 8, 1760

Maine
(Massachusetts)

NOVA SCOTIA

Ft. Frontenac
Aug. 27, 1758

Crown Point
July 31, 1759

L. Champlain

Ft. Ticonderoga
July 8, 1758

L. Ontario

Ft. Wm. Henry
Aug. 9, 1757

Ft. Niagara
July 25, 1759

Ft. Oswego
Aug. 4, 1756

New Hampshire

L. Erie

New York

Massachusetts

Connecticut

Ft. Duquesne
Nov. 25, 1758

Pennsylvania

Rhode Island

Battle of Monongahela
July 9, 1755

New Jersey

ATLANTIC OCEAN

N

Ft. Necessity
July 1754

Maryland

Delaware

Virginia

0   200 Miles

0   200 Kms

★ British victory

✦ French victory

command of all British forces in North America. Arriving in February 1755, Braddock made plans to recapture Fort Duquesne and led an expedition of 1,300 British regulars and 450 Virginia militia against it. On 9 July 1755, in the Battle of the MONONGAHELA, a few miles from his goal, Braddock's superior force was ambushed by some 900 French and allied Indians. Braddock's command suffered 50 percent casualties before disengaging and retreating. Braddock, mortally wounded, died during the retreat.

Despite open warfare between Britain and France in America, war was not formally declared between the two states until 1756, with the start of the Seven Years' War in Europe. Fighting in America was largely inconclusive; however, the French kept the upper hand by capturing FORT OSWEGO and FORT WILLIAM HENRY. Despite these setbacks, the British remained active, attacking a Delaware Indian village at Kittanning and rescuing 24 prisoners.

British fortunes began to change in 1758 as British prime minister William Pitt poured additional resources into the struggle. The British army executed a three-pronged attack on the French, against LOUISBOURG on Cape Breton Island, Fort Carillon (FORT TICONDEROGA) on Lake Champlain, and FORT FRONTENAC on Lake Ontario. The attack on Carillon failed, but Louisbourg and Frontenac fell to British sieges.

In Pennsylvania, many of the Indians abandoned their French allies. By July the French had had to abandon FORT DUQUESNE to British brigadier general John Forbes. For the first time the British controlled the Ohio Valley, the Great Lakes, and the mouth of the St. Lawrence River.

Throughout 1759 French forts continued to fall; the British secured CROWN POINT and FORT NIAGARA. The key to the American interior, the French stronghold at QUEBEC on the St. Lawrence River, was regarded as the strongest fortress in Canada. The British foresaw that capturing it would bring French resistance to an end.

In early 1759 the British planned the largest military operation on the war, a combined force of 9,000 regulars and militia commanded by Major General James Wolfe, supported by 20 warships under Vice Admiral Charles Saunders. The ships carried the men from Louisbourg to Orleans Island, just below Quebec. The French commander, Major General Louis-Joseph, marquis de Montcalm-Gozon de Saint-Véran, had 14,000 troops and allied Indians for the defense of the fortress.

Quebec lay high on cliffs above the St. Lawrence, and for two months Wolfe's efforts to gain a foothold near the city were foiled. Saunders, nervous over the prospect of his ships' being caught in ice by the approaching winter, threatened to leave. Finally, the British discovered a footpath up the cliffs just north of the city. On the night of 12–13 September, Wolfe sent a battalion of provincial rangers up the path under the command of Colonel William Howe, followed by four regular battalions of infantry. By dawn the next day Wolfe had 4,000 men drawn up in line of battle above the city on the Plains of Abraham.

Believing he could not hold the city if the British controlled this position, Montcalm attacked Wolfe, but he did so without artillery, which the governor of the city withheld. The battle saw both commanders mortally wounded but the British victorious. Quebec surrendered on 18 September. It was the turning point of the war, making eventual British victory all but certain. By the end of 1760 both MONTREAL and Detroit were also in British hands. Montreal fell to Major General Jeffrey Amherst and Detroit to colonial major Robert ROGERS and his famed Rangers. The French and Indian War left the British in control of North Africa. This fact was confirmed in the 1763 Treaty of PARIS.

See also AMERICAN INDIAN WARFARE, OVERVIEW OF; MILITIA, ORGANIZATION AND ROLE OF.

Further reading: Anderson, Fred. *Crucible of War: The Seven Years' War and the Fate of Empire in British North America, 1754–1766.* New York: Knopf, 2000; Jennings, Francis. *Empire of Fortune: Crowns, Colonies and Tribes in the Seven Years' War in America.* New York: Norton, 1988; Rafert, Stewart. *The Miami Indians of Indiana: A Persistent People, 1654–1994.* Bloomington: Indiana University Press, 1999; Schwartz, Seymour I. *The French and Indian War: The Imperial Struggle for North America.* New York: Simon and Schuster, 1994.

— Patrick R. Jennings

frigates *Warship type in the age of sail, forerunner of the modern cruiser*
Frigates were ship rigged (three masts, each with crossed yards). They had a single gun deck and mounted their heavy ordnance on it; the lighter guns were carried on the open spar deck. Smaller frigates might carry 24–30 guns, the larger ones as many as 60 guns.

Frigates were the workhorses of the age of fighting sail, performing a wide variety of functions. They scouted ahead of the main fleet to provide warning of the approach of enemy ships. They were also detached as merchant-ship raiders (*GUERRE DE COURSE*), and they served as escorts. Frigates grew in size over time. By the beginning of the 18th century they were 175 feet in length and 2,000 tons or more.

During the American Revolutionary War, in December 1775, the Continental Congress authorized construction of 13 frigates. They were in three classes of 24, 28, and 32 guns; their construction was distributed by contract among the colonies. They amassed an indifferent war record. The Americans also obtained frigates from the French, the most famous of these being the converted East Indiaman BON-HOMME RICHARD, commanded by John Paul JONES.

After the war Congress disbanded the navy. In 1794, however, with the beginning of the wars of the French Revolution and Napoleon, and with rising problems with the Barbary states, Congress authorized the construction of six frigates, four 44s and two 36s: the CONSTITUTION, CONSTELLATION, UNITED STATES, PRESIDENT (all 44s), and the CHESAPEAKE and Congress (36s). The Constitution was (and is) 204 feet in length overall (gun-deck length 175 feet); 45 feet, two inches in beam; and 2,200 tons in displacement. It mounted 14-pounders as the main battery when the preferred armament for contemporary British frigates was 18-pounders. Nonetheless, the ships were strongly built, with live oak sides, and were superior to their British counterparts.

The new American frigates gave impressive service during the QUASI-WAR with France and especially during the War of 1812 when a number of them scored victories in individual ship contests. Sailing frigates continued in service up through the Civil War; the Constitution remains in commission at the Charlestown Navy Yard in Boston.

Sailing frigates began to be replaced in the 1850s with the new Merrimack class of steam frigates, one of the best known of which was the lead ship in the class, the Merrimack, rebuilt during the Civil War by the Confederates as the ironclad VIRGINIA.

The term frigate survived in large "destroyer leaders" of the World War II era and was later applied to antisubmarine escorts. In the mid-1970s the Bronstein, Brooke, and Garcia destroyer escorts were redesignated "frigates," followed by Knox-class frigates. Today the U.S. Navy operates the Oliver Hazard Perry class of guided-missile frigates, begun in 1975. Modern frigates patrol littorals, conduct convoy operations, and escort carrier battle groups.

See also DESTROYER.

Further reading: Canney, Donald L. *The Old Steam Navy.* Vol. 1, *Frigates, Sloops, and Gunboats, 1815–1885.* Annapolis, Md.: Naval Institute Press, 1990; Chapelle, Howard. *The History of the American Sailing Navy: The Ships and Their Development.* New York: Norton, 1949; Silverstone, Paul H. *The Sailing Navy, 1775–1854.* Annapolis, Md.: Naval Institute Press, 2000; Tucker, Spencer C. *Handbook of 19th Century Naval Warfare.* Annapolis, Md.: Naval Institute Press, 2000.

— A. J. L. Waskey

frontier posts *Military installations on the western frontier*
The earliest European settlers in North America relied on forts for protection against Indians and Old World rivals. As settlement moved westward into more hostile environments, forts became essential to survival, as both points of safety and centers of commerce. After the U.S. government assumed responsibility for frontier defense, forts not only continued to offer safety and promote commerce but also served as bases of operation for federal soldiers. Forts thus became integral parts, and permanent fixtures, of the American frontier experience.

Once settlement spread across the Mississippi to remote areas, far from major centers and main avenues of communication and into the lands of the mobile Plains Indians, the need for semipermanent military installations rose accordingly. The annexation of Texas, followed quickly by the opening of the Oregon Territory and the Mexican cession, placed great demands on the small standing army. Texas alone, with its extensive western frontier, proximity to Indian Territory, and long border with Mexico, required dozens of posts. During the 12 years before and 25 years after the Civil War, an extensive network of forts supported government efforts to control the Indians of the American West.

Despite images portrayed in motion pictures, few frontier posts were of the enclosed-stockade variety. Only those in the most exposed and vulnerable situations, such as Forts Phil Kearny and C. F. Smith on the Bozeman Trail, afforded such protection. The vast majority resembled small villages. Laid out around a broad parade ground were officers' quarters and enlisted men's barracks, a post headquarters, a hospital, corrals, workshops, kitchens, laundress huts, and post traders' stores.

Because of fiscal restraints, most forts were constructed by soldiers, usually of locally available materials, such as rock, adobe, or wood. Because of the shifting frontier, most of the forts were considered transitory and therefore received few improvements. They could be inhospitable—drafty, leaky, vermin infested, and unbearably cold or intolerably hot.

Over time many forts, those that were poorly located or obsolete, were closed in favor of new posts. Frequently, temporary posts or camps were upgraded to forts, just as existing forts could be relegated to subpost status.

Fort and camp garrisons performed many roles, often simultaneously. Most forts housed only a few companies of troops at a time, usually a combination of cavalry and infantry. Rarely did a post support a full regiment or more. Forts served as staging areas for major campaigns, but more often than not garrisons performed such routine duties as guarding travel routes, mail shipments, and surveying parties. Many garrisons were called upon to watch over reservations or protect friendly Indians. Mostly, life at frontier forts was boring, monotonous, and unpleasant. More importantly, however, forts became economic engines, attracting new settlement and new enterprise, such as saloons, hotels, gambling and prostitution, and retail establishments. These spawned communities that in many cases outlived the forts and became vital towns and cities.

As the Indian Wars came to a close, the government abandoned obsolete posts and concentrated forces in viable forts, which received upgrades in accordance with their new missions. Several frontier forts remained in productive service until World War II. Others, such as Forts Leavenworth and Riley in Kansas, Fort Sill in Oklahoma, Fort Huachuca in Arizona, and Fort Bliss in Texas, continue as active military bases.

See also AMERICAN INDIAN WARS, OVERVIEW; ARMY, U.S.; FETTERMAN DISASTER; RED RIVER WAR; SIOUX WARS.

Further reading: Frazer, Robert W. *Forts of the West.* Norman: University of Oklahoma Press, 1965; Utley, Robert M. *Frontier Regulars: The United States Army and the Indian, 1866–1891.* New York: Macmillan, 1973.

— David Coffey

Fulton, Robert (1765–1815) *Painter and engineer*

Born on 14 November 1765 on a farm near Lancaster, Pennsylvania, Robert Fulton at an early age showed talent for painting and mechanics. After his father died Fulton proceeded to Philadelphia, soon establishing himself as a painter. In 1787, armed with letters of reference, he began a 20-year sojourn in Europe. He was practically adopted in London by the famous American painter Benjamin West and his wife.

The 1790s saw Fulton move from painting to mechanical pursuits, inventing a saw for cutting marble, a rope-making machine, and machines for hauling boats along canals—all illustrated by engineering drawings. In early summer 1797 he went to Paris to obtain patents for a canal system. While in France he conceived the idea of a functional submarine, the *Nautilus*, which on 12 December 1797 he offered to the Directory, for a fee, with which to destroy the British navy. He met and was strongly influenced by the rich American writer, poet, and liberal statesman Joel Barlow, who encouraged him to build his submarine and helped finance it. Finally securing French government support, Fulton built his *Nautilus* and saw it pass tests on the surface and submerged in the Seine and also in the Atlantic Ocean off Le Havre. For various reasons Fulton disassembled his submarine, and French government support ended.

Fulton then took his inventive genius to Britain. In a test demonstration, he blew up a brig with a mine. Actual employment of his mines against the French fleet in Boulogne in 1804 and 1805 did little damage, and British financial support ended. Fulton returned to America and devoted himself to designing a steamboat. In 1807 his *Clermont* steamed up the Hudson River.

Fulton continued his experiments in underwater warfare and sought to interest the U.S. government in his weapons. On 20 July 1807, one of his torpedoes (mines) sank a 200-ton brig in 20 seconds. Congress appropriated $5,000 for testing his mines against a fully manned ship in New York Harbor. So well defended was the target ship that his torpedo failed to strike it, and a committee of investigation rejected an anchored version meant for harbor defense. He then served on a committee to consider the feasibility of a canal in the upper regions of New York State. He was also the first to operate steamboats on the Ohio and Mississippi Rivers and catamaran ferries between New York and New Jersey.

During the WAR OF 1812, Fulton designed the revolutionary DEMOLOGOS, the first steam warship in history, laid down on 20 June 1814. It had a catamaran hull 130 feet long and five-foot oak sides. He placed the boilers and a 130-horsepower engine below the waterline and the paddle wheel in between, where it was protected from shot and shell. Designed for the protection of New York Harbor, it was not completed until after the war ended. Renamed the *Fulton* in honor of its designer, the vessel was destroyed by an internal explosion in 1829.

Robert Fulton *(Library of Congress)*

In February 1815 Fulton rescued a friend who had fallen through the ice on the Hudson. He subsequently contracted pneumonia and died on 21 February.

See also MINES, SEA; NAVY, U.S.; SUBMARINES.

Further reading: Hutcheon, Wallace, Jr. *Robert Fulton: Pioneer of Undersea Warfare.* Annapolis, Md.: Naval Institute Press, 1981; Philip, Cynthia Owen. *Robert Fulton: A Biography.* New York: Franklin Watts, 1985; Sale, Kirkpatrick. *The Fire of His Genius: Robert Fulton and the American Dream.* New York: Free Press, 2001.

— Paolo E. Coletta

Funston, Frederick (1865–1917) *U.S. Army general*
Born on 9 November 1865 at New Carlisle (near Springfield), Ohio, Frederick Funston was raised on a farm near Iola, Kansas. Funston's father was a U.S. congressman. After college and several jobs, including that of schoolteacher, Funston became a botanist with the Department of Agriculture and took part in several expeditions in the American West and Alaska.

Funston began his military career in 1896 as a "filibuster," or mercenary, fighting with Cuban rebels in the 1895–98 insurrection against Spanish rule. The non–Spanish speaking Funston rose steadily as an artillery officer in the Cuban insurgent forces. Wounded numerous times, he earned battlefield promotions through lieutenant colonel before being captured by the Spanish. Released, he returned to the United States in 1898, just prior to the SPANISH-AMERICAN WAR.

Funston secured a commission as colonel and commander of the 20th Kansas Volunteer Infantry Regiment. To his dismay, however, the regiment was sent to San Francisco rather than Cuba. After the war ended Funston deployed with his unit to the Philippines, where he took part in the 1899–1902 PHILIPPINE-AMERICAN WAR. Funston's regiment distinguished itself as part of Major General Arthur MACARTHUR's 2d Division, and Funston was awarded the Medal of Honor for his heroic action at Calumpit in Central Luzon on 27 April 1899.

Returning with his unit to Kansas, Funston was promoted to brigadier general of U.S. Volunteers. He returned to the Philippines to command a brigade. Later he planned and took part in the March 1901 operation that captured Filipino rebel leader Emilio AGUINALDO and helped to end the war. For this action in April Funston was appointed a brigadier general in the regular army.

Serving in the Departments of the Colorado and of the Columbia (1901–1905), he went to the Department of California in 1905 and was the senior military commander during the 1906 earthquake; he was publicly touted as "the man who saved San Francisco." From 1908 to 1910 he commanded the Army Service Schools at Fort Leavenworth, Kansas. He then returned to the Philippines to command the Department of Luzon (1911–13) and then the Hawaiian Department (1913–14). In 1914 he was military governor of VERACRUZ during the U.S. occupation of that Mexican city. Promoted to major general, Funston returned to the Mexican border in 1916 and sent the PUNITIVE EXPEDITION INTO MEXICO under Brigadier General John J. PERSHING. Funston might have commanded the AMERICAN EXPEDITIONARY FORCE sent to France in 1917 had he not died of a heart attack in San Antonio, Texas, on 19 February 1917.

Further reading: Crouch, Thomas W. *A Yankee Guerrillero: Frederick Funston and the Cuban Insurrection, 1896–1897.* Memphis: Memphis State University Press, 1975; Bain, David Haward. *Sitting in Darkness: Americans in the Philippines.* Boston: Houghton Mifflin, 1984.

— J. G. D. Babb

Index

★ ────────────────────────────────────

Note: Page numbers in **boldface** indicate main topics; *italic* page numbers denote illustrations.

Helbing